Preface

The success of Modular FORTRAN 77 and the resulting user feedback from that edition provided invaluable insight into the needs and diversity of the community of FORTRAN instructors. This feedback indicated a clearly defined segment of the teaching community that wants modular concepts to be introduced on "day one" of their course and sustained throughout the semester. This text is specifically written to meet this need.

Like Modular FORTRAN 77, this alternate edition uses a practical, applications approach rather than a theoretical approach. It differs in being more rigorous in its enforcement of modular program design. Where more flexibility is needed as to when and how much modularity can be introduced I recommend Modular FORTRAN 77.

This text also differs from Modular FORTRAN 77 in that features of the new ANSI standard are integrated throughout the entire text, suitably annotated and beginning in Chapter 1, rather than placed entirely in a separate chapter. Additionally, a demanding set of laboratory projects has been added to the text and the option of introducing data files earlier in a course (Chapter 5 rather than Chapter 9) is provided. I have also made use of the experience and feedback provided by adopters of the first edition to "clean up" the usual number of errors inherent in any first edition. For these errors I both apologize and accept responsibility.

I continue to believe that FORTRAN is still one of the most powerful and easy to use high-level computer languages available for engineering and scientific applications. As such it will continue to be the premier engineering and scientific programming language for new applications. Additionally, the vast inventory of currently existing FORTRAN programs and algorithms make it almost certain that professional engineers and scientists will encounter the language during their careers.

Finally, the need to keep FORTRAN current, using modular constructs and new data types, such as pointers, has been ably met by the new FORTRAN standard. I feel it imperative that we, as teachers, remain true to the continuing development and evolving nature of FORTRAN by presenting it as the structured language it has become.

Distinctive Features of This Book

Modularity This book stresses modular programming from beginning to end. The concept of subprograms is introduced in Chapter 1 and argument passing in Chapter 4. Thereafter, every program is written within the context of driver/subprogram code.

ANSI Fortran 90 Features Although FORTRAN 77 is the default version of FORTRAN used throughout the text, FORTRAN 90 features are integrated and highlighted throughout the entire book. Although the new standard recommends that, except for FORTRAN 66 and FORTRAN 77, the name of the language be spelled as Fortran, we will use the notation FORTRAN 77 and FORTRAN 90 for consistency. (A forthcoming edition devoted to FORTRAN 90 will adhere to the recommended lowercase spelling.)

WRITE and FORMAT Statements The list-directed WRITE statement is introduced in Chapter 1 and is used in preference to the PRINT statement throughout the text. This provides for an early introduction to output unit numbers, which is easily transferable to file writing and is not possible with the PRINT statement. Formatted output is also introduced early, in Chapter 2, which provides students with the ability to both think about and create professional looking output.

Early (Optional) Introduction to Files Text (formatted) files are introduced in the second-half of Chapter 5, immediately after the DO statement. This provides for rather straight-forward and extremely meaningful applications of the DO statement using only a change in unit numbers for the WRITE statement introduced in Chapter 1 and the READ statement introduced in Chapter 3. This gives the instructor an option to present students with a more realistic idea of how data is stored and processed early in the course, and provides the opportunity of presenting students with meaningful sets of data for project work. The file material in the latter half of Chapter 5, however, may be delayed until later in the course and introduced wherever the instructor sees it as appropriate.

Cumulative Lab Projects Cumulative lab exercises are provided at the end of selected chapters. These projects require a deeper understanding of FORTRAN and necessitate an integration of input, processing, and output concepts for their completion. They require the students to prepare a documented and formatted report in a professional manner. Both sample data and report structures are provided.

Closer Look Sections Given the many different emphases that can be applied to the teaching of FORTRAN, I have added a number of Closer Look sections to most of the chapters in this text. These allow you to provide different emphasis with different students or different sections of the FORTRAN class.

Flexible Introduction to Control Structures The presentation of control structures permits a variety of teaching approaches. Although the DO statement is presented in Chapter 5, followed by Selection and Conditional Loops in Chapters 6 and 7, this ordering of topics may easily be altered to suit an individual instructor's preference for presenting control structures. The following chart illustrates possible course alternatives.

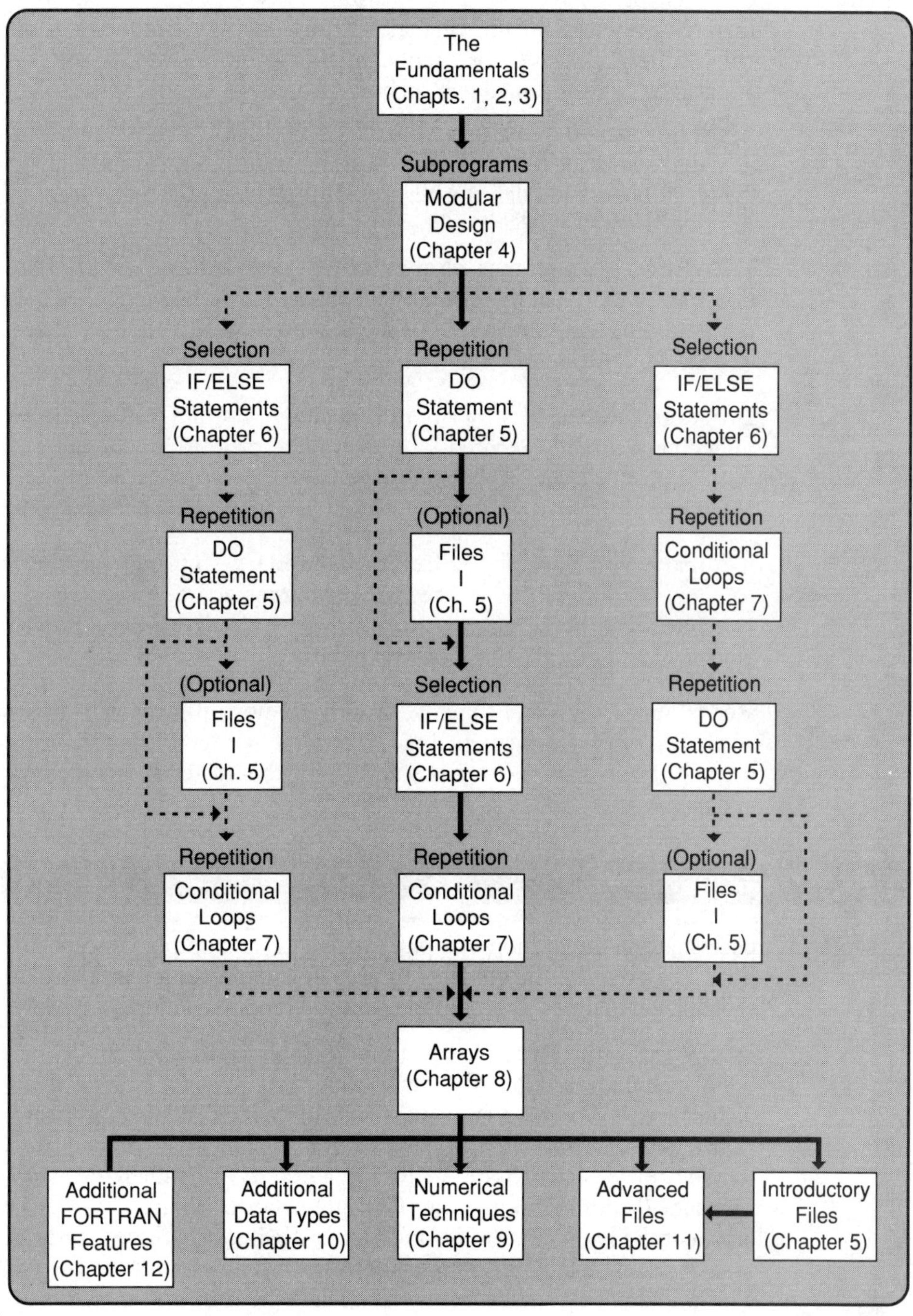

Applications Engineering and scientific examples are used throughout the text to both motivate and illustrate concepts presented in the text. Additionally the majority of the chapters have a section consisting of two specific applications relating to the material presented in the chapter. Many of the applications are of the "tried and true" variety and are not unique to this book. However, some interesting new applications have been added, such as the study of acid rain, the calculation of pollen counts, telephone switching networks, and the construction of a user-written random number generator that are not typically found in introductory texts. Additionally, Chapter 9 is completely devoted to numerical applications and is a mini introduction to numerical techniques in and of itself.

Exercises A wide range of exercises are included at the end of almost every section, rather than just at the end of each chapter. They range from skill builders, to programming assignments, to debugging exercises. In addition there are many program modification assignments.

Program Testing Every single FORTRAN program in this text has been successfully compiled and executed by myself. The majority of these are included on the diskette provided with the text. Additional, many of the programs have also been run independently by reviewers or the Consulting Editors, using different computer systems.

Comparative Charts for Different Compilers Throughout this text I have tried to allow for differences between the different computing environments in which FORTRAN can be taught. As a result, I have displayed these differences in a table whenever a significant variation seemed to occur.

Readability The one thing I have found most important in my own teaching is regardless of what is written about, it must be written so that students can read it. As a result, I have taken every precaution for this material to be clear, unambiguous, and deliberate.

Acknowledgements

Modern FORTRAN 77/90: The Alternate Edition is a direct result of the success (and the limitations) of its "sister" edition, Modular FORTRAN 77.

Users of Modular FORTRAN 77 who provided feedback from their teaching experiences with that text made an invaluable contribution to the quality of this text. They include Shui Lam (Cal State Long Beach); Mary Kay Frohock (University of Kansas); Kris Froehlke (Indianapolis University/Purdue University); Josef Zurada (University of Louisville); Robert Kenyon (University of Illinois at Chicago); Terry Thul (New Mexico State University); Randy Odendahl (SUNY Oswego);Chris Connant (Broome Community College); Martha Tillman (College of San Mateo) and Scott Bailey, Peter Smith, and Ginter Trybus (Cal State Northridge).

Personal telephone conversations with five users of Modular FORTRAN 77 had a profound on this text. I deeply appreciate the time and thoughts of Josann Duane

(Ohio State University); S. Srinivasan (University of Louisville); Richard Martin (Southwest Missouri State); Neil Sorensen (Weber State University); and Kent Dunham (University of Idaho). Many of their suggestions for improving Modular FORTRAN 77 were also incorporated into Modern FORTRAN 77/90: The Alternate Edition.

Non-adopters of Modular FORTRAN 77 who did not adopt the text because "it didn't go far enough" in the direction of modularity had an equally definitive impact on this text. They include Henry Todd (BYU), Judy Hankins (Middle Tennessee State), Richard Lejk (UNC - Charlotte), and Judy Gersting (University of Hawaii). Michael Clancy (University of California) graciously permitted my editor to tape-record their conversation regarding ways in which this text could improve. The transcription of this unusual method of reviewing was quite illuminating.

I was also fortunate to have four consulting editors whose teaching environments and orientations were different and complimentary to my own. Each of them contributed trenchant and thoughtful criticisms, as well as original work of their own, towards completion of this text. Judy Cain (Tompkins-Cortland Community College), John Lyon (University of Arizona), Wesley Scruggs (Brazoport College), and Howard Silver (Fairleigh Dickinson University) have been a privilege to work with.

No acknowledgement would be complete without also mentioning my brother, Dr. Richard Bronson, who distilled the issue of modularity in FORTRAN for me originally, and thus had a profound influence on this text. My Dean, Dr. Paul Lerman, and my Chairman Dr. Naadimuthu, also provided direct encouragement and support. Without their support this text could not have been written. A special thanks also goes to Ed Brodhead of FDU, who frequently was more concerned than I that the manuscript reach its destination on time.

It has also been a privilege to work with my friend and publisher Richard Jones, who has been in spirit what every author wishes their publisher was: a partner. Acknowledgement also goes to Jane Scott-Jones for keeping Richard within the bounds of sanity and allowed him to approach this project with some degree of rationality. Pat Rogondino, the production editor at Rogondino & Associates has also been wonderful to work with. Her attention to detail and high standards have helped in many ways to improve the quality of this book. My deep appreciation and love also go to my son David for designing the cover of this text; I also am very appreciative of the efforts of Professor Marvin Goldstein and Ankush Narula for making this cover design a reality.

Finally, I deeply appreciate the patience, understanding, and love provided by my friend, wife, and partner, Rochelle.

Gary Bronson

Contents

Preface iv

Chapter One Getting Started 1

1.1 Introduction to Programming 1
1.2 Introduction to Modularity 9
1.3 How Program Units Are Built 15
1.4 Writing Complete Programs 23
1.5 Common Programming Errors 31
1.6 Things to Remember 32
1.7 A Closer Look: Computer Hardware and Storage 34

Chapter Two Data and Operations 39

2.1 Data Constants and Arithmetic Operations 40
2.2 Variables and Declaration Statements 50
2.3 Assignment Statements 60
2.4 Formatted Output 71
2.5 Top-Down Program Development 89
2.6 Applications 96
2.7 Common Programming Errors 104
2.8 Things to Remember 105
2.9 A Closer Look: Errors, Testing, and Debugging 107

Chapter Three Completing the Basics 113

3.1 Intrinsic Functions 113
3.2 The List-Directed READ Statement 122
3.3 The Formatted READ Statement* 135
3.4 Named Constants: The PARAMETER Statement 144
3.5 Applications 150
3.6 Common Programming Errors 159
3.7 Things to Remember 160
3.8 A Closer Look: Program Life Cycle 161

LAB SET FOR CHAPTERS 1–3 165

Chapter Four Modularity Using Subprograms 169

4.1 Subroutine Program Units 170
4.2 Program Development Using Subroutines 185
4.3 Subprogram Functions 198
4.4 Statement Functions 209
4.5 Applications 212
4.6 Common Programming Errors 227
4.7 Things to Remember 229
4.8 A Closer Look: Programming Costs 230

Chapter Five DO Loops and Data Files 235

5.1 DO Loops 236
5.2 DO Loop Programming Techniques 248
5.3 Nested Loops 258
5.4 List-Directed Data Files* 263
5.5 User-Formatted Data Files 274
5.6 Applications 283
5.7 Common Programming Errors 294
5.8 Things to Remember 294
5.9 Enrichment Study: Writing Control Codes 297

LAB SET for Chapters Four and Five 301

Chapter Six Selection 307

6.1 Relational Expressions 307
6.2 The IF-ELSE Structure 313
6.3 The IF-ELSEIF Structure 328
6.4 The CASE Structure 333

6.5 Applications 338
6.6 Common Programming Errors 347
6.7 Things to Remember 348

Chapter Seven Conditional Loops 351
7.1 The FORTRAN 77 DO WHILE Structure 351
7.2 The FORTRAN 90 DO WHILE Construct 362
7.3 REPEAT-UNTIL Loops 372
7.4 Applications 375
7.5 Common Programming Errors 385
7.6 Things to Remember 386

LAB SET for Chapters Six and Seven 388

Chapter Eight Arrays 395
8.1 Single Dimension Arrays 396
8.2 The DATA Statement and Array Initialization 407
8.3 Two Dimension Arrays 411
8.4 Arrays as Arguments 418
8.5 Applications 425
8.6 Common Programming Errors 435
8.7 Things to Remember 436
8.8 A Closer Look: Sorting Methods 438

Lab Set for Chapter 8 445

Chapter Nine Numerical Techniques and Applications 451
9.1 Solving Simultaneous Linear Equations 451
9.2 Root Finding 463
9.3 Numerical Integration 454
9.4 Common Programming Errors 504
9.5 Things to Remember 506

Chapter Ten Additional Data Types 507
10.1 Double Precision Data 507
10.2 Complex Data 512
10.3 String and Substring Processing 515
10.4 Data Structures as Parallel Arrays 519
10.5 Applications 526
10.6 Common Programming Errors 532
10.7 Things to Remember 535

Chapter Eleven Additional Data File Capabilities 535
11.1 Text (Formatted) Files 536
11.2 Binary (Unformatted) Files* 539
11.3 File Statements 541
11.4 Direct Access Files 548
11.5 Internal Files 552
11.6 Exercises 554
11.7 Common Programming Errors 556
11.8 Things to Remember 556

Chapter Twelve Additional FORTRAN Features 559
12.1 COMMON Blocks 559
12.2 New FORTRAN 90 Features 566
12.3 Pointers and Targets 569
12.4 Structures 573
12.5 Linked Lists 580
12.6 Things to Remember 588

Appendix A A-1

Appendix B B-1

Appendix C C-1

Appendix D D-1

Appendix E E-1

Appendix F F-1

Solutions S-1

Index 591

1 Getting Started

Chapter One

1.1 Introduction to Programming

1.2 Introduction to Modularity

1.3 How Program Units Are Built

1.4 Writing Complete Programs

1.5 Common Programming Errors

1.6 Things to Remember

1.7 A Closer Look: Computer Hardware and Storage

1.1 Introduction to Programming

A computer is a machine, and like other machines, such as automobiles and lawn mowers, it must be turned on and then driven, or controlled, to do the task it was meant to do. In an automobile, for example, control is provided by the driver, who sits inside of and directs the car. In a computer, the driver is a set of instructions called a program. More formally, a *computer program* is a sequence of instructions used to operate a computer to produce a specific result. *Programming* is the process of writing these instructions in a language to which the computer can respond and that other programmers can understand. The set of instructions that can be used to construct a program is called a *programming language.*

On a fundamental level, all computer programs do the same thing (Figure 1-1); they direct a computer to accept data (input), to manipulate the data (process), and to produce reports (output). This implies that all computer programming languages must provide essentially the same capabilities for performing these operations, and such is indeed the case. The fundamental set of instructions provided by such high-

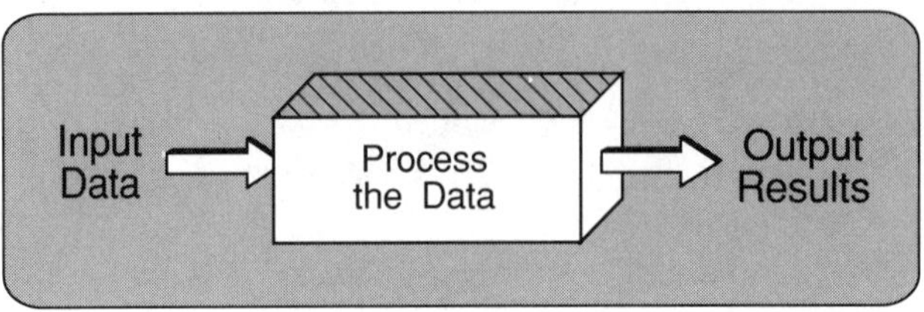

Figure 1-1 All Programs Perform the Same Operations

level procedure-oriented computer languages as FORTRAN, BASIC, COBOL, and Pascal is listed in Table 1-1. The term *high-level* means that the statements in these languages resemble English statements. The term *procedure-oriented* means that these languages are primarily used to describe procedures for producing specific results.

If all programming languages provide essentially the same features, why are there so many of them? There are so many languages because there are vast differences in the types of input data, calculations needed, and required output reports. For example, scientific and engineering applications usually require high-precision numerical outputs that are accurate to many decimal places. In addition, these applications typically use many algebraic or trigonometric formulas to produce their results. For example, the determination of a rocket's reentry point, as illustrated in Figure 1-2, requires a trigonometric formula and a high degree of numerical accuracy. For such applications, the FORTRAN programming language, with its algebra-like instructions, is ideal. FORTRAN (an acronym derived from FORmula TRANslation) was introduced commercially in 1957. Originally designed for translating formulas into computer-readable form, FORTRAN was the first high-level language to be developed. The current standard for FORTRAN is maintained by the American National Standards Institute (ANSI).

Table 1-1 Programming Language Instruction Summary

Operation	FORTRAN	BASIC	COBOL	Pascal
Input (get the data)	READ	INPUT	READ	READ
		READ/DATA	ACCEPT	READLN
Processing (use the data)	=	LET	COMPUTE	:=
	IF/ELSE	IF/ELSE	IF/ELSE	IF/ELSE
	DO	FOR	PERFORM	FOR
				WHILE
				REPEAT
Output (display the data)	WRITE	PRINT	WRITE	WRITE
	PRINT	PRINT/USING	DISPLAY	WRITELN

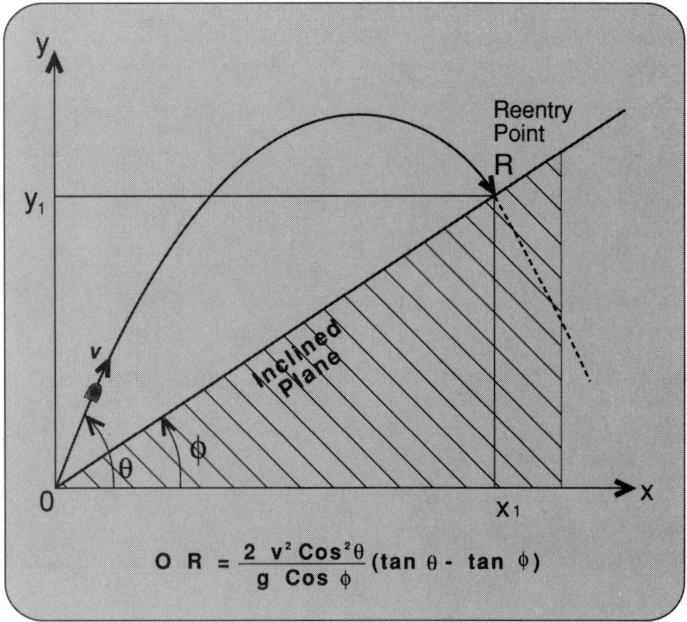

Figure 1-2 FORTRAN is Ideal for Scientific and Engineering Applications

Algorithms

Before a program is written, the programmer must have a clear understanding of the desired result and how the proposed program is to produce it. In this regard, it is useful to realize that a computer program describes a procedure for converting a given set of input data into a desired set of outputs.

In computer science, such a procedure is called an algorithm. More specifically, an *algorithm* is defined as a step-by-step sequence of instructions that describes how a computation or task is to be performed. In essence, an algorithm answers the question "What method will be used to solve this problem?" Only after the specific steps required to produce the desired result are known and the algorithm clearly understood can the program be written. Seen in this light, programming is the translation of the selected algorithm into a language that the computer can use.

To illustrate an algorithm, we shall consider a simple requirement. Assume that a program must calculate the sum of all whole numbers from 1 through 100. Figure 1-3 illustrates three methods we could use to find the required sum. Each method constitutes an algorithm.

Clearly, most people would not bother to list the possible alternatives in a detailed step-by-step manner, as is done in Figure 1-3, and then select one of the algorithms to solve the problem. But then most people do not think algorithmically; they tend to think heuristically. For example, if you had to change a flat tire on your car, you would not think of all the steps required—you would simply change the tire or call someone else to do the job. This is an example of heuristic thinking.

Method 1. Columns: Arrange the numbers from 1 to 100 in a column and add them:

```
   1
   2
   3
   4
   .
   .
  98
  99
+100
----
5050
```

Method 2. Groups: Arrange the numbers in convenient groups that sum to 100. Multiply the number of groups by 100, then add any unused numbers to the total:

```
 0 + 100 = 100 ┐
 1 +  99 = 100 │
 2 +  98 = 100 │  50 groups
 3 +  97 = 100 ├──────┐
 .          .  │      ↓
 .          .  │     (50 x 100) + 50 = 5050
 .          .  │                  ↑
49 +  51 = 100 ┘                  │
50 +   0 =  50 ───────────────────┘
               One unused number
```

Method 3. Formula: Use the formula Sum = n/2 x (a + b) where

n = number of terms to be added (100)
a = first number to be added (1)
b = last number to be added (100)

Sum = 100/2 x (1 + 100) = 5050

Figure 1-3 Summing the Numbers 1 Through 100

Unfortunately, computers do not respond to heuristic commands. A general statement such as "add the numbers from 1 to 100" means nothing to a computer, because it can only respond to algorithmic commands written in an acceptable language such as FORTRAN. To program a computer successfully, you must clearly understand this difference between algorithmic and heuristic commands. A computer is an "algorithm-responding" machine; it is not a "heuristic-responding" machine. A computer will not understand if you tell it to change a tire or to add the numbers from 1 through 100. Instead, you must give the computer a detailed, step-by-step set of instructions that collectively forms an algorithm. For example, the set of instructions:

```
Set n equal to 100
Set a = 1
Set b equal to 100
Calculate sum = n/2 * (a + b)
Print the sum
```

forms a detailed method, or algorithm, for determining the sum of the numbers from 1 through 100. Notice that these instructions are not a computer program. Unlike a program, which must be written in a language to which the computer can respond, an algorithm can be written or described in various ways. When English-like phrases are used to describe the algorithm (processing steps), as in this example, the description is called *pseudocode.* When mathematical equations are used, the description is called a *formula.* When pictures that employ specifically defined shapes are used, the description is called a *flowchart.* A flowchart provides a pictorial representation of the algorithm using the symbols shown in Figure 1-4. Figure 1-5 illustrates the use of these symbols in depicting an algorithm for determining the average of three numbers.

Because flowcharts are cumbersome to revise, the use of pseudocode to express the logic of an algorithm has gained increasing acceptance among programmers in recent years. Unlike flowcharts, where standard symbols are defined, there are no standard rules for constructing pseudocode. Any short English phrases may be used

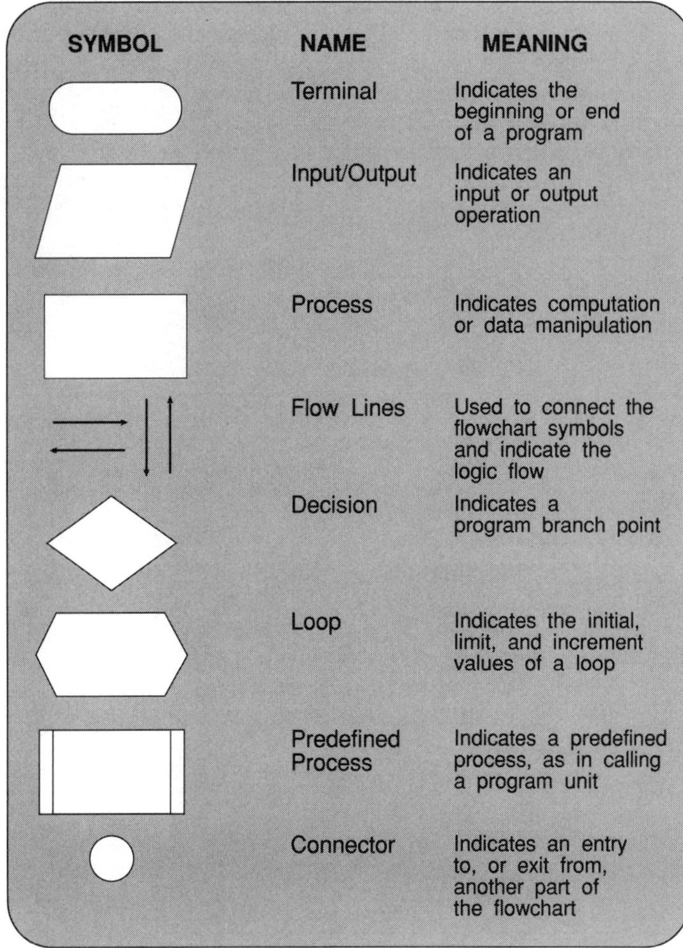

Figure 1-4 Flowchart Symbols

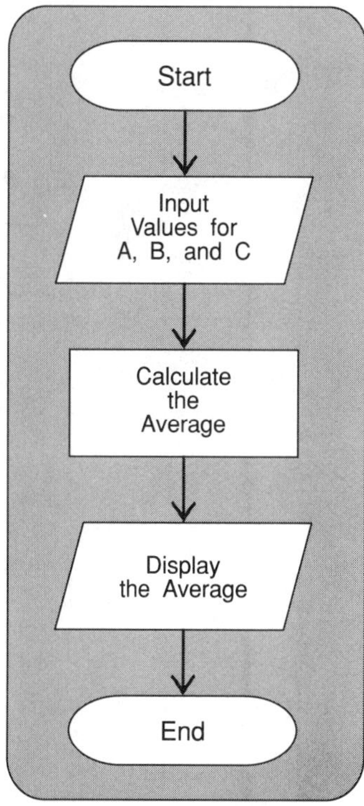

Figure 1-5 Flowchart for Calculating the Average of Three Numbers

to describe an algorithm using pseudocode. For example, acceptable pseudocode for describing the steps needed to compute the average of three numbers is:

```
Input the three numbers into the computer
Calculate the average by adding the numbers and
dividing the sum by three
Display the average
```

A more recent alternative to both flowcharts and pseudocode, which combines the pictorial aspects of flowcharts with the language aspects of pseudocode, are Nassi-(rhymes with sassy) Schneiderman charts. Figure 1-6 illustrates the four shapes used in constructing Nassi-Schneiderman charts. As each of these shapes corresponds to one of the four basic language statements defined in a high-level language such as FORTRAN, these shapes can be used to describe any FORTRAN program. For example, Figure 1-7 illustrates the Nassi-Schneiderman chart describing the steps needed to compute the average of three numbers.

The Nassi-Schneiderman chart illustrated in Figure 1-7 contains an outer process block that describes the purpose of the algorithm, which is *Average three numbers*. Within this outer block are three internal process blocks, with each block containing a pseudocode description of the block's purpose. As with pseudocode, the chart is read from top to bottom.

Although Nassi-Schneiderman charts essentially provide the same information as pseudo-code, they additionally provide a visual element that pseudocode lacks. The usefulness of this visual attribute in clearly identifying an equivalent FORTRAN statement must, however, wait until each corresponding FORTRAN statement is described.

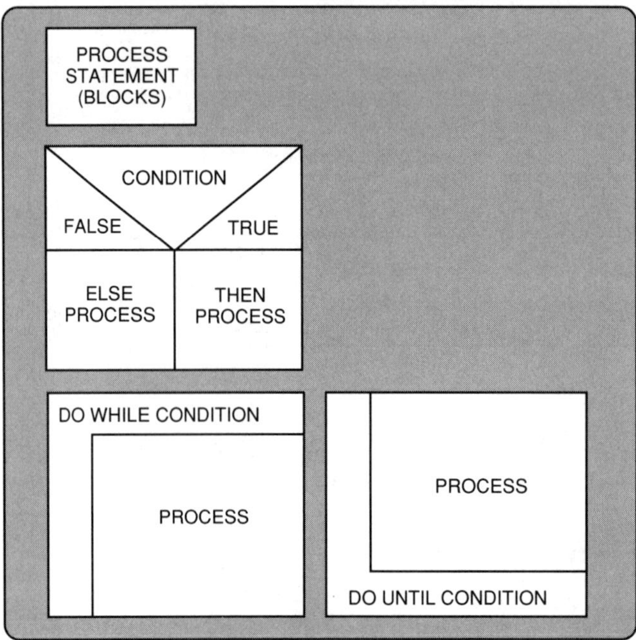

Figure 1-6 Nassi-Schneiderman Symbols

Only after the programmer has selected an algorithm, described it clearly, and understands the steps required can he or she write the algorithm using computer-language statements. When computer-language statements are used to describe the algorithm, the description is called a *computer program.*

From Algorithms to Programs

After an algorithm has been selected, the programmer must convert it into a form that can be used by a computer. The conversion of an algorithm into a computer program, using a language such as FORTRAN, is called *coding* the algorithm (see Figure 1-8). Much of the remainder of this text is devoted to showing you how to code algorithms into FORTRAN.

Program Translation

Once a program is written in FORTRAN, it still cannot be executed on a computer without further translation. This is because the internal language of all computers consists of a series of 1s and 0s, called the computer's *machine language.* To generate a machine-language program that can be executed by the computer requires that the FORTRAN program, referred to as a *source program,* be translated into the computer's machine language (see Figure 1-9).

The translation into machine language can be accomplished in two ways. When each statement in a high-level-language source program is translated individually and executed immediately, the programming language used is called an *interpreted language,* and the program doing the translation is called an *interpreter.*

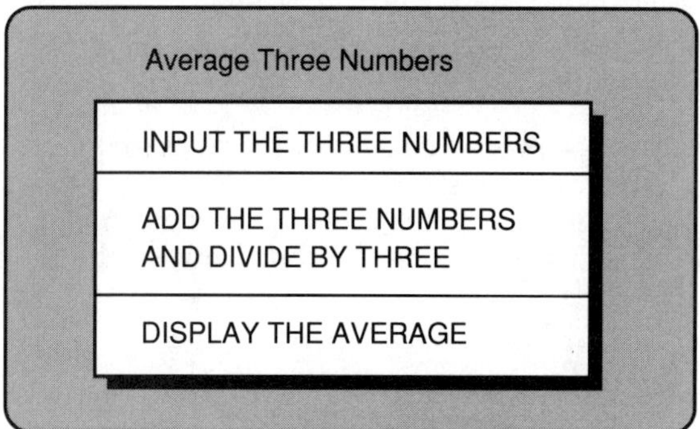

Figure 1-7 Nassi-Schneiderman Chart for Calculating the Average of Three Numbers

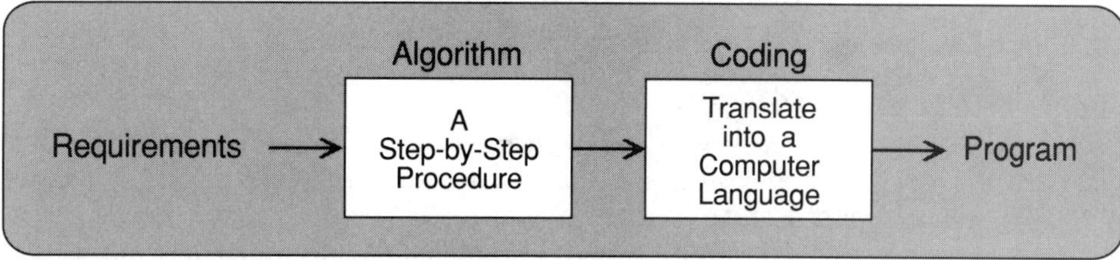

Figure 1-8 Coding an Algorithm

Figure 1-9 Source Programs Must Be Translated

When all the statements in a source program are translated before any one statement is executed, the programming language used is called a *compiled language*, and the program doing the translation is called a *compiler*. FORTRAN is a compiled language. With FORTRAN, the source program is translated as a unit into machine language. The machine-language version of the original source program is a separate entity called the *object program*. (See Appendix A for a complete description of entering, compiling, and running a FORTRAN program.)

Skill Builder Exercises

1. Define the terms:

a. computer program
b. programming
c. program language
d. FORTRAN
e. algorithm
f. pseudocode
g. flowchart
h. high-level language
i. source program
j. object program
k. compiler
l. interpreter

2. Determine a step-by-step procedure and list the steps to do each of the following tasks. (*Note:* There is no single correct answer for any of these tasks. The exercise is designed to give you practice in converting heuristic commands into equivalent algorithms and in making the shift between the thought processes involved in the two types of thinking.)

a. fix a flat tire
b. make a telephone call
c. go to the store and purchase a loaf of bread
d. roast a turkey

3. Determine and write an algorithm (list the steps) to interchange the contents of two cups of liquid. Assume that a third cup is available to hold the contents of either cup temporarily. Each cup should be rinsed before any new liquid is poured into it.

4. Write a detailed set of instructions, in English, to calculate the dollar amount of money in a piggybank that contains h half-dollars, q quarters, n nickels, d dimes, and p pennies.

5. Write a set of detailed, step-by-step instructions, in English, to find the smallest number in a group of three integer numbers.

6. a. Write a set of detailed, step-by-step instructions, in English, to calculate the change remaining from a dollar after a purchase is made. Assume that the cost of the goods purchased is less than a dollar. The change received should consist of the smallest number of coins possible.
   b. Repeat Exercise 6a, but assume the change is to be given only in pennies.
7. a. Write an algorithm to locate the first occurrence of the name JONES in a list of names arranged in random order.
   b. Discuss how you could improve your algorithm for Exercise 7a if the list of names were arranged in alphabetical order.
8. Write an algorithm to determine the total occurrences of the letter e in any sentence.
9. Determine and write an algorithm to sort four numbers into ascending (from lowest to highest) order.

1.2 Introduction to Modularity

A well-designed program is constructed using a design philosophy similar to that used to construct a well-designed building. It doesn't just happen but depends on careful planning and execution for the final design to accomplish its intended purpose. Just as for a building, an integral part of the design of a program is its structure.

In programming, the term *structure* has two interrelated meanings. The first meaning refers to the program's overall construction, which is the topic of this section. The second meaning refers to the form used to carry out the individual tasks within the program, which is the topic of Chapters 4 and 5. In relation to the first meaning, programs whose structure consists of interrelated segments, arranged in a logical and easily understandable order to form an integrated and complete unit, are referred to as *modular programs* (Figure 1-10). Not surprisingly, modular programs are noticeably easier to develop, correct, and modify than programs constructed otherwise. In general programming terminology, the smaller segments used to construct a modular program are referred to as *modules.*

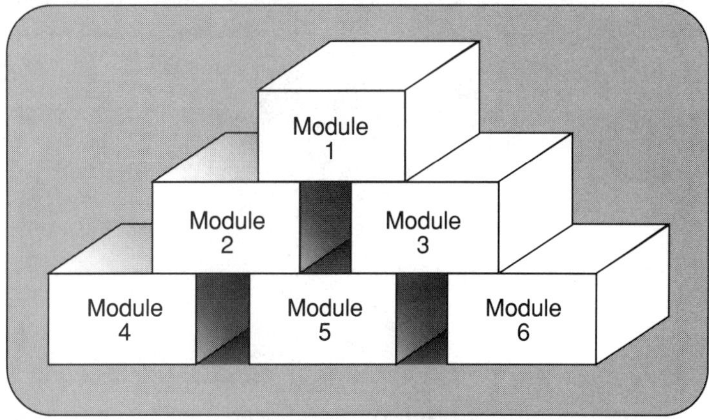

Figure 1-10 A Well-Designed Program Is Built Using Modules

In a modular program each module is designed and developed to perform a clearly defined, specific task. This task can be tested and modified without disturbing other modules in the program. The final program is constructed by connecting as many modules as necessary to produce the desired result. Unfortunately, each programming language has its own specific name for modules. In FORTRAN, a module is referred to as a *program unit.*

Program Units

A program unit is essentially a small program in its own right. As such, it must be capable of doing what is required of all programs: receive data, operate on the data, and produce a result (see Figure 1-11). Unlike a larger program, however, a program unit performs only limited operations. Typically, each program unit performs a single task required by the larger program of which it is a part.

A complete program is constructed by combining as many program units as necessary to produce the desired result. The advantage to this modular construction is that the overall design of the program can be developed before any single program unit is written. Once the requirements for a program unit are finalized, it can be programmed and integrated within the overall program as the unit is completed.

FORTRAN provides three common types of program units: the MAIN, SUBROUTINE, and FUNCTION unit types.* Each of these program unit types performs a specific type of task. We shall learn and use all of these unit types as we progress.

It is useful to think of a program unit, regardless of its type, as a small machine that transforms the data it receives into a finished product. For example, Figure 1-12 illustrates a program unit that accepts three numbers and calculates their average to produce an output.

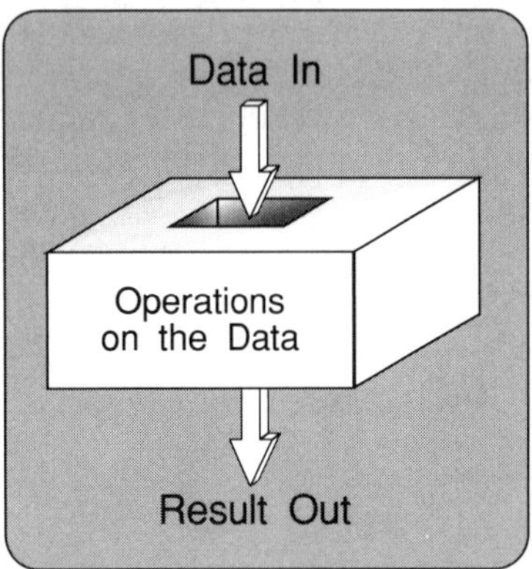

Figure 1-11 A Program Unit Receives Data, Operates on the Data, and Produces a Result

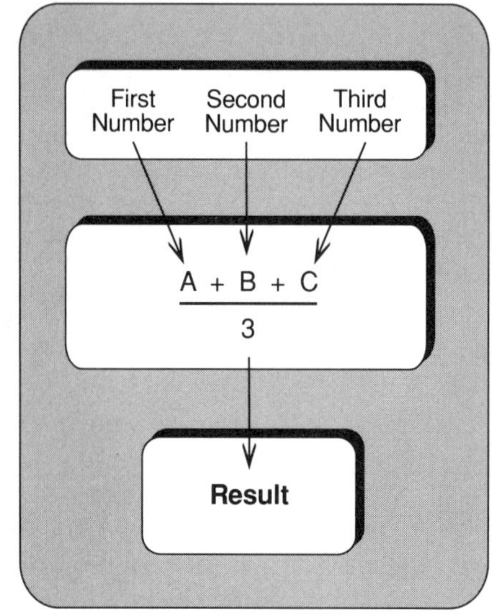

Figure 1-12 A Program Unit That Averages Three Numbers

* The fourth and last type, BLOCK DATA progam units, described in Section 12.1 is rarely used.

The MAIN Program Unit

A distinct advantage to using program units in FORTRAN is that we can plan the overall structure of the program, including making provisions for testing and verifying the operation of individual units, in advance. We first determine the individual tasks required of each unit and establish how the units will be combined. Only after the overall structure of the program has been designed is each program unit written to perform its required task.

To provide for the orderly placement and execution of individual program units, every FORTRAN program must have one, and only one, MAIN program unit (Figure 1-13). This MAIN unit is frequently referred to as the *driver unit*, because of its function of telling all other program units the sequence in which they are to be executed.

Figure 1-14 illustrates a complete MAIN program unit. The first line in the program unit, PROGRAM TEST, is called a *header line*. The word PROGRAM in the header line identifies the beginning of a MAIN program unit. The word TEST is a user-selected name for this MAIN unit. The rules for choosing your own program unit names are presented at the end of this section.

The end of a MAIN unit is always designated by the word END written on a line by itself. The words PROGRAM, STOP, and END are examples of FORTRAN keywords. A *keyword* is a word that takes on a special meaning when it is used in a particular way. When the keyword END is placed on a line by itself, it becomes an END statement, which is required as the last statement in the MAIN program unit. Unlike most other programming languages, FORTRAN's keywords are not reserved words (FORTRAN has no reserved words). A *reserved word* is a word that is set aside by the compiler for a special purpose and can be used only in the manner specified by the compiler. Since FORTRAN's keywords are not reserved, it is possible, although not advisable, to use a keyword such as END for other purposes than an END statement (for example, as the name of a MAIN unit).

Statements following the program header, up to and including the END statement, are collectively referred to as a program unit's body. The *body* of a program unit determines what the unit does. Typically, each statement in the unit's

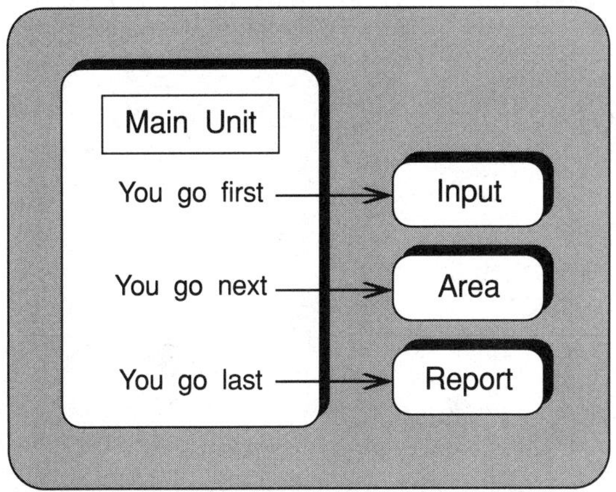

Figure 1-13 The MAIN Program Unit Directs All Other Units

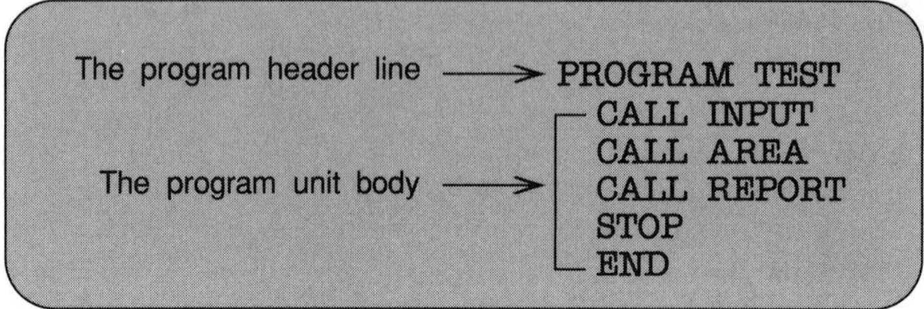

Figure 1-14 A Sample MAIN Program Unit

body resides on a line by itself, although a single statement can, as we will see, continue across multiple lines. In no case, however, can multiple FORTRAN 77 statements be written on the same line. Multiple statements are allowed in FORTRAN 90 but must be separated by semicolons (;).

The body of the MAIN program unit illustrated in Figure 1-14 consists of five statements. The keywords CALL in each of the first three statements are commands to execute SUBROUTINE program units. The first statement in the unit's body, CALL INPUT, calls a SUBROUTINE program unit named INPUT into execution. The word CALL informs the compiler that a transfer to a SUBROUTINE program unit is being requested and that the following word, INPUT, is the name of the requested unit.

When the INPUT program unit is finished executing, the AREA program unit is called. After the AREA unit is completed the REPORT program unit is called. The fourth statement is the STOP command. Although the MAIN program unit is complete as written, the SUBROUTINE program units INPUT, AREA, and REPORT must still be written for the whole program to be executed. After these four program units are written, the program, consisting of MAIN, INPUT, AREA, and REPORT, is complete. In the next section we will see how SUBROUTINE program units are constructed.

Symbolic Names

Program unit names such as TEST, INPUT, AREA, and REPORT are all examples of FORTRAN symbolic names. In FORTRAN 77 a symbol*ic name* is any combination of letters and digits that:

1. begins with an uppercase letter
2. contains only uppercase letters and digits following the initial letter (no blanks or other symbols allowed)
3. consists of at most six characters (up to 21 characters, including the underscore (_) are permitted in FORTRAN 90)

Examples of valid symbolic names are:

NETPAY AVERAG TOTL ADD3 NEWBAL BESSEL SUM1

ANSI Fortran 90 Features. "Although FORTRAN 77 is the default version of FORTRAN used throughout the text, Fortran 90 features are integrated and highlighted throughout the entire book. Although the new standard recommends that, except for FORTRAN 66 and FORTRAN 77, the name of the language be spelled as Fortran, we will use the notation FORTRAN 77 and FORTRAN 90 for consistency. (A forthcoming edition devoted to Fortran 90 will adhere to the recommended lowercase spelling.)"

mbolic names are:

ns with a number, which violates Rule 1)
ns with a lowercase letter, which violates Rule 1)
ains a blank space, which violates Rule 2)
ains a special character, which violates Rule 2)
ains lowercase letters, which violates Rule 2)
ains too many characters, which violates Rule 3)

ne should also be a mnemonic when used as a program unit memory aid used to convey information about what the name ble, the program unit name SQUARE is a mnemonic if it is the unit that calculates the square of a number or the area of a elf gives some indication of what the program unit does. Exam unit names that are not mnemonics are:

A HOWARD R2D2 C3P0 GOFOR X4 D

c symbolic names should not be used as program unit names no information about what the program unit does.

l feature you may encounter is the support of symbolic names x characters. Another non-standard extension to FORTRAN is case letters in symbolic names. Although lowercase letters are TRAN 77 standard for symbolic names, many compilers allow ilers are then either case sensitive or case insensitive.

e compiler does not differentiate between uppercase and lowern compilers symbolic names such as TOTAL, total, and TotAL epresent the same name. *Case sensitive* compilers consider these nct and different entities. In this text we will conform to the rd and use only uppercase letters in symbolic names. We reco the same. This ensures that your programs will run on any g the FORTRAN 77 standard.

ises

the following are valid FORTRAN 77 program unit names. If , state whether they are mnemonic names. If they are invalid hy.

ENSITY	M123$	NEWBAL	1234	ABCD
ANGENT	ABSVAL	MARRIED	B34A	34AB
2-B3	NEWBAL	MIN_VAL	SINE	$SINE
NVOICES	NETPAY	BALANCE	SOLD	AVERAGE

e following subroutine program units have been written:

AXES, NETPAY, and OUTPUT

MAIN program unit that calls these subroutine program units in that they are listed.

eir names, what do you think each subroutine program unit in 2a does?

3. Assume that the following subroutine program units have been written:

   ITEMS, SALETX, BALNCE

   a. Write a MAIN program unit that calls these program units in the order that they are listed.
   b. From their names, what do you think each program unit in Exercise 3a does?

4. Create valid names for subroutine program units that do the following:

   a. find the average of a set of numbers
   b. find the area of a rectangle
   c. find the value of a polynomial
   d. find the density of a steel door
   e. find the maximum value of a set of numbers.
   f. sort a set of numbers from lowest to highest.

5a. Assuming a case-insensitive compiler, determine which of these program unit names are equivalent:

AVERAG	averag	MODE	BESSEL	Mode
Total	besseL	TeMp	Densty	TEMP
denSTY	MEAN	total	mean	moDE

   b. Redo Exercise 5a assuming a case sensitive compiler.
   c. If the compiler adheres strictly to the FORTRAN 77 standard, determine which of the symbolic names in Exercise 5a are invalid.

6. Explain the relationship between an algorithm and a program's modular structure.

Project Structuring Exercises

Most projects, both programming and nonprogramming, can be structured into smaller subtasks or units of activity. These smaller subtasks can often be delegated to different people so that when all the tasks are finished and integrated, the project or program is completed. For Exercises 7 through 12, determine a set of subtasks that, taken together, complete the project. Be aware that there are many possible solutions for each exercise. The only requirement is that the set of subtasks selected completes the required task.

(*Note:* The purpose of these exercises is to have you consider the different ways that complex tasks can be structured. Although there is no one correct solution to these exercises, there are incorrect solutions and solutions that are better than others. An incorrect solution is one that does not fully specify the task. One solution is better than another if it more clearly or easily identifies what must be done.)

7. You are given the task of wiring and installing lights in the attic of your house. Determine a set of subtasks that, taken together, will accomplish this. (*Hint:* The first subtask would be to determine the placement of the light fixtures.)

8. You are given the job of preparing a complete meal for five people next weekend. Determine a set of subtasks that, taken together, accomplish this. (*Hint:* One subtask, not necessarily the first one, would be to buy the food.)

9. You are a sophomore in college and are planning to go to graduate school for a master's degree in electrical engineering. List a set of major objectives that you must fulfill to meet this goal. (*Hint:* One objective is "Take the right courses.")

10. You are given the job of planning a surprise birthday party. Determine a set of subtasks to accomplish this. (*Hint:* One such subtask would be to create a guest list.)

11. You are responsible for planning and arranging the family camping trip this summer. List a set of subtasks that, taken together, accomplish this objective successfully. (*Hint:* One subtask would be to select the campsite.)

12a. A national electrical supply distribution company desires a computer system to prepare its customer invoices. The system must be capable of creating each day's invoices. Additionally, the company wants the capability to retrieve and output a printed report of all invoices that meet certain criteria: for example, all invoices sent in a particular month with a net value of more than a given dollar amount, all invoices sent in a year to a particular client, or all invoices sent to firms in a particular state. Determine three or four major program units into which this system could be separated. (*Hint:* One program unit is "Prepare invoices" to create each day's invoices.)

b. Suppose someone enters incorrect data for a particular invoice, and the error is discovered after the data has been entered and stored by the system. What program unit is needed to take care of correcting this problem? Discuss why such a program unit might or might not be required by most commercial systems.

c. Assume a program unit exists that allows a user to change data that has been incorrectly entered and stored. Discuss the need for including an "audit trail" that would allow for a later reconstruction of the changes made, when they were made, and who made them.

1.3 How Program Units Are Built

A complete FORTRAN program is constructed using one or more program units. Each program unit, regardless of its type, must be constructed using the same form as the MAIN program unit introduced in Section 1.2. Specifically, this includes a program unit header line and a program unit body, as illustrated in Figure 1-15.

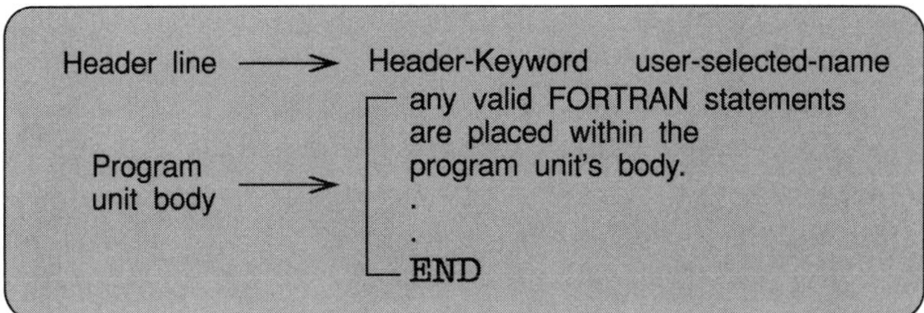

Figure 1-15 A Sample MAIN Program Unit

Program Unit Header Lines

The header line of each program unit is what determines the unit's type. A MAIN program unit is explicitly identified by the header keyword PROGRAM, a SUBROUTINE program unit is identified by the header keyword SUBROUTINE, and a FUNCTION program unit is identified by the header keyword FUNCTION.

Examples of valid MAIN program unit header lines are:

```
PROGRAM TEST
PROGRAM GRAPH
PROGRAM MAIN
PROGRAM SLOPE
```

Each of these header lines identifies the program unit as a MAIN unit. Additionally, a user-selected name must be included on each header line to identify the name of the unit. In the previous examples the first MAIN unit has been named TEST, the second MAIN unit has been named GRAPH, the third MAIN unit has been named MAIN, and the fourth MAIN unit has been named SLOPE. Since each FORTRAN program can have only one MAIN unit, these header lines could not appear together in a single program.

Examples of SUBROUTINE program unit header lines are:

```
SUBROUTINE INPUT
SUBROUTINE AVERGE
SUBROUTINE DISPLY
```

Examples of FUNCTION program unit header lines are:

```
FUNCTION SHOW( )
FUNCTION HYPER( )
```

As illustrated, FUNCTION program units require that parentheses be placed after the function's name. In Chapter 2 we will see the purpose of these parentheses. SUBROUTINE and FUNCTION program units are also referred to as *subprogram units*, or subprograms, for short.

Program Unit Bodies

The body of each program unit consists of valid FORTRAN statements and must end with the keyword END, placed on a line by itself. Every program unit statement must conform to certain rules and forms, which collectively are called the language's *syntax*. One of these syntax rules is that every program unit statement (including the header line) must be placed in a certain position on a line. These line positions are referenced by column number, with column number 1 being the first position on the line, column number 2 the second position, and so on.

Figure 1-16 illustrates FORTRAN's coding form, which defines the prescribed form for each line in every program unit. Specifically, as illustrated in Figure 1-16, each line consists of a label field (which includes the comment indicator column), a continuation field, a statement field, and an identification/sequence field. A requirement of FORTRAN is that each statement in a program must have a statement field entry. If a particular statement does not contain any of the other fields, those fields are left blank.

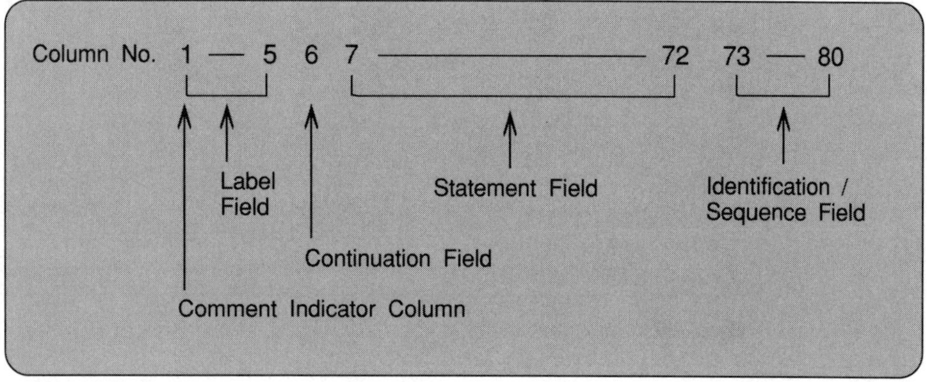

Figure 1-16 The FORTRAN Coding Form

For example, each line in the program previously shown in Figure 1-14 uses only the statement field. Thus, when this program is entered into a computer, each statement must be typed within columns 7 through 72, which constitute the statement field. More typically, the program would be typed using the positioning indicated in Figure 1-17. The additional indentation beyond column 7 of the statements following the program header line is strictly for clarity. This indentation within the statement field is of great help in quickly isolating and locating a specific program unit's header line for programs consisting of many program units.

To reinforce the idea that all FORTRAN 77 programs must conform to the FORTRAN coding form, the column heading shown in Figure 1-17 will be retained for all subsequent sample programs listed in this and the next chapter. By Chapter 3 we will assume that you have become familiar with correctly positioning program lines, and the column headings will be dropped. As the identification/sequence field (columns 73–80) is rarely used in any statement, this field will be excluded in all program listings, as it is in Figure 1-17. Each of the fields on the coding form is now explained.

Label Field

The label field, consisting of the first five columns in a line, is used for statement numbers. A *statement number* is any integer from 1 to 99999 that is typed into the label field. Although the program statements shown in Figure 1-17 contain no statement numbers, certain statements require a statement number so they may be referenced by other statements in the same program unit (more about this later). If a line does not require a statement number, the label field should be left blank.

Column 1 of the label field is also referred to as the comment indicator column. If either an asterisk ( ) or a C is placed in this column, the line becomes a *comment line*. For example,

```
123456789————Column Number ——————————————72 73—80
* THIS IS A COMMENT LINE
*       THIS PROGRAM PRINTS OUT A MESSAGE
*           THIS PROGRAM CALCULATES THE SLOPE OF A LINE
```

```
Column Number
123456789 . . . . . . . . . . . . . 72
      PROGRAM MAIN
        CALL INPUT
        CALL AREA
        CALL REPORT
        END
```

Figure 1-17 Using the FORTRAN Coding Form

are all comment lines. Comment lines can be placed anywhere within a program, without restriction, and have no effect on program execution. The compiler ignores all comment lines—they are there strictly for the convenience of anyone reading the program. When used carefully, comment lines can be very helpful in clarifying what a complete program is about, what an individual program unit does, what a specific group of statements is meant to accomplish, or what one line is intended to do.

Continuation Field

An individual FORTRAN statement can consist of up to twenty lines. The first line is always called the *initial line*, and any succeeding lines of the same statement are called *continuation lines*. Initial lines are designated either by leaving column 6, the continuation field, blank or by placing a zero (0) in this field. Continuation lines are specified by placing any nonblank character except zero in column 6. When a statement is continued beyond an initial line, the label field of all continuation lines must be left blank. Comment lines cannot be continued across two lines using the continuation field; every line in a comment must begin with either a * or a C in column 1.

Statement Field

The third field in each line, consisting of columns 7 through 72, is reserved for the actual FORTRAN statement. A statement can be placed anywhere within the statement field. It is customary to write program unit header statements starting in column 7 and to indent each statement in a unit's body by at least two more columns to improve program readability. Every line in a FORTRAN program, except for comment lines, must have an entry in the statement field.

Identification/Sequence Field

The last field of the FORTRAN coding form, consisting of columns 73 through 80, is always ignored by a FORTRAN compiler and is rarely used anymore. This field is a holdover from the early days of FORTRAN, when statements were typed on punched cards consisting of 80 columns. By typing either an identification or a sequence number in this field, a programmer could correctly reorder a deck of cards that was inadvertently dropped or shuffled. The advent of keyboard input has made the need for keeping cards in order, and hence for using the identification/sequence field, obsolete.

FORTRAN 90 Free-Form Source Coding

F90

In FORTRAN 90 free-form source coding is allowed. In free-form source coding each source line may contain from zero to 132 characters and there are no restrictions on where a statement may appear on a line. Although the free-form source code exists in addition to the fixed-form FORTRAN 77 source code, the forms may not be intermixed in the same program.

In free-form source coding spaces may be inserted freely within a line, except within keywords. Additionally, comments may appear anywhere on a line and are signified by an exclamation point. For example, the program header line

```
PROGRAM MAIN !THIS IS A PROGRAM HEADER LINE
```

contains the comment `THIS IS A PROGRAM HEADER LINE`. In all cases the comment extends to the end of the source line. If the first nonblank character on the line is an exclamation point, the line is called a comment line. A line containing all blanks is also considered a comment line in FORTRAN 90 and does not require the ! symbol.

The ampersand character, &, in FORTRAN 90 free-form source coding is used to indicate that the current line is continued on the next line that is not a comment line. Thus, in free-form source entry, the continuation mark is placed on the line being continued rather than on the continuation line, as in the fixed-form source code required in all earlier versions of FORTRAN. In no case can a statement in FORTRAN 90 have more than 39 continuation lines, and comment lines cannot be continued.

Statement Categories

You will have many statements at your disposal in constructing your FORTRAN source programs. All statements, however, belong to one of two broad categories: executable statements and nonexecutable statements. An *executable statement* causes some specific action to be performed by the computer. For example, a statement that tells the computer to add or subtract a number is an executable statement. A *nonexecutable statement* is a statement that describes some feature of either the program or its data but does not cause the computer to perform any action. An example of a nonexecutable statement is a program unit header. A header statement explicitly defines the beginning of a program unit but causes no specific action to be taken by the computer when the program is executed. As the various FORTRAN statements are introduced in the coming sections, we will point out which ones are executable and which are nonexecutable.

Skill Builder Exercises

Note for Exercises 1–3: Assume that the following are valid statements from a FORTRAN program. Using the FORTRAN fixed-form coding form, show how each statement should be placed on each line entered into the computer.

1.
```
PROGRAM MAIN
CALL GROPAY
CALL TAXES
CALL NETPAY
CALL DISPLAY
STOP
END
```

2.
```
* THIS PROGRAM CALCULATES THE AREA OF A CIRCLE
PROGRAM MAIN
* THE EXECUTABLE STATEMENTS IN THE PROGRAM ARE THE FOLLOWING
CALL RADIUS
CALL AREA
CALL OUTPUT
STOP
END
```

3.
```
* THIS PROGRAM DISPLAYS A FOUR-LINE POEM
PROGRAM MAIN
CALL POEM
STOP
END
SUBROUTINE POEM
* THE NUMBERS 10, 20, 30, AND 40 IN THE NEXT FOUR STATEMENTS
* ARE STATEMENT LABELS THAT BELONG IN THE LABEL FIELD
10 PRINT *, 'COMPUTERS, COMPUTERS EVERYWHERE'
20 PRINT *, ' AS FAR AS I CAN SEE'
30 PRINT *, 'I REALLY, REALLY LIKE THOSE THINGS'
40 PRINT *, ' OH JOY, OH JOY FOR ME'
RETURN
END
```

4.
```
PROGRAM MAIN
CALL TEST
STOP
END
SUBROUTINE TEST
* THE NUMBER 100 IN THE NEXT STATEMENT IS A
* STATEMENT LABEL THAT BELONGS IN THE LABEL FIELD
100 FORMAT(1X,A,1X,I5)
* THE 100 IN THE NEXT TWO STATEMENTS ARE PART OF THE
* STATEMENTS AND BELONG IN THE STATEMENT FIELD
PRINT 100, '30/5 = ', 30/5
PRINT 100, 'THE SUM OF 2 + 12 IS ', 2 + 12
RETURN
END
```

5.
```
PROGRAM MAIN
CALL TEST
STOP
END
SUBROUTINE TEST
* THE NUMBERS 100 AND 200 IN THE NEXT TWO STATEMENTS ARE
* LABELS THAT BELONG IN THE LABEL FIELD
100 FORMAT(1X,A,2X,A)
200 FORMAT(1X,I5,2X,F5.3)
* THE FOLLOWING TWO STATEMENTS ARE CALLED
* DECLARATION STATEMENTS
REAL VALUE
INTEGER COUNT
PRINT 100, 'VALUE', 'SIN'
PRINT 100, '-----', '---'
DO 10 COUNT = 1, 20
* FOR APPEARANCE ONLY, BEGIN THE NEXT TWO STATEMENTS
* IN COLUMN 11
VALUE = 0.1 * I
PRINT 200, VALUE, SIN(VALUE)
* THE 10 IN THE NEXT STATEMENT IS A STATEMENT NUMBER
10 CONTINUE
RETURN
END
```

Debugging Exercises

Note for Exercises 6-14: A program "bug" is an error in a program. Some of the most common bugs occur because of the misplacement of statements within the columns of each program line or the misspelling of keywords. Determine the bug in each of the following statements.

6.
```
123456789———Column Number ——————————————72 73——80
PROGRAM MAIN
```

7.
```
123456789———Column Number ——————————————72 73——80
       PROGAM MAIN
```

8.
```
123456789———Column Number ——————————————72 73——80
     *THIS IS A COMMENT LINE
```

9.
```
123456789———Column Number ——————————————72 73——80
       100 FORMAT(1X,I5)
```

10.
```
123456789———Column Number ——————————————72 73——80
                                         CALL REPORT
```

11.
```
123456789———Column Number ——————————————72 73——80
CALL REPORT
```

12.
```
123456789———Column Number ——————————————72 73——80
     10  CALL REPORT
```

13.
```
123456789————Column Number ————————————————————72 73——80
      C THE NEXT LINE IS AN INITIAL LINE OF A STATEMENT
    PRINT 100, 'THE AVERAGE IS',
      C AND THE NEXT LINE IS A CONTINUATION LINE
 1 AVERAGE
```

14.
```
123456789————Column Number ————————————————————72 73——80
      PRGRAM MAIN
      * THIS PROGRAM CALCULATES THE SINE OF AN
        ANGLE
      CALL SINE
      STOP
      END
```

Expanding Your Skills

15. Determine the procedures required to enter a program on your computer system. Also determine how to save the program and re-load it from the storage system connected to your computer.

16. Using the procedures determined in Exercise 15, enter and store the following program (make sure to enter the program in accordance with the FORTRAN coding form, as illustrated):

```
123456789————Column Number ——————————————————————72
      PROGRAM MAIN
        CALL DISPLY
        STOP
        END
      SUBROUTINE DISPLY
        PRINT *, 'THIS IS A MESSAGE'
        PRINT *, 'THAT WAS DISPLAYED UNDER THE DIRECTION'
        PRINT *, 'OF A FORTRAN PROGRAM'
        RETURN
        END
```

17a. Determine the procedures required to compile and execute a FORTRAN program on your system.

b. Using the procedures determined in Exercises 15 and 17a, enter, compile, and execute the program listed in Exercise 16. Make sure to enter the program in accordance with the FORTRAN fixed-form coding form.

18. Using the procedures in Exercises 15 and 17a, enter, compile, and execute the following program. Make sure to enter the program in accordance with the FORTRAN fixed-form coding form:

```
123456789————Column Number ——————————————————————72
      PROGRAM MAIN
        CALL SHOW
        STOP
        END
```

```
      SUBROUTINE SHOW
        REAL ANGLE
        INTEGER I
        PRINT *, 'ANGLE SIN(ANGLE)'
        PRINT *, '----- ----------'
        DO 10 I = 1, 20
          ANGLE = 0.1 * I
          PRINT *, ANGLE, SIN(ANGLE)
   10 CONTINUE
      RETURN
      END
```

1.4 Writing Complete Programs

It is now time to put together the information we have learned in the previous sections and write a complete, working program. A particularly easy program to write is one that displays a message on the standard system display device connected to the computer. Generally, this display device is either a video screen or a printer and is formally referred to as the computer's *standard output device.* Either a PRINT or a WRITE statement can be used to send a message to the standard output device. Both of these statements can be used for either *list-directed output,* in which the placement of the display is under the direction of the FORTRAN compiler, or *user-formatted output,* in which the programmer explicitly controls the positioning of the output display. In this section the list-directed forms of both the PRINT and the WRITE statement are introduced and used within the context of a complete program.

The List-Directed WRITE Statement

The general form of the list-directed WRITE statement is:

```
WRITE(unit number, *) list of items
```

The asterisk before the closing parenthesis in the WRITE statement tells the compiler to use its own default format for displaying the list of items in the statement. The unit number within the WRITE statement's parentheses designates where the message is to be displayed. Table 1-2 lists the unit numbers assigned to the standard output display device by the more commonly used FORTRAN compilers. A space has been left in the table for you to enter the unit numbers used by your compiler to identify your system's standard output device.

One of the simplest items to display on the standard system output device is a single message. A message is any combination of letters, numbers, and special characters (such as dollar signs, exclamation points, periods, etc.) enclosed within apostrophes ('), which are also called single quotes, to mark both the beginning and the end of the message. For example, on a DEC-VAX computer, the statement:

```
WRITE(6,*) 'HELLO THERE WORLD!'
```

is a command to display the message HELLO THERE WORLD! on the computer's standard output device. The equivalent statement for a Prime computer is:

```
WRITE(1,*) 'HELLO THERE WORLD!'
```

Table 1-2 Standard Output Device Unit Numbers

Compiler	Unit Number	Example
AT&T PHILON	6 or *	WRITE(6,*) 'HELLO' or WRITE(*,*) 'HELLO'
AUSTEC (R/M)	6 or *	WRITE(6,*) 'OKAY' or WRITE(*,*) 'OKAY'
DEC-VAX	5, 6 or *	WRITE(6,*) 'BYE' or WRITE(*,*) 'BYE'
DTSS	0, 6, or *	WRITE(0,*) 'BYE' or WRITE(6,*) 'BYE' or WRITE(*,*) 'BYE'
IBM	6 or *	WRITE(6,*) 'OKAY' or WRITE(*,*) 'OKAY'
MICROSOFT	6 or *	WRITE(6,*) 'BYE' or WRITE(*,*) 'BYE'
PRIME	1 or *	WRITE(1,*) 'HELLO' or WRITE(*,*) 'HELLO'
Your System:		

The asterisk (*) in both of these statements tells the compiler to use its own default format for creating the display. For messages, the default format is, as you might expect, to display the message exactly as it is written within the apostrophes. (In Chapter 2 we will see how to replace the asterisk with a reference to an explicit user-defined format for controlling the output display.)

More formally, a message in FORTRAN is referred to as a *literal* because it contains literal information consisting of any sequence of numbers, letters, and special characters, such as the dollar sign ($). Literals are also called *character constants*, and the two terms are used interchangeably.

Except for messages within apostrophes and certain specific cases that will be noted as they occur, FORTRAN ignores all *white space* (any combination of blank spaces and tabs). Therefore, blank spaces may be freely inserted within a statement to improve its appearance. For example, all three of the following WRITE statements produce the same result.

```
WRITE(6,*) 'HELLO'
WRITE(6,*)'HELLO'
WRITE (6, *) 'HELLO'
```

Page 24

Comparative Charts for Different Compilers. Throughout this text, "I have tried to allow for differences between the different computing environments in which FORTRAN can be taught. As a result, I have displayed these differences in a table whenever a significant variation seemed to occur."

hough the spaces separating the parentheses, unit number, comma, asterisk, sage are optional and have no effect on the output, spaces within the apos- lo affect the display. For example, the statement:

```
WRITE(6,*) 'HELLO'
```

a different display than the statement:

```
WRITE(6,*) 'H E L L O'
```

st case the message HELLO is displayed, with no spaces between the letters, second case the message H E L L O is displayed, with a space separating r from the next.

v let's put this all together into a working FORTRAN program that can be ur computer. Consider Program 1-1:*

```
Column Number ——————————————————————72

Y

SPLY
'HELLO THERE WORLD!'
```

that Program 1-1 follows the program structure introduced in the last program has only one main program unit, all header lines and program nts are contained within columns 7 through 72, and each statement is ine by itself. It also conforms to a modular program structure where the am unit is used to call other program units that produce the required the only result produced by Program 1-1 is a message, only a single needed. When Program 1-1 is compiled and executed, the message is ayed on your terminal, as shown in Figure 1-18.

ram 1-1 is our first complete, working program, we will analyze it in detail to lisplay is produced. The first program unit in Program 1-1 is a MAIN unit, s the start of the FORTRAN program. In this program the MAIN unit is used utine named DISPLY. Here, the name of the called subroutine is selected by ner according to the rules presented in Section 1.2 for symbolic names. end of the MAIN program unit is a single SUBROUTINE program unit. The ader line is:

```
SUBROUTINE DISPLY
```

of the subroutine consists of the three statements

```
WRITE(6,*) 'HELLO THERE WORLD!'
RETURN
END
```

---

ter, the unit number 6 in the WRITE statement must be replaced by 1.

```
HELLO THERE WORLD!
```

Figure 1-18 The Output of Program 1-1

The WRITE statement in this subroutine causes the message HELLO THERE WORLD! to be displayed, the RETURN statement returns control to the MAIN unit, and the END statement terminates the subroutine. Although the display produced by the DISPLY subroutine is extremely simple, it does illustrate the correct structure of a modular program using a single subroutine.*

Although Program 1-1 displays only a single message, we can add additional WRITE statements within the subroutine to display more than one message. See if you can read Program 1-2 and determine what it does.**

Program 1-2

```
123456789 —— Column Number ——————————72
      PROGRAM MAIN
        CALL TELLIT
        STOP
        END
*
      SUBROUTINE TELLIT
        WRITE(6,*) '          WELCOME TO THE GUESS A NUMBER GAME PROGRAM'
        WRITE(6,*) 'I WILL THINK OF A NUMBER BETWEEN 1 AND 100.'
        WRITE(6,*) '  YOU WILL HAVE SEVEN TRIES TO GUESS THE NUMBER.'
        WRITE(6,*) 'AFTER EACH GUESS I WILL TELL YOU IF YOU WERE'
        WRITE(6,*) 'EITHER HIGH, LOW, OR GUESSED THE CORRECT NUMBER.'
        WRITE(6,*) '                   HAVE FUN AND GOOD LUCK!'
        RETURN
        END
```

When program 1-2 is compiled and run, the following message is displayed.

```
          WELCOME TO THE GUESS A NUMBER GAME PROGRAM
I WILL THINK OF A NUMBER BETWEEN 1 AND 100.
  YOU WILL HAVE SEVEN TRIES TO GUESS THE NUMBER.
AFTER EACH GUESS I WILL TELL YOU IF YOU WERE
EITHER HIGH, LOW, OR GUESSED THE CORRECT NUMBER.
                   HAVE FUN AND GOOD LUCK!
```

* If the RETURN statement is omitted, the subroutine's END statement causes a return to the MAIN unit.

** Again, if this program is to be run on a Prime computer, the unit number in the WRITE statements must be changed to a 1.

WRITE and FORMAT Statements. "The list-directed WRITE statement is introduced in Chapter 1 and is used in preference to the PRINT statement throughout the text. This provides for an early introduction to output unit numbers, which is easily transferable to file writing and is not possible with the PRINT statement. Formatted output is also introduced early, in Chapter 2, which provides students with the ability to both think about and create professional looking output."

As you might have guessed, each WRITE statement in the TELLIT subroutine causes a new line to be displayed. Since the subroutine has six WRITE statements, six individual lines are produced. In each case the message in the WRITE statement is displayed exactly as it appears within the enclosing apostrophes, including spaces. Thus, the leading spaces in the first, third, and sixth messages are retained in the displayed output.

Also notice the sequence in which Program 1-2 is executed. The program begins with the MAIN program unit's nonexecutable program header statement and continues sequentially, statement by statement, until the STOP statement is encountered. The CALL statement transfers control to the TELLIT subroutine, which consists of seven executable statements. The statements within the body of this unit are also executed sequentially, with each WRITE statement producing a single line of output. The next-to-last statement in the subroutine is a RETURN statement, which terminates the subroutine's execution and causes control to be passed back to the MAIN unit. The remaining statements in the MAIN program unit are a STOP and an END statement. The STOP statement transfers control back to the computer's operating system. The END statement signals the end of the MAIN program unit for compilation purposes.*

Altering the placement of any of the WRITE statements in the TELLIT subroutine automatically alters the display produced by the complete program. For example, if the statements in Program 1-2 were written in the order shown in Program1-3, the output shown in Figure 1-19 would be produced.

Although all of the messages illustrated have used only uppercase letters, this is not required in FORTRAN. Messages can contain any characters, including lowercase letters, percent signs (%), ampersands (&), exclamation points (!), and any other symbol supported by your computer. These characters are allowed within messages because the compiler attributes no significance to them other than to store and display them exactly as they appear in the message. Messages can even include an apostrophe, as long as we indicate that the apostrophe is to be displayed and does not signify the end of the message. This is done by using two consecutive apostrophes. For example, the statement:

```
WRITE(6,*) 'Joe''s grade'
```

* Although a MAIN program unit may contain both a STOP and END statement at the end of the unit, the STOP statement is not required immediately before an END statement on most FORTRAN 77 and FORTRAN 90 compilers, as it was in earlier FORTRAN versions. In these earlier versions, a STOP statement was the last statement actually compiled and translated into machine language. The END statement, in these earlier versions, was a nonexecutable statement that marked the physical end of the program to the compiler and told the compiler to terminate reading any more statements and begin the actual compilation. In FORTRAN 77 and FORTRAN 90, the END statement is an executable one that performs both functions; it informs the compiler of the program's physical end and gets translated into machine language. As such, the STOP statement is no longer required immediately before the END statement. For this reason, the convention adopted by this book will be to discontinue using a STOP statement immediately before an END statement in all subsequent MAIN program units. However, if your computer displays either an error or warning message when the STOP statement is omitted, continue to include them in your programs.

Also note that all program units may contain several STOP statements, whereas the END statement must always be the last statement in all program units. For example, a STOP statement might be located within a program unit to halt execution when a detectable error is encountered by the program. The use of a STOP statement in this context requires the selection statements described in Chapter 6.

Program 1-3

```
123456789 —— Column Number ——————————————————————————————————72
      PROGRAM MAIN
        CALL TELLIT
        END
*
      SUBROUTINE TELLIT
        WRITE(6,*) '                 HAVE FUN AND GOOD LUCK!'
        WRITE(6,*) 'I WILL THINK OF A NUMBER BETWEEN 1 AND 100.'
        WRITE(6,*) '  YOU WILL HAVE SEVEN TRIES TO GUESS THE NUMBER.'
        WRITE(6,*) 'AFTER EACH GUESS I WILL TELL YOU IF YOU WERE'
        WRITE(6,*) 'EITHER HIGH, LOW, OR GUESSED THE CORRECT NUMBER.'
        WRITE(6,*) '          WELCOME TO THE GUESS A NUMBER GAME PROGRAM'
        RETURN
       END
```

```
                 HAVE FUN AND GOOD LUCK!
 I WILL THINK OF A NUMBER BETWEEN 1 AND 100.
   YOU WILL HAVE SEVEN TRIES TO GUESS THE NUMBER.
 AFTER EACH GUESS I WILL TELL YOU IF YOU WERE
 EITHER HIGH, LOW, OR GUESSED THE CORRECT NUMBER.
          WELCOME TO THE GUESS A NUMBER GAME PROGRAM
```

Figure 1-19 The Output From Program 1-3

produces the display:

```
Joe's grade
```

Finally, it is possible to use the WRITE statements with no output. For example, the statement:

```
WRITE(6,*)
```

causes a blank line to be displayed. Thus, the sequence of statements:

```
WRITE(6,*) 'THE SLOPE OF THE LINE'
WRITE(6,*)
WRITE(6,*) '     Y = 5X + 3'
WRITE(6,*)
WRITE(6,*) '       IS 5.'
```

causes the following double-spaced display:

```
THE SLOPE OF THE LINE
      Y = 5X + 3
        IS 5.
```

The List-Directed PRINT Statement

The unit number in a WRITE statement permits output to be written to units other than the standard output display device. For example, the display can be written directly to a disk or tape unit if the appropriate unit number is used. The routing of results to the standard output device is so common, however, that all FORTRAN 77 and FORTRAN 90 compilers, including those listed in Table 1-1, provide an alternative form for the list-directed WRITE statement. This form is the list-directed PRINT statement, which has the general form:

```
PRINT *, list of items
```

For example, the statement:

```
PRINT *, 'HELLO THERE WORLD!'
```

causes the message `HELLO THERE WORLD!` to be displayed on the standard output device. In this statement the term `PRINT *,` is equivalent to the term `WRITE(1,*)` for Prime computers and can be used in place of the term `WRITE(6,*)` for the other computers listed in Table 1-1. Since, by definition, the PRINT statement can only direct its display to the standard output device, an explicit unit number designating the standard output device is unnecessary. Program 1-4 uses this PRINT statement in place of the WRITE statement used in Program 1-1. Both programs produce the output shown in Figure 1-18.

Program 1-4

```
123456789 ——— Column Number ———————————————72
      PROGRAM MAIN
        CALL DISPLY
        END
      SUBROUTINE DISPLY
        PRINT *, 'HELLO THERE WORLD!'
        END
```

As with the WRITE statement, the PRINT statement can be used to produce blank lines. For example, the statement:

```
PRINT *
```

causes a blank line to be displayed (note that there is no comma after the asterisk). Finally, on all computer systems the statement:

```
PRINT *, 'message in here'
```

is equivalent to the statement:

```
WRITE(*,*) 'message in here'
```

As before, the asterisk in the PRINT statement is equivalent to the second asterisk in the WRITE statement and selects the compiler's default formats for the placement of the display. The first asterisk in the WRITE statement is a unit designator (see Table 1-2) that selects the standard output device assigned by the system for output display. For example, on a DEC-VAX computer the following three statements all produce the same display:

```
PRINT *, 'HELLO THERE WORLD!'
WRITE(*,*) 'HELLO THERE WORLD!'
WRITE(6,*) 'HELLO THERE WORLD!'
```

In the remainder of the book we will use the WRITE statement almost exclusively for output since this statement can be carried directly over to writing to files (introduced in Chapter 5) or any other output device, which cannot be done with the PRINT statement.

On Using One or More Modules

The number and size of each module in a program depend, respectively, on the number of tasks required by the program and the complexity of each individual task. Even for extremely simple programs it is important to practice writing modular FORTRAN programs to develop the facility of "thinking modular." This ability will benefit the programmer when much larger programs requiring numerous subroutines and more involved tasks must be designed.

By definition, however, modular does not mean that a program must contain a subroutine; it simply means that each program consists of one or more modules appropriate to solving the task at hand. For many programs a single module consisting of only a MAIN program unit is sufficient. This is especially true when a program is written to illustrate a specific feature of the FORTRAN language.

Using only a single program unit, a FORTRAN program has the form:

```
123456789 ——— Column Number ——————————————————72
      PROGRAM name
        valid FORTRAN statements in here
        END
```

For example, Program 1-4, which displays a single message, can be written in this form as:

```
123456789 ——— Column Number ——————————————————72
      PROGRAM MAIN
        WRITE(6,*) 'HELLO THERE WORLD!'
        END
```

Notice that this form of the program is obtained by removing the second, third, and fourth lines in Program 1-4. For the remainder of the text, programs that are used to illustrate individual features of the FORTRAN language will adhere to a single program unit format, while more complex programming tasks will be coded using multiple program units.

Additional Exercises for Chapter 1

Skill Builder Exercises

1a. Using either PRINT or WRITE statements, write a FORTRAN program that calls a subroutine to print your name on one line, your street address on a second line, and your city, state, and zip code on the third line.

b. Compile and run the program you have written for Exercise 1a on a computer. (Note: To do this, you must understand the procedures for entering, compiling, and running a FORTRAN program on the particular computer you are using.)

2a. Using either PRINT or WRITE statements, write a FORTRAN program that calls a subroutine to print out the following:

```
THE COSECANT OF AN ANGLE
  IS EQUAL TO ONE OVER
     THE SINE OF THE SAME ANGLE.
```

b. Compile and run the program you have written for Exercise 2a.

3a. How many PRINT or WRITE statements should be used to display the following?

```
DEGREES       RADIANS
    0          0.0000
   90          1.5708
  180          3.1416
  270          4.7124
  360          6.2832
```

b. Write a complete FORTRAN program to produce the output illustrated in Exercise 3a.

c. Compile and run the program you have written for Exercise 3b on a computer.

Expanding Your Skills

4. When a PRINT or WRITE statement is used to display a message, the first character in the message is displayed at the beginning of a new line. This character positioning actually represents two distinct operations. What are they?

5a. Most computer operating systems provide the capability for redirecting output intended for the standard output device to some other device. For example, if the standard output device is a video screen, redirection to either a printer or directly to a floppy or hard disk file may be possible. Determine if your computer supports this redirection capability.

b. If your computer supports output redirection, run the program written for Exercise 2a using this feature. Have the display produced by your program redirected to a disk file named DEGREE.

c. If the standard output device for your computer is a video screen, and your system supports output redirection to a printer, run the program written for Exercise 2a using this redirection feature.

1.5 Common Programming Errors

Part of learning any programming language is making the elementary mistakes made by most beginning students. These mistakes can be quite frustrating, since each language seems to have its own set of traps waiting for the unwary. Following are the more common errors made when initially programming in FORTRAN.

1. Starting a statement in either column 1 or column 6 rather than in column 7 or beyond.

2. Continuing a statement beyond column 72. For example, the statement:

```
1234567 ——————— Column Number ————————————————————————72 73 —— 80
      WRITE(6,*) 'THIS IS A WONDERFUL DAY BECAUSE THE SUN IS OUT'
```

   causes a compiler error message. The message is generated because the statement has no closing apostrophe (recall that characters typed in columns 73 through 80 are ignored by the compiler).
3. Using lowercase rather than uppercase letters. (Some compilers permit lowercase letters. In case-insensitive compilers, the lowercase letter can be used in place of its corresponding uppercase equivalent; in case-sensitive compilers, lowercase letters are recognized as distinct from their uppercase equivalents.)
4. Inadvertently misspelling keywords such as PRINT and WRITE: for example, typing PINT instead of PRINT.
5. Omitting the comma after the asterisk in a PRINT statement (except when a blank line is printed using the statement PRINT *).
6. Continuing a comment line over two lines without placing either an asterisk or a C in column 1 of the second line. For example, the comment:

```
123456789 ——————— Column Number
* THIS COMMENT WILL CAUSE AN ERROR BECAUSE IT INCORRECTLY EXTENDS
OVER TWO LINES
```

   results in a FORTRAN error message. This comment is correct when written as:

```
123456789 ——————— Column Number
* THIS COMMENT IS NOW VALID EVEN
*   THOUGH IT EXTENDS OVER TWO LINES
```

7. Forgetting the keyword SUBROUTINE in a subroutine's header line.
8. Incorrectly typing the letter O for the number zero (0), or vice versa.
9. Incorrectly typing the lowercase letter l or the uppercase letter I for the number 1, or vice versa.

The first seven of these errors are initially the most common but tend to diminish as the programmer gains experience. The last two errors are more persistent and plague even experienced programmers. We suggest that you write a program and specifically introduce each of these errors, one at a time, to see what error messages are produced by your compiler. Later, when these error messages appear due to inadvertent errors in your programming, you will have had experience in understanding the messages and correcting the errors.

1.6 Things to Remember

1. An *algorithm* is a step-by-step procedure that describes how a computation or task is to be performed.
2. A computer program is a description of an algorithm written in a language that can be used by a computer.

3. FORTRAN provides three commonly used types of program units: the MAIN, SUBROUTINE, and FUNCTION types. Each of these unit types performs a particular type of task.
4. A complete FORTRAN program consists of one or more program units. One of these program units must be a MAIN program unit. The MAIN unit is also called a driver unit when it is primarily used to call other program units.
5. Program units have a header line and a program unit body. The header line includes a header keyword that identifies the type of program unit and contains a user-selected name for the unit. The header keywords for MAIN and SUBROUTINE program units are PROGRAM and SUBROUTINE, respectively. The last statement in a program unit is the keyword END placed on a line by itself.
6. SUBROUTINE and FUNCTION program units are referred to as *subprogram* units.
7. All program unit statements, including the header line, must comply with the FORTRAN coding form illustrated below:

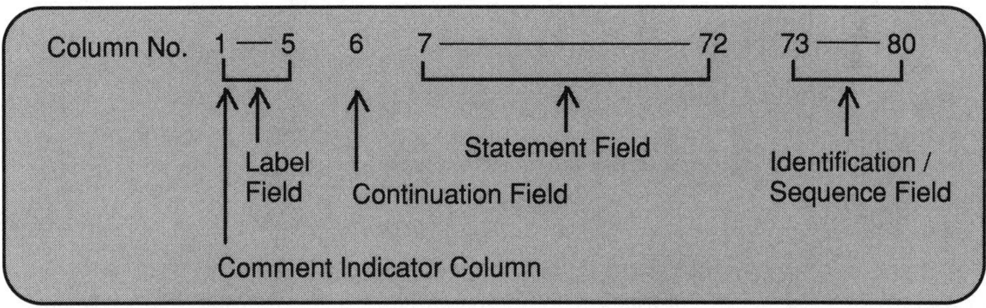

8. If an asterisk (*) or the letter C is placed in column 1, the line becomes a comment line. Comment lines can be placed anywhere in a program unit and are used to clarify either the purpose of the program unit itself or individual sections and lines of code within the program unit.
9. A FORTRAN statement can be continued across multiple lines. When this is done, a nonblank character other than 0 must be placed in column 6 of each continuation line. In no case may multiple statements be placed on the same line.
10. A computer's *standard output device* is the default display device (video terminal or printer) used by your system for the display of text.
11. In *list-directed* output, the placement of the display produced by either a WRITE or a PRINT statement is determined by the compiler's default format specifications.
12. Both PRINT and WRITE statements can be used to display messages on a computer's standard output device. The form of the list-directed PRINT statement for displaying messages is:

```
PRINT *, 'message'
```

The form of the list-directed WRITE statement for displaying messages is:

```
WRITE(unit number, *) 'message'
```

where each compiler has its own unit number for determining where the message is to be displayed. IBM, Prime, and DEC-VAX compilers use unit numbers 6, 1, and either 5 or 6, respectively, as their standard output device numbers. An asterisk may also be used in place of the unit number to designate the standard output device.

The message displayed by PRINT and WRITE statements can include any character supported by your computer. Two consecutive apostrophes ('') are used to designate a single apostrophe within a message.

13. The statement `PRINT *` causes a blank line to be displayed on the standard output device. The equivalent WRITE statement is `WRITE(n,*)`, where *n* is the unit number assigned by your system to its standard output device.

14. In a modular program each task performed by the program is accomplished using an individual program unit. The simplest modular FORTRAN program consists of a MAIN program unit only. The program has the form:

```
123456789 ———— Column Number ————————————————72
      PROGRAM name
        valid FORTRAN statements in here
        END
```

An example of such a program is:

```
123456789 ———— Column Number ————————————————72
      PROGRAM SHOW
        WRITE(6,*) 'HELLO THERE WORLD!'
        END
```

An example of a modular program that uses one subroutine in addition to the required MAIN unit is:

```
123456789 ———— Column Number ————————————————72
      PROGRAM MAIN
        CALL DISPLY
        END
      SUBROUTINE DISPLY
        WRITE(6,*) 'HELLO THERE WORLD!'
        END
```

Both programs display the message `HELLO THERE WORLD!` on the computer's standard output device. The latter program illustrates how a subroutine is called and adheres to the strict usage of a MAIN program unit as a *driver* unit that is only used to call other program units.

15. All statements in a program unit are executed sequentially, one after another, unless a statement causing an alteration of this normal sequence is encountered. There is no "look ahead" capability, where one statement can anticipate the result of another statement later in the program unit.

1.7 A Closer Look: Computer Hardware and Storage

All computers, from large supercomputers costing millions of dollars to smaller desktop personal computers, must perform a minimum set of functions and provide the capability to:

1. accept input
2. display output
3. store information in a logically consistent format (traditionally binary)

4. perform arithmetic and logic operations on either the input or stored data
5. monitor, control, and direct the overall operation and sequencing of the system

Figure 1-20 illustrates the computer hardware components that support these capabilities. Specifically, this hardware consists of arithmetic and logic, control, memory, and input/output units.

The *arithmetic and logic unit* (*ALU*) performs all the arithmetic and logic functions, such as addition, subtraction, and so on, provided by the system.

The *control unit* directs and monitors the overall operation of the computer. It keeps track of where in memory the next instruction resides, issues the signals needed to both read data from and write data to other units in the system, and executes all instructions.

The *memory unit* stores information in a logically consistent format. Typically, both instructions and data are stored in memory, usually in separate and distinct areas.

The *input* and *output* (*I/O*) *units* provide access to and from the computer. These units are the interface to which peripheral devices such as keyboards, cathode ray screens, printers, and card readers are attached.

In the first commercially available computers of the 1950s, all hardware units were built using relays and vacuum tubes. The resulting computers were extremely large pieces of equipment, each capable of making thousands of calculations per second and costing millions of dollars.

With the introduction of transistors in the 1960s, both the size and the cost of computer hardware were reduced. The transistor was approximately one-twentieth the size of its vacuum tube counterpart. The transistor's small size allowed manufacturers to combine the arithmetic and logic unit with the control unit into a single new unit. This combined unit is called the *central processing unit* (*CPU*). The combination of the ALU and control units into one CPU made sense because a majority of control signals generated by a program are directed to the ALU in response to arithmetic and logic instructions within the program. Combining the ALU with the control unit simplified the interface between these two units and provided improved processing speed.

The mid-1960s saw the introduction of integrated circuits (ICs), which resulted in still another significant reduction in the space required for a CPU. Initially,

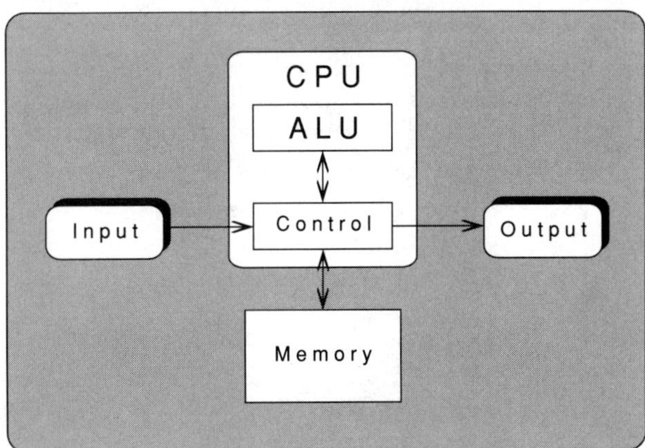

Figure 1-20 Basic Hardware Units of a Computer

integrated circuits were manufactured with up to 100 transistors on a single 1-cm^2 chip of silicon. Such devices are referred to as small-scale integrated (SSI) circuits. Current versions of these chips contain from hundreds of thousands to over a million transistors and are referred to as very large-scale integrated (VLSI) chips.

VLSI chip technology has provided the means of transforming the giant computers of the 1950s into today's desktop personal computers. Each individual unit required to form a computer (CPU, memory, and I/O) is now manufactured on an individual VLSI chip, and the single-chip CPU is referred to as a *microprocessor*. Figure 1-21 illustrates how the chips are connected internally within current personal computers, such as IBM PCs.

Concurrent with the remarkable reduction in computer hardware size have been an equally dramatic decrease in cost and increase in processing speeds. Equivalent computer hardware that cost over $1 million in 1950 can now be purchased for less than $500. If the same reductions had occurred in the automobile industry, for example, a Rolls-Royce could now be purchased for $10! The processing speeds of current computers have also increased by a factor of a thousand over their 1950s predecessors, with the computational speeds of current machines being measured in both millions of instructions per second (MIPS) and billions of instructions per second (BIPS).

Computer Storage

It would be very convenient if a computer stored numbers and letters in its memory and arithmetic and logic units the way that people do. The number 126, for example, would then be stored as 126, and the letter A stored as the letter A. Unfortunately, because of their physical components, computers store information differently than people do.

The smallest and most basic data item in a computer is called a bit. Physically, a bit is really a switch that can be either open or closed. By convention, the open and closed positions of each switch are represented as a 0 and a 1, respectively.

A single bit that can represent the values 0 and 1 by itself has limited usefulness. All computers, therefore, group a set number of bits together for both storage and transmission. The grouping of eight bits to form a larger unit is an almost universal computer standard. Such groups are commonly referred to as bytes. A single byte consisting of eight bits, where each bit is either a 0 or a 1, can represent any one of 256 distinct patterns. These consist of the pattern 00000000 (all eight switches open), the pattern 11111111 (all eight switches closed), and all possible

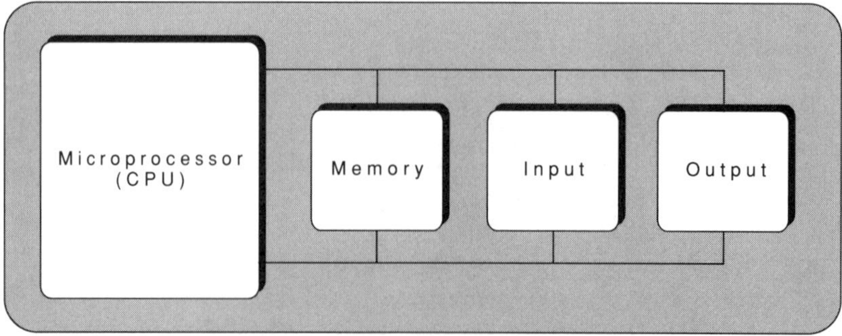

Figure 1-21 VLSI Chip Connections for a Desktop Computer

combinations of 0s and 1s in between. Each of these patterns can be used to represent either a letter of the alphabet; other single characters, such as a dollar sign, comma, and so on; a single digit; or numbers containing more than one digit. The patterns of 0s and 1s used to represent letters, single digits, and other single characters are called *character codes* (two such codes, called the ASCII and EBCDIC codes, are presented in Section 2.1). The patterns used to store numbers are called *number codes*, one of which is presented below.

Two's Complement Numbers

The most common number code for storing integer values inside a computer is called the *two's complement* representation. Using this code, the integer equivalent of any bit pattern, such as 10001101, is easy to determine and can be found for either positive or negative integers with no change in the conversion method. For convenience, we will assume byte-sized bit patterns consisting of a set of eight bits each, although the procedure carries over directly to larger-size bit patterns.

The easiest way to determine the integer represented by each bit pattern is to first construct a simple device called a value box. Figure 1-22 illustrates such a box for a single byte. Mathematically, each value in the box illustrated in Figure 1-22 represents an increasing power of two. Since two's complement numbers must be capable of representing both positive and negative integers, the leftmost position, in addition to having the largest absolute magnitude, also has a negative sign.

Conversion of any binary number, for example, 10001101, simply requires inserting the bit pattern in the value box and adding the values having ones under them. Thus, as illustrated in Figure 1-23, the bit pattern 10001101 represents the integer number –115.

The value box can also be used in reverse, to convert a base 10 integer number into its equivalent binary bit pattern. Some conversions, in fact, can be made by inspection. For example, the base 10 number –125 is obtained by adding 3 to –128. Thus, the binary representation of –125 is 10000011, which equals –128 + 2 + 1. Similarly, the two's complement representation of the number 40 is 00101000, which is 32 plus 8.

Although the value box conversion method is deceptively simple, it is directly related to the underlying mathematical basis of two's complement binary numbers. The original name of the two's complement code was the weighted-sign code, which correlates directly to the value box. As the name *weighted sign* implies, each bit position has a weight, or value, of two raised to a power and a sign. The signs of all bits except the leftmost bit are positive, and the sign of the leftmost bit is negative.

In reviewing the value box, it is evident that any two's complement binary number with a leading 1 represents a negative number, and any bit pattern with a leading 0 represents a positive number. Using the value box, it is easy to determine the most positive and negative values capable of being stored. The most negative

-128	64	32	16	8	4	2	1

Figure 1-22 An Eight-Bit Value Box

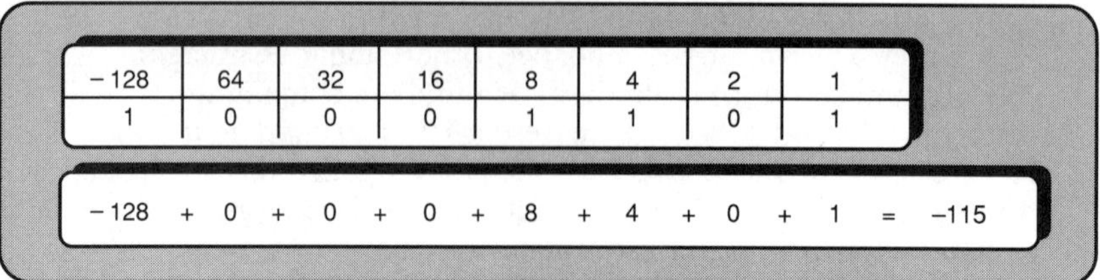

Figure 1-23 Converting 10001101 to a Base 10 Number

value that can be stored in a single byte is the decimal number –128, which has the bit pattern 10000000. Any other nonzero bit will simply add a positive amount to the number. Additionally, it is clear that a positive number must have a 0 as its leftmost bit. From this you can see that the largest positive eight-bit two's complement number is 01111111, or 127.

Words and Addresses

One or more bytes may themselves be grouped into larger units, called *words*, which facilitate faster and more extensive data access. For example, retrieving a word consisting of four bytes from a computer's memory results in more information than would be obtained by retrieving a word consisting of a single byte. Such a retrieval is also considerably faster than four individual byte retrievals. This increase in speed and capacity, however, is achieved by an increase in the computer's cost and complexity.

Early personal computers, such as the Apple IIe and Commodore machines, internally stored and transmitted words consisting of single bytes. AT&T 6300 and IBM PC/XTs use word sizes consisting of two bytes; Digital Equipment, Data General, Prime, and other minicomputers store and process words consisting of four bytes each. Supercomputers, such as the CRAY-1 and Control Data 7000, have six- and eight-byte words, respectively.

The number of bytes in a word determines the maximum and minimum values that can be represented by the word. Table 1-3 lists these values for 1-, 2-, and 4-byte words (each of the values listed can be derived using 8-, 16-, and 32-bit value boxes, respectively).

Table 1-3 Integer Values and Word Size

Word size	Maximum integer value	Minimum integer value
1 byte	127	–128
2 bytes	32,767	–32,768
4 bytes	2,147,483,647	–2,147,483,648

In addition to representing integer values, computers must also store and transmit numbers containing decimal points. Such numbers are mathematically referred to as real numbers. The codes used for real numbers, which are more complex than those used for integers, are presented in Appendix D.

2 Data and Operations

Chapter Two

2.1 Data Constants and Arithmetic Operations

2.2 Variables and Declaration Statements

2.3 Assignment Statements

2.4 Formatted Output

2.5 Top-Down Program Development

2.6 Applications

2.7 Common Programming Errors

2.8 Things to Remember

2.9 A Closer Look: Errors, Testing, and Debugging

FORTRAN programs can process different types of data in different ways. For example, calculating the trajectory of a rocket requires that mathematical operations be performed using numerical data, while sorting a list of names requires comparison operations using alphabetic data.

In this chapter we introduce the basic types of data that can be used in FORTRAN programs, with emphasis on numerical data and the mathematical operations (addition, subtraction, multiplication, division, etc.) that can be performed on it. Information is also presented for displaying the results of these calculations using the PRINT and WRITE statements. This information provides us with the ability to write complete FORTRAN programs for elementary engineering and scientific applications.

2.1 Data Constants and Arithmetic Operations

FORTRAN recognizes six basic types of data: integers, real numbers, character strings, logical values, double precision numbers, and complex numbers. The first four of these data types, expressed as constants, are described below. Complex data and double precision data are presented in Chapter 10.

Integer Constants

An *integer constant* in FORTRAN is any positive or negative number without a decimal point. Examples of valid integer constants are:

6 –12 +35 1000 186 –6755821 +42

As these examples illustrate, integers may either be signed (have a leading + or – sign) or unsigned (no leading + or – sign). Commas, decimal points, or special symbols, such as the dollar sign, are not allowed. Examples of invalid integer constants are:

$187.62 3,532 4. 8,634,941 2,371.98 +7.0

The largest (most positive) and smallest (most negative) integer values that can be used in a program depend on the amount of storage each computer sets aside for integer values. For IBM 370, DEC-VAX, and Prime computers the most positive integer allowed is 2147483647, and the most negative integer is –2147483648.*

Real Constants

A *real constant* is any number that contains a decimal point. Examples of real constants are:

+12.125 7. –8.3 0.0 1351.76 0.66 –6.67 +5.

Notice that the numbers 7., 0.0, and +5. are classified as real constants in FORTRAN, while the same numbers written without a decimal point (7, 0, +5) are classified as integer constants.

The distinction between real and integer constants is made because of the different internal representations that computers use to store these data types. An integer requires storing of the sign and magnitude of the number; a real number requires storing of the sign, integer, and fractional parts of the number. (The interested reader can refer to Appendix D for a more complete explanation of the various internal data representations used for real values.)

Although real numbers can be signed or unsigned, special symbols, such as the dollar sign and the comma, are not permitted. Examples of invalid real constants that contain such special characters are:

5,326.25 6,459. $10.29

* It is interesting to note that in all cases the magnitude of the most negative integer allowed is always one more than the magnitude of the most positive integer. This is because of the method most commonly used to represent integers, called two's complement representation. (For an explanation of two's complement representation see Section 1.7.)

Exponential Notation

Real numbers can be written in an exponential notation, which is useful in expressing both very large and very small numbers in compact form. The following examples illustrate how numbers with decimals can be expressed in exponential notation.

Decimal Notation	Exponential Notation
1837.	1.837E3
57641.	5.7641E4
234.26	2.3426E2
.00849	8.49E-3
.000265	2.65E-4

In exponential notation, the letter E stands for exponent. The number following the E represents a power of 10 and indicates the number of places the decimal point should be moved to obtain the standard decimal value. The decimal point is moved to the right if the number after the E is positive. It is moved to the left if the number after the E is negative. For example, the E2 in the number 2.3426E2 means move the decimal point two places to the right, so that the number represented is 234.26. The E-3 in the number 8.49E–3 means move the decimal point three places to the left, so that 8.49E–3 is equal to .00849.

Character Constants

The third basic data constant recognized by FORTRAN is the character constant. This data constant is also referred to as either a message, string, or literal and was introduced in Chapter 1. To review, a character constant consists of one or more characters that are enclosed within apostrophes (single quotes). Examples of valid character constants are:

```
'A'
'**&!##!!'
'$3,256.22'
'VELOCITY'
'HELLO THERE WORLD!'
'THE SINE OF THE ANGLE IS:'
```

The number of characters within a character constant is the *length* of the constant. For example, the length of the character constant '$3,256.22' is nine, and the length of the character constant 'A' is one. If an apostrophe is required within a character constant, two apostrophes are used. For example, the string 'DR. JOHNSON''S DOG' is a character constant of length 17 consisting of the characters:

```
DR.(space)JOHNSON'S(space)DOG
```

Character constants are typically represented in a computer using either the ASCII or the EBCDIC code. ASCII, pronounced "As-Key," is an acronym for American Standard Code for Information Interchange. EBCDIC, pronounced "Ebb-sih-dick," is an acronym for Extended Binary Coded Decimal Interchange Code. Each of these codes assigns individual characters to a specific pattern of 0s and 1s. Table 2-1 lists the correspondence between bit patterns and the uppercase letters of the alphabet used by the ASCII and EBCDIC codes.

Using Table 2-1, we can determine how the character constant 'SMITH', for example, is stored inside a computer that uses the ASCII character code. Using the ASCII code, this sequence of characters requires five bytes of storage (one byte for each letter) and would be stored as illustrated in Figure 2-1.

Logical Constants

There are only two logical data values in FORTRAN. These are the logical constants:

`.TRUE.` and `.FALSE.`

Table 2-1 The ASCII and EBCDIC Uppercase Letter Codes

Letter	ASCII code	EBCDIC code	Letter	ASCII code	EBCDIC code
A	01000001	11000001	N	01001110	11010101
B	01000010	11000010	O	01001111	11010110
C	01000011	11000011	P	01010000	11010111
D	01000100	11000100	Q	01010001	11011000
E	01000101	11000101	R	01010010	11011001
F	01000110	11000110	S	01010011	11100010
G	01000111	11000111	T	01010100	11100011
H	01001000	11001000	U	01010101	11100100
I	01001001	11001001	V	01010110	11100101
J	01001010	11010001	W	01010111	11100110
K	01001011	11010010	X	01011000	11100111
L	01001100	11010011	Y	01011001	11101000
M	01001101	11010100	Z	01011010	11101001

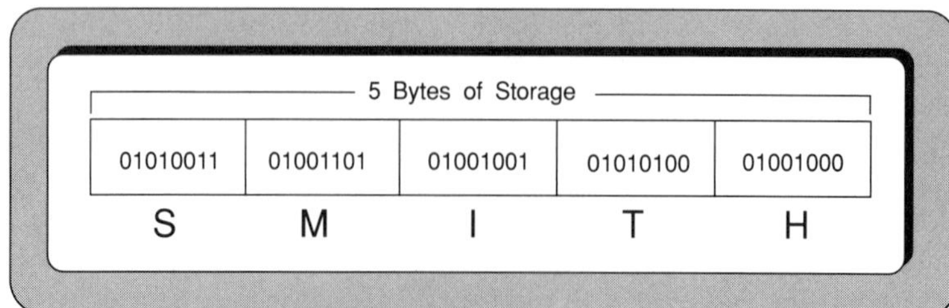

Figure 2-1 The Letters SMITH Stored Inside a Computer Using the ASCII Code

The periods surrounding the words TRUE and FALSE are part of the constants. Without the periods the words become symbolic names rather than logical values.

Logical data is useful in programming because all computers have the ability to select a course of action based on the state of a programmer-specified condition. Any condition has one of two possible outcomes: either the condition is satisfied, or it is not. In computer and mathematical terms, a condition that is satisfied is considered to be true; a condition that is not satisfied is considered to be false. The two logical constants in FORTRAN correspond to these outcomes and are used extensively in programs that incorporate decision-making statements.

Arithmetic Operations

Integers and real numbers may be added, subtracted, multiplied, divided, and raised to a power. The symbols for performing arithmetic operations in FORTRAN are shown in Table 2-2.

A *simple arithmetic expression* consists of an arithmetic operator connecting two arithmetic operands in the form:

```
operand operator operand
```

Examples of simple arithmetic expressions are:

```
16 + 2
17 - 5
2.75 + 9.3
.06 * 14.8*
26.7 / 3.0
3.1416 ** 2
```

The spaces around the arithmetic operators in these examples are inserted strictly for clarity. They may be omitted without affecting the value of the expression.

Table 2-2 FORTRAN's Arithmetic Operators

Operator	Operation
+	Addition
–	Subtraction
*	Multiplication
/	Division
**	Exponentiation (raising to a power)

The value of any arithmetic expression can be displayed using either a PRINT or a WRITE statement. For example, the value of the expression `.06 * 14.8` can be displayed using the statement:

```
PRINT *, .06 * 14.8
```

Here, the expression, with no surrounding apostrophes, is included directly in the PRINT statement. When this statement is executed, the indicated multiplication is performed, and the output, .888000, is displayed on the standard output device. As this output shows, six digits to the right of the decimal point are displayed. For real number output using list-directed PRINT or WRITE statements, the exact number of decimal digits is compiler dependent. If the value to be displayed does not have the requisite number of decimal digits, zeros are added to the number to fill the fractional part. If the number has more than the default number of decimal digits (six, in this example), the fractional part is rounded to the default number of decimal places.

In addition to calculating and displaying the value of an expression, the list of items in both PRINT and WRITE statements can also include a message. For example, the WRITE statement:

```
WRITE(6,*) 'THE VALUE OF THE EXPRESSION .06 * 14.8 IS ', .06*14.8
```

contains two items in its output list. The first item is a message, which is enclosed in apostrophes, and the second item is an arithmetic expression. When this statement is executed within a complete FORTRAN program, the display:

```
THE VALUE OF THE EXPRESSION .06 * 14.8 is     .888000
```

is produced. See if you can determine the output that is produced by the following sequence of statements:

```
WRITE(6,*) '.06 * 14.8'
WRITE(6,*) .06 * 14.8
WRITE(6,*) '06 * 14.8 IS', .06 * 14.8
```

The first WRITE statement contains a message, which is enclosed in apostrophes. As the message consists of the characters .06 * 14.8, these characters will be displayed by the WRITE statement when it is executed. The second WRITE statement does not contain a message because no apostrophes are used. Thus, the value of the expression .06 * 14.8, which is .888000, is calculated and displayed when this statement is executed. Finally, the third WRITE statement contains both a message and an expression. When this statement is executed, the message will be displayed first, and the value of the arithmetic expression will be calculated and displayed next. This produces the output:

```
.06 * 14.8 IS    .888000
```

Program 2-1 illustrates using a WRITE statement to display the results of simple arithmetic expressions within the context of a complete program.

* Some compilers require a leading digit before a decimal point. For such compilers .06 must be written as 0.06. The ANSI standard (77 and 90) specifies a leading zero.

Program 2-1

```
PROGRAM SHOWOP
  WRITE(6,*) 'OPERATION          VALUE'
  WRITE(6,*) '15.2 + 2.0', 15.2 + 2.0
  WRITE(6,*) '15.2 - 2.0', 15.2 - 2.0
  WRITE(6,*) '15.2 * 2.0', 15.2 * 2.0
  WRITE(6,*) '15.2 / 2.0', 15.2 / 2.0
  WRITE(6,*) '15.2 ** 2.0', 15.2 ** 2.0
  END
```

The output of Program 2-1 is:

```
OPERATION          VALUE
15.2 + 2.0       17.200000
15.2 - 2.0       13.200000
15.2 * 2.0       30.400000
15.2 / 2.0        7.600000
15.2 ** 2.0     231.040000
```

Notice that when a WRITE (or PRINT) statement is used to display more than one item, as in the statement:

```
WRITE(6,*)'15.0 + 2.0', 15.0 + 2.0
```

the individual items must be separated by commas. In this case the first item is a message enclosed within apostrophes. The second item is an arithmetic expression, the result of which is also displayed by the WRITE statement.

Expression Types

An expression that contains only integer operands is called an *integer expression*, and the result of the expression is an integer value. Similarly, an expression containing only real operands is called a *real expression*, and the result of a real expression is a real value. An expression containing both integer and real operands is called a *mixed-mode expression*. Although it is better not to mix integer and real operands when performing an arithmetic operation (the one exception being raising a real value to an integer power), predictable results are obtained when integer and real values are used together in a mixed-mode expression. A simple arithmetic expression containing both an integer and real data value is evaluated by converting the integer value to a real number, with the result of the operation being real. For example,

```
5 + 3. =  5. + 3. = 8.  (a real value)
16 * 1.  = 16. * 1. = 16. (a real value)
42. / 2  = 42. / 2. = 21. (a real value)
```

Integer Division

A trap for the unwary in FORTRAN can occur when an integer value is divided by another integer value. In such a case the result of the integer expression, as has already been mentioned, will be an integer. For example, dividing the integer 7 by the integer 2 yields an integer result. Since integers cannot contain a fractional part, the anticipated result, 3.5, is not obtained. In FORTRAN, the fractional part of the result obtained when dividing two integers is dropped (truncated). For example,

```
7/2 is 3
9/4 is 2
7/5 is 1
```

Operator Precedence and Associativity

Besides such simple expressions as 5 + 12 and .08 * 26.2, we frequently need to create more complex arithmetic expressions. FORTRAN, like most other programming languages, requires that certain rules be followed in the writing of expressions containing more than one arithmetic operator. These rules are:

1. Two arithmetic operators must never be placed adjacent to one another. For example, 5 / * 6 is invalid because the two operators / and * are placed next to each other. The expression 5 ** 6, however, is valid and does not violate this rule because the double asterisk is the exponentiation operator.
2. Any expression, real or integer, may be raised to an integer power, but only positive real expressions may be raised to a real power. For example, (–2.5) ** 3 is valid and (–2.5) ** 3.5 is invalid.
3. Parentheses may be used to form groupings, and all expressions enclosed within parentheses are evaluated first. For example, in the expression (6 + 4) / (2 + 3), the 6 + 4 and 2 + 3 are evaluated first to yield 10 / 5. The 10 / 5 is then evaluated to yield 2.

   Sets of parentheses may also be enclosed by other parentheses. For example, the expression (2 * (3 + 7)) / 5 is valid. When parentheses are used within parentheses, the expressions in the innermost parentheses are always evaluated first.

   The evaluation continues from innermost to outermost parentheses until the expressions of all parentheses have been evaluated. The number of right-facing parentheses, (, must always equal the number of left-facing parentheses,), so that there are no unpaired sets.
4. Parentheses cannot be used to indicate multiplication. The multiplication operator, *, must be used. For example, the expression (3 + 4) (5 + 1) is invalid. The correct expression is (3 + 4) * (5 + 1).

As a general rule, parentheses should be used to specify logical groupings of operands and to indicate clearly, to both the computer and any programmer reading the expression, the intended order of arithmetic operations. In the absence of parentheses, expressions containing multiple operators are evaluated by the priority, or precedence, of each operator. Table 2-3 shows the precedence and lists the associativity of the operators considered in this section.

The precedence of an operator establishes its priority relative to all other operators. Operators at the top of Table 2-3 have a higher priority than operators at the bottom of the table. In expressions with multiple operators, an operator with higher precedence is used before an operator with lower precedence. For example, in the expression 6 + 4 / 2 + 3, the division is done before the addition, yielding an intermediate result of 6 + 2 + 3. The additions are then performed, left to right, to yield a final result of 11.

When the minus sign precedes an operand, as in the expression –*A* ** *B*, the minus sign negates (reverses the sign of) the number, usually with the same priority level as subtraction.* For example, the expression –6 ** 2 is calculated as –(6**2), which equals –36.

Expressions containing operators with the same precedence are evaluated according to their associativity. This means that evaluation for addition and subtraction, as well as multiplication and division, is from left to right, and successive exponents are evaluated from right to left as each operator is encountered. For example, in the expression 8 + 40 / 8 * 2 + 4, the multiplication and division operators are of higher precedence than the addition operator and are evaluated first. Both the multiplication and division operators, however, are of equal priority. Therefore, these operators are evaluated according to their left-to-right associativity, yielding:

```
8 +  40 / 8 * 2 + 4  =
8 +       5 * 2 + 4  =
8 +          10 + 4
```

The addition operations are now performed, again from left to right, yielding:

```
18 + 4 = 22
```

When two exponentiation operations occur sequentially, the resulting expression is evaluated from right to left. Thus, the expression 2**2**4 is evaluated as 2**16, which equals 65,536.

Note that in evaluating an expression with more than one operator, the result of each intermediate calculation is determined by the data types of the values used in the calculation. For example, 5/2. * 3 evaluates to the real number 7.5, while 5/2 * 3.0 evaluates to the real number 6.0.

Table 2-3 Operator Precedence and Associativity

Operator	Associativity
**	right to left
* /	left to right
+ –	left to right

* The precedence of the unary minus tends to be machine dependent.

In both expressions the division is done before the multiplication (left-to right-associativity). In the first expression, however, the division of an integer and a real value is involved. The result of this mixed-mode operation is the real number 2.5. Multiplying the real number 2.5 by the integer number 3 results in a second mixed-mode operation whose result is the real number 7.5. In the second expression the division involves two integers. The intermediate result produced by this integer expression is the integer value 2; multiplying this integer by the real number 3.0 results in a final real value of 6.0.

Skill Builder Exercises

1. Determine data types appropriate for the following data:
   a. the average of four grades
   b. the number of days in a month
   c. the length of the Golden Gate Bridge
   d. the numbers in a state lottery
   e. the distance from Brooklyn, New York, to Newark, New Jersey
   f. the names in a mailing list

2. Convert the following numbers into standard decimal form:

```
6.34E5    1.95162E2    8.395E1    2.95E-3    4.623E-4
```

3. Write the following decimal numbers using exponential notation:

```
126.    656.23    3426.95    4893.2    .321    .0123    .006789
```

4. Using the system reference manuals for your computer, determine the character code used by your computer.

5a. Show how the name MARTHA would be stored inside a computer that uses the ASCII code. That is, draw a figure similar to Figure 2-1 for the letters KINGSLEY.

b. Show how the name MARTHA would be stored inside a computer that uses the EBCDIC code.

6a. Repeat Exercise 5a using the letters of your own last name.

b. Repeat Exercise 5b using the letters of your own last name.

7. Listed below are correct algebraic expressions and incorrect FORTRAN expressions corresponding to them. Find the errors and write corrected FORTRAN expressions.

Algebra	FORTRAN expression
a. $(2)(3) + (4)(5)$	`(2)(3) + (4)(5)`
b. $\frac{6 + 18}{2}$	`6 + 18 / 2`
c. $\frac{4.5}{12.2 - 3.1}$	`4.5 / 12.2 - 3.1`

d. 4.6(3.0 + 14.9) `4.6(3.0 + 14.9)`

e. (12.1 + 18.9)(15.3 – 3.8) `(12.1 + 18.9)(15.3 - 3.8)`

8. Determine the value of the following integer expressions:

a. 3 + 4 * 6
b. 3 * 4 / 6 + 6
c. 2 * 3 / 12 * 8 / 4
d. 10 * (1 + 7 * 3)
e. 20 – 2 / 6 + 3
f. 20 – 2 / (6 + 3)
g. (20 – 2) / 6 + 3
h. (20 – 2) / (6 + 3)

9. Determine the value of the following real expressions:

a. 3.0 + 4.0 * 6.0
b. 3.0 * 4.0 / 6.0 + 6.0
c. 2.0 * 3.0 / 12.0 * 8.0 / 4.0
d. 10.0 * (1.0 + 7.0 * 3.0)
e. 20.0 – 3.0 / 6.0 + 3.0
f. 20.0 – 3.0 / (6.0 + 3.0)
g. (20.0 – 2.0) / 6.0 + 3.0
h. (20.0 – 2.0) / (6.0 + 3.0)

10. Evaluate the following mixed-mode expressions and list the data types of the results. In evaluating the expressions, be aware of the data types of all intermediate calculations.

a. 10.0 + 15 / 2 + 4.3
b. 10.0 + 15.0 / 2 + 4.3
c. 3.0 * 4 / 6 + 6
d. 3 * 4.0 / 6 + 6
e. 20.0 – 2 / 6 + 3
f. 10 + 17 * 3 + 4
g. 10 + 17 / 3. + 4

11. Assuming that AMOUNT has the integer value 1, M has the integer value 50, N has the integer value 10, and P has the integer value 5, evaluate the following expressions:

a. N / P + 3
b. M / P + N – 10 * AMOUNT
c. M – 3 * N + 4 * AMOUNT
d. AMOUNT / 5
e. 18 / P
f. –P * N
g. –M / 20
h. (M + N) / (P + AMOUNT)
i. M + N / P + AMOUNT

12. Repeat Exercise 11 assuming that AMOUNT has the real value 1.0, M has the real value 50.0, N has the real value 10.0, and P has the real value 5.0.

Expanding Your Skills

13. Enter, compile, and run Program 2-1 on your computer system.

14. Rewrite Program 2-1 so that it contains one subroutine (*Hint:* Review Program 1-1 in Chapter 1.)

15. Since computers use different representations for storing integer, real, and character values, discuss how a program might alert the computer to the data types of the various values it will be using.

Note: For the following exercise you should have an understanding of basic computer storage concepts. Specifically, if you are unfamiliar with the concept of a byte, refer to Section 1.7 before doing the next exercise.

16. Although the total number of bytes varies from computer to computer, memory sizes of 65,536 to more than 4 million bytes are common. In computer language, the letter K is used to represent the number 1024, which is 2 raised to the 10th power. Thus, a memory size of 64K is really 64 times 1024, or 65,536 bytes, and a memory size of 512K consists of 512 times 1024, or 524,288 bytes. Using this information, calculate the actual number of bytes in:

a. a memory containing 64K bytes
b. a memory containing 128K bytes
c. a memory containing 192K bytes
d. a memory containing 256K bytes
e. a memory consisting of 64K words, where each word consists of 2 bytes
f. a memory consisting of 64K words, where each word consists of 4 bytes
g. a floppy diskette that can store 360K bytes

2.2 Variables and Declaration Statements

All integer, real, character, and logical values used in a computer program are stored and retrieved from the computer's memory unit. Conceptually, individual memory locations in the memory unit are arranged like the rooms in a large hotel. Like hotel rooms, each memory location has a unique address ("room number"). Before high-level languages such as FORTRAN existed, memory locations were referenced by their addresses. For example, storing the integer values 45 and 12 in the memory locations 1652 and 2548 (see Figure 2-2), respectively, required instructions equivalent to:

put a 45 in location 1652

put a 12 in location 2548

To add the two numbers just stored and save the result in another memory location, for example, at location 3000, required a statement comparable to:

add the contents of location 1652
to the contents of location 2548
and store the result in location 3000

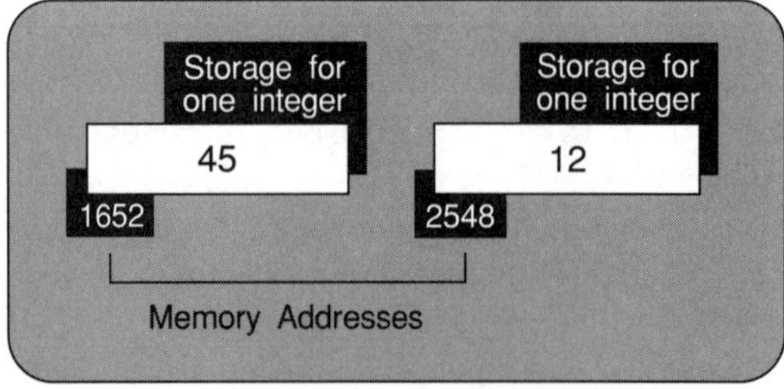

Figure 2-2 Enough Storage for Two Integers

Clearly, this method of storage and retrieval is cumbersome. In high-level languages such as FORTRAN, symbolic names are used in place of actual memory addresses. Symbolic names used in this manner are called *variables.* A variable is simply a name given by the programmer to a memory storage location. The term *variable* is used because the value stored in the variable can change, or vary. For each name that the programmer uses, the computer keeps track of the actual memory address corresponding to that name. In our hotel room analogy, this is equivalent to putting a name on the door of a room, for example, BLUE room, and referring to the room by this name rather than using the actual room number.

In FORTRAN the selection of variable names is left to the programmer as long as the variable name is chosen according to the rules used for selecting symbolic names given in Chapter 1. A variable name can thus consist of from one to six uppercase letters or digits, the first of which must be a letter, with no embedded special characters.

As with program unit names, variable names should be mnemonics that give some indication of the variable's use. For example, a good name for a variable used to store a value that is the total of some other values would be SUM or TOTAL. Similarly the variable name WIDTH is a good choice if the value stored in the variable represents a width. Variable names that give no indication of the value stored, such as R2D2, LINDA, BILL, and GETUM, should not be selected.

Now assume the first memory location illustrated in Figure 2-2, that has address 1652, is given the name FIRST. Also assume that memory location 2548 is given the variable name SECOND, and memory location 3000 is given the variable name TOTAL, as illustrated in Figure 2-3.

Using these variable names, storing 45 in location 1652 and 12 in location 2548 and adding the contents of these two locations is accomplished by the FORTRAN statements:

```
FIRST = 45
SECOND = 12
TOTAL = FIRST + SECOND
```

Each of these three statements is called an assignment statement because it tells the computer to assign (store) a value into a variable. Assignment statements always

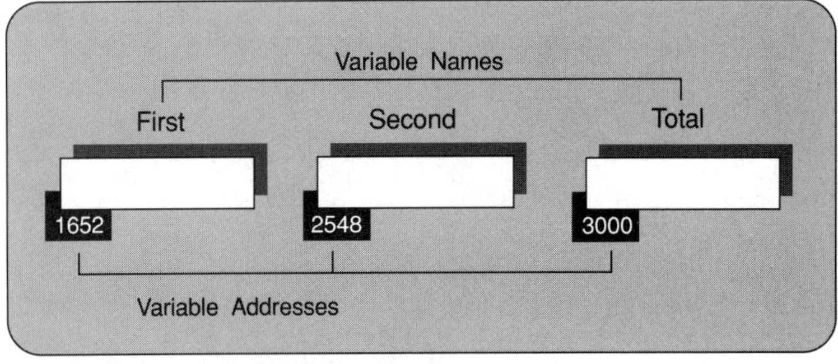

Figure 2-3 Naming Storage Locations

have an equal (=) sign and one variable name immediately to the left of the equal sign. The value on the right of the equal sign is determined first; this value is assigned to the variable on the left of the equal sign. The blank spaces in the assignment statements are inserted for readability. We will have more to say about assignment statements in the next section, but for now we can use them to store values in variables.

A variable name is useful because it frees the programmer from concern over where data is physically stored inside the computer. We simply use the variable name and let the computer deal with where in memory the data are actually stored. Before storing a value into a variable, however, we must clearly define the type of data to be stored in it. This requires telling the computer in advance the names of the variables that will be used for integers, the names that will be used for real numbers, and the names that will be used to store the other FORTRAN data types.

Declaration Statements

Naming a variable and specifying the data type that can be stored in it are accomplished using declaration statements. Declaration statements, which are also called specification statements, are nonexecutable statements that have the general form:

```
data type   variable name
```

where data type designates a valid FORTRAN data type (INTEGER, REAL, CHARACTER, etc.), and variable name is a user-selected variable name. For example, variables used to hold integer values are declared using the declaration statement:

```
INTEGER variable name
```

Thus, the declaration statement:

```
INTEGER TOTAL
```

declares TOTAL as the name of a variable capable of storing an integer value. Declaration statements must be placed after the program unit's header line and before any other statements contained within the program unit's body. For example, if the variable TOTAL is to be used in a MAIN program unit, its declaration statement would be placed in the unit as:

```
123456789 ——— Column Number ———————————————————72
      PROGRAM MAIN
        INTEGER TOTAL
```

Notice that the declaration statement is written on a line by itself within columns 7 through 72 (the statement field).

Variables used to hold real values are declared using the keyword REAL, variables used to hold character data are declared using the keyword CHARACTER, and variables used for logical data are declared using the key word LOGICAL. For example, the statement:

```
REAL AVERGE
```

declares that AVERGE is a variable name that will be used to store a real value.

Program 2-2

```
123456789 ——— Column Number ———————————————————72
      PROGRAM DECLAR
************************************************************
*         THIS PROGRAM DECLARES FOUR REAL VARIABLES. THE       *
*         TOTAL AND AVERAGE OF THE FIRST TWO VARIABLES ARE     *
*         COMPUTED.                                            *
************************************************************
        REAL GRADE1
        REAL GRADE2
        REAL TOTAL
        REAL AVERGE
*
        GRADE1 = 85.5
        GRADE2 = 97.0
        TOTAL = GRADE1 + GRADE2
        AVERGE = TOTAL/2.0
        WRITE(6,*) 'THE AVERAGE OF THE GRADES IS ', AVERGE
        END
```

Program 2-2 illustrates the declaration and use of four real variables. The list-directed WRITE statement is then used to display the contents of one of these variables.

The placement of the declaration statements in Program 2-2 is straightforward, although we will shortly see that the four individual declarations can be combined into a single declaration. Note that the statements within the box of asterisks, including the box itself, are comment lines because of the asterisks in column 1. When Program 2-2 is run, the following output is displayed:

```
THE AVERAGE OF THE GRADES IS        91.250000
```

Two comments about the WRITE statement made in Program 2-2 should be made. First, as was also noted with respect to Program 2-1, if more than one item is to be displayed using the WRITE statement, the individual items in the list must be separated by commas. Second, if a variable name is one of the items in the display list, as in Program 2-2, the value stored in the variable is displayed rather than the variable name. When the WRITE statement sees a variable name in its output list, it first goes to the variable and retrieves the value stored. It is this value that is displayed. The same is true for the equivalent PRINT statement. For example, the statement:

```
PRINT*, 'THE AVERAGE OF THE GRADES IS ', AVERGE
```

displays the same two items as Program 2-2. The first item printed is the message and the second item is the value stored in the variable AVERGE. As with the WRITE statement, the two items in the PRINT statement are separated by a comma. Since the compiler's default format, as specified by the asterisk in both the PRINT and the WRITE statements, is used, the spacing of the output display and the number of digits displayed to the right of the decimal point depend on the default format of the compiler (in Section 2.4 we will see how to explicitly designate our own output formats).

Just as integer and real variables must be declared before they can be used, variables used to store logical values and character constants must also be suitably declared. Logical variables are declared using the keyword LOGICAL. For example, the declaration statement:

```
LOGICAL BINARY
```

declares that the variable name BINARY will be used to hold a logical value. This means that either the value .TRUE. or the value .FALSE. can be stored in this variable.

Character variables are declared using the keyword CHARACTER. Since character constants can be of varying length, the declaration of a character constant should include the maximum number of characters that the variable will store. If the string length is omitted, a default length of one is assumed. For example, the declaration:

```
CHARACTER CH
```

declares CH to be a character variable capable of holding a single character. By adding a length specifier, as in either the declaration statement:

```
CHARACTER*14 TITLE
```

or the declaration statement

```
CHARACTER TITLE*14
```

the variable TITLE is declared to be a character variable capable of holding 14 characters.

Multiple Declarations

Variables having the same data type always can be grouped together and declared using a single declaration statement. The general form of such a declaration statement is:

```
data type variable list
```

where data type must be a valid FORTRAN data type (INTEGER, REAL, CHARACTER, etc.), and the list is replaced by a list of variable names. For example, the four separate declarations:

```
REAL GRADE1
REAL GRADE2
REAL TOTAL
REAL AVERGE
```

can be replaced by the single declaration statement:*

* Some systems require that all variables of the same data type must be declared using a single declaration statement.

```
REAL GRADE1, GRADE2, TOTAL, AVERGE
```

In the case of a CHARACTER declaration, the optional length specifier applies to each variable in the list. For example, the declaration:

```
CHARACTER*20  CODE, TITLE
```

declares both CODE and TITLE to be variables of length 20. A separate length specifier can also be designated for any individual character variable in the declaration list, regardless of the general length specifier given for the complete list. For example, the declaration:

```
CHARACTER*15 NAME, STREET, CITY, STATE*2, ZIP*5, CODE
```

specifies the variables NAME, STREET, CITY, and CODE as character variables of length 15, STATE to be a character variable of length 2, and ZIP to be a character variable of length 5.

Notice that declaring multiple variables in a single declaration statement requires that the data type of the variables be given only once and that all the variables in the list be separated by commas. The space after each comma is inserted for readability and is not required.

F90

In FORTRAN 90 a variable may have an attribute as well as a data type. To include the attribute, the general form of variable declaration statements in FORTRAN 90 is:

```
data type ,attribute 1 ,attribute 2  .... :: list of variables
```

where the comma before each attribute and the :: (two colons with no intervening space) symbol are only required if an attribute is included (attributes are described in Chapter 12). For example, since the declaration:

```
REAL SUM
```

has no attributes, the comma immediately after the data type and the :: symbol do not have to be included. The :: symbol, however, can always be used in FORTRAN 90, resulting in the equivalent declaration:

```
REAL :: SUM
```

Multiple variables can still be declared in FORTRAN 90 as they are in earlier versions of FORTRAN. Thus, in FORTRAN 90 the following two declarations are equivalent:

```
INTEGER NUM1, NUM2, NUM3
INTEGER :: NUM1, NUM2, NUM3
```

Another feature of FORTRAN 90 is the way in which character variables are declared. In the new version of FORTRAN the length of a character variable can be specified by including the term (LEN = n) after the CHARACTER type designation. Thus, the declarations:

```
CHARACTER*20 NAME
CHARACTER(LEN = 20) NAME
CHARACTER*20 :: NAME
CHARACTER(LEN = 20) :: NAME
```

are all equivalent.

Implicit Declarations

Specifying the data type of a variable using a declaration statement is referred to as *explicit data typing.* Programming languages that require all variables be declared before they can be used are called *strongly typed languages.* In this regard FORTRAN is considered a *weakly typed language* because it does not require a declaration for every variable. In the absence of a declaration, FORTRAN assumes the following data typing: any variable beginning with an I, J, K, L, M, or N is an integer variable, and any variable not beginning in one of these letters is a real variable. For example, if the variables ALPHA, BETA, INTVAL, and ICOUNT were used in a program without being explicitly declared, INTVAL and ICOUNT would be created as integer variables and ALPHA and BETA as real variables. FORTRAN's implicit declaration feature can be disabled by including the statement IMPLICIT NONE before any variable declarations are made.

Despite the fact that FORTRAN allows default data declarations for real and integer variables, it is good programming practice to explicitly declare all variables used in a program. An explicit declaration provides the programmer with the opportunity to carefully decide on the names of the variables that will be used and the data types that will be stored within them. It also provides a summary of all variables that have been used, which is extremely helpful if additional variables need to be named. All of the programs in this text will adhere to the programming practice of explicitly declaring all variable names.

Specifying Storage Allocation

Declaration statements perform both a software and a hardware function. From a software perspective, declaration statements always provide a convenient, up-front list of all variables and their data types. In addition to this software role, declaration statements also serve a distinct hardware task. Since each data type has its own storage requirements (an integer uses less room than a real number, for example), the computer can allocate sufficient storage for a variable only after it knows the variable's data type. Because variable declarations provide this information, they also inform the computer of the physical memory storage that must be reserved for each variable. (In the hotel analogy introduced at the beginning of this section, this is equivalent to connecting adjoining rooms to form larger suites.)

Figure 2-4 illustrates the series of operations set in motion by declaration statements in performing their memory allocation function. As illustrated, declaration statements both cause sufficient memory to be allocated for each data type and "tag" the reserved memory locations with a name. This name is, of course, the variable's name.

Within a program, the declared variable name is used by a programmer to reference the contents of the variable (that is, the variable's value). Where in memory this value is stored is generally of little concern to the programmer. The computer, however, must be concerned with where each value is stored. In this task the computer uses the variable's name to locate the desired value. Knowing the variable's data type allows the computer to access the correct number of locations for each type of data.

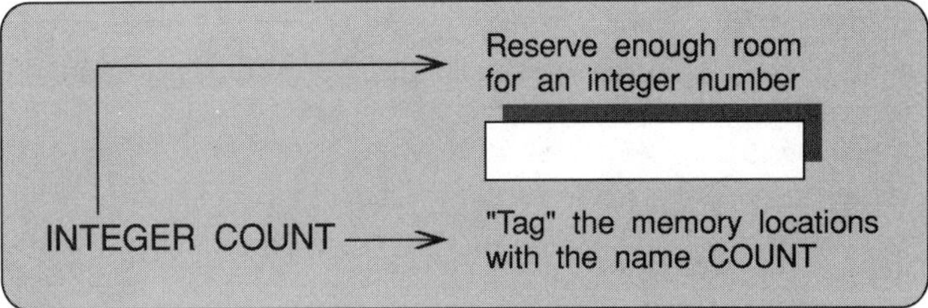

Figure 2-4(a) Defining the INTEGER Variable Named COUNT

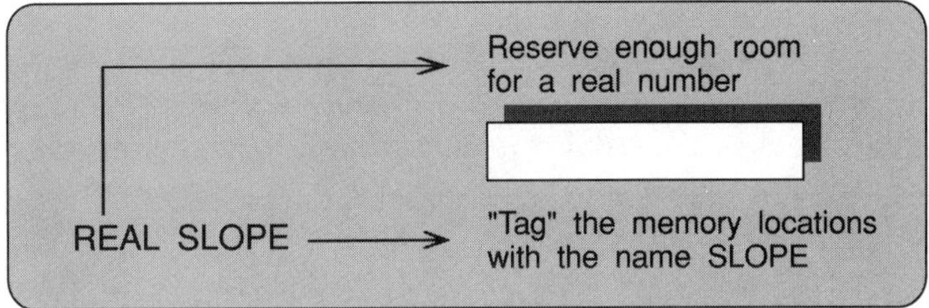

Figure 2-4(b) Defining the REAL Variable Named SLOPE

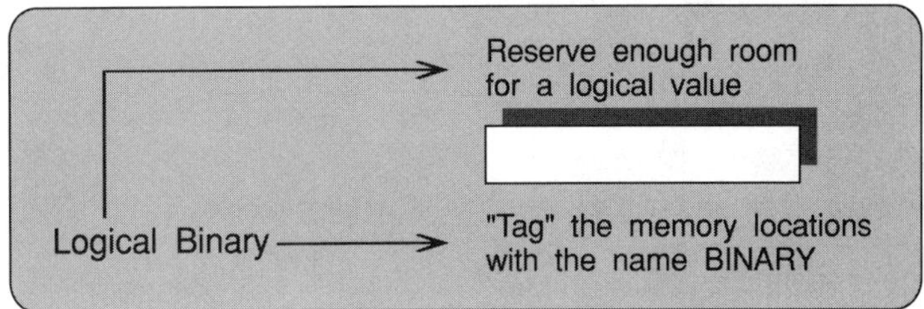

Figure 2-4(c) Defining the LOGICAL Variable Named BINARY

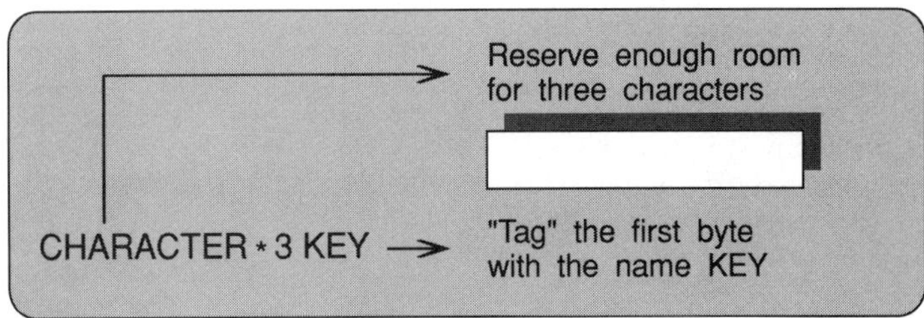

Figure 2-4(d) Defining the CHARACTER Variable Named KEY

Skill Builder Exercises

1. State whether the following variable names are valid or not in FORTRAN 77. If they are invalid, state the reason why.

```
PROD-A      C1234      ABCD       -C3        12345
NEWBAL      WATTS      $TOTAL     NEW$AL     A1B2C3D4
9AB6        SUM.OF     AVERAGE    GRADE1     FINGRAD
```

2a. State whether the following variable names are valid or not FORTRAN 77. If they are invalid, state the reason why.

```
SLSTAX      A243       R2D2       FIRST_NUM  CC-A1
HARRY       SUE        C3P0       TOTAL      SUM
MAXNUM      OKAY       A          AWSOME     GOFOR
3SUM        FOR        TOT.A1     C$FIVE     NETPAY
```

b. List which of the valid variable names found in Exercise 2a normally should not be used because they convey no information about the variable.

3a. Write a declaration statement to declare that the variable COUNT will be used to store an integer.

b. Write a declaration statement to declare that the variable GRADE will be used to store a real number.

c. Write a declaration statement to declare that the variable KEYCH will be used to store a single character.

4. For each of the following, write a single declaration statement:
   a. NUM1, NUM2, and NUM3 used to store integer numbers
   b. GRADE1, GRADE2, GRADE3, and GRADE4 used to store real numbers
   c. CH, LET1, LET2, LET3, and LET4 used to store character types of sizes 1, 3, 3, 7, and 9 respectively.

5. For each of the following, write a single declaration statement:
   a. FIRNUM and SECNUM used to store integers
   b. PRICE, YIELD, and COUPON used to store real numbers
   c. MATRTY to store a character constant consisting of nine letters

6. Rewrite each of these declaration statements as three individual declarations:
   a. INTEGER MONTH, DAY, YEAR
   b. REAL HOURS, RATE, OTIME
   c. REAL PRICE, AMOUNT, TAXES
   d. CHARACTER INKEY, CH, CHOICE
   e. CHARACTER*5, CODE, CITY*10, ZIP

7. Every variable has at least two items associated with it. What are these two items?

Expanding Your Skills

8. Rewrite Program 2-2 so that it uses only a single declaration statement; then enter, compile, and run the program on your computer system.

Note for Exercises 9 through 11: These exercises assume you are familiar with the material presented in Section 1.7. For these exercises assume that a character requires one byte of storage, an integer two bytes, and a real number four bytes and that variables are assigned consecutive storage locations in the order they are declared. Memory bytes are shown in Figure 2-5.

9a. Using Figure 2-5 and assuming that the variable name RATE is assigned to the byte having memory address 159, determine the addresses corresponding to each variable declared in the following statements:

```
REAL RATE
CHARACTER CH1, CH2, CH3, CH4
INTEGER NUM, COUNT
```

b. Repeat Exercise 9a, but substitute the actual bit patterns that a computer using the ASCII code would use to store the characters in the variables `CH1`, `CH2`, `CH3`, and `CH4` assuming the following assignment statements. (*Hint:* Use Table 2-1.)

```
CH1 = 'O'
CH2 = 'K'
CH3 = 'A'
CH4 = 'Y'
```

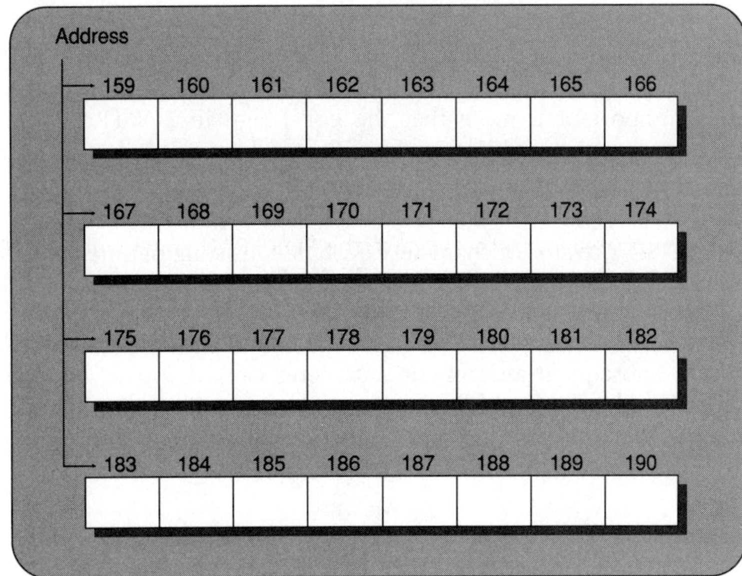

Figure 2-5 Memory Bytes for Exercises 9, 10, and 11

10. Using Figure 2-5 and assuming that the variable named `CN1` is assigned to the byte at memory address 159, determine the addresses corresponding to each variable declared in the following statements:

```
CHARACTER CN1, CN2, CN3, CN4, CN5
CHARACTER*2 CN6, CN7, KEY*1, SCH*4
CHARACTER*4 INC1
```

11. Using Figure 2-5 and assuming that the variable name `MILES` is assigned to the byte at memory address 159, determine the addresses corresponding to each variable declared in the following statements:

```
REAL MILES
INTEGER COUNT, NUM
CHARACTER KEY1, KEY2*3, KEY3
```

2.3 Assignment Statements

The most basic FORTRAN statement for both assigning values to variables and performing computations is the assignment statement. This statement has the general form:

```
VARIABLE = expression
```

The simplest arithmetic expression in FORTRAN is a single constant, and in each of the following assignment statements, the expression to the right of the equal sign is a constant:

```
LENGTH = 25
WIDTH = 17.5
```

In these assignment statements, the value of the constant to the right of the equal sign is assigned to the variable on the left side of the equal sign. It is extremely important to note that the equal sign in FORTRAN does not have the same meaning as an equal sign in algebra. The equal sign in an assignment statement tells the computer to first determine the value of the expression to the right of the equal sign and then to store (or assign) that value in the variable to the left of the equal sign. In this regard, the FORTRAN statement LENGTH = 25 is read "LENGTH is assigned the value 25." The blank spaces in the assignment statement are inserted for readability only.

When a value is assigned to a variable for the first time, the variable is said to be *initialized.* Subsequent assignment statements can, of course, be used to change the value assigned to a variable. For example, assume the following statements are executed one after another:

```
SLOPE = 3.7
SLOPE = 6.28
```

The first assignment statement assigns the value of 3.7 to the variable named SLOPE. Since this is the first time a value is assigned to this variable, it is also correct to say that SLOPE is initialized to 3.7. The next assignment statement causes the computer to assign a value of 6.28 to SLOPE. The 3.7 that was in SLOPE is erased and replaced with the new value of 6.2, because a variable can store only one value at a time. In this regard it is sometimes useful to think of the variable to the left of the equal sign as a temporary parking spot in a huge parking lot. Just as an individual parking spot can only be used by one car at a time, each variable can store only one value at a time. The "parking" of a new value in a variable automatically causes the computer to remove any value previously parked there.

In its most general form, a FORTRAN expression is any combination of constants and variables that can be evaluated to yield a result. Thus, the expression in an assignment statement can be used to perform calculations using the arithmetic operators introduced in Section 2.1 (see Table 2-2). Examples of assignment statements using expressions containing these operators are:

```
SUM = 3 + 7
DIFF = 15 - 6
PRODUC = .05 * 14.6
TALLY = COUNT + 1
NEWTOT = 18.3 + TOTAL
TAXES = .06 * AMOUNT
TOTWET = WEIGHT * FACTOR
AVERGE = SUM / ITEMS
NEWVAL = NUMBER ** POWER
```

As always in an assignment statement, the equal sign directs the computer first to calculate the value of the expression to the right of the equal sign and then to store this value in the variable to the left of the equal sign. For example, in the assignment statement TOTWET = WEIGHT * FACTOR, the expression WEIGHT * FACTOR is first evaluated to yield a result. This result, which is a number, is then stored in the variable TOTWET.

In writing assignment statements, you must be aware of two important considerations. Since the expression to the right of the equal sign is evaluated first, all variables used in the expression must be initialized if the result is to make sense. For example, the assignment statement TOTWET = WEIGHT * FACTOR will only cause a valid number to be stored in TOTWET if the programmer first takes care to put valid numbers in WEIGHT and FACTOR. Thus, the sequence of statements:

```
WEIGHT = 155.0
FACTOR = 1.06
TOTWET = WEIGHT * FACTOR
```

ensures that we know the values being used to obtain the result that will be stored in the variable to the left of the equal sign. Figure 2-6 illustrates the values stored in the variables WEIGHT, FACTOR, and TOTWET.

The second consideration to keep in mind is that since the value of an expression is stored in the variable to the left of the equal sign, there must only be one variable listed in this position. For example, the assignment statement:

```
AMOUNT + EXTRA = 1462 + 10 - 24
```

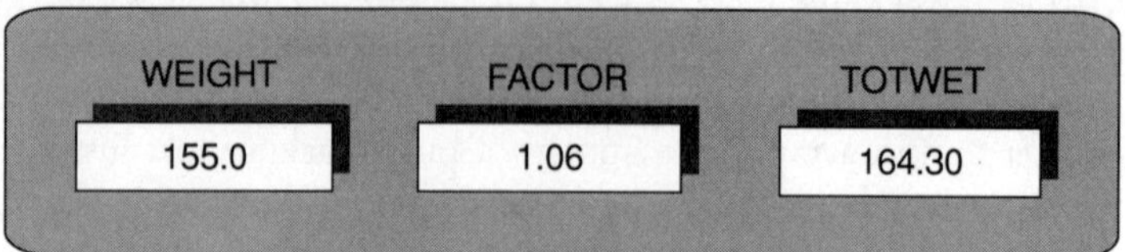

Figure 2-6 Values Stored in the Variables

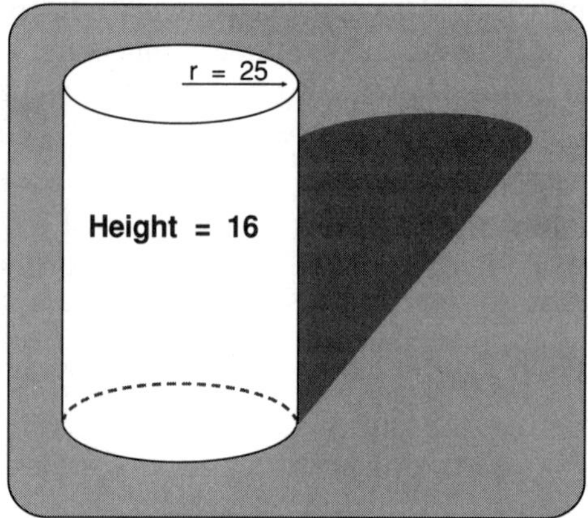

Figure 2-7 Determining the Volume of a Cylinder

is invalid. The right-side expression evaluates to the integer 1448, which can only be stored in a variable. Since AMOUNT + EXTRA is not the valid name of a memory location (it is not a valid variable name), the computer does not know where to store the value 1448. Program 2-3 illustrates the use of assignment statements to calculate the volume of a cylinder. As illustrated in Figure 2-7, the volume of a cylinder is determined by the formula $Volume = pi\ r^2h$, where r is the radius of the cylinder, h is the height, and *pi* is the constant 3.1416 (accurate to four decimal places).

Program 2-3

```
12345678 ------------ Column Number ---------------------72
      PROGRAM CYLVOL
***     THIS PROGRAM CALCULATES THE VOLUME OF A CYLINDER,
***     GIVEN ITS RADIUS AND HEIGHT
        REAL RADIUS, HEIGHT, VOLUME
        RADIUS = 2.5
        HEIGHT = 16.0
        VOLUME = 3.1416 * RADIUS **2 * HEIGHT
        WRITE(6,*) 'THE VOLUME OF THE CYLINDER IS ', VOLUME
        END
```

When Program 2-3 is compiled and executed, the output is:

```
THE VOLUME OF THE CYLINDER IS 314.160000
```

Notice the order in which statements are executed in Program 2-3. The program begins with the program header line and continues sequentially, statement by statement, until the END statement is encountered. All computer programs execute in this manner. The computer works on one statement at a time, executing that statement with no knowledge of what the next statement will be. This explains why all variables used in an expression must have values assigned to them before the expression is evaluated.

When the computer executes the statement VOLUME = 3.1416 * RADIUS **2 * HEIGHT in Program 2-3, it uses whatever value is stored in the variables RADIUS and HEIGHT at the time the assignment statement is executed. If no values have been specifically assigned to these variables before they are used in the assignment statement, the computer uses whatever values happen to occupy these variables when they are referenced (on some systems all variables are automatically initialized to zero). The computer does not look ahead to see if you assign values to these variables later in the program.

Assignment Variations

Although only one variable is allowed immediately to the left of the equal sign in an assignment expression, the variable on the left of the equal sign can also be used on the right of the equal sign. For example, the assignment statement TOTAL = TOTAL + 20 is valid. Clearly, in algebra, TOTAL could never be equal to itself plus 20. But in FORTRAN, the statement TOTAL = TOTAL + 20 is not an equation — it is a statement that is evaluated in two distinct steps. The first step is to calculate the value of TOTAL + 20. The second step is to store the computed value in TOTAL. See if you can determine the output of Program 2-4.

Program 2-4

```
123456789 ——————————— Column Number ————————————————72
      PROGRAM MAIN
        INTEGER TOTAL
        TOTAL = 15
        WRITE(6,*) 'THE NUMBER STORED IN TOTAL IS ', TOTAL
        TOTAL = TOTAL + 25
        WRITE(6,*) 'THE NUMBER NOW STORED IN TOTAL IS ', TOTAL
        END
```

The assignment statement TOTAL = 15 initializes the value in TOTAL to the number 15, as shown in Figure 2-8.

The first WRITE statement causes both a message and the value stored in TOTAL to be displayed. The output produced by this statement is:

```
THE NUMBER STORED IN TOTAL IS       15
```

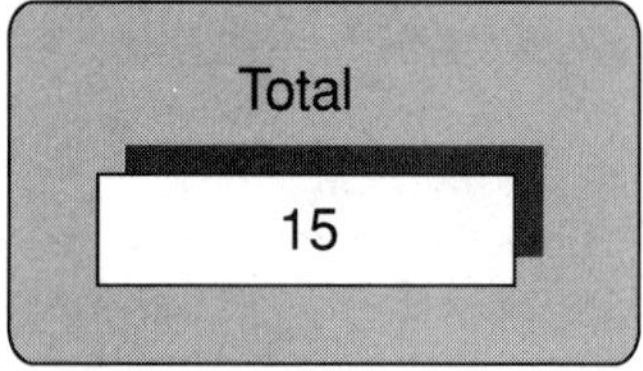

Figure 2-8 The Integer 15 is Stored in TOTAL

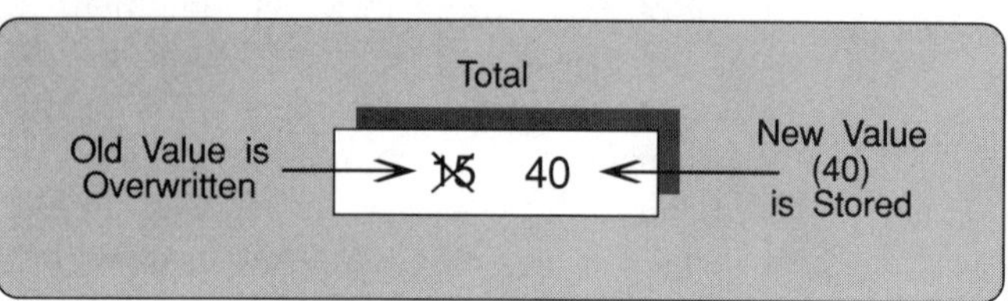

Figure 2-9 TOTAL = TOTAL + 25 Causes a New Value to Be Stored in TOTAL

The second assignment statement in Program 2-4, TOTAL = TOTAL + 25, causes the computer to retrieve the 15 stored in TOTAL and add 25 to this number, yielding the number 40. The number 40 is then stored in the variable on the left side of the equal sign, which is the variable TOTAL. The 15 that was in TOTAL is overwritten and replaced with the new value of 40, as shown in Figure 2-9.

Accumulating

Assignment expressions like TOTAL = TOTAL + 25 are very common in programming and are required in accumulating subtotals when data are entered one number at a time. For example, if we want to add the numbers 62, 40, 55, and 90 in calculator fashion, the following statements could be used:

Statement	Value in TOTAL
`TOTAL = 0`	0
`TOTAL = TOTAL + 62`	62
`TOTAL = TOTAL + 40`	102
`TOTAL = TOTAL + 55`	157
`TOTAL = TOTAL + 90`	247

The first statement initializes TOTAL to 0. This removes any number ("garbage" value) stored in the memory locations corresponding to TOTAL and ensures we start with 0. (This is equivalent to clearing a calculator before doing any computations.) As each number is added, the value stored in TOTAL is increased accordingly. After completion of the last statement, TOTAL contains the total of all the added numbers.

Program 2-5 illustrates the effect of these statements by displaying TOTAL's contents after each addition is made.

The output produced by Program 2-5 is:

```
THE VALUE OF TOTAL IS INITIALLY SET TO          0
  TOTAL IS NOW          62
  TOTAL IS NOW         102
  TOTAL IS NOW         157
  THE FINAL VALUE IN TOTAL IS          247
```

Although it is clearly easier to add the numbers by hand than to use the sequence of assignment statements listed, these statements do illustrate the subtotaling

Program 2-5

```
123456789 ———————————— Column Number ———————————————72
      PROGRAM MAIN
        INTEGER TOTAL
        TOTAL = 0
        WRITE(6,*) 'THE VALUE OF TOTAL IS INITIALLY SET TO ', TOTAL
        TOTAL = TOTAL + 62
        WRITE(6,*) '  TOTAL IS NOW ', TOTAL
        TOTAL = TOTAL + 40
        WRITE(6,*) '  TOTAL IS NOW ', TOTAL
        TOTAL = TOTAL + 55
        WRITE(6,*) '  TOTAL IS NOW ', TOTAL
        TOTAL = TOTAL + 90
        WRITE(6,*) '  THE FINAL VALUE IN TOTAL IS ', TOTAL
        END
```

effect of repeated assignment statements having the form:

```
VARIABLE = VARIABLE + added value
```

We will find many uses for this type of statement when we become more familiar with the repetition statements introduced in Chapter 5.

Counting

A variation of the accumulating assignment statement is the counting statement. Counting statements have the form:

```
VARIABLE = VARIABLE + fixed number
```

Examples of counting statements are:

```
I = I + 1
N = N + 1
ICOUNT = ICOUNT + 1
J = J + 2
M = M + 2
KK = KK + 3
```

In each of these examples the same variable is used on both sides of the equal sign. After the statement is executed, the value of the respective variable is increased by a fixed amount. In the first three examples, the variables I, N, and ICOUNT have all been increased by one. In the next two examples, the respective variables have been increased by two, and in the final example the variable KK has been increased by three. Variable names beginning in I, J, K, L, M, or N are conventionally used for counter variables to stress their integer nature (recall that variable names beginning in these letters are implicitly specified as integer variables). The following sequence of statements illustrate the use of a counter.

Statement	Value in ICOUNT
`ICOUNT = 0`	0
`ICOUNT = ICOUNT + 1`	1
`ICOUNT = ICOUNT + 1`	2
`ICOUNT = ICOUNT + 1`	3
`ICOUNT = ICOUNT + 1`	4

Skill Builder Exercises

1. Write an assignment statement to calculate the circumference of a circle. The equation for determining the circumference, c, of a circle is $c = 2\ pi\ r$, where r is the radius, and *pi* equals 3.1416.
2. Write an assignment statement to calculate the area of a circle. The equation for determining the area, a, of a circle is $a = pi\ r^2$, where r is the radius and $pi = 3.1416$.
3. Write an assignment statement to convert temperature in degrees Fahrenheit to degrees Celsius. The equation for this conversion is *Celsius* = 5/9 (*Fahrenheit* –32).
4. Write an assignment statement to calculate the round trip distance, d, in feet, of a trip that is s miles long, one way.
5. Write an assignment statement to calculate the elapsed time, in minutes, that it takes to make a trip. The equation for computing elapsed time is *elapsed time = total distance / average speed.* Assume that the distance is in miles and the average speed is in miles/hour.
6. Write an assignment statement to calculate the nth term in an arithmetic sequence. The formula for calculating the value, v, of the nth term is $v = a + (n-1)d$, where a is the first number in the sequence and d is the difference between any two numbers in the sequence.
7. Write an assignment statement to calculate the maximum height, h, of a projectile. The formula for determining the maximum height is $h = (v^2 \sin^2 \theta)/2g$, where v is the initial velocity of the projectile, θ is the angle at which the projectile is fired, and g is the gravitational constant equal to 32.2 ft/sec^2.
8. Write an assignment statement to calculate the linear expansion in a steel beam as a function of temperature increase. The formula for linear expansion, l, is $l = l_o[1+a(T_f-T_o)]$, where l_o is the length of the beam at temperature T_o, a is the coefficient of linear expansion, and T_f is the final temperature of the beam.
9. Coulomb's law states that the force F, acting between two electrically charged spheres, is given by the formula $F = k\ q_1\ q_2/\ r^2$, where q_1 is the charge on the first sphere, q_2 is the charge on the second sphere, r is the distance between the centers of the two spheres, and k is a proportionality constant. Write an assignment statement to calculate the force F.
10. Write an assignment statement to determine the maximum bending moment, M, of a beam. The formula for maximum bending moment is

$M = X W (L - X) / L$, where X is the distance from the end of the beam that a weight, W, is placed, and L is the length of the beam.

11. Determine the output of the following program:

```
      PROGRAM MAIN
*** A PROGRAM ILLUSTRATING INTEGER TRUNCATION ***
        INTEGER NUM1, NUM2
        NUM1 = 9/2
        NUM2 = 17/4
        WRITE(6,*) 'THE FIRST INTEGER DISPLAYED IS', NUM1
        WRITE(6,*) 'THE SECOND INTEGER DISPLAYED IS', NUM2
        END
```

12. Determine the output produced by the following program:

```
PROGRAM MAIN
  REAL AVERGE
  AVERGE = 26.27
  WRITE(6,*) 'THE AVERAGE IS', AVERGE
  AVERGE = 682.3
  WRITE(6,*) 'THE AVERAGE IS', AVERGE
  AVERGE = 1.968
  WRITE(6,*) 'THE AVERAGE IS', AVERGE
  END
```

13. Determine the output produced by the following program:

```
PROGRAM MAIN
  REAL SUM
  SUM = 0.0
  WRITE(6,*) 'THE SUM IS', SUM
  SUM = SUM + 26.27
  WRITE(6,*) 'THE SUM IS', SUM
  SUM = SUM + 1.968
  WRITE(6,*) 'THE FINAL TOTAL IS', SUM
  END
```

14a. Determine what each statement causes to happen in the following program:

```
PROGRAM MAIN
  INTEGER NUM1
  INTEGER NUM2
  INTEGER TOTAL
  NUM1 = 25
  NUM2 = 30
  TOTAL = NUM1 + NUM2
  WRITE(6,*) NUM1, '+', NUM2, '=', TOTAL
  END
```

b. What is the output that will be produced when the program listed in Exercise 14a is compiled and executed?

Debugging Exercises

Note for Exercises 15 through 18: Identify the errors in the sections of code listed in each exercise:

15.
```
PROGRAM MAIN
  INTEGER LENGTH, WIDTH, AREA
  WIDTH = 20
  AREA = LENGTH * WIDTH
```

16.
```
PROGRAM MAIN
  AREA = LENGTH * WIDTH
  LENGTH = 15
  WIDTH = 20
```

17.
```
PROGRAM MAIN
  INTEGER LENGTH, WIDTH, AREA
  LENGTH = 16
  WIDTH = 24
  LENGTH * WIDTH = AREA
```

18.
```
PROGRAM MAIN
  INTEGER LENGTH = 20, WIDTH = 10, AREA
  AREA = LENGTH * WIDTH
```

19. By mistake a student reordered the statements in Program 2-5 as follows:

```
PROGRAM MAIN
  INTEGER TOTAL
  TOTAL = 0
  TOTAL = TOTAL + 62
  TOTAL = TOTAL + 40
  TOTAL = TOTAL + 55
  TOTAL = TOTAL + 90
  WRITE(6,*) 'THE VALUE OF TOTAL IS INITIALLY SET TO ', TOTAL
  WRITE(6,*) '   TOTAL IS NOW ', TOTAL
  WRITE(6,*) '   TOTAL IS NOW ', TOTAL
  WRITE(6,*) '   TOTAL IS NOW ', TOTAL
  WRITE(6,*) '   THE FINAL VALUE IN TOTAL IS ', TOTAL
  END
```

Determine the output that this program produces.

Programming Exercises

20a. Enter, compile, and execute Program 2-3 on your computer system.

b. Rewrite Program 2-3 so that it contains one subroutine.

c. Execute the program written for Exercise 20b on a computer.

21a. Enter, compile, and execute Program 2-4 on your computer system.

b. Rewrite Program 2-4 so that it contains one subroutine.

c. Execute the program written for Exercise 21b on a computer.

22. Enter, compile, and execute Program 2-5 on your computer system.

23. Using Program 2-3, determine the volume of cylinders having the following radii and heights:

Radius (in.)	Height (in.)
1.62	6.23
2.86	7.52
4.26	8.95
8.52	10.86
12.29	15.35

24. Modify Program 2-3 to calculate the weight, in pounds, of the steel cylinder whose volume was found by the program. The formula for determining the weight is $weight = .28\ (pi)(r^2)(h)$, where r is the radius (in inches) and h is the height (in inches) of the cylinder.

25. The circumference of an ellipse (see Figure 2-10) is given by the formula:

$$Circumference = pi * \sqrt{2(a^2 + b^2)}$$

Using this formula, write a FORTRAN program to calculate the circumference of an ellipse having a minor radius of 2.5 inches and a major radius of 6.4 inches. (*Hint:* The square root can be taken by raising the real quantity $2(a^2 + b^2)$ to the 0.5 power.)

26a. The combined resistance of three resistors connected in parallel, as shown in Figure 2-11, is given by the equation:

$$Combined\ resistance = \frac{1}{\frac{1}{R_1} + \frac{1}{R_2} + \frac{1}{R_3}}$$

Write a FORTRAN program to calculate and display the combined resistance when the three resistors $R_1 = 1000$, $R_2 = 1000$, and $R_3 = 1000$ are connected in parallel. Your program should produce the display THE COMBINED

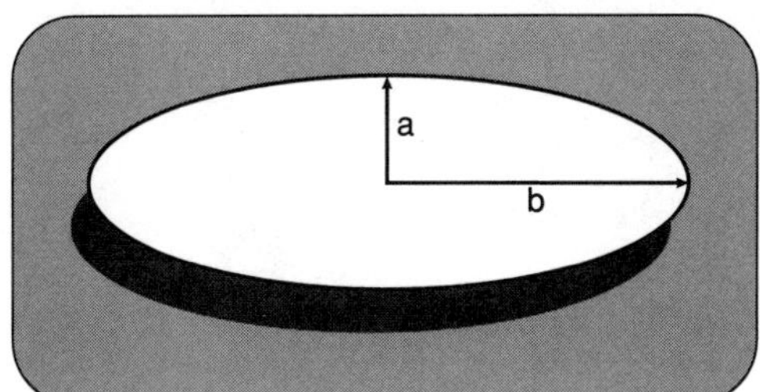

Figure 2-10 The Minor Radius *a* and the Major Radius *b* of an Ellipse

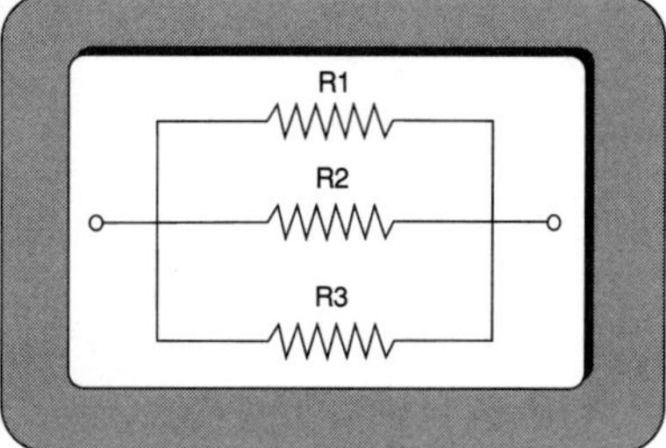

Figure 2-11 Three Resistors Connected in Parallel

RESISTANCE, IN OHMS, IS xxxxx, where the *x*s are replaced by the value of the combined resistance computed by your program.

b. How do you know that the value calculated by your program is correct?

c. Once you have verified the output produced by your program, modify it to determine the combined resistance when the resistors $R_1 = 1500$, $R_2 = 1200$, and $R_3 = 2000$ are connected in parallel.

27a. Write a FORTRAN program to calculate and display the value of the slope of the line connecting the two points whose coordinates are (3,7) and (8,12). Use the fact that the slope between two points having coordinates (x_1,y_1) and (x_2,y_2) is $slope = (y_2 - y_1) / (x_2 - x_1)$. Your program should produce the display THE SLOPE IS xxxx, where the *x*s are replaced by the value calculated by your program.

b. How do you know that the result produced by your program is correct?

c. Once you have verified the output produced by your program, modify it to determine the slope of the line connecting the points (2,10) and (12,6).

28a. Write a FORTRAN program to calculate and display the coordinates of the midpoint of the line connecting the two points given in Exercise 27a. Use the fact that the coordinates of the midpoint between two points having coordinates (x_1,y_1) and (x_2,y_2) are $((x_1+x_2)/2,\ (y_1+y_2)/2)$. Your program should produce the following display:

```
THE X MIDPOINT COORDINATE IS xxx
THE Y MIDPOINT COORDINATE IS xxx
```

where the *x*s are replaced with the values calculated by your program.

b. How do you know that the midpoint values calculated by your program are correct?

c. Once you have verified the output produced by your program, modify it to determine the midpoint coordinates of the line connecting the points (2,10) and (12,6).

29a. For the electrical circuit shown in Figure 2-12, the branch currents I_1, I_2, and I_3 can be determined using the formulas

$$I_1 = \frac{E_2R_3 + E_1(R_1 + R_3)}{(R_1 + R_3)\,(R_2 + R_3) - (R_3)^2}$$

$$I_2 = \frac{E_1R_3 + E_2(R_1 + R_3)}{(R_1 + R_3)\,(R_2 + R_3) - (R_3)^2}$$

$$I_3 = I_1 - I_2$$

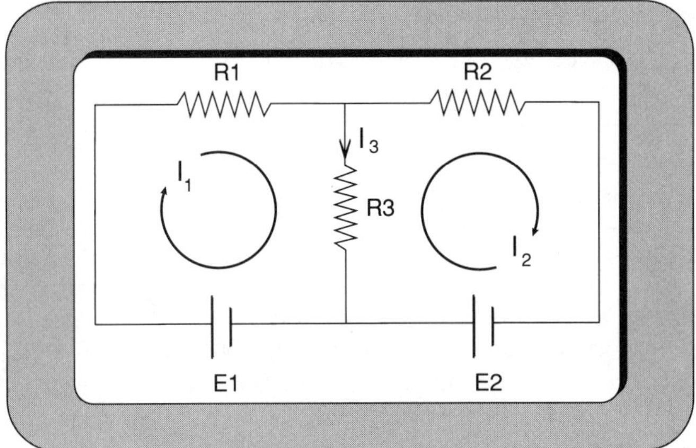

Figure 2-12 An Electrical Circuit

Using these formulas, write a FORTRAN program to compute the branch currents when R_1 = 10 ohms, R_2 = 4 ohms, R_3 = 6 ohms, E_1 = 12 volts, and E_2 = 9 volts. The display produced by your program should be:

```
BRANCH CURRENT 1 IS xxxx
BRANCH CURRENT 2 IS xxxx
BRANCH CURRENT 3 IS xxxx
```

where the *x*s are replaced by the values determined in your program.

b. How do you know that the branch currents calculated by your program are correct?

c. Once you have verified the output produced by your program, modify it to determine the branch currents for the values R_1 = 1500, R_2 = 1200, R_3 = 2000, E_1 = 15, and E_2 = 12.

2.4 Formatted Output

Besides calculating correct results, it is extremely important for a program to present its results clearly and attractively. Typically, in fact, most users of a program judge it based on the perceived ease of data entry and the style and presentation of the output. For many applications, especially when a program is being developed, the list-directed PRINT and WRITE statements introduced in Chapter 1 are sufficient. Occasions do arise, however, that require more explicit programmer control of the output format. This explicit control is provided using *user-formatted* output, where the spacing and appearance of the display are directly specified by the programmer.

User-Formatted PRINT and WRITE Statements

The output display produced by both PRINT and WRITE statements can be explicitly defined using the user-formatted version of these statements rather than their list-directed versions. In fact, both list-directed and user-formatted versions are variations of more general forms for these statements. For the WRITE statement, this more general form is:

```
WRITE (unit number, format identifier) expression list
```

The expression list is a list of any valid FORTRAN expressions, which include constants, variables, and arithmetic expressions including both constants and variables. The format identifier in the WRITE statement allows us to control the precise form in which items in the expression list are displayed. Specifically, the format identifier can be:

1. an asterisk
2. a format specification enclosed in parentheses and apostrophes
3. a reference to a FORMAT statement that contains a format specification

An asterisk, as we have already seen, selects the compiler's list-directed (default) format. In place of the asterisk, an explicit format specification can be used. A more useful approach is to place this explicit format specification in a separate FORMAT statement that is referenced by the WRITE statement. This approach allows the same format control to be referenced by any number of WRITE statements and is the approach we will adopt. Using this approach, the required form of the user-formatted WRITE statement is:

```
WRITE (unit number, n) expression list
```

where the unit number, as before, designates where the display is to be sent, *n* is a number from 1 to 99999 that refers to a FORMAT statement, and the expression list is a list of FORTRAN expressions, as in the list-directed version. The FORMAT statement referenced by the WRITE statement must use the same number, *n*, in its label field. For example, a sample user-formatted WRITE statement and its associated FORMAT statement are:

```
123456789 ——— Column Number ——————————————————72
      WRITE (6, 10) AVERGE
   10 FORMAT(' ','THE AVERAGE IS',F5.2)
```

The statement label 10 was chosen arbitrarily, and any other valid integer between 1 and 99999 could have been selected.

The same options available to the WRITE statement are also provided by the PRINT statement. Specifically, the general form of the PRINT statement that references a FORMAT statement is:

```
PRINT n, expression list
```

where *n* is the label number of a FORMAT statement. For example, assuming that unit number 6 designates the standard output device, the statement pair:

```
      PRINT 10, AVERGE
10    FORMAT(' ','THE AVERAGE IS',F5.2)
```

produces the same output as the statements

```
      WRITE(6,10) AVERGE
10    FORMAT(' ','THE AVERAGE IS',F5.2)
```

FORMAT Statements

FORMAT statements referenced by the user-formatted versions of both the PRINT and WRITE statements consist of a statement label, the keyword FORMAT, and a format specification list having the general form:

```
n    FORMAT (specification list)
```

where *n* is a statement label, which is a number from 1 to 99999, that is placed in columns 1 through 5 (the label field). As we have already seen, the statement label in the FORMAT statement is used to connect the format specification to a corresponding PRINT or WRITE statement. The specification list in the statement designates both the vertical and horizontal positioning of the display. The vertical positioning specifies whether the displayed line is placed at the top of the next printed page (for displays printed on paper), on the next line, double spaced, or with no vertical spacing (called overprinting). Horizontal positioning determines the number of items displayed on a single line, the spacing between items on the same line, and the number of digits that are displayed for each value. An example of a FORMAT statement is:

```
10 FORMAT(' ','THE AVERAGE IS',F5.2)
```

The specification list in this FORMAT statement consists of three items, each of which must be separated from the others by a comma.

The first item in a specification list is called the *carriage control character* and specifies the vertical positioning of the line to be printed. Table 2-4 lists the most commonly used carriage control characters and the effect each produces.

For example, the carriage control character specified by the FORMAT statement:

```
10 FORMAT(' ','THE AVERAGE IS',F5.2)
```

is the character constant `' '`. The space within apostrophes, as listed in Table 2-4, specifies that single spacing has been selected.

Carriage control characters, as their name implies, were originally designed for controlling the carriage of a standard printer. When used with a printer, the top-of-page carriage control character causes the current page to be ejected and the top of the next page to be placed under the print mechanism. The overprint control causes no motion of the carriage; this causes the new line to print on top of the existing one,

Table 2-4 Carriage Control Characters

Character	Effect
+	No vertical spacing: return to column 1 of the current line and overprint the current display.
a blank space	Single spacing: advance to the next space line before displaying any data.
0	Double spacing: advance two lines before displaying any data.
1	Top-of-page (paper output only): advance to the top of the next page before displaying any data.

which is called overprinting. With video screens these two specifiers do not have the same effect. Generally, the top-of-page has no effect on a video screen, and the overprint erases the existing line before the next line is displayed.

Before actually displaying a line of text on an output device, the computer first constructs the line internally within its memory unit. The memory area reserved for constructing the line is called a *buffer* (see Figure 2-13). The buffer is automatically cleared (filled with blanks) before being used to construct a new line. Once the line is constructed, the contents of the buffer are sent out for display as a complete entity. The first location of the buffer is used to store the carriage control character. When the complete contents of the buffer are sent to the display unit, the carriage control character tells the display device where to vertically position the next line. *Thus, the second character in the buffer becomes the first character actually displayed.*

The same buffer mechanism is employed for list-directed output, except that the compiler places a blank space in the first buffer position (single spacing) and fills the rest of the buffer with the indicated data in accordance with its own format specifications. Following are the more common FORMAT specifications for explicit user control of how data is entered into the buffer and ultimately displayed. A complete listing of all format specifications is presented in Appendix B.

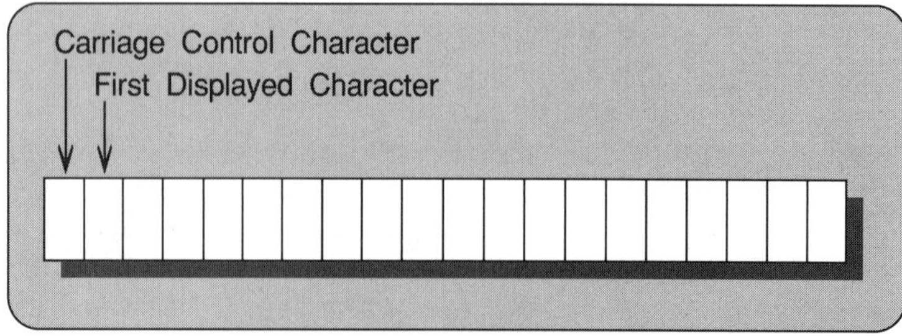

Figure 2-13 An Output Buffer

Literal Specification

A literal specification consists of one or more characters enclosed within apostrophes and permits the direct placement of the enclosed characters in the memory buffer. Thus, carriage control characters can be placed in the buffer by enclosing the selected carriage control character within apostrophes and placing the resulting character constant as the first item in the specification list. Similarly, any other character constant can be entered in the buffer using a literal specification. For example, the FORMAT statement:

```
10 FORMAT (' ','INVENTORY REPORT:')
```

sets the carriage control for single spacing and places the 17 characters INVENTORY REPORT: in positions 2 through 18 of the buffer. When referenced by a WRITE statement, as in the combination of statements

```
     WRITE(6,10)
10   FORMAT (' ','INVENTORY REPORT:')
```

the following display is produced:

```
INVENTORY REPORT:
12345678911111111
         01234567
```

The italicized numbers under the display correspond to the column positions that the characters above would occupy on the output line. Thus, the I is displayed in column 1, and the colon, :, is placed in column 17.

When no carriage control character is included in a format specifier, the first character intended for display by default fills the first position of the output buffer and becomes the carriage control character. For example, what do you think the display produced by the sequence of statements:

```
     WRITE(6,10)
10   FORMAT ('1999 PROFIT PROJECTIONS')
```

would be?

Here the carriage control specification was omitted. Since the computer always uses the first character in the specification list as a carriage control, the 1 in the number 1999 is used for this purpose. The actual message, displayed at the top of a new page, becomes:

```
999 PROFIT PROJECTIONS
1234567891111111111222
         0123456789012
```

As before, the numbers under the display indicate the column position of each displayed character. It should be noted that since FORMAT statements are nonexecutable, the actual placement of a FORMAT statement can come before or after the PRINT or WRITE statement that references it. Some programmers prefer to place all FORMAT statements together, at either the beginning or end of a program (before the END statement), while other programmers prefer to place an individual FORMAT statement close to the PRINT or WRITE statement that references it. All of these approaches are appropriate.

Although literal specifications are extremely useful for specifying carriage control characters and messages that can be used for report or column headings, this specification does not permit us to display numeric values stored in variables. For this we need two format specifiers, one for integers (I) and another for real numbers (F).

The I Specification

The I specification is required for displaying the contents of an integer variable under user-formatting control. The general form of this specification is:

```
Iw
```

where the I specifies that an integer number will be displayed, and the *w* designates the maximum field width size to be filled. For example, assuming the variables ICOUNT, MINVAL, and MAXVAL contain the values shown in Figure 2-14, the combination of statements:

```
      WRITE(6,20) ICOUNT, MINVAL, MAXVAL
   20 FORMAT(' ',I3,I4,I5)
```

produces the display:

```
  8  12   16
123456789111
         012
```

The numbers 3, 4, and 5 in the I specifications are all field width specifiers. The 3 causes the first integer to be displayed in a total field width of three spaces, in this case, two blank spaces followed by the number 8. The field width specifier in the second integer specification, I4, causes two blank spaces and the number 12 to be printed for a total field width of four spaces. The last field width specifier causes the 16 to be printed in a field of five spaces, which includes three blanks and the number 16. As illustrated, for field widths that are large enough to contain the desired integer, the number is right-justified within the designated field. If the field width specifier is too small for the integer to be displayed, the field is filled with asterisks. For example, assuming the number 28194 is stored in the variable ITOTAL, the statements:

```
      WRITE (6,30) ITOTAL
   30 FORMAT(' ',I4)
```

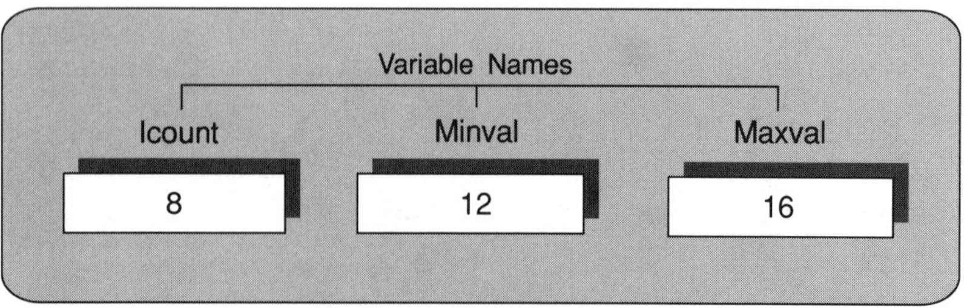

Figure 2-14 The Variables ICOUNT, MINVAL, and MAXVAL in Memory

produce the display:

```
****
```

Here the field width of four is not large enough to contain the integer, so the field is filled with asterisks. If the integer to be displayed is a negative number, the field width must be large enough to contain both the minus sign and the magnitude of the number, or asterisks will be printed.

An extremely useful display is produced by combining a literal message specification with a numerical specification. For example, the sequence of statements:

```
      INTEGER IPOWER
      IPOWER = 2**10
      WRITE (6,30) IPOWER
30    FORMAT(' ','2 RAISED TO THE 10TH = ',I4)
```

produces the display:

```
2 RAISED TO THE 10TH = 1024
1234567891111111111222222222
         0123456789012345
```

Here the display not only presents the results of a calculation but also gives an indication of what the numerical value represents.

The F Specification

The F specification (the F stands for floating point) defines the format of the output for displaying values of real variables and expressions in decimal (as opposed to exponential) form. The general form of this specification is:

```
Fw.d
```

The F in the specification must be present and designates that a decimal number will be displayed. In addition, the two field width specifiers, denoted as *w* and *d*, separated by a period, must also be present. The first specifier (*w*) determines the total width of the display, including space for a sign and the number's decimal point. The second specifier (*d*) determines how many digits are printed to the right of the decimal point. For example, the statements:

```
      SLOPE = 25.67
      PRINT 16, SLOPE
16    FORMAT(' ',F9.3)
```

produce the display:

```
   25.670
123456789
```

As before, field position numbers have been placed under the output to clearly mark the display field. The specification F9.3 tells the computer to display a real number in a total field width of 9 spaces, with three digits displayed to the right of the decimal point. Since the number contains only two digits to the right of the decimal point, the decimal part of the number is padded with a trailing zero. Numbers are always right-justified in the field.

If the portion of the total field width allocated to the integer portion of a decimal number is too small to fit the integer part of the number, the display is filled with asterisks. For field widths that can accommodate the integer portion of a decimal number, the fractional part of the number is always displayed with the number of specified digits. If the fractional part contains fewer digits than specified, the number is padded with trailing zeros; if the fractional part contains more digits than called for in the specifier, the number is rounded to the indicated number of decimal places. Program 2-6 illustrates these effects using WRITE statements to display the values of two floating point arithmetic expressions.

Program 2-6

```
123456789 ——————————— Column Number ——————————————————72
      PROGRAM MAIN
        WRITE(6,10) 16.3 + 2.1
        WRITE(6,10) 18.621 + 2.116
 10     FORMAT(' ','THE VALUE OF THE EXPRESSION IS ',F5.2)
        END
```

The output of Program 2-6 is:

```
THE VALUE OF THE EXPRESSION IS 18.40
THE VALUE OF THE EXPRESSION IS 20.74
123456789111111111122222222223333333
         012345678901234567890123456
```

Notice that the values displayed on both lines of the output are contained within individual fields five spaces wide with two positions beyond the decimal point. The first value displayed has been padded with a trailing zero to fill the fractional part of the field, and the second value has been rounded to two decimal places. Also notice that both WRITE statements in the program reference the same FORMAT statement.

One caution should be mentioned here. The FORMAT statement does check the values it is given. Thus, if an integer specification is used (I3, for example), and the value given the statement is a real number, the program will display an error message on output. Similarly, if a real specification is used (F5.2, for example), and the corresponding number is an integer, an error message on output will also be produced.

The X Specification

The X specification is used to create blank fields by causing the computer to skip over a specified number of spaces. To illustrate the usefulness of creating a blank field first, consider the FORMAT statement:

```
100 FORMAT (' ',I3,I4)
```

This statement defines two integer fields with no intervening space between them. The first field occupies columns 1, 2, and 3 and is immediately followed by the second field. Using the X edit descriptor, we can insert any desired number of blank spaces in the output before a field is used. The general form of the X edit specification is:

```
nX
```

where *n* is an integer number defining how many spaces should be skipped over (left blank). For example, the FORMAT statement:

```
100 FORMAT (' ',1X,I3,2X,I3)
```

causes a single space to be skipped over before the first integer field is used. After the first integer is displayed, two additional spaces are skipped over, and then the second integer field is used. For example, the following sequence of statements:

```
      INTEGER NUM1, NUM2
      NUM1 = 726
      NUM2 = 345
      WRITE(6,100) NUM1, NUM2
100   FORMAT (' ',1X,I3,2X,I3)
```

produces the display:

```
 726  345
123456789
```

The X specification may also be used as a substitute for the single-space carriage control specification, ' '. For example, the 1X in the FORMAT statement:

```
10 FORMAT(1X,I4)
```

causes one blank space to fill the first position in the memory buffer in the same manner as the ' ' literal specification. Thus, the literal specification ' ' and the 1X specification can be used interchangeably for carriage control purposes. Additionally, since FORTRAN defaults to single spacing when an unrecognized control character is used, any noncontrol code placed in the first buffer position also causes single spacing to occur. For example, both of the following FORMAT statements produce single-spaced output lines:

```
45 FORMAT('7',I5)
66 FORMAT(30X,'HELLO WORLD!')
```

The first FORMAT statement specifies that an integer is to be displayed in a field with a width of 5, starting at column 1. Because a separate carriage control specification has not been included in the second FORMAT statement, this statement specifies that the message `HELLO WORLD!` is to be displayed after 29 blank spaces (not 30) have been skipped over. The first blank space designated by the specification 30X is used as the carriage control.

The A Specification

The A specification (the A stands for alphanumeric) defines the output format for displaying character data. The most common form of this specification is:

```
Aw
```

where the A designates that alphanumeric data will be displayed and the *w* is an optional field width specifier designating the maximum character size of the display. For example, the statements:

```
      PRINT 10, 'HAVE A HAPPY DAY'
10    FORMAT (' ',A25)
```

includes both the A edit specification and a field width specifier of 25. This specification causes the character constant HAVE A HAPPY DAY to be displayed in a field width of 25, as follows:

```
        HAVE A HAPPY DAY
1234567891111111111222222
         0123456789012345
```

As illustrated, if the specified field width is larger than the character constant to be displayed, the constant is right-justified in the field and padded with leading blanks. If the field width specifier is too small for the string to be displayed, only the first *w* characters of the constant will be output. For example, the statements:

```
      PRINT 10, 'HELLO THERE WORLD!'
10    FORMAT (' ',A5)
```

produce the display:

```
HELLO
12345
```

When the A edit specification is used without a field width specifier, the output is displayed in a field sufficiently large to hold the required number of characters. Thus, the statements:

```
      PRINT 10, 'HAVE A HAPPY DAY'
10    FORMAT (' ',A)
```

produce the display:

```
HAVE A HAPPY DAY
1234567891111111
         0123456
```

In using the A specification it is the programmer's responsibility to ensure that character data are actually being used. Attempting to display a number, either real or integer, using the A specification will produce an error message or an unpredictable display.

Additional Format Control Characters

Many other format specifications exist in addition to the literal, I, F, A, and X specifications. The more useful of these additional specifications include repeat specifications, multiple line control, and tab control. The specifications providing these features are now described (a complete list of format specifications is presented in Appendix B).

Repeat Counts

A repeat count allows both single and groups of format specifications to be repeated. For example, the specification:

```
10 FORMAT (' ',F5.2,F5.2,F5.2)
```

uses the same specifier, F5.2, three times in succession. Using a repeat count of 3, this statement can be rewritten as:

```
10 FORMAT (' ',3F5.2)
```

Notice that the repeat count simply allows us to shorten the format specifier by eliminating the need to retype the same specifier explicitly. In addition to repeating a single format specifier, a repeat count also can be used with larger groupings of specifications. For example, the statement:

```
20 FORMAT (' ',1X,I3,2X,I3,2X,I3,2X,F4.2,1X,F5.2,1X,F5.2)
```

repeats the sequence I3,2X three times and the sequence 1X,F5.2 twice. Enclosing these sequences in parentheses and using repeat counts of 3 and 2, respectively, results in the following equivalent FORMAT statement.

```
20 FORMAT (' ',1X,3(I3,2X),F4.2,2(1X,F5.2))
```

All of the format specifiers presented so far (I, F, A, and X) may use repeat counts. The following format specifiers are nonrepeatable.

The Slash (/) Specification

The slash (/) specification, which can be placed anywhere within a specification list, forces the output buffer to display its contents immediately and then to clear itself. For example, the statements:

```
   PRINT 65
65 FORMAT(' ','HELLO',/,' ','THERE',//,' ','WORLD!')
```

produce the following display:

```
HELLO
THERE
WORLD!
```

This display is produced as follows: The carriage control ' ' and the word HELLO in the format specifier initially fill the first six locations of the output buffer with a blank and the characters H, E, L, L, and O. The first slash then forces the contents of the buffer to be displayed, producing the first output line. The buffer is then cleared and is filled with a blank followed by the characters T, H, E, R, and E. The next slash causes the contents of the buffer to be displayed again, producing the second line of output, and the buffer is again cleared. The second slash in the sequence // once again causes the contents of the buffer to be displayed. Since there is nothing in the buffer, a blank line is displayed. Finally, the buffer is filled with a blank space and the characters W, O, R, L, D, and !. The closing parenthesis of the format specifier then forces the contents of the buffer to be displayed, producing the last output line.

Two facts with respect to the slash edit descriptor should be kept in mind. First, since the slash causes the contents of the buffer to be displayed and the buffer cleared, the first character following a sequence of one or more slashes should be a carriage control character. Second, the commas enclosing the slash edit descriptor are always optional. For example, omitting the commas surrounding the slashes in the previous format statement produces the equivalent statement:

```
65 FORMAT(' ','HELLO'/' ','THERE'//' ','WORLD!')
```

Tab Specifications

The tab specifications provide tab capabilities and permit display fields to begin at any specified position. The first form of this specification is:

```
Tc
```

where *c* is an integer representing an absolute column number in the buffer at which the next field is to begin. For example, the FORMAT statement:

```
30 FORMAT (' ',T15,I3,T45,F5.2)
```

causes the first field, I3, to be placed at column 15 in the buffer and the second field, F5.2, to be placed at column 45 in the buffer. Thus, on the output display the first field will be displayed in column 14 and the second field in column 44. Tabbing "backward" usually is permitted. For example, the FORMAT statement:

```
35 FORMAT(' ',T24,I5,T10,I2,T30,I6)
```

will cause the first integer field, I5, to begin at column 24 in the buffer and the second field to begin at column 10. Finally, the last integer field, I6, begins at column 30 in the buffer.

In addition to absolute tabbing provided by the T edit descriptor, the TL and TR edit descriptors provide left (backward) and right (forward) relative positioning. The general form of the tab left (backward) specification is:

```
TLn
```

where *n* is an integer denoting how many spaces to the left, relative to the current position, should be backspaced. The general form of the tab right (forward) specification is:

```
TRn
```

where *n* is an integer denoting how many spaces to the right, relative to the current position, should be skipped over. For example, the statements:

```
   WRITE (6,22) 123,'HELLO',4567
22 FORMAT(' ',T8,I3,TL9,A5,TR4,I4)
```

produce the output:

```
HELLO 1234567
1234567891111
         0123
```

The first tab in the format, T8, causes the display to tab over to column 8 in the buffer, which corresponds to column 7 on the screen or paper. The number 123 is entered into this field position, at which point the current paper column position is 10. Tabbing back from column 10 with the TL9 descriptor places the starting column of the second field, A5, at column 1 on the paper output. After the word HELLO is displayed in columns 1 through 5, the current column position becomes 6. Tabbing forward from this position four spaces places the starting position of the last field at column 10.

Since relative tabbing to the right is the same as skipping over spaces, the conversion sequences TR*n* and *n*X can be used interchangeably. For example, the statement:

```
10 FORMAT(' ',I3,TR5,F6.2)
```

produces the same display as does the statement:

```
20 FORMAT(' ',I3,5X,F6.2)
```

Skill Builder Exercises

1. Write out the display produced by the following statements (assume that unit number 6 designates the standard output device):

a.
```
      NUM1 = 7
      WRITE(6,10) NUM1
   10 FORMAT (' ',1X,I1)
```
b.
```
      NUM1 = 7
      WRITE(6,20) NUM1
   20 FORMAT (' ',1X,I4)
```
c.
```
      NUM1 = 29876
      WRITE(6,30) NUM1
   30 FORMAT (' ',1X,I4)
```
d.
```
      SECNUM = 7.92
      WRITE(6,40) SECNUM
   40 FORMAT (1X,F5.2)
```
e.
```
      SECNUM = 5.762
      WRITE(6,50) SECNUM
   50 FORMAT (1X,F5.2)
```
f.
```
      SECNUM = 82.625
      WRITE(6,60) SECNUM
   60 FORMAT (1X,F5.2)
```

g.
```
      SECNUM = 523.462
      WRITE(6,70) SECNUM
   70 FORMAT (1X,F5.2)
```
h.
```
      SECNUM = 924.
      WRITE(6,80) SECNUM
   80 FORMAT (1X,F5.2)
```
i.
```
      WRITE(6,10) 'The number is ', 26.27
      WRITE(6,10) 'The number is ', 682.3
      WRITE(6,10) 'The number is ', 1.968
   10 FORMAT (1X,A,1X,F6.2)
```
j.
```
      WRITE (6,20) 26.27
      WRITE (6,20) 682.3
      WRITE (6,20) 1.968
      WRITE (6,30)
      WRITE (6,20) 26.27 + 682.3 + 1.968
   20 FORMAT(1X,F6.2)
   30 FORMAT(1X,'---')
```
k.
```
      WRITE (6,30) 26.27
      WRITE (6,30) 682.3
      WRITE (6,30) 1.968
      WRITE (6,40)
      WRITE (6,30) 26.27 + 682.3 + 1.968
   30 FORMAT (' ',3X,F6.2)
   40 FORMAT (' ',T4,'---')
```
l.
```
      WRITE (6,50) 34.164
      WRITE (6,50) 10.003
      WRITE (6,60)
      WRITE (6,50) 34.164 + 10.003
   50 FORMAT (' ',8X,F5.2)
   60 FORMAT (' ',T9,'---')
```

2. Determine the output produced by the following program:

```
      PROGRAM MAIN
       REAL AVERAGE
       AVERGE = 26.27
       WRITE(6,10) AVERGE
       AVERGE = 682.3
       WRITE(6,10) AVERGE
       AVERGE = 1.968
       WRITE(6,10) AVERGE
 10    FORMAT (1X,'THE AVERAGE IS',1X,F6.2)
       END
```

3. Determine and write out the display produced by the following statements:

a.
```
      NUM1 = 7
      PRINT 10, NUM1
   10 FORMAT (' ',1X,I1)
```
b.
```
      NUM1 = 7
      PRINT 20, NUM1
   20 FORMAT (' ',1X,I4)
```
c.
```
      NUM1 = 29876
      PRINT 30, NUM1
   30 FORMAT (' ',1X,I4)
```
d.
```
      SECNUM = 7.92
      PRINT 40, SECNUM
   40 FORMAT (1X,F5.2)
```
e.
```
      SECNUM = 5.762
      PRINT 50, SECNUM
   50 FORMAT (1X,F5.2)
```
f.
```
      SECNUM = 82.625
      PRINT 60, SECNUM
   60 FORMAT (1X,F5.2)
```
g.
```
      SECNUM = 523.462
      PRINT 70, SECNUM
   70 FORMAT (1X,F5.2)
```
h.
```
      SECNUM = 924.
      PRINT 80, SECNUM
   80 FORMAT (1X,F6.2)
```
i.
```
      PRINT 10, 'THE NUMBER IS ', 26.27
      PRINT 10, 'THE NUMBER IS ', 682.3
      PRINT 10, 'THE NUMBER IS ', 1.968
   10 FORMAT (1X,A,1X,F6.2)
```
j.
```
      PRINT 20, 26.27
      PRINT 20, 682.3
      PRINT 20, 1.968
      PRINT 30
      PRINT 20, 26.27 + 682.3 + 1.968
   20 FORMAT(1X,F6.2)
   30 FORMAT(1X,'---')
```
k.
```
      PRINT 30, 26.27
      PRINT 30, 682.3
      PRINT 30, 1.968
      PRINT 40
      PRINT 30, 26.27 + 682.3 + 1.968
   30 FORMAT(' ',3X,F6.2)
   40 FORMAT(' ',T4,'---')
```

l.
```
      PRINT 50, 34.164
      PRINT 50, 10.003
      PRINT 60, '---'
      PRINT 50, 34.164 + 10.003
   50 FORMAT (' ',8X,F5.2)
   60 FORMAT (' ',T9,A)
```

4a. Determine the output displayed by the following program:

```
      PROGRAM MAIN
      REAL PRICE, SALSTX, TOTAL
      PRICE = 36.0
      SALSTX = .05 * PRICE
      TOTAL = PRICE + SALSTX
      PRINT 55, SALSTX
      PRINT 60, TOTAL
   55 FORMAT (1X,'THE SALES TAX IS $',F7.3)
   60 FORMAT (1X,'THE TOTAL BILL IS $',F7.3)
      END
```

b. Rewrite the FORMAT statements in the program listed in Exercise 4a to produce the display:

```
THE SALES TAX IS $ 1.80
THE TOTAL BILL IS $37.80
```

c. Compile and execute the program written for Exercise 4b to verify the output.

5. Determine and write out the display produced by the following statements.

a.
```
      INUM = 4
      WRITE (6,10) INUM
   10 FORMAT (1X,I1)
```

b.
```
      INUM = 4
      WRITE (6,20) INUM
   20 FORMAT (1X,I4)
```

c.
```
      INUM = 32736
      WRITE (6,30) INUM
   30 FORMAT (1X,I4)
```

d.
```
      TNUM = 8.64
      WRITE (6,40) TNUM
   40 FORMAT (1X,F5.2)
```

e.
```
      TNUM = 7.562
      WRITE (6,50) TNUM
   50 FORMAT (1X,F5.2)
```

f.
```
      TNUM = 87.735
      WRITE (6,60) TNUM
   60 FORMAT (1X,F5.2)
```

g.
```
      TNUM = 523.462
      WRITE (6,70) TNUM
   70 FORMAT (1X,F5.2)
```

h.
```
      TNUM = 863.
      WRITE (6,80) TNUM
   80 FORMAT (1X,F5.2)
```

Programming Exercises

6. Using either PRINT or WRITE statements, write a FORTRAN program that displays the results of the expressions (3.0 * 5.0), (7.1 * 8.3 – 2.2), and (3.2 / (6.1 * 5)) on three separate lines. Each value displayed should be limited to two decimal positions to the right of the decimal point. Calculate the value of these expressions manually to verify that the displayed values are correct.

7. The combined resistance of three resistors connected in parallel, as shown in Figure 2-15, is given by the equation

$$\textit{Combined resistance} = \frac{1}{\frac{1}{R_1} + \frac{1}{R_2} + \frac{1}{R_3}}$$

Using this formula, write a FORTRAN program to calculate and display the combined resistance when the three resistors R_1 = 1000, R_2 = 1000, and R_3 = 1000 are connected in parallel. The output should produce the display: THE COMBINED RESISTANCE IS xxxx.xx OHMS, where xxxx.xx denotes that the calculated value should be placed in a field width of 7 columns, with two positions to the right of the decimal point.

8. Write a FORTRAN program to calculate and display the value of the slope of the line connecting the two points whose coordinates are (3,7) and (8,12). Use the fact that the slope between two points having coordinates (x_1,y_1) and (x_2,y_2) is slope = $(y_2 - y_1) / (x_2 - x_1)$. The display produced by your program should be: THE VALUE OF THE SLOPE IS xxx.xx, where xxx.xx denotes that the calculated value should be placed in a field wide enough for three places to the left of the decimal point and two places to the right of it.

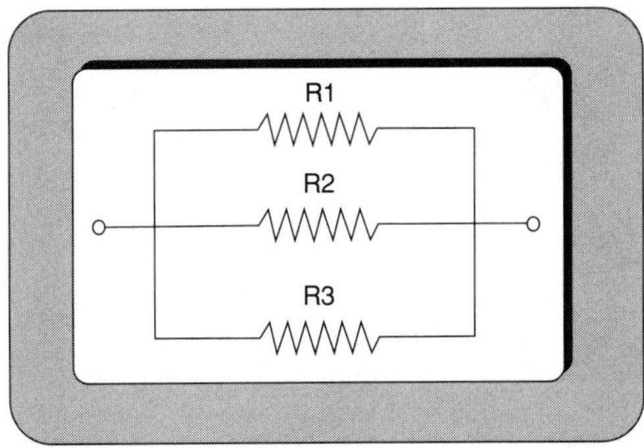

Figure 2-15 Three Resistors Connected in Parallel

9. Write a FORTRAN program to calculate and display the coordinates of the midpoint of the line connecting the two points given in Exercise 8. Use the fact that the coordinates of the midpoint between two points having coordinates (x_1,y_1) and (x_2,y_2) are $((X_1+X_2)/2, (Y_1+Y_2)/2)$. The display produced by your program should be:

```
THE X COORDINATE OF THE MIDPOINT IS xxx.xx
THE Y COORDINATE OF THE MIDPOINT IS xxx.xx
```

where xxx.xx denotes that the calculated value should be placed in a field wide enough for three places to the left of the decimal point and two places to the right of it.

10. Write a FORTRAN program to calculate and display the maximum bending moment, *M*, of a beam, which is supported on both ends (see Figure 2-16). The formula for maximum bending moment is $M = X\ W\ (L - X) / L$, where *X* is the distance from the end of the beam that a weight, *W*, is placed, and *L* is the length of the beam. Let $W = 500$ lbs., $X = 10$ ft., and $L = 25$ ft. The display produced by your program should be:

```
THE MAXIMUM BENDING MOMENT IS xxxx.xxxx
```

where xxxx.xxxx denotes that the calculated value should be placed in a field wide enough for four places each to the right and to the left of the decimal point.

11. For the electrical circuit shown in Figure 2-17, the branch currents I_1, I_2, and I_3 can be determined using the formulas:

$$I_1 = \frac{E_2R_3 + E_1(R_1 + R_3)}{(R_1 + R_3)(R_2 + R_3) - (R_3)^2}$$

$$I_2 = \frac{E_1R_3 + E_2(R_1 + R_3)}{(R_1 + R_3)(R_2 + R_3) - (R_3)^2}$$

$$I_3 = I_1 - I_2$$

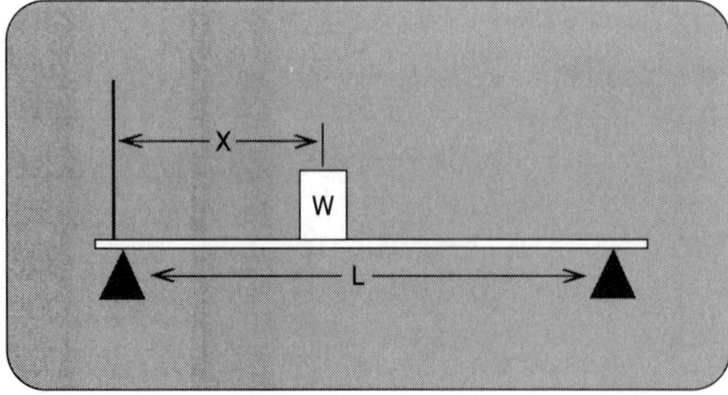

Figure 2-16 Calculating the Maximum Bending Moment

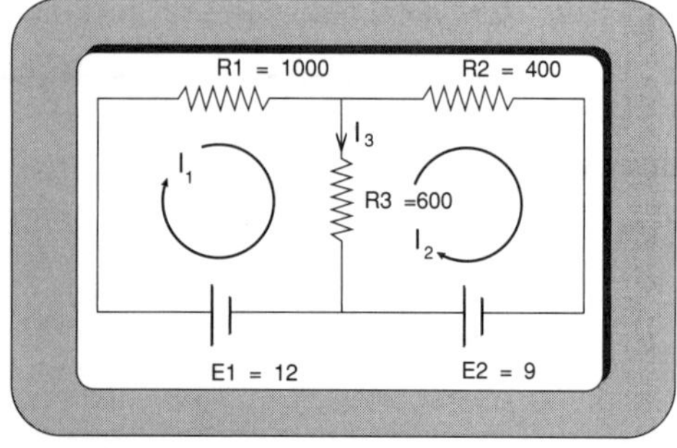

Figure 2-17 Calculating Loop Currents in an Electrical Circuit

Using these formulas, write a FORTRAN program to compute the branch currents when R_1 = 1000 ohms, R_2 = 400 ohms, R_3 = 600 ohms, E_1 = 12 volts, and E_2 = 9 volts. The display produced by your program should be:

```
BRANCH CURRENT 1 IS xx.xxxx
BRANCH CURRENT 2 IS xx.xxxx
BRANCH CURRENT 3 IS xx.xxxx
```

where xx.xxxx denotes that the calculated value should be placed in a field wide enough for two places to the left of the decimal point and four places to the right of it.

2.5 Top-Down Program Development

Recall from Section 1.1 that writing a FORTRAN program is essentially the last step in the programming process. The first step in the process is determining what is required and selecting the algorithm to be coded into FORTRAN. In this section we present a five-step program development procedure, called top-down development, for converting programming problems into working FORTRAN programs. To make this development procedure more meaningful, we first apply it to a simple programming problem. The key part of the development procedure, called top-down design, is then applied to a more complicated program requirement. As we will see, designing a program using a top-down approach results in a modular program design.

The five steps in the top-down development procedure are to:

1. determine the desired output items that the program must produce
2. determine the input items
3. design the program as follows:
   a. either select an algorithm for transforming the input items into the desired outputs or design one using a top-down design technique
   b. check the chosen algorithm, by hand, using specific input values
   c. determine variable names for the selected algorithm
4. code the algorithm into FORTRAN
5. test the program using selected test data

Formally, steps 1 and 2 in the development procedure are referred to as the program *analysis phase*; step 3 is called the *design phase*, step 4 the *coding phase*, and step 5 the *testing phase*.

In the analysis phase of program development (steps 1 and 2), we are concerned with extracting the complete input and output information supplied by the problem. Together these two items are referred to as the problem's Input/Output, or I/O. Only after a problem's I/O has been determined is it possible to select an algorithm for transforming the inputs into the desired outputs. For example, consider the following simple programming problem:

The electrical resistance of a metal wire, in ohms, is given by the formula $R = (mL)/A$, where m is the resistivity of the metal; L is the length of the wire, in feet; and A is the cross-sectional area of the wire, in circular mils. Using this information, write a FORTRAN program to calculate the resistance of a wire that is 125 feet long, has a cross-sectional area of 500 circular mils, and is copper. The resistivity of copper is 10.4.

Step 1: Determine the Desired Output

The first step in developing a program for this problem statement is determining the required outputs (step 1 of the development procedure). Frequently, the statement of the problem will use such words as *calculate*, *print*, *determine*, *find*, or *compare*, which can be used to determine the desired outputs.

For our sample problem statement, the key phrase is "to calculate the resistance of a wire." This clearly identifies an output item. Since there are no other such phrases in the problem, only one output item is required.

Step 2: Determine the Input Items

After the desired output has been clearly identified, step 2 of the development process requires that all the input items be identified. It is essential at this stage to distinguish between input items and input values. An input item is the name of an input quantity, while an input value is a specific number or quantity that the input item can be. For example, in our sample problem statement the input items are the resistivity, m, the length of the wire, L, and the cross-sectional area of the wire, A. Although these input items have specific numerical values, these input item values are generally not of importance in step 2.

The reason that input values are not needed at this point is that the initial selection of an algorithm typically is independent of specific input values; the algorithm depends on knowing what the output and input items are and if there are any special limits. Let us see why this is so, as we determine a suitable algorithm for our sample problem statement.

Step 3a: Determine an Algorithm

From the problem statement it is clear that the algorithm for transforming the input items to the desired output is given by the formula $R = (mL)/A$. Notice that this formula can be used regardless of the specific values assigned to m, L, and A. Although we cannot produce an actual numerical value for the output item, resistance, unless we have actual numerical values for the input items, the correct relationship between inputs and outputs is expressed by the formula. Recall that this is precisely what an algorithm provides: a description of how the inputs are to be transformed into outputs that work for all inputs. Thus, the complete algorithm, in pseudocode, for solving this problem is:

Assign values to m, L, and A
Calculate the resistance using the formula R = (mL)/A
Display the result

Step 3b: Do a Hand Calculation

After an algorithm is selected, the next step in the design procedure, step 3b, is to check the algorithm manually using specific data. Performing a manual calculation, either by hand or using a calculator, helps to ensure that you really do understand the problem. An added feature of doing a manual calculation is that the results can be used later to verify the operation of your program in the testing phase. Then, when the final program is used with other data, you will have established a degree of confidence that a correct result is being calculated.

Doing a manual calculation requires that we have specific input values that can be applied to the algorithm to produce the desired output. For this problem three input values are given: a resistivity of 10.4, a cross-sectional area of 500 circular mils, and a length of 125 feet. Substituting these values into the formula, we obtain a resistance of 2.6 ohms for the copper wire.

Step 3c: Select Variable Names

The last step in the design phase (step 3c) is to choose the names of variables to hold the input, output, and any intermediate calculated items determined in the analysis phase (steps 1 and 2). Let us use the variables named RESTVY, AREA, and LENGTH for the input items resistivity, area, and length, respectively; and a variable named RESIST for the calculated output, the resistance of the wire. All of these names are arbitrary, and any valid symbolic names can be used in their place.

Step 4: Write the Program

After variable names for the chosen algorithm have been selected, all that is required of our program is to declare these variables, initialize the input variables appropriately, compute the resistance variable, and print the calculated resistance value. Program 2-7 performs these steps.

Program 2-7

```
123456789 <————————————— Column Number
      PROGRAM OHMS
***     THIS PROGRAM CALCULATES THE RESISTANCE, IN OHMS, OF A WIRE
        REAL RESTVY, AREA, LENGTH, RESIST
        RESTVY = 10.4
        AREA = 500
        LENGTH = 125
***     DETERMINE THE WIRE'S RESISTANCE
        RESIST = (RESTVY * LENGTH) / AREA
        WRITE(6,*) 'THE RESISTANCE OF THE WIRE (IN OHMS) IS', RESIST
        END
```

When program 2-7 is executed, the following output is produced:

```
THE RESISTANCE OF THE WIRE (IN OHMS) IS   2.600000
```

Once a working program that produces a result has been written, the final step in the development process, testing the program, can begin.

Step 5: Test the Program

The purpose of testing is to verify that a program works correctly and actually fulfills its requirements. Once testing has been completed, the program can be used to calculate outputs for differing input data without the need for retesting. This is, of course, the real value in writing a program; the same program can be used over and over with new input data.

In theory, testing would reveal all existing program errors (in computer terminology, a program error is called a *bug*). In practice, this would require checking all possible combinations of statement execution. Because of the time and effort required, this is usually an impossible goal except for extremely simple programs such as Program 2-7. (We illustrate why this is generally an impossible goal in Chapter 6, which describes FORTRAN's IF statements.)

The inability to completely test most programs has led to various testing methodologies. The simplest of these methods is to verify the program's operation for carefully selected sets of input data. One set of input data that always should be used is the data that was selected for the hand calculation made previously in step 3b of the development procedure. If testing reveals an error (bug), the process of debugging, which includes locating, correcting, and verifying the correction, can be initiated. It is important to realize that although this type of verification testing may reveal the presence of an error, it does not necessarily indicate the absence of one. Thus, the fact that a test does not reveal an error does not indicate that another bug is not lurking somewhere else in the program.

Modularity and Top-Down Design

The design of Program 2-7 was relatively simple. The design of a more complex program's structure can be considerably more involved. Designing a program in its more elaborate form is similar to receiving the pieces of a puzzle (the inputs) and deciding how to arrange them to form a completed structure (the desired output). Unlike a jigsaw puzzle, however, the pieces of a program design puzzle can be arranged in many different ways, depending on the algorithm chosen for transforming the inputs into the desired outputs. In this regard, the program designer is very similar to an architect who must draw up the plans for a house.

The general procedure for designing programs (step 3 in our development procedure) is called *top-down design*. The purpose of top-down design is to design an algorithm in such a way that the program structure corresponding to the algorithm is modular. To achieve this goal, the design starts from the highest-level requirement and proceeds to the parts that must be constructed. As an example, consider an inventory reporting program that is required to keep track of the number of parts in inventory. The required output for this program is a description of all parts carried in inventory and the number of units of each item in stock; the given inputs are the initial inventory quantity of each part, the number of items sold, the number of items returned, and the number of items purchased.

For these I/O specifications, a designer initially could organize the requirements for the program into the three sections illustrated in Figure 2-18. This is called a *first-level structure diagram* because it represents the first overall structure of the program selected by the designer.

In top-down design, the lower boxes in the structure diagram are refined until the tasks indicated in the boxes are small enough to be programmed as individual program units. For example, both the data entry and report sections shown in Figure 2-18 would be further refined into suitable segments. The data entry section certainly must include provisions for entering the data. Since it is the system designer's responsibility to plan for contingencies and human error, provisions also must be made for changing incorrect data after an entry has been made and for deleting a previously entered value altogether. Similar subdivisions for the report section also can be made. Figure 2-19 illustrates a second-level structure diagram for an inventory tracking system that includes these further refinements.

The process of refinement continues until the last level of tasks can be coded using individual program units. Notice that the design produces a tree-like structure whose levels branch out as we move from the top of the structure to the bottom. When the design is complete, it specifies both how many program units are needed and the calling sequence of each unit (that is, lower-level units are called from higher-level ones). The individual algorithms specified for each box on the final structure diagram, which are coded using separate subprograms, are frequently described using either flowcharts or pseudocode.

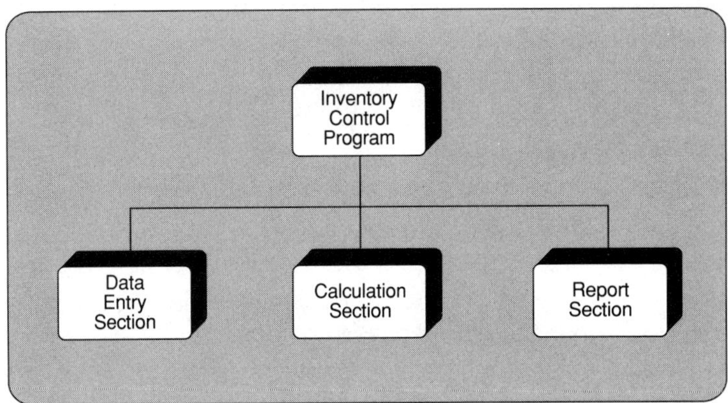

Figure 2-18 First-Level Structure Diagram

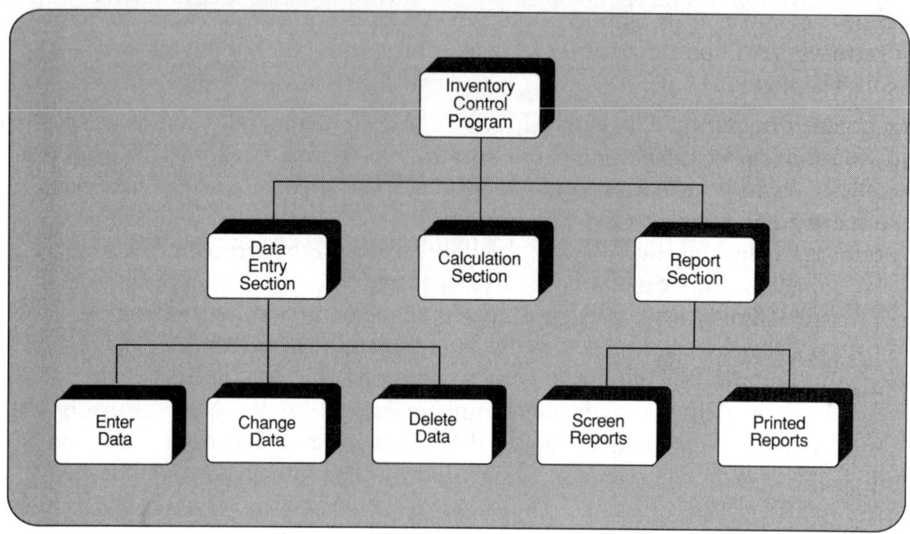

Figure 2-19 Second-Level Structure Diagram

Exercises

Note: In each of these exercises a programming problem is given. Read the problem statement first and then answer the questions pertaining to the problem.

1. Write a FORTRAN program that calculates the amount, in dollars, contained in a piggybank. The bank contains half-dollars, quarters, dimes, nickels, and pennies.
   a. For this programming problem, how many outputs are required?
   b. How many inputs does this problem have?
   c. Determine an algorithm for converting the input items into output items.
   d. Test the algorithm written for part c using the following sample data: half-dollars = 0, quarters = 17, dimes = 24, nickels = 16, and pennies = 12.
2. Write a program to calculate the value of *Distance*, in miles, given the relationship:

   Distance = *Rate* * *Elapsed time*

   a. For this programming problem, how many outputs are required?
   b. How many inputs does this problem have?
   c. Determine an algorithm for converting the input items into output items.
   d. Test the algorithm written for part c using the following sample data: *Rate* is 55 miles per hour and *Elapsed time* is 2.5 hours.
   e. How must the algorithm you determined in part c be modified if the elapsed time was given in minutes instead of hours?

3. Write a program to determine the value of *Ergies*, given the relationships:

   $Ergies = Fergies \sqrt{Lergies}$

   $Lergies = 2\pi e\mu$

   a. For this programming problem, how many outputs are required?
   b. How many inputs does this problem have?
   c. Determine an algorithm for converting the input items into output items.
   d. Test the algorithm written for part c using the following sample data: *Fergies* = 14.65, $\pi = 3.1416$, $\mu = 1.672$, and $e = 2.7818$.

4. Write a program to display the following name and address:

   Mr. J. Knipper
   63 Seminole Way
   Dumont, NJ 07030

   a. For this program problem, how many lines of output are required?
   b. How many inputs does this problem have?
   c. Determine an algorithm for converting the input items into output items.

5. Write a FORTRAN program to determine how far a car has traveled after 10 seconds assuming the car is initially traveling at 60 miles per hour and the driver applies the brakes to uniformly decelerate at a rate of 12 miles/sec^2. Use the fact that $distance = st - (1/2)dt^2$, where s is the initial speed of the car, d is the deceleration, and t is the elapsed time.

   a. For this programming problem, how many outputs are required?
   b. How many inputs does this problem have?
   c. Determine an algorithm for converting the input items into output items.
   d. Test the algorithm written for part c using the data given in the problem.

6. Consider the following programming problem: in 1627, Manhattan Island was sold to the Dutch settlers for approximately $24. If the proceeds of that sale had been deposited in a Dutch bank paying 5 percent interest, compounded annually, what would the principal balance be at the end of 1995? A display is required as follows: Balance as of December 31, 1995, is xxxxxx, where xxxxxx is the amount calculated by your program.

   a. For this programming problem, how many outputs are required?
   b. How many inputs does this problem have?
   c. Determine an algorithm for converting the input items into output items.
   d. Test the algorithm written for part c using the data given in the problem statement.

7. Write a program that calculates and displays the weekly gross pay and net pay of two individuals. The first individual is paid an hourly rate of $8.43, and the second individual is paid an hourly rate of $5.67. Both individuals have 20 percent of their pay withheld for income tax purposes, and both pay 2 percent of their net pay, before taxes, for medical benefits.

a. For this programming problem, how many outputs are required?
b. How many inputs does this problem have?
c. Determine an algorithm for converting the input items into output items.
d. Test the algorithm written for part c using the following sample data: the first person works 40 hours during the week, and the second person works 35 hours per week.

8. The formula for the standard normal deviation z, used in statistical applications is:

$$z = \frac{x - \mu}{r}$$

where μ refers to a mean value and r to a standard deviation. Using this formula, write a program that calculates and displays the value of the standard normal deviation when $x = 85.3$, $\mu = 80$, and $r = 4$.

a. For this programming problem, how many outputs are required?
b. How many inputs does this problem have?
c. Determine an algorithm for converting the input items into output items.
d. Test the algorithm written for part c using the data given in the problem.

9. The equation of the normal (bell-shaped) curve used in statistical applications is:

$$y = \frac{1}{r\sqrt{2pi}}\ e^{-1/2[(x-\mu)/r]2}$$

Using this equation, write a FORTRAN program to calculate the value of y.

a. For this programming problem, how many outputs are required?
b. How many inputs does this problem have?
c. Determine an algorithm for converting the input items into output items.
d. Test the algorithm written for part c assuming $\mu = 90$, $r = 4$, $x = 80$, and $\pi = 3.1416$.

2.6 Applications

In this section we apply the top-down development procedure presented in the previous section to two specific applications. Although each application is different, the top-down development procedure can be applied to any programming problem to produce a completed program.

Application 1: Pendulum Clocks

Pendulums used in clocks keep relatively accurate time because when the length of a pendulum is relatively large compared to the maximum arc of its swing, the time to complete one swing is independent of both the pendulum's weight and the maximum displacement of the swing. When this condition is satisfied, the relationship between the time to complete one swing and the length of the pendulum is given by the formula:

$$length = g\ [time/(2\ \pi)]^2$$

where π, accurate to four decimal places, is equal to 3.1416 and g is the gravitational constant equal to 32.2 ft/sec^2. When the time of a complete swing is given in seconds, the length of the pendulum is in feet. Using the given formula, write a FORTRAN program to calculate and display the length of a pendulum needed to produce a swing that will be completed in one second. The length should be displayed in inches.

Program Development

Using our five-step development procedure, we have:

Step 1: Determine the Desired Outputs

For this problem, a single output is required by the program: the length of the pendulum. The problem also specifies that the actual value be displayed in units of inches.

Step 2: Determine the Input Items

The input items required for this problem are the time to complete one swing, the gravitational constant, g, and π.

Step 3: Design the Program

a. The algorithm for transforming the three input items into the desired output item is given by the formula $length = g\ [time/(2\ \pi)]^2$. Since this formula calculates the length in feet, we will have to multiply the result by 12 to convert the answer into inches.
b. A hand calculation, using the data that $g = 32.2$, $time = 1$, and $\pi = 3.1416$, yields a length of 9.78 inches for the pendulum.
c. We select the variable name TIME for the time and LENGTH for the length. As g and π are constants that do not change, we will not assign them to variables; instead, their values will be directly incorporated in the assignment statement used to determine the pendulum's length.

Step 4: Write the Program

Program 2-8 provides the necessary code.

Program 2-8

```
PROGRAM MAIN
  REAL TIME, LENGTH
  TIME = 1.0
  LENGTH = 12 * 32.2 * (TIME/(2*3.1416))**2
  WRITE(6,*) 'THE LENGTH OF THE PENDULUM (IN INCHES) MUST BE', LENGTH
  END
```

Program 2-8 begins with a program header line and ends with an *END* statement. Additionally, Program 2-8 contains a variable declaration statement, two assignment statements, and one output statement. The assignment statement TIME = 1.0 is used to initialize the TIME variable. The assignment statement:

```
LENGTH = 12 * 32.2 * (TIME/(2*3.1416))**2
```

calculates a value for the variable LENGTH. Notice that the 12 is used to convert the calculated value from feet into inches. Also notice the placement of parentheses in the expression (TIME/(2*3.1416)). Both sets of parentheses are needed. The inner set of parentheses ensures that the value of π is multiplied by 2 before the division is performed. If these parentheses were not included, the value of TIME would first be divided by 2, and then the quantity TIME/2 would be multiplied by 3.1416. Finally, the outer parentheses ensure that the total quantity (TIME/(2*3.1416)) is squared. When Program 2-8 is compiled and executed, the following output is produced:

```
THE LENGTH (IN INCHES) OF THE PENDULUM MUST BE  9.787582
```

Step 5: Test the Program

The last step in the development procedure is testing the output of the program. Since the displayed value agrees with our previous hand calculation, we have established a degree of confidence in the program. This permits us to use the program for different values of time. It should be noted that if the parentheses were not correctly placed in the assignment statement that calculated a value for LENGTH, the displayed value would not agree with our previous hand calculation. This would have alerted us to the fact there was an error in the program.

Application 2: Telephone Switching Networks

A directly connected telephone network is one in which all telephones in the network are directly connected and do not require a central switching station to establish calls between two telephones. For example, financial institutions on Wall Street use such a network to maintain direct and continuously open phone lines between institutions.

The number of direct lines, L, needed to maintain a directly connected network for N telephones is given by the formula:

$$L = N(N-1)/2$$

For example, directly connecting four telephones, without the use of a central switching station, requires six individual lines (see Figure 2-20). Adding a fifth telephone to the network illustrated in Figure 2-20 would require an additional four lines, for a total of 10 lines.

Using the given formula, write a program that determines the number of direct lines required for 100 subscribers and the additional lines required if 10 new subscribers are added to the network.

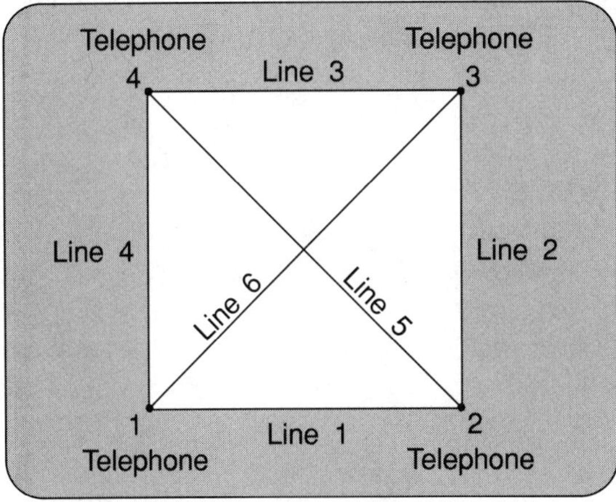

Figure 2-20 Directly Connecting Four Telephones

Program Development

Using our five-step development procedure, we have:

Step 1: Determine the Desired Outputs

For this program, two outputs are required: the number of direct lines for 100 telephones and the additional number of lines needed when 10 new telephones are added into the existing network.

Step 2: Determine the Input Items

The input items required for this problem are the number of subscribers, denoted as N in the formula.

Step 3: Design the Program

a. The first output is easily obtained using the formula $L = (N-1)/2$. Although there is no formula given for additional lines, we can use the given formula to determine the total number of lines needed for 110 subscribers. Subtracting the number of lines for 100 subscribers from the number of lines needed for 110 subscribers will then yield the number of additional lines required. Thus, the complete algorithm for our program, in pseudocode, is:

Calculate the number of direct lines for 100 subscribers
Calculate the number of direct lines for 110 subscribers
Calculate the additional lines needed, which is the difference between the second and first calculation
Display the number of lines for 100 subscribers
Display the additional lines needed

b. A hand calculation, using the data given yields that:
$L = 100(100 - 1)/2 = 100(99)/2 = 4950$ lines
for 100 subscribers and that $L = 5995$ direct lines needed for 110 subscribers. Thus, an additional 1045 lines would be needed to directly connect the 10 additional telephones into the existing network.

c. We select the variable name NUMIN for the initial number of 100 subscribers, NUMFIN for the final number of 110 subscribers, LINES1 for the initial number of lines, and LINES2 for the final number of lines.

Step 4: Write the Program

Program 2-9 provides the necessary code.

Program 2-9

```
123456789 ———————————— Column Number ————————————
      PROGRAM MAIN
        INTEGER NUMIN, NUMFIN, LINES1, LINES2
        NUMIN = 100
        NUMFIN = 110
        LINES1 = NUMIN*(NUMIN - 1)/2
        LINES2 = NUMFIN*(NUMFIN - 1)/2
        WRITE(6,*)'THE NUMBER OF LINES ORIGINALLY NEEDED IS ', LINES1
        WRITE(6,*)' THERE ARE ', LINES2 - LINES1, ' NEW LINES NEEDED'
        END
```

As before, the FORTRAN program begins with a program header line and ends with an END statement. Since the number of lines between subscribers must be an integer (a fractional line is not possible) the variables LINES1 and LINES2 are specified as integer variables. The first two assignment statements initialize the variables NUMIN and NUMFIN. The next assignment statement calculates the number of lines needed for 100 subscribers, and the last assignment statement calculates the number of lines for 110 subscribers. The first WRITE statement is used to display a message and the result of the first calculation. The second WRITE statement is used to display the difference between the two calculations. The following output is produced when Program 2-9 is compiled and executed:

```
THE NUMBER OF LINES ORIGINALLY NEEDED IS  4950
 THERE ARE  1045 NEW LINES NEEDED
```

Additional Exercises for Chapter Two

1a. Modify Program 2-8 to calculate the length of a pendulum that produces an arc that takes two seconds to complete.

b. Compile and execute the program written for Exercise 1a on a computer.

c. Rewrite Program 2-8 so that it contains one subroutine.

2a. Modify Program 2-8 to determine the time it takes a three-foot pendulum to complete one swing. Your program should produce the following display:

```
THE TIME TO COMPLETE ONE SWING (IN SECONDS) IS  xxxx
```

where xxxx is replaced by the actual value calculated by your program.

b. Compile and execute the program written for Exercise 2a on a computer. Make sure to do a hand calculation so that you can verify the results produced by your program.

c. After you have verified the results of the program written in Exercise 2a, modify the program to calculate the time it takes a four-foot pendulum to complete one swing.

d. Rewrite the program written for Exercise 2a so that it contains one subroutine.

3a. Modify Program 2-9 to calculate and display the total number of lines needed to directly connect 1000 individual phones to each other.

b. Compile and execute the program written for Exercise 3a on a computer.

4a. Modify Program 2-9 so that the variable NUMFIN is initialized to 10, which is the additional number of subscribers to be connected to the existing network. Make any other changes in the program so that the program produces the same display as does Program 2-9.

b. Compile and execute the program written for Exercise 4a on a computer. Check that the display produced by your program matches the display shown in the text.

c. Rewrite the program written for Exercise 4a so that it contains one subroutine.

5a. Write, compile, and execute a FORTRAN program to convert temperature in degrees Fahrenheit to degrees Celsius. The equation for this conversion is *Celsius* = 5.0/9.0 (*Fahrenheit* – 32.0). Have your program convert and display the Celsius temperature corresponding to 98.6 degrees Fahrenheit. Your program should produce the display:

```
FOR A FAHRENHEIT TEMPERATURE OF xxxx  DEGREES
THE CELSIUS TEMPERATURE IS xxxx DEGREES
```

where appropriate values are inserted by your program in place of the *x*s.

b. Check the values computed by your program. After you have verified that your program is working correctly, modify it to convert 86.5 degrees Fahrenheit into its equivalent Celsius value.

6a. Write, compile, and execute a FORTRAN program to calculate the dollar amount contained in a piggybank. The bank currently contains 12 half-dollars, 20 quarters, 32 dimes, 45 nickels, and 27 pennies. Your program should produce the following display:

```
THE VALUE OF MONEY, IN DOLLARS, IS xxxx
```

where xxxx is replaced by the actual value calculated by your program.

b. Check the values computed by your program. After you have verified that your program is working correctly, modify it to determine the dollar value of a bank containing no half-dollars, 17 quarters, 19 dimes, 10 nickels, and 42 pennies.

7a. Write, compile, and execute a FORTRAN program to calculate the elapsed time it took to make a 183.67-mile trip. The equation for computing elapsed time is *elapsed time = total distance / average speed.* Assume that the average speed during the trip was 58 miles/hour. Your program should produce the display:

```
THE TIME FOR THE TRIP WAS xxxx HOURS
```

where the *x*s are replaced with the value calculated by your program.

b. Check the values computed by your program. After you have verified that your program is working correctly, modify it to determine the elapsed time it takes to make a 372-mile trip at an average speed of 67 miles/hour.

8a. Write, compile, and execute a FORTRAN program to calculate the sum of the numbers from 1 to 100. The formula for calculating this sum is $sum = (n/2)\ (2^*a + (n-1)d)$, where n is the number of terms to be added, a is the first number, and d is the difference between each number. Your program should produce the display:

```
THE SUM OF THE NUMBERS IS xxxx
```

where the xs are replaced by the sum computed by your program.

b. Check the values computed by your program. After you have verified that your program is working correctly, modify it to determine the sum of the integers from 100 to 1000.

9a. Newton's law of cooling states that when an object with an initial temperature T is placed in a surrounding substance of temperature A, it will reach a temperature *TFIN* in t minutes according to the formula:

$$\text{TFIN} = (T - A)\, e^{-kt} + A$$

In this formula e is the irrational number 2.71828 rounded to five decimal places (commonly known as Euler's number), and k is a thermal coefficient, which depends on the material being cooled. Using this formula, write, compile, and execute a FORTRAN program that determines the temperature reached by an object after 20 minutes when it is placed in a glass of water whose temperature is 60 degrees. Assume that the object initially has a temperature of 150 degrees and has a thermal coefficient of 0.0367. Your program should produce the display:

```
THE FINAL TEMPERATURE IS xxxx
```

where the *x*s are replaced by the value calculated by your program.

b. Check the value computed by your program. After you have verified that your program is working correctly, modify it to determine the temperature reached by an object after 10 minutes when it is placed in a glass of water whose temperature is 50 degrees.

10a. Given an initial deposit of money, A, in a bank that pays interest annually, the amount of money at a time N years later is given by the formula:

$$AMOUNT = A * (1 + I)^N$$

where I is the interest rate as a decimal number (e.g., 9.5 percent is .095). Using this formula, write, compile, and execute a FORTRAN program that determines the amount of money that will be available in four years if $10,000 is deposited in a bank that pays 10 percent interest annually. Your program should produce the display:

```
THE VALUE AFTER xx YEARS IS yyyyy
```

where the *x*s are replaced by the number of years and the *y*s by the value of money calculated by your program.

b. Check the value computed by your program by hand. After you have verified that your program is working correctly, modify it to determine the amount of money available if $24 is invested at 4 percent for 300 years.

11a. If an initial deposit of A dollars is made in a bank, and the interest, I, is compounded M times a year, the amount of money available after N years is given by the expression:

$$A * (1 + I/M)^{M*N}$$

Using this expression, write, compile, and run a FORTRAN program to determine the amount of money available after 10 years if $5000 is invested in a bank paying 6 percent interest compounded quarterly ($M = 4$).

b. Check the value computed by your program. After you have verified that your program is working correctly, modify it to determine the amount of money available if $1000 is invested at 8 percent, compounded quarterly, for 10 years.

12a. Effective annual interest is the rate that must be compounded annually to generate the same interest as a stated rate compounded over a stipulated conversion period. For example, a stated rate of 8 percent compounded quarterly is equivalent to an effective annual rate of 8.24 percent. The relationship between the effective annual rate, E, and the stated rate, I, compounded M times a year is $E = (1 + I/M)^M - 1$. Using this formula, write, compile, and execute a FORTRAN program to determine the effective annual rate for a stated rate of 6 percent compounded four times a year (quarterly). Your program should produce the display:

```
THE EFFECTIVE INTEREST IS xxxx
```

where the *x*s are replaced by the value calculated by your program.

b. Check the value computed by your program. After you have verified that your program is working correctly, modify it to determine the effective annual rate for a stated rate of 8 percent compounded monthly.

13a. The present value of a dollar amount is the amount of money that must be deposited in a bank account today to yield a specified dollar amount in the future. For example, if a bank is currently paying 8 percent interest annually, you would have to deposit $6,947.90 in the bank today to have $15,000 in 10 years. Thus, the present value of the $15,000 is $6,947.90. Using this information, write, compile, and execute a FORTRAN program that calculates how much must be deposited in a bank today to provide exactly $8,000 in 9 years at an annual interest rate of 8 percent. Use the formula:

$$\textit{Present value} = \textit{Future amount} / (1.0 + \textit{annual interest rate})^{\textit{Years}}$$

b. Check the value computed by your program. After you have verified that your program is working correctly, modify it to determine the amount of money that must be invested in a bank today to yield $15,000 in eighteen years at an annual rate of 6 percent.

14a. The set of linear equations:

$$a_{11}X_1 + a_{12}X_2 = c_1$$
$$a_{21}X_1 + a_{22}X_2 = c_2$$

can be solved using Cramer's rule as:

$$X_1 = \frac{c_1 a_{22} - a_{12} c_2}{a_{11} a_{22} - a_{12} a_{21}}$$

$$X_2 = \frac{c_2 a_{11} - a_{21} c_1}{a_{11} a_{22} - a_{12} a_{21}}$$

Using these equations, write, compile, and execute a FORTRAN program to solve for the X_1 and X_2 values that satisfy the following equations:

$$3X_1 + 4X_2 = 40$$
$$5X_1 + 2X_2 = 34$$

b. Check the values computed by your program. After you have verified that your program is working correctly, modify it to solve the following set of equations:

$$3X_1 + 12.5X_2 = 22.5$$
$$4.2X_1 - 6.3X_2 = 30$$

2.7 Common Programming Errors

The common programming errors associated with the material presented in this chapter are:

1. Forgetting to separate variable names with commas in all declaration, PRINT, and WRITE statements.
2. Using a variable in an expression before the variable has been initialized. In such a case, whatever value happens to be in the variable will be used when the expression is evaluated, and the result will be meaningless.
3. Misspelling a variable's name within a program. For example, assume that the following declaration is made:

```
REAL VOLTS, CURRNT, RESIST
```

Now assume that the variable CURRNT is misspelled in the assignment statement:

```
VOLTS = CURNT * RESIST
```

The program would treat CURNT as a new REAL variable and use whatever value happened to be in the variable's storage locations (see previous error), effectively assigning a "garbage" value to VOLTS. Finding this error or even knowing that one occurred could be extremely troublesome.

4. Storing an incorrect data type in a variable. This error is not detected by the compiler. Here, the assigned value is converted to the data type of the variable to which it is assigned. For example, if LENGTH has been declared an integer variable, the assignment LENGTH = 26.95894 assigns the value 26 to LENGTH.
5. Dividing integer values incorrectly. This error usually is disguised within a larger expression and can be very troublesome to detect. For example, the expression 7.26 + 4/5 + 8.95 yields the same result as the expression 7.26 + 8.95 because the integer division of 4/5 is 0.
6. Mixing data types in the same expression without clearly understanding the effect produced. Since FORTRAN allows expressions with "mixed" data types, it is important to be clear about the order of evaluation and the data type of all intermediate calculations. As a general rule, data types should never be mixed in an expression unless a specific effect is desired.
7. Not using parentheses to clarify the intended order of computation in an expression.
8. Attempting multiple assignments within one statement. For example, the statement $A = B = C = 10$ is an invalid assignment statement.
9. Specifying a field width in a FORMAT statement that does not include sufficient space for both the decimal point and sign of a real number.

2.8 Things to Remember

1. The six basic types of data recognized by FORTRAN are integer, real, double precision, character, logical, and complex data. Each of these types of data is typically stored in a computer using different amounts of memory.
2. Every variable in a FORTRAN program should be declared with the type of value it can store. Declarations within a program unit must be placed as the first statements within the unit. Variables of the same type should be declared using a single declaration statement.
3. An *expression* is any combination of constants and/or variables that can be evaluated to yield a result.
4. Assignment statements are used to store values into variables. The general form of an assignment statement is:

```
VARIABLE = expression
```

5. PRINT and WRITE statements are used to display the values of expressions. In *list-directed* output, the format of the display is determined by the compiler. In *user-formatted* output, the format of the display is explicitly specified by the programmer.
6. The general form of the list-directed PRINT statement is:

```
PRINT *, item list
```

where the item list can contain any number of valid FORTRAN expressions. The equivalent WRITE statement is:

```
WRITE(unit number,*) item list
```

where the unit number is an integer number that designates where the output is to be displayed.
7. The general form of the user-formatted version of the PRINT statement is:

```
PRINT n, item list
```

where *n* is the statement number of a FORMAT statement and the item list can consist of any number of valid FORTRAN expressions. The equivalent WRITE statement is:

```
WRITE(unit number, n) item list
```

8. A FORMAT statement consists of a statement label, the keyword FORMAT, and a format specification list. The general form of this statement is:

```
n   FORMAT (specification list)
```

where *n* is a statement label that is referenced by either a PRINT or a WRITE statement. When used with a PRINT or a WRITE statement, the first character in the specification list is a carriage control character that determines the vertical spacing of the output. The remaining specification determines the horizontal spacing and form of the output.
9. A simple FORTRAN program using only a MAIN program unit has the form:

```
123456789 ——— Column Number ————————————————72
      PROGRAM HEADER LINE
        declaration statements
        all other statements
        END
```

This general form is also valid for subroutine program units. For example, the program:

```
123456789 ——— Column Number ————————————————72
      PROGRAM SHOW
        CALL TEST
        END
```

```
*
        SUBROUTINE TEST
          declaration statements
          all other statements
          END
```

consists of two program units, both of which follow the general form required of all program units.

10. Although assignment and output statements can be placed in any order within a program unit after the declaration statements, it only makes sense to use PRINT or WRITE statements for displaying the contents of a variable after a proper value has been assigned to it. Similarly, a variable should only be used in an expression after the variable has been properly initialized. Comment statements may be placed anywhere in the program and have no effect on program execution.

2.9 A Closer Look: Errors, Testing, and Debugging

The ideal in programming is to efficiently produce readable, error-free programs that work correctly and can be modified or changed with a minimum of testing required for reverification. In this regard it is useful to know the different types of errors that can occur, when they are detected, and how they can be corrected.

Compile-time and Run-time Errors

An error in a program can be detected either before a program is compiled, while the program is being compiled, while it is being run, after the program has been executed and the output is being examined, or not at all. Errors that are detected by the compiler are formally referred to as compile-time errors and errors that occur while the program is being run are formally referred to as *run-time* errors.

Although there is no formal name for errors that are detected either before a program is compiled or after a program is executed, there are methods for locating errors at these times. The method for detecting errors after a program has been executed is formally referred to as *program verification and testing.* The method for detecting errors before a program is compiled is called *desk checking.* Desk checking refers to the procedure of checking a program, by hand, at a desk or table for syntax and logic errors, which are described next.

Syntax and Logic Errors

Computer literature distinguishes between two primary types of errors, called syntax and logic errors, respectively. A *syntax error* is an error in the structure or spelling of a statement. For example, the statement:

```
WRITE 6,* 'THERE ARE FIVE ERRORS HERE
WRITEE (6 *) 'CAN YOU FIND TEM?'
VOLUME = LENGTH * WIDTH
```

contains four syntax errors. These errors are:

1. The parentheses around the unit number and format control are missing from the first line
2. The closing apostrophe is missing in the first line
3. The keyword WRITE is misspelled in the second line
4. There is a comma missing after the number 6 in the second line

All of these errors will be detected by the compiler when the program is compiled. This is true of all syntax errors — since they violate the basic rules of FORTRAN, if they are not discovered by desk checking, the compiler will detect them and display an error message indicating that a syntax error exists.* In some cases the error message is extremely clear and the error is obvious, and in other cases it takes a little detective work to understand the error message displayed by the compiler. Since all syntax errors are detected at compile time, the terms *compile-time* and *syntax errors* are frequently used interchangeably. Strictly speaking, however, compile-time refers to when the error was detected and syntax refers to the type of error detected.

Note that the misspelling of the word THEM in the second WRITE statement and the calculation of a volume as length times width are not syntax errors. As far as the compiler is concerned these errors do not violate any syntactical rules.

Logic errors are characterized by erroneous, unexpected, or unintentional errors that are a direct result of some flaw in the program's logic. These errors, which are never caught by the compiler, may either be detected by desk-checking, by program testing, by accident when a user obtains an obviously erroneous output, while the program is executing, or not at all. If the error is detected while the program is running, a run-time error occurs that results in an error message being generated and/or abnormal and premature program termination.

Since logic errors may not be detected by the computer, they are always more difficult to detect than syntax errors. If not detected by desk checking, a logic error typically reveals itself in two predominant ways. In one instance the program abruptly terminates during execution, while in the second case the program runs to completion but produces incorrect or unintended results. For example, calculating the volume of a rectangle as length * width or misspelling the word THEM in the code illustrated previously are errors that cause incorrect and undesirable program output, but do not stop the program from running. More generally, logic errors of this type include:

No output
This is either caused by an omission of a WRITE statement or a sequence of statements that inadvertently bypasses a WRITE statement.

Unappealing or misaligned output
This is always caused by an error in either a PRINT or WRITE statement.

* They may not, however, all be detected at the same time. Frequently, one syntax error "masks" another error and the second error is only detected after the first error is corrected.

Incorrect numerical results
This is always caused by either incorrect values assigned to the variables used in an expression, the use of an incorrect arithmetic expression, an omission of a statement, roundoff error or the use of an improper sequence of statements.

See if you can detect the logic error in Program 2-10.

Program 2-10

```
123456789 ------------------ Column Number ---------------------------72
* COMPOUND INTEREST PROGRAM
      PROGRAM MAIN
        CALL COMPND
        END
*
      SUBROUTINE COMPND
        INTEGER NYEARS
        REAL CAPTAL, AMOUNT, RATE
        WRITE(6,*) 'THIS PROGRAM CALCULATES THE AMOUNT OF MONEY'
        WRITE(6,*) 'IN A BANK ACCOUNT FOR AN INITIAL DEPOSIT'
        WRITE(6,*) 'INVESTED FOR N YEARS AT AN INTEREST RATE R.'
        WRITE(6,*)
        WRITE(6,*) ' ENTER THE INITIAL AMOUNT IN THE ACCOUNT: '
        READ (5,*) AMOUNT
        WRITE(6,*) ' ENTER THE INTEREST RATE (EX. 5 FOR 5%): '
        READ (5,*) RATE
        CAPTAL = AMOUNT * (1 + RATE/100.) ** NYEARS
        WRITE(6,*) ' THE FINAL AMOUNT OF MONEY IS ', CAPTAL
        RETURN
        END
```

Following is a sample run of Program 2-10.

```
THIS PROGRAM CALCULATES THE AMOUNT OF MONEY
IN A BANK ACCOUNT FOR AN INITIAL DEPOSIT
INVESTED FOR N YEARS AT AN INTEREST RATE R.

 ENTER THE INITIAL AMOUNT IN THE ACCOUNT:
1000.
 ENTER THE INTEREST RATE (EX. 5 FOR 5%):
5
 THE FINAL AMOUNT OF MONEY IS     1000.00000000
```

As indicated in the output, the final amount of money is identical to the initial amount input. Did you spot the error in Program 2-10 that produced this apparently erroneous output?

Unlike a misspelled output message, the error in Program 2-10 causes a mistake in a computation. Here the error is that the program does not initialize the variable NYEARS before this variable is used in the calculation of CAPTAL. When the assignment statement that calculates CAPTAL is executed, the computer uses whatever value is stored in NYEARS. On those systems that initialize all variables to zero, the value zero will be used for NYEARS. However, on those systems that do not initialize all variables to zero, whatever "garbage" value that happens to occupy the storage locations corresponding to the variable NYEARS will be used (the manuals supplied with your compiler will indicate which of these two actions your compiler takes). In either case an error is produced.

The second major type of logic error is one that may cause the program to prematurely terminate execution, and almost always results in a system error message being displayed. Examples of this type of error are attempts to divide by zero or take the square root of a negative number. When this type of logic error occurs, it becomes a run-time error.

Testing and Debugging

In theory, a comprehensive set of test runs would reveal all logic errors and ensure that a program will work correctly for any and all combinations of input and computed data. In practice this requires checking all possible combinations of statement execution. Due to the time and effort required, this is an impossible goal except for extremely simple programs. Let us see why this is so. Consider Program 2-11.

Program 2-11

```
PROGRAM MAIN
 CALL SUB1
 CALL SUB2
 CALL SUB3
 CALL SUB4
 END
```

Program 2-11 calls five different subroutines when the program is run. For purposes of illustration, assume that each subroutine has 32 possible computation possibilities. (Although the method of producing such a subroutine is currently beyond our capability, it can be constructed using five simple IF-ELSE statements of the type introduced in Chapter 6.) If there are 32 possible paths through each subroutine, there will be 1,048,576 (32^4) different computational possibilities for the complete program.

The time needed to create individual test data to exercise each computational possibility and the actual computer run time required for all of the test data clearly become prohibitive. For this and larger programs the complete testing of all program paths, referred to as *exhaustive testing*, is a practical impossibility.

The inability to fully test all combinations of statement execution sequences has led to the programming proverb that "There is no error-free program." It has also led to the realization that any testing that is done should be well thought out to maximize the possibility of locating errors. An important corollary to this is the realization that although a single test can reveal the presence of an error, it does not verify the absence of one. The fact that one error is revealed by testing does not indicate that another error is not lurking somewhere else in the program; the fact that one test revealed no errors does not indicate that there are no errors.

Once an error is discovered, however, the programmer must locate where the error occurs, and then fix it. In computer jargon, a program error is referred to as a "bug" and the process of isolating, correcting, and verifying the correction is called "debugging."

Although there are no hard and fast rules for isolating the cause of an error, some useful techniques can be applied. The first of these is a preventive technique. Frequently many errors are simply introduced by the programmer in the rush to code and run a program before fully understanding what is required and how the result is to be achieved. A symptom of this haste to get a program entered into the computer is the lack of an outline of the proposed program (pseudocode or flowcharts) or a handwritten program itself. Many errors can be eliminated simply by checking a copy of the program before it is ever entered or compiled by desk-checking the program.

A second useful technique is to mimic the computer and execute each statement, by hand, as the computer would. This means writing down each variable as it is encountered in the program and listing the value that should be stored in the variable as each input and assignment statement is encountered. Doing this also sharpens your programming skills, because it requires that you fully understand what each statement in your program causes to happen. Such a check is called *program tracing*.

A third and very powerful debugging technique is to use one or more diagnostic PRINT statements to display the values of selected variables. For example, consider again Program 2-10. Since this program produced an incorrect value for CAPTAL, it is worthwhile placing a PRINT statement immediately before the assignment statement for CAPTAL to display the value of all variables used in the computation. If the displayed values are correct, then the problem is in the assignment statement; if the values are incorrect, we must determine where the incorrect values were actually obtained. Once the program has been determined to operate correctly, all of the PRINT statements can be easily located and removed.

In this same manner, another use of PRINT statements in debugging is to immediately display the values of all input data. This technique is referred to as *echo printing*, and is useful in establishing that the computer is correctly receiving and interpreting the input data.

Finally, no discussion of debugging is complete without mentioning the primary ingredient needed for successful isolation and correction of errors. This is the attitude and spirit you bring to the task. Since you wrote the program your natural assumption is that it is correct or you would have changed it before it was compiled. It is extremely difficult to back away and honestly test and find errors in your own software. As a programmer you must constantly remind yourself that just because you *think* your program is correct does not make it so. Finding errors in your own programs is a sobering experience, but one that will help you become a master programmer. It can also be exciting and fun if approached as a detection problem with you as the master detective.

3 Completing the Basics

Chapter Three

3.1 Intrinsic Functions

3.2 The List-Directed READ Statement

3.3 The Formatted READ Statement

3.4 Named Constants: The PARAMETER Statement

3.5 Applications

3.6 Common Programming Errors

3.7 Things to Remember

3.8 A Closer Look: Program Life Cycle

In the first two chapters we explored how results are displayed using FORTRAN's output statements and how numerical data is stored and processed using variables and assignment statements. In this chapter we complete our introduction to FORTRAN by presenting additional processing and input capabilities.

3.1 Intrinsic Functions

As we have seen, assignment statements can be used to perform arithmetic computations. For example, the assignment statement:

```
PWATTS = RESIST * CURRNT ** 2
```

squares the value in CURRNT, multiplies by the value in RESIST, and then assigns the resulting value to PWATTS. Although raising a number to a power is easily done using the exponentiation operator (**), finding a trigonometric value using FORTRAN's arithmetic operators is not as simple. To facilitate the calculation of trigonometric, logarithmic, and other mathematical calculations frequently required in scientific and engineering programs, FORTRAN provides standard preprogrammed routines, called *intrinsic functions*, that can be included in a program.

Before using a FORTRAN intrinsic function, the programmer must know:

- the name of the desired intrinsic function
- what the intrinsic function does
- the type of data required by the intrinsic function
- the data type of the result returned by the intrinsic function

To illustrate the use of FORTRAN's intrinsic functions, consider the intrinsic function named SQRT, which calculates the square root of a number. The square root of a number is computed using the expression:

```
SQRT(number)
```

where the intrinsic function name, in this case SQRT, is followed by parentheses containing the number for which the square root is desired. The purpose of the parentheses following the function name is to provide a funnel through which data can be passed to the function (see Figure 3-1). The items that are passed to the function through the parentheses are called *arguments* of the function and constitute its input data. For example, the following expressions are used to compute the square root of the arguments 4.0, 17.0, 25.0, 1043.29, and 6.4516:

```
SQRT(4.0)
SQRT(17.0)
SQRT(25.0)
SQRT(1043.29)
SQRT(6.4516)
```

The argument to the function named SQRT must be a positive real value. The SQRT function computes the square root of its argument, and the returned result is itself a real value. The values returned by the previous expressions are:

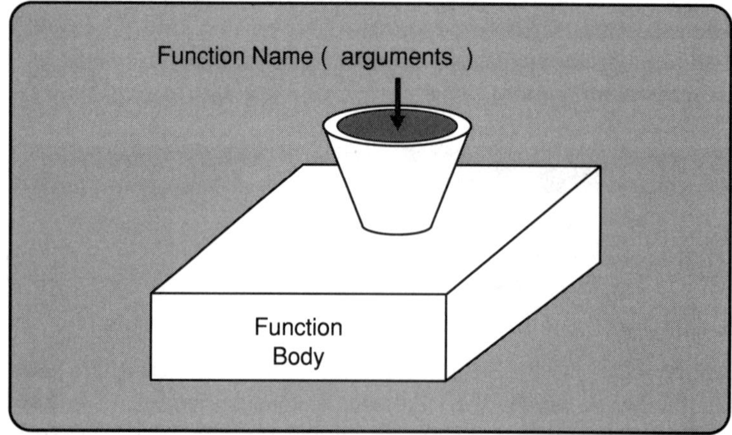

Figure 3-1 Passing Data to a Function

Expression	Value returned
`SQRT(4.0)`	`2.000000`
`SQRT(17.0)`	`4.123106`
`SQRT(25.0)`	`5.000000`
`SQRT(1043.29)`	`32.300000`
`SQRT(6.4516)`	`2.540000`

Table 3-1 lists the more commonly used intrinsic functions provided in FORTRAN in addition to the SQRT function. Although some of the intrinsic functions listed require more than one argument, all functions, by definition, return a single value. Table 3-2 lists the value returned by selected functions using example arguments. Note that the argument types for the examples agree with those given in Table 3-1 for the specified function.

Whenever an intrinsic function is used, it is called into action by giving the name of the function and passing any data to it within the parentheses following the function's name (see Figure 3-2).

The arguments that are passed to a function need not be single constants. Expressions can also be arguments, provided that the expression can be computed to yield a value of the required data type. For example, the following arguments are valid for the given functions:

```
SQRT(4.0 + 5.3 * 4.0)          ABS(2.3 * 4.6)
SQRT(16.0 * 2.0 - 6.7)         SIN(THETA - PHI)
SQRT(X * Y - Z/3.2)            COS(2.0 * OMEGA)
```

Table 3-1 Common FORTRAN Functions

Function name and argument(s)	Argument type(s)	Returned value	Description
ABS(R)	REAL	REAL	Absolute value of R
IABS(I)	INTEGER	INTEGER	Absolute value of I
INT(R)	REAL	INTEGER	Integer part of R
REAL(I)	INTEGER	REAL	Convert an integer to a real
FLOAT(I)	INTEGER	REAL	Same as REAL(I)
MOD(I1,I2)	INTEGER	INTEGER	Integer remainder of I1 / I2
SQRT(R)	REAL	REAL	Square root of R
SIN(R)	REAL	REAL	Sine of R (R in radians)
COS(R)	REAL	REAL	Cosine of R (R in radians)
TAN(R)	REAL	REAL	Tangent of R (R in radians)
EXP(R)	REAL	REAL	e raised to the R power
ALOG(R)	REAL	REAL	Natural log of R
ALOG10(R)	REAL	REAL	Common log (base 10) of R
MAX0(I1,I2,..,IN)	INTEGER	INTEGER	Returns largest argument
AMAX1(R1,R2,..,RN)	REAL	REAL	Returns largest argument
MIN0(I1,I2,..,IN)	INTEGER	INTEGER	Returns smallest argument
AMIN1(R1,R2,..,RN)	REAL	REAL	Returns smallest argument

Table 3-2 Selected Function Examples

Examples	Returned value
ABS(-7.362)	7.3620000
IABS(-3)	3
INT(-16.892)	-16
REAL(29)	29.000000
MOD(17,3)	2
MOD(9,5)	4
MAX0(5, 1, 6, 9, 2)	9
AMAX1(3.67, 9.8, 2.456)	9.800000
MIN0(5, 1, 6, 9, 2)	1
AMIN1(3.67, 9.8, 2.456)	2.4560000

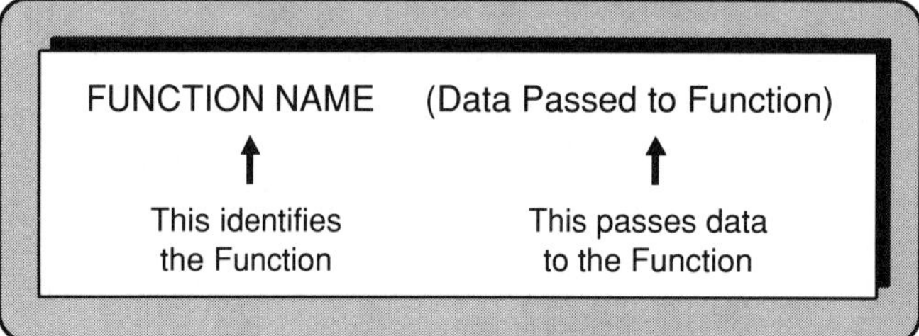

Figure 3-2 Using and Passing Data to a Function

The expressions in parentheses are first evaluated to yield a specific value. Thus, values would have to be assigned to the variables X, Y, Z, THETA, PHI, and OMEGA before their use in the above expressions. After the value of the argument is calculated, it is passed to the function.

Functions may be included as part of larger expressions. The value returned by the function is computed before any other operation is performed, for example:

```
4 * SQRT(4.5 * 10.0 - 9.0) - 2.0 =
         4 * SQRT(36.000000) - 2.0 =
                  4 * 6.000000 - 2.0 =
                      24.000000 - 2.0 = 22.000000
```

and:

```
3.0 * ALOG(30 * .514) =
     3.0 * ALOG(15.42) =
         3.0 * 2.735665 = 8.206995
```

The step-by-step evaluation of:

```
3.0 * SQRT(5 * 33 - 13.71) / 5
```

is:

Step	**Result**
1. Perform multiplication in argument	`3.0 * SQRT(165 - 13.71) / 5`
2. Complete argument calculation	`3.0 * SQRT(151.290000) / 5`
3. Return a function value	`3.0 * 12.300000 / 5`
4. Perform the multiplication	`36.900000 / 5`
5. Perform the division	`7.380000`

Program 3-1 illustrates the use of the SQRT function to determine the time it takes a ball to hit the ground after it has been dropped from an 800-foot tower. The mathematical formula used to calculate the time, in seconds, that it takes to fall a given distance, in feet, is:

$$time = sqrt\ (2 * distance / g)$$

where g is the gravitational constant equal to 32.2 ft/sec^2.

Program 3-1

```
PROGRAM MAIN
  REAL TIME, HEIGHT
  HEIGHT = 800
  TIME = SQRT(2.0 * HEIGHT / 32.2)
  WRITE(6,*) 'IT WILL TAKE ', TIME, ' SECONDS'
  WRITE(6,*) ' TO FALL ', HEIGHT, ' FEET.'
  END
```

Following is the output of Program 3-1.

```
IT WILL TAKE 7.049074 SECONDS
TO FALL 800.000000 FEET.
```

As used in Program 3-1, the value returned by the SQRT function is assigned to the variable TIME. The value returned by any function may always be used as any other value of the same type. This means that the returned value may be assigned to a variable (as in Program 3-1), included within larger expressions, or even used as an argument to another function. For example, the expression:

```
SQRT (SIN (ABS (THETA) ) )
```

is valid. Since parentheses are present, the computation proceeds from the inner to the outer pairs of parentheses. Thus, the absolute value of *THETA* is computed first and used as an argument to the SIN function. The value returned by the SIN function is then used as an argument to the SQRT function.

It must be noted that the arguments of all intrinsic trigonometric functions (SIN, COS, etc.) must be in radians. Thus, to obtain the sine of an angle that is given in degrees, you must first convert the angle to radian measure. This is accomplished easily by multiplying the angle by the term (3.1416/180.). For example, to obtain the sine of 30 degrees, the expression SIN(30 * 3.1416/180.) should be used.

Skill Builder Exercises

1. Write function calls to determine:
   a. the square root of 6.37
   b. the square root of $X - Y$
   c. the sine of 30 degrees
   d. the sine of 60 degrees
   e. the integer part of the number 19.37
   f. the absolute value of $A^2 - B^2$
   g. the remainder of 7 divided by 2
   h. the value of e raised to the third power
2. For $A = 10.6$, $B = 13.9$, $C = -3.42$, determine the value of:
   a. `INT(A)`
   b. `INT(C)`
   c. `ABS(A) + ABS(B)`
   d. `SQRT(ABS(A - B))`
   e. `AMIN1(A,B)`
   f. `AMIN1(A,B,C)`
   g. `AMAX1(A,B,C)`
   h. `AMAX1(2*SQRT(A),B-C)`
   i. `MIN0(INT(A), INT(B), INT(ABS(C)))`
   j. `MOD(9,4)`
   k. `MOD(17,3)`
   l. `MOD(3,17)`
3. Write FORTRAN statements for the following:
   a. $b = \sin x - \cos x$
   b. $b = \sin^2 x - \cos^2 x$
   c. $area = (c * b * \sin a)/2$
   d. $c = \sqrt{a^2 + b^2}$
   e. $p = \sqrt{|m - n|}$
   f. $sum = \dfrac{a(r^n - 1)}{r - 1}$
   g. x is the largest value of the real variables P, Q, R, S, and T
   h. y is the smallest value of the real variables P, Q, R, S, and T

Programming Exercises

4. Write, compile, and execute a program that calculates and returns the fourth root of the number 81.0, which is 3. When you have verified that your program works correctly, use it to determine the fourth root of 1,728.8964. Your program should make use of the SQRT function.

5. Write, compile, and execute a FORTRAN program that calculates the distance between two points whose coordinates are (7,12) and (3,9). Use the fact that the distance between two points having coordinates (x_1, y_1) and (x_2, y_2) is *distance* = *sqrt*($[x_1 - x_2]^2 + [y_1 - y_2]^2$). When you have verified that your program works correctly by calculating the distance between the two points manually, use your program to determine the distance between the points (–12,–15) and (22,5).

6. If a 20-foot ladder is placed on the side of a building at a 75-degree angle, as illustrated in Figure 3-3, the height at which the ladder touches the building can be calculated as *height* = 20 * *sin* 75°. Calculate this height by hand and then write, compile, and execute a FORTRAN program that determines and displays the value of the height. When you have verified that your program works correctly, use it to determine the height of a 25-foot ladder placed at an angle of 85 degrees.

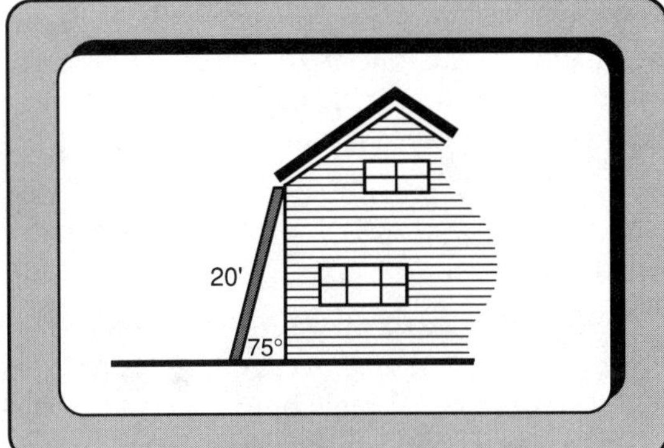

Figure 3-3 Calculating the Height of a Ladder Against a Building

7. The maximum height reached by a ball thrown with an initial velocity v, in meters/sec, at an angle of θ is given by the formula *height* = $(.5 * v^2 * \sin^2 \theta) / 9.80$. Using this formula, write, compile, and execute a FORTRAN program that determines and displays the maximum height reached when the ball is thrown at 15 meters/sec at an angle of 60 degrees. Calculate the maximum height manually and verify the result produced by your program. After you have verified that your program works correctly, use it to determine the height reached by a ball thrown at 7 miles/hour at an angle of 45 degrees.

8. For small values of x, the value of sin(x) can be approximated by the power series:

$$x - \frac{x^3}{6} + \frac{x^5}{120}$$

As with the SIN function, the value of x must be in radians. Using this power series, write, compile, and execute a FORTRAN program that approximates the sine of 180/3.1416 degrees, which equals 1 radian. Additionally, have your program use the SIN function to calculate the sine and display both calculated values and the absolute difference of the two results. Verify the approximation produced by your program. After you have verified that your program is working correctly, use it to approximate the value of the sine of 62.2 degrees.

9. The polar coordinates of a point consist of the distance, r, from a specified origin and an angle, θ, with respect to the x axis. The x and y coordinates of the point are related to its polar coordinates by the formulas:

$$x = r \cos \theta$$
$$y = r \sin \theta$$

Using these formulas, write a FORTRAN program that calculates the x and y coordinates of the point whose polar coordinates are $r = 10$ and $\theta = 30$ degrees. Verify the results produced by your program by calculating the results manually. After you have verified that your program is working correctly, use it to convert the polar coordinates $r = 12.5$ and $\theta = 67.8$ degrees into rectangular coordinates.

10. A model of worldwide population growth, in billions of people, since 1985, is given by the equation:

$$population = 4.88e^{.02\,[\text{Year} - 1985]}$$

Using this formula, write, compile, and execute a FORTRAN program to estimate the worldwide population in the year 1995. Verify the result displayed by your program by calculating the answer manually. After you have verified that your program is working correctly, use it to estimate the world's population in the year 2012.

11. A model to estimate the number of grams of a certain radioactive isotope left after N years is given by the formula:

$$Remaining\ material = (Original\ material)\ e^{-.00012\,N}$$

Using this formula, write, compile, and execute a FORTRAN program to determine the amount of radioactive material remaining after 1000 years, assuming an initial amount of 100 grams. Using a hand calculation, verify the display produced by your program. After you have verified that your program is working correctly, use it to determine the amount of radioactive material remaining after 275 years, assuming an initial amount of 250 grams.

12. The number of years that it takes for a certain isotope of uranium to decay to one-half of an original amount is given by the formula:

$$Half\text{-}life = \ln(2)/k$$

where k equals .00012. Using this formula, write, compile, and execute a FORTRAN program that calculates and displays the half-life of this uranium isotope. Using a hand calculation, verify the result produced by your program. After you have verified that your program is working correctly, use it to determine the half-life of a uranium isotope having a $k = .00026$.

13. The amplification of electronic circuits is measured in units of decibels, which is calculated as:

$$10\ \text{LOG}\ (P_O/P_I)$$

where P_O is the power of the output signal and P_I is the power of the input signal. Using this formula, write, compile, and execute a FORTRAN program that calculates and displays the decibel amplification in which the output power is 50 watts and the input power is 1 watt. Using a hand calculation, verify the result displayed by your program. After you have verified that your program is working correctly, use it to determine the amplification of a circuit whose output power is 4.639 watts and input power is 1 watt.

14. The loudness of a sound is measured in units of decibels, calculated as:

$$10\ \text{LOG}\ (SL/RL)$$

where *SL* is intensity of the sound being measured and *RL* is a reference sound intensity level. Using this formula, write a FORTRAN program that calculates and displays the decibel loudness of a busy street having a sound intensity of 10,000,000 *RL*. Using a hand calculation, verify the result produced by your program. After you have verified that your program is working correctly, use it to determine the sound level, in decibels, of the following sounds:

a. a whisper of sound intensity 200 *RL*

b. a rock band playing at a sound intensity of 1,000,000,000,000 *RL*

c. an airplane taking off at a sound intensity of 100,000,000,000,000 *RL*

15. The dollar change remaining after an amount PAID is used to pay a restaurant check of amount CHECK can be calculated using the following FORTRAN statements:

```
* DETERMINE THE AMOUNT OF PENNIES IN THE CHANGE
      CHANGE = (PAID - CHECK)*100

* DETERMINE THE NUMBER OF DOLLARS IN THE CHANGE
      DOLLAR = INT(CHANGE/100)
```

a. Using the previous statements as a starting point, write a FORTRAN program that calculates the number of dollar bills, quarters, dimes, nickels, and pennies in the change when $10 is used to pay a bill of $6.07.

b. Without compiling or executing your program, check the effect, by hand, of each statement in the program and determine what is stored in each variable as each statement is encountered.

c. When you have verified that your algorithm works correctly, compile and execute your program. Verify that the result produced by your program is correct. After you have verified that your program is working correctly, use it to determine the change when a check of $12.36 is paid using a $20 bill.

16a. For display purposes, the F FORMAT specification allows the programmer to round all outputs to the desired number of decimal places. However, this can yield seemingly incorrect results when used in financial programs that require all monetary values to be displayed to the nearest penny. For example, the display produced by the statements:

```
      REAL A, B
      A = 1.674
      B = 1.322
      WRITE(6,100) A
      WRITE(6,100) B
      WRITE(6,110)
      C = A + B
      WRITE(6,100) C
  100 FORMAT(1X,F4.2)
  110 FORMAT(1X,'----')
```

is:

```
1.67
1.32
----
3.00
```

Clearly, the sum of the displayed numbers should be 2.99 and not 3.00. The problem is that although the values in A and B have been displayed with two decimal digits, they were added internal to the program as three-digit numbers. The solution is to round the values in A and B before they are added by the statement C = A + B. Using the INT function, devise a method to round the values in the variables A and B to the nearest hundredth (penny value) before they are added.

b. Include the method you have devised for exercise 16a into a working program that produces the following display:

```
1.67
1.32
----
2.99
```

3.2 The List-Directed READ Statement

Data for programs that are going to be executed only once may be included directly in the program. For example, if we wanted to multiply the numbers 300.0 and .05, we could use Program 3-2.

Program 3-2

```
PROGRAM MAIN
  REAL FIRNUM, SECNUM, PRODCT
  FIRNUM = 300.0
  SECNUM = .05
  PRODCT = FIRNUM * SECNUM
  WRITE(6,*) FIRNUM,' TIMES ', SECNUM,' IS ', PRODCT
  END
```

The output displayed by Program 3-2 is:

```
300.000000 TIMES .050000 IS 15.000000
```

Program 3-2 can be shortened, as illustrated in Program 3-3. Both programs, however, suffer from the same basic problem in that they must be rewritten in order to multiply different numbers.

Except for the practice provided to the programmer in writing, entering, and running the program, programs that do the same calculation only once, on the same set of numbers, are clearly not very useful. After all, it is simpler to use a calculator to multiply two numbers than to enter and run either Program 3-2 or 3-3.

Program 3-3

```
PROGRAM MAIN
  WRITE(6,*) '300.00 TIMES .05 IS ', 300.00 * .05
  END
```

To overcome the necessity of rewriting and compiling a program for each new set of data, a READ statement can be used. The READ statement permits data to be entered into a program while it is executing. Just as the PRINT and WRITE statements display a copy of the value stored inside a variable, the READ statement allows the user to enter a value at the terminal while the program is executing (see Figure 3-4).

The entered value is then stored directly in a variable. Additionally, like its output statement counterparts, the READ statement has both list-directed and user-formatted versions. In this section the list-directed version is presented. The user-formatted version of the READ statement is described in Section 3.3.

The list-directed READ statement is used to accept data from a terminal, card reader, or auxiliary storage device such as a disk without the need of an explicit format specifier. FORTRAN 77 provides two distinct forms for its list-directed READ statement. The most general of these forms is:

```
READ (unit number, *) list of variables
```

The asterisk (*) in the READ statement specifies that the compiler's list-directed format is to be used. The *unit number* within the statement's parentheses designates where the input is coming from. Initially, we will only be reading data from either the keyboard or card reader connected to the computer, referred to as the computer's *standard input device.* Table 3-3 lists the unit numbers assigned to the standard input device by the more commonly used FORTRAN compilers. A space has been left in the table for you to enter your system's standard input unit number.

For example, assuming that unit number 5 denotes the standard input device, the statement READ (5,*) FIRNUM tells the computer to read its standard input device for a single value that is to be stored in the variable FIRNUM.

When a statement such as READ (5,*) FIRNUM is encountered, the computer stops program execution and waits for a number to be entered at the computer's standard input device (for the remainder of the text we assume this is a keyboard). When a number is typed and the ENTER key is pressed, the READ statement stores

Figure 3-4 READ Is Used to Enter Data; PRINT and WRITE Are Used to Display Data

Table 3-3 Standard Input Device Unit Numbers

Compiler	Unit number	Example
AT&T Philon	5 or *	READ (5,*) FIRNUM or READ (*,*) FIRNUM
AUTEC (R/M)	5 or *	READ (5,*) SECNUM or READ (*,*) SECNUM
DEC-VAX	5, 6 or *	READ (5,*) SLOPE or READ (6,*) SLOPE or READ (*,*) SLOPE
DTSS	0, 5, or *	READ (0,*) FIRNUM or READ (5,*) FIRNUM or READ (*,*) FIRNUM
IBM	5 or *	READ (5,*) SECNUM or READ (*,*) SECNUM
Microsoft	5 or *	READ (5,*) SLOPE or READ (*,*) SLOPE
Prime	1 or *	READ (1,*) FIRNUM or READ (*,*) FIRNUM
Your System		

the entered value in the variable FIRNUM. The program then continues execution with the next statement following the READ. To see this, consider Program 3-4, where we have assumed that unit number 5 designates the keyboard.

The first WRITE statement in Program 3-4 displays a message that tells the person at the terminal what should be typed. When a message is used in this manner it is called a *prompt.* In this case the prompt tells the user to type a number. The computer then executes the next statement, which is a READ statement. The READ statement puts the computer into a temporary pause (or wait) state for as long as it takes the user to type a value. The user signals the READ statement that input is ready for reading by pressing the RETURN key after the value has been typed. The entered value is stored in the variable whose name is in the READ statement, and the computer is taken out of its paused state. Program execution then proceeds with the next statement, which in Program 3-4 is a WRITE statement. This statement causes

Program 3-4

```
PROGRAM MAIN
  REAL FIRNUM, SECNUM, PRODCT
  WRITE(6,*) 'PLEASE TYPE IN A NUMBER: '
  READ (5,*) FIRNUM
  WRITE(6,*) 'PLEASE TYPE IN ANOTHER NUMBER: '
  READ (5,*) SECNUM
  PRODCT = FIRNUM * SECNUM
  WRITE(6,*) FIRNUM,' TIMES ', SECNUM,' IS ', PRODCT
  END
```

the next message to be displayed. The next READ statement again puts the computer into a temporary wait state while the user types a second value. This second number is stored in the variable SECNUM.

The following sample run was made using Program 3-4:

```
PLEASE TYPE IN A NUMBER:
300.
PLEASE TYPE IN ANOTHER NUMBER:
0.05
300.00000 TIMES 0.050000 IS 15.000000
```

In Program 3-4, each READ statement is used to store one value into a variable. The READ statement, however, can be used to enter and store as many values as there are variables in the variable list. For example, again assuming that unit number 5 designates the standard input device, the statement:

```
READ (5,*) FIRNUM, SECNUM
```

results in two values being read from the terminal and assigned to the variables FIRNUM and SECNUM. If the data entered at the terminal were:

```
0.052 245.79
```

the variables FIRNUM and SECNUM would contain the values 0.052 and 245.79, respectively. When actually entering numbers such as 0.052 and 245.79, you must leave at least one space between the numbers or separate them with a comma. The space or comma between the entered numbers clearly indicates where one number ends and the next begins. Inserting more than one space between numbers has no effect on the READ statement. In this sense, list-directed input provides a kind of free-form input.

Any number of READ statements may be included in a program, and any number of values may be input using a single READ statement. *When entering a character value in response to a list-directed* READ *statement, however, the entered data must be enclosed in apostrophes.* Program 3-5 illustrates using the READ statement to input three numbers from the standard input device. The program then calculates and displays the average of the numbers entered.

Program 3-5

```
PROGRAM MAIN
  INTEGER NUM1, NUM2, NUM3
  REAL AVERGE
  WRITE(6,*) 'ENTER THREE INTEGER NUMBERS: '
  READ (5,*) NUM1, NUM2, NUM3
  AVERGE = (NUM1 + NUM2 + NUM3) / 3.0
  WRITE(6,*) 'THE AVERAGE OF THE NUMBERS IS: ',AVERGE
  END
```

The following sample run was made using Program 3-5:

```
ENTER THREE INTEGER NUMBERS:
22, 56, 73
THE AVERAGE OF THE NUMBERS IS: 50.333333
```

Note that the data entered at the standard input device for this sample run consist of the input:

```
22, 56, 73
```

In response to this line of input, Program 3-5 stores the value 22 in the variable NUM1, the value 56 in the variable NUM2, and the value 73 in the variable NUM3 (see Figure 3-5). Since the average of three integer numbers can be a real number, the variable AVERGE, which is used to store the average, is declared as a real variable. Note also that the parentheses are needed in the assignment statement AVERGE = (NUM1 + NUM2 + NUM3) / 3.0. Without these parentheses, the only value that would be divided by 3.0 would be the integer in NUM3 (since division has a higher precedence than addition). As previously noted, the commas in the input are not required as long as one or more spaces separate the individual data items.

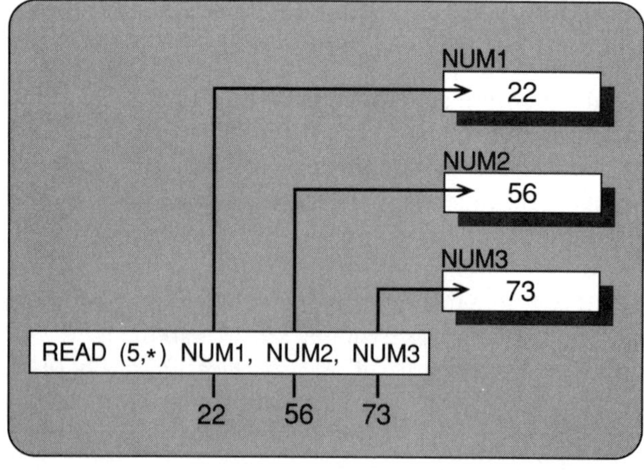

Figure 3-5 Reading Data into the Variables NUM1, NUM2, and NUM3

Had the user inadvertently entered real values instead of integers in response to the prompt in Program 3-5, the real values would have been truncated to integers. This happens because the READ statement is "clever" enough to make a few data type conversions. Thus, if a real number is entered when an integer is expected, the READ statement only uses the integer part of the number. Similarly, if an integer is entered in response to a READ statement that expects a real number, the READ statement automatically adds a decimal point at the end of the integer before storing the number. For example, assume that REANUM has been declared as a real variable, INTNUM as an integer variable, and the statement:

```
READ (5,*) REANUM,INTNUM
```

is being executed. For purposes of illustration, assume that the following line of data is entered at the standard input device:

```
22 26.75 45.62
```

The READ statement converts the 22 to the real number 22.0 and stores this value in the variable REANUM. The statement continues reading the input, expecting an integer value. As far as READ is concerned, the fractional part of the number 26.75 is extraneous input and is ignored. Thus, the integer number 26 is stored in INTNUM.* The remaining data entered on the same line, 45.62, is extra input and is ignored. However, if less data is entered than the number of variables in the READ statement, the READ statement will continue to make the computer pause until sufficient data has been entered.

Default to Standard Input

The input of data from the standard input device is so common that FORTRAN 77 provides a second form of the READ statement that automatically defaults to this device for its data entry. This second form of the list-directed READ statement is:

```
READ *, list of variables
```

Here the term READ * is equivalent to the term READ (*n*,*), where *n* is the standard input device's unit number. Since, by definition, this second form of the READ statement can accept its input only from the standard input device, the unit number is omitted from the statement. In both forms of the READ statement the asterisk tells the compiler that list-directed (free-form) input is to be used. Program 3-6 illustrates this second form of the READ statement. In this program the user is prompted to enter the temperature in degrees Fahrenheit. The entered value is converted to degrees Celsius using the algorithm *Celsius* = (5.0 / 9.0) * (*Fahrenheit* – 32.0), and the equivalent Celsius temperature is displayed.

* On some systems a "type mismatch" error is displayed.

Program 3-6

```
      PROGRAM TEMPCN
*** THIS PROGRAM CONVERTS AN ENTERED FAHRENHEIT
*** TEMPERATURE INTO AN EQUIVALENT CELSIUS VALUE
        REAL FAHREN, CELSUS
        WRITE(6,*) 'ENTER THE TEMPERATURE IN DEGREES FAHRENHEIT:
        READ *, FAHREN
        CELSUS = (5.0/9.0)* (FAHREN - 32.0)
        WRITE(6,*) ' THE EQUIVALENT CELSIUS TEMPERATURE IS ',CELSUS
        END
```

Following is a sample run using Program 3-6. In response to the prompt, a Fahrenheit temperature of 212 degrees, which corresponds to the boiling point of water, was entered. In Celsius this corresponds to 100 degrees, which agrees with the output produced by the program.

```
ENTER THE TEMPERATURE IN DEGREES FAHRENHEIT
212
THE EQUIVALENT CELSIUS TEMPERATURE IS 100.000000
```

Table 3-4 summarizes the various forms provided for list-directed input from the standard input device. Also included are corresponding forms for list-directed output to the standard output device. All of the READ statements in the table perform an identical input function, and all of the WRITE and PRINT statements accomplish an identical output function. Additionally, any of the statements listed in the table can be freely intermixed within a single program.

Notice from the table that all of the READ statements in the first column are equivalent, just as all of the WRITE statements in the second column are equivalent. For example, on an IBM computer the statement:

```
READ (5,*) NUM1
```

can be replaced by the statement:

```
READ *, NUM1
```

Table 3-4 Summary of Standard Input and Output List-Directed Statements

Input	Output
READ (*n*,*) variable list	WRITE (*k*,*) expression list
READ (*,*) variable list	WRITE (*,*) expression list
READ *, variable list	PRINT *, expression list

Note: *n* is the standard input device number and *k* is the standard output device number and both of these statements can be replaced by:

```
READ (*,*) NUM1
```

The first asterisk in this last statement is a unit designator (see Table 3-3) that selects the computer's standard input device. The second asterisk selects the compiler's default formats for the entry of the data. As with user-formatted output, this asterisk can be replaced with an explicit format specification, the topic of the next section.

Skill Builder Exercises

1. For each of the following declaration statements, write a single list-directed READ statement, using either form of the READ statement, that will cause the computer to pause while data for the declared variables is entered by a user.
   a. `INTEGER NUMBER`
   b. `REAL GRADE`
   c. `CHARACTER KEYVAL*8`
   d. `INTEGER MONTH, YEAR`
      `REAL SCORE`
   e. `CHARACTER CH*4`
      `INTEGER NUM1, NUM2`
   f. `REAL CAPTAL, RATE, AMOUNT`
   g. `CHARACTER*4 LETTR1, LETTR2, KEY*8`
      `INTEGER NUM1, NUM2, NUM3`
   h. `REAL OHMS1, OHMS2, OHMS3, VOLTS1, VOLTS2, VOLTS3`
2. Given the following declaration statements:

```
INTEGER NUM1,NUM2
REAL TEMP, AMBINT
CHARACTER*5 VAL1, VAL2
```

   determine and correct the errors in the following READ statements, assuming that the first form of the READ statement presented in the text is to be used.
   a. `READ * (NUM1, NUM2, VAL2)`
   b. `READ (NUM1, NUM2), *`
   c. `READ (NUM1,I4)`
   d. `READ INTO TEMP AND AMBINT`
   e. `READ VAL1, VAL2`
   f. `READ * NUM1, TEMP`
3. Redo Exercise 2 assuming that the second form of the READ statement (default to standard input) presented in the text is to be used.

Programming Exercises

4a. Modify Program 3-6 to convert Celsius degrees into equivalent Fahrenheit values. Make sure that an appropriate prompt and output line are displayed and that the conversion algorithm is suitably altered.

b. Compile and execute the program written for Exercise 4a. Verify your program by calculating by hand, and then using your program, the Fahrenheit equivalent of the following test data:

Test data set 1: 0 degrees Celsius
Test data set 2: 50 degrees Celsius
Test data set 3: 100 degrees Celsius

When you are sure your program is working correctly, use it to complete the following table:

Celsius	Fahrenheit
45	
50	
55	
60	
65	
70	

5. Write, compile, and execute a FORTRAN program that displays the following prompt:

```
ENTER THE RADIUS OF A CIRCLE:
```

After accepting a value for the radius, your program should calculate and display the area of the circle. (*Note:* area = 3.1416 * radius^2.) For testing purposes, verify your program using a test input radius of 3 inches. After manually checking that the result produced by your program is correct, use your program to complete the following table:

Radius (inches)	Area (square inches)
1.0	
1.5	
2.0	
2.5	
3.0	
3.5	

6a. Write, compile, and execute a FORTRAN program that displays the following prompts:

```
ENTER THE MILES DRIVEN:
ENTER THE GALLONS OF GAS USED:
```

After each prompt is displayed, your program should use a READ statement to accept data from the keyboard for the displayed prompt. After the gallons of gas used has been entered, your program should calculate and display miles per gallon obtained. This value should be included in an appropriate message and calculated using the equation *miles per gallon = miles / gallons used.* Verify your program using the following test data:

Test data set 1: miles = 276, gas = 10 gallons
Test data set 2: miles = 200, gas = 15.5 gallons

When you have completed your verification, use your program to complete the following table:

Miles driven	Gallons used	MPG
250	16	
275	18	
312	19.54	
296	17.39	

b. For the program written for Exercise 6a, determine how many verification runs are required to ensure the program is working correctly and give a reason supporting your answer.

7a. Write, compile, and execute a FORTRAN program that displays the following prompts:

```
ENTER A NUMBER:
ENTER A SECOND NUMBER:
ENTER A THIRD NUMBER:
ENTER A FOURTH NUMBER:
```

After each prompt is displayed, your program should use a READ statement to accept a number from the keyboard for the displayed prompt. After the fourth number has been entered, your program should calculate and display the average of the numbers. The average should be included in an appropriate message. Check the average displayed by your program using the following test data:

Test data set 1: 100, 100, 100, 100
Test data set 2: 100, 0, 100, 0

When you have completed your verification, use your program to complete the following table:

Numbers	Average
92, 98, 79, 85	
86, 84, 75, 86	
63, 85, 74, 82	

b. Repeat Exercise 7a, making sure that you use the same variable name, NUMBER, for each number input. Also use the variable SUM for the sum of the numbers. (*Hint:* To do this, you must use the statement SUM = SUM + NUMBER after each number is accepted. Review the material on accumulating presented in Section 2.3.)

8a. Write, compile, and execute a FORTRAN program that computes and displays the value of the second order polynomial $ax^2 + bx + c$ for any user-input values of the coefficients a, b, c, and the variable x. Have your program first display a message informing the user as to what the program will do and then display suitable prompts to alert the user to enter the desired data. (*Hint:* Use a prompt such as ENTER THE COEFFICIENT OF THE X SQUARED TERM:)

b. Check the result produced by your program using the following test data:

Test data set 1: a = 0, b = 0, c = 22, x = 56
Test data set 2: a = 0, b = 22, c = 0, x = 2
Test data set 3: a = 22, b = 0, c = 0, x = 2

Test data set 4: a = 2, b = 4, c = 5, x = 2
Test data set 5: a = 5, b = –3, c = 2, x = 1

When you have completed your verification, use your program to complete the following table:

a	*b*	*c*	*x*	**polynomial value**
2	17	–12	1.3	
3.2	2	15	2.5	
3.2	2	15	–2.5	
–2	10	0	2	
–2	10	0	4	
–2	10	0	5	
–2	10	0	6	
5	22	18	8.3	
4.2	–16	–20	–5.2	

9. The number of bacteria, B, in a certain culture that is subject to refrigeration can be approximated by the equation $B = 300{,}000\ e^{-.032t}$, where t is the time, in hours, that the culture has been refrigerated. Using this equation, write, compile, and execute a single FORTRAN program that prompts the user for a value of time, calculates the number of bacteria in the culture, and displays the result. For testing purposes, check your program using a test input of 10 hours. When you have verified the operation of your program, use it to determine the number of bacteria in the culture after 12, 18, 24, 36, 48, and 72 hours.

10. Write, compile, and execute a program that calculates and displays the square root value of a user-entered real number. Recall that the square root of a number can be found by either using the SQRT function or by raising the number to the 1/2 power. (*Hint:* Do not use integer division—can you see why?) Verify your program by calculating the square roots of the following data: 25, 16, 0, and 2. When you have completed your verification, use your program to determine the square root of 32.25, 42, 48, 55, 63, and 79.

11. Write, compile, and execute a program that calculates and displays the fourth root of a user-entered number. Recall from elementary algebra that the fourth root of a number can be found either by using the SQRT function twice or by raising the number to the 1/4 power. (*Hint:* Do not use integer division—can you see why?) Verify your program by calculating the fourth root of the following data: 81, 16, 1, and 0. When you have completed your verification, use your program to determine the fourth root of 42, 121, 256, 587, 1240, and 16,256.

12. For the series circuit shown in Figure 3-6, the voltage drop, V_2, across resistor R_2 and the power, P_2, delivered to this resistor are given by the equations $V_2 = I\ R_2$ and $P_2 = I\ V_2$, where $I = E/(R_1 + R_2)$. Using these equations, write, compile, and execute a FORTRAN program that prompts the user for values of E, R_1, and R_2, calculates the voltage drop and power delivered to R_2, and displays the results. Check your program using the test data E = 10 volts,

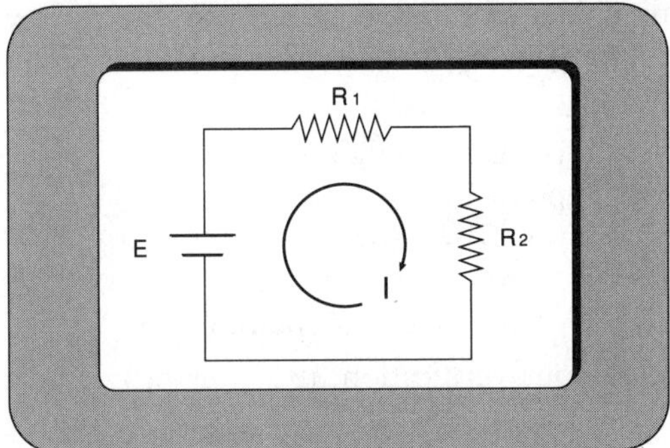

Figure 3-6 Calculating the Voltage Drop

R_1 = 100 ohms, and R_2 = 200 ohms. When you have completed your verification, use your program to complete the following table:

E (volts)	R_1 (ohms)	R_2 (ohms)	Voltage drop (volts)	Power delivered (watts)
10	100	100		
10	100	200		
10	200	200		
20	100	100		
20	100	200		
20	200	200		

13. Write, compile, and execute a FORTRAN program that computes the combined resistance of three parallel resistors. The values of each resistor should be accepted using a READ statement (use the formula for combined resistance given in Exercise 26 of Section 2.3). Verify the operation of your program by using the following test data:

Test data set 1: R_1 = 1000, R_2 = 1000, and R_3 = 1000
Test data set 2: R_1 = 1000, R_2 = 1500, and R_3 = 500

When you have completed your verification, use your program to complete the following table:

R_1 (ohms)	R_2 (ohms)	R_3 (ohms)	Combined resistance (ohms)
3000	3000	3000	
6000	6000	6000	
2000	3000	1000	
2000	4000	5000	
4000	2000	1000	
10000	100	100	

14. Using READ statements, write, compile, and execute a FORTRAN program that accepts the x and y coordinates of two points. Have your program determine and display the midpoints of the two points (use the formula given in Exercise 28 of Section 2.3 on page 79). Verify your program using the following test data:

Test data set 1: point 1 = (0,0), point 2 = (16,0)
Test data set 2: point 1 = (0,0), point 2 = (0,16)
Test data set 3: point 1 = (0,0), point 2 = (–16,0)
Test data set 4: point 1 = (0,0), point 2 = (0,–16)
Test data set 5: point 1 = (–5,–5), point 2 = (5,5)

When you have completed your verification, use your program to complete the following table.

Point 1	Point 2	Midpoint
(4,6)	(16,18)	
(22,3)	(8,12)	
(–10,8)	(14,4)	
(–12,2)	(14,–4)	
(–4,–6)	(20,16)	
(–4,-6)	(–16,–18)	

15. Write, compile, and execute a FORTRAN program that calculates and displays the amount of money, A, available in N years when an initial deposit of X dollars is deposited in a bank account paying an annual interest rate of R percent. Use the relationship that $A = X(1.0 + R/100)^N$. The program should prompt the user to enter appropriate values and use READ statements to accept the data. In constructing your prompts, use statements such as ENTER THE AMOUNT OF THE INITIAL DEPOSIT. Verify the operation of your program by calculating, by hand, the amount of money available for the following test data:

Test data set 1: $1000 invested for 10 years at 0 percent interest
Test data set 2: $1000 invested for 10 years at 6 percent interest

When you have completed your verification, use your program to determine the amount of money available for the following cases:

a. $1000 invested for 10 years at 8 percent interest
b. $1000 invested for 10 years at 10 percent interest
c. $1000 invested for 10 years at 12 percent interest
d. $5000 invested for 15 years at 8 percent interest
e. $5000 invested for 15 years at 10 percent interest
f. $5000 invested for 15 years at 12 percent interest
g. $24 invested for 300 years at 4 percent interest

16. Program 3-4 prompts the user to input two numbers, where the first value entered is stored in FIRNUM and the second value is stored in SECNUM. Using this program as a starting point, write a program that swaps the values stored in the two variables.

17. Write a FORTRAN program that prompts the user to type in an integer number. Have your program accept the number as an integer and immediately display the integer using a WRITE statement. Run your program three times. The first time you run the program, enter a valid integer number, the second time enter a real number, and the third time enter a character constant (recall that a character constant must be surrounded by apostrophes). Using the output display, see what number your program actually accepted from the data you entered. What happened, if anything, and why?

18. Repeat Exercise 17 but have your program declare the variable used to store the number as a real variable. Run the program four times. The first time enter an integer, the second time enter a decimal number with less than six decimal places, the third time enter a number having more than six decimal places, and the fourth time enter a character constant (recall that a character constant must be surrounded by apostrophes). Using the output display, keep track of what number your program actually accepted from the data you typed in. What happened, if anything, and why?

19. Repeat Exercise 17 but have your program declare the variable used to store the number as a character variable having a length of four characters. Run the program four times. The first time enter character data having four or fewer characters (recall that input character data must be surrounded by apostrophes), the second time enter a character constant having more than four characters, the third time enter an integer, and the fourth time enter a decimal number. Using the output display, keep track of what value your program actually accepted from the data you typed in. What happened, if anything, and why?

20a. Why do you think that most successful applications programs contain extensive data input validity checks? (*Hint:* Review Exercises 17, 18, and 19.)

b. What do you think is the difference between a data type check and a data reasonableness check?

c. Assume that a program requests that the velocity and acceleration of a car be entered by the user. What are some checks that could be made on the data entered?

3.3 The Formatted READ Statement*

Just as the list-directed output statements PRINT and WRITE have their user-formatted counterparts, the list-directed READ statements do also. As with the list-directed READ statements, the user-formatted counterparts come in two forms. The most general of these forms is:

```
READ (unit number, format specifier) variable list
```

where unit number designates where the input will be entered and the format

* This topic may be omitted on first reading without loss of subject continuity.

specifier designates the specific spacing of the input data on the input unit. Acceptable format specifiers include:

1. an asterisk, which specifies a list-directed format
2. the statement number of a FORMAT statement
3. a format specification, enclosed in parentheses surrounded by apostrophes

For user-selected input formatting, the last two options are used. For example, assuming that the variables NUM1 and NUM2 have been declared as integers, the statement:

```
READ (5,10) NUM1, NUM2
```

specifies that the two integers are to be read from unit number 5 using the format defined in FORMAT statement 10. For purposes of illustration, assume the following FORMAT statement:

```
10 FORMAT(I2,3X,I4)
```

This FORMAT statement specifies that the input line consists of two integer fields separated by three spaces. The first integer must occupy columns 1 and 2 of the line and the second 6 through 9.

Using this format demands that the entered data conform exactly to the fields specified. For example, assuming that unit number 5 corresponds to the standard input device, consider the sequence of statements:

```
      INTEGER NUM1, NUM2
      READ (5,10) NUM1, NUM2
   10 FORMAT(I2,3X,I4)
```

If the data entered is:

```
45   6732     ← data entered
123456789     ← column number
```

the value 45 is assigned to the variable NUM1 and the value 6732 is assigned to NUM2. If instead the data entered is placed as follows:

```
4    673 2  ← data entered
123456789   ← column number
```

the number 4 is assigned to NUM1 and the number 732 is assigned to NUM2. Note that the blanks embedded in each field are effectively ignored.*

As illustrated by this example, a FORMAT statement by itself is neither an input nor a output format. The format refers to an input line only because it is referenced by a READ statement. Additionally, when a format specification is used for input, the first character is not interpreted as a carriage control code. Carriage control only has meaning in a format specification used for output. The format specifications for reading integer, real, and character data and for skipping over designated input fields, as expected, are essentially the same as those used for writing these items and are presented at the end of this section.

* Some FORTRAN compilers consider embedded blanks to be zeros, in which case NUM1 = 40, NUM2 = 7302.

Default to Standard Input

In addition to the more general form of the user-formatted READ statement that can receive input from any device, an alternate form is provided in FORTRAN 77 and FORTRAN 90 for standard input data entry. This alternate form is:

```
READ k, list of variables
```

Here, the term READ *k*, is equivalent to the term READ (*n*,*k*), where *n* is the unit number of the standard input device, and *k* is a reference to a FORMAT statement. As an example of this alternate form, consider the sequence of statements:

```
      INTEGER NUM1, NUM2
      READ 10, NUM1, NUM2
   10 FORMAT(I4,I3)
```

This form of the READ statement designates that the data will be entered at the standard input device. The referenced FORMAT statement specifies that the input line entered at the standard input device consists of two integer fields, the first of which occupies columns 1 through 4 of the line and the second of which occupies columns 5, 6, and 7.

Assuming that the keyboard is the standard input unit, if the data entered at the keyboard in response to these statements is:

```
4567329     ← data entered
1234567     ← column number
```

the value 4567 is assigned to the variable NUM1 and the value 329 is assigned to NUM2. If instead the following data is entered:

```
4567 123     ← data entered
123456789    ← column number
```

the number 456, which is the contents of columns 1 through 4, is assigned to NUM1, and the contents of columns 5, 6, and 7, which is interpreted as the number 71, is assigned to NUM2.* Note that the blank in column 6 is effectively ignored.

In the early days of FORTRAN, during the 1960s and 1970s, the standard input device was almost always a card reader. For these devices, which read a standard card having 80 columns, explicit user-designated formatting was the preferred method of data entry. Such formatting allowed cards to be prepared by data entry clerks using a standard format. The cards were then read by the program using an appropriate FORMAT statement. Although user-formatted input is still defined for keyboard input, it is rarely used for this purpose because of the additional level of complexity that is not present in its free-form list-directed counterpart. Nevertheless, user-formatted input does have its place. Typically, it is used with the first form of the READ statement presented for reading data stored on a medium such as a magnetic disk or tape. The use of user formatting for these storage mediums can result in

* For compilers that consider embedded blanks to be zeros, NUM2 would be assigned the number 701.

savings of storage space due to the fixed-form field widths employed. The saving of storage space will become clearer when we encounter user-formatted input of data files in Chapter 5.

Input Edit Descriptors

The commonly used edit descriptors for user-formatted input are essentially the same as those used for user-formatted output. They are presented below as they relate to data input.

Integer Input

The I edit descriptor is used for reading user-formatted integer data. The form of this descriptor, which is the same as for user-formatted integer data output, is:

```
rIw
```

where *r* is the repeat factor, I denotes an integer, and *w* is the width of the integer field. For example, the statements:

```
      INTEGER I, J, K
      READ (5,10) I, J, K
   10 FORMAT(I3,I4,I5)
```

specify an input line of three integer fields having lengths of 3, 4, and 5 columns, respectively. For the following input line:

```
678 -3 4  29
123456789111
         0123
↑
Column number 1
```

the number 678 is assigned to *I*, –3 to *J*, and 429 to *K*. Note that blanks are ignored in an input field, and a number can be placed in any position within a field.*

Real Number Input

The F edit descriptor can be used for reading real numbers. The form of this descriptor, which is the same as for user-formatted real data output, is:

```
rFw.d
```

where *r* is the repeat factor, F denotes a real number, *w* denotes total field width, and *d* denotes the number of digits to the right of the decimal point. If a decimal point is included in the input number, the number can be placed anywhere within the defined field. For example, the statements:

* Again, some compilers interpret embedded blanks as zeros.

```
      REAL A, B, C
      READ (2,10) A, B, C
   10 FORMAT(F6.2,2F4.1)
```

define three input fields: the first has a field width of 6, and the next two, because of the repeat count, both have field widths of 4. For the following input line:

```
 54.23 6.1 9.6
12345678911111
         01234
↑
Column number 1
```

the value 54.23 within the first field is assigned to *A*, the value 6.1 in the second field is assigned to *B*, and the value 9.6 in the third field is assigned to *C*. Within the three fields, each number can be placed in any position without affecting the values assigned to the variables *A*, *B*, and *C*.

The decimal point actually can be omitted from a user-formatted real number. When the decimal point is omitted in the input data, the *d* format specification automatically assigns the last *d* positions in the field as the fractional part of the number. For example, if the previous input line was:

```
  5423  61  96
12345678911111
         01234
↑
Column number 1
```

the same values as before are assigned to the variables *A*, *B*, and *C*.

Real values may also be entered in scientific notation using the F edit descriptor. For example, the numbers 1.79E2, .925E+2, and 26.7E–3 may all be placed in fields described by the F descriptor. When the exponent is preceded by a sign, as in the numbers .925E+2 and 26.7E–3, the E can be omitted. Thus, these two numbers can also be stored in their defined fields as .925+2 and 26.7–3.

Character Input

The A edit descriptor is used for reading formatted character data. As with output, the input version of the A edit descriptor has the two forms:

```
rA and rAw
```

where *r* is a repeat factor, A denotes character data, and *w* is an optional field width specifier. In the first form, the character field is determined by the length declared for the variable in its CHARACTER declaration. For example, the statements:

```
      CHARACTER STRNG1*3, STRNG2*4, STRNG3*5
      READ (2,10) STRNG1, STRNG2, STRNG3
   10 FORMAT(3A)
```

define three character variables of length 3, 4, and 5, respectively, and three corresponding field lengths. For the following input line:

```
NOW IS THE TIME
123456789111111
         012345
↑
```

Column number 1

the character constant NOW is assigned to STRNG1, the constant bISb (where b denotes a blank space) is assigned to STRNG2, and the constant THEbT is assigned to STRNG3. As with all data input, any extra data on a line are ignored. Note that character data entered in response to a user-formatted input statement do not require apostrophes surrounding the input data. (As noted previously, apostrophes are required when entering data in response to a list-directed READ statement.)

When a field width is used with the A edit descriptor, it defines the width of the input character field. If this field width is larger than the length declared for the character variable, the rightmost characters in the input field up to the number of characters declared for the variable are used. If the field width is smaller than the length declared for the character variable, the input characters are stored, left-justified in the character variable, and the remaining positions in the variable are padded with trailing blanks. For example, the statements:

```
   CHARACTER*4 STRNG1, STRNG2, STRNG3
   READ (2,10) STRNG1, STRNG2, STRNG3
10 FORMAT(A4,A6,A2)
```

define three character variables of length 4, and three input fields of widths 4, 6, and 2, respectively. For the following input line:

```
RAREEARTHMETALS
123456789111111
         012345
↑
```

Column number 1

the characters RARE in the first field of four are assigned to STRNG1. In the second field of six, the rightmost four characters, RTHM, are assigned to STRNG2, and the first two characters in the field are ignored. Finally, the two characters ET in the third field are padded with two trailing blank spaces and assigned to STRNG3. The rest of the characters on the line are considered extra input and are ignored.

Positional Editing

The X, T, and TR positional edit descriptors can be used to skip over designated columns of input data. For example, the statement:

```
10 FORMAT(1X,I4,3X,F5.2)
```

specifies four input fields. The first field consists of one column, the second is an integer field four spaces wide, the third is a field of three columns, and the fourth is a real field five spaces wide. Fields specified by the X edit descriptor are skipped over on input. This means that any data in these fields is ignored.

The TR (tab right) edit descriptor works in the same manner as the X edit descriptor. For example, the statement:

```
20 FORMAT(TR4,F5.2,TR7,F7.3)
```

is exactly equivalent to the statement:

```
20 FORMAT(4X,F5.2,7X,F7.3)
```

Finally, the T edit descriptor specifies an absolute column position in the input line. For example, the statement:

```
20 FORMAT(T20,I4)
```

specifies that the designated integer field begins at column 20 in the line.

Exercises

1. For the following READ statements, write appropriate variable declaration statements.

a.
```
      READ (1,10) WATTS
   10 FORMAT(F8.2)
```
b.
```
      READ (5,20) TEMP
   20 FORMAT(F5.2)
```
c.
```
      READ (*,30) COUNT
   30 FORMAT(I4)
```
d.
```
      READ (1,40) NUM1, NUM2, VALUE, CH1
   40 FORMAT(I4,I5,F3.2,A6)
```
e.
```
      READ (5,50) COUNT, VOLTS, OHMS
   50 FORMAT(I2,2F6.2)
```
f.
```
      READ (*,60) AVERGE, IFLAG, KEY, CODE
   60 FORMAT(F7.3,I1,2A6)
```

2. Given the following declaration statements:

```
INTEGER NUM1,NUM2
REAL TEMP, AMBINT
CHARACTER*5 VAL1, VAL2
```

determine and correct the errors in the following statements. Assume that the maximum integer value that will be read into NUM1 and NUM2 is 9999 and that the real variables TEMP and AMBINT have a maximum integer part of 999 with at most three digits to the right of the decimal point.

a.
```
      READ (1,10,NUM1)
```
b.
```
      READ (5,20) (NUM1,NUM2,NUM3)
```
c.
```
      READ (*,30),TEMP,AMBINT
```
d.
```
      READ (1,10) NUM1
```
e.
```
      READ (5,20) NUM1, TEMP, VAL1
   20 FORMAT(3I4)
```

f.
```
      READ (*,30) NUM1, AMBINT, VAL1
   30 FORMAT(A,I2,F7.4)
```

3. List the starting and ending column numbers for all input fields defined by the following statements:

   a. `10 FORMAT(I4,F5.2,I5)`
   b. `20 FORMAT(F5.3,I6,A8)`
   c. `30 FORMAT(1X,F5.2,2X,A20)`
   d. `40 FORMAT(2(1X,I5))`
   e. `60 FORMAT(1X,2(I3,2X),F5.2,2(1X,I3))`

4. The following is a valid FORTRAN program.

```
      PROGRAM MAIN
        INTEGER NUM1, NUM2
        READ(*,10)NUM1, NUM2
   10   FORMAT(I4,I3)
        WRITE(*,*) NUM1, NUM2
        END
```

   When this program is run, the user enters the data 1 234 5. For this data input, determine the output produced by the program.

5. Determine if the following program will work. Discuss what should be changed in the program, if anything.

```
      PROGRAM MAIN
        CHARACTER*8, MESSGE
        INTEGER NUM1, NUM2
        READ (5,10) MESSGE, NUM1, NUM2
        WRITE(6,10) MESSGE, NUM1, NUM2
   10   FORMAT(1X,A,2(1X,I3))
        END
```

6a. Write, compile, and run a FORTRAN program that accepts two integer numbers from the standard input device using the FORMAT statement:

```
   10 FORMAT(I2,I4)
```

The program should display the numbers entered to verify correct data input.

b. Determine what your program will display for the following data input line:

```
45678      ← data entered
123456     ← column number
```

c. Verify your answer to Exercise 6b by running your program and entering the designated input line.

7a. Write, compile, and run a FORTRAN program that accepts two real numbers from the standard input device using the FORMAT statement:

```
   10 FORMAT(1X,F7.2,2X,F5.2)
```

The program should display the numbers entered to verify correct data input.

b. Determine what your program will display for the following data input line:

```
     6.78     23.4   ← data entered
   12345678911111
            01234
   ↑
   Column number 1
```

c. Determine what your program will display for the following data input line:

```
6.78     23.4   ← data entered
123456789111
         012
↑
Column number 1
```

d. Determine what your program will display for the following data input line:

```
      678 234     ← data entered
12345678911111
         012345
↑
Column number 1
```

e. Verify your answers to Exercises 7b, 7c, and 7d by running your program and entering the designated input line.

f. Run the program written for Exercise 7a using the following data input line:

```
  678         234  ← data entered
12345678911111
         01234
↑
Column number 1
```

Using the display produced by your program, determine how your compiler interprets trailing blank spaces in an input field.

8. Write, compile, and execute a FORTRAN program that accepts four real numbers from the standard input device using the FORMAT statement:

```
10 FORMAT(4(1X,F5.2))
```

Your program should read the input, determine the average of the four numbers read, and display the average. Verify the output produced by your program using the following test data:

Test data set 1: 100, 100, 100, 100
Test data set 2: 100, 0, 100, 0

When you have completed your verification, use your program to complete the following table:

Numbers	**Average**
92, 98, 79, 85	
86, 84, 75, 86	
63, 85, 74, 82	

9. Using the FORMAT statement:

```
10 FORMAT(4(1X,F6.2))
```

write, compile, and execute a FORTRAN program that reads an input line and interprets the first and second numbers on the input line as the coordinates of one point and the third and fourth numbers as the coordinates of a second point. Using the formula given in Exercise 28 of Section 2.3, have your program compute and display the midpoint of the two points entered. Verify your program using the following test data:

Test data set 1: point 1 = (0,0), point 2 = (16,0)
Test data set 2: point 1 = (0,0), point 2 = (0,16)
Test data set 3: point 1 = (0,0), point 2 = (–16,0)
Test data set 4: point 1 = (0,0), point 2 = (0,–16)
Test data set 5: point 1 = (–5,–5), point 2 = (5,5)

When you have completed your verification, use your program to complete the following table:

Point 1	**Point 2**	**Midpoint**
(4, 6)	(16, 18)	
(22, 3)	(8, 12)	
(6.3, 8.2)	(18.25, 24.32)	
(4.0, 4.0)	(10.0, –5.0)	
(–2.0, 5.0)	(4.0, 5.0)	

3.4 Named Constants: The PARAMETER Statement

Certain constants used within a program may have a more general meaning that is recognized outside the context of the program. Examples of these types of constants include the number 3.1416, which is the value of *pi* accurate to four decimal places; 32.2 ft/sec^2, which is the gravitational constant (see, for example, Program 3-1); and the number 2.71828, which is Euler's number accurate to five decimal places.

The meaning of certain other constants appearing in a program is defined strictly within the context of the application being programmed. For example, in a program to determine bank interest charges, the value of the interest rate takes on a special meaning. Similarly, in determining the weight of various-sized objects, the density of the material being used takes on a special significance. Numbers such as these are referred to by programmers as *magic numbers*. By themselves the numbers are quite ordinary, but in the context of a particular application they have a special ("magical") meaning. Frequently, the same magic number appears repeatedly within the same program. This recurrence of the same constant throughout a program is a potential source of error should the constant have to be changed. For example, if the interest rate changes, or a new material is employed with a different density, the programmer will have the cumbersome task of changing the value of the magic number everywhere it appears in the program. Multiple changes, however, are subject to error: if just one value is overlooked and not changed, the result obtained when the program is run will be incorrect.

To avoid the problems of having a magic number spread throughout a program and to clearly permit identification of more universal constants, such as *pi*, FORTRAN allows the programmer to give these constants their own symbolic names. Then, instead of using the constant throughout the program, the symbolic name is used instead. In the case of magic numbers, should the number ever need to be changed, the change can be made once at the point where the symbolic name is equated to the actual constant value.

Equating constants to symbolic names is accomplished using the PARAMETER statement. The general form of this statement is:

```
PARAMETER (name1 = expression, name2 = expression, etc.)
```

For example, the number 3.1416 can be equated to the symbolic name PI using the PARAMETER statement:

```
PARAMETER (PI = 3.1416)
```

Constants named in this fashion are called both *named constants* and *symbolic constants*, and we shall use both terms interchangeably.

Once a constant has been named, the name can be used in any FORTRAN statement in place of the number itself. For example, the assignment statement:

```
CIRCUM = 2 * PI * RADIUS
```

makes use of the named constant PI. This statement must, of course, appear after PI has been named in a PARAMETER statement. As with variables, the names of the symbolic constants must be declared prior to being used in a PARAMETER statement. For example, the naming of PI would be used with a declaration statement as follows:

```
REAL PI
PARAMETER (PI = 3.1416)
```

Other than the requirement that a PARAMETER statement must appear after the declarations for its named constants, PARAMETER and declaration statements can be freely intermixed. Both types of statements must, however, be placed at the top of a program unit immediately following the program unit's header line. Program 3-7 illustrates the use of a PARAMETER statement to calculate the weight of a steel cylinder. The density of the steel is 0.284 lb/in^3.

Notice in Program 3-7 that a single PARAMETER statement defines two named constants: PI and DENSTY. The following run was made using Program 3-7 to determine the weight of a cylinder with a radius of 3 inches and a height of 12 inches.

```
ENTER THE RADIUS OF THE CYLINDER
3
ENTER THE HEIGHT OF THE CYLINDER
12
 THE CYLINDER WEIGHS      96.359150 POUNDS.
```

The advantage of using the named constant PI in Program 3-7 is that it clearly identifies the value 3.1416 in terms recognizable to most people. The advantage of using the named constant DENSTY is that it permits a programmer to change the

Program 3-7

```
      PROGRAM MAIN
*** THIS PROGRAM DETERMINES THE WEIGHT OF A STEEL CYLINDER
*** BY MULTIPLYING THE VOLUME OF THE CYLINDER TIMES ITS DENSITY
*** THE VOLUME OF A CYLINDER IS (PI * RADIUS**2 * HEIGHT)
        REAL PI, DENSTY, RADIUS, HEIGHT, WEIGHT
        PARAMETER (PI = 3.1416, DENSTY = 0.284)
        WRITE(6,*) 'ENTER THE RADIUS OF THE CYLINDER'
        READ *, RADIUS
        WRITE(6,*) 'ENTER THE HEIGHT OF THE CYLINDER'
        READ *, HEIGHT
        WEIGHT = DENSTY * PI * RADIUS**2 * HEIGHT
        WRITE(6,*) ' THE CYLINDER WEIGHS ', WEIGHT, ' POUNDS.'
        END
```

value of the density for another material without having to search through the program to see where the density is used. Of course, if many different materials are to be considered, the density should be changed from a named constant to a variable. A natural question arises, then, as to the difference between named constants and variables.

The value of a variable can be altered anywhere within a program. By its nature a named constant is a constant value that must not be altered after it is defined. Naming a constant rather than assigning the value to a variable ensures that the value in the constant cannot be subsequently altered. Whenever a named constant appears in an instruction, it has the same effect as the constant it represents. Thus, DENSTY in Program 3-7 is simply another way of representing the number 0.284. Since DENSTY and the number 0.284 are equivalent, the value of DENSTY may not be changed subsequently within the program. Once DENSTY has been defined as a constant, an assignment statement such as:

```
DENSTY = 0.156
```

is meaningless and will result in an error message, because DENSTY is not a variable. Since DENSTY is only a substitute for the value 0.284, this statement is equivalent to writing the invalid statement 0.284 = 0.156.

In addition to using the PARAMETER statement to name constants, as in Program 3-7, this statement can also be used to equate the value of a constant expression to a symbolic name. A *constant expression* is an expression consisting of operators and constants only. For example, the statement:

```
PARAMETER (CONVRT = 3.1416/180.0)
```

equates the value of the constant expression 3.1416/180.0 to the symbolic name CONVRT. The symbolic name, as always, can be used in any statement following its definition. For example, since the expression 3.1416/180.0 is required for converting degrees to radians, the symbolic name selected for this conversion factor can be conveniently used whenever such a conversion is required. Thus, in the assignment statement:

```
HEIGHT = DISTNC * SIN(ANGLE*CONVRT)
```

the symbolic constant CONVRT is used to convert the value in ANGLE to radian measure.

A previously defined named constant can also be used in a subsequent PARAMETER statement. For example, the following sequence of statements is valid:

```
REAL PI, CONVRT
PARAMETER (PI = 3.1416, CONVRT = PI/180.)
```

Since the constant 3.1416 has been equated to the symbolic name PI, it can be used legitimately in any subsequent definition, even within the same PARAMETER statement. Program 3-8 uses the named constant CONVRT to convert a user-entered angle, in degrees, into its equivalent radian measure for use by the SIN function.

Program 3-8

```
PROGRAM MAIN
  REAL PI, CONVRT, ANGLE
  PARAMETER (PI = 3.1416, CONVRT = PI/180.0)
  WRITE(6,*) 'ENTER THE ANGLE (IN DEGREES)'
  READ *, ANGLE
  WRITE(6,*) ' THE SINE OF THE ANGLE IS ', SIN(ANGLE*CONVRT)
  END
```

Following is a sample run using Program 3-8:

```
ENTER THE ANGLE (IN DEGREES)
30
 THE SINE OF THE ANGLE IS 5.000000 E-01
```

The use of PARAMETER statements is not restricted to integer and real constants. A constant of any data type can be named, with the only requirement being that the data type of the named constant be declared and a constant of the correct type be equated to the declared name. For example, the pair of statements:

```
CHARACTER*7 UNITS
PARAMETER (UNITS = 'NANOSEC')
```

declares UNITS to be a symbolic name of type CHARACTER. Its use in the PARAMETER changes its status to a symbolic constant (it no longer can be used as a variable) and equates a constant of the correct data type to it.

A useful feature in defining a symbolic character constant is that the length of the constant need not be specified in the declaration statement. If the "dummy" length specifier, (*), is used in the declaration statement, the actual length of the character constant is determined by the compiler when the PARAMETER statement is encountered. Thus, the previous declaration for UNITS can be replaced by the declaration:

```
CHARACTER*(*) UNITS
```

The use of the "dummy" length specifier makes subsequent modifications to the named constant much easier because it eliminates the need to count the length of each character string. For example, if it is required to change UNITS to 'NANO-SECONDS', all that needs to be modified is the PARAMETER statement. The new PARAMETER statement becomes:

```
PARAMETER (UNITS = 'NANOSECONDS')
```

and no change to the declaration for UNITS is necessary.

Statement Ordering

We have introduced a variety of statements. In using the various statement types, certain placement rules must be followed. For the statements we have presented these rules are:

1. The END statement must be the last statement of every program unit. This statement consists of the keyword END with no spaces allowed between any of the letters (on some compilers spaces are permitted).
2. Comment lines may appear anywhere in a program unit, except as the last line of a program unit.
3. FORMAT statements may appear anywhere between the program header line and the END statement.
4. PARAMETER and declaration statements, which collectively (along with additional statements to be introduced) are referred to as *specification* statements, may be intermixed and must appear before all executable statements. Executable statements, which may be freely intermixed, include all assignment, WRITE, PRINT, and READ statements.

A review of Programs 3-7 and 3-8 will verify that they adhere to these statement placement rules. Any violations of these rules will result in a compiler error message.

Figure 3-7 summarizes the relationships described by these statement placement rules. Horizontal lines in the figure indicate statement types that cannot be

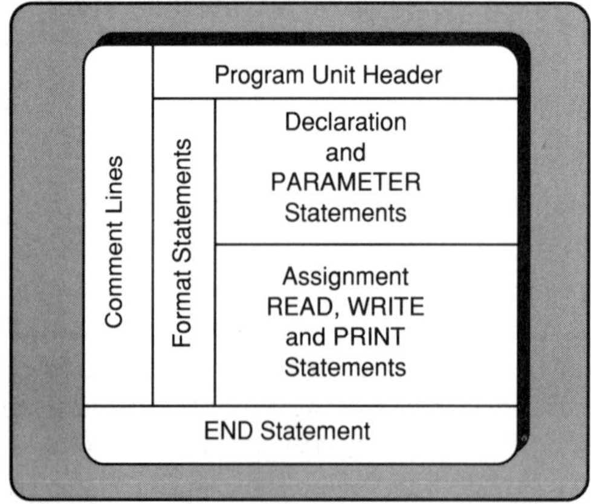

Figure 3-7 Required Statement Placement

intermixed. For example, the line between PARAMETER and assignment statements indicates that these two types of statements must not be intermixed. Since PARAMETER statements appear above the line, all PARAMETER statements in a program unit must appear before any assignment statement is used. Similarly, all of the other statements below this same line, such as the PRINT statement, cannot be intermixed with any statement above the line. Thus, PRINT statements cannot be intermixed with either program header lines or PARAMETER statements, and all PRINT statements must appear after the last PARAMETER statement in a program unit.

Statements separated by dashed vertical lines in Figure 3-7 can be freely intermixed. Thus, comment lines can be intermixed with any statement in a program unit except for an END statement. Similarly, FORMAT statements may appear anywhere between the program header line and END statement and may be intermixed with any other statement within these two bounds.

Exercises

1. Modify Program 3-1 to use the named constant GRAV in place of the value 32.2 used in the program. Compile and execute your program to verify that it produces the same result as shown in the text.
2. Modify Program 3-6 to use the named constant FACTOR in place of the expression (5.0/9.0) used in the program. Compile and execute your program to verify that it produces the same result as shown in the text.
3. Rewrite the following program using a PARAMETER statement for the constant 3.1416.

```
PROGRAM MAIN
  REAL RADIUS, CIRCUM, AREA
  PRINT *, 'ENTER A RADIUS'
  READ *, RADIUS
  CIRCUM = 2.0 * 3.1416 * RADIUS
  AREA = 3.1416 * RADIUS**2
  WRITE(6,*) 'THE CIRCUMFERENCE IS ', CIRCUM
  WRITE(6,*) 'THE AREA IS ', AREA
  END
```

4. Rewrite the following program so that the variable PRIME is changed to a named constant.

```
PROGRAM MAIN
  REAL PRIME, AMOUNT, INTRST
  PRIME = 0.08
  WRITE(6,*) 'ENTER THE AMOUNT' READ *, AMOUNT
  INTRST = PRIME * AMOUNT
  WRITE(6,*) 'THE INTEREST EARNED IS ', INTRST
  END
```

3.5 Applications

In this section we present two applications to further illustrate both the use of READ statements to accept user input data and the use of intrinsic functions for performing calculations.

Application 1: Acid Rain

The use of coal as the major source of steam power began with the Industrial Revolution. Currently, coal is one of the principal sources of generating electrical power in many industrialized countries.

Since the middle of the nineteenth century it has been known that the oxygen used in the burning process combines with the carbon and sulfur in the coal to produce both carbon dioxide and sulfur dioxide. When these gases are released into the atmosphere, the sulfur dioxide combines with the water and oxygen in the air to form sulfuric acid, which itself is transformed into separate hydronium ions and sulfates (see Figure 3-8). It is the hydronium ions in the atmosphere that fall to earth, either as components of rain or as a dry deposit, which changes the acidity level of lakes and forests.

The acid level of rain and lakes is measured on a pH scale using the formula:

$$\text{pH} = -\text{Log}_{10}\,(\text{concentration of hydronium ions})$$

where the concentration of hydronium ions is measured in units of moles/liter. A pH value of 7 indicates a neutral value (neither acid nor alkaline), while levels below 7

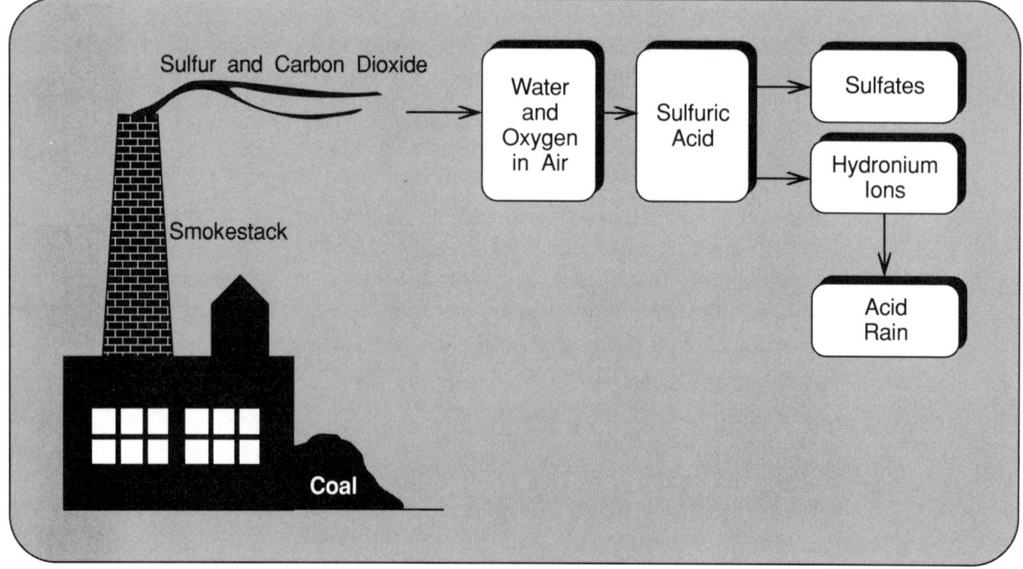

Figure 3-8 The Formation of Acid Rain

indicate the presence of an acid, and levels above 7 indicate the presence of an alkaline substance. For example, sulfuric acid has a pH value of approximately 1, lye has a pH value of approximately 13, and water typically has a pH value of 7. Marine life usually cannot survive in water with a pH level below 4.

Using the formula for pH, we will write a FORTRAN program that calculates the pH level of a substance based on a user-input value for the concentration of hydronium ions.

Program Development

Using the top-down development procedure described in Chapter 2, we have:

Step 1: Determine the Desired Outputs

Although the statement of the problem provides technical information on the composition of acid rain, from a programming viewpoint this is a rather simple problem. Here there is only one required output: a pH level.

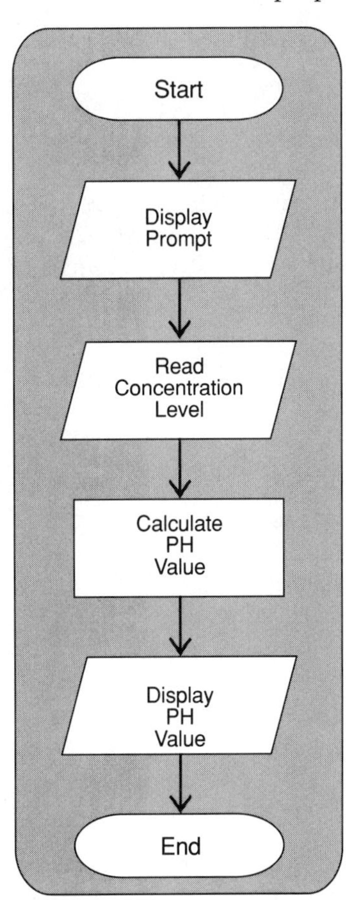

Figure 3-9 The Selected Algorithm as a Flowchart

Step 2: Determine the Input Items

For this problem there is only one input item, the concentration level of hydronium ions.

Step 3a: Determine an Algorithm

The processing required to transform the input to the required output is a rather straightforward use of the pH formula provided. The flowchart representation of the complete algorithm for entering the input data, processing the data to produce the desired output, and displaying the output is illustrated in Figure 3-9.

The pseudocode representation of the algorithm depicted in Figure 3-9 is:

Display a prompt to enter an ion concentration level
Read a value for the concentration level
Calculate a pH level using the given formula
Display the calculated value

Step 3b: Do a Hand Calculation

To ensure that we understand the formula used in the algorithm, we will do a hand calculation. We can use the result of this calculation to verify the result produced by the program.

Assuming a hydronium concentration of .0001 (any value would do), the pH level is calculated as $-\ \mathrm{LOG}_{10}\ 10^{-4}$. Either by knowing that the logarithm of 10 raised to a power is the power itself, or by using a log table, the value of this expressions is found to be $-(-4) = 4$.

Step 3c: Select Variable Names

The last step required before the selected algorithm is described in FORTRAN is to select variable names for the input, output, and any intermediate variables required by the algorithm. For this problem we will select the variable names HYDRON for the input variable and PHLEVL for the calculated pH level (any valid variable name could have been selected).

Step 4: Write the Program

Program 3-9 describes the selected algorithm in FORTRAN using the variable names chosen in Step 3c.

Program 3-9 begins with a program header line and a declaration statement that declares two real variables, HYDRON and PHLEVL. The program then displays a prompt requesting input data from the user.

Program 3-9

```
PROGRAM MAIN
  REAL HYDRON, PHLEVL
  WRITE(6,*) 'ENTER THE HYDRONIUM ION CONCENTRATION LEVEL:
  READ *, HYDRON
  PHLEVL = - ALOG10(HYDRON)
  WRITE(6,*) 'THE PH LEVEL IS: ',PHLEVL
  END
```

After the prompt is displayed, a READ statement is used to store the entered data in the variable HYDRON. Finally, a value for PHLEVL is calculated, using the intrinsic logarithmic function, and displayed. As always, the program is terminated with an END statement.

Step 5: Test the Program

A test run using Program 3-9 produced the following:

```
ENTER THE HYDRONIUM ION CONCENTRATION LEVEL:
0.0001
THE PH LEVEL IS: 4.000000
```

As the program performs a single calculation, and the result of this test run agrees with our previous hand calculation, the program has been completely tested. It now can be used to calculate the pH level of other hydronium concentrations with confidence that the results being produced are accurate.

Application 2: Sine Approximation

The sine of an angle x, in radians, can be approximated using the polynomial:

$$x - \frac{x^3}{6} + \frac{x^5}{120}$$

Using this polynomial, write a program that approximates the sine of a user-entered angle using the first, second, and third terms, respectively, of the approximating polynomial. For each approximation, display the value calculated by FORTRAN's intrinsic sine function, the approximate value, and the absolute difference between the two. Make sure to verify your program using a hand calculation. Once the verification is complete, use the program to approximate the sine of 62.5 degrees.

Program Development

Using the top-down development procedure described in Chapter 2, we have:

Step 1: Determine the Desired Outputs

This program requires a total of nine outputs, arrived at as follows: the statement of the problem specifies that three approximations are to be made, using one, two, and three terms of the approximating polynomial, respectively. For each approximation to the sine, three output values are required: the value of the sine produced by the intrinsic SIN function, the approximation value, and the absolute difference between the two values. Figure 3-10 illustrates, in symbolic form, the structure of the required output display.

The output indicated in Figure 3-10 can be used to get a feel for what the program must look like. Realizing that each line in the display can be produced only by executing either a PRINT or a WRITE statement, it should be clear that three such statements must be executed. Additionally, since each output line contains three computed values, each PRINT or WRITE statement executed will have three items in its expression list.

Step 2: Determine the Input Items

The only input to the program consists of the angle whose sine is to be approximated. This will require a single prompt and a READ statement to input the necessary value.

Step 3a: Determine an Algorithm

Before any output item can be calculated, it will be necessary to have the program prompt the user for an input angle and then have the program accept a user-entered value. Since this angle will be in degrees, and both the SIN function and the approximating polynomial require radian measure, the input angle will have to be converted into radians.

Sine	Approximation	Difference
Intrinsic Function Value	1st Approximate Value	1st Difference
Intrinsic Function Value	2nd Approximate Value	2nd Difference
Intrinsic Function Value	3rd Approximate Value	3rd Difference

Figure 3-10 Required Output Display

The actual output display consists of two header lines followed by three lines of calculated data. The heading lines can be produced using two PRINT or WRITE statements. Now let us see how the actual data being displayed is produced.

The first item on the first data output line illustrated in Figure 3-10, the sine of the angle, can be obtained using the SIN( ) function. The second item on this line, the approximation to the sine, can be obtained by using the first term in the polynomial that was given in the program specification. Finally, the third item on the line can be calculated using the ABS( ) function on the difference between the first two items. When all of these items are calculated, a single PRINT or WRITE statement can be used to display the three results on the same line.

The second output line illustrated in Figure 3-10 displays the same type of items as the first line, except that the approximation to the sine requires using two terms of the approximating polynomial. Notice also that the first item on the second line, the sine of the angle, is the same as the first item on the first line. This means that this item does not have to be recalculated, and the value calculated for the first line can simply be displayed a second time. Once the data for the second line has been calculated, a single PRINT or WRITE statement can be used to display the required values.

Finally, only the second and third items on the last output line shown in Figure 3-10 need to be recalculated, since the first item on this line is the same as previously calculated for the first line. The second item on the third line is calculated using all three terms of the polynomial, and the last item on this line is obtained as the absolute difference between the first two items. Once the data for this last line has been calculated, a single PRINT or WRITE statement can be used to display the complete line.

Thus, for this problem, the complete algorithm described in pseudocode is:

Display a prompt for the input angle
Read an angle in degrees
Convert the angle to radian measure
Display the heading lines
Calculate the sine of the angle
Calculate the first approximation
Calculate the first difference
Print the first output line
Calculate the second approximation
Calculate the second difference
Print the second output line
Calculate the third approximation
Calculate the third difference
Print the third output line

Step 3b: Do a Hand Calculation

To ensure that we understand the processing used in the algorithm, we will do a hand calculation. We can use the result of this calculation to verify the result produced by the program that we write. For test purposes, any angle will do, and we will select a value of 30 degrees. Converting this angle to radian measure requires multiplying it by the factor 3.1416/180.0, which corresponds to 0.523600 radians.

For this test value the following approximations to the sine are obtained:

Using the first term of the polynomial the approximation is:

$$0.523600$$

Using the first two terms of the polynomial, the approximation is:

$$0.523600 - (0.523600)^3 / 6 = .499675$$

Using all three terms of the polynomial, the approximation is:

$$0.499675 + (0.523600)^5 / 120 = .500003$$

Notice that in using all three terms of the polynomial, that it was not necessary to recalculate the value of the first two terms. Instead, we used the value previously calculated in our second approximation. All of the approximations are extremely close to 0.5, which is the actual sine of 30 degrees.

Step 3c: Select Variable Names

The last step required before the selected algorithm is described in FORTRAN is to select variable names for the input, output, and any intermediate variables required by the algorithm. For this problem we select the variable names ANGLE for the input angle entered by the user and RADIAN for its equivalent radian measure. The conversion factor 3.1416/180.0 to convert the input angle from degrees into radians will be given the name CONVRT and constructed as a named constant using the PARAMETER statement. Finally, the variable names SINE, APPROX, and DIF will be declared for the sine of the angle, the approximation to the sine, and the difference between these two quantities, respectively. As always, any valid variable names could have been selected.

Step 4: Write the Program

Program 3-10 represents a description of the selected algorithm in FORTRAN.

Program 3-10

```
      PROGRAM MAIN
*** THIS PROGRAM APPROXIMATES THE SINE OF AN ANGLE, IN DEGREES
*** USING ONE, TWO, AND THREE TERMS OF AN APPROXIMATING POLYNOMIAL
        REAL ANGLE RADIAN, CONVRT, SINE, APPROX, DIF
        PARAMETER (CONVRT = 3.1416/180.0)
        WRITE(6,*) 'ENTER AN ANGLE (IN DEGREES)'
        READ *, ANGLE
*** CONVERT THE ANGLE TO RADIAN MEASURE
        RADIAN = CONVRT * ANGLE
*** WRITE TWO HEADER LINES
```

(Continued on the next page)

Program 3-10 *(Continued from the previous page)*

```
      WRITE(6,*)' SINE         APPROXIMATION DIFFERENCE'
      WRITE(6,*)' ------------ ------------- ----------'
*** CALCULATE THE SINE USING THE INTRINSIC FUNCTION
      SINE = SIN(RADIAN)
*** CALCULATE THE FIRST APPROXIMATION AND DISPLAY A LINE
      APPROX = RADIAN
      DIF = ABS(SINE - APPROX)
      WRITE(6,*) SINE, APPROX, DIF
*** CALCULATE THE SECOND APPROXIMATION AND DISPLAY A LINE
      APPROX = APPROX - (RADIAN ** 3 / 6.0)
      DIF = ABS(SINE - APPROX)
      WRITE(6,*) SINE, APPROX, DIF
*** CALCULATE THE THIRD APPROXIMATION AND DISPLAY A LINE
      APPROX = APPROX + (RADIAN ** 5 / 120.0)
      DIF = ABS(SINE - APPROX)
      WRITE(6,*) SINE, APPROX, DIF
      END
```

Notice that the input angle is immediately converted to radians after it is read. The two header lines are then printed prior to any approximations being made. The value of the sine is then computed using the intrinsic sine function and is assigned to the variable SINE. This assignment permits this value to be used in the three difference calculations and be displayed three times without the need for recalculation.

Since the approximation to the sine is "built up" using more and more terms of the approximating polynomial, only the new term for each approximation is calculated and added to the previous approximation. Finally, to permit the same variables to be reused, the values in them are immediately printed before the next approximation is made. Following is a sample run produced by Program 3-10.

```
ENTER AN ANGLE (IN DEGREES)
30
SINE             APPROXIMATION       DIFFERENCE
------------     -------------       ------------
5.000011E-01     5.236000E-01        2.359891E-02
5.000011E-01     4.996752E-01        3.258522E-04
5.000011E-01     5.000032E-01        2.098380E-06
```

Step 5: Test the Program

The first two columns of output data produced by the sample run agree with our hand calculation. (If you are unfamiliar with exponential notation, review Section 2.1.) A hand check of the last column verifies that it contains the correct value differences between the first two columns.

As the program only performs seven calculations, and the result of the test run agrees with our hand calculations, the program has been completely tested. It can now be used with other input angles with confidence that the results it produces are correct.

Additional Exercises for Chapter Three

1a. Enter, compile, and run Program 3-9 on your computer system.

b. Rewrite Program 3-9 using formatted READ and PRINT statements.

2. Enter, compile, and run Program 3-10 on your computer system.

3. By mistake a student wrote Program 3-10 as follows:

```
      PROGRAM MAIN
*** THIS PROGRAM APPROXIMATES THE SINE OF AN ANGLE, IN DEGREES
*** USING ONE, TWO, AND THREE TERMS OF AN APPROXIMATING POLYNOMIAL
        REAL ANGLE RADIAN, CONVRT, SINE, APPROX, DIF
        PARAMETER (CONVRT = 3.1416/180.0)
*** WRITE TWO HEADER LINES
        WRITE(6,*)' SINE         APPROXIMATION DIFFERENCE'
        WRITE(6,*)' ------------ ------------- ----------'
        WRITE(6,*) 'ENTER AN ANGLE (IN DEGREES)'
        READ *, ANGLE
*** CONVERT THE ANGLE TO RADIAN MEASURE
        RADIAN = CONVRT * ANGLE
*** CALCULATE THE SINE USING THE INTRINSIC FUNCTION
        SINE = SIN(RADIAN)
*** CALCULATE THE FIRST APPROXIMATION AND DISPLAY A LINE
        APPROX = RADIAN
        DIF = ABS(SINE - APPROX)
        WRITE(6,*) SINE, APPROX, DIF
*** CALCULATE THE SECOND APPROXIMATION AND DISPLAY A LINE
        APPROX = APPROX - (RADIAN ** 3 / 6.0)
        DIF = ABS(SINE - APPROX)
        WRITE(6,*) SINE, APPROX, DIF
** CALCULATE THE THIRD APPROXIMATION AND DISPLAY A LINE
        APPROX = APPROX + (RADIAN ** 5 / 120.0)
        DIF = ABS(SINE - APPROX)
        WRITE(6,*) SINE, APPROX, DIF
        END
```

Determine the output that will be produced by this program.

4a. The formula for the standard normal deviation, z, used in statistical applications is:

$$z = \frac{X - \mu}{6}$$

where μ refers to a mean value and r to a standard deviation.

Using this formula, write a program that calculates and displays the value of the standard normal deviation when $X = 85.3$, $\mu = 80$, and $r = 4$.

b. Rewrite the program written in Exercise 4a to accept the values of x, μ, and r as user inputs while the program is executing.

5a. The equation of the normal (bell-shaped) curve used in statistical applications is:

$$y = \frac{1}{r\sqrt{2\pi}} e^{-(1/2)[(x-\mu)/r]^2}$$

Using this equation, and assuming $\mu = 90$ and $r = 4$, write a program that determines and displays the value of y when $x = 80$.

b. Rewrite the program written in Exercise 5a to accept the values of x, μ, and r as user inputs while the program is executing.

6a. Write, compile, and execute a program that calculates and displays the gross pay and net pay of two individuals. The first individual works 40 hours and is paid an hourly rate of $8.43. The second individual works 35 hours and is paid an hourly rate of $5.67. Both individuals have 20 percent of their pay withheld for income tax purposes, and both pay 2 percent of their gross pay, before taxes, for medical benefits.

b. Redo Exercise 6a assuming that the individuals' hours and rate will be entered when the program is run.

7. The volume of oil stored in a underground 200-foot deep cylindrical tank is determined by measuring the distance from the top of the tank to the surface of the oil. Knowing this distance and the radius of the tank, the volume of oil in the tank can be determined using the formula *Volume* = π *radius*^{2} (200 – distance). Using this information, write, compile, and execute a FORTRAN program that accepts the radius and distance measurements, calculates the volume of oil in the tank, and displays the two input values and the calculated volume. Verify the results of your program by doing a hand calculation using the following test data: radius is 10 feet, distance is 12 feet.

8. The perimeter, underground surface area, and volume of an in-ground pool are given by the following formulas:

Perimeter = 2(*length* + *width*)
Volume = *length* * *width* * *average depth*
Underground surface area = 2(*length* + *width*)*average depth* + *length* * *width*

Using these formulas as a basis, write a FORTRAN program that accepts the length, width, and average depth measurements, calculates the perimeter, volume, and underground surface area of the pool, and produces the following display:

```
                                                      UNDERGROUND
LENGTH    WIDTH    DEPTH    PERIMETER    VOLUME    SURFACE AREA
------    -----    -----    ---------    ------    ------------
xxxxx     xxxxx    xxxxx    yyyyy        yyyyy     yyyyy
```

where xxxxx and yyyyy represent input and calculated quantities, respectively. In writing your program, make the following two calculations immediately after the input data has been entered: *length * width* and *length + width*. The results of these two calculations should then be used, as appropriate, in the assignment statements for determining the perimeter, volume, and underground surface area. Verify the results of your program by doing a hand calculation using the following test data: length is 25 feet, width is 15 feet, and average depth is 5.5 feet. When you have verified that your program is working, use it to complete the following table.

LENGTH	WIDTH	DEPTH	PERIMETER	VOLUME	UNDERGROUND SURFACE AREA
25	10	5			
25	10	5.5			
25	10	6			
25	10	6.5			
30	12	5			
30	12	5.5			
30	12	6			
30	12	6.5			

3.6 Common Programming Errors

The errors commonly associated with the material presented in this chapter are:

1. Forgetting to separate with commas all variable names within a READ statement.
2. Using an intrinsic function without providing the correct number of arguments having the proper data type.
3. Incorrectly defining a FORMAT specification that does not correctly correspond to the data items being displayed. For example, specifying a field width too small to accommodate the displayed item. In its most common occurrence, this usually takes the form of not specifying sufficient room for a real number's decimal point and a possible leading negative sign.
4. A major programming error is the rush to code and run a program before the programmer fully understands what is required and the algorithms and procedures that will be used to produce the desired result. A symptom of this haste to get a program entered into the computer is the lack of either an outline of the proposed program or a written program itself (see the Section 3.8). Many problems can be caught just by checking a copy of the program, either handwritten or listed from the computer, before it is compiled.
5. Another error is the unwillingness to test a program in depth. After all, since you wrote the program, you assume it is correct, or you would have changed it before it was compiled. It is extremely difficult to back away and test your own software honestly. As a programmer, you must constantly remind yourself that just because you think your program is correct does not make it so. Finding

errors in your own program is a sobering experience, but one that will help you become a master programmer.

3.7 Things to Remember

1. FORTRAN provides intrinsic functions for calculating trigonometric, logarithmic, and other mathematical computations typically required in scientific and engineering programs.
2. Data passed to an intrinsic function are called *arguments* of the function. Arguments are passed to an intrinsic function by including each argument, separated by commas, within the parentheses following the function's name. Each intrinsic function has its own requirements for the number and data types of the arguments that must be provided.
3. Each intrinsic function operates on its arguments to calculate a single value.
4. Functions may be included within larger expressions.
5. The READ statement is used for data input. The general form of this statement is:

   ```
   READ(n, fmt) list of variables
   ```

   where *n* is a unit number designating from where the input will be read and *fmt* specifies the format of the input. When an asterisk (*) is used for the unit number, the computer's standard input unit is specified. If an asterisk is used for the format specification, the compiler's list-directed format is selected.
6. For standard unit input, an alternative form of the READ statement can be used. This alternative form is:

   ```
   READ fmt, list of variables
   ```

   The *fmt* in this statement can either be an asterisk, which designates list-directed input, an explicit format control specification, or the statement label of a FORMAT statement. In the latter two instances, user-designated formatting is selected.
7. When the computer encounters a READ statement, it temporarily suspends further statement execution until sufficient data has been entered for the number of variables contained in the READ statement.
8. It is a good programming practice to display a message, prior to a READ statement, that alerts the user as to the type and number of data items to be entered. Such a message is called a *prompt.*
9. A PARAMETER statement is used to equate a constant to a symbolic name. The general form of the PARAMETER statement is:

   ```
   PARAMETER (name1 = expression, name2 = expression, etc.)
   ```

For example, the number 3.1416 can be equated to the symbolic name PI using the PARAMETER statement:

```
PARAMETER (PI = 3.1416)
```

Once a symbolic name has been equated to a value, another value may not be assigned to the symbolic name.

10. When using FORTRAN's various statement types, certain placement rules must be followed. These rules are:

i. The END statement must be the last statement of every program unit. This statement consists of the keyword END with no spaces between any of the letters.

ii. Comment lines may appear anywhere in a program unit, except as the last line of a program unit.

iii. FORMAT statements may appear anywhere between the program header line and the END statement.

iv. PARAMETER and declaration statements, which collectively (along with additional statements to be introduced) are referred to as *specification* statements, may be intermixed and must appear before all executable statements. Executable statements, such as assignment, WRITE, PRINT, and READ statements, may be freely intermixed with each other.

3.8 A Closer Look: Program Life Cycle

Just as people and products have a life cycle, so do programs. A program's life cycle is divided into three main stages, as illustrated in Figure 3-11. These stages consist of program development, program documentation, and program maintenance.

The development stage is where a program is initially developed. It is at this stage that requirements must be understood and the structure of the program planned

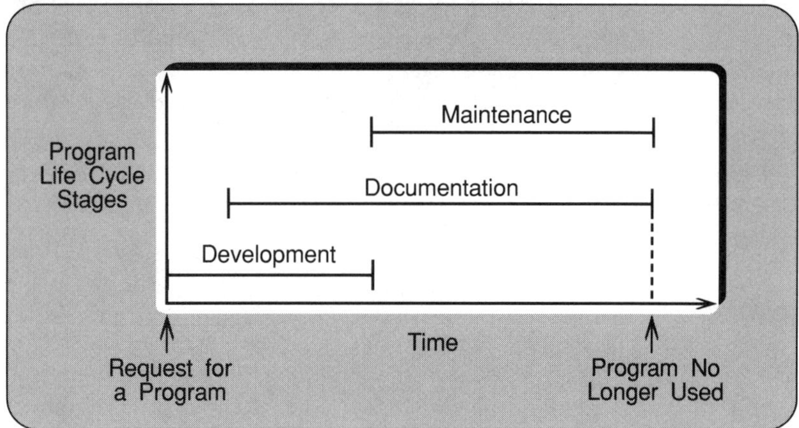

Figure 3-11 A Program's Life Cycle

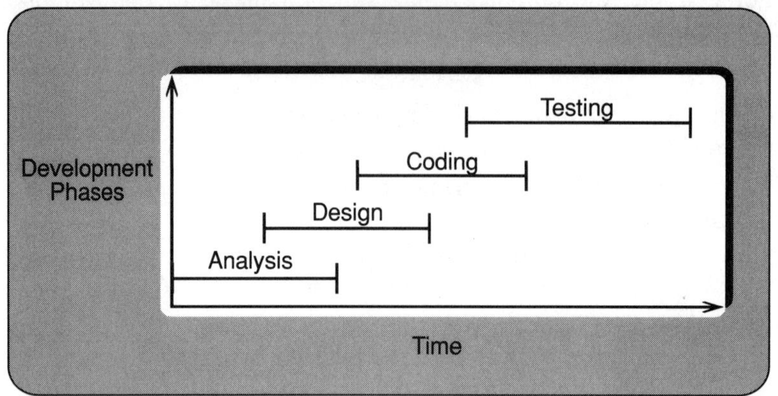

Figure 3-12 The Phases of Program Development

using the top-down development procedure presented in Section 2.5. The documentation stage, as its name implies, consists of creating, both within the program and in separate documents, sufficient user and programmer support references and explanations. At the maintenance stage, the program is modified or enhanced as new demands and requirements are obtained or program errors are detected. Complete courses and textbooks are devoted to each of these three program stages. Our purpose in listing them is to put the actual writing of a program in perspective with the total effort needed to produce professional engineering and scientific software.

The writing of a program in a computer language is formally called *coding* (informally, of course, it is called programming). And that, after all, is what we have been doing—writing programs in a language, or code, that can be decoded and used by the computer. As we saw in Section 2.5, the coding of a program is but one component in the program's development stage. The total development effort is composed of four distinct phases, as illustrated in Figure 3-12.

Listed below are both the steps in the top-down development procedure corresponding to each development phase and the relative amount of effort that typically is expended on each phase in large engineering and scientific programming projects. As can be seen from this listing, the coding phase is not the major effort in overall program development.

Phase	**Top-down development step**	**Effort**
Analysis	Steps 1 and 2	10%
Design	Step 3	20%
Coding	Step 4	20%
Testing	Step 5	50%

Many new programmers have trouble because they spend the majority of their time coding the program without first spending sufficient time understanding and designing it. In this regard, it is worthwhile to remember the programming saying "It is impossible to write a successful program for a problem or application that is not fully understood."

It is for this reason that the analysis phase is one of the most important, because if the requirements are not fully and completely understood before programming begins, the results are almost always disastrous. Once a program structure is created and the program is written, new or reinterpreted requirements often cause havoc. An analogy with house construction is useful to illustrate this point.

Imagine designing and building a house without fully understanding the architect's specifications. After the house is completed, the architect tells you that a bathroom is required on the first floor, where you have built a wall between the kitchen and the dining room. In addition, that particular wall is one of the main support walls for the house and contains numerous pipes and electrical cables. In this case, adding one bathroom requires a major modification to the basic structure of the house.

Experienced programmers know the importance of analyzing and understanding a program's requirements before coding, if for no other reason than that they too have constructed programs that later had to be entirely dismantled and redone. The following exercise should give you a sense of this experience.

Figure 3-13 illustrates the outlines of six individual shapes from a classic children's puzzle. Assume that as one or more shapes are given, starting with shapes A and B, an easy-to-describe figure must be constructed.

Typically, shapes A and B are initially arranged to obtain a square, as illustrated in Figure 3-14. Next, when shape C is considered, it is usually combined with the existing square to form a rectangle, as illustrated in Figure 3-15. Then, when pieces D and E are added, they are usually arranged to form another rectangle, which is placed alongside the existing rectangle to form a square, as shown in Figure 3-16.

Figure 3-13 Six Individual Shapes

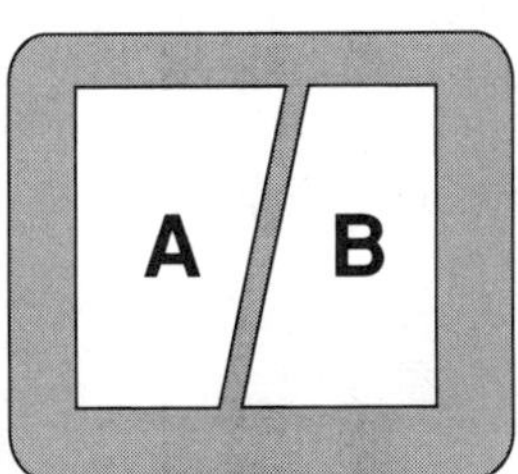

Figure 3-14 Typical First Figure

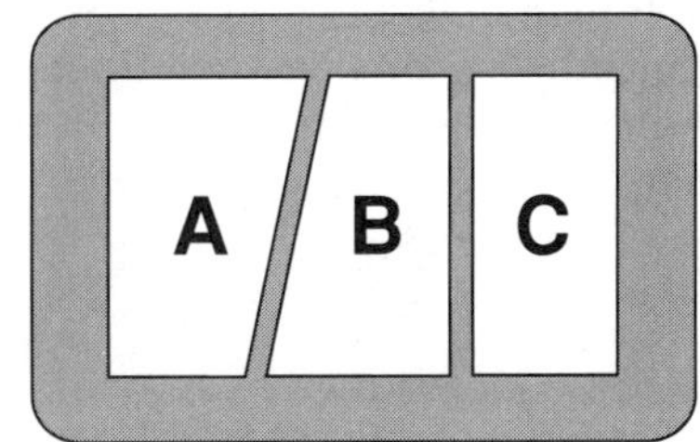

Figure 3-15 Typical Second Figure

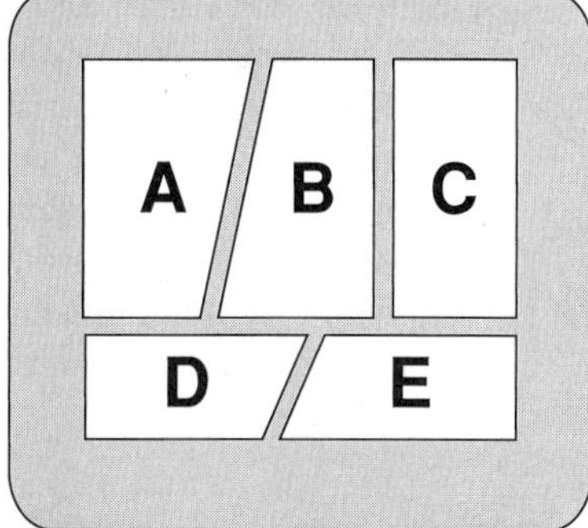

Figure 3-16 Typical Third Figure

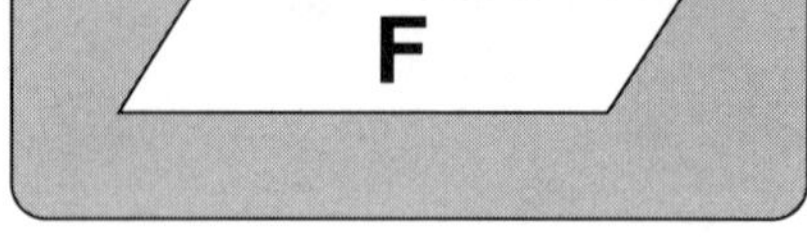

Figure 3-17 The Last Piece

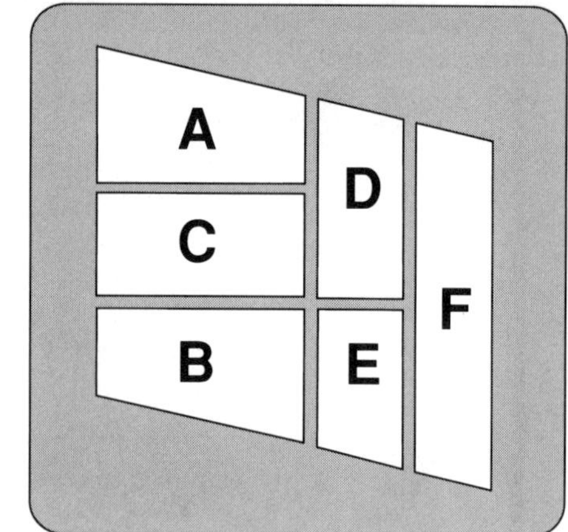

Figure 3-18 Including All the Pieces

The process of adding new pieces onto the existing structure is identical to constructing a program and then adding to it as each subsequent requirement is understood. The problem arises when the program is almost finished and a requirement is added that does not fit easily into the established pattern. For example, assume that the last shape (shape F) is now to be added (see Figure 3-17). This last piece does not fit into the existing pattern that has been constructed. In order to include this piece with the others, the pattern must be completely dismantled and restructured.

Unfortunately, many programmers structure their programs in the same manner used to construct Figure 3-16. Rather than taking the time to understand the complete set of requirements, new programmers frequently start coding based on the understanding of only a small subset of the total requirements. Then, when a subsequent requirement does not fit the existing program structure, the programmer is forced to dismantle and restructure either parts or all of the program.

Now, let's approach the problem of creating a figure from another view. If we started by arranging the first set of pieces as a parallelogram, all the pieces could be included in the final figure, as illustrated in Figure 3-18.

It is worthwhile observing that the piece that caused us to dismantle the first figure (Figure 3-16) actually sets the pattern for the final figure illustrated in Figure 3-18. This is often the case with programming requirements. The requirement that seems to be the least clear is frequently the one that determines the main interrelationships of the program. Thus, it is essential to include and understand all the known requirements before coding is begun. In practical terms, this means doing the analysis and design before attempting any coding.

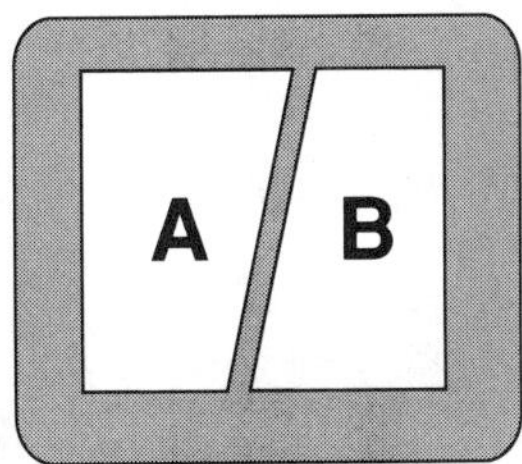

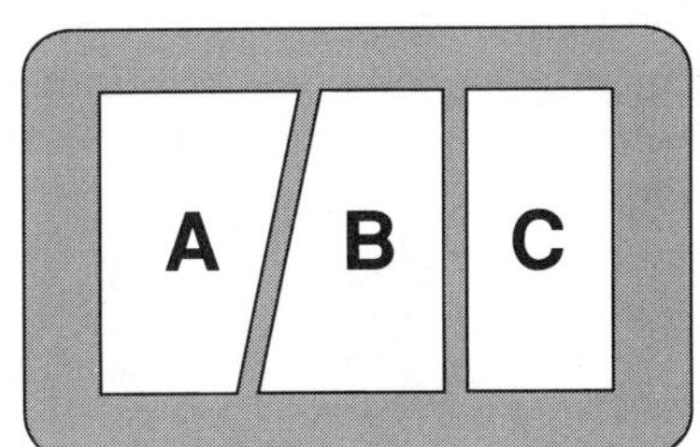

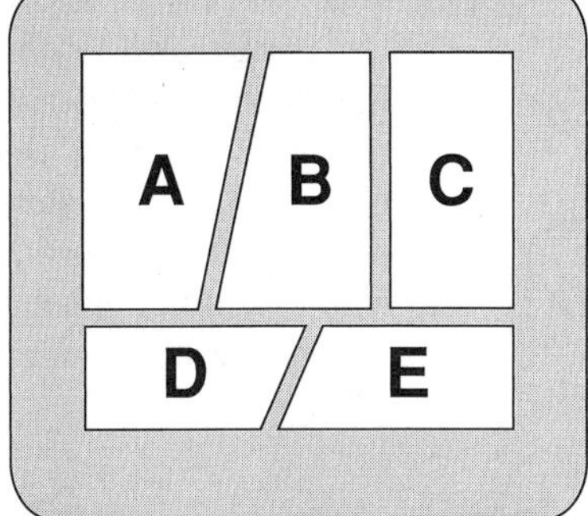

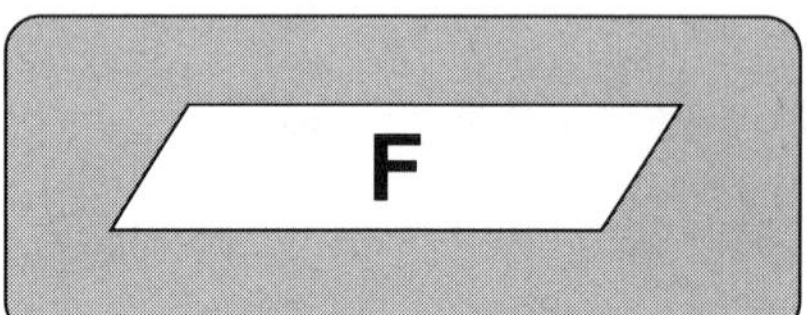

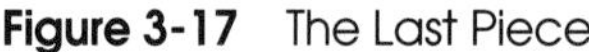

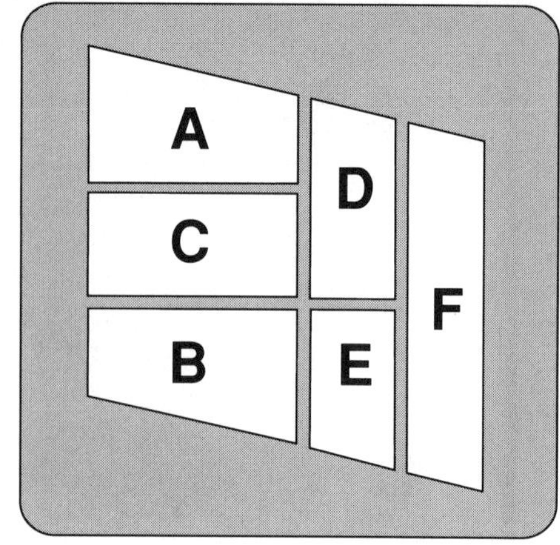

LAB SET FOR CHAPTERS 1–3

LAB ASSIGNMENT 1

1. Show the values displayed by each WRITE statement.

```
      INTEGER N
      REAL A, B, C, D, X, Y,Z
      X = 3/2
      Y = 3/2.0
      Z = 3.0 /2.0
      WRITE(6,*) X,Y,Z,N              ________ ________ ________ ________
*
      A = 2.0
      B = 3.0
      C = 4.0
      D = 5.0
*
      X = A + B / C + D
      Y = (A + B) / C + D
      Z = (A + B) / (C + D)
      WRITE(6,*) X, Y, Z                       ________ ________ ________
*
      X = A * B / C * D
      Y = (A * B) / C * D
      Z = (A * B) / (C * D)
      WRITE(6,*) X, Y, Z                       ________ ________ ________
*
      X = D/C/A
      Y = A**B**C
      Z = C*B**A
      WRITE(6,*) X, Y, Z                       ________ ________ ________
```

2. (Circle the correct answer) What value is assigned to X for the following FORTRAN code:

```
      INTEGER J, K
      REAL X
      J = 3
      K = -2
      X = 5*J / 4* K
```

a. -1.875000 b. -6 c. -6.000000 d. -7.500000

3. Circle the arithmetic operation that produces a result different from the other choices:

a. `A * B + C / D`

b. `(A * B) + C / D`

c. `(A * B + C) / D`

d. `A * B + (C / D)`

e. `(A * B) + (C / D)`

4. Write FORTRAN expressions for the following algebraic expressions:

a. $X^2 + 2AX + B$

b. $P(1 + \frac{I}{2})^{NM}$

c. $\frac{A^2B^2}{2}$

d. $\sqrt{A^2 + b^2}$

LAB ASSIGNMENT 2

1. Familiarize yourself with your computer system as well as the file creation and editing features provided by the system. Specifically, create a file called SCHEDULE.TXT and type your class schedule in an appropriate form. When you are satisfied with it, obtain a printout. Hand in the printout.

2. The following FORTRAN payroll calculation program was entered by a careless typist:

```
      PROGRAM MAIN
        CALL PAYROL
        END
*
      SUBROUTINE PAYROL
        REAL RATE, HOURS, PAY
        RATE = 5.50
        HOURS = 5.0
        PAY = RAT * HOURS
        WRITEE (6,*) 'AMOUND TO BE PAID = ', PAY
        RETURN
        END
```

a. Create a file called PAYROLL.FOR and type the program exactly as shown. Try to compile the program. What does the error message tell you?

b. Enter the editor and correct the spelling of WRITE. Compile the program. Assuming there are no compile errors, link and run your program. Explain the answer displayed.

c. Repeat part b, correcting all the remaining errors.

LAB ASSIGNMENT 3

You are to write the three programs below, then enter, compile, link, and execute them. Once you have all three of them working you will need to obtain a copy of them to turn in.

Program 1: Construct a program that prints your name and address as they would appear on a mailing label, using the formatted WRITE statement. An example of your program's output is:

```
WESLEY E SCRUGGS
500 COLLEGE DRIVE
LAKE JACKSON TX 77566
```

Program 2: Write a program to print your name, height, age, and weight using the formatted READ statement to enter the data and formatted WRITE statement to display the data. A sample output would be:

```
PLEASE ENTER YOUR NAME
WESLEY SCRUGGS

PLEASE ENTER YOUR HEIGHT, AGE, AND WEIGHT
60, 35, 145

NAME: WESLEY SCRUGGS
HEIGHT:  60 INCHES
AGE:     35 YEARS
WEIGHT: 145 LBS
```

Program 3: Suppose your checking account balance is $23.49 and this month you cashed two checks, one for $14.23 and one for $5.00. Write a program that outputs your new balance. Use assignment statements to assign the first amount to CHECK1 and the second amount to CHECK2; then use an assignment statement to calculate NEWBAL. Use a formatted WRITE statement to output your data with two decimal places. Your output should be:

```
ORIGINAL BALANCE: $ 23.49
CHECKS WRITTEN  :   19.23
NEW BALANCE     :    4.26
```

LAB ASSIGNMENT 4

The volume of a powdered raw material stored in an underground rectangular tank is estimated by measuring the distance, D, from the top of the tank to the surface of the powder.

The distance, D, the height, H, the length, L, and the width, W of the tank are to be input by the user when the program is run. The volume, V, of the powder should then be calculated using the formula V = L * W * (H-D). The output should be printed on a single-spaced line. Column headings are optional (if you know how to print column headings, however, do so). The items to be output are the length, width, distance, height, and volume.

Use comments at the beginning of the program to identify the programmer, lab assignment number, date, and the purpose of the program. Do not use any comments in the body of your program.

Your data can be read in as real or integer data. Run your program at least five times with the following data. Check your answers; to help you check your output, the first two volumes are 7000 and 5000. (Hint: Be careful with your assignent statements.) You may wish to check your other volumes by hand.

D	L	W	H
05	10	20	40
15	10	20	40
15	20	10	40
00	20	10	40
15	10	20	15

LAB ASSIGNMENT 5

A steel door is 3 feet wide, 5 feet high, and 1.5 inches thick. The weight density of steel is 0.283 lbs. per cubic inch. Write a FORTRAN program that performs the following:

a. reads the width and height of the door in feet and the density in lbs. per cubic inch. Appropriate prompts should be provided to the user.
b. computes the volume and weight of the door after proper conversion of units.
c. displays the volume and weight clearly labeled with appropriate units.

Use comments at the beginning of the program to identify the programmer, lab assignment number, date, and the purpose of the program. Do not use any comments in the body of your program.

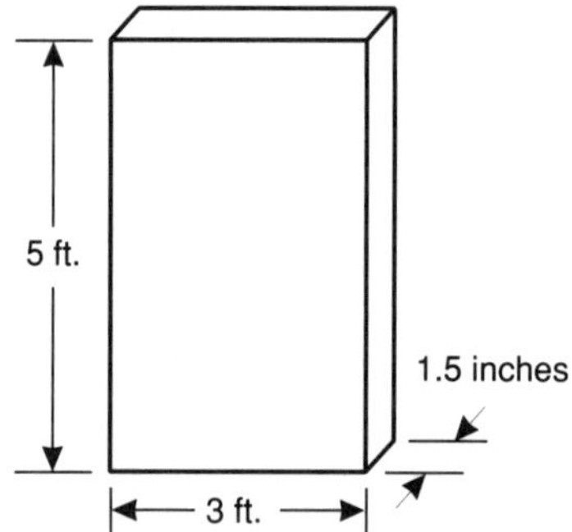

Page 445

Cumulative Lab Projects. "Cumulative lab exercises are provided at the end of selected chapters. These projects require a deeper understanding of FORTRAN and necessitate an integration of input, processing, and output concepts for their completion. They require the students to prepare a documented and formatted report in a professional manner. Both sample data and report structures are provided."

y Using
ıms

tines

ineering sciences are designed, built, and tested very
of modules that are integrated to perform a completed
his is an automobile where one major module is the
ission, a third the braking system, a fourth the body,
lules is linked together and ultimately placed under the
can be compared to a supervisor or main program
rates as a complete unit, able to do useful work, such as
the assembly process, each module is individually con-
be free of defects (bugs) before it is installed in the final

might do if you wanted to improve your car's perfor-
xisting engine or remove it altogether and bolt in a new

engine. Similarly, you might change the transmission or tires or shock absorbers, making each modification individually as your time and budget allowed. In each case the majority of the other modules can stay the same, but the car now operates differently.

In this analogy, each of the major components of a car can be compared to a subroutine. For example, the driver calls on the engine when the gas pedal is pressed. The engine accepts inputs of fuel, air, and electricity to turn the driver's request into a useful product—power, and then sends this output to the transmission for further processing. The transmission receives the output of the engine and converts it to a form that can be used by the drive axle. An additional input to the transmission is the driver's selection of gears (drive, reverse, neutral, etc.).

In each case, the engine, transmission, and other modules only "know" the universe bounded by their inputs and outputs. The driver need know nothing of the internal operation of the engine, transmission, drive axle, and other modules that are being controlled. The driver simply "calls" on a module, such as the engine, brakes, air conditioning, and steering when that module's output is required. Communication between modules is restricted to passing needed inputs to each module as it is called upon to perform its task, and each module operates internally in a relatively independent manner. This same modular approach is used by engineers to create and maintain reliable FORTRAN programs using program units.

As we have seen, each FORTRAN program must contain a MAIN program unit. In addition to this required unit, FORTRAN programs may also contain any number of additional program units, which are collectively referred to as subprograms. Each FORTRAN subprogram must begin with one of the keywords FUNCTION, SUBROUTINE, or BLOCK DATA. In this chapter we learn how to write SUBROUTINE and FUNCTION subprograms, pass data to them, process the passed data, and return a result. Additionally, in section 4-8 we present the underlying economic motivation for constructing modular programs.

4.1 Subroutine Program Units

As we have already seen in Chapter 1, a subroutine is a distinct program unit in its own right, similar to a MAIN program unit. Its purpose is to receive data, operate on the data, and return as few or as many values as required. A subroutine's name is simply a user-selected name that contains no more than six characters (thirty-one in FORTRAN 90), the first of which must be a letter.

As we also saw in Chapter 1, a subroutine is called into action using a CALL statement. For example, the statement:

```
CALL CIRCUM
```

initiates the execution of a subroutine named CIRCUM. This statement is used in Program 4-1 to call a subroutine that determines the circumference of a circle.

Program 4-1

```
      PROGRAM MAIN
        CALL CIRCUM
        END
*
      SUBROUTINE CIRCUM
        REAL RADIUS, CCUM
        RADIUS = 2.24
        CCUM = 2.0 * 3.1416 * RADIUS
        WRITE(6,*) 'THE CIRCUMFERENCE IS ',CCUM
        RETURN
        END
```

When Program 4-1 is compiled and executed the following output is obtained:

```
THE CIRCUMFERENCE IS       14.074370
```

As written, Program 4-1 makes no provision for the MAIN program unit to either pass data into the subroutine or receive data back from it. Let us see how to rectify this situation so that data can be exchanged between these two program units.

In exchanging data between two program units we must be concerned with both the sending and receiving sides of the data exchange. Let us look at the sending of data into a subroutine first.

In its most general form, a subroutine is called into action using a CALL statement having the form:

CALL *subroutine-name (argument list)*

Except for the addition of the parentheses and the argument list, this is identical to the CALL statement introduced in Chapter 1. As always, the keyword CALL tells the computer that a transfer into a subroutine is to take place. The subroutine name, as illustrated in Figure 4-1, identifies the subroutine that is to be executed, and the argument list is used to exchange data with the called subroutine.

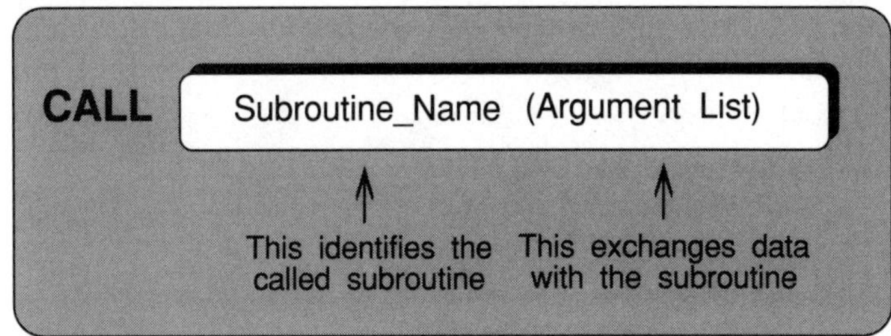

Figure 4-1 Calling a Subroutine

The arguments in a CALL statement are referred to as *actual arguments* and can be either constants, variables, or expressions that can be evaluated to yield a value at the time of the CALL. For example, the statement

```
CALL AREA(3.5)
```

both calls a subroutine named AREA and makes the number 3.5 available to it. Here the argument list consists of a single actual argument, the constant 3.5. Similarly, the statement

```
CALL DISPLY(2.67, 8)
```

calls a subroutine named DISPLY and makes two actual arguments, the real constant 2.67 and the integer constant 8, available to the called subroutine. In the following CALL statement:

```
CALL CIRCUM(RADIUS)
```

the subroutine CIRCUM is called using a variable named RADIUS as an actual argument. To illustrate the use of this CALL statement within a main program unit consider program 4-2. Included within the program is an appropriate CIRCUM subroutine to receive the transmitted data. The complete program, consisting of both main and subroutine program units, produces the same output as Program 4-1.

The CALL statement in Program 4-2 both calls the CIRCUM subroutine into action and makes one actual argument available to it. Let's now see how the subroutine CIRCUM has been constructed to correctly receive this argument.

Like all program units, a subroutine consists of two parts, a subroutine header and a subroutine body, as illustrated in Figure 4-2. In addition to naming the subroutine, the subroutine header is used to exchange data between the subroutine and its calling program unit. The purpose of the subroutine body is to process the passed data and produce any values that are to be returned to the calling program unit.

Program 4-2

```
      PROGRAM MAIN
        REAL RADIUS
        RADIUS = 2.24
        CALL CIRCUM(RADIUS)
        END
*
      SUBROUTINE CIRCUM(R)
        REAL R, CCUM
        CCUM = 2.0 * 3.1416 * R
        WRITE(6,*) 'THE CIRCUMFERENCE IS ', CCUM
        RETURN
        END
```

```
The Subroutine Header --->   SUBROUTINE name (argument list)
                             - argument and variable declarations
The Subroutine Body -->    |   any other FORTRAN statements
                           |   RETURN
                             - END
```

Figure 4-2 General Format of a Subroutine

The subroutine header line must include the keyword SUBROUTINE, the name of the subroutine, and the names of any arguments that will be used by it, in the general form:

```
SUBROUTINE  name(argument  list)
```

The arguments in a subroutine header line are referred to as either *formal* or *dummy arguments*. These two terms are synonymous and we will use them interchangeably in the remainder of the text. For example, the header line of the subroutine in Program 4-1:

```
SUBROUTINE CIRCUM(R)
```

contains a single formal argument named R. The names of formal arguments are selected by the programmer according to the same rules used to select variable names. It should be noted that the names selected for formal arguments may, but do not have to, be the same as the actual argument names used in the CALL statement.

The purpose of the formal arguments in a subroutine header is to provide names by which the subroutine can access values transmitted through the CALL statement. Thus, the argument name R is used within the subroutine to refer to the value transmitted by the CALL statement. In this regard, it is extremely useful to visualize arguments as containers or pipelines through which values can be transmitted between called and calling program units. As illustrated in Figure 4-3, the formal argument named R effectively opens one side of the container through which values will be passed between the MAIN and CIRCUM program units. Within the MAIN program unit the same container is known as the argument named RADIUS, which is also a variable of the calling program unit.

Subroutines do not know where the values made available to it come from. As far as the CIRCUM( ) subroutine is concerned, the dummy argument R can be treated as a variable that has been initialized externally. As such, however, dummy arguments must still be declared, either explicitly using a declaration statement or implicitly using FORTRAN's implicit data typing rules.

When an explicit argument declaration statement is used, as it is in Program 4-2, it is placed immediately after the subroutine's header line. Once declared, an argument can be used anywhere within the subroutine in the same manner as a variable. Also, as illustrated in Program 4-2, variables used by the subroutine (in this

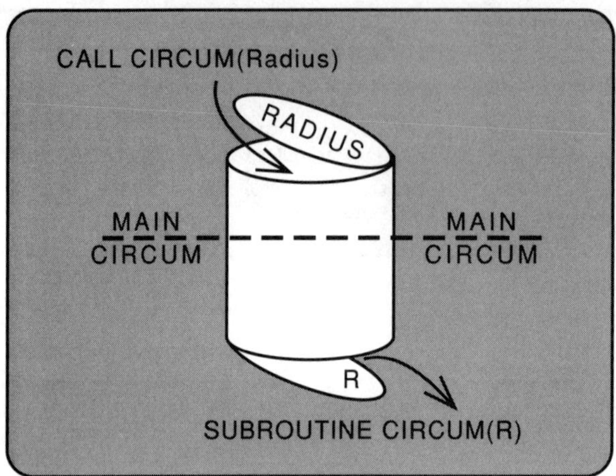

Figure 4-3 Exchanging Data with a Subroutine

case the variable CCUM) must also be declared. The variable declarations can be made on a line by themselves, or included within the declarations of the dummy arguments. Although the arguments and variables within a declaration statement can be listed in any order, it makes for clearer reading if all dummy arguments are declared before any variables.

Caution

Since an actual argument and its corresponding dummy argument both reference the same memory locations (see Figure 4-3), the rule concerning the correspondence between numbers and data types of actual and dummy arguments is simple: they must MATCH! If there are two actual arguments in a subroutine call, there must be two dummy arguments in the subroutine argument list. The first actual argument becomes the first dummy argument, and the second actual argument becomes the second dummy argument.

Additionally, the individual data types of each argument must be the same. Thus, if a subroutine's first dummy argument is declared as an integer, an integer variable, integer constant, or integer expression must be used as an actual argument when the subroutine is called. If the subroutine's second dummy argument has been declared as REAL, then the second actual argument must also be REAL. Table 4-1 illustrates how arguments used in CALL statements match dummy arguments used in subroutine program units.

Notice from Table 4-1 that when a character string is received as a dummy argument by a subprogram, the length of the dummy string can be specified by the "dummy" length specifier (*). This is because the actual length of the string has already been previously declared by the calling module.

Argument mismatches typically do not result in compile-time errors, although some compilers will report a TYPE MISMATCH error if both calling program unit

Table 4-1 Matching Actual and Dummy Arguments

Calling Module	Subroutine Headers and Declarations

`INTEGER NUM`
`REAL SIZE`
`CALL SUB1(NUM, SIZE)`
	`SUBROUTINE SUB1(N, SZ)`
	`  INTEGER N`
	`  REAL SZ`

`REAL AREA`
`CHARACTER STR*10, CHTR`
`CALL SUB2(AREA, STR, CHTR, 4.5)`
	`SUBROUTINE SUB2(A, ST, CH, VAL)`
	`  REAL A, VAL`
	`  CHARACTER ST*(*), CH`

`INTEGER NUM`
`CALL SUB3(10, 'HELLO', NUM)`
	`SUBROUTINE SUB3(N1, STR, N2)`
	`  INTEGER N1, N2`
	`  CHARACTER STR*(*)`

`REAL V, ANG`
`PARAMETER(LN = 'HELLO')`
`CALL SUB4(V**2, LN, SIN(ANG)`
	`SUBROUTINE SUB4(X, Y, Z)`
	`  REAL X, Z`
	`  CHARACTER Y*(*)`

and subroutine are compiled together. Argument mismatches typically do cause errors when a program is run or, worse, go undetected and produce incorrect results.

Although it is easy to make argument mismatch errors, they can be very hard to find later on because there is no conversion between data types when a mismatch occurs. If the data type of an actual and formal argument do not match, the subroutine simply interprets the internal computer code for the actual argument using the coding scheme for the declared formal argument data type, and the received value will bear no obvious relationship to the transmitted value. To avoid this error it is worthwhile initially displaying the values received by the subroutine. Once it has been verified that correct values have been received, the display can be removed.

Returning Values

In addition to receiving inputs when it is called, every subroutine has the capability of returning one or more values to its calling routine. The mechanism for doing this relies on the correspondence between actual arguments used in the CALL statement and the dummy arguments used in the subroutine header. To illustrate how this correspondence can be used to return values from a subroutine, consider program 4-3.

Program 4-3

```
      PROGRAM MAIN
        REAL FIRNUM, SECNUM
        WRITE(6,*) 'ENTER TWO NUMBERS: '
        READ (5,*)  FIRNUM, SECNUM
        WRITE(6,*) 'THE VALUE IN FIRNUM IS: ',FIRNUM
        WRITE(6,*) 'THE VALUE IN SECNUM IS: ',SECNUM
        CALL NEWVAL(FIRNUM, SECNUM)
        WRITE(6,*)
        WRITE(6,*) 'THE VALUE IN FIRNUM IS NOW:', FIRNUM
        WRITE(6,*) 'THE VALUE IN SECNUM IS NOW:', SECNUM
        END
*
      SUBROUTINE NEWVAL(XNUM,YNUM)
        REAL XNUM, YNUM
        XNUM = 89.5
        YNUM = 99.5
        RETURN
        END
```

In calling the NEWVAL( ) subroutine within Program 4-3 it is extremely important to understand the connection between the actual arguments used in the CALL statement and the dummy arguments used in the subroutine header. *Both reference the same data items.* The significance of this is that the value in the actual (calling) argument can be altered by the subroutine using the dummy argument name and provides the basis for returning values from a subroutine. Thus, the dummy arguments XNUM and YNUM do not store copies of the values in FIRNUM and SECNUM, but directly access the locations in memory set aside for these two arguments. This type of subroutine call, where a subroutines' dummy arguments reference the same memory locations as the actual arguments of the calling unit, is formally referred to as a *call by reference.* The equivalence between argument names used in Program 4-3 is illustrated in Figure 4-4. As before, it is useful to consider both actual and formal argument names as different names referring to the same container. The calling program unit refers to the container using an actual argument name while the subroutine refers to the same container using its formal argument name.

The following sample run was obtained using Program 4-3:

```
ENTER TWO NUMBERS:
22.5 33.0
THE VALUE IN FIRNUM IS:      22.500000
THE VALUE IN SECNUM IS:      33.000000

THE VALUE IN FIRNUM IS NOW:      89.500000
THE VALUE IN SECNUM IS NOW:      99.500000
```

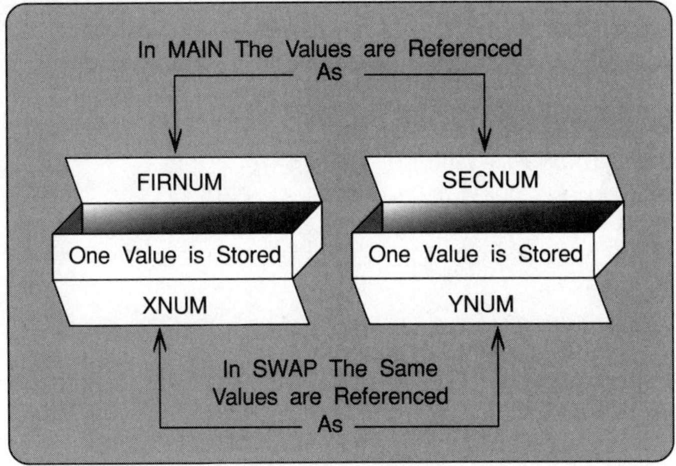

Figure 4-4 The Equivalence of Actual and Dummy Arguments in Program 4-3

In reviewing this output notice that the values displayed for the variables FIRNUM and SECNUM have been changed immediately after the call to the NEWVAL( ) subroutine. This is because these two variables were used as actual arguments in the CALL statement, which gives NEWVAL( ) access to them. Within NEWVAL( ) these arguments are known as XNUM and YNUM, respectively. As illustrated by the final displayed values, the assignment of values to XNUM and YNUM within NEWVAL( ) is reflected in MAIN as the altering of FIRNUM's and SECNUM's values.

The equivalence between actual calling arguments and dummy subroutine arguments illustrated in Program 4-3 provides the basis for returning any number of values from a subroutine. For example, assume that a subroutine is required to accept three values, compute these values' sum and product, and return these computed results to the calling routine. Naming the subroutine CALC( ) and providing five dummy arguments (three for the input data and two for the returned values), the following subroutine can be used.

```
SUBROUTINE CALC(X,Y,Z,TOTAL,PROD)
  REAL X,Y,Z,TOTAL,PROD
  TOTAL = X + Y + Z
  PROD = X*Y*Z
  RETURN
  END
```

This subroutine has five dummy arguments, named X, Y, Z, TOTAL, and PROD, all declared as real arguments. Within the subroutine only the last two arguments are altered. The value of the fourth argument, TOTAL, is calculated as the sum of the first three arguments, and the last argument, PROD, is computed as the product of the arguments X, Y, and Z. Program 4-4 includes this subroutine in a complete program.

Program 4-4

```
      PROGRAM MAIN
        REAL FIRNUM, SECNUM, THRNUM, SUM, PRDCT
        WRITE(6,*) 'ENTER THREE NUMBERS: '
        READ *, FIRNUM, SECNUM, THRNUM
        CALL CALC(FIRNUM, SECNUM, THRNUM, SUM, PRDCT)
        WRITE(6,*) 'THE SUM OF THE ENTERED NUMBERS IS: ',SUM
        WRITE(6,*) 'THE PRODUCT OF THE ENTERED NUMBERS IS: ',PRDCT
        END
*
      SUBROUTINE CALC(X,Y,Z,TOTAL,PROD)
        REAL X,Y,Z,TOTAL,PROD
        TOTAL = X + Y + Z
        PROD = X*Y*Z
        RETURN
        END
```

Within the main program unit, subroutine CALC( ) is called using the five actual arguments FIRNUM, SECNUM, THRNUM, SUM, and PRDCT. As required, these arguments agree in number and data type with the dummy arguments declared by subroutine CALC( ). Of the five actual arguments passed, only FIRNUM, SECNUM, and THRNUM have been assigned values when the call to CALC( ) is made. The remaining two arguments have not been initialized and will be used to receive values back from CALC( ). Depending on the compiler used in compiling the program, these arguments will initially contain either zeros or "garbage" values. Figure 4-5 illustrates the relationship between actual and formal argument names and the values they contain after the return from CALC( ) for the following sample run using Program 4-4:

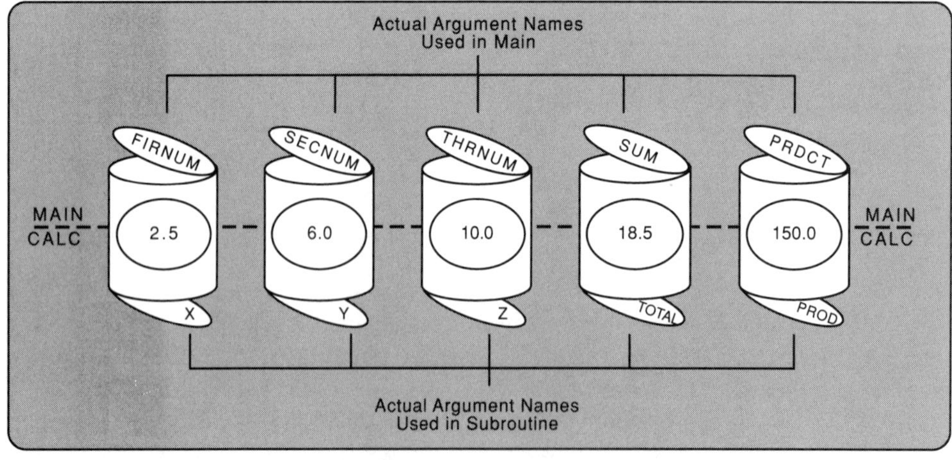

Figure 4-5 Relationship Between Actual and Formal Arguments

```
ENTER THREE NUMBERS:
2.5 6.0 10.0
THE SUM OF THE ENTERED NUMBERS IS:        18.500000
THE PRODUCT OF THE ENTERED NUMBERS IS:      150.000000
```

Once CALC( ) is called, it uses its first three arguments to calculate values for TOTAL and PROD and then returns control to MAIN. Because of the order of its actual calling arguments, the MAIN program unit knows the values calculated by CALC( ) as SUM and PRDCT, which are then displayed.

Although all of the examples we have used have illustrated calling a subroutine from a main program unit, this is not required in FORTRAN. A subroutine can be called by any program unit, including another subroutine, with one exception: a subroutine must never call itself, either directly or indirectly. Thus, the following subroutine is invalid because it calls itself.

```
SUBROUTINE DOIT(A,B,C)
   .
   .
   CALL DOIT(X,Y,Z)
   .
   .
   END
```

Similarly, the following sequence of subroutines is invalid because the first subroutine references itself indirectly through the second subroutine.

```
SUBROUTINE ONE( )
   .
   .
   CALL TWO( )
   END
SUBROUTINE TWO( )
   .
   .
   CALL ONE( )
   .
   .
   END
```

The actual arguments used in calling a subroutine can be variables, as illustrated in Program 4-4, single constants, or more complex expressions yielding the correct argument data type. For example, a valid call to CALC( ) using constant and variable arguments in Program 4-4 is:

```
CALL CALC(2.0,3.0,6.2,SUM,PROD)
```

When an actual argument is either a constant value or an expression that yields a constant value, the corresponding dummy argument in the called subroutine must never be used on the left-hand side of an assignment statement. To do so would be an attempt to change the value of a constant within the calling program unit.

In addition to its dummy arguments, a subroutine may declare as many variables as needed to complete its task. These variable declarations can either be made on a line by themselves, or included within the declarations of the dummy arguments.* For example, if I, J, and K are integer dummy arguments and KOUNT and MAXVAL are integer variables within a subroutine named FINMAX( ), a valid subroutine heading and declaration statement is:

```
SUBROUTINE FINMAX(I,J,K)
  INTEGER I, J, K, KOUNT, MAXVAL
```

Alternatively, the variable declarations can be made on a line by themselves using the following arrangement:

```
SUBROUTINE FINMAX(I,J,K)
  INTEGER I, J, K
  INTEGER KOUNT, MAXVAL
```

Although FORTRAN permits both arguments and variables to be intermingled in any order within a declaration statement, for program clarity arguments should always be declared prior to variables.

Variable Scope

By their very nature, FORTRAN subroutines are constructed to be independent modules. The implication of this is that variables declared in one program unit cannot be accessed by another program unit unless specific provisions are made to allow such access. As we have seen, one such access is provided through a subroutine's argument list. Seen in this light, an appropriate analogy for a subroutine is a closed box, with slots at the top to exchange values with the calling program unit.

The metaphor of a closed box is useful because it emphasizes the fact that what goes on inside the subroutine, except for the altering of an argument's value, is hidden from the view of all other program units. This includes any variables declared within the subroutine. These internally declared variables, which are available only to the subroutine itself, are said to be local to the subroutine, or *local variables*. This term refers to the scope of a variable, where scope is defined as the section of the program where the variable is valid or "known." Local variables are meaningful only

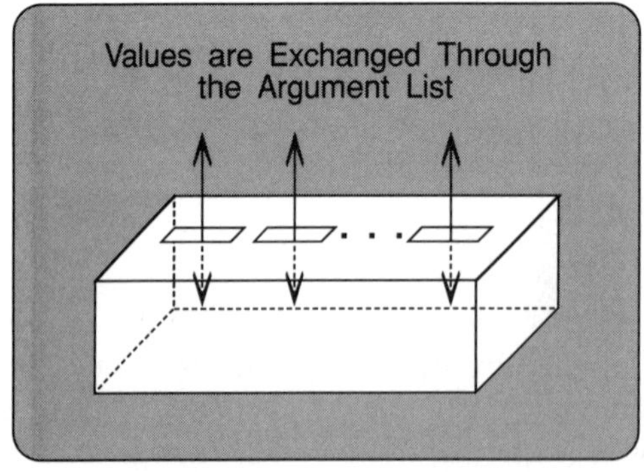

Figure 4-6 A Subroutine Can Be Considered a Closed Box

* Some compilers require that all variables and arguments of the same data type be declared using a single declaration statement.

when used in expressions or statements inside the subroutine that declared them. This means that the same variable name can be declared and used in more than one subroutine. For each subroutine that declares the variable, a separate and distinct variable is created. For example, consider Program 4-5.

Program 4-5

```
   PROGRAM MAIN
      INTEGER INUM
      INUM = 20
      WRITE(6,*) 'THE VALUE IN INUM, WITHIN MAIN IS ', INUM
      CALL SHOW
      WRITE(6,*) 'THE VALUE IN INUM, AGAIN FROM MAIN IS ', INUM
      END
*
     SUBROUTINE SHOW
      INTEGER INUM
      INUM = 0
      WRITE(6,*) '  THE VALUE IN INUM, WITHIN SHOW IS ', INUM
      RETURN
      END
```

Program 4-5 contains two separate local variables, both named INUM. Storage for the INUM variable used in the main program unit is created by the declaration statement located in this unit. A different storage area for the INUM variable used in the subroutine named SHOW is created by the declaration statement located in the subroutine (see Figure 4-7).

Each of the variables named INUM is local to the program unit in which it is declared, and each of these variables can be used only from within the appropriate program unit. Thus when INUM is used in the main program unit, the storage area referenced by the first declaration statement is accessed, and when INUM is used in the SHOW subroutine the storage area referenced by its declaration statement is accessed. The following output is produced when Program 4-5 is executed.

```
THE VALUE IN INUM, WITHIN MAIN IS          20
  THE VALUE IN INUM, WITHIN SHOW IS          0
THE VALUE IN INUM, AGAIN FROM MAIN IS        20
```

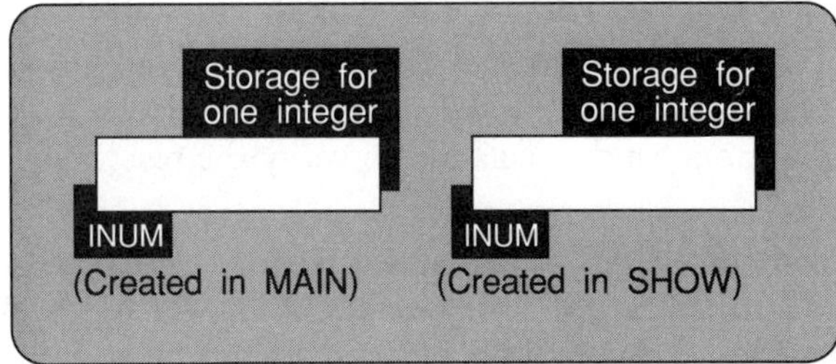

Figure 4-7 The Storage Areas Created by Program 4-5

Since each program unit only "knows" its own local variables, the main program unit can only display the value of its INUM variable, which is 20. This display is made both before and after the call to the SHOW subroutine. From within SHOW the value displayed for its INUM variable has no connection with any variable declared outside of this subroutine, regardless of the similarity in names. The value displayed for INUM within SHOW is zero because of the assignment statement INUM = 0 contained within this subroutine. The setting of this variable to zero, however, has no effect on the INUM declared in the main unit. As illustrated, this variable still retains its value of 20 after the call to SHOW has been completed.

By definition, since all FORTRAN variables are declared within a program unit, all FORTRAN variables are local variables. FORTRAN does, however, provide two different means of extending the scope of a local variable from one program unit into another. One way is to use a variable as an argument in a CALL statement. For lengthy argument lists that must be shared between many subroutines this becomes awkward and cumbersome. The second method is to use a COMMON block, which is the subject of Section 12.1.

Exercises

1. Write subroutine headers, argument declarations, and CALL statements for the following:

a. A subroutine named TEST( ) having a real dummy argument named EXPER. The corresponding actual argument used in calling TEST( ) is named VALUE.

b. A subroutine named MINUTE( ) having an integer dummy argument named ITIME. The corresponding actual argument used in calling MINUTE( ) is named LSECND.

c. A subroutine named KEY( ) having a character dummy argument named CODE. The corresponding actual argument used in calling KEY( ) is also named CODE.

d. A subroutine named YIELD( ) having a real dummy argument named RATE and an integer dummy argument named N. The actual arguments used in calling YIELD( ) are named COUPON and IYEARS.

e. A subroutine named RAND( ) having two real dummy arguments named SEED and RANDNO, respectively. The actual arguments used in calling RAND( ) are named SEED and RVAL.

2a. Write a subroutine named AREA( ) that accepts two dummy real arguments named WIDTH and XLENTH. The subroutine should calculate the area of a rectangle by multiplying the passed data and then display the calculated area.

b. Include the AREA( ) subroutine written for Exercise 2a in a working program. The main program unit should correctly call and pass the values 4.4 and 2.0 to AREA( ). Make sure to do a hand calculation to verify the result displayed by your program.

3a. Write a subroutine named TOTAMT( ) that accepts four actual integer arguments named IQUART, IDIMES, NICKEL, and IPENNY, which represent the number of quarters, dimes, nickels, and pennies in a piggybank. The subroutine should determine the dollar value of the number of quarters, dimes, nickels, and pennies passed to it and display the calculated value.

b. Include TOTAMT( ) subroutine written for Exercise 3a in a working program. The main program unit should correctly call and pass the values of 26 quarters, 80 dimes, 100 nickels, and 216 pennies to TOTAMT( ). Make sure to do a hand calculation to verify the result displayed by your program.

4a. The time in hours, minutes, and seconds is to be passed to a subroutine named TOTSEC( ). Write TOTSEC( ) to accept these values, determine the total number of seconds in the passed data, and display the calculated value.

b. Include the TOTSEC( ) subroutine written for Exercise 4a in a working program. The main program unit should correctly call TOTSEC( ) and display the value returned by the subroutine. Use the following test data to verify your program's operation: hours = 10, minutes = 36, and seconds = 54. Make sure to do a hand calculation to verify the result displayed by your program.

5a. Write a subroutine named TAX( ) that accepts a dollar amount and a tax rate as formal arguments, and returns the tax due on the dollar amount. For example, if the numbers 100.00 and .06 are passed to the subroutine, the value returned should be 6.00, which is 100.00 times .06.

b. Include the TAX( ) subroutine written for Exercise 5a in a working program. The main program unit should correctly call FMAX( ) and display the value returned by the subroutine.

6a. Write a subroutine named CHANGE( ) that accepts a real number and four actual integer arguments named QUART, DIMES, NICKEL, and PENNY. The subroutine should determine the number of quarters, dimes, nickels, and pennies in the number passed to it and write these values directly to the calling program unit.

b. Include the CHANGE( ) subroutine written for Exercise 6a in a working program. The main program unit should correctly call CHANGE( ) and display the values returned by the subroutine.

7a. The time in hours, minutes, and seconds is to be passed to a subroutine named TOTSEC( ). Write TOTSEC( ) to accept these values, determine the total number of seconds in the passed data, and return the calculated value to the calling program unit.

b. Include the TOTSEC( ) subroutine written for Exercise 7a in a working program. The main program unit should correctly call TOTSEC( ) and display the value returned by the subroutine.

8a. Write a subroutine named TIME( ) that accepts an integer number of seconds named in the dummy argument named TOTSEC and returns the number of hours, minutes, and seconds corresponding to the total seconds in the three dummy integer arguments named HOURS, MIN, and SEC.

b. Include the TIME( ) subroutine written for Exercise 8a in a working program. The main program unit should correctly call TIME( ) and display the three values returned by the subroutine.

9. Write a subroutine named DAYCNT( ) that accepts a month, day, and year as its input arguments, calculates an integer representing the total number of days from the turn of the century corresponding to the passed date, and returns the calculated integer to the calling program unit. For this problem assume that each year has 365 days and each month has 30 days. Test your subroutine by verifying that the date 1/1/00 returns a day count of one.

10. Write a subroutine named LIQUID( ) that is to be called using the statement CALL LIQUID(CUPS, GALONS, QUARTS, PINTS). The subroutine is to determine the number of gallons, quarts, pints, and cups in the passed value named CUPS, and directly alter the respective arguments in the calling subroutine. Use the relationships of two cups to a pint, four cups to a quart, and 16 cups to a gallon.

11a. A clever and simple method of preparing to sort dates into either ascending (increasing) or descending (decreasing) order is to first convert a date having the form month/day/yr into an integer number using the formula date = year * 10000 + month * 100 + day. For example, using this formula the date 12/6/88 converts to the integer 881206 and the date 2/28/90 converts to the integer 900228. Sorting the resulting integer numbers automatically puts the dates into the correct order. Using this formula, write a subroutine named CONVRT( ) that accepts a month, day, and year, converts the passed data into a single date integer, and returns the integer to the calling program unit.

b. Include the CONVRT( ) subroutine written for Exercise 11a in a working program. The main program unit should correctly call CONVRT( ) and display the integer returned by the subroutine.

12a. Write a subroutine named DATE( ) that accepts an integer of the form described in Exercise 11a, determines the corresponding month, day, and year, and returns these three values to the calling program unit. For example, if DATE( ) is called using the statement

```
CALL DATE(901116,MONTH,DAY,YEAR)
```

the number 11 should be returned in MONTH, the number 16 in DAY, and the number 90 in YEAR.

b. Include the DATE( ) subroutine written for Exercise 12a in a working program. The main program unit should correctly call DATE( ) and display the three values returned by the subroutine.

13. The following program uses the same variable names in both the calling and called subroutine. Determine if this causes any problem for the computer.

```
PROGRAM MAIN
  INTEGER MIN, HOUR, SEC
  WRITE(6,*) 'ENTER TWO NUMBERS :'
  READ(5,*) MIN, HOUR
  CALL TIME(MIN,HOUR,SEC)
  WRITE(6,*) 'THE TOTAL NUMBER OF SECONDS IS ', SEC
  END
```

```
*
      SUBROUTINE TIME(MIN,HOUR,SEC)
        INTEGER MIN, HOUR, SEC
        SEC = (HOUR * 60 + MIN) * 60
        RETURN
        END
```

14. An extremely troublesome logic error occurs when the data types of actual and formal arguments are mismatched. For example, consider the following program that intentionally introduces this error:

```
      PROGRAM MAIN
        REAL FIRNUM, SECNUM
        INTEGER SUM
        FIRNUM = 22.2
        SECNUM = 10.3
        CALL ADDIT(FIRNUM, SECNUM, SUM)
        WRITE(6,*) 'THE SUM OF 22.2 AND 10.3 IS ', SUM
        END
*
      SUBROUTINE ADDIT(A,B,C)
        REAL A, B, C
        C = A + B
        RETURN
        END
```

In the subroutine ADDIT( ), the formal arguments A and B are used to access values supplied by the calling program unit and C is used to return a value. The subroutine thus accepts two real values and correctly returns their sum. On the receiving side the sum is referenced as the integer variable SUM. Although you might think that the returned real value would be truncated and converted to an integer value, this does not happen. Run this program on your computer to determine what value is received by the main program unit. Explain why you received the answer that you did.

4.2 Program Development Using Subroutines

A well designed computer program starts like a well designed term paper, with an outline. Just as a term paper begins with an initial outline that lists the paper's main topics, a computer program's initial outline provides a listing of the primary tasks that the program must accomplish.

A computer program's initial outline is typically either a pseudocode description (see Section 1.1) or a first-level structure diagram (see Section 2.5). This initial outline begins the process of defining a more complicated problem into a set of smaller, more manageable tasks. Each of these tasks can be further subdivided, or refined, into even smaller tasks, if required. Once the tasks are well defined, the

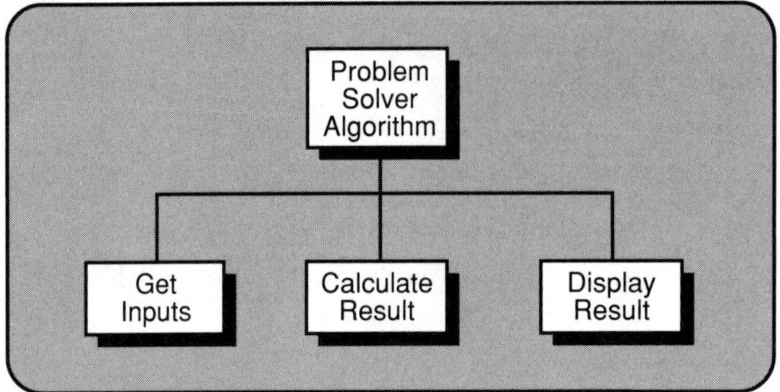

Figure 4-8 First-Level Structure Diagram of the Problem-Solver Algorithm

actual work of coding can begin, starting with any task, in any order. If there are more tasks than can be handled by one programmer, they can be distributed among as many programmers as required. This is equivalent to having many people work on a large research project, with each person responsible for an individual topic.

In its most general form, a typical outline applicable to most simple FORTRAN programs is the following algorithm:

Get the inputs to the problem
Calculate the desired result
Report the results of the calculation

These three tasks are the primary responsibilities of every program, and we shall refer to this algorithm as the Problem-Solver Algorithm. A first-level structure diagram of this algorithm is shown in Figure 4-8.

Each task in the Problem-Solver Algorithm can be worked on independently as a subprogram—a sort of "mini" FORTRAN program that typically is easier to complete than a whole program. Each of these subprogram tasks can be refined and coded in any desired order, although completing the input section first usually makes testing and development easier. We now apply this development procedure to an actual programming problem.

A Programming Problem

Assume that we must write a FORTRAN program to convert the rectangular (X,Y) coordinates of a point into polar form. That is, given an X and Y position on a Cartesian coordinate system, as illustrated in Figure 4-9, we must calculate the distance from the origin, r, and the angle from the x-axis, θ, specified by the point. The values of r and θ are referred to as the point's *polar coordinates*.

When the X and Y coordinates of a point are known, the equivalent r and θ coordinates can be calculated using the formulas:

$$r = \sqrt{X^2 + Y^2}$$

$$\theta = \tan^{-1}(Y/X), \quad X \neq 0$$

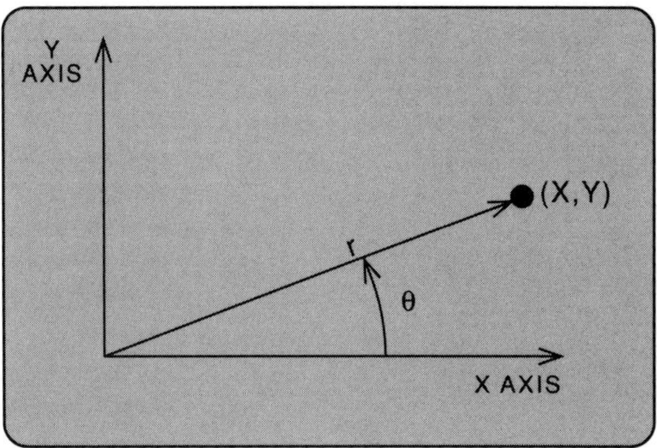

Figure 4-9 Correspondence Between Polar (Distance and Angle) and Cartesian (X,Y) Coordinates

We begin the development of our program with an outline of what the program is to accomplish. An initial pseudocode description of the desired program can be constructed using our Problem-Solver Algorithm as it pertains to the specifics of this application. For this application the required inputs are an X and Y coordinate, the calculation is to convert the input values to their polar coordinate form, and the display is the calculated polar coordinates. Thus the initial pseudocode description is:

Get the X and Y coordinate values
Calculate the Polar (r and θ) coordinate values
Display the Polar coordinate values

The equivalent first- or top-level structure diagram for this algorithm is illustrated in Figure 4-10.

As this is a relatively simple program and each task described by the algorithm needs no further refinement, coding of each task can begin. To illustrate that any task may be coded independently of any other task, we will arbitrarily start coding the subroutine that performs the calculation of polar coordinates. As an added fea-

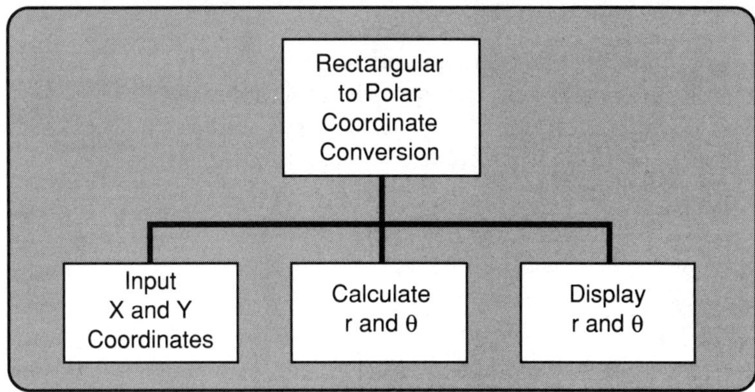

Figure 4-10 Top-Level Structure Diagram

ture, we will have this subroutine return the angle θ in degrees rather than the radian measure returned by the ATAN( ) function. Since this subroutine must receive two inputs, the X and Y coordinates, and return two outputs, the r and θ coordinates, we provide the subroutine with four arguments, two for its inputs and two for its outputs. Arbitrarily selecting the argument names of X, Y, R, and THETA, and naming the subroutine POLAR, the following code performs the required calculation of polar coordinates.

```
SUBROUTINE POLAR(X, Y, R, THETA)
  REAL X, Y, R, THETA
  PARAMETER (TODEG = 180.0 / 3.142593)
  R = SQRT(X**2 + Y**2)
  THETA = ATAN(Y / X) * TODEG
  RETURN
  END
```

The code of the subroutine POLAR( ) is rather straightforward and adheres to the standard form of a subroutine program unit introduced in the previous section. In the POLAR( ) subroutine each of its arguments is declared as a REAL and the named constant TODEG is defined in a PARAMETER statement as the factor 180.0 / 3.142593. The next two assignment statements use the two arguments X and Y to assign values to the arguments R and THETA. As written, the POLAR( ) subroutine may be compiled to check for any compile-time errors.

For a complete understanding of arguments it is worthwhile realizing that POLAR( ) can also be written using only two arguments. For example, the following version of POLAR( ) is also valid:

```
SUBROUTINE POLAR(A, B)
  REAL A, B, C
  PARAMETER (TODEG = 180.0 / 3.142593)
  C = A
  A = SQRT(A**2 + B**2)
  B = ATAN(B / C) * TODEG
  RETURN
  END
```

In this version the arguments A and B are used for both receiving and returning values. To understand this version it is helpful to think of the arguments A and B as containers (or variables) that are initialized from outside of the subroutine, when it is called. For example, the sequence of statements:

```
X = 3.0
Y = 4.0
CALL POLAR(X,Y)
```

would initialize the arguments as illustrated in Figure 4-11.

As illustrated in Figure 4-11, viewing arguments as containers through which values may be passed in either direction is helpful in understanding the fundamental characteristics of arguments: *they simply provide the ability for both a called and calling program unit to access the same storage area using different names.*

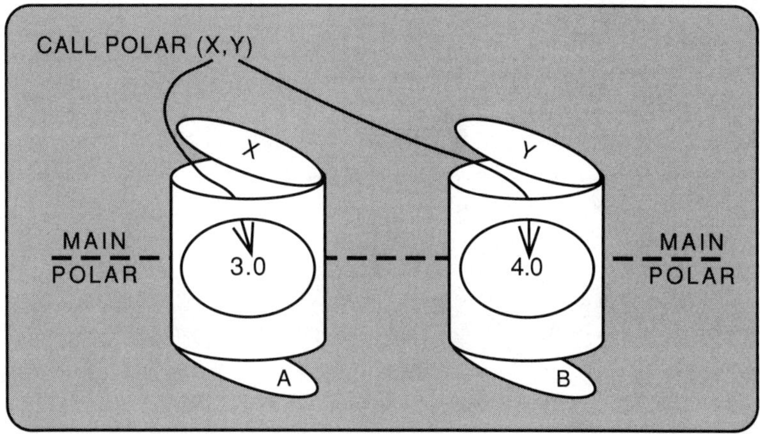

Figure 4-11 Argument Values when POLAR( ) is Called

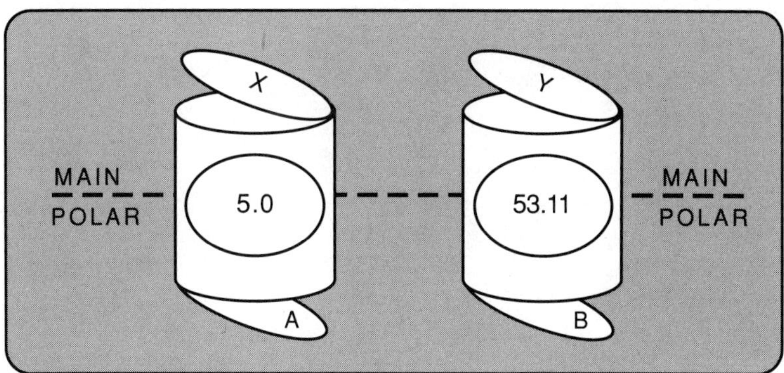

Figure 4-12 Values in A and B Set Internally by POLAR( )

Internal to our second version of the POLAR( ) subroutine, the values placed into the arguments by the calling routine are accessed using the names A and B. The first assignment statement, A = SQRT(A**2 + B**2), retrieves the values in A and B, and assigns a new value to A. Similarly, the next assignment statement alters the value in B. After these statements are executed the values in the arguments are as shown in Figure 4-12, assuming the initialization of arguments illustrated in Figure 4-11.

The values assigned to A and B can be accessed by the calling routine with the actual argument names, X and Y, that were used in the calling statement. It should be noted, however, that if the call to our second version of POLAR( ) were made by the statement CALL POLAR(3.0,4.0), an error would result. This error is caused by the attempt of POLAR( ) to change the value of the constants 3 and 4 in the calling routine. To avoid this possible error and to explicitly separate input and output arguments, our subroutines will typically use distinct arguments for input and output purposes. Thus, we will use our first version of POLAR( ) to complete the conversion program.

Testing the Subroutine

Once POLAR( ) is written it can be tested independently of any other subroutine. This is done by either writing a dedicated driver program that only calls POLAR( ), or by using program stubs. We will consider a dedicated driver program first, and discuss program stubs at the end of this section.

Program 4-6 provides a dedicated driver program that can be attached to the subroutine POLAR( ) for testing purposes.

Program 4-6

```
      PROGRAM MAIN
        REAL DIST, ANGLE
        CALL POLAR(3.0, 4.0, DIST, ANGLE)
        WRITE(6,*) 'DIST = ', DIST
        WRITE(6,*) 'ANGLE = ', ANGLE
        END
*
      SUBROUTINE POLAR(X, Y, R, THETA)
        REAL X, Y, R, THETA
        PARAMETER (TODEG = 180.0 / 3.142593)
        R = SQRT(X ** 2 + Y **2)
        THETA = ATAN(Y / X) * TODEG
        RETURN
        END
```

Notice that in the MAIN program unit we pass the constants 3.0 and 4.0 into POLAR( ). The subroutine accepts these inputs as the arguments X and Y, and uses these arguments in calculating values for the arguments R and THETA. Within MAIN, these last two arguments are known as DIST and ANGLE, whose values are displayed immediately after the CALL statement. The output produced when Program 4-6 is executed is:

```
DIST =          5.000000
ANGLE =         53.113190
```

These are the same results that would be obtained from a hand calculation. As the subroutine performs only two calculations, and the result displayed by our test program agrees with those obtained from a hand calculation, the subroutine has been completely tested by itself. It still remains to be group tested with the remaining two subroutines required for the complete program to ensure that correct argument values are exchanged between each subroutine.

Completing the Program

The structure diagram for our complete program (Figure 4-11) requires that subroutines also be written for accepting two rectangular coordinates and displaying the calculated polar coordinates, respectively. The following subroutine, GETREC( ), can be used to accept the input data.

```
SUBROUTINE GETREC(X, Y)
  REAL X, Y
  WRITE(6,*) 'RECTANGULAR TO POLAR COORDINATE CONVERSION PROGRAM'
  WRITE(6,*)
  WRITE(6,*) 'ENTER THE X COORDINATE'
  READ(5,*) X
  WRITE(6,*) 'ENTER THE Y COORDINATE'
  READ(5,*) Y
  RETURN
  END
```

In this subroutine the formal arguments X and Y are used to return the values that are entered in response to the two READ statements. As with the POLAR( ) subroutine, this subroutine may be tested by itself using a small dedicated driver program. The subroutine with its driver program is illustrated in Program 4-7.

Program 4-7

```
      PROGRAM MAIN
        REAL XVAL, YVAL
        CALL GETREC(XVAL, YVAL)
        WRITE(6,*) 'THE ENTERED VALUE FOR XVAL IS: ', XVAL
        WRITE(6,*) 'THE ENTERED VALUE FOR YVAL IS: ', YVAL
        END
*
      SUBROUTINE GETREC(X, Y)
        REAL X, Y
        WRITE(6,*) 'RECTANGULAR TO POLAR COORDINATE CONVERSION PROGRAM'
        WRITE(6,*)
        WRITE(6,*) 'ENTER THE X COORDINATE'
        READ(5,*) X
        WRITE(6,*) 'ENTER THE Y COORDINATE'
        READ(5,*) Y
        RETURN
        END
```

Notice that the dedicated driver program, which is also referred to as a "front-end" driver, has been used to both call GETREC( ) and display the values returned by this subroutine. The following output produced by Program 4-7 verifies the correct operation of the GETREC( ) subroutine:

```
RECTANGULAR TO POLAR COORDINATE CONVERSION PROGRAM

ENTER THE X COORDINATE
3.0
ENTER THE Y COORDINATE
4.0
THE ENTERED VALUE FOR XVAL IS:          3.000000
THE ENTERED VALUE FOR YVAL IS:          4.000000
```

In a similar manner, the subroutine for displaying two polar coordinates is constructed. Program 4-8 contains both the subroutine, which we have named SHOWIT( ), and a front-end driver used for testing the subroutine. Notice that the formal argument names used in the header line for SHOWIT( ) need not be the same as those used in any other subroutine. SHOWIT( ) is constructed to simply display the values in its two arguments, which in this case have been named RADIUS and ANGLE.

Program 4-8

```
      PROGRAM MAIN
        CALL SHOWIT(5.0, 53.11319)
        END
*
      SUBROUTINE SHOWIT(RADIUS, ANGLE)
        REAL RADIUS, ANGLE
        WRITE(6,*)
        WRITE(6,*) 'THE POLAR COORDINATES ARE:'
        WRITE(6,*) '  DISTANCE FROM ORIGIN: ', RADIUS
        WRITE(6,*) '  ANGLE (IN DEGREES) FROM X-AXIS: ', ANGLE
        RETURN
        END
```

The output of Program 4-8, which follows, verifies that SHOWIT( ) correctly displays the values passed to it.

```
THE POLAR COORDINATES ARE:
  DISTANCE FROM ORIGIN:          5.000000
  ANGLE (IN DEGREES) FROM X-AXIS:         53.113190
```

It now remains to create one MAIN driver program that calls each of the developed subroutines in the correct order. This is done in Program 4-9, which also includes the subroutines GETREC( ), POLAR( ), and SHOWIT( ). Although all three subroutines have been included in Program 4-9, it is important to note that this is not necessary. The driver program and each of the individual subroutines can be written and compiled individually, and then linked together just prior to run time, as described in Appendix A.

Program 4-9

```
***********************************************************************
*  THIS PROGRAM CONVERTS RECTANGULAR COORDINATES TO POLAR COORDINATES *
*  SUBROUTINES USED:                                                  *
*    GETREC - OBTAIN THE RECTANGULAR COORDINATES                      *
*    POLAR  - CALCULATE THE POLAR COORDINATES                         *
*    SHOWIT - DISPLAY THE POLAR COORDINATES                           *
***********************************************************************
*
      PROGRAM MAIN
        REAL X, Y, DIST, ANGLE
        CALL GETREC(X, Y)
        CALL POLAR(X, Y, DIST, ANGLE)
        CALL SHOWIT(DIST, ANGLE)
        END
*
      SUBROUTINE GETREC(X, Y)
        REAL X, Y
        WRITE(6,*) 'RECTANGULAR TO POLAR COORDINATE CONVERSION PROGRAM'
        WRITE(6,*)
        WRITE(6,*) 'ENTER THE X COORDINATE'
        READ(5,*) X
        WRITE(6,*) 'ENTER THE Y COORDINATE'
        READ(5,*) Y
        RETURN
        END
*
      SUBROUTINE POLAR(X, Y, R, THETA)
        REAL X, Y, R, THETA
        PARAMETER (TODEG = 180.0 / 3.142593)
        R = SQRT(X ** 2 + Y **2)
        THETA = ATAN(Y / X) * TODEG
        RETURN
        END
*
      SUBROUTINE SHOWIT(RADIUS, ANGLE)
        REAL RADIUS, ANGLE
        WRITE(6,*)
        WRITE(6,*) 'THE POLAR COORDINATES ARE:'
        WRITE(6,*) '  DISTANCE FROM ORIGIN: ', RADIUS
        WRITE(6,*) '  ANGLE (IN DEGREES) FROM X-AXIS: ', ANGLE
        RETURN
        END
```

The following output was produced from one run using Program 4-9:

```
RECTANGULAR TO POLAR COORDINATE CONVERSION PROGRAM

ENTER THE X COORDINATE
3.0
ENTER THE Y COORDINATE
4.0

THE POLAR COORDINATES ARE:
  DISTANCE FROM ORIGIN:           5.000000
  ANGLE (IN DEGREES) FROM X-AXIS:          53.113190
```

Program Stubs

An alternative to writing individual front-end driver programs for each subroutine, as the subroutine is developed, is to write the MAIN driver program first, and add the subroutines later, as they are developed. The problem that arises with this approach is that the program cannot be run until all of the subroutines are written. For example, consider the driver program used in Program 4-9, and repeated below, minus the initial comment lines:

```
PROGRAM MAIN
  REAL X, Y, DIST, ANGLE
  CALL GETREC(X, Y)
  CALL POLAR(X, Y, DIST, ANGLE)
  CALL SHOWIT(DIST, ANGLE)
  END
```

Now assume that the I/O subroutines have been written but you haven't as yet figured out the details of the calculating subroutine POLAR( ). Thus, with the addition of the input subroutine GETREC( ) and the output subroutine SHOWIT( ), the almost complete program becomes:

```
      PROGRAM MAIN
        REAL X, Y, DIST, ANGLE
        CALL GETREC(X, Y)
        CALL POLAR(X, Y, DIST, ANGLE)
        CALL SHOWIT(DIST, ANGLE)
        END
*
      SUBROUTINE GETREC(X, Y)
        REAL X, Y
        WRITE(6,*) 'RECTANGULAR TO POLAR COORDINATE CONVERSION PROGRAM'
        WRITE(6,*)
        WRITE(6,*) 'ENTER THE X COORDINATE'
        READ(5,*) X
```

```
      WRITE(6,*) 'ENTER THE Y COORDINATE'
      READ(5,*) Y
      RETURN
      END
*
    SUBROUTINE SHOWIT(RADIUS, ANGLE) L RADIUS, ANGLE
      WRITE(6,*)
      WRITE(6,*) 'THE POLAR COORDINATES ARE:'
      WRITE(6,*) '  DISTANCE FROM ORIGIN: ', RADIUS
      WRITE(6,*) '  ANGLE (IN DEGREES) FROM X-AXIS: ', ANGLE
      RETURN
      END
```

This program would be complete if there were a subroutine definition for POLAR( ). But we really don't need a correct POLAR( ) subroutine to test and run what has been written, we just need a subroutine that acts like it is: a "fake" POLAR( ) that returns values of the proper form for the subroutine call is all that is required to allow initial testing. This fake subroutine is called a stub. A *stub is* the beginning of a final program unit that can be used as a place-holder for the final unit until the unit is completed. A stub for POLAR( ) is as follows:

```
SUBROUTINE POLAR(X, Y, R, THETA)
  REAL X, Y, R, THETA
  R = 10.0
  THETA = 20.0
  RETURN
  END
```

This stub subroutine can now be compiled and linked with the previously completed code. When it is developed, the "real" code will replace the stub portion.

The minimum requirement of a stub subroutine is that it compile and link with its calling module. In practice, it is a good idea to have a stub display a message that it has been entered successfully or display its received arguments. An example of the former is shown in BIGSUB( ), a stub simulating an unfinished subroutine receiving several arguments.

```
SUBROUTINE BIGSUB(NUM1, NUM2, NUM3, X, Y, Z)
  INTEGER NUM1, NUM2, Z
  REAL NUM3, X, Y
  WRITE(6,*) 'BIGSUB ENTERED'
  RETURN
  END
```

As the subprogram is refined, you let it do more and more, perhaps allowing it to return intermediate or incomplete results. This incremental, or stepwise, refinement is an important concept in efficient program development that provides you with the means of running a program that does not yet meet all of its final requirements.

Exercises

1a. The volume, v, and surface area, s, of a cylinder are given by the formulas:

$$v = \pi r^2 l \quad \text{and} \quad s = 2\pi r l$$

where r is the cylinder's radius and l is its length. Using these formulas write and test a subroutine named CYLIN( ) that accepts the radius and length of a cylinder and returns its volume and surface area.

b. Write a structure chart for a program that accepts the values of r and l from the user, calculates the volume and surface area of a cylinder, and displays the calculated value.

c. Write and run a FORTRAN program for the structure chart developed in Exercise 1b.

2a. A geometric sequence is a set of numbers of the form a, ar, ar^2, ar^3, ..., where a is the first term and r is called the common ratio. Thus, after the first term, each subsequent number can be obtained by multiplying the preceding number by r, and the nth is calculated as ar^{n-1}. For example, in the sequence 4, 12, 36, 108, ..., the first term, a, is 4, and the common ratio, r, is 3. Using this information, write and test a FORTRAN subroutine that accepts the first term, and common ratio, and an integer number, N, to denote the term that is desired. The subroutine should then calculate and return the Nth and (N+1)st terms of the sequence.

b. Write a structure chart for a program that accepts the values of the first term, common ratio, and desired term the user, calculates the Nth and (N+1)st term, and displays the calculated values.

c. Write and run a FORTRAN program for the structure chart developed in Exercise 2b.

3. Modify Program 4-9 to accept the rectangular coordinates of two points (X_1, Y_1) and (X_2, Y_2), calculate the distance of each point from the origin, and the distance between the two points. The distance, d, between two points is given by the formula

$$d = \sqrt{(x_2 + x_1)^2 + (y_2 - y_1)^2}$$

4a. An algorithm to round any real number, P, to N decimal places is the following:

Step 1: Multiply P by 10^N

Step 2: Add 0.5 to the result of Step 1

Step 3: Truncate the value obtained in Step 2

Step 4: Divide the result of Step 3 by 10^N

For example, if P is the number 4.567692 and we desire to round this value to 3 decimal places (N = 3), applying the algorithm produces the following results:

Step 1: $4.567692 * 10^3 = 4.567692 * 1000 = 4567.692$

Step 2: $4567.692 + 0.5 = 4568.192$

Step 3: 4568

Step 4: 4568 / 1000 = 4.568

Write a subroutine named ROUND( ) that accepts P and N as inputs and returns the rounded value of P in the formal argument named PRND. Test your subroutine using a dedicated driver program unit.

b. Modify the subroutine written for Exercise 4a so that the same formal argument, P, is used for the original number and the returned rounded number.

c. Write a structure chart for a program that accepts the values of P and N from the user, calculates the rounded value of P, and displays the calculated value.

d. Write and run a FORTRAN program for the structure chart developed in Exercise 4c.

5a. Write a subroutine that calculates the radius, R, and area, A, of a circle when its circumference, C, is given. The relevant formulas are: $R = C/2\pi$ and $A = \pi R^2$. Test your subroutine using a program having a dedicated driver program unit.

b. Write a structure chart for a program that accepts the value of the circumference from the user, calculates the radius and area, and displays the calculated values.

c. Write and run a FORTRAN program for the structure chart developed in Exercise 5b.

6a. A recipe for making enough acorn squash for 4 people requires the following ingredients:

2 acorn squashes
2 teaspoons of lemon juice
1/4 cup of raisins
1 1/2 cups of applesauce
1/4 cup of brown sugar
3 tablespoons of chopped walnuts

Using this information, write and test a subroutine that accepts the number of people that must be served and returns the amount of each ingredient required.

b. Write a structure chart for a program that accepts the number of people to be served, calculates the quantity of each ingredient needed, and displays the calculated values.

c. Write and run a FORTRAN program for the structure chart developed in Exercise 6b.

7a. The owner of a strawberry farm has made the following arrangement with a group of students: they may pick all the strawberries they want. When they are through picking, the strawberries will be weighed: the farm will retain 50% of the strawberries and the students will divide the remainder evenly between them. Using this information, write and test a FORTRAN subroutine named STRAW( ) that accepts the number of students and the total pounds picked as input arguments, and returns the number of pounds and the approximate number of strawberries that the owner of the farm and one student receive. Assume that a strawberry weighs approximately one ounce. There are 16 ounces to a pound.

b. Write a structure chart for a program that accepts the number of students and total pounds of strawberries picked in one subroutine; calculates the number of pounds and approximate number of strawberries received by the farm owner and each student in a second subroutine; and displays the calculated values in a third subroutine.

c. Write and run a FORTRAN program for the structure chart developed in Exercise 7b.

8a. The determinant of the 2 by 2 matrix

$$\begin{vmatrix} a_{11} & a_{12} \\ a_{21} & a_{22} \end{vmatrix}$$

is $a_{11}a_{22} - a_{21}a_{12}$. Similarly, the determinant of a 3 by 3 matrix

$$\begin{vmatrix} a_{11} & a_{12} & a_{13} \\ a_{21} & a_{22} & a_{23} \\ a_{31} & a_{32} & a_{33} \end{vmatrix} =$$

$$a_{11}\begin{vmatrix} a_{22} & a_{23} \\ a_{32} & a_{33} \end{vmatrix} - a_{21}\begin{vmatrix} a_{12} & a_{13} \\ a_{32} & a_{33} \end{vmatrix} + a_{31}\begin{vmatrix} a_{12} & a_{13} \\ a_{22} & a_{23} \end{vmatrix}$$

Using this information write and test two subroutines, named DET2( ) and DET3( ). The DET2( ) subroutine should accept the four coefficients of a 2 by 2 matrix and return its determinant. The DET3( ) subroutine should accept the nine coefficients of a 3 by 3 matrix and return its determinant by calling DET2( ) to calculate the required 2 by 2 determinants.

b. Write a structure chart for a program that accepts the nine coefficients of a 3 by 3 matrix in one subroutine, passes these coefficients to DET3( ), and uses a third subroutine to display the calculated determinant.

c. Write and run a FORTRAN program for the structure chart developed in Exercise 8b.

4.3 Subprogram Functions

FORTRAN provides three types of functions: intrinsic, subprogram, and statement. We are already familiar with intrinsic functions, such as ABS( ), SQRT( ), EXP( ), etc., that are provided as an intrinsic part of the FORTRAN language. Both subprogram and statement functions perform in an identical manner to intrinsic functions, except that they are user-written. A subprogram function is a distinct program unit, like a subroutine, while a statement function is a single FORTRAN statement, much like an assignment statement, that is contained within other program units.

The purpose of all functions, be they intrinsic, subprogram, or statement, is to receive data, operate on the data, and return a single value, as illustrated in Figure 4-13. In using a function, we must be concerned with both the function itself and how

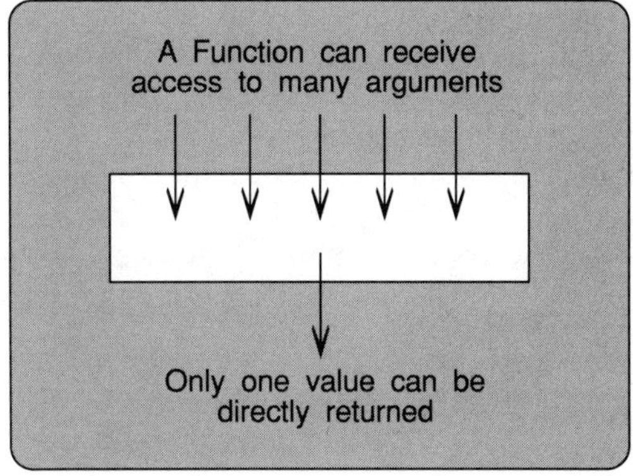

Figure 4-13 A Function Returns a Single Value

it is called by other program units. We first show how a subprogram function is created, and then turn our attention to how it is called by other program units.

Like all program units, a subprogram function consists of two parts, a function header and a function body, and has the general form:

```
data-type FUNCTION function-name(list of arguments)
  argument and variable declarations
  executable statements
  function-name = some expression
  RETURN
  END
```

The purpose of the function header line, which is the first line of the function, is to identify the data type returned by the function, provide the function with a name, and specify the number and order of arguments expected by the function. The purpose of the function body is to declare the data-type of the function's arguments and then operate on the passed data and return a single value back to the calling function.

Beyond the obvious difference of the keyword FUNCTION instead of SUBROUTINE in the header line, notice that a function's header line includes a data type. The data type contained within the header line declares the data type of the value that will be returned by the function, and can be any of the data types we've studied.* The argument names in the header line are referred to as either formal or dummy arguments (the two names are synonymous) and are used to pass data into the function. For example, the following function header line can be used for a subprogram function named FMAX( ) that is to receive two values and return a single REAL value.

```
REAL FUNCTION FMAX(X,Y)
```

The names of the arguments in the function declaration line, in this case X and Y, are chosen by the programmer. Since the header declaration for FMAX( ) includes two arguments, this function expects to receive two data items when it is

* Instead of declaring the data type in the header, it can be declared with the function's arguments, internal to the function. As this is less readable in clearly identifying the data type of the return value, we will always declare the function's data type in its header line.

called. Instead of the argument names X and Y, any two valid variable names could have been used. The dummy arguments are used internal to the function to refer to the data passed to the function. If a function does not have any arguments, the parentheses following the function name must still be included.

Although a function without any arguments is extremely limited, one such function can be constructed to return a value for π that is accurate to the maximum number of decimal places allowed by your computer. This value is obtained by taking the arcsine of 1.0, which is π/2, and multiplying the result by 2. Naming this function PI( ) we have:

```
REAL FUNCTION PI( )
  PI = 2.0 * ASIN(1.0)
  RETURN
  END
```

The PI( ) function illustrates two important requirements of all function program units. The first requirement, which is a new feature, is that the function must contain a statement that assigns a value to the function name. This is typically accomplished using an assignment statement of the form:

```
function-name = expression
```

In our PI( ) function this statement takes the specific form:

```
PI = 2.0 * ASIN(1.0)
```

The value assigned to PI, the name of the function, is the value returned by the function. The expression in this statement may include the formal arguments, any variables declared and assigned values within the function, or other function calls. In no case, however, may a function reference itself within its body. (Functions that internally reference themselves are referred to as *self-referential* or *recursive* functions and are not permitted in FORTRAN.)

The second requirement illustrated by our PI( ) function is the inclusion of a RETURN statement. When this statement is executed the value assigned to the function name is returned to the calling function. As with all program units, the END statement is the last statement used to close the unit. Unlike earlier versions of FORTRAN, the END statement in both FORTRAN 77 and FORTRAN 90 subprogram functions actually performs two tasks: it both marks the physical end of the program unit and acts as a RETURN statement. Although this makes an explicit RETURN statement immediately before an END statement theoretically unnecessary, we will include it in all of our functions.*

* Including a RETURN statement is done for two reasons. First, some compilers require it. Thus, if you are using such a compiler, the RETURN statement is mandatory. For these compilers the END statement is considered a nonexecutable statement that is used to mark the physical end of a program unit. In this role the END statement tells the compiler to stop reading any more statements and begin the actual compilation. Here the last statement to be compiled and translated into machine language is the statement immediately preceding the END statement, which is the RETURN statement. During program execution it is the machine language version of the RETURN that is actually executed. The second reason for including a RETURN is one of programming style. Many programmers feel that the RETURN statement clearly indicates a subprogram function's exit point. As subprogram functions can have multiple exit points, it is felt that all return points in a function, including the one at the end of the function, should clearly be marked with a RETURN statement.

Unlike our PI( ) function, a function typically has one or more arguments to work with, such as FORTRAN's intrinsic functions. For example, the square root function SQRT(X) returns the square root of its argument, X, and MOD(M,N) returns the remainder after dividing M by N using integer division. Let us now create a function that uses arguments.

As a specific application, we will create a function that rounds the fractional part of a real number to "N" digits to the right of the decimal place. This is a common requirement, for example, when dealing with monetary values, where a result such as \$3.9764 typically would be rounded to two decimal places (N = 2) to produce an acceptable result of \$3.98. An algorithm to perform this rounding task on any arbitrary real number, P, is:

Step 1: Multiply P by 10^N
Step 2: Add 0.5 to the result of Step 1
Step 3: Truncate the result of Step 2
Step 4: Divide the result of Step 3 by 10^N

For example, if P is 3.9764 and N is 2, which means round P to 2 decimal places, the algorithm produces the following results:

Step 1: $3.9764 * 10.0^2 = 3.9764 * 100 = 397.64$
Step 2: $397.64 + 0.5 = 398.14$
Step 3: Truncating the above value yields 398.
Step 4: $398. / 100. = 3.98$

Expressing this algorithm as a subprogram function named ROUNDN( ) produces the following:

```
      REAL FUNCTION ROUNDN(P,N)
        REAL P, TEMP
        INTEGER N
*
        TEMP = INT(P * 10.0 ** N + 0.5)
        ROUNDN = REAL(TEMP / 10.0 ** N)
        RETURN
        END
```

Notice that the ROUNDN( ) function is declared as returning a real value and has two formal arguments, P and N. Within the function P and N are declared as a REAL and an INTEGER argument, respectively. Additionally, a variable named TEMP is declared as a REAL variable. Although the declaration of the arguments can be made in any order (that is, N can be declared before P), the placement of the formal arguments within the header line's parentheses is important. As written, ROUNDN( ) expects to receive two arguments, the first of which must be real and the second of which must be an integer. From a programming viewpoint, arguments can be considered as variables whose values are assigned outside of the function and passed to the function when it is called.

Within the ROUNDN( ) function the assignment statement for TEMP performs Steps 1, 2, and 3 of the rounding algorithm. The last assignment statement performs Step 4 of the algorithm and assigns the calculated value to ROUNDN, which is the name of the function. The function is then completed with the RETURN and END statements.

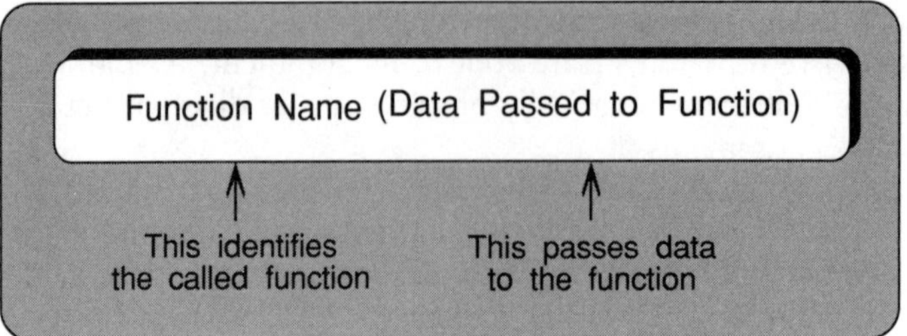

Figure 4-14 Calling and Passing Data to a Function

Calling a Subprogram Function

Having written two subprogram functions, PI( ) and ROUNDN( ), we now turn our attention to how these functions can be called by other program units. Unlike subroutines, subprogram functions are not called using a CALL statement. Rather, they are called in the same manner as intrinsic functions—by giving the function's name and passing any data to it in the parentheses following the function name (see Figure 4-14). At the same time the function is called, provision must also be made to correctly use its calculated value.

To clarify the process of sending data to a function and using its returned value, consider Program 4-10, which calls the function ROUNDN( ).

Program 4-10

```
      PROGRAM MAIN
        REAL NUMBER, NUMX, ROUNDN
        INTEGER PLACES
        WRITE(6,*) 'ENTER A DECIMAL NUMBER'
        READ(5,*) NUMBER
        WRITE(6,*) 'ENTER THE NUMBER OF DECIMAL PLACES FOR ROUNDING'
        READ (5,*) PLACES
        NUMX = ROUNDN(NUMBER,PLACES)
        WRITE(6,*) 'THE ROUNDED NUMBER IS', NUMX
        END
*
      REAL FUNCTION ROUNDN(P,N)
        REAL P, TEMP
        INTEGER N
*
        TEMP = INT(P * 10.0 ** N + 0.5)
        ROUNDN = REAL(TEMP / 10.0 ** N)
        RETURN
        END
```

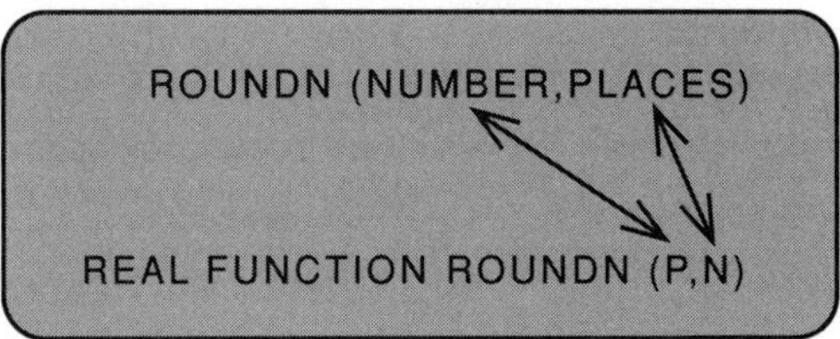

Figure 4-15 Assigning Actual Arguments to Formal Arguments

As illustrated in Program 4-10, calling a function is rather trivial. All that is required is that the name of the function be used and that any data passed to the function be enclosed within the parentheses following the function name. The items enclosed within the parentheses are called *actual arguments* of the called function. As illustrated in Figure 4-15, the formal arguments P and N within ROUNDN( ) reference the values in the actual arguments NUMBER and PLACES, respectively, in MAIN. The function itself does not know which program unit made the function call. The calling program unit must, however, provide actual arguments that match in number, order, and data type to the formal arguments declared by the function. As with subroutines, no data type conversions are made between actual and formal arguments.

At the time that a function is called, provision must also be made to use the value that is provided by the function. To use the returned value we must either provide a variable to store the value or use the value directly in an expression. Storing the returned value in a variable is accomplished using a standard assignment statement. For example, the assignment statement in Program 4-10

```
NUMX = ROUNDN(NUMBER,PLACES)
```

can be used to store ROUNDN( )'s returned value in the variable named NUMX. This assignment statement does two things. First, the right-hand side of the assignment statement calls ROUNDN( ), then the result returned by the ROUNDN function is stored in the variable NUMX. Since the value returned by ROUNDN( ) is real, the variable NUMX must also be declared as a REAL variable within the calling function's variable declarations.

The second method of calling a function and using its returned value is to include the function within any valid FORTRAN expression. For example, the statement:

```
WRITE(6,*) ROUNDN(NUMBER,PLACES)
```

can be used to directly call ROUNDN( ) and display its value. It must be noted, however, that if a function is used either within a WRITE or PRINT statement the function itself cannot contain an output statement to the same device. This would be considered a recursive output call that causes a run-time error. Invoking a function using an expression such as 2 * ROUNDN(NUMBER, PLACES) is also valid, as long as the expression is correctly used within a complete FORTRAN statement. In both of these function calls, the variables NUMBER and PLACES have been used as actual arguments. More generally, any valid FORTRAN expression can be used as an actual argument.

The last item that must be provided for is to ensure that the calling program unit "knows" the data type of the value returned by the function. One method of specifying a function's data type is to explicitly declare the function name within the calling program unit in the same way that a variable is declared. Note that in Program 4-10 ROUNDN has been declared as a REAL, which means that ROUNDN returns a REAL value. In the absence of an explicit declaration, the compiler will assign a data type in accordance with FORTRAN's implicit typing rules—see Section 2.2). Notice that the declaration of ROUNDN within MAIN uses the function's name only and the parentheses are omitted.

The placement of the FMAX( ) function after the MAIN program unit in Program 4-10 is a matter of choice. Some programmers prefer to put all subprogram functions at the top of a program and make MAIN the last function listed. We prefer to list the MAIN program unit first because it is the driver function that should give anyone reading the program an idea of what the complete program is about before encountering the details of each function. Either placement approach is acceptable in FORTRAN and you will encounter both styles in your programming work.

As a last example of constructing and calling a function program unit, consider Program 4-11.

Program 4-11

```
      PROGRAM MAIN
        REAL FAHREN, TEMVER
        WRITE(6,*) 'ENTER A FAHRENHEIT TEMPERATURE: '
        READ *, FAHREN
        WRITE(6,*) 'THE CELSIUS EQUIVALENT IS:', TEMVER(FAHREN)
        END
*
      REAL FUNCTION TEMVER(INTEMP)
*   THE FOLLOWING FUNCTION CONVERTS A FAHRENHEIT TEMPERATURE
*   INTO ITS EQUIVALENT CELSIUS VALUE
        REAL INTEMP
        TEMVER = (5.0/9.0) * (INTEMP - 32.0)
        RETURN
        END
```

In reviewing Program 4-11 it is important to note the major items introduced in this section, as they relate to the function TEMVER( ). The first item is the declaration of TEMVER within MAIN. This alerts MAIN to the data type that TEMVER( ) will be returning. The second item to notice in MAIN is the call to TEMVER( ) within the WRITE statement.

The last two items of note concern the coding of the TEMVER( ) function. The first line of TEMVER( ) declares that the function will return a REAL value, and within TEMVER( ) a value of the correct type is assigned to TEMVER. Thus,

TEMVER( ) is internally consistent in sending a real value back to MAIN, and MAIN has been correctly alerted to receive and use the returned integer.

It should also be noted that because subprogram functions are independent program units in their own right, formal argument names, variable names, and statement numbers within a function may be identical to those used in both the MAIN program unit and any other user-written function or subroutine. No confusion exists because each program unit is treated as a separate entity by the compiler. In fact, since individual program units are, by definition, independent, they may even be stored in separate files and compiled separately from any other units. Doing this requires that all the program units be explicitly linked together before the complete program can be run. A discussion of linking separate files is contained in Appendix A.

Caution

It is important to know that when a variable is used as an actual calling argument, the called function receives direct access to the variable. This means that the function can inadvertently alter a calling program unit's variable. For example, the calling statement ROUNDN(NUMBER,PLACES) in Program 4-10 gives ROUNDN( ) access to MAIN's variables NUMBER and PLACES, even though these variables are "known" as P and N within ROUNDN( ). Thus, if the assignment statement P = 22.5 is contained in the function, both the value in P and the value in NUMBER, within MAIN, are changed. The reason for this, as illustrated in Figure 4-16, is that both NUMBER and P refer to the same storage location and are simply different names for the same variable. Similarly, both PLACES and N refer to the same variable stored in memory. Because of this equivalence it is important that functions never assign values to their arguments.

If a function must use an argument in a way that will alter its value, the argument should first be assigned to a new variable declared within the function. This variable name should then be used in subsequent expressions in place of the argument name. Then, any change to the variable inside the function, even if the variable has the same name as a variable in another program unit, has no effect outside of the function.

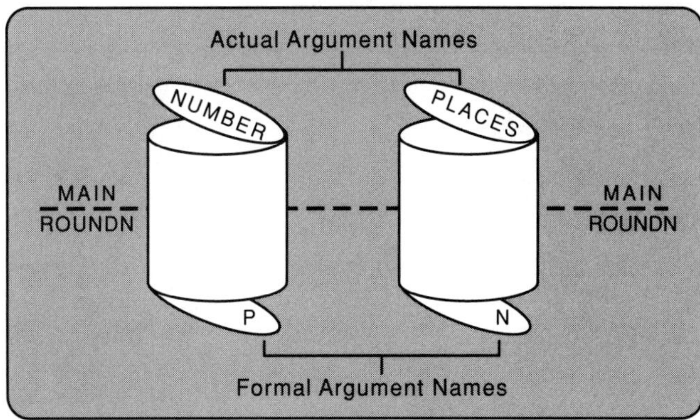

Figure 4-16 The Relationship between Actual and Formal Arguments

Skill Builder Exercises

1. For the following function header and argument declarations, determine the number, type, and order (sequence) of the values that must be passed to the function:

a.
```
INTEGER FUNCTION FTORAL(N)
   INTEGER N
```
b.
```
REAL FUNCTION PRICE(TYPE, YIELD, MATRTY)
   INTEGER TYPE
   REAL YIELD, MATRTY
```
c.
```
REAL FUNCTION YIELD(TYPE, PRICE, MATRTY)
   CHARACTER TYPE
   REAL PRICE, MATRTY
```
d.
```
CHARACTER FUNCTION FLAG(INTRST, PRICE, TIME)
   CHARACTER
   INTRST INTEGER PRICE, TIME
```
e.
```
INTEGER FUNCTION TOTAL(RATE, AMOUNT)
   REAL RATE, AMOUNT
```
f.
```
REAL FUNCTION ROI(A,B,C,D,E,F)
   INTEGER A,D,F
   CHARACTER B
   REAL C,E
```
g.
```
REAL FUNCTION GETVAL(ITEM, ITER, DFLAG, DELIM)
   CHARACTER ITEM, DFLAG
   REAL ITER
   INTEGER DELIM
```
h.
```
CHARACTER FUNCTION LOCASE(C)
   CHARACTER C
```

2. For each of the function headers listed in Exercise 1, write function declarations that should be included in a program unit that calls the listed function.

3. For the following sections of code, write a variable declaration that should be included in the function for the variable ABNUM.

a.
```
REAL FUNCTION ITEM(A,B,C,D)
         .
         .
   ITEM = ABNUM
   RETURN
   END
```
b.
```
REAL FUNCTION SIM(NUM)
         .
         .
    SIM = ABSNUM
    RETURN
    END
```
c.
```
CHARACTER FUNCTION KEY(LETTER)
         .
         .
    KEY = ABSNUM
```

```
      RETURN
      END
```

d.
```
      INTEGER FUNCTION FACTOR(N)
            .
            .
      FACTOR = ABSNUM
      RETURN
      END
```

4. For each section of code listed in Exercise 3, write a function declaration, variable declaration, and assignment statement that could be used by a calling function to correctly call the above functions and store the returned value.

Programming Exercises

5a. Write a FORTRAN program that returns the fractional part of any user entered number. For example, if the number 256.879 is entered, the number .879 should be displayed. (Hint: Use the INT( ) function.)

b. Enter, compile, and execute the program written for Exercise 5a.

6a. Write a FORTRAN program that accepts an integer argument and determines whether the passed integer is even or odd. (Hint, use the MOD( ) function.)

b. Enter, compile, and execute the program written for Exercise 6a.

7a. Write a function named CHECK, which has three arguments. The first argument should accept an integer number, the second argument a real number, and the third argument a double precision number. The body of the function should just display the values of the data passed to the function when it is called.

(Note: When tracing errors in functions, it is very helpful to have the function display the values it has been passed. Quite frequently, the error is not in what the body of the function does with the data, but in the data received and stored. This type of error occurs when a different data type is passed to the function than the data type specified for the arguments.)

b. Include the function written in Exercise 7a in a working program. Make sure your function is called from the MAIN program unit. Test the function by passing various data to it.

8. As stated in the text, the actual arguments passed to a function must match in number, order, and data type to the formal arguments declared in a function's header line. The program below deliberately creates a data type mismatch both in its arguments and returned value. Enter this program on your system. If your compiler does not detect these errors, note the results when it is run. Try to explain what is happening.

```
*****************************************************************
* THE FOLLOWING DEMONSTRATES THAT DATA TYPES ARE NOT CONVERTED IN *
* FUNCTION CALLS                                                  *
*****************************************************************
```

```
      PROGRAM MAIN
        INTEGER NUM, ANSWER, TRICKY
        REAL SIZE
        NUM = 10
        SIZE = 20.9
        WRITE(6,*) 'BEFORE TRICKY, NUM = ', NUM, 'SIZE = ', SIZE
        ANSWER = TRICKY(NUM,SIZE)
        WRITE(6,*) ' AFTER TRICKY, NUM = ', NUM, 'SIZE = ', SIZE
        WRITE(6,*) ' TRICKY RETURNED AN ANSWER OF ', ANSWER
        END
*
      REAL FUNCTION TRICKY(NUM,SIZE)
        REAL NUM
        INTEGER SIZE
*   THE CALLING PROGRAM UNIT THINKS TRICKY AND NUM ARE INTEGERS
*   AND SIZE IS REAL
        WRITE(6,*) 'IN TRICKY NUM AND SIZE CAME IN AS', NUM, SIZE
        WRITE(6,*) 'IN TRICKY NUM AND SIZE ARE SET TO', NUM, SIZE
        TRICKY = 100.678
        RETURN
        END
```

9a. A second-degree polynomial in x is given by the expression $ax^2 + bx + c$, where a, b, and c are known numbers and a is not equal to zero. Write a function named POLY2(A,B,C,X) that computes and returns the value of a second-degree polynomial for any passed values of a, b, c, and x.

b. Include the function written in Exercise 8a in a working program. Make sure your function is called from the MAIN program unit and test the function by passing various data to it.

10. The programming language Pascal has neither a tangent nor arcsine function. It does, however, have SIN(X) and COS(X). Use the fact that the tangent of an angle is the sine of the angle divided by the cosine to write a subprogram function named MYTAN( ), that returns the tangent of its single angle argument ANG. Test your function by calling it from a program that asks the user for an angle in radians, then prints the results of MYTAN( ) and the intrinsic function TAN( ), for comparison. What values of ANG cause the function to fail?

11. Rewrite the subroutine TOTSEC( ) of Exercise 4 in Section 4.1 as a function of the same name. The function should accept integer arguments of hours, minutes, and seconds and return the total sum of seconds in these arguments. Test your function by calling it from a MAIN program unit that writes the returned value for various inputs.

12. Rewrite the subroutine CONVRT( ) of Exercise 11 in Section 4.1 as a function of the same name. The function should accept integer arguments of day, month, and year and return a single integer value. The return value is obtained by multiplying the year by 10,000, the month by 100, and adding the results to the day. Test the function in a program that prints the day count for various input dates.

13. Functions can return values of any data type, including character strings. To demonstrate this, write the function GETNM( ), a character function with no arguments. GETNM( ) should prompt the user for their name and return what is entered. Make the data type of the function a character with a length specifier of 20. Inside the function, READ directly into the function's name. Test the function in a program that prints the returned name.
14. Although FORTRAN's trigonometric functions, such as SIN( ), COS( ), and TAN( ) expect their arguments in radian measure, angles are more commonly measured in degrees. Write a function named DEGRAD( ) that has a real input argument representing an angle in degrees and returns the radian equivalent. Recall that there are pi radians in 180 degrees. Use this fact and have your function use the PI( ) function developed in this section. Test your function by calling it from a program that prints the radian equivalent of an angle read in as degrees.

4.4 Statement Functions

Frequently the value computed by a function can be calculated using a single statement. These functions are generally simple mathematical statements such as:

```
C = 5.0/9.0 * (F - 32)
RAD = (3.1459 / 180.) * ANGLE
```

$$Y = 6X^2 + 2X + 9$$

$$M = 5XY - 3Z + 24W$$

For functions that can be expressed as a formula in one line, FORTRAN provides a special one-line *statement function.* The general form of a statement function is:

```
function-name(argument list) = expression
```

A statement function has no header line, declaration section, RETURN or END statement. It must be a "one-liner" that is an exact mimic of the formula it is used to evaluate. The function name can be any valid FORTRAN symbolic name, such as the names used for variables. The *argument list* is a list of zero or more variables, where multiple variables must be separated by commas. A variable included in the argument list is referred to as either a *formal* or *dummy* argument (the terms are synonymous). Finally the expression can be any valid FORTRAN expression using constants, the formal arguments of the function, and any other valid variables or functions except the one being defined.

Examples of valid statement functions are

```
FTOC(INTEMP) = 5.0 /9.0 * (INTEMP - 32.0)
PERIM(LENGTH, WIDTH) = LENGTH * WIDTH
TESTD(A,B,C) = A**2 - 4.0 * B * C
```

The first statement function has one formal argument, the second function has two formal arguments, and the third function has three such arguments. As with

FORTRAN's subprogram functions, statement functions cannot reference themselves. Thus, the statement function

```
FACTOR(N) = N * FACTOR(N-1)
```

is invalid.

Unlike subprogram functions, which are independent program units, statement functions cannot be placed in their own separately compiled files. They must be included in the program unit (MAIN, subroutine, or function subprogram) where they are used (called). The statement function's data type and the data type of all its dummy arguments are declared in, and only in, the calling program unit. The statement function is placed after all declaration statements and before any of the calling unit's executable statements. Once this is done, the function can be used in the same manner as all of FORTRAN's intrinsic functions. Program 4-12 illustrates the use of the statement function FTOC( ) within a MAIN program unit.

Program 4-12

```
      PROGRAM MAIN
         REAL FTOC, INTEMP, FAHREN
* HERE IS THE STATEMENT FUNCTION
         FTOC(INTEMP) = 5.0/9.0 * (INTEMP - 32.0)
         WRITE(6,*) 'ENTER A FAHRENHEIT TEMPERATURE: '
         READ *, FAHREN
         WRITE(6,*) 'THE CELSIUS EQUIVALENT IS:', FTOC(FAHREN)
         END
```

The key points to note in Program 4-12 are the declaration statement and the statement immediately following that defines the function FTOC( ). Once the statement function is properly defined, it is called within Program 4-12 in the same manner as both intrinsic and subprogram functions.

One last feature: statement functions can make use of any variable, named constant, intrinsic function, subprogram function whose data type has been declared in the calling program unit's declarations, or other statement function defined earlier in the calling program unit. Using other functions within a statement function is sometimes useful but can make programs less readable.

Exercises

1. Write a statement function named CTOF( ) that converts a Celsius temperature to its equivalent Fahrenheit value making use of the formula *Fahrenheit = 9.0 /5.0 Celsius + 32*. Include CTOF( ) in a MAIN program unit that passes various values to the function and displays the returned value. Compile and execute your program and manually verify the converted temperatures displayed.

2. Write a statement function named MULT( ) that accepts two real numbers as arguments, multiplies these two numbers, and returns the result. Include MULT( ) in a MAIN program unit that passes various values to the function and displays the returned value. Manually verify that the displayed value is correct.

3. Write a statement function named HYPTNS( ) that accepts the lengths of two sides of a right triangle and determines the triangle's hypotenuse. (The hypotenuse of a right triangle is equal to the square root of the sum of each side squared.)

   Include HYPTNS( ) in a MAIN program unit and verify that the function works properly by passing various values to it, displaying the returned value, and checking that the displayed value is correct.

4. Write a statement function named POLY(A,B,C,X) that computes and returns the value of the polynomial $ax^2 + bx + c$, for any passed values of a, b, c, and x. Include the function POLY( ) in a working program and test the function by passing various data to it, displaying the returned value, and checking that the displayed value is correct.

5. Write a statement function named ABSDIF(X,Y) that returns the absolute value of the difference between two real numbers. For example, the function call ABSDIF(-1,-10) should return the value 9, and the call ABSDIF(-2,10) should return the value 12. Include the function ABSDIF( ) in a MAIN program unit and test the function by passing various numbers to it, displaying the returned value, and checking that the displayed value is correct.

6a. Write a statement function named FRACPT( ) that returns the fractional part of any real number passed to the function. For example, if the number 256.879 is passed to FRACPT( ), the number 0.879 should be returned. Have the function FRACPT( ) call the intrinsic function INT( ). The number returned by FRACPT( ) can then be determined as the number passed to it less its integer part.

b. Include the function written in Exercise 6a in a working program. Make sure your function is called from MAIN and correctly returns a value to MAIN. Have MAIN use a WRITE statement to display the returned value. Test the function by passing various data to it and verifying the displayed value.

7a. Write a statement function named ROUND( ) that rounds any real value to two decimal places. Rounding to two decimal places is obtained using the following steps:

Step 1: Multiply the passed number by 10**2
Step 2: Add 0.5 to the number obtained in Step 1
Step 3: Take the integer part of the number obtained in Step 3
Step 4: Divide the result of Step 3 by 10**2

b. Include the function written in Exercise 7a in a working program. Make sure your function is called from MAIN and correctly returns a value to MAIN. Have MAIN use a WRITE statement to display the returned value. Test the function by passing various data to it and verifying the displayed value.

8a. Modify the statement function written for Exercise 7a to accept two values. The second passed value is the number of decimal places that the first passed value should be rounded to. For example, ROUND(27.6485,2) should return the value 27.65 and ROUND(27.6485,3) should return the value 27.649.

b. Include the function written in Exercise 8a in a working program. Make sure your function is called from MAIN and correctly returns a value to MAIN. Have MAIN use a WRITE statement to display the returned value. Test the function by passing various data to it and verifying the displayed value.

4.5 Applications

In this section we present two applications using subprograms. In the first application we create a random number generator subroutine. In the second application a complete program using subroutines, subprogram functions, and statement functions is presented to calculate age norms.

Application 1: Random Number Generation

There are many mathematical and engineering problems in which probability must be considered or statistical sampling techniques must be used. For example, in simulating automobile traffic flow or telephone usage patterns, statistical models are required. Additionally, applications such as simple computer games and more involved "strategy games" in business and science can only be described statistically. All of these statistical models require the generation of random numbers. Conventionally, random number generators are used to produce random numbers within the range 0.0 to 1.0, which means that any number within this range is as likely to occur as any other number.

One method of generating random numbers is the power residue method. In one version of this method a suitable n digit "seed" number, where n is an even number, is multiplied by the value $(10^{n/2} - 3)$. Using the lowest n digits of the result (the "residue") produces a new seed. Dividing the new seed by 10^n creates a random number within the range 0.0 to 1.0. Continuing this procedure produces a series of random numbers and new seeds, with each new seed number used as the seed for the next random number. If the original seed has four or more digits (n equal to or greater than 4) and is not divisible by either two or five, this procedure yields $5 \times 10^{(n-2)}$ random numbers before a sequence of numbers repeats itself. For example, starting with a 6-digit seed (n = 6), such as 654321, a series of $5 \times 10^4 = 50{,}000$ random numbers can be generated. Using a power residue algorithm, we will write a subroutine random number generator. This subroutine will be used in subsequent chapters to simulate a coin tossing and other statistical experiments.

The specific power residue algorithm employed consists of the following steps:

1. Have the subroutine accept a six-digit integer seed that will be used to generate a random number.

2. Multiply the seed number by 997, which is 10^3 - 3.
3. Extract the lower 6 digits of the result produced by step 2. Use this random number as the next seed.
4. Divide the result of step 3 by 10^6 to force the random number within the range 0.0 to 1.0.

Thus, if the user-entered seed number is 654321 (step 1), the first random number generated is calculated as follows:

2. 654321 * 997 = 652358037
3. Extract the lower 6 digits of the number obtained in step 2. This is accomplished using a standard programming "trick". The trick involves:
   3a. Dividing the number by 10^6 = 1000000
       For example, 652358037 / 1000000 = 652.358037
   3b. Taking the integer part of the result of step 3a.
       For example, INT(652.358037) = 652
   3c. Multiplying the previous result by 10^6
       For example, 652×10^6 = 652000000
   3d. Subtracting this result from the original number
       For example, 652358037 - 652000000 = 358037
       This value is returned as the new seed.
4. 358037 / 10^6 = .358037, which is the random number generated between 0.0 and 1.0. This value is also returned by the subroutine.

   All of these steps can be incorporated into the subroutine RANDOM( ).

```
SUBROUTINE RANDOM(SEED,RANDX)
  INTEGER SEED
  REAL RANDX
  SEED = 997.0 * SEED - INT(997.0 * SEED/1.E6)*1.E6
  RANDX = SEED / 1.E6
  RETURN
  END
```

In this subroutine, steps 2 and 3 of the algorithm are performed by the expression *997.0 * SEED - INT(997.0 * SEED/1.E6)*1.E6* used on the right-hand side of the first assignment statement. Assigning the value obtained from this expression to the argument SEED alters the value in this dummy argument. Thus, this argument is used for both input and output from the subroutine. The second assignment statement in the subroutine scales the random number in SEED to be within the desired range of 0.0 to 1.0.

Program 4-13 provides a driver unit for the RANDOM( ) subroutine to initially verify its operation.

Program 4-13

```
      PROGRAM MAIN
        INTEGER SD
        REAL RNDNUM
        SD = 654321
        CALL RANDOM(SD,RNDNUM)
        WRITE(6,10) RNDNUM
   10   FORMAT(1X,'THE RETURNED RANDOM NUMBER IS ', F8.6)
        END
*
      SUBROUTINE RANDOM(SEED,RANDX)
        INTEGER SEED
        REAL RANDX
        SEED = INT(997.0 * SEED - INT(997.0 * SEED/1.E6)*1.E6)
        RANDX = SEED / 1.E6
        RETURN
       END
```

Following is a sample run using Program 4-13.

```
THE RETURNED RANDOM NUMBER IS  .358037
```

In Chapter 6, we will see how to expand Program 4-13 to produce a series of random numbers. This series, which will vary depending on the initial SEED value passed to RANDOM( ), can then be used to simulate a variety of statistical applications. In practice, the original SEED value is itself obtained randomly, such as the time of day, so that no two identical series of random numbers are generated.

Application 2: Age Norms

A fairly common procedure in child development is to establish normal ranges for height and weight as they relate to a child's age. These normal ranges are frequently referred to as *age norms*. In this application we develop a program for calculating both the expected height of a child between the ages of six and 11 and the deviation of this height norm to an actual child's height.

For our application let us assume that as a part of a study on child development we have gathered various statistics on a group of normally maturing children between the ages of six and 11 years. From this data we have developed the following formula to predict the normal height, in inches, of a child in this age group:

$$\text{Normal Height} = -0.25\,(\text{Age} - 6)^2 + 3.5\,(\text{Age} - 6) + 45$$

Using this formula we now develop a program to calculate and display the normal height for a child between six and 11 years old, and the percent difference from a child's actual height. The percent difference is given by the formula:

$$\text{Percent Difference} = (100)\ \frac{|\text{Actual Height - Normal Height}|}{\text{Normal Height}}$$

This problem, with a few minor but important conversion issues, is a classic application of the Problem Solver Algorithm presented in Section 4.2. For this particular application the algorithm takes the form:

Get the child's age and height as inputs
Calculate a normal height and percent difference
Display the calculated values

The top-level structure diagram corresponding to this algorithm is shown in Figure 4-17. As each module is developed and refined, additional program units may be called from these top-level modules.

Although the modular approach permits us to develop modules in any order, the input module is typically constructed first to ensure that we understand the data that we will be working with. For this problem we require two inputs, the age and height of a child. There is one complication here, because age is typically given in years and months, while the formula for the normal height requires age in years. To convert an age input as years and months, we will construct a one-line statement function that is contained within our input subroutine. Following is a subroutine named GETKID( ) that performs the required input task, including the age conversion function.

```
      SUBROUTINE GETKID(AGE, HEIGHT)
        INTEGER YRS, MOS, HEIGHT, Y, M
        REAL AGE, YEARS
* STMT FUNCTION TO CONVERT YEARS AND MONTHS TO DECIMAL NO. OF YRS
        YEARS(Y,M) = REAL(Y) + REAL(M)/12.0
        WRITE(6,*) 'HOW OLD (IN YEARS) IS THIS CHILD?'
        READ(5,*) YRS
        WRITE(6,*) 'HOW MANY MONTHS SINCE THE CHILD''S BIRTHDAY?'
        READ(5,*) MOS
        AGE = YEARS(YRS,MOS)
        WRITE(6,*) 'ENTER THE CHILD''S HEIGHT (IN INCHES): '
        READ(5,*) HEIGHT
        RETURN
        END
```

The subroutine GETKID( ) is rather straightforward. It prompts the user for a child's age, in years and months, and the child's height. Using the statement function YEARS, it converts the entered age data into a decimal number, and returns the age and height to its calling program unit via its two dummy arguments AGE and HEIGHT. We will test GETKID( ) by constructing a driver program for the complete program structure illustrated in Figure 4-17, using stubs for the remaining two subroutines.

The requirements for this MAIN program unit is that it first call GETKID( ) to obtain the child's age and height. It must then pass these two values, as inputs, to a calculation module that will return two values: a normal height and percent difference between the calculated normal height and actual height. Finally, the MAIN program unit must pass the two calculated values to a display program unit. Arbi-

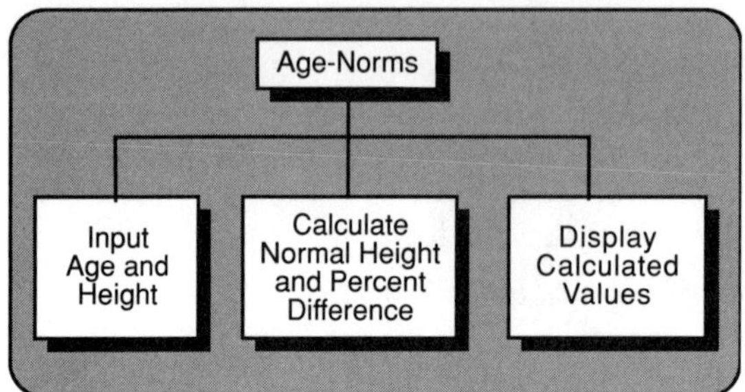

Figure 4-17 Top-Level Structure Diagram for AGE-NORMS Program

trarily naming the calculation and display subroutines as NORMS( ) and SHOWIT( ), respectively, permits us to write the "skeleton" driver unit contained in Program 4-14.

Program 4-14

```
      PROGRAM MAIN
        INTEGER HEIGHT, NORMHT
        REAL AGE, DIFFHT
        CALL GETKID(AGE, HEIGHT)
        CALL NORMS(AGE, HEIGHT, NORMHT, DIFFHT)
        CALL SHOWIT(NORMHT, DIFFHT)
        END
***
      SUBROUTINE GETKID(AGE, HEIGHT)
        INTEGER YRS, MOS, HEIGHT, Y, M
        REAL AGE, YEARS
* STMT FUNCTION TO CONVERT YEARS AND MONTHS TO DECIMAL NO. OF YRS
        YEARS(Y,M) = REAL(Y) + REAL(M)/12.0
        WRITE(6,*) 'HOW OLD (IN YEARS) IS THIS CHILD?'
        READ(5,*) YRS
        WRITE(6,*) 'HOW MANY MONTHS SINCE THE CHILD''S BIRTHDAY?'
        READ(5,*) MOS
        AGE = YEARS(YRS,MOS)
        WRITE(6,*) 'ENTER THE CHILD''S HEIGHT (IN INCHES): '
        READ(5,*) HEIGHT
        RETURN
        END
*** THE FOLLOWING IS A STUB FOR NORMS( )
      SUBROUTINE NORMS(AGE, HEIGHT, NORMHT, DIFFHT)
        INTEGER HEIGHT, NORMHT
        REAL AGE, DIFFHT
        WRITE(6,*) 'INTO NORMS'
        WRITE(6,*) ' AGE = ', AGE, '    HEIGHT = ', HEIGHT
```

(continued on next page)

(continued from previous page)

```
          NORMHT = 10
          DIFFHT = 2.5
          RETURN
          END
*** THE FOLLOWING IS A STUB FOR SHOWIT( )
        SUBROUTINE SHOWIT(NORMHT, DIFFHT)
          INTEGER NORMHT
          REAL DIFFHT
          WRITE(6,*) 'INTO SHOWIT'
          WRITE(6,*) ' NORMHT = ', NORMHT, '     DIFFHT = ', DIFFHT
          RETURN
          END
```

Notice that the MAIN program unit in Program 4-14 uses two arguments to accept the data returned by GETKID( ). It then calls NORMS( ) with four arguments, two of which will be used to pass the data received from GETKID( ), AGE and HEIGHT, and two new argument names, NORMHT and DIFFHT, that will be used to return the calculated normal height and percent difference. Finally it calls SHOWIT( ) to display the two arguments calculated in NORMS( ). The program is then completed by using two stub subroutines, one for NORMS( ) and one for SHOWIT( ). These stubs are constructed to individually display both a message indicating that each subroutine has been called and the values of any passed arguments. Additionally, the stub for NORMS( ) sets arbitrary values into the arguments NORMHT and DIFFHT. When NORMS( ) is fully developed, these values will be replaced by appropriate calculated values. For now, however, the values can be passed on to SHOWIT( ) to verify correct argument transmission and receipt.

The following is the output from a sample run of Program 4-14.

```
HOW OLD (IN YEARS) IS THIS CHILD?
10
HOW MANY MONTHS SINCE THE CHILD'S BIRTHDAY?
6
ENTER THE CHILD'S HEIGHT (IN INCHES):
50
INTO NORMS
AGE =       10.500000     HEIGHT =           50
INTO SHOWIT
NORMHT =             10     DIFFHT =          2.500000
```

As this output shows, the GETKID( ) program unit is working properly in obtaining an age and height, converting an age of 10 years and 6 months to an equivalent decimal value of 10.5, and returning the age and height to MAIN. Similarly, NORMS( ) correctly receives the transmitted age and height and returns two values. These values, in turn, are successfully passed to SHOWIT( ) for display.

To complete the program requires that the subroutines NORMS( ) and SHOWIT( ) be fully developed. Since SHOWIT( ) is the simpler of the two subroutines, we will develop it first. This "out of order" development is not unusual; in fact, it is the same technique used by motion picture producers to complete a movie. Here we take advantage of the fact that displaying the results is rather trivial if someone else did the actual calculations. Besides, completing the output section gives us the means to verify the calculation section when it is completed. Following is the SHOWIT( ) subroutine:

```
      SUBROUTINE SHOWIT(NORMHT, DIFFHT)
        INTEGER NORMHT
        REAL DIFFHT
        WRITE(6,10) NORMHT
        WRITE(6,20) DIFFHT
10      FORMAT(1X,'THE AVERAGE HEIGHT IN INCHES IS: ', I3)
20      FORMAT(1X,'  THE ACTUAL HEIGHT DEVIATES BY: ', F6.2,'%')
        RETURN
        END
```

The SHOWIT( ) subroutine can either be placed in its own file and compiled separately, or placed directly into Program 4-14 as a replacement for the SHOWIT( ) stub. Now we are ready to work on the final subroutine NORMS( ).

We want NORMS( ) to return both the calculated normal height and the percent difference of the child's actual height from normal. Following is the NORMS( ) subroutine:

```
        SUBROUTINE NORMS(AGE, HEIGHT, NORMHT, DIFFHT)
         INTEGER HEIGHT, NORMHT
         REAL AGE, DIFFHT, AGEDIF, PCDIFF, MINAGE
         PARAMETER(MINAGE = 6.0)
* CALCULATE THE "NORMAL" HEIGHT
         AGEDIF = AGE - MINAGE
         NORMHT = INT(-0.25*(AGEDIF**2) + 3.5*AGEDIF + 45.0)
* CALCULATE THE PERCENT DIFFERENCE FROM THE "NORMAL" HEIGHT
         DIFFHT = PCDIFF(HEIGHT, NORMHT)
         RETURN
         END
***
         REAL FUNCTION PCDIFF(ACTUAL, NORMAL)
         INTEGER ACTUAL, NORMAL
         PCDIFF = ABS(REAL(ACTUAL - NORMAL)) / REAL(NORMAL) * 100.0
         RETURN
         END
```

NORMS( ) illustrates a typical calculation subroutine. It uses two "in" arguments to supply data for the desired calculations and it returns its results in the last two "out" arguments. NORMS( ), has the ability, of course, to alter any of its arguments, including the first two. This is the reason for using the local variable, which was named AGEDIF: if the assignment statement AGE = AGE - MINAGE were used in NORMS( ) the variable AGE in the MAIN program unit would have been changed also.* Such an undesirable modification to an argument's value is called a *side effect*, which is usually avoided through the use of locally declared variables. Also notice that NORMS( ) has its own locally PARAMETERized constant, the "base" age of six years old. Additionally, NORMS( ) calls a function subprogram to calculate the percent difference of the child's actual height from normal. The reason for this is that the calculation of a percent difference is a general computation that can be used in other applications. Thus, the PCDIFF( ) function can be separately compiled and linked to any future module needing this computation. It could even be used once again by our NORMS( ) subroutine, if this program unit was expanded to calculate a normal weight and percent difference of normal to actual weights (see Exercise 16).

Internally, the PCDIFF( ) function declares its arguments as integers, but uses the type conversion function REAL( ) to avoid integer division. Within NORMS( ), the PCDIFF( ) function is declared as returning a real value and then is used in the same manner as an intrinsic function.

Once NORMS( ) has been developed, the complete program, using the final versions of GETKID( ), NORMS( ), SHOWIT( ), and PCDIFF( ) can be run. Program 4-15 illustrates the use of these subroutines within a complete program.

Program 4-15

```
***********************************************************************
* GROWTH: SHOW HOW CLOSE A CHILD'S HEIGHT (AGES 6 - 11) IS TO         *
*   "NORMAL" VALUES"                                                  *
* SUBROUTINES USED:                                                   *
*   GETKID - OBTAIN CHILD'S AGE AND HEIGHT                            *
*   NORMS  - CALCULATE NORMAL HEIGHT AND PERCENT DIFFERENCE           *
*   SHOWIT - DISPLAY THE RESULTS                                      *
***********************************************************************
      PROGRAM GROWTH
        INTEGER HEIGHT, NORMHT
        REAL AGE, DIFFHT
        CALL GETKID(AGE, HEIGHT)
        CALL NORMS(AGE, HEIGHT, NORMHT, DIFFHT)
        CALL SHOWIT(NORMHT, DIFFHT)
        END
***
      SUBROUTINE GETKID(AGE, HEIGHT)
        INTEGER YRS, MOS, HEIGHT
        REAL AGE, YEARS
```

(continued on next page)

* Clearly, the expression AGE - MINAGE could have been used directly in the calculation of NORMHT, eliminating the need for AGEDIF altogether. Doing this results in the assignment statement NORMHT = INT(-0.25*((AGE - MINAGE)**2) + 3.5*(AGE - MINAGE) + 45.0), which is not as clear and requires a continuation line.

(continued from previous page)

```
* STMT FUNCTION TO CONVERT YEARS AND MONTHS TO DECIMAL NO. OF YRS
      YEARS(Y,M) = REAL(Y) + REAL(M)/12.0
      WRITE(6,*) 'HOW OLD (IN YEARS) IS THIS CHILD?'
      READ(5,*) YRS
      WRITE(6,*) 'HOW MANY MONTHS SINCE THE CHILD''S BIRTHDAY?'
      READ(5,*) MOS
      AGE = YEARS(YRS,MOS)
      WRITE(6,*) 'ENTER THE CHILD''S HEIGHT (IN INCHES): '
      READ(5,*) HEIGHT
      RETURN
      END
***
      SUBROUTINE NORMS(AGE, HEIGHT, NORMHT, DIFFHT)
      INTEGER HEIGHT, NORMHT
      REAL AGE, DIFFHT, AGEDIF, PCDIFF, MINAGE
      PARAMETER(MINAGE = 6.0)
* CALCULATE THE "NORMAL" HEIGHT
      AGEDIF = AGE - MINAGE
      NORMHT = INT(-0.25*(AGEDIF**2) + 3.5*AGEDIF +45.0)
* CALCULATE THE PERCENT DIFFERENCE FROM THE "NORMAL" HEIGHT
      DIFFHT = PCDIFF(HEIGHT, NORMHT)
      RETURN
      END
***
      REAL FUNCTION PCDIFF(ACTUAL, NORMAL)
      INTEGER ACTUAL, NORMAL
      PCDIFF = ABS(REAL(ACTUAL - NORMAL)) / REAL(NORMAL) * 100.0
      RETURN
      END
***
      SUBROUTINE SHOWIT(NORMHT, DIFFHT)
      INTEGER NORMHT
      REAL DIFFHT
      WRITE(6,10) NORMHT
      WRITE(6,20) DIFFHT
   10 FORMAT(1X,'THE AVERAGE HEIGHT IN INCHES IS: ', I3)
   20 FORMAT(1X,'  THE ACTUAL HEIGHT DEVIATES BY: ', F6.2, '%')
      RETURN
      END
```

Following is a sample run using Program 4-15.

```
HOW OLD (IN YEARS) IS THIS CHILD?
10
HOW MANY MONTHS SINCE THE CHILD'S BIRTHDAY?
6
ENTER THE CHILD'S HEIGHT (IN INCHES):
50
THE AVERAGE HEIGHT IN INCHES IS:  55
  THE ACTUAL HEIGHT DEVIATES BY:   9.09%
```

Figure 4-18 shows the final structure diagram for Program 4-15.

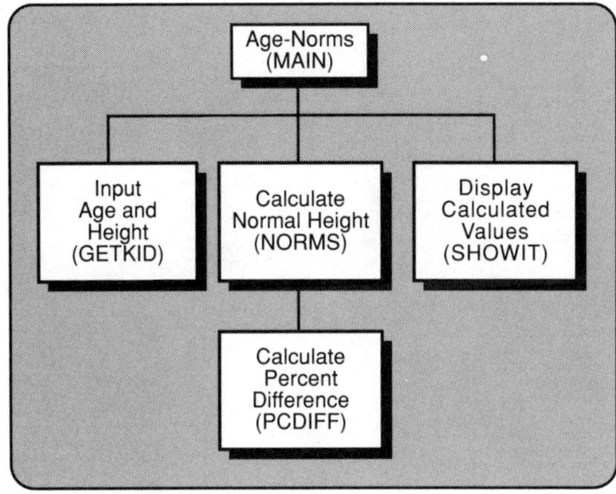

Figure 4-18 Structure Diagram for Program 4-15

Additional Exercises for Chapter 4

1. In relation to the variable and constant declarations and the executable code of a module, where must a statement function definition be placed?
2. Comment on this statement: "All subroutines could be written as function subprograms and all function subprograms could be written as subroutines."
3. Comment on this statement: "You must declare the data type of invoked subprograms in the calling module to avoid type mismatch errors caused by FORTRAN's implicit typing mechanism."
4. Comment on this statement: "The data types of actual and corresponding dummy arguments must match except that FORTRAN will convert reals to integers and vice-versa if required."
5. Assume you have declared the real variable AREA in your MAIN program and a real variable AREA in a subroutine which is not a dummy argument of the subroutine. If you alter the value of AREA in the subroutine, does it alter the value of AREA in the main program?

6. Assume the variables of the previous question refer to corresponding actual and dummy arguments used in a CALL to the subroutine. What effect does altering the value of AREA in the subroutine have on the variable AREA in the main program?

7. Assume you forget to include the statement that assigns a value to the function's name in an integer function named INTVAL that uses no arguments. The compiler does not report this as an error. Assume you call the function with this statement:

```
RESULT = INTVAL( )
```

where RESULT has been declared to be an integer variable. What is the likely value of RESULT after this call?

8. Study the following code. What values are printed?

```
      PROGRAM MAIN
        REAL A, B
        A = 2.4
        B = 5.6
        CALL SWAP(A, B)
        WRITE(6,*) A, B
        END
*
      SUBROUTINE SWAP(X,Y)
        REAL X, Y
        X = Y
        Y = X
        RETURN
        END
```

9. Study the following code. What values are printed?

```
      PROGRAM MAIN
        REAL A, B
        A = 2.4
        B = 5.6
        CALL SWAP(A, B)
        WRITE(*, *) A, B
        END
*
      SUBROUTINE SWAP(X,Y)
        REAL X, Y , TEMP
        TEMP = X
        X = Y
        Y = TEMP
        RETURN
        END
```

10. Instead of using a local variable TEMP inside the SWAP( ) subroutine used in Exercise 9, a programmer decided to pass TEMP as an argument in the following version of SWAP( ). What is the output?

```
      PROGRAM MAIN
        REAL A, B, TEMP
        A = 2.4
        B = 5.6
        CALL SWAP(A, B, TEMP)
        WRITE(*, *) A, B
        END
*
      SUBROUTINE INTSWP(A, B, C)
        REAL A, B, C
        C = A
        A = B
        B = C
        RETURN
        END
```

11. Study the following code. What values are printed?

```
      PROGRAM MAIN
        INTEGER NUM, SNEEKY
        NUM = 3
        WRITE(*, *) SNEEKY(NUM), SNEEKY(NUM), SNEEKY(NUM)
        END
*
      INTEGER FUNCTION SNEEKY(N)
        INTEGER N
        SNEEKY = N + 2
        N = N + 2
        RETURN
        END
```

12. What can you say about the following statement: "A MAIN program unit can directly call a statement function contained in a subroutine it uses."

13. Is the following statement true? "Subroutines and function subprograms cannot make use of MAIN program unit PARAMETERized constants unless they are passed to the subprograms as arguments."

14. True or false? "You can PARAMETERize a dummy argument's value inside a function subprogram to protect its value."

15. What is the output of this program?

```
      PROGRAM MAIN
        REAL VAL1, VAL2, VAL3
        INTEGER RESULT
        VAL1 = 2.0
        VAL2 = 16.0
        VAL3 = 110.56
        CALL DOIT(VAL1, VAL2, VAL3, RESULT)
        WRITE(*, *) RESULT
        END
```

```
*
      SUBROUTINE DOIT(FIRST, SCOND, THIRD, THENBR)
        INTEGER THENBR
        REAL FIRST, SCOND, THIRD
        THNBR = INT(FIRST ** 5 + SQRT(SCOND) + INT(LOG10(THIRD)))
        RETURN
        END
```

Programming Exercises

16. Modify Program 4-15 to calculate a child's normal weight and the percent weight difference, in addition to the calculated height values. Assume the formula for predicting normal weight, in pounds, is given by the formula:
Normal Weight = 0.5 (Age - 6) + 5.0 (Age - 6) + 48

17. By now you have probably realized the intrinsic trigonometric functions SIN(A), COS(A) and TAN(A) sometimes need a little help. Angle measurements are often in degrees, not radians, and it's a nuisance (and potential source of error) remembering to apply the conversion factor. Some extensions of FORTRAN have built-in trig functions that handle input in degrees, but in case yours doesn't, write the functions SINDEG(A), COSDEG(A) and TANDEG(A) that accept angle measurements in degrees and return the appropriate trigonometric relation. Use the user-defined function PI( ), developed in Section 3.3, in your versions.

18. It's just as useful to have inverse trigonometric functions ASINDG(SINE), ACOSDG(COSN) and ATANDG(TNGT) that return angle measurements in degrees instead of radians. Write these functions, using the function subprogram PI( ), developed in Section 4.3, in your versions.

19. An important concept (one that's often needed) in programming is that of a "mirror image" to conversion procedures. In other words, if something is easy to do, it should be just as easy to undo. With this in mind, write the companion subroutine to POLAR( ) used in program 4-19 that's CALLed with the two polar coordinates RAD, ANG (where ANG is an angle in degrees) and returns the rectangular coordinates XCOORD, YCOORD. Use the functions SINDEG and COSDEG you developed in Exercise 17 in your answer. Be sure to test your subroutine with a set of program modules similar to those used to test POLAR( ).

20. In 3-dimensional space, the position of a coordinate can be given by x-y-z rectangular coordinates or by r-θ-φ spherical coordinates. Subroutines to convert from one to the other could be part of a program used in air traffic control radar. Figure 4-19 illustrates the relationship between these coordinate systems.

Conversions from rectangular to spherical are given by:

$$r = \sqrt{x^2 + y^2 + 2^2}$$

$$\theta = \mathrm{TAN}^{-1} \frac{y}{x} \quad x \neq 0$$

$$\phi = \mathrm{COS}^{-1} \left(\frac{Z}{\sqrt{x^2 + y^2 + Z^2}}\right)$$

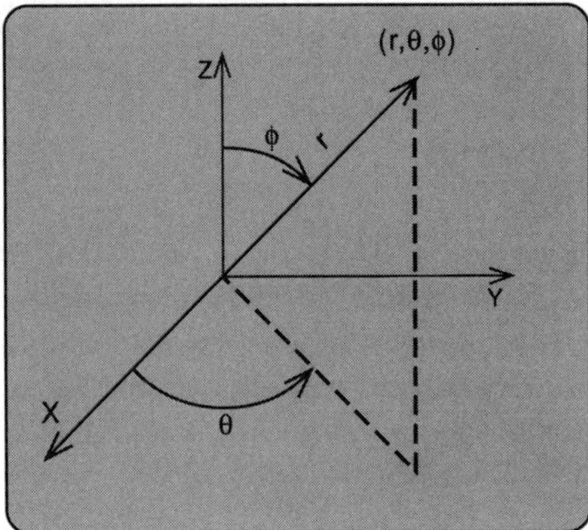

Figure 4-19 Relationship Between Rectangular Spherical Coordinates

and the conversions from spherical to rectangular are:

$$x = \text{r SIN } \phi \text{ COS } \theta$$
$$y = \text{r SIN } \phi \text{ COS } \theta$$
$$z = \text{r COS } \phi$$

a. Write and test the subroutine RCTOSP(X, Y, Z, R, THETA, PHI). Have your subroutine return angles in degree measurement and make use of the functions you developed in Exercise 2.

b. Write and test the companion subroutine SPTORC(R, THETA, PHI, X, Y, Z). Your subroutine should accept input in degree measurement using the functions developed in Exercise 18.

> **Programming Pointer:** We've used a "building-block" approach in Exercises 17 -20. With PI( ) in our library, it was simple to write the trigonometric functions that use degrees. With these functions completed, the rectangular to polar/spherical conversions are more easily developed. Make free use of this technique as you develop programs. It simplifies program development, improves reliability and provides a framework for future growth.

21. When working in the fields of engineering or science, you often need the roots of quadratic equations, equations of the form:

$$f(x) = \text{A}x^2 + \text{B}x + \text{C}$$

These roots can be evaluated by using the quadratic formula:

$$\frac{-\text{B} \pm \sqrt{\text{B}^2 + 4\text{AC}}}{2\text{A}}, \text{A} \neq 0$$

Write the subroutine QROOTS(A, B, C, ROOT1, ROOT2) that returns the two real roots of a quadratic equation if $\text{B}^2 > 4\text{AC}$.

Add this subroutine to your utility module file after testing.

22. The volume of a right circular cylinder is given by its radius squared times its height times π. Assume you've written the function subprogram PI that returns the real value for c. Write the function subprogram that takes two real arguments: RAD, the radius of a cylinder, and HGT, the cylinder's height, and returns the cylinder's volume.

23. Rewrite the function subprogram developed in Exercise 20 as a statement function. Assume all names have been properly declared in the enclosing program module, including the real function PI.

24. Assume there was no intrinsic absolute value function ABS(X) in FORTRAN. Write the real function ABSR that returns the absolute value of its single real argument. Your function must not alter the value of the argument. (Hint: think what happens when you square a number. There's a better way to do this but we haven't gotten to selection yet.)

25. A value that is sometimes useful is the greatest common divisor of two integers N1 and N2. A famous mathematician, Euclid, discovered an efficient method to do this over two thousand years ago. We'll be able to write it in FORTRAN soon, but for now we'll have to settle for a stub. Write the integer function subprogram stub GCD(N1, N2). For now, have it return a value that suggests it received its arguments correctly. (N1 + N2 is a good choice of return values. Why isn't N1 / N2 a good choice?)

26. Write the subroutine ROTATE(I1, I2, I3) that shifts the integer values contained in I1, I2 and I3 to the left by performing a circular shift. A left circular shift means I1 takes on I2's value, I2 takes on I3's value and I3 takes on I1's value (before it was replaced by I2). This may seem to be pointless, but circular shifters are common computer components. Usually, before a piece of hardware is constructed, it is tested out in a software simulation.

27. Write the function subprogram PMT that has three arguments PRI, INT, and MOS. PRI is the amount financed, INT is the yearly percentage rate of interest and MOS is the number of months financed. PMT returns the monthly payment according to the following formula:

$$\text{PMT} = \frac{\text{P}}{\left[\frac{1-(1+i)^{-n}}{i}\right]}$$

where P = principle financed, i = monthly interest rate (not a percentage) and n = months financed. Test your function. What argument values cause it to malfunction (and should not be input)?

28. You are bracing a tower with three supporting members as shown in Figure 4-20. The supports descend toward the ground at an angle of θ from the horizontal (in degrees) and are attached to the tower at HGT feet above the ground. You are interested in the length of each support LEN and the distance from the base of the tower SPAN to place each lower support footing. Write the subroutine TOWER that takes HGT and THETA as input arguments and returns LEN and SPAN.

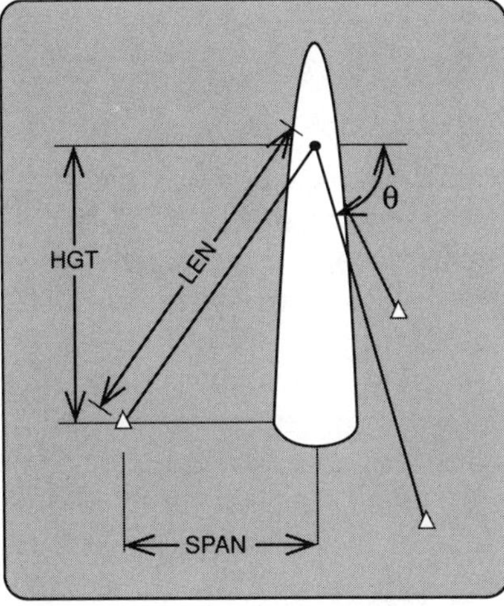

Figure 4-20

29. Write the subroutine SEPRAT( ) that has one real input argument VALUE and two output arguments WHOLPT and FRACPT. SEPRAT returns the whole number portion of VALUE in the integer argument WHOLPT and the fractional part of VALUE in the real argument FRACPT.

30. Write the statement function FTOCEL that converts a Fahrenheit temperature to a Celsius temperature. Assume all names used have been properly declared in the using program. Use the formula

$$\text{Celsius} = \frac{5}{9}\ (\text{Fahrenheit} - 32)$$

4.6 Common Programming Errors

1. The most common and most difficult error to detect and correct is a mismatch between actual and dummy arguments. These errors fall into the following categories:

a. The count of actual arguments is not the same as the count of dummy arguments.

b. The order of actual arguments and intended corresponding dummy arguments does not match. This transposition can lead to very confusing errors, especially if the argument data types are identical.

c. The failure to explicitly declare the data type of all arguments in both the calling and called module. FORTRAN's implicit typing mechanism can cause a type mismatch.

d. The data type of each actual argument does not exactly match the type of each corresponding dummy argument. There is no type conversion, even between reals and integers. To illustrate what does happen when a mismatch occurs, assume that a subroutine named CIRCLE has the header line:

```
SUBROUTINE CIRCLE(RADIUS)
```

where RADIUS is declared as a real argument. Now assume that this subroutine is inadvertently called by the statement

CALL CIRCLE(IRAD)

where IRAD is an integer variable. Although you might expect that CIRCLE would convert the passed integer argument into a real value, this is not what happens at all. What does happen is illustrated in Figure 4-2

As illustrated in Figure 4-21, the actual argument IRAD and its equivalent dummy argument within the subroutine, RADIUS, both reference the same starting location in memory. Thus, the computer's internal code for the calling unit's actual integer argument is interpreted within the subroutine as the code of a real value. This creates a number within the subroutine that bears no obvious relationship to the calling unit's actual integer argument.

The simplest way to prevent these errors is to display all passed values within a subroutine's body before any calculations are made. Once the verification has taken place, the display can be dispensed with. Similarly, all values passed back to the calling unit should be initially displayed to ensure that correct values have been received from the subroutine.

2. Failure to correctly declare the data type of a user-defined function in the calling module and failure to declare the function's type in its definition. They must match. A mismatch can cause bizarre return values but is sometimes detected during linking.
3. Failure to assign a return value to a function before a RETURN statement is encountered or failure to assign values to dummy return argument in subroutines. The return value of a function is undefined in this case. Arguments that were not altered retain their previous values.
4. Failure to include an empty parentheses in both the call and definition of a function without arguments. FORTRAN will treat the function name as an ordinary variable, not a function.
5. Failure to use the keywords SUBROUTINE or FUNCTION in the definition of these subprograms. This causes a compiler error.

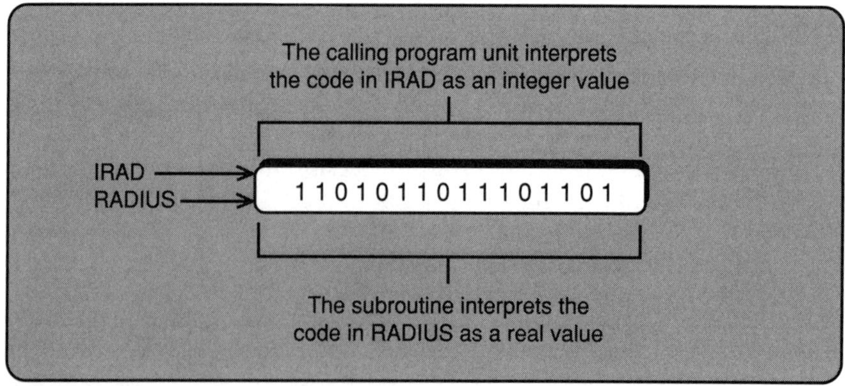

Figure 4-21 Argument Type Mismatch Error

6. Failure to link all needed subprogram definitions with the MAIN program unit. The linker will report an error.
7. Inadvertently changing the value of a dummy argument inside a subprogram when the calling module did not expect the change. This is an unwanted side effect that can be detected by writing all actual argument values after the return from the call.
8. Using a WRITE statement inside a function whose return value is directly printed in a WRITE statement in the calling module. Overcome this error by assigning the return value to a calling module variable, then print the value of the variable.
9. An attempt to change the value of a dummy argument inside a subprogram when the actual argument is either an expression, function result or constant. This usually causes a run-time error.
10. Inadvertently having a subprogram call itself or establishing a circular chain of calls that lead back to the original subprogram. This causes either a compile error or a run-time error.

4.7 Things to Remember

1. The general form of a subroutine is:

```
SUBROUTINE name(arg1, arg2, ...)
  declarations
  executable statements
  RETURN
  END
```

   The arguments of a subroutine are referred to as either *formal* or *dummy arguments*. The declaration of the formal arguments determines the data type of these arguments.
2. A subroutine is called using a CALL statement having the form

```
CALL subroutine-name(arg1, arg2, ...)
```

   The arguments in the CALL statement are referred to as *actual arguments*. The data type, number, and order of the actual arguments used in the CALL statement must agree with the data type, number, and order of the corresponding dummy arguments in the subroutine's argument list. Actual arguments are usually variables, constants, expressions, or function results.
3. The general form of a subprogram function is:

```
type FUNCTION name(arg1, arg2, ...)
  declarations
  executable statements
  name = expression
  RETURN
  END
```

4. Function statements are defined at the beginning of a program unit, immediately following the last declaration statement, and have the general form:

   ```
   function-name(argument list) = expression
   ```

   For example, the function statement

   ```
   AREA(BASE,HEIGHT) = 0.5 * BASE * HEIGHT
   ```

   can be used to calculate the area of a triangle.
5. All functions (intrinsic, statement, and subprogram) calculate and return a single value.
6. A function's type determines the data type of the value returned by the function.
7. Both subprogram and statement functions are called by giving the function name and passing any data to it in the parentheses following the name.
8. The data type of statement and subprogram functions should be declared in the calling function and determines the type of value received by the calling program. In the absence of an explicit specification, the data type of the returned value is implicitly typed using FORTRAN's implicit typing rule. This rule types any function or variable beginning in either I, J, K, L, M, or N as an integer and all other names as reals.
9. The arguments passed to a function must agree in type, order, and number with the function's formal arguments.
10. Scope: Every name (argument, variable, named constant, and statement function) used in a program has a scope, which determines where in the program the name can be used. The scope of all names declared within a program unit is *local.* This means that the name only has meaning within the program unit that declared it. If the same variable name is used in two different program units, two distinct variables are created.
11. Use: Use a function when a single return value is needed. Use a subroutine in all other situations. Each subprogram should be designed to perform one logical task, not many tasks. If a subprogram starts to become complicated by performing many tasks, break it into smaller subprogram units. A rule of thumb is that the length of a subprogram should not exceed one standard page (see Section 4.8).
12. Development Strategies: Use the top-down approach. Refine and test program modules in stages. Use stubs to help in intermediate testing. Include generalized program units in a separate program utility file for future use.

4.8 A Closer Look: Programming Costs

Any project that requires a computer incurs both hardware and software costs. The costs associated with the hardware consist of all costs relating to the physical components used in the system. These components include the computer itself, peripherals, and any other items, such as air conditioning, cabling, and associated equipment

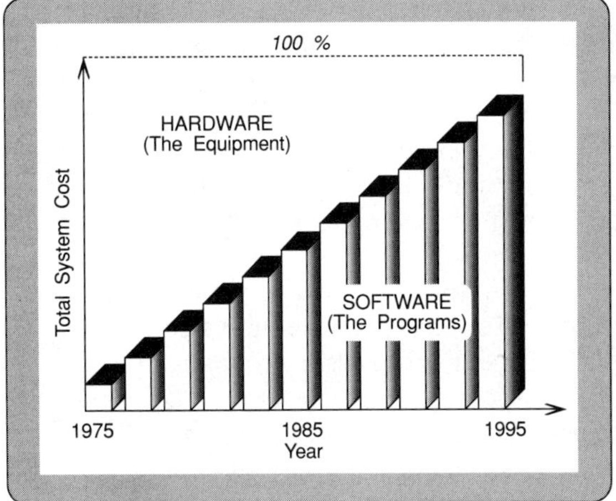

Figure 4-22 Software Is the Major Cost of Most Engineering Projects

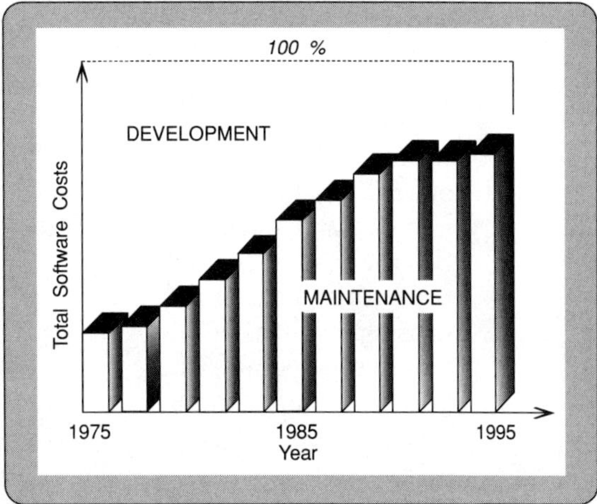

Figure 4-23 Maintenance Is the Predominant Software Cost

required by the project. The software costs include all costs associated with initial program development and subsequent program maintenance. As illustrated in Figure 4-22, the major cost of most engineering projects, be they research or development, has become the software costs.

The reason that software costs contribute so heavily to total project costs is that these costs are closely related to human productivity (labor intensive), while hardware costs are more directly related to manufacturing technologies. For example, microchips that cost over $500 per chip ten years ago can now be purchased for under $1 per chip.

It is far easier, however, to dramatically increase manufacturing productivity by a thousand, with the consequent decrease in hardware costs, than it is for people to double either the quantity or quality of their thought output. So as hardware costs have plummeted, software productivity and their associated costs have remained rather constant. Thus, the percentage of software costs to total system costs (hardware plus software) has increased dramatically.

Looking at just software costs (see Figure 4-23), we find that the maintenance of existing programs accounts for approximately 75 percent of these costs. Maintenance includes the correction of newly found errors and the addition of new features and modifications to existing programs.

Students generally find it strange that maintenance is the predominant software cost because they are accustomed to solving a problem and moving on to a different one. Science and engineering fields do not operate this way. In these fields, one application or idea is typically built on a previous one, and may require months or years of work. This is especially true in programming. Once a program is written, new features become evident. Advances in technology such as networking, fiber optics, genetic engineering, and graphical displays also open up new software possibilities.

How easily a program can be maintained (debugged, modified, or enhanced) is related to the ease with which the program can be read and understood, which is directly related to the modularity with which the program was constructed. Modular programs are constructed using one or more program units, each of which performs a clearly defined and specific task. If each program unit (module) is clearly structured internally and the relationship between program units clearly specified, each unit can be tested and modified with a minimum of disturbance or undesirable interaction with the other units in the program.

Just as hardware designers frequently locate the cause of a hardware problem by using test methods designed to isolate the offending hardware subsystem, modular software permits the software engineer to similarly isolate program errors to specific software units.

Once a bug has been isolated, or a new feature needs to be added, the required changes can be confined to appropriate program units, without radically affecting other program units. Only if the affected unit requires different input data or produces different outputs are its surrounding program units affected. Even in this case the changes to the surrounding modules are clear; they must either be modified to output the data needed by the changed module or changed to accept the new output data. Modules help the programmer determine where the changes must be made, while the internal structure of the module itself determines how easy it will be to make the change.

Although there are no hard and fast rules for well-written program units, specific guidelines do exist. The total number of instructions in a unit generally should not exceed 50 lines. This allows the complete program unit to fit on a standard 8 1/2-by-11-inch sheet of paper for ease of reading. Each program unit should have one entrance point and one exit point. This makes it easy to trace the flow of data when errors are detected.

As we have stressed throughout the text, the instructions contained within a module should use variable names that describe the data and are self-documenting. This means that they tell what is happening without a lot of extra comments. For example, the statement

```
X = (A - B) / (C - D)
```

does not contain intelligent variable names that give an indication of what is being calculated. A more useful set of instructions, assuming that a slope is being calculated, is:

```
SLOPE = (Y2 - Y1) / (X2 - X1)
```

Here, the statement itself "tells" what the data represents, what is being calculated, and how the calculation is being performed. Always keep in mind that the goal is to produce programs that make sense to any programmer reading them, at any time. The use of mnemonic data names makes excessive comments unnecessary. The program should, however, contain a sufficient number of comments explaining what a program unit does and any other pertinent information that would be helpful to other programmers; but excessive comments are usually a sign of insufficient program design or poorly constructed coding.

Another sign of a good program is the use of indentation to alert a reader to nested statements and indicate where one statement ends and another begins. Consider the pseudocode listed in the module "What to Wear" shown in Figure 4-24.

```
if it is below 60 degrees
if it is snowing
wear your lined raincoat
else
wear a topcoat
if it is below 40 degrees
wear a sweater also
if it is below 30 degrees
wear a jacket also
else if it is raining
wear an unlined raincoat
```

Figure 4-24 Version 1— What to Wear

Because the if and else statement matchings are not clearly indicated, the instructions in the module are open to multiple interpretations. For example, using Figure 4-24, try to determine what to wear if the temperature is 35 degrees and it is raining. Now consider Version 2 of "What to Wear" in Figure 4-25.

```
if it is below 60 degrees
   if it is snowing
      wear your lined raincoat
   else
      wear a topcoat
   if it is below 40 degrees
   wear a sweater also
      if it is below 30 degrees
         wear a jacket also
 else if it is raining
   wear an unlined raincoat
```

Figure 4-25 Version 2 — What to Wear

Version 2 is indented, making it clear what the selection criteria are. If it is below 60 degrees the set of instructions indented underneath the first if will be executed, else the condition `if it is raining` will be checked.

It should be noted that this second version of the module "What to Wear" is not the only possible interpretation of how the if-else statements of Version 1 could be matched. We leave it as an exercise to construct additional versions of "What to Wear."

5 DO Loops and Data Files

Chapter 5

5.1 DO Loops

5.2 DO Loop Programming Techniques

5.3 Nested Loops

5.4 List-Directed Data Files

5.5 User-Formatted Data Files

5.6 Applications

5.7 Common Programming Errors

5.8 Things to Remember

5.9 A Closer Look: Writing Control Codes

The programs examined so far have been useful in illustrating the correct structure of FORTRAN programs and in introducing fundamental input, output, and assignment capabilities. By this time you should have gained enough experience to be comfortable with the concepts and mechanics of the FORTRAN programming process. It is now time to move up a level in our knowledge and abilities.

The real power of most computer programs resides in their ability to repeat the same calculation or sequence of instructions many times over, each time using different data, without the necessity of rerunning the program for each new set of data. In the first part of this chapter we show how to construct DO loops using FORTRAN's DO statement. A DO loop permits any processing task to be repeated a given number of times. In the second part of this chapter we introduce the concept of a Data File, which provides the programmer with the ability to store data on a computer independent of any program. As we will see, the structure of most data files makes them ideal candidates for processing using DO loops.

5.1 DO Loops

Many programming problems involve the need to repeat a task a given number of times. For example, suppose we wanted to input and convert five Fahrenheit temperatures to their Celsius equivalent. To do this we could repeat the following three lines of code five times:

```
WRITE(6,*) 'ENTER A FAHRENHEIT TEMPERATURE'
READ(5,*) FAHREN
CELSUS = (5.0/9.)*(FAHREN - 32.0)
WRITE(6,*) '  THE EQUIVALENT CELSIUS VALUE IS: ', CELSUS
```

A much easier approach to this problem, since it involves repeating the same task five times, is to use a DO loop. In pseudocode a DO loop is described as follows:

```
Do the following statements n times
 statement 1
 statement 2
    .
    .
 statement m
Enddo
```

As indicated by the pseudocode, one statement is needed to define how many times the task is to be repeated and one statement is needed to mark the last statement in the repeated task. In FORTRAN the statement that defines the number of repetitions is a DO statement and the statement commonly used to mark the end of the task is a CONTINUE statement. (In both FORTRAN 90 and DEC-VAX compilers, an END DO statement can be used as the last statement of the loop.) Using a CONTINUE statement, the general form of a FORTRAN DO loop is:

```
DO k counter = initial-value, final-value, increment-value
     statement 1
     statement 2
         .
         .
    statement n
k   CONTINUE
```

As indicated, a DO statement is the first statement of the loop and a CONTINUE statement is the last statement of the loop. The statements between the DO and CONTINUE constitute the task that is to be repeated. Figure 5-1 illustrates both the Nassi-Schneiderman and flowchart representations of this loop.

Although the DO loop looks a little complicated, it is really quite simple if we consider each of its parts separately. The k in the DO statement is the numeric label of the last executable statement in the loop and must be the same numeric label in front of the CONTINUE statement.* Following the label in the DO statement are five items: a variable name, an equal sign, an initial value, a final value, and an

* If an END DO statement is permitted by your computer in place of a CONTINUE statement, the label k must be omitted from the DO statement.

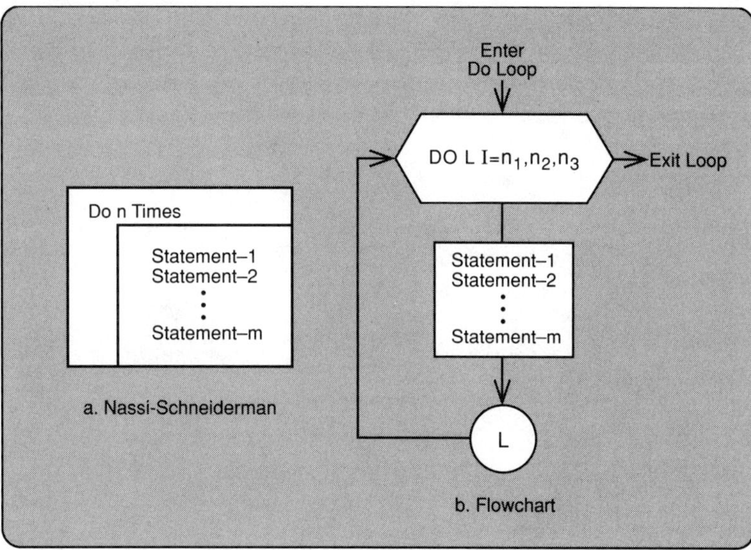

Figure 5-1 DO Loop Representations

increment value. Except for the increment, each of these items must be present in a DO statement, including the comma used to separate the initial and final values. If an increment is included, a comma must also be used to separate the increment value from the final value. Here is what these items are used for:

1. The variable name can be any valid FORTRAN name and is referred to as the *loop counter* (typically the counter is chosen as an integer variable).
2. The *initial-value* is the starting (initializing) value assigned to the counter and can be either a constant, variable, numeric expression, or function result.
3. The *final-value* is the maximum value the counter can have and determines when the loop is finished. It can either be a constant, variable, numeric expression, or function result.
4. The *increment-value*, which can be a constant, variable, numeric expression, or function result, is a value that is added or subtracted from the counter each time the loop is executed. If the increment is omitted it is assumed to be 1. Examples of valid DO statements are:

```
DO 5 COUNT = 1, 7, 1
DO 25 I = 5, 15, 2
DO 16 KK = 1, 20
```

In the first DO statement the counter variable is named COUNT, the initial value assigned to COUNT is 1, the loop will be terminated when the value in COUNT exceeds 7, and the increment value is 1. In the next DO statement the counter variable is named I, the initial value of I is 5, the loop will be terminated when the value in I exceeds 15, and the increment is 2. In the last DO statement the counter variable is named KK, the initial value of KK is 1, the loop will be terminated when the value of KK exceeds 20, and a default value of 1 is used for the increment.

Since there are restrictions on the last statement in a DO loop, a CONTINUE statement is typically used in this position to avoid any problems. The CONTINUE statement is simply a "place-holder" statement that is used where a statement is syntactically required but no action is called for. The general form of this statement is

```
k CONTINUE
```

where *k* is a statement number. When placed at the end of a DO loop, the value of *k* must be the same as the value referenced in the DO statement. As a specific example of a DO loop consider the following section of code:

```
      DO 10 COUNT = 1,5
        WRITE(6,*) 'ENTER A FAHRENHEIT TEMPERATURE'
        READ(5,*) FAHREN
        CELSUS = (5.0/9.0)*(FAHREN - 32.0)
        WRITE(6,*) '  THE EQUIVALENT CELSIUS VALUE IS: ', CELSUS
   10 CONTINUE
```

Here the DO statement is the first statement of the loop and determines how many times the statements in the loop are to be repeated. The CONTINUE statement performs no action but determines the end of the loop and causes a transfer back to the beginning of the loop. The statements within the loop are indented for readability only to clearly delineate the task that is being repeated; indentation is not required but strongly suggested for readable programs. Execution of the loop is as follows:

The initial value assigned to the counter variable COUNT is 1. Since the value in COUNT does not exceed the final value of 5, the statements up to and including the CONTINUE statement are executed. The execution of the first WRITE statement within the loop produces the prompt:

```
ENTER A FAHRENHEIT TEMPERATURE
```

The next statement, which is a READ statement, causes the computer to pause and wait for data to be entered. Assum, for purposes of illustration that the number 212.0 is entered by the user. The third statement within the DO loop, which is an assignment statement, calculates and assigns a value to the variable CELSUS. This value is then displayed by the last WRITE statement, which produces the display:

```
THE EQUIVALENT CELSIUS VALUE IS:  100.000000
```

The CONTINUE statement is then encountered, which signals that the end of the task to be repeated has been reached. This signals the computer to transfer control back to the DO statement at the top of the loop. The DO statement then increments the value in COUNT to 2, and the process is repeated. Since the value in COUNT does not exceed the final value of 5, the statements up to and including the CONTINUE statement, are once again executed. This process continues until the value in COUNT exceeds the final value of 5. Program 5-1 contains this DO loop in a complete program.

Program 5-1

```
      PROGRAM MAIN
        CALL SHOWDO
        END
*
      SUBROUTINE SHOWDO
        INTEGER COUNT
        REAL FAHREN, CELSUS
        DO 10 COUNT = 1,5
          WRITE(6,*) 'ENTER A FAHRENHEIT TEMPERATURE'
          READ(5,*) FAHREN
          CELSUS = (5.0/9.0)*(FAHREN - 32.0)
          WRITE(6,*) '  THE EQUIVALENT CELSIUS VALUE IS: ', CELSUS
   10   CONTINUE
        RETURN
        END
```

Following is a complete run using Program 5-1, including the user values input in response to the prompt:

```
ENTER A FAHRENHEIT TEMPERATURE
212.0
  THE EQUIVALENT CELSIUS VALUE IS:      100.000000
ENTER A FAHRENHEIT TEMPERATURE
32.0
  THE EQUIVALENT CELSIUS VALUE IS:    0.000000E+00
ENTER A FAHRENHEIT TEMPERATURE
60.0
  THE EQUIVALENT CELSIUS VALUE IS:       15.555560
ENTER A FAHRENHEIT TEMPERATURE
80.0
  THE EQUIVALENT CELSIUS VALUE IS:       26.666670
ENTER A FAHRENHEIT TEMPERATURE
90.0
  THE EQUIVALENT CELSIUS VALUE IS:       32.222230
```

Notice in Program 5-1 that the loop counter, COUNT, has been used simply to keep track of how many times statements within the DO loop are executed, which in this case is five. Although this is always the primary job of the loop counter, the counter may also be used within the loop, as long as its value is not altered in any way. (Altering the counter's value within the loop would adversely affect the count being automatically maintained by the DO statement). For example, consider Program 5-2.

Program 5-2

```
      PROGRAM MAIN
        CALL TABLE
        END
*
      SUBROUTINE TABLE
        INTEGER I
        WRITE(6,*) '         NUMBER    SQUARE ROOT'
        WRITE(6,*) '         ------    -----------'
        DO 20 I = 1, 10
          WRITE(6,*) I, SQRT(I)
 20     CONTINUE
        RETURN
        END
```

When Program 5-2 is executed, the following display is produced:

```
NUMBER      SQUARE ROOT
------      -----------
     1        1.000000
     2        1.414214
     3        1.732051
     4        2.000000
     5        2.236068
     6        2.449490
     7        2.645751
     8        2.828427
     9        3.000000
    10        3.162278
```

The first two lines displayed by the program are produced by the two WRITE statements placed before the DO statement. The remaining output is produced by the DO loop. This loop begins with the DO statement and ends with the CONTINUE statement (note that the CONTINUE statement's label number matches that given in the DO statement). Notice also that the variable used for the loop counter in Program 5-2 has been named I. This loop is executed as follows:

The initial value assigned to the counter variable I is 1. Since the value in I does not exceed the final value of 10, the statements in the loop, including the CONTINUE statement, are executed. The execution of the WRITE statement within the loop produces the display

```
1        1.00000000
```

The CONTINUE statement is then encountered and control is transferred back to the DO statement. The DO statement then increments the value in I to 2, tests if I is greater than 10, and repeats the loop, producing the display:

```
2        1.41421354
```

Program 5-3

```
      PROGRAM MAIN
        CALL TEST
        END
      SUBROUTINE TEST
        INTEGER TESTER
        DO 15 TESTER = 12, 20, 2
          WRITE(6,*) TESTER
15      CONTINUE
        RETURN
        END
```

This process continues until the value in I exceeds the final value of 10, producing the complete table. See if you can determine the output produced by Program 5-3.

Did you figure it out? The loop starts with TESTER initialized to 12, stops when TESTER exceeds 20, and increments TESTER in steps of two. The actual statements executed include all statements following the DO statement up to and including the CONTINUE statement. The output of Program 5-10 is:

```
12
14
16
18
20
```

DO Loop Structure

Now that we have seen a few simple examples of DO loop structures, it is useful to summarize the rules that all DO loops must adhere to:

1. The last statement in a DO loop can actually be any executable statement except a GO TO, IF, END, STOP, RETURN, or another DO statement. By always placing a CONTINUE statement as the last statement of a DO loop we ensure that this rule is not violated.
2. The DO loop counter variable may be either a real or integer variable.
3. The initial, final, and increment values, which are referred to as *parameters* of the DO statement, may be constants, variables, expressions, or function results. If a variable is used, it must have a value previously assigned to it. Likewise, any expression must yield a numeric value. For example, the DO statement:

   ```
   DO 10 IDCOUNT = BEGIN, BEGIN + 10.0, AUGMNT
   ```

   is valid and can be used as long as values have been assigned to the variables BEGIN, and AUGMNT before this statement is encountered in a program.

4. The initial, final, and increment values may be positive or negative, but the loop will not be executed at all if:*

   a. the initial value is greater than the final value and the increment is positive

   b. the initial value is less than the final value and the increment is negative

   c. the increment is zero.

   Once a DO loop is correctly structured, it is executed as follows:**

   Step 1. The initial value is assigned to the counter variable.

   Step 2. The value in the counter is compared to the final value. If the value is less than or equal to the final value, then:

   Step 2a. All loop statements are executed

   Step 2b. The counter is incremented and Step 2 is repeated

   Else

   the loop is terminated.

Figure 5-2 illustrates this flow of control. In understanding the operation of the DO loop it is extremely important to realize that no statement within the loop should ever alter the value in the counter. The value in the counter may itself be displayed, as in Programs 5-2 and 5-3, or used in an expression to calculate some other variable. It must never, however, be used on the left-hand side of an assignment statement within the loop. The value contained in the counter when a DO loop is completed is system dependent. Generally, however, the counter contains the last value that exceeds the final tested value.

Notice that Figure 5-2 illustrates the internal workings of the DO loop. To avoid the necessity of always illustrating these steps, the simplified flowchart or Nassi-Schneiderman symbol previously illustrated in Figure 5-1 is more commonly used.

To understand the enormous power of DO loops, consider the task of printing a table of numbers from 1 to 10, including their squares and cubes, as is done in Program 5-4.

---

* This is referred to as a pre-test loop. On some compilers the value of the loop counter is compared to the final value at the end of the loop, in which case the loop always executes at least once. This later type of operation is called a post-test loop. To determine the test performed by your compiler, you can run the following loop.

```
      DO 5 I = 10, 1, 1
         WRITE(6,*) I
10    CONTINUE
```

This loop will either execute once, or not at all. If a value of I is printed, your compiler uses a post-test. If no printout is obtained, your compiler performs a pre-test.

** The number of times that a DO loop is executed is determined by the expression

```
INT((final value - initial value + increment)/increment)
```

If this expression results in a negative value, the loop is not executed.

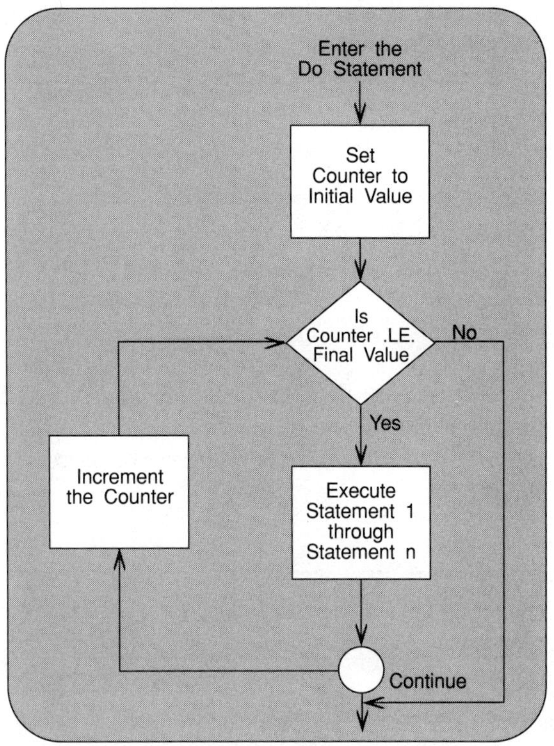

Figure 5-2 DO Loop Flowchart

Program 5-4

```
      PROGRAM MAIN
        CALL TAB3
        END
*
      SUBROUTINE TAB3
        INTEGER NUM
        WRITE(6,*) '          NUMBER      SQUARE       CUBE'
        WRITE(6,*) '          ------      ------       ----'
        DO 30, NUM = 1,10
          WRITE(6,*) NUM, NUM**2, NUM**3
   30   CONTINUE
        RETURN
        END
```

When Program 5-4 is run, the display produced is:

```
NUMBER        SQUARE        CUBE
------        ------        ----
     1             1           1
     2             4           8
     3             9          27
     4            16          64
     5            25         125
     6            36         216
     7            49         343
     8            64         512
     9            81         729
    10           100        1000
```

Simply changing the number 10 in the DO statement of Program 5-4 to 1000 creates a loop that is executed 1000 times and produces a table of numbers from 1 to 1000. Thus, a small change in the code produces an immense increase in the processing and output provided by the program.

Skill Builder Exercises

1. Write individual DO statements for the following cases:

a. Use a counter named I that has an initial value of 1, a final value of 20, and an increment of 1.

b. Use a counter named ICOUNT that has an initial value of 1, a final value of 20, and an increment of 2.

c. Use a counter named J that has an initial value of 1, a final value of 100, and an increment of 5.

d. Use a counter named ICOUNT that has an initial value of 20, a final value of 1, and an increment of -1.

e. Use a counter named ICOUNT that has an initial value of 20, a final value of 1, and an increment of -2.

f. Use a counter named COUNT that has an initial value of 1.0, a final value of 16.2, and an increment of 0.2.

g. Use a counter named XCNT that has an initial value of 20.0, a final value of 10.0, and an increment of -0.5.

2. Determine the number of times that each DO loop is executed for the DO statements written for Exercise 1.

3. Determine the value in TOTAL after each of the following loops is executed.

a.
```
   TOTAL = 0
   DO 10 I = 1, 10
     TOTAL = TOTAL + I
10 CONTINUE
```

b.
```
   TOTAL = 1
   DO 10 COUNT = 1, 10
     TOTAL = TOTAL * 2
10 CONTINUE
```

c.
```
   TOTAL = 0
   DO 10 I = 10, 15
     TOTAL = TOTAL + I
10 CONTINUE
```

d.
```
   TOTAL = 50
   DO 15 I = 1, 10
     TOTAL = TOTAL - I
15 CONTINUE
```

e.
```
   TOTAL = 1
   DO 20 ICNT = 1, 8
     TOTAL = TOTAL * ICNT
20 CONTINUE
```

f.
```
   TOTAL = 1.0
   DO 25 J = 1, 5
     TOTAL = TOTAL / 2.0
25 CONTINUE
```

4. Determine the errors in the following DO statements:

a. `DO I = 1,10`

b. `DO 10 COUNT 5,10`

c. `DO 5 JJ = 1 10 2`

d. `DO 15 KK = 1, 10, -1`

e. `DO 20 KK = -1, -20`

5. Determine the output of the following program.

```
      PROGRAM MAIN
        INTEGER I
        DO 10 I = 20, 0, -4
          WRITE(6,*) I
10      CONTINUE
        END
```

6. Modify Program 5-4 to produce a table of the numbers zero through 20 in increments of 2, with their squares and cubes.

7. Modify Program 5-4 to produce a table of numbers from 10 to 1, instead of 1 to 10 as it currently does.

Programming Exercises

8. Write and run a FORTRAN program that accepts ten individual values of gallons, one at a time, and converts each value entered to its liter equivalent before the next value is requested. Use a DO loop in your program. There are 3.785 liters in one gallon.

9. Write and run a FORTRAN program that displays a table of 20 temperature conversions from Fahrenheit to Celsius. The table should start with a Fahrenheit value of 20 degrees and be incremented in values of 4 degrees. Recall that Celsius = (5.0/9.0) * (Fahrenheit - 32).

10. The expansion of a steel bridge as it is heated to a final Celsius temperature, TF, from an initial Celsius temperature, T0, can be approximated using the formula

    ```
    Increase in length = α * L * (TF-T0)
    ```

    where α is the coefficient of expansion, which for steel is 11.7 E-6, and L is the length of the bridge at temperature T0.

    Using this formula, write a FORTRAN program that displays a table of expansion lengths for a steel bridge that is 7365 feet long at zero degrees Celsius, as the temperature increases to 40 degrees in five degree increments.

11. The probability that an individual telephone call will last less than t minutes can be approximated by the exponential probability function

    Probability that a call lasts less than t minutes $= 1 - e^{-t/a}$

    where a is the average call length and e is Euler's number (2.71828). For example, assuming that the average call length is 2.5 minutes, the probability that a call will last less than one minute is calculated as $1 - e^{-1/2.5} = 0.3297$.

    Using this probability function, write a FORTRAN program that calculates and displays a list of probabilities of a call lasting less than one to less than 10 minutes, in one-minute increments.

12. The arrival rate of customers in a busy New York bank can be estimated using the Poisson probability function

    $$P(x) = \frac{a^x e^{-a}}{x!}$$

    where

    x = the number of customer arrivals per minute

    a = the average number of arrivals per minute

    and

    e = Euler's number (2.71828)

    For example, if the average number of customers entering the bank is three customers per minute, then a is equal to three. Thus, the probability of 0 customers arriving in any one minute =

    $$P(x=0) = \frac{3^0 e^{-3}}{0!} = .0498$$

    and

    the probability of 1 customer arriving in any one minute =

    $$P(x=1) = \frac{3^1 e^{-3}}{1!} = .1494$$

Using the Poisson probability function, write a FORTRAN program that calculates and displays the probability of 0 to 20 customer arrivals in a minute when the average arrival rate is 3 customers per minute.

b. The formula given in Exercise 12a is also applicable for estimating the arrival rate of planes at a busy airport (here, an arriving "customer" is an incoming airplane). Using this same formula, modify the program written in Exercise 10a to accept the average arrival rate as an input data item. Then run the modified program to determine the probability of zero to ten planes attempting to land in any one- minute period at an airport during peak arrival times. Assume that the average arrival rate for peak arrival times is one plane per two minutes.

13. Write and run a program that calculates and displays the amount of money available in a bank account that initially has $1,000 deposited in it and that earns 8 percent interest a year. Your program should display the amount available at the end of each year for a period of ten years. Use the relationship that the money available at the end of each year equals the amount of money in the account at the start of the year plus .08 times the amount available at the start of the year.

14. A machine purchased for $28,000 is depreciated at a rate of $4,000 a year for seven years. Write and run a FORTRAN program that computes and displays a depreciation table for seven years. The table should have the form:

```
               Depreciation Schedule
                            End-of-year    Accumulated
      Year   Depreciation      value       depreciation
       1         4000          24000           4000
       2         4000          20000           8000
       3         4000          16000          12000
       4         4000          12000          16000
       5         4000           8000          20000
       6         4000           4000          24000
       7         4000              0          28000
```

15. A well-regarded manufacturer of widgets has been losing 4 percent of its sales each year. The annual profit for the firm is 10 percent of sales. This year the firm has had $10 million in sales and a profit of $1 million. Determine the expected sales and profit for the next 10 years. Your program should complete and produce a display as follows:

```
                Sales and Profit Projection
      Year     Expected sales     Projected profit
       1       $10000000.00        $1000000.00
       2       $ 9600000.00        $ 960000.00
       3                   .                  .
       .                   .                  .
       .                   .                  .
       .                   .                  .
      10                   .                  .
     Totals:   $           .       $          .
```

5.2 DO Loop Programming Techniques

In this section we present three common programming techniques associated with DO loops. All of these techniques are common knowledge to experienced FORTRAN programmers.

Technique 1: Variable Parameters

As described in the previous section, the initial, final and increment values in a DO statement are formally referred to as the parameters of the DO statement. Although each parameter (the initial, final, and increment value) must be known and set before the DO statement is executed, these values may be set using variables rather than constant values. For example, the four statements

```
I = 5
J = 10
K = 1
DO 20 COUNT = I, J, K
```

produce the same effect as the single statement

```
DO 20 COUNT = 5,10,1
```

The advantage of the first DO statement, where variables are used for the counter, initial, and final parameters, is that it allows us to assign values to these variables external to the DO statement. This is especially useful when READ statements are used to set the actual values. To make this a little more tangible, consider Program 5-5.

Program 5-5

```
*******************************************************************
* THIS PROGRAM DISPLAYS A TABLE OF NUMBERS, THEIR SQUARE AND CUBE *
* ROOTS STARTING FROM THE NUMBER 1. THE FINAL NUMBER IN THE TABLE *
* IS DECIDED BY THE USER                                          *
*******************************************************************
      PROGRAM MAIN
        CALL SCTABL
        END
*
      SUBROUTINE SCTABL
        INTEGER NUM, IFINAL
        WRITE(6,*) 'ENTER THE FINAL NUMBER:'
        READ(5,*) IFINAL
        WRITE(6,*) '         NUMBER      SQUARE       CUBE'
        WRITE(6,*) '         ------      ------       ----'
        DO 30, NUM = 1, IFINAL
          WRITE(6,*) NUM, NUM**2, NUM**3
  30    CONTINUE
        RETURN
        END
```

In Program 5-5, we have used a variable name for the final parameter only. Since this parameter must be set before the DO statement is executed, a READ statement has been placed before the DO statement to allow the user to decide what the final value should be. Notice that this arrangement permits the user to set the size of the table at run time, rather than having the programmer set the table size at compile time. This also makes the program more general, since it now can be used to create a variety of tables without the need for reprogramming and recompiling.

Technique 2: Accumulating Within a DO Loop

One of the most powerful uses of a DO loop is to total a list of numbers. To introduce the concept involved, consider Program 5-6 where a DO loop is used to accept and then display four user-entered numbers, one at a time. Although it uses a very simple idea, the program highlights the flow of control concepts needed for totaling the entered numbers.

Program 5-6

```
      PROGRAM MAIN
        CALL ACCUM
        END
*
      SUBROUTINE ACCUM
        INTEGER COUNT
        REAL NUM
        WRITE(6,*) 'THIS PROGRAM WILL ASK YOU TO ENTER SOME NUMBERS.'
        DO 50 COUNT = 1, 4
          WRITE(6,*) 'ENTER A NUMBER: '
          READ(5,*)  NUM
          WRITE(6,*) '    THE NUMBER JUST ENTERED IS ', NUM
 50     CONTINUE
        RETURN
        END
```

Following is a sample run of Program 5-6, including numbers input in response to the appropriate prompts.

```
THIS PROGRAM WILL ASK YOU TO ENTER SOME NUMBERS.
ENTER A NUMBER:
10
   THE NUMBER JUST ENTERED IS      10.000000
ENTER A NUMBER:
18.3
   THE NUMBER JUST ENTERED IS      18.300000
ENTER A NUMBER:
291
   THE NUMBER JUST ENTERED IS     291.000000
ENTER A NUMBER:
83
  THE NUMBER JUST ENTERED IS      83.000000
```

Let us review the program to clearly understand how the output was produced. The first message displayed is caused by the execution of the first WRITE statement. This statement is outside and before the loop, so it is executed once before any statement within the loop.

Once the DO loop is entered, the statements within it are executed as long as the value in the loop counter does not exceed the final loop value. The first time through the loop the message `ENTER A NUMBER:` is displayed. The program then executes the READ statement, which forces the computer to wait for a number to be entered at the keyboard. Once a number is typed and the RETURN key is pressed, the second WRITE in the loop displays the number that was entered. The end of the loop is then encountered and the variable COUNT is automatically incremented by one. This process continues until four passes through the loop have been made. Each pass causes the message `ENTER A NUMBER:` to be displayed, the READ statement to be executed, and the message `THE NUMBER JUST ENTERED IS` to be displayed. Figure 5-3 illustrates the flow of control for Program 5-6.

Rather than simply displaying the entered numbers, Program 5-6 can be modified to process the entered data. For example, let us add the numbers entered and display the total. To do this, we must be very careful how we add the numbers, since the same variable, NUM, is used for each number entered. Because of this the entry of a new number in Program 5-6 automatically causes the previous number stored in NUM to be lost. Thus, each number entered must be added to the total before another number is entered. The required sequence is:

```
enter a number
add the number to the total
```

How do we add a single number to a total? A statement such as `TOTAL = TOTAL + NUM` does the job perfectly. This is the accumulating statement introduced in Section 2.3. After each number is entered, the accumulating statement adds the number into the TOTAL, as illustrated in Figure 5-4. The complete flow of control required for adding the numbers is illustrated in Figure 5-5.

In reviewing Figure 5-5, observe that we have made a provision for initially setting TOTAL to zero before the DO loop is entered. If we were to clear TOTAL inside the DO loop, it would be set to zero each time the loop was executed and any previously stored value would be erased.

Program 5-7 incorporates the necessary modifications to Program 5-6 to total the entered numbers. As indicated in the flow diagram shown in Figure 5-4, the statement `TOTAL = TOTAL + NUM` is placed immediately after the READ state-

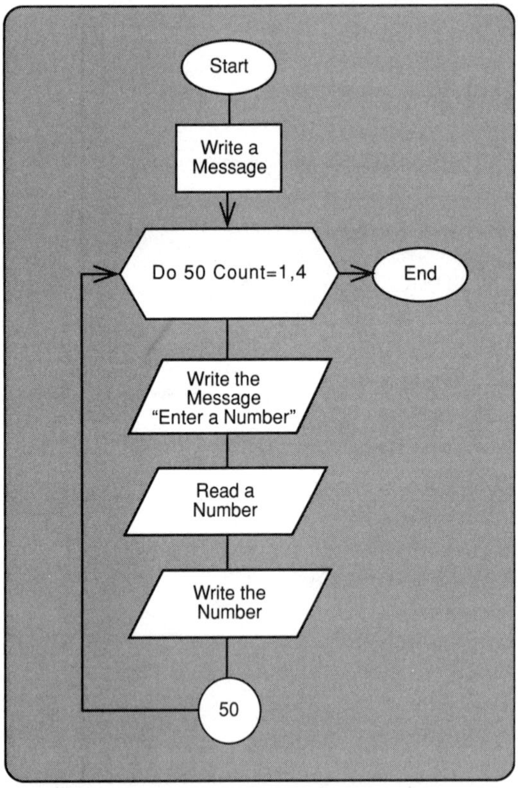

Figure 5-3 Flowchart for Program 5-6

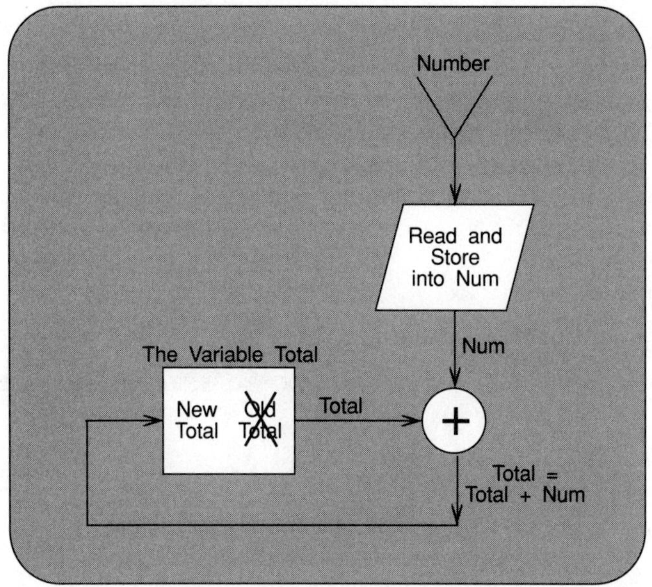

Figure 5-4 Accepting and Adding a Number to a Total

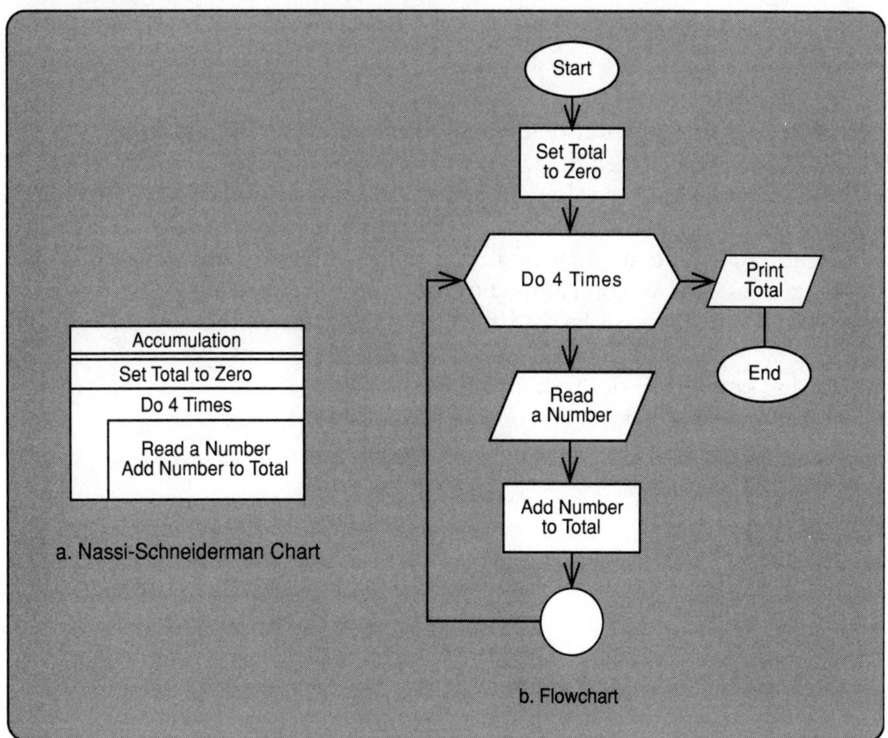

Figure 5-5 Summing Numbers Using a DO Loop

ment. Putting the accumulating statement at this point in the program ensures that the entered number is immediately 'captured' into the total.

Program 5-7

```
      PROGRAM MAIN
        CALL ACCUM
        END
*
      SUBROUTINE ACCUM
        INTEGER COUNT
        REAL NUM, TOTAL
        WRITE(6,*) 'THIS PROGRAM WILL ASK YOU TO ENTER SOME NUMBERS.'
        TOTAL = 0.0
        DO 50 COUNT = 1, 4
          WRITE(6,*) 'ENTER A NUMBER: '
          READ(5,*)  NUM
          TOTAL = TOTAL + NUM
          WRITE(6,*) '    THE TOTAL IS NOW ', NUM
   50   CONTINUE
        WRITE(6,*) 'THE FINAL TOTAL IS ', TOTAL
        RETURN
        END
```

Let us review Program 5-7. The variable TOTAL was created to store the total of the numbers entered. Prior to entering the DO loop TOTAL is initialized to zero. This ensures that any previous value present in the storage locations assigned to this variable is erased. When the DO loop is entered, the statement `TOTAL = TOTAL + NUM` is used to add the value of the entered number into TOTAL. As each value is entered, it is added into the existing TOTAL to create a new TOTAL. Thus, TOTAL becomes a running subtotal of all the values entered. Only when all numbers are entered does TOTAL contain the final sum of all the numbers.

After the DO loop is finished, the last WRITE statement displays the final sum.

Using the same data that was entered in the sample run for Program 5-6, the following sample run of Program 5-7 was made:

```
THIS PROGRAM WILL ASK YOU TO ENTER SOME NUMBERS.
ENTER A NUMBER:
10
   THE TOTAL IS NOW       10.000000
ENTER A NUMBER:
18.3
   THE TOTAL IS NOW       28.300000
ENTER A NUMBER:
291
   THE TOTAL IS NOW      319.300000
ENTER A NUMBER:
83
   THE TOTAL IS NOW      402.300000
THE FINAL TOTAL IS      402.300000
```

Having used an accumulating assignment statement to add the numbers entered, we can now go further and calculate the average of the numbers. First, however, we must decide where to calculate the average—within the DO loop or outside it?

Calculating an average requires that both a final total and the number of items in that total be available. The average is then computed by dividing the final total by the number of items. Thus, we must ask, "At what point in the program are both the correct total and the number of items available?" In reviewing Program 5-7 we see that the final total is available after the DO loop is finished. In fact, the whole purpose of the DO loop is to ensure that the numbers are entered and correctly added to produce a correct total. Thus, after the loop is finished is the correct point for calculating the average. With this as background, see if you can read and understand Program 5-8.

Program 5-8

```
      PROGRAM MAIN
        CALL ACCUM
        END
*
      SUBROUTINE ACCUM
        INTEGER COUNT, NUMS
        REAL NUM, TOTAL, AVERGE
        PARAMETER(NUMS = 4)
        WRITE(6,*) 'THIS PROGRAM WILL ASK YOU TO ENTER SOME NUMBERS.'
        TOTAL = 0.0
        DO 50 COUNT = 1, NUMS
          WRITE(6,*) 'ENTER A NUMBER: '
          READ(5,*)  NUM
          TOTAL = TOTAL + NUM
 50     CONTINUE
        AVERGE = TOTAL / NUMS
        WRITE(6,*) 'THE AVERAGE OF THE NUMBERS IS ', AVERGE
        RETURN
        END
```

Program 5-8 is almost identical to Program 5-7, except for the calculation of the average and the use of the PARAMETERized constant NUMS. The repeating display of the total within the loop and the final display of the total after the loop have also been eliminated.

The DO statement in Program 5-8 creates a loop that is executed four times. The user is prompted to enter a number each time through the loop. After each number is entered, it is immediately added to the total. Notice that TOTAL is initialized to zero before the DO statement is executed. The loop in Program 5-8 is executed as long as the value in COUNT is less than or equal to NUMS, which is 4. Thus, to obtain the proper average, the four entered numbers are divided by NUMS after the loop is completed. The usefulness of using a named constant is that the program can easily be changed to read and calculate the average of any number of values by simply changing the value of NUMS in the PARAMETER statement. If a named constant were not used, altering the program would require locating every occurrence of the number 4 and changing it to the desired value.

Following is a sample run using Program 5-8:

```
THIS PROGRAM WILL ASK YOU TO ENTER SOME NUMBERS.
ENTER A NUMBER:
10
ENTER A NUMBER:
18.3
ENTER A NUMBER:
291
ENTER A NUMBER:
83
THE AVERAGE OF THE NUMBERS IS     100.575000
```

Technique 3: Evaluating Functions of One Variable

DO loops can be conveniently constructed to determine and display the values of single variable functions for a set of values over any specified interval. For example, assume that we want to know the values of the function

$$Y = 10X^2 + 3X - 2$$

for integer values of X between two and five. Assuming that X has been declared as an integer variable, the following DO loop can be used to calculate the required values.

```
      DO 10 X = 2, 5
        Y = 10 * X ** 2 + 3 * X - 2
        WRITE(6,*) X, Y
   10 CONTINUE
```

Program 5-9

```
      PROGRAM MAIN
        CALL VALFUN
        END
*
      SUBROUTINE VALFUN
        INTEGER X,Y
        WRITE(6,*)'        X VALUE      Y VALUE'
        WRITE(6,*)'        -------      -------'
        DO 10 X = 2,5
           Y = 10 * X ** 2 + 3 * X - 2
           WRITE(6,*) X, Y
   10   CONTINUE
        RETURN
        END
```

For this loop we have used the variable X as both the counter variable and the unknown (independent variable) in the function. For each value of X from two to five a new value of Y is calculated and displayed. This DO loop is contained within Program 5-9, which also displays appropriate headings for the written values.

The following is displayed when Program 5-9 is executed:

```
X VALUE          Y VALUE
-------          -------
   2                44
   3                97
   4               170
   5               263
```

Two items are of importance here. The first is that any equation with one unknown can be evaluated using a single DO loop. The method requires substituting the desired equation into the DO loop in place of the equation used in Program 5-9, and adjusting the counter values to match the desired solution range.

The second item of note is that we are not constrained to using integer values for the counter variable. For example, by specifying a non-integer increment, solutions for fractional values can be obtained. This is shown in Program 5-9a, where the equation $Y = 10X^2 + 3X - 2$ is evaluated in the range X = 2 to X = 6 in increments of 0.5.

Program 5-9a

```
      PROGRAM MAIN
        CALL VALFUN
        END
*
      SUBROUTINE VALFUN
        REAL X, Y
        WRITE(6,*)'          X VALUE          Y VALUE'
        WRITE(6,*)'          -------          -------'
        DO 10 X = 2.0, 6.0, 0.5
           Y = 10.0 * X ** 2 + 3.0 * X - 2.0
           WRITE(6,*) X, Y
10      CONTINUE
        RETURN
        END
```

Notice that X and Y have been declared as REALs in Program 5-9a, to allow these variables to take on fractional values. The following is the output produced by this program.

```
X VALUE          Y VALUE
-------          -------
2.000000        44.000000
2.500000        68.000000
3.000000        97.000000
3.500000       131.000000
4.000000       170.000000
4.500000       214.000000
5.000000       263.000000
5.500000       317.000000
6.000000       376.000000
```

Exercises

1. Rewrite Program 5-7 to compute the total of eight numbers.
2. Rewrite Program 5-7 to display the prompt:

```
PLEASE TYPE IN THE TOTAL NUMBER OF DATA VALUES TO BE ADDED:
```

In response to this prompt, the program should accept a user-entered number and then use this number to control the number of times the DO loop is executed. Thus, if the user enters 5 in response to the prompt, the program should request the input of five numbers and display the total after five numbers have been entered.

3. By mistake, a programmer put the statement AVERGE = TOTAL / NUMS within the DO loop immediately after the statement TOTAL = TOTAL + NUM in Program 5-8. Thus, the DO loop becomes:

```
      DO 50 COUNT = 1, NUMS
        WRITE(6,*) 'ENTER A NUMBER: '
        READ(5,*)  NUM
        TOTAL = TOTAL + NUM
        AVERGE = TOTAL / NUMS
 50   CONTINUE
```

Will the program yield the correct result with this DO loop? From a programming perspective, which DO loop is better to use, and why?

4. Rewrite Program 5-8 to compute the average of ten numbers.
5. Rewrite Program 5-8 to display the prompt:

```
PLEASE TYPE IN THE TOTAL NUMBER OF DATA VALUES TO BE AVERAGED:
```

In response to this prompt, the program should accept a user-entered number and then use this number to control the number of times the DO loop is executed. Thus, if the user enters 6 in response to the prompt, the program should request the input of six numbers and display the average of the next six numbers entered.

6. In addition to the arithmetic average of a set of numbers, both a geometric and harmonic mean can be calculated. The geometric mean of a set of n numbers $x_1, x_2, \ldots x_n$ is defined as

$$\sqrt[n]{x_1 \cdot x_2 \cdot \cdots \cdot x_n}$$

and the harmonic mean as

$$\frac{n}{\frac{1}{x_1} + \frac{1}{x_2} + \cdots + \frac{1}{x_n}}$$

Using these formulas, write a FORTRAN program that accepts ten numbers, and then calculates and displays both the geometric and harmonic means of the entered numbers.

7. Write a FORTRAN program that converts Fahrenheit to Celsius temperature in increments of 5 degrees. The initial value of the Fahrenheit temperature and the

total conversions to be made are to be requested as user input during program execution. Recall that Celsius = (5.0/9.0) * (Fahrenheit - 32.0)

8. Modify Program 5-9a to produce a table of Y values for the following:

a. $Y = 3X^5 - 2X^3 + X$

for X between 5 and 10 in increments of .2

b. $Y = 1 + x + \frac{x^2}{2} + \frac{x^3}{6} + \frac{x^4}{24}$

for X between 1 and 3 in increments of .1

c. $Y = 2e^{.8t}$ for t between 4 and 10 in increments of .2

9. A model of world wide population, in billions of people, is given by the equation

Population $= 4.88(1 + e^{.02t})$

where t is the time in years (t = 0 represents January 1985 and t = 1 represents January 1986). Using this formula, write a FORTRAN program that displays a monthly population table for the months January 1990 through December 1991.

10. The x and y coordinates, as a function of time, t, of a projectile fired with an initial velocity v at an angle of θ with respect to the ground is given by

$$x = v\,t\cos(\theta)$$
$$y = v\,t\sin(\theta)$$

Using these formulas, write a FORTRAN program that displays a table of x and y values for a projectile fired with an initial velocity of 500 ft/sec at an angle of 22.8 degrees. (Hint: Remember to convert to radian measure.) The table should contain values corresponding to the time interval 0 to 10 seconds in increments of one-half seconds.

11a. The following data were collected on a recent automobile trip.

	Mileage	**Gallons**
Start of trip:	22495	Full tank
	22841	12.2
	23185	11.3
	23400	10.5
	23772	11.0
	24055	12.2
	24434	14.7
	24804	14.3
	25276	15.2

Write a FORTRAN program that accepts a mileage and gallons value and calculates the miles-per-gallon (mpg) achieved for that segment of the trip. The miles-per-gallon is obtained as the difference in mileage between fill-ups divided by the number of gallons of gasoline used in the fill-up.

b. Modify the program written for Exercise 11a to additionally compute and display the cumulative mpg achieved after each fill-up. The cumulative mpg is calculated as the difference between each fill-up mileage and the mileage at the start of the trip divided by the sum of the gallons used to that point in the trip.

12a. A bookstore summarizes its monthly transactions by keeping the following information for each book in stock:

Book identification number
Inventory balance at the beginning of the month
Number of copies received during the month
Number of copies sold during the month

Write a FORTRAN program that accepts this data for each book and then displays the book identification number and an updated book inventory balance using the relationship:

New Balance = Inventory balance at the beginning of the month
+ Number of copies received during the month
- Number of copies sold during the month

Your program should use a DO loop with a fixed count condition so that information on only three books is requested.

b. Run the program written in Exercise 12a on a computer. Review the display produced by your program and verify that the output produced is correct.

13a. The outstanding balance on Rhona Karp's car loan is $8,000. Each month Rhona is required to make a payment of $300, which includes both interest and principal repayment of the car loan. The monthly interest is calculated as .10/12 of the outstanding balance of the loan. After the interest is deducted the remaining part of the payment is used to pay off the loan. Using this information, write a FORTRAN program that produces a table indicating the beginning monthly balance, the interest payment, the principal payment, and the remaining loan balance after each payment is made. Your output should resemble and complete the entries in the following table until the outstanding loan balance is zero.

```
  Beginning       Interest      Principal     Ending Loan
   Balance        Payment        Payment        Balance
8000.00000000   66.66666667  233.33333333   7766.66666667
7766.66666667   64.72222223  235.27777777   7531.38888890
7531.38888890        .             .              .
      .              .             .              .
      .              .             .              .
      .              .             .          0.00000000
```

b. Modify the program written in Exercise 13a to display the total of the interest and principal paid at the end of the table produced by your program.

5.3 Nested Loops

There are many situations in which it is very convenient to have a loop contained within another loop. Such loops are called nested loops. A simple example of a nested loop is:

```
      DO 10 I = 1, 4                        ← Start of Outer Loop
        WRITE(6,*) 'I IS NOW ', I
        DO 5  J = 1, 3                      ← Start of Inner Loop
          WRITE(6,*) '   J = ', J
 5      CONTINUE                            ← End of Inner Loop
10    CONTINUE                              ← End of Outer Loop
```

The first loop, controlled by the value of I, is called the outer loop. The second loop, controlled by the value of J, is called the inner loop. Notice that all statements in the inner loop are contained within the boundaries of the outer loop and that we have used a different variable to control each loop. For each single trip through the outer loop, the inner loop runs through its entire sequence. Thus, each time the I counter increases by one, the inner DO loop executes completely. This situation is illustrated in Figure 5-6.

Program 5-10 includes the above code in a working program.

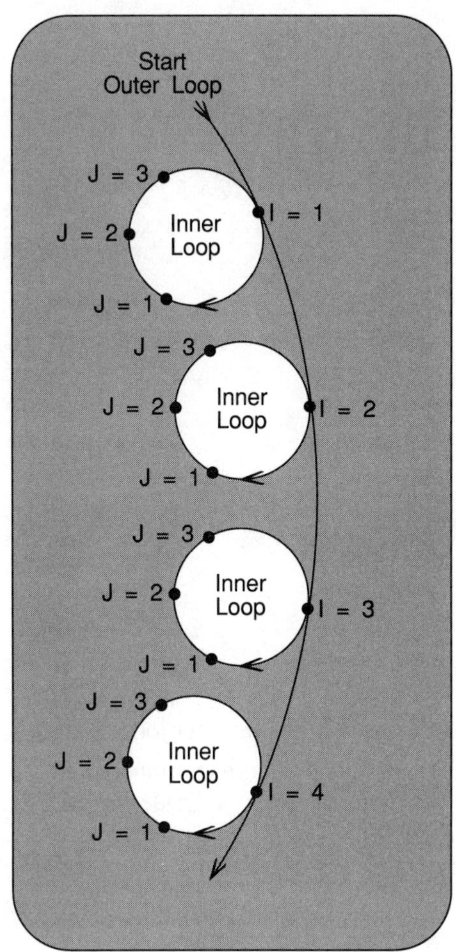

Figure 5-6 For Each I, J Makes a Complete Loop

Program 5-10

```
      PROGRAM MAIN
        CALL NESTED
        END
*
      SUBROUTINE NESTED
        INTEGER I,J
***     START OF OUTER LOOP
        DO 10 I = 1,4
          WRITE(6,*) 'I IS NOW ',I
***       START OF INNER LOOP
          DO 5 J = 1,3
            WRITE(6,*) '  J = ',J
    5     CONTINUE
   10   CONTINUE
        RETURN
        END
```

Following is the output of a sample run of Program 5-10:

```
I IS NOW  1
  J =  1
  J =  2
  J =  3
I IS NOW  2
  J =  1
  J =  2
  J =  3
I IS NOW  3
  J =    1
  J =    2
  J =    3
I IS NOW  4
  J =    1
  J =    2
  J =    3
```

The only requirements that must be adhered to in creating nested loops are:

1. An inner loop must be fully contained within an outer loop.
2. An outer loop counter variable must not be altered within an inner loop.

Let us use a nested loop to compute the average grade for each student in a class of 20 students. Each student has taken four exams during the course of the semester. The final grade for each student is calculated as the average of the four examination grades.

Program Analysis

The pseudocode for this example is

Do 20 times
Set student total to zero
Do 4 times
read in a grade
add the grade to the student total
End Inner Do
Calculate student's average grade
Print student's average grade
End Outer Do

As described in the pseudocode, an outer loop consisting of 20 passes will be used to calculate the average for each student. The inner loop will consist of four passes, with one examination grade entered in each inner loop pass. As each grade is entered it is added to the total for the student, and at the end of the loop the average is calculated and displayed. Program 5-11 uses a nested loop to make the required calculations.

Program 5-11

```
      PROGRAM MAIN
        CALL AVGRAD
        END
*
      SUBROUTINE AVGRAD
*** THIS SUBROUTINE CALCULATES THE AVERAGE GRADE FOR 20 STUDENTS
        INTEGER I, J
        REAL GRADE, TOTAL, AVERGE
*** THIS IS THE START OF THE OUTER LOOP
        DO 30 I = 1, 20
          TOTAL = 0.0
          DO 15 J = 1,4
            WRITE(6,*) 'ENTER AN EXAM GRADE FOR THIS STUDENT: '
            READ(5,*) GRADE
            TOTAL = TOTAL + GRADE
  15      CONTINUE
        AVERGE = TOTAL / 4.0
        WRITE(6,*) 'THE AVERAGE FOR THIS STUDENT IS ', AVERGE
  30    CONTINUE
        RETURN
        END
```

In reviewing Program 5-11, pay particular attention to the initialization of TOTAL within the outer loop, before the inner loop is entered. TOTAL is initialized 20 times, once for each student. Also notice that the average is calculated and displayed immediately after the inner loop is finished. Since the statements that compute and print the average are also contained within the outer loop, 20 averages are calculated and displayed. The entry and addition of each grade within the inner loop use summation techniques we have seen before, which should now be familiar to you.

Programming Exercises

1. Modify subroutine AVGRAD in Program 5-11 to make it more general. The modified subroutine should have two formal arguments, named NUMSTU and NUMGRD. NUMSTU should be used to accept the number of students whose average grade will be calculated and NUMGRD should be used to accept the number of grades that will be averaged for a student. Thus, the statement CALL AVGRAD(20,4) would indicate to the AVGRAD routine that the average of 20 students is to be calculated, with each average consisting of four grades. Test your subroutine using a dedicated driver program.
2. Four experiments are performed, each experiment consisting of six test results. The results for each experiment are given below. Write a program using a nested loop to compute and display the average of the test results for each experiment.

1st experiment results:	23.2	31.5	16.9	27.5	25.4	28.6
2nd experiment results:	34.8	45.2	27.9	36.8	33.4	39.4
3rd experiment results:	19.4	16.8	10.2	20.8	18.9	13.4
4th experiment results:	36.9	39.5	49.2	45.1	42.7	50.6

3. Modify the program written for Exercise 2 so that the number of test results for each experiment is entered by the user. Write your program so that a different number of test results can be entered for each experiment.

4a. A bowling team consists of five players. Each player bowls three games. Write a FORTRAN program that uses a nested loop to enter each player's individual scores and then computes and displays the average score for each bowler. Assume that each bowler has the following scores:

1st bowler:	286	252	265
2nd bowler:	212	186	215
3rd bowler:	252	232	216
4th bowler:	192	201	235
5th bowler:	186	236	272

b. Modify the program written for Exercise 4a to calculate and display the average team score. (Hint: Use a second variable to store the total of all the players' scores.)

5. Rewrite the program written for Exercise 4a to eliminate the inner loop. To do this, you will have to input three scores for each bowler rather than one at a time. Each score must be stored in its own variable name before the average is calculated.
6. Write a program that calculates and displays values for Y when

```
Y = XZ/(X-Z)
```

Your program should calculate Y for values of X ranging between 1 and 5 and values of Z ranging between 2 and 6. X should control the outer loop and be incremented in steps of 0.2 and Z should be incremented in steps of 0.5.

7. Write a program that calculates and displays the yearly amount available if \$1,000 is invested in a bank account for 10 years. Your program should display

Early (Optional) Introduction to Files. "Text (formatted) files are introduced in the second-half of Chapter 5, immediately after the DO statement. This provides for rather straight-forward and extremely meaningful applications for the DO statement using only a change in unit numbers for the WRITE statement introduced in Chapter 1 and the READ statement introduced in Chapter 3. This gives the instructor an option to present students with a more realistic idea of how data is stored and processed early in the course, and provides the opportunity of presenting students with meaningful sets of data for project work."

the amounts available for interest rates from percent to 12 percent inclusively, at 1 percent increments. Use a nested loop, with the outer loop having a fixed count of seven and the inner loop a fixed count of 10. The first iteration of the outer loop should use an interest rate of 6 percent and display the amount of money available at the end of the first 10 years. In each subsequent pass through the outer loop, the interest rate should be increased by 1 percent. Use the relationship that the money available at the end of each year equals the amount of money in the account at the start of the year, plus the interest rate times the amount available at the start of the year.

5.4 List-Directed Data Files*

The data for the programs we have seen so far has either been assigned internally within the programs or entered interactively during program execution. In this section we learn how to store data outside of a program. This external data storage permits a program to use the data without having to recreate it each time the program is run. Additionally, it provides the basis for sharing data between programs, so that the data output by one program can be input directly to another program. As we will also see, the structure of data files makes them unusually good candidates for processing using DO loops.

Any collection of data that is stored together under a common name on a storage medium other than the computer's main memory is called a *data file*. Typically data files are stored on floppy diskettes, hard disks, or magnetic tapes. This section describes the FORTRAN statements needed to create and process data files.

A data file is physically stored by a computer using a unique file name. Typically, most computers require that the file name consist of no more than eight characters followed by an optional period and an extension of up to three characters.** Using this convention, the following are all valid computer data file names:

```
MATH.DAT   DJAVG.STK    RECORDS
INFOR.DAT  EXPER1.DAT   RESULTS.MEM
```

Computer data file names should be chosen to indicate the file's informational content. For data files the first eight characters typically are used to describe the data and the three characters after the decimal point are used to describe either the application or are set equal to DAT to indicate a data file. For example, the file name EXPER1.DAT is useful for describing a file of data pertaining to experiment number one. Similarly, the filename DJAVG.STK could be used for Dow Jones averages required in a stock related program.

Within a FORTRAN program a file is always referenced using a unit number rather than the file's actual name. The unit number is a programmer-selected posi-

* This section introduces data files, which permits the assignment of exercises using data contained in such files. If such exercises are not to be assigned until later in the course, this material and the remaining sections of this chapter may be omitted on first reading without loss of subject continuity.

** Although this convention has been adopted by most computer systems, the maximum number of characters allowed for a file name is system dependent.

tive integer that corresponds to the file's computer name. The correspondence between unit number and computer file name is assigned by an OPEN statement.

An OPEN statement is an executable statement that performs two tasks. First, it physically opens a data file for use by a program. Second, opening a file equates the data file's name to the integer unit number used by the program to reference the file. The simplest form of the OPEN statement that accomplishes these tasks is:

```
OPEN(unit number, FILE = filename)
```

The keyword OPEN and the parentheses are required and identify this as an OPEN statement. As indicated, the OPEN statement requires a user-selected unit number, which is either a constant or an integer expression that evaluates to a number between 1 and 63, and the name of the data file assigned to this unit number. The file name can either be a character constant, in which case it must be enclosed in apostrophes, or a character variable. For example, the statement

```
OPEN(1,FILE = 'EXPER1.DAT')
```

opens a file named EXPER1.DAT and assigns this to unit number one. The number 1 is a programmer-selected value for the file, and represents how the file is referenced within the FORTRAN program containing the OPEN statement.

As an executable statement, an OPEN statement can be placed anywhere within a program unit after the unit's declaration statements. When an OPEN statement is encountered the computer checks whether the file currently exists on the system. If a file having the indicated file name exists, the file is opened. If the file does not exist, a blank file having the indicated name is created.

Writing to a File

After a file is opened, data can be written to it using any WRITE statement that correctly references the file's unit number (the PRINT statement cannot be used because it implicitly references the system's standard output unit). The general form of a file WRITE statement is identical to the WRITE statement introduced in Section 2.4 and has the form:

```
WRITE(unit number, n) expression list
```

For example, the statement

```
WRITE(4,*) WEIGHT, FACTOR, BALNCE
```

causes the values of the variables WEIGHT, FACTOR, BALNCE to be written to a file previously opened as unit number four. The asterisk in this WRITE statement indicates that values will be written using the system's list-directed default format. Similarly, the statement

```
WRITE(4,15) WEIGHT, FACTOR, BALNCE
```

causes these same three variable values to be written to file number four using the format specified in FORMAT statement 15.

Notice that these file WRITE statements are used in the same manner as a WRITE statement used to display values on the system's standard output device, with the replacement of the standard output unit number with the file's unit number. The file unit number directs the output to a specific file instead of to the standard display device. Program 5-12 illustrates the use of an OPEN statement and two subsequent WRITE statements for writing data to an opened file.

When Program 5-12 is executed, a file named TEST.DAT is created by the computer. After the file is opened two WRITE statements are used to write two lines to the TEST.DAT file. The file produced by this program consists of the following two lines:

```
165.000000
  7.500000        2.062500
```

The WRITE statements in Program 5-12 uses the system's list-directed format, designated by the asterisk before the closing parentheses, to write values into the file. If an explicit user-selected format is desired, the asterisk must be replaced by either a FORMAT statement label or a format character string contained within apostrophes (see Section 2.4).

Program 5-12

```
      PROGRAM MAIN
        CALL OPFILE
        END
*
      SUBROUTINE OPFILE
         REAL WEIGHT, SLOPE, FACTOR
         WEIGHT = 165.0
         SLOPE = 7.5
         FACTOR = 2.0625
         OPEN(4,FILE = 'TEST.DAT')
         WRITE(4,*) WEIGHT
         WRITE(4,*) SLOPE, FACTOR
         RETURN
         END
```

As illustrated in Program 5-12, writing to a file is essentially the same as writing to the standard output device, except for the explicit designation of the file's unit number in the WRITE statement. This means that all of the techniques you have learned for creating standard output displays apply to file writes as well. For example, Program 5-13 illustrates storing data read in from the standard input device to a file opened as unit number 3.

Program 5-13

```
      PROGRAM MAIN
        CALL GRPOST
        END
*
      SUBROUTINE GRPOST
        INTEGER I
        REAL GRADE
        OPEN(3,FILE = 'GRADES.DAT')
        DO 10 I = 1, 5
          WRITE(6,*) 'ENTER A GRADE'
          READ(5,*) GRADE
          WRITE(3,*) I, GRADE
          WRITE(6,*) '  THIS GRADE HAS BEEN WRITTEN TO THE FILE'
10      CONTINUE
        CLOSE(3)
        RETURN
        END
```

When Program 5-13 is executed, a file named GRADES.DAT is opened by the computer (if the file does not exist it is automatically created). After the file is opened a DO loop is used to write five lines to the file, with each line containing two items. Assuming that the values 95.0, 83.0, 100.0, 85.0, and 97.0 were entered when the program was run, the file produced by this program would consist of the following five lines:

```
1    95.000000
2    83.000000
3   100.000000
4    85.000000
5    97.000000
```

Closing a File

Included in Program 5-13 is a CLOSE statement. This statement is used to formally break the link established by the OPEN statement and releases the unit number, which can then be used for another file. The simplest form of this statement is

```
CLOSE(n)
```

where n is the unit number assigned to the data file when it was opened. Since all computers have a limit on the maximum number of files that can be open at one time, closing files that are no longer needed makes good sense. In the absence of a specific CLOSE statement, as in Program 5-12, any open files existing at the end of normal program execution are automatically closed by the operating system.

When a file is closed, a special end-of-file (EOF) marker is automatically placed by the operating system as the last character in the file. The EOF character has a unique numerical code that has no equivalent representation as a printable character. This special numerical value, which is system dependent, ensures that the EOF character can never be confused with a valid character contained internally within the file. As we will see in the next section, this EOF character is frequently useful in determining if the end of a file has been reached when the exact number of items in the file is not known beforehand.

Reading and Processing a File

Once a file has been created and written to, READ statements can be used to read data from the file. Reading data from a file is almost identical to reading data from a standard keyboard, with the addition of an explicit file unit number to indicate where the data is coming from. For example, the statement

```
READ(3,*) A,B,C
```

causes three values to be read from file 3, using the system's list-directed format, while the statement

```
READ(3,10) A,B,C
```

causes values to be read into the variables A, B, and C using FORMAT statement 10.

The format designated for reading data from a file requires that the programmer knows how the data was written originally to the file. This is necessary for correct "stripping" of the data from the file into appropriate variables for storage. Thus, for example, if list-directed formatting was used in writing a file, list-directed formatting would be used for reading the file. Program 5-14 illustrates this by using a list-directed READ statement to read the data in the GRADES.DAT file created by Program 5-13.

Program 5-14

```
      PROGRAM MAIN
        CALL GRREAD
        END
*
      SUBROUTINE GRREAD
        INTEGER I, N
        REAL GRADE
        OPEN(3,FILE = 'GRADES.DAT')
        DO 10 I = 1, 5
          READ(3,*) N, GRADE
          WRITE(6,*) N, GRADE
   10   CONTINUE
        CLOSE(3)
        RETURN
        END
```

Program 5-14 reads five lines from the GRADES.DAT file. Each time the file is read, an integer and a real value are input to the program. The display produced by Program 5-14 is:

```
1   95.000000
2   83.000000
3   100.000000
4   85.000000
5   97.000000
```

A few general comments are in order in reference to reading and writing to files. Any attempt to read a newly created blank file always results in a run-time error message. More troublesome is the attempt to write to an existing file containing data. Writing to an existing file automatically erases all existing lines after the written line. This means that if a write is made to an existing file before any reads are made, all of the information in the file is effectively erased. This occurs because the first line written to a newly opened file is, by default, written at the start of the file. These constraints on reading and writing to a file are a result of the defaults assumed by the OPEN statement we have been using. In Chapter 11 these default settings are described in detail and options for overriding them are presented.

Rather than simply reading and displaying data from an existing file, as is done in Program 5-14, data read from a file can be processed in the same manner as data read from the standard input device. For example, Program 5-15 computes the average of the grades in the GRADES.DAT file using the algorithm:

Open the file
Initialize the total to zero
Do five times
Read an integer and a grade
Add the grade to the total
Enddo
Calculate the average grade
Display the average grade

Notice that this is essentially the same algorithm previously used in Program 5-7 for determining the average of four numbers entered at the keyboard, except that now the data is being read from a file.

Program 5-15

```
      PROGRAM MAIN
        CALL GRREAD
        END
*
      SUBROUTINE GRREAD
        INTEGER I, N
        REAL TOTAL, GRADE, AVERGE
        TOTAL = 0.0
```

(Continued on the next page)

(Continued from the previous page)

```
      OPEN(3,FILE = 'GRADES.DAT')
      DO 10 I = 1, 5
        READ(3,*) N, GRADE
        TOTAL = TOTAL + GRADE
10    CONTINUE
      AVERGE = TOTAL / N
      WRITE(6,*) 'THE AVERAGE OF THE GRADES IN THE FILE IS ', AVERGE
      CLOSE(3)
      RETURN
      END
```

Using the GRADES.DAT file created by Program 5-13, the following output was produced by Program 5-15:

```
THE AVERAGE OF THE GRADES IN THE FILE IS        92.000000
```

Rewinding and Backspacing

The data files we have created have all been sequential files. The term *sequential* refers both to the placement of data in the file and the method in which this data is subsequently accessed. In *sequential access* the data is read and written in a sequential manner. This means that data items are read and written one after another, in order, with no skipping or jumping over items. Thus, for example, to read the fifth value in a sequential access file, the previous four values must be read first.

The position in a file of the next item to be read or written is maintained by a system file pointer, which is created automatically by the computer system and set to the start of the file whenever a file is opened. Reading from a file does not alter the values in the file, but each time an item is read the computer's internal file pointer is moved to the next item in the file. Similarly, each time a value is written to a file the file pointer is updated.

The FORTRAN statements BACKSPACE and REWIND can be used to alter the normal sequential access to a file. The REWIND statement resets the current position to the start of the file. REWIND requires the file's unit number as its only argument. For example, the statement

```
REWIND(1)
```

resets file number 1 to the start of the file. A REWIND is done automatically each time a file is opened.

The BACKSPACE statement allows the programmer to move the computer's internal file pointer back one line. For example, if a file has been opened and three lines of the file have been read or written to, the file pointer is automatically incremented and points to line four. This is the next line to be read or written. If a BACKSPACE statement is now executed, the internal file pointer is decremented and points to line three. A second BACKSPACE decrements the file pointer to line two, and so on. Once the file pointer is set to the first line in the file, either by opening the file, using a REWIND statement, or by using a BACKSPACE statement, a subsequent BACKSPACE statement has no effect. Program 5-16 illustrates the use of the REWIND and BACKSPACE statements.

Program 5-16

```
      PROGRAM MAIN
        CALL RETEST
        END
*
      SUBROUTINE RETEST
        INTEGER I, N
        REAL VAL
        OPEN(1,FILE = 'GRADES.DAT')
        DO 10 I = 1,3
          READ (1,*) N, VAL
   10   CONTINUE
        READ (1,*) N, VAL
        WRITE(6,*) N, VAL
        BACKSPACE(1)
        BACKSPACE(1)
        READ (1,*) N,VAL
        WRITE(6,*) N, VAL
        REWIND(1)
        READ (1,*) N, VAL
        WRITE(6,*) N, VAL
        CLOSE(1)
        RETURN
        END
```

Assuming the file GRADES.DAT contains the following data:

```
1   95.000000
2   83.000000
3  100.000000
4   85.000000
5   97.000000
```

The output of Program 5-16 is

```
4   85.000000
3  100.000000
1   95.000000
```

This output is produced as follows: The DO loop in Program 5-16 causes the first three lines in the file to be read. Upon completion of the DO loop the computer's internal file pointer points to the fourth line in the file. The READ statement immediately after the DO loop reads this line, which is then displayed by the next WRITE statement. The computer's internal file pointer now points to the fifth line. The first BACKSPACE statement then moves the file pointer back to the start of the fourth line, and the second BACKSPACE sets the pointer to the start of the third line. This line is then read and displayed. The REWIND statement then sets the file pointer to the start of the file. The final READ statement reads this first line, which is then displayed by the final WRITE statement.

Physical Device Files

The unit numbers we have used are called logical unit numbers. A *logical unit number* is one that references a file of logically related data that has been saved under a common name; that is, a data file. In addition to logical unit numbers, FORTRAN also supports physical unit numbers. A *physical unit number* references a hardware device, such as a keyboard, screen, or printer.

As we have already seen, the physical device assigned to your program for data entry is formally called the standard input file. Usually this is a keyboard. When a program is run, this standard input device is automatically opened and assigned a unit number, typically 1 or 5. Similarly, the output device used for display is also automatically opened and assigned a unit number, typically either 1 or 6. These unit numbers are always available for programmer use without the need for a formal OPEN statement.

In addition to the standard input and output devices, other devices can be used for input or output if the name assigned to them by the system is known. For example, on most IBM or IBM-compatible personal computers a video screen is the standard output device. Frequently, however, an application requires that a report or graph be displayed on the printer.

Since the IBM personal computer operating system (DOS) assigns the names PRN and LPT1 to the printer, these names can be used within an OPEN statement to connect the printer to a FORTRAN program. For example, the statement OPEN(1, FILE = 'PRN') makes the printer available for direct output from the program as file number 1. Any subsequent WRITE statement of the form WRITE(1,k) will cause its display to be sent to the printer. As always, the value of k determines the format of the output: if k is an integer number between 1 and 99999, it references a user-determined FORMAT statement and if k is an asterisk (*), list-directed output is selected for the display.

Exercises

1. Using the reference manuals provided with your computer's operating system, determine:

a. the maximum number of characters that can be used to name a file for storage by the computer system

b. the maximum number of data files that can be open at the same time

c. the file numbers that are reserved by the computer system and the file numbers that are available for programmer use

2. Would it be appropriate to call a saved FORTRAN program a file? Why or why not?
3. Write individual OPEN statements to link the following data file names to the corresponding unit numbers:

External Name	Unit Number
MATH.DAT	2
BOOK.DAT	3
RESIST.DAT	4
EXPER2.DAT	7
PRICES.DAT	8
RATES.MEM	9

4. Write CLOSE statements for each of the files opened in Exercise 3.

5a. Write a FORTRAN program that stores the following numbers into a file named RESULT.DAT: 16.25, 18.96, 22.34, 18.94, 17.42, 22.63

b. Write a FORTRAN program to read the data in the VALUE.DAT file created in Exercise 5a and display the data. Additionally, your program should compute and display the sum and average of the data. Check the sum and average displayed by your program using a hand calculation.

6a. Write a FORTRAN program that prompts the user to enter five numbers. As each number is entered the program should write the number into a file named VALUE.DAT.

b. Write a FORTRAN program that reads the data in the VALUE.DAT file created in Exercise 6a and displays each individual data item.

7a. Create a file containing the following car numbers, number of miles driven, and number of gallons of gas used by each car:

Car No.	Miles Driven	Gallons Used
54	250	19
62	525	38
71	123	6
85	1,322	86
97	235	14

b. Write a FORTRAN program that reads the data in the file created in Exercise 7a and displays the car number, miles driven, gallons used, and the miles per gallon for each car. The output should additionally display the total miles driven, total gallons used, and average miles per gallon for all the cars. These totals should be displayed at the end of the output report.

8a. Create a file with the following data containing the part number, opening balance, number of items sold, and minimum stock required:

Part Number	Initial Amount	Quantity Sold
310	95	47
145	320	162
514	34	20
212	163	150

b. Write a FORTRAN program to create an inventory report based on the data in the file created in Exercise 8a. The display should consist of the part number, initial amount, quantity sold, and current balance, where *current balance = initial amount - quantity sold.*

9a. Create a file containing the following data:

Identification Number	Rate	Hours
10031	6.00	40
10067	5.00	48
10083	6.50	35
10095	8.00	50

b. Write a FORTRAN program that uses the information contained in the file created in Exercise 9a to produce a pay report. The pay report should consist of identification number, rate, hours, and gross pay, where *gross pay = rate * hours.*

10a. Store the following data in a file:

```
5 96 87 78 93 21 4 92 82 85 87 6 72 69 85 75 81 73
```

b. Write a FORTRAN program to calculate and display the average of each group of numbers in the file created in Exercise 10a. The data is arranged in the file so that each group of numbers is preceded by the number of data items in the group. Thus, the first number in the file, 5, indicates that the next five numbers should be grouped together. The number 4 indicates that the following four numbers are a group, and the 6 indicates that the last six numbers are a group. (Hint: Use a nested loop. The outer loop should be executed three times.)

11. Enter and execute Program 5-13 so that the GRADES.DAT file created by this program exists on your computer system. Then, using the BACKSPACE statement, write a FORTRAN program that reads and displays the contents of the GRADES.DAT file in reverse line order.

12. Rotech Systems is a distributor of high-speed memory devices for specialized computer applications. Each memory device in stock is stored by tolerance. Having just completed an annual check of inventory in stock, Rotech has found it has the following quantities of memory devices in stock:

Device Number	5% Tolerance	2% Tolerance	1% Tolerance
SRAM4016	464	612	129
SRAM4314	742	1,215	375
SRAM4311	517	820	298
SRAM4364	684	105	22
SRAM4464	771	200	358

First create a file containing this inventory data. Then write a FORTRAN program that uses the information contained in the file to produce an inventory report. The inventory report should consist of device number, amounts in each tolerance level, and a total amount for each device category. Additionally, an estimate of the inventory's value is to be calculated and displayed. For this estimate assume an average value of $10 for each memory device and use the formula *Estimated Inventory Value = Average Value * Total Memory Devices in Stock.*

13a. Write a FORTRAN program that uses either the random number generator described in Section 4.5 or one supplied by your computer system to select

1,000 random numbers having values between 1 and 100. As each number is selected it should be written to a file called NUMBER.

b. Using the NUMBER file created in Exercise 13a, write a FORTRAN program that reads the data in the file and computes the average of the 1,000 data items.

14. Instead of using an actual file name in an OPEN statement, a character variable can be used. For example, the statement

```
OPEN (7, FILE = FNAME)
```

equates unit number 7 to the file name assigned to the variable FNAME. Here the variable FNAME must be declared as a character variable of sufficient length to hold a valid file name. The following code illustrates how this OPEN statement could be used in practice.

```
CHARACTER*12 FNAME
WRITE(6,*) 'ENTER A FILE NAME: '
READ (*,'(A)') FNAME
OPEN(7,FILE = FNAME)
```

The variable declaration statement in this code creates a character variable named FNAME having a length of twelve characters. This length was chosen because it is large enough to hold an actual file name consisting of eight initial characters, a period, and three extension characters. The code then requests that the file name be entered by the user. The entered name is stored in the character variable FNAME, which then is used by the OPEN statement. (Note: the entered name does not have to be enclosed in single quotes because user-formatting is used by the READ statement. If the list-directed statement, READ *, FNAME were used, the entered name would have to be enclosed in single quotes.)

a. Using this code, rewrite Program 5-13 so that the name of the data file is entered when the program is executed.

b. Modify the READ statement used in the program written for Exercise 11a so that it references a FORMAT statement rather than including the format directly within the READ statement.

5.5 User-Formatted Data Files

In addition to the list-directed format we have been using for writing and reading file data, explicit user-designated formats may also be used. In this section we present both the user-formatted READ and WRITE statements as they relate to data files.

Writing Formatted Files

The WRITE statement required to produce a user-formatted data file is identical to the WRITE statement used to produce user-formatted standard display output. As presented in Sections 2.4 and 5.4, the general form of this statement is:

```
WRITE(unit number, format specifier) expression list
```

For writing to a file the unit number in the WRITE statement must be either an integer number designating a previously opened file or an integer expression that evaluates to a valid integer file number. The format specifier designates the specific placement of the data written to the file. Acceptable format specifiers for file writes are the same as those for writing to the standard output device. These include:

1. An asterisk, which specifies a list-directed format
2. The statement number of a FORMAT statement
3. A literal format control character constant enclosed in parentheses that are themselves contained within apostrophes

For user-selected formatting the last two options are used. For example, the statement

```
WRITE(1,15) VALUE, SLOPE, NUMBER
```

references FORMAT statement 15, and the statement

```
WRITE(1,'(I4,1X,I3,2X,I3)') VALUE, SLOPE, NUMBER
```

includes a literal format character constant directly within the WRITE statement. The format specifications for writing to a file are identical to the format specifications previously described in Section 2.4 for standard output units. It is the unit number in the WRITE statement that directs the formatted output to a disk or tape unit rather than the standard output unit. There is one difference, however, in sending data to a disk or tape unit than to a display unit such as a video screen or printer: disk and tape units do not respond to the carriage control characters required by video screens and printers. Thus, if carriage control characters are written to a file, they will have no effect on the file, except to be stored with any other file data. The creation of a user-formatted file using a formatted WRITE statement is illustrated in Program 5-17.

Program 5-17

```
      PROGRAM MAIN
        CALL WRFILE
        END
*
      SUBROUTINE WRFILE
        INTEGER I
        REAL RESULT
        OPEN(1,FILE='TEST.DAT')
        DO 10 I = 1,5
          WRITE(6,*) 'ENTER A NUMBER'
          READ(5,*) RESULT
          WRITE(1,20) I, RESULT
 10     CONTINUE
 20     FORMAT(5X,I2,3X,F5.2)
        RETURN
        END
```

```
     1   26.50
     2   18.00
     3   44.75
     4   33.25
     5   52.00
123456789111111
         012345
```

Column Number One

Figure 5-7 The Structure of the TEST.DAT File

Program 5-17 uses the format specification `5X,I2,3X,F5.2` contained in FORMAT statement 20 for writing an integer and real value to each record in the TEST.DAT file. This format specifies that each line written will include a blank field of five spaces (note that the first space is not taken as a carriage control character), followed by an integer placed in a field consisting of two spaces, followed by a blank field of three spaces, followed by a real value with two decimal positions to the right of its decimal point placed within a field width of five spaces. Assuming the values 26.5, 18.0, 44.75, 33.25, and 52.0 were entered when the program was run, the file produced by Program 5-17 is illustrated in Figure 5-7. The italicized numbers in the figure indicate the column position occupied by each data item.

The Complete WRITE Statement

The WRITE statement we have been using for output is an abbreviated form of the more complete WRITE statement

```
WRITE (UNIT=u, FMT=fmt, IOSTAT=var, ERR=stl) expression list
```

where *u* and *fmt* are a unit number and format specifier, respectively. The terms UNIT, FMT, IOSTAT and ERR are optional keywords that may be placed in any order within the parentheses, *var* is a user-specified integer variable, and stl is a user-specified statement label (blank spaces may be used freely within the parentheses). If the keyword UNIT is not explicitly included in the statement, the unit number must be the first item in parentheses. If the FMT keyword is omitted, the format specifier must be the second item in the list and the keyword UNIT must also be omitted.

If the IOSTAT keyword is present it must be followed by an equal sign and an integer variable name (scalar or array element). The value assigned to the variable depends on the output status produced by the WRITE statement. The value assigned to the integer variable is zero if the WRITE statement executed without an error, or a positive value if an error was encountered (the actual positive value assigned to the variable is compiler dependent). The value assigned to the variable may be displayed using either a PRINT or WRITE statement. For example, the sequence of statements

```
WRITE(1, 20, IOSTAT=IVAL) A, B, C
WRITE(6,*) 'IVAL = ', IVAL
```

will output the values of the variables A, B, and C to file number 1 using format statement 20 and assign an I/O status value to the variable IVAL. The value of IVAL is then displayed on the standard output unit using a WRITE statement.

The ERR option specifies a statement label that control is transferred to if any error condition is encountered during the WRITE. If the ERR option is omitted and an output error does occur, a run-time error will be produced.

Formatted READ Statements

Both user-formatted and list-directed input from a file require a READ statement that permits designation of the file's unit number. As previously described in Section 3.3, the most commonly used form of this statement is:

```
READ (unit, fmt) variable list
```

where *unit* is a file unit number and *fmt* is a format specifier. The unit number, as always, designates the unit supplying the data. For data files the unit number must be either an integer number corresponding to an open file or an integer expression yielding such an integer. Just as in the WRITE statement, the fmt contained in the READ statement can be either

1. An asterisk, which specifies a list-directed format
2. The statement number of a FORMAT statement
3. A literal format control character constant enclosed in parentheses that are themselves contained within apostrophes

List-directed input, as we have seen, is especially convenient for keyboard input of numerical values because it recognizes spaces and commas as data separators. User-formatted input is typically used for reading data files where the format is the same for every line in the file. For example, assume that the variables NUM1 and NUM2 have been declared as integers. Then, the statement

```
READ(2,10) NUM1,NUM2
```

specifies that two integers are to be read from file number 2 using the format defined in FORMAT statement 10. For purposes of illustration, assume the following FORMAT statement:

```
10 FORMAT(I2,3X,I4)
```

This FORMAT statement specifies that the input record consists of two integer fields separated by three spaces. The first integer must occupy columns 1 and 2 of the record and the second 6 through 9. Using this format demands that the data in the file conform exactly to the fields specified. For example, consider the sequence of statements:

```
      INTEGER NUM1, NUM2
      OPEN(2,FILE='TEST.DAT')
      READ (2,10) NUM1, NUM2
   10 FORMAT(I2,3X,I4)
```

If the data stored in the TEST.DAT file is

```
45    6732     ← data in the file
123456789      ← column number
```

the value 45 is assigned to the variable NUM1 and the value 6732 is assigned to NUM2. If, on the other hand, the data in the file is

```
4    673 2     ← data in the file
123456789      ← column number
```

the number 4 is assigned to NUM1 and the number 732 is assigned to NUM2. Note that this assumes blanks embedded in each field are effectively ignored. (Some compilers are configured to interpret blank spaces as zeros.) The format specifications for reading integer, real, and character data, and for skipping over designated input fields are the same as those used for writing these items previously described in Section 3.3.

The Complete READ Statement

The READ statement we have used for inputting data from a file is n abbreviated form of the more complete READ statement

```
READ(UNIT=u,FMT=fmt,IOSTAT=var,ERR=st1,END=st2)  variable  list
```

where *u* and *fmt* are a unit number and format specifier, respectively. The words UNIT, FMT, IOSTAT, ERR, and END are optional keywords that may be placed in any order within the parentheses, *var* is a user-selected integer variable (scalar or subscripted), and *st1* and *st2* are statement labels (blank spaces may be used freely within the parentheses and have no effect on the statement). If the keyword UNIT is not explicitly included in the statement, the unit number must be the first item in parentheses. If the FMT keyword is omitted, the format specifier must be the second item in the list and the keyword UNIT must also be omitted. The IOSTAT, ERR, and END keywords provide optional error recovery from specific exceptional conditions.

If the IOSTAT keyword is present it must be followed by an equal sign and an integer scalar or array variable. The value assigned to the variable depends on the I/O status produced by the READ statement. The value assigned to the integer variable is zero if the READ statement executed without an error, it is assigned a negative number if an end-of-file was detected, and is assigned a positive value for any other detected error condition. The actual value assigned to the variable (not the signs, which are defined by the FORTRAN 77 standard) are compiler dependent and may be displayed using either a PRINT or WRITE statement. Thus, the sequence of statements

```
READ(5, 30, IOSTAT=IVAL) A, B, C
WRITE(6,*) 'IVAL = ', IVAL
```

will input three values from file number 5 into the variables A, B, and C, and assign an I/O status value to the variable IVAL. The value of IVAL is then displayed on the standard output unit using a WRITE statement.

The ERR option specifies a statement label that control is transferred to if any error condition is encountered except an end-of-file, while the END option specifies a statement label for transfer of control when the end of the file is detected. The statement labels specified by the ERR and END options can be the same. If the ERR option is omitted, an input error will produce a run-time error. For example, the statement:

```
READ(3,*, ERR = 10, END = 20) I, VAL
```

will read values for I and VAL *unless* an input error or the end of the file has been reached. In the case of an error control is transferred to statement number 10, while detection of the end-of-file (EOF) marker results in a transfer to statement number 20. The ERR and END options are very useful in providing graceful termination from unexpected input conditions in place of a more abrupt run-time error. For example, consider Program 5-18, which expects to read and display 50 lines from the TEST.DAT file.

Program 5-18

```
      PROGRAM MAIN
        CALL SHFILE
        END
*
      SUBROUTINE SHFILE
        INTEGER I, N
        REAL RESULT
 5      FORMAT(5X,I2,3X,F5.2)
        OPEN(1,FILE='TEST.DAT')
        WRITE(6,*) '        EXPERIMENT'
        WRITE(6,*) '          NUMBER      RESULT'
        WRITE(6,*) '        ---------------------'
        DO 10 I = 1, 50
          READ(1,5, ERR=20, END=30) N, RESULT
          WRITE(6,*) N, RESULT
10      CONTINUE
          RETURN
20      STOP 'ERROR IN FILE READ'
30      STOP 'END OF FILE WAS DETECTED'
       END
```

The READ statement in the DO loop will read an integer and real valued number 50 times, unless either a data error is detected (such as character data in the file when numeric data is expected) or the end-of-file is reached. Until these latter two conditions are detected the READ statement executes as if both the ERR and END options are not present. If an error is detected control is transferred to statement 20, which stops the program and displays an error message. Similarly, if the end-of-file marker is detected, control is transferred to statement 30. Using the TEST.DAT file created by Program 5-17, which contains only five lines, the output produced by Program 5-18 is:

```
          EXPERIMENT
            NUMBER        RESULT
          ------------------------
                1        26.500000
                2        18.000000
                3        44.750000
                4        33.250000
                5        52.000000
      END OF FILE WAS DETECTED
```

Exercises

1. List the starting and ending column numbers for all input fields defined by the following statements.

 a. `10 FORMAT(I2,F6.3,I4)`
 b. `20 FORMAT(F7,2,I2,A6)`
 c. `30 FORMAT(5X,F5.2,7X,A25)`
 d. `40 FORMAT(3(2X,I4))`
 e. `60 FORMAT(6X,3(I2,3X),F6.2,3(3X,I2))`

2. The following is a valid FORTRAN program.

```
      PROGRAM MAIN
        CALL SHFILE
        END
*
      SUBROUTINE SHFILE
        INTEGER NUM1, NUM2
        OPEN (3, FILE = 'TEST.DAT')
        READ(3,10) NUM1, NUM2
10      FORMAT(I4,I3)
        WRITE(6,*) NUM1, NUM2
        RETURN
        END
```

Assuming that the following data is stored in the file named TEST.DAT

```
1 23 45
1234567
↑
 Column Number 1
```

determine the output produced by the program.

3a. The following is a valid FORTRAN program.

```
      PROGRAM MAIN
        CALL  TESTIT
        END
*
        SUBROUTINE TESTIT
          INTEGER I
          REAL NUM1, NUM2
          OPEN (3, FILE = 'TEST.DAT')
          DO 20 I = 1,4
            READ(3,30) NUM1, NUM2
            WRITE(6,*) NUM1, NUM2
20        CONTINUE
30        FORMAT(1X,F7.2,2X,F5.2)
          RETURN
          END
```

Determine the output produced by this program assuming that the following data is stored in the file named TEST.DAT

```
 6.78    23.4
6.78    23.4
    678     345
678         234
123456789111111
        012345
↑
```

Column Number 1

b. Verify your answers for Exercise 3a by first creating the TEST.DAT file given in the problem and then running the listed program. (You may create TEST.DAT either by using an editor or writing a FORTRAN program that reads the data from the keyboard and writes it to the file.) Using the display produced by your program, determine whether your compiler ignores blank spaces within an input field or considers them as zeros.

4. Determine the output produced by the following program

```
      PROGRAM MAIN
        CALL RETEST
        END
*
      SUBROUTINE RETEST
        INTEGER NUM1, NUM2
        OPEN(1,FILE='TEST.DAT')
        NUM1 = 45
        NUM2 = 67
        NUM3 = 32
        WRITE(1,5) NUM1, NUM2, NUM3
5       FORMAT(3(1X,I2))
        REWIND(1)
        READ(1,10)NUM1, NUM2
```

```
10      FORMAT(1X,I2,1X,I4)
        WRITE(6,*) NUM1, NUM2
        RETURN
        END
```

5. Determine if the following program will work. Discuss what should be changed in the program, if anything.

```
      PROGRAM MAIN
        CALL WRFILE
        END
*
      SUBROUTINE WRFILE
        CHARACTER*8, MESSGE
        INTEGER NUM1, NUM2
        OPEN(2,FILE='RESULT.DAT'
        READ(2,10) MESSGE, NUM1, NUM2
        WRITE(6,10) MESSGE, NUM1, NUM2
10      FORMAT(1X,A,2(1X,I3))
        RETURN
        END
```

6a. Rewrite Program 5-17 to include the format specification as a literal character constant directly within the WRITE statement.

b. Rewrite Program 5-17 using list-directed formatting for records written to the TEST.DAT file.

c. Rewrite Program 5-18 to input and display the data in the file produced by the program written for Exercise 6b.

7a. Write a FORTRAN program that writes the four real numbers 92.65, 88.72, 77.46, and 82.93 to a file named RESULT using the FORMAT statement

```
10 FORMAT(4(1X,F5.2))
```

After writing the data to the file your program should read the data from the file, determine the average of the four numbers read, and display the average.

b. Compile and run the program written for Exercise 7a. Additionally, verify the output produced by your program by manually calculating the average of the four input numbers.

8a. Using the FORMAT statement

```
10 FORMAT(4(1X,F5.2))
```

write a FORTRAN program that creates a file named POINTS and writes the following numbers to the file:

```
 6.3  8.2  18.25  24.32    ← 1st line
 4.0  4.0  10.0   -5.0     ← 2nd line
-2.0  5.0   4.0    5.0     ← 3rd line
```

b. Using the data in the POINTS file created in Exercise 8a, write a FORTRAN program that reads each record and interprets the first and second numbers in each record as the coordinates of one point and the third and fourth numbers as the coordinates of a second point. Using the formulas given in Exercise 8 and 9 of Section 2.4, have your program compute and display the slope and midpoint of the two points entered. Your program should include the END option of the formatted READ statement.

c. Compile, run, and manually verify the output produced by the program written for Exercise 8b.

9a. Using the FORMAT statement

```
10 FORMAT(4(I3,2X))
```

write a FORTRAN program that creates a file named GRADES and writes the following numbers to the file:

```
100, 100, 100, 100
100, 0, 100, 0
86, 83, 89, 94
78, 59, 77, 85
89, 92, 81, 88
```

b. Using the data in the GRADES file created in Exercise 9a, write, compile, and run a FORTRAN program that reads each line in the GRADES file, computes the average for each line, and displays the average.

10. Redo Exercise 12 of Section 5.4 using a formatted file. Your first task is to create a file containing the inventory data. Each line in the file should consist of a device number, and the three inventory levels for that part number should be written using the FORMAT statement

```
10 FORMAT(A8,3(2X,I4))
```

After the file has been created write, compile, and run a FORTRAN program that reads the information contained in the file and produces an inventory report. The inventory report should consist of device number, amounts in each tolerance level, and a total amount for each device category.

5.6 Applications

In this section two applications are presented to further illustrate using files to store data and DO loops to process the data in the files. The first application uses a file as a data base for storing the ten most recent pollen counts, which are used in the summer as allergy "irritability" measures. As a new reading is obtained, a new file is created to contain the ten most recent readings.

In the second application a program is constructed to accept a set of grades from a file and determine the average and standard deviation of the stored data.

Application 1: Pollen Counts

Pollen count readings, which are taken from August through September in the northeastern region of the United States, measure the number of ragweed pollen grains in the air. Pollen counts in the range of 10 to 200 grains per cubic meter of air are typical during this time of year. Typically, pollen counts above 10 begin to affect a small percentage of hay fever sufferers, counts in the range of 30 to 40 will noticeably bother approximately 30 percent of hay fever sufferers, while counts between 40 and 50 adversely affect over 60 percent of all hay fever sufferers.

A program is to be written that creates a new file containing the ten most recent pollen counts. The ten values in the file must consist of the last nine pollen counts in the current file plus the newest pollen count entered by the user. (This type of data storage is formally referred to as a first-in first-out (FIFO) list, also called a *queue*. If the list is maintained in last-in first-out order (LIFO), it is called a *stack*.) Additionally, the average of the new file's data is to be calculated and displayed. For purposes of illustration, assume that a file name POLL1, containing the data shown in Figure 5-8, has already been created.

```
 30 ← oldest pollen count (to be deleted)
 60
 40
 80
 90
120
150
130
160
170 ← last pollen count
```

Figure 5-8 Data Currently in the POLL1 File

The pseudocode for the file update program is:

Display a message indicating what the program does
Request the name of the existing data file
Request the name of the new data file to be created
Request a new pollen count reading
Initialize a total with the new pollen count reading
Open both existing and new files
Read the first POLLEN count in the existing file
Do for the next nine POLLEN records in the existing file
Read a pollen count
  Add the count to the total
  Write the count to the new file
Enddo
Write the new pollen count to the new file
Close both files
Calculate and display the current ten day average.

The construction of the new data file from the existing data file and the new pollen count, as described by this algorithm, is illustrated in Figure 5-9. Program 5-19 expresses this algorithm in FORTRAN.

Program 5-19

```
      PROGRAM MAIN
        CALL RENEW
        END
*
      SUBROUTINE RENEW
        INTEGER PCOUNT, NEWCNT, SUM, I
        REAL AVERGE
        CHARACTER*12 CURNAM, NEWNAM
*** GET THE DATA FILE NAMES AND MOST RECENT POLLEN COUNT
        WRITE(6,*)'      THIS PROGRAM CREATES A NEW POLLEN COUNT FILE'
        WRITE(6,*)'         AND CALCULATES A NEW TEN COUNT AVERAGE'
        WRITE(6,*)
        WRITE(6,*) 'ENTER THE CURRENT POLLEN FILE NAME (IN APOSTROPHES): '
        READ (5,*) CURNAM
        WRITE(6,*) 'ENTER THE NEW POLLEN FILE NAME (IN APOSTROPHES): '
        READ (5,*) NEWNAM
        WRITE(6,*) 'ENTER THE NEW POLLEN COUNT READING: '
        READ (5,*) NEWCNT
        SUM = NEWCNT
*** OPEN THE FILES AND WRITE THE NEW FILE
        OPEN(1,FILE = CURNAM)
        OPEN(2,FILE = NEWNAM)
*** READ THE OLDEST POLLEN COUNT - DO NOTHING WITH IT
        READ(1,*, ERR = 20, END = 30) PCOUNT
*** READ AND USE THE REMAINING POLLEN COUNTS
        DO 5 I = 1,9
          READ(1,*, ERR = 20, END = 30) PCOUNT
          SUM = SUM + PCOUNT
          WRITE(2,*) PCOUNT
    5   CONTINUE
*** WRITE THE LATEST POLLEN COUNT TO THE NEW FILE
        WRITE(2,*) NEWCNT
        WRITE(6,*) '    AN UPDATED DATA FILE HAS BEEN WRITTEN'
        CLOSE(1)
        CLOSE(2)
*** COMPUTE AND DISPLAY THE NEW AVERAGE
        AVERGE = REAL(SUM)/10.0
        WRITE(6,*) '     THE NEW 10 COUNT AVERAGE IS: ', AVERGE
        RETURN
   20   STOP 'ERROR IN READING EXISTING POLLEN FILE'
   30   STOP 'END OF EXISTING POLLEN FILE REACHED'
        END
```

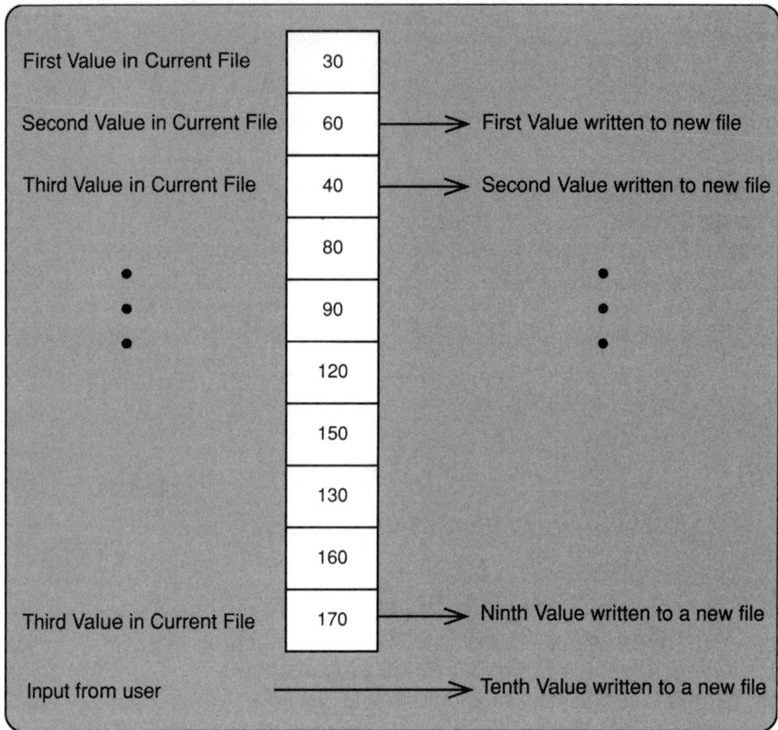

Figure 5-9 The Update Process

Following is a sample run using Program 5-19:

```
        THIS PROGRAM CREATES A NEW POLLEN COUNT FILE
           AND CALCULATES A NEW TEN COUNT AVERAGE
  ENTER THE CURRENT POLLEN FILE NAME (IN APOSTROPHES):
  'POLL1'
  ENTER THE NEW POLLEN FILE NAME (IN APOSTROPHES):
  'POLL2'
  ENTER THE NEW POLLEN COUNT READING:
  200
     AN UPDATED DATA FILE HAS BEEN WRITTEN
      THE NEW 10 COUNT AVERAGE IS:       120.000000
```

The updated file created by Program 5-19 is illustrated in Figure 5-10. In reviewing the contents of this file notice that the most current reading has been added to the end of the file and that the other counts are obtained from the original file shown in Figure 5-9, but moved up one position in the file.

Notice also that the names of the existing data files were entered using apostrophes. This is required when character data is entered in response to list-directed input. If a formatted READ statement were used, the names of the files would be entered without the enclosing apostrophes.

```
 60 <— oldest count
 40
 80
 90
120
150
130
160
170
200 <— most recent reading
```

Figure 5-10 The Updated POLL1 File

Application 2: Grade Analysis

A program is to be developed that accepts a list of grades, contained in a file named GRADES.DAT, as input and calculates both the average and standard deviation of the grades.

Program Development

For this program we will apply the complete top-down development procedure described in Chapter 2 to ensure that you understand the required processing.

Step 1: Determine the Desired Output
The statement of the problem indicates that two output values are required: an average and standard deviation.

Step 2: Determine the Input Items
The input item defined in the problem statement is a list of grades contained in a file. Because the size of the list is not specified in the problem statement and to make our program as general as possible, it will be designed to handle any size list, with the actual number of grades in the file entered at run time by the user. Additionally, we will design the program to accept the name of the file at run time as a user-entered data item.

Step 3a: Determine an Algorithm
This problem is again a classic application of the Problem Solver Algorithm presented in Section 4.2. For this particular application the algorithm takes the form:

Obtain the data file name and number of grades in the file
Read the file and calculate an average and standard deviation
Display the calculated values

A first-level structure diagram corresponding to this algorithm is illustrated in Figure 5-11. Using a modular design approach, each of the tasks specified in the structure is coded in its own subroutine program unit.

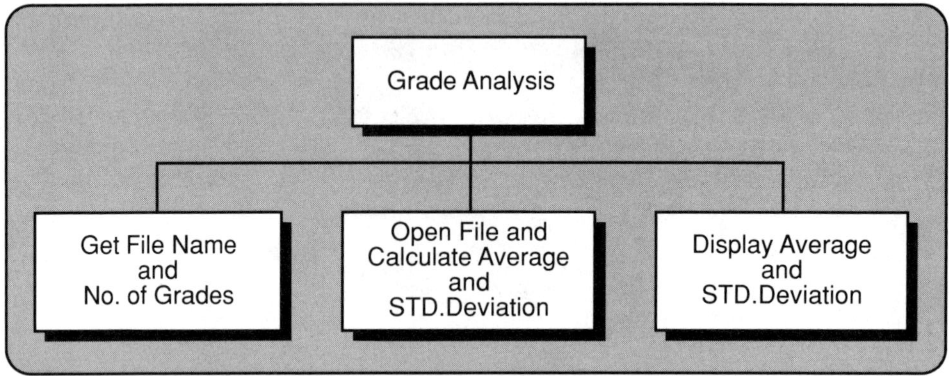

Figure 5-11 First-Level Structure Diagram for Application 2

As the determination of a standard deviation is new to us, we must be careful to describe and understand the algorithm to be used for this calculation. The calculation of a standard deviation requires that the average be known. The complete algorithm for the standard deviation, which includes the computation of an average, is:

Calculate the average as follows:
Do for each grade in the file:
Read a grade
Add the grade to a total
Enddo
Divide the final total by the number of grades in the file.
Calculate the standard deviation as follows:
Rewind the grades file
Do for each grade in the file
Read a grade
Subtract the average from the grade. The resulting value is called a deviation.
Square the deviation just calculated
Add the squared deviation to a total
Enddo
Divide the sum of the squared deviations by the number of grades
The square root of the number found in the previous step is the standard deviation

Step 3b: Do a Hand Calculation

To ensure that we understand the required processing we will do a hand calculation. For this calculation we will arbitrarily assume that the average and standard deviation of the following ten grades are to be determined: 98, 82, 67, 54, 78, 83, 95, 76, 68, and 63.

The average of this data is determined as

$$\text{Average} = (98 + 82 + 67 + 54 + 78 + 83 + 95 + 76 + 68 + 63)/10 = 76.4$$

The standard deviation is calculated by first determining the sum of the squared deviations. The standard deviation is then obtained by dividing the resulting sum by 10 and taking its square root.

$$\begin{aligned}\text{Sum of squared deviations} &= (98 - 76.4)^2 + (82 - 76.4)^2 \\ &+ (67 - 76.4)^2 + (54 - 76.4)^2 \\ &+ (78 - 76.4)^2 + (83 - 76.4)^2 \\ &+ (95 - 76.4)^2 + (76 - 76.4)^2 \\ &+ (68 - 76.4)^2 + (63 - 76.4)^2 \\ &= 1730.400700\end{aligned}$$

$$\text{Standard Deviation is } \sqrt{1730.4007/10} = \sqrt{173.04007} = 13.154470$$

Step 3c: Select Variable and Argument Names

For this problem we will use the argument names FNAME and NUMEL for the file name and number of elements, and the names AVERGE and STDDEV for the calculated average and standard deviation, respectively. Internal to the subroutine used for reading and processing the grades file we will use a variable named GRADE for each grade, SUMGRD for the summing the grades, and the variable named SUMDEV for summing the squared deviations.

Step 4: Write the Required Subroutines

The input subroutine for entering the file name and number of values in the file is rather straight forward, and is written as follows:

```
      SUBROUTINE GET(FNAME, NUMEL)
        INTEGER NUMEL
        CHARACTER FNAME*12
        WRITE(6,*) 'ENTER THE FILE NAMES FOR THE GRADES:'
        READ(5,10) FNAME
 10     FORMAT(A12)
        WRITE(6,*) 'ENTER THE NUMBER OF GRADES IN THE FILE:'
        READ(5,*) NUMEL
        RETURN
        END
```

This subroutine asks the user to supply both a file name and the number of values in the file, which are passed to the calling routine as arguments. Notice that the file name is read using a formatted READ statement, which allows the user to enter the file name without enclosing them in apostrophes. The subroutine used for displaying the calculated average and standard deviation is also a simple one. This program unit, which must accept two passed arguments and display their values, is written as follows:

```
      SUBROUTINE SHOW(AVERGE, STDDEV)
        REAL AVERGE, STDDEV
        WRITE(6,10) AVERGE
        WRITE(6,20) STDDEV
 10     FORMAT(1X,'THE AVERAGE OF THE DATA IS: ', F6.2)
 20     FORMAT(1X,'THE STANDARD DEVIATION OF THE DATA IS: ', F6.2)
        RETURN
        END
```

The subroutine for reading the data file and calculating the average and standard deviation, which is the most challenging subprogram of this program, now follows:

The header line for this subroutine, which we will name STATS, must include four arguments: one for receiving the file name, one for receiving the number of grades in the file, one for returning the calculated average, and one for returning the calculated standard deviation. Using the argument names selected in Step 3c, the subroutine header becomes

```
SUBROUTINE STATS(FNAME, NUMEL, AVERGE, STDDEV)
```

The order of the arguments within the argument list is entirely arbitrary. For convenience we have placed those arguments that will be used as input to the subroutine first, and those arguments that will be used to return the average and standard deviation last. (Keep in mind, however, that from FORTRAN's standpoint each of the four arguments really provides a two-way swinging door in which values may be exchanged in any direction between the calling program unit and the subroutine.)

The appropriate declarations for the subroutine's arguments becomes:

```
INTEGER NUMEL
REAL AVERGE, STDDEV
CHARACTER FNAME*12
```

The remaining body of the subroutine simply calculates the average and standard deviation according to the algorithm described in Step 3a of the Development Procedure. Thus, the completed subroutine becomes

```
      SUBROUTINE STATS(FNAME, NUMEL, AVERGE, STDDEV)
        INTEGER NUMEL, I
        REAL AVERGE, STDDEV, SUMGRD, SUMDEV, GRADE
        CHARACTER FNAME*12
        OPEN(1, FILE = FNAME)
***   CALCULATE THE AVERAGE     ***
        SUMGRD = 0.0
        DO 10 I = 1, NUMEL
          READ(1,*) GRADE
          SUMGRD = SUMGRD + GRADE
   10   CONTINUE
        AVERGE = SUMGRD / NUMEL
***   CALCULATE THE STANDARD DEVIATION     ***
        REWIND(1)
        SUMDEV = 0.0
        DO 20 I = 1, NUMEL
          READ(1,*) GRADE
          SUMDEV = SUMDEV + (GRADE - AVERGE)**2
   20   CONTINUE
        STDDEV = SQRT(SUMDEV/NUMEL)
        CLOSE(1)
        RETURN
        END
```

Notice that the calculation portion of the subroutine uses one DO loop to sum the individual grades and a second DO loop to determine the sum of the squared deviations. Because calculation of the squared deviations requires the average, the standard deviation can be calculated only after the average has been computed. Notice also that the termination value of the loop counter in both DO loops is NUMEL, which is the number of grades that is passed to the subroutine through the argument list. The use of this argument gives the subroutine its generality and allows it to be used for lists of any number of grades. Adding an appropriate MAIN program unit to our three subroutines results in Program 5-20.

Program 5-20

```
      PROGRAM MAIN
        INTEGER NUMEL
        REAL AVERGE, STDDEV
        CHARACTER*12 FNAME
        CALL GET(FNAME, NUMEL)
        PRINT *, FNAME, NUMEL
        CALL STATS(FNAME, NUMEL, AVERGE, STDDEV)
        CALL SHOW(AVERGE, STDDEV)
        END
      SUBROUTINE GET(FNAME, NUMEL)
        INTEGER NUMEL
        CHARACTER FNAME*12
        WRITE(6,*) 'ENTER THE FILE NAMES FOR THE GRADES:'
        READ(5,10) FNAME
 10     FORMAT(A12)
        WRITE(6,*) 'ENTER THE NUMBER OF GRADES IN THE FILE:'
        READ(5,*) NUMEL
        RETURN
        END
      SUBROUTINE STATS(FNAME, NUMEL, AVERGE, STDDEV)
        INTEGER NUMEL, I
        REAL AVERGE, STDDEV, SUMGRD, SUMDEV, GRADE
        CHARACTER FNAME*12
        OPEN(1, FILE = FNAME)
***   CALCULATE THE AVERAGE      ***
        SUMGRD = 0.0
        DO 10 I = 1, NUMEL
          READ(1,*) GRADE
          SUMGRD = SUMGRD + GRADE
 10     CONTINUE
        AVERGE = SUMGRD / NUMEL
***   CALCULATE THE STANDARD DEVIATION     ***
        REWIND(1)
        SUMDEV = 0.0
        DO 20 I = 1, NUMEL
          READ(1,*) GRADE
          SUMDEV = SUMDEV + (GRADE - AVERGE)**2
```

(Continued on the next page)

(Continued from the previous page)

```
 20      CONTINUE
         STDDEV = SQRT(SUMDEV/NUMEL)
         CLOSE(1)
         RETURN
         END
       SUBROUTINE SHOW(AVERGE, STDDEV)
         REAL AVERGE, STDDEV
         WRITE(6,10) AVERGE
         WRITE(6,20) STDDEV
  10     FORMAT(1X,'THE AVERAGE OF THE DATA IS: ', F6.2)
  20     FORMAT(1X,'THE STANDARD DEVIATION OF THE DATA IS: ', F6.2)
         RETURN
         END
```

Step 5: Test the Program

Testing Program 5-20 requires running it with the data previously used in our hand calculation. This data was first written to a file named GRADES. A test run using Program 5-20 with the GRADES data file resulted in the following:

```
ENTER THE FILE NAMES FOR THE GRADES:
GRADES
ENTER THE NUMBER OF GRADES IN THE FILE:
10
THE AVERAGE OF THE DATA IS:  76.40
THE STANDARD DEVIATION OF THE DATA IS:  13.15
```

Since this result agrees with our previous hand calculations and the STATS( ) subroutine contains no additional calculations that have not been verified, the program has been completely tested.

Additional File Exercises

1. Write a FORTRAN program to create the POLL1 file illustrated in Figure 5-8.
2. Modify Program 5-19 to calculate both the old and new pollen count average.
3. Modify Program 5-20 to count the number of grades in the file as it is being READ. (Hint: This will require using the END option of the READ statement to stop READing the file when it is out of data.)

4a. A file named POLAR.DAT contains the polar coordinates needed in a graphics program. Currently this file contains the following data:

Distance (Inches)	Angle (Degrees)
2	45
6	30
10	45
4	60
12	55
8	15

Write a FORTRAN program to create this file on your computer system.

b. Using the POLAR.DAT file created in Exercise 4a, write a FORTRAN program that accepts distance and angle data from the user and adds the data to the end of the file.

c. Using the POLAR.DAT file created in Exercise 4a, write a FORTRAN program that reads this file and creates a second file named XYCORD.DAT. The entries in the new file should contain the rectangular coordinates corresponding to the polar coordinates in the POLAR.DAT file. Polar coordinates are converted to rectangular coordinates using the equations

$$x = r\ cos(theta)$$
$$y = r\ sin(theta)$$

where r is the distance coordinate and *theta* is the radian equivalent of the angle coordinate in the POLAR.DAT file.

5a. Write a FORTRAN program to create a data file containing the following information:

Student ID Number	Student Name	Course Name	Course Credits	Course Grade
2333021	BOKOW, R.	NS201	3	4.0
2333021	BOKOW, R.	MG342	3	4.0
2333021	BOKOW, R.	FA302	1	3.5
2333021	BOKOW, R.	MK106	3	2.0
2574063	FALLIN, D.	MA208	3	3.0
2574063	FALLIN, D.	CM201	3	2.0
2574063	FALLIN, D.	CP101	2	3.0
2574063	FALLIN, D.	QA140	3	4.0
2663628	KINGSLEY, M.	CM245	3	3.0
2663628	KINGSLEY, M.	EQ521	3	4.0
2663628	KINGSLEY, M.	MK341	3	4.0
2663628	KINGSLEY, M.	CP101	2	3.5

b. Using the file created in Exercise 5a, write a FORTRAN program that creates a student grade reports. The grade report for each student should contain the student's name and identification number, a list of courses taken, the credits and grade for each course, and a semester grade point average. For example, the grade report for the first student is:

```
STUDENT NAME: BOKOW, R.
STUDENT ID NUMBER:

Course        Credits   Grade
NS201            3        4.0
MG342            3        4.0
FA302            1        3.5
MK106            3        2.0
TOTAL SEMESTER COURSE CREDITS COMPLETED: 10
SEMESTER GRADE POINT AVERAGE: 3.35
```

The semester grade point average is computed in two steps. First, the sum of each course's grade value times the credits for each course is computed. This sum is then divided by the total number of credits taken during the semester. (Hint: You will need a nested DO loop for this problem.)

6a. Write a FORTRAN program to create a data file containing the following information:

StudentStudent ID Number	Course Name	Cumulative Credits	Grade Point Average (GPA)
2333021	BOKOW, R.	48	4.0
2574063	FALLIN, D.	12	1.8
2663628	KINGSLEY, M.	36	3.5

b. Using the file created in Exercise 6a as one file and the file created in Exercise 5a as a second file, write a program that creates a third file containing the data from both files, in the proper order. That is, the data for each student should be grouped together before the data for the next student is encountered.

c. Using the file created in Exercise 6a, write a program that calculates and displays the student grade report shown in Exercise 5b.

5.7 Common Programming Errors

The common programming errors made in using DO loops are:

1. Modifying a DO statement's counter variable within the DO loop.
2. Using the value of the counter after the loop has completed executing (the final value is computer dependent).
3. Using uninitialized variable names as DO statement parameters.
4. Failing to initialize an accumulator variable prior to entering a DO loop when the loop is used for summing purposes.
5. Failing to enclose an inner DO loop entirely within the outer DO loop.
6. Forgetting to use the same statement label for the CONTINUE statement as was used in the DO statement.

The common programming errors made when using files are:

1. Incorrect use of the OPEN statement. As a minimum this statement must include a unit number and the FILE = 'filename' specifier.
2. Forgetting to use the file's unit number when using a file READ or WRITE statement. Programmers used to writing these statements for standard input and output devices sometimes forget to change the unit number when accessing data files.
3. Attempting to use a PRINT statement for file writing by replacing the list-directed asterisk with a unit number. The PRINT statement can only access the standard output device. If a unit number is used in this statement, the compiler will consider it to be a FORMAT statement label.

5.8 Things to Remember

1. The DO statement is extremely useful in creating loops that must be executed a fixed number of times. The initializing value, final value, and increment used by the loop

counter are all included within the DO statement. The general form of a DO loop is:

```
        DO k counter = initial, final, increment
          statement 1
          statement 2
              .
              .
          statement n
    k   CONTINUE
```

2. The initial, final, and increment values of the DO statement, which are referred to as *parameters* of the statement, may be constants, variables, expressions, or returned function values.
3. If the increment parameter of a DO statement is positive, the initial value must be less than the final value for the loop to operate correctly. If the increment parameter is negative, the initial value must be greater than the final value for the loop to operate correctly.
4. The value of the counter variable must not be altered within a DO loop.
5. The value of the counter variable after the loop has finished executing is system dependent, and should not, therefore, be used in any expression.
6. A *data file* is any collection of data stored together on an external storage medium under a common name. Formally, each line of data stored on the file is called a *record*.
7. The manner in which records are written to and read from a file is called the file's access method. In a sequentially accessed file each record must be accessed in a sequential manner. This means that the second record in the file cannot be read until the first record has been read, the third record cannot be read until the first and second records have been read, and so on until the last record is read. Similarly, a record cannot be written until all previous records have been written and a record cannot be replaced without destroying all following records.
8. A file can be either a formatted or unformatted file.

a. A *formatted file* is one in which each data item in the file is formatted, using either explicit user-designated formats or the compiler's list-directed format. A formatted file is also referred to a text file and is the type of file presented in this chapter.

b. An *unformatted file* is one is which each data item in the file is stored using the computer's internal binary code. An unformatted file is also referred to as a *binary* file and is the subject of Chapter 11.

9. An OPEN statement is required to connect a file name to a program unit number. The most basic form of the OPEN statement is:

```
OPEN (unit number, FILE = 'filename')
```

This form of the OPEN statement, by default, designates the file as both sequential and formatted. If the file does not exist, the OPEN statement creates a file having the indicated name.

10. Data is written to a file using a WRITE statement. The most basic form of this statement for writing to a sequential, formatted file is:

```
WRITE(unit number, format specifier) expression list
```

The unit number in all WRITE statements must either be an integer number designating a previously opened file or an integer expression that evaluates to a valid integer file number. The format specifier can be either an asterisk, which specifies a list-directed format, the statement number of a FORMAT statement, or a literal format control character constant enclosed in parentheses and surrounded by apostrophes.

11. Data is read from an existing file using a READ statement. The most basic form of this statement for reading from a sequential, formatted file is

```
READ(unit number, format specifier) variable list
```

The unit number in all READ statements must either be an integer number designating a previously opened file or an integer expression that evaluates to a valid integer file number. The format specifier can be either an asterisk, which specifies a list-directed format, the statement number of a FORMAT statement, or a format control character constant contained within in apostrophes.

12. In addition to files opened explicitly within a program, the standard input and output files are automatically opened when a FORTRAN program is executed. The standard input file corresponds to the physical device used for data entry, and the standard output file is the physical device used for data display. Each of these files is assigned a unit number by the system. On many systems an asterisk can be used in place of a unit number to designate the standard I/O device. This asterisk is distinct from the asterisk used to select list-directed formatting.

13. The REWIND statement, which has the general form:

```
REWIND(file-number)
```

sets the file to its first record. A REWIND is done automatically when a file is opened.

14. The BACKSPACE statement, which has the general form:

```
BACKSPACE(file-number)
```

moves the current position in the file back one record.

15. Files are formally closed using a CLOSE statement. The most common form of this statement is:

```
CLOSE(file-number)
```

All opened files are automatically closed when the program they are opened is finished executing.

5.9 Enrichment Study: Writing Control Codes

In addition to responding to the codes for letters, digits, and special punctuation symbols, which are collectively referred to as printable characters, physical device files such as printers and CRT screens can also respond to a small set of control codes. Because control codes have no equivalent character that can be displayed, they are also referred to as non-printable characters.

Four of these codes that are extremely useful in applications are the bell, page eject, line feed, and carriage return control codes. When a page eject control code is sent to a printer a page of paper is ejected and printing begins on the next sheet of paper. If care is taken to align the printer to the top of a new page when printing is started, the page eject control character can be used as an equivalent "top-of-page" command. The bell code is used to sound the bell or speaker contained within every display terminal, the line feed code is used to advance the output display by one line, and the carriage return code moves the display cursor or print head to column one on the current line.

Sending control codes to an output device is done in a similar manner as sending a printable character to a file. Instead of sending an actual character to the output device, the numerical value of the control code is used. For computers that use the ASCII code, this amounts to substituting the equivalent ASCII numerical value for the appropriate letter. Referring to Table 2.1 in Section 2.1, we see that the ASCII code for an A, for example, is the binary value 01000001, which corresponds to the decimal number 65. This numerical value can be converted to a character by using FORTRAN's intrinsic CHAR( ) function. Thus, the statement `WRITE(6,*) CHAR(65)`, for example, causes an A to be output to the standard output unit. This statement produces the same display as the statement `WRITE(6,*) 'A'`.

The importance of using the CHAR( ) function and the numerical code for the letter is only realized when a control code, rather than a character code, must be transmitted. Since no equivalent character exists for control codes, the numerical value for the code must be used within the CHAR( ) function. For all computers that use the ASCII code, the bell, line feed, and carriage return code correspond to the decimal numbers 7, 10, and 13 respectively. For most printers the decimal page eject code is a decimal 12. For example, using this code and assuming the printer is the standard output device, the statement

```
WRITE(6,*)  CHAR(12)
```

causes the printer to eject the current page. Similarly, if the CRT is the standard output device the code

```
      WRITE(6,*) CHAR(7), CHAR(7), CHAR(7)
      DO 10 I = 1,25
        WRITE(6,*) CHAR(10)
10    CONTINUE
```

causes the bell to be "beeped" three times and the screen cleared. The clearing of the screen is accomplished by sending 25 consecutive line feeds to it. Program 5-21 illustrates how this code could be included in a working program, using individual subroutines to sound the bell and clear the screen. In each subroutine the appropriate codes have been equated to more meaningful character variable names.

Program 5-21

```
      PROGRAM MAIN
        CALL BELL3
        CALL CLEAR
        END
*
      SUBROUTINE BELL3
        CHARACTER BELL
        BELL = CHAR(7)
        WRITE(6,*) BELL, BELL, BELL
        RETURN
        END
*
      SUBROUTINE CLEAR
        CHARACTER LINEFD
        LINEFD = CHAR(10)
        DO 10 I = 1,25
          WRITE(6,*) LINEFD
 10     CONTINUE
        RETURN
        END
```

Program 5-21 will also work if the printer is the standard output device, except that 66 line feeds would be required to eject a standard page. For printers, however, it is easier to send the single page eject code. If the printer is not the standard output device it must first be opened before the eject code is transmitted.

For IBM personal computers the printer has the file name PRN. Program 5-22 illustrates using this name to open a printer connected to an IBM or IBM-compatible personal computer and then send a page eject code to it.

Program 5-22

```
      PROGRAM MAIN'CALL NEWPG
        END
      *
      SUBROUTINE NEWPG
        CHARACTER EJECT
        EJECT = CHAR(12)
        OPEN (1, FILE = 'PRN')
        WRITE (6,*) EJECT
        RETURN
        END
```

LAB SET FOR CHAPTERS FOUR AND FIVE

LAB ASSIGNMENT 6

1. For the following program, show what is displayed on the screen.

```
      PROGRAM MAIN
        CALL SHOWIT
        END
*
      SUBROUTINE SHOWIT
        INTEGER X, Y
        WRITE(*,*) 'X', 'Y'
        DO 20 X = 1,4
        Y = X**2 + 3*X + 1
        WRITE(*,*) X, Y
 20   CONTINUE
        RETURN
        END
```

2. What is the value of SUM displayed after the following program is run? (Note: This is a trick question.)

```
      PROGRAM MAIN
        CALL TEST
        END
*
      SUBROUTINE TEST
        INTEGER SUM, M, N
        SUM = 0
        DO 10 M = 1,3
          DO 20 N = 1,2
            SUM = SUM + N ** M
20         CONTINUE
10    CONTINUE
        RETURN
        END
```

Answer: ________________

3. How many times is the WRITE statement executed in the following program?

```
      PROGRAM MAIN
        CALL TEST
        END
*
      SUBROUTINE TEST
        INTEGER N, I, J
        N = 5
        DO 10 I = 1, N-1
          DO 20 J = 1, N-1
            WRITE(*,*) I, J
 20         CONTINUE
 10   CONTINUE
        RETURN
        END
```

Answer: ________________

4. Determine the values of T and S that are printed by the following program:

```
      PROGRAM MAIN
        CALL TEST
        END
*
      SUBROUTINE TEST
        INTEGER I
        REAL S, T
        S = 1.0/2.0
        T = 40.0
        DO 10 I = 1, 6
        T = T - I
        S = S * I
 10   CONTINUE
        WRITE(*,*) T, S
        RETURN
        END
```

______ (T value) ______ (S Value)

5. What values of L and M are displayed when the program below is run?

```
      PROGRAM MAIN
        CALL TEST
        END
*
      SUBROUTINE TEST
        INTEGER I, J, K, L, M, F
        I = 2
        J = 12
        K = 2
        L = F(I,J,K)
        M = F(J,L,K)
        WRITE (*,*) L, M
        RETURN
        END
*
      INTEGER FUNCTION F(A,B,C)
        INTEGER I, A, B, C, D
        D = 1024
        DO 5 I = A, B, C
          D = D/2
  5     CONTINUE
        F = D
        RETURN
        END
```

______ (L value) ______ (M value)

LAB ASSIGNMENT 7

A cylindrical water tank with a 2 ft. radius is filled with water to an initial height of h feet. A small orifice of 0.6 inch diameter at the bottom of the tank allow water to drain out. The average velocity, vel, of the water draining out of the orifice and the time, t, (in seconds) for the water to drain from the tank are given by the formulas:

$$vel = \sqrt{2gh}/2$$

and

$$t = \frac{h(r_t / r_o)}{vel}$$

where

$g = 32.2$ ft/sec^2
r_t is the radius of the tank (in inches)
r_o is the radius of the orifice (in inches)

Using these formulas write a FORTRAN program to accomplish the following:

a. Calculate the time, in hours, for all the water to drain from the tank using initial heights of 1, 2, 3, 4, 5, 6 7, 8, 9, and 10 feet. (Note that the formula for t, above, gives the time in seconds.) As a check on your program, it takes 1.401 hours to drain the tank if it is initially filled to a height of 10 feet, and it takes 0.443 hours to train the tank if it is initially filled to a height of one foot.

b. Display the initial height (in feet) and the time (in hours)by including in your write-up a neatly plotted graph (prepared by hand from the output of your program) of time as a function of initial water height, h. Be sure to label the axes properly and title the graph. Draw a smooth curve through the data points.

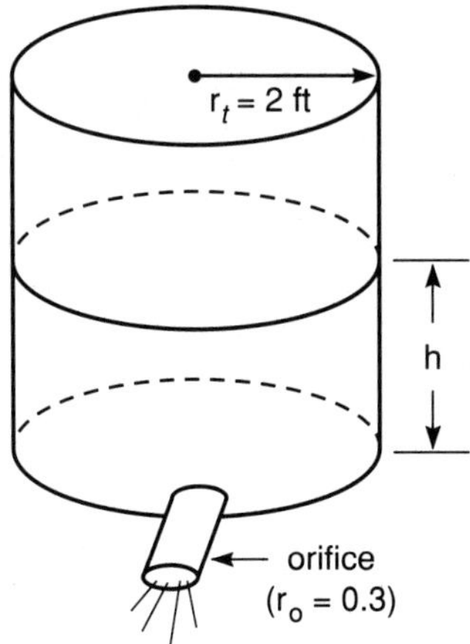

LAB ASSIGNMENT 8

The location of the center of gravity for the water displaced by a ship with a triangular hull is given by the following two-part formula:

If D is less than or equal to A

$$X = \frac{2D}{3}$$

If D is greater than A

$$X = \frac{D^2 - (A^2/3)}{2D - A}$$

where:

D is the depth of the water
A is the distance to the keel
X is the distance form the keel to the center of gravity

Use comments at the beginning of the program to identify the programmer, lab assignment number, date, and the purpose of the program. Do not use any comments in the body of your program.

Your data can be read in as real or integer data. Run your program at least four times with the following data (if you are using data files, first create a data file with the data). Check your answers; to help you check your output the first and third values of X are 13.00 and 10.00, respectively.

D	A
20	15
13	10
15	20
30	40

(Hint: Notice that in the first two sets of data points D is greater than A, while in the last two sets D is less than A. Use two DO loops in your program.)

The program should call a subroutine to print your name at the top of the report and triple spaced below this should be your columnar field headings. All headings should be displayed by a subroutine.

LAB ASSIGNMENT 9

There are 15 employees at the local Widget Company. Each employee is paid \$9.00 per hour for 40 hours of work and \$13.50 per hour for any overtime work. The management would like to know the regular, overtime, and total payroll made to each department. Additionally, it would like the total regular pay, overtime pap, and payroll made for all the departments to be included on the report. Write a program to produce this report, which should have the following form:

```
  DEPARTMENT          EMPLOYEE      REGULAR       OVERTIME      TOTAL
    NUMBER             NUMBER         PAY            PAY          PAY
2301
2301
2301
2301
2301
                                   -------       --------      -----
    DEPT. TOTALS:

2302
   .
   .
2302
                                   -------       --------      -----
DEPT. TOTALS:

2303
   .
   .
 2302
                                   -------       --------      -----
DEPT. TOTALS:
      GRAND TOTALS:                -------       --------      -----
                                   -------       -------       -----
```

Following is the input data. Place this data in a data file before running your program, and have your program read the data file for its input data.

DEPT	EMPLOYEE NUMBER	HOURS WORKED
2301	12893	46
2301	12765	40
2301	14947	52
2301	16899	40
2301	16756	45
2302	12264	40
2302	13456	40
2302	14398	45
2302	15789	50
2302	16555	48
2303	10432	42
2303	11988	45
2303	12764	46
2303	14876	48
2303	15228	50

Processing:

1. Be sure and set all accumulators to zero.

2. Modify the heading subroutine you created in Lab Assignment 8 so that the page number is passed as an argument and the subroutine outputs the following:

   Your Name Page xx

3. Use a nested DO loop in your program. Notice that there are three departments, that each department has five employees, and all employees work at least 40 hours.
4. Using a PARAMETER statement define the hourly rate and the overtime rate as the named constants REGRAT and OTRATE, respectively.

LAB ASSIGNMENT 10

The Fog index is an index used by editors to gauge the reading level difficulty of an article, and is described in detail in the article reproduced on the next page.

For this assignment obtain a samples of at least 100 words from any four text books you are currently using. For each of these samples manually determine the number of sentences, words, and big words (these are defined in the accompanying article) contained in the sample. Write these values into a file, using the format:

```
TEXTBOOK SUBJECT  WORDS  BIG WORDS  SENTENCES
```

For example, the first record in your file might be

```
CALCULUS  110  15  7
```

Processing:

1. Create the data file as described above.
2. Write a program that reads the file you created and displays both the subject and the Fog index calculated for this subject.
3. Modify the heading subroutine you created in Lab Assignment 8 so that the page number is passed as an argument and the subroutine outputs the following:

Your Name Page xx

The following article is from a recent edition of the NLA NEWS*.

Editors worry about the reading level of their publications. For example, the Wall Street Journal aims for a Fog index of 11, The New York Times about 15, and the New York Daily News 9. The Fog index is a formula generally used to find an approximate reading grade level by measuring the sentence length and the fraction of words with three or more syllables. While reading difficulty is critically dependent on concepts and the presentation, neither factor enters the Fog index.

We looked at one recent issue of NLA News and worked out the Fog index for several articles:

Quantitative Methods:	10
Museum staff member:	12
Political scientist:	18
Sociologist:	19

In other words, the last sample is read easily by someone reading at grade 19 level (roughly the doctorate).

To find the Fog index, pick a sample of at least 100 words. Omit all proper names, and then:

1. Count the number of sentences. Clauses separated by colons or semicolons are treated as separate sentences.

2. Count the number of "Big Words" — words of three or more syllables. Do not include words that reach three syllables because of "es" or "ed" endings, or because they are compounds of simple words, such as everything or seventeen).

3. Substitute into the formula:

$$\text{Fog index} = 0.4\left(\frac{\text{Number of words}}{\text{Number of sentences}} + 100\,\frac{\text{Number of Big words}}{\text{Number of words}}\right)$$

As an example, we look at the first three paragraphs of this article. After we leave out numbers and proper names, we have the sample shown in the box below. There are 102 words, 6 sentences, and 19 big words (italicized in box on next page). in box).

* The NLA NEWS, Vol. 7, No. 9, May 1991. Permission to reproduce this article was kindly granted by Dr. John Truxal, Co-director of the New Liberal Arts Program of the Alfred P. Sloan Foundation.

Editors worry about the reading level of their *publications*. For *example*, the aims for a index of about and the. The index is a *formula generally* used to find an *approximate* reading grade level by measuring the sentence length and the fraction of words with three or more *syllables*. While reading *difficulty* is *critically dependent* on concepts and the *presentation*, neither factor enters the Fog index.

We looked at one recent issue of NLA News and worked out the Fog index for *several* articles: *Quantitative* Methods *Museum* staff member *Political scientist Sociologist*.

In other words, the last sample is read *easily* by someone reading at grade level (roughly the *doctorate*).

Then, the formula gives

$$0.4 * (102/6 + 100 * 19/102) = 14$$

The reading level is grade 14 (college sophomore).

In applying the Fog index to an "I Can Read It All By Myself" book, we find an index of 2 — second grade reading level.

6 Selection

Chapter Six

6.1 Relational Expressions
6.2 The IF-ELSE Structure
6.3 The IF-ELSEIF Structure
6.4 The CASE Structure
6.5 Applications
6.6 Common Programming Errors
6.7 Things to Remember

The field of programming, as a distinct discipline, is still a relatively new activity. It should not be surprising, then, that many advances have occurred in the theoretical foundations of this field. One of the most important of these advances was the recognition in the late 1960s that any algorithm, no matter how complex, could be constructed using combinations of standardized sequence, selection, and repetition *flow of control* structures.

The term *flow of control* refers to the order in which a program's statements are executed. Unless directed otherwise, the normal flow of control for all programs is *sequential.* This means that statements are executed in sequence, one after another, in the order in which they are placed within the program.

Selection and repetition structures permit the sequential flow of control to be altered in precisely defined ways. As you might have guessed, the selection structure is used to select which statements are to be performed next, and the repetition structure is used to repeat a set of statements. In this chapter we present FORTRAN's selection statements. As selection requires choosing between alternatives, we begin this chapter with a description of FORTRAN's selection criteria.

6.1 Relational Expressions

Besides providing computational capabilities (addition, subtraction, multiplication, division, etc.), all computers have the ability to compare quantities. Because many seemingly "intelligent" decision-making situations can be reduced to the level of choosing between two quantities, this comparison capability can be used to create a remarkable intelligencelike facility.

The expressions used to compare quantities are called *relational expressions.* A simple relational expression consists of a relational operator connecting two variable and/or constant operands, as shown in Figure 6-1.

FORTRAN's relational operators are listed in Table 6-1. These relational operators may be used with all of FORTRAN's data types but must be typed exactly as shown. Thus, while the following examples:

```
AGE .GT. 40                 2.0 .GT. 3.3
3 .LT. 4                    TEMP .GT. 98.6
DAY .NE. 5                  IDNUM .EQ. 682
LENGTH .LE. 50              HOURS .GT. 40
FLAG .EQ. DONE
```

are all valid, the following:

```
LENGTH LT 50          (periods are missing)
2.0 > 3.3             (invalid operator)
FLAG .EQUAL. DONE     (invalid operator)
```

are invalid.

Relational expressions are also called *conditions*, and we will use both terms interchangeably. Like all FORTRAN expressions, relational expressions are evaluated to yield a result. For relational expressions this result is either the logical constant .TRUE. or .FALSE. For example, the value of the expression 3 .LT. 4 is always .TRUE., and the value of the expression 2.0 .GT. 3.3 is always .FALSE.

FORTRAN displays the value of a relational expression as either a T or an F, where T denotes a true value and F a false value.

Thus, the statements:

```
WRITE(6,*) 'THE VALUE OF 3 .LT. 4 IS', 3 .LT .4
WRITE(6,*) 'THE VALUE OF 2.0 .GT. 3.0 IS', 2.0 .GT. 3.3
```

can be used to display the value of the expressions 3 .LT. 4 and 2.0 .GT. 3.3, respectively, and produce the display:

```
THE VALUE OF 3 .LT. 4 IS T
THE VALUE OF 2.0 .GT. 3.0 IS F
```

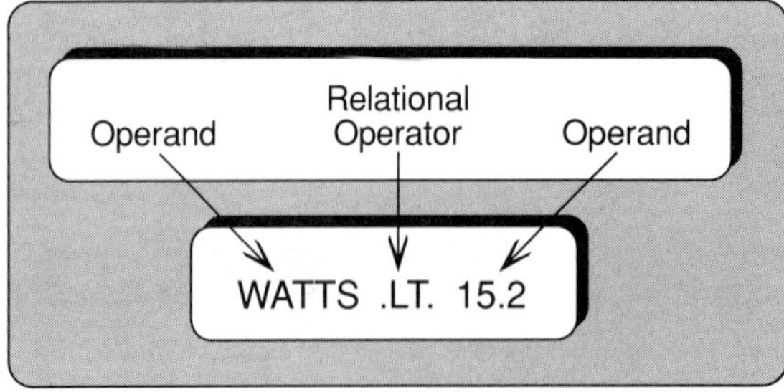

Figure 6-1 Anatomy of a Simple Relational Expression

Table 6-1 FORTRAN's Relational Operators

Relational operator	Meaning	Example
.LT.	Less than	AGE .LT. 30
.GT.	Greater than	HEIGHT .GT. 6.2
.LE.	Less than or equal to	TAXBLE .LE. 20000
.GE.	Greater than or equal to	TEMP .GE. 98.6
.EQ.	Equal to	GRADE .EQ. 100
.NE.	Not equal to	NUMBER .NE. 250

The value of a condition such as HOURS .GT. 40 depends on the value stored in the variable HOURS. In a FORTRAN program, a condition such as this is typically used as part of a selection statement. In these statements, which are presented in the next section, the selection of which statement is to be executed next is based on the value of the condition (true or false).

Character data can also be compared using relational operators. For example, in both the ASCII and the EBCDIC codes the letter A is stored using a code having a lesser numerical value than the letter B, the code for a B is lesser in value than the code for a C, and so on. For character sets coded in this manner, the following conditions are evaluated as listed below.

Expression	Value
'A' .GT. 'D'	.FALSE.
'E' .LE. 'M'	.TRUE.
'G' .EQ. 'K'	.FALSE.
'J' .GE. 'M'	.FALSE.
'F' .NE. 'P'	.TRUE.

Comparing letters is essential in alphabetizing names or using characters to select a particular choice in decision-making situations.

Logical Operators

In addition to simple relational expressions as conditions, more complex conditions can be created using the logical operations AND, OR, and NOT. These operations are represented by the respective symbols:

```
.AND.
.OR.
.NOT.
```

When the AND operator, .AND., is used between two relational expressions, the resulting condition is called a *logical expression* and is true only if both single relations are true by themselves. Thus, the logical condition:

```
(VOLTGE .GT. 48) .AND. (MILAMP .LT. 10)
```

is true only if VOLTGE is greater than 48 and MILAMP is less than 10. The parentheses surrounding the individual relational expressions are used for clarity only, because the logical .AND. operator has a lower precedence than the relational operators (.GT., .LT., .EQ., etc.).

The logical OR operator, .OR., must also be applied between two relational expressions, and the resulting expression referred to as a logical expression. With the .OR. operator, the resulting condition is true if either one or both of the two individual conditions is true. Thus, the condition:

```
(VOLTGE .GT. 48) .OR. (MILAMP .LT. 10)
```

is true if either VOLTGE is greater than 48, or MILAMP is less than 10 or if both conditions are true. Again, the parentheses around the relational expressions are used only for clarity, since the .OR. operator has a lower precedence than all relational operators.

For the declarations:

```
INTEGER I,J
REAL A,B,COMPLET
```

the following represent valid logical expressions:

```
A .GT. B
I .EQ. J .OR. A .LT. B .OR. COMPLET .GT. B
A/B .GT. 5.0 .AND. I .LE. 20
```

Before these complex conditions can be evaluated, the values of A, B, I, J, and COMPLET must be known. Assuming A = 12.0, B = 2.0, I = 15, J = 30, and COMPLET = 0.0, the previous expressions yield the following results:

Expression	Value
`A .GT. B`	`.TRUE.`
`I .EQ. J .OR. A .LT. B .OR. COMPLET .GT. B`	`.FALSE.`
`A/B .GT. 5.0 .AND. I .LE. 20`	`.TRUE.`

Although it is better not to construct relational or logical expressions using different data types, FORTRAN will automatically convert integer operands to real values when they are compared to real values. Numerical operands, however, should not be compared to either character or logical operands. Similarly, character operands should be compared to only character operands and logical operands compared to only logical operands.

The NOT operator is used to change a relational or logical expression to its opposite state. That is, if an expression is true, then .NOT.*expression* is false. Similarly, if an expression is false to begin with, then .NOT.*expression* is true. For example, assuming the number 26 is stored in the variable VOLTGE, the expression VOLTGE .GT. 48 is false, and the expression .NOT.(VOLTGE .GT. 48) is true.

Both relational and logical operators have a hierarchy of execution similar to that for the arithmetic operators. Table 6-2 lists the precedence of these operators in relation to the other operators we have used.

Table 6-2 Operator Precedence and Associativity (from Highest to Lowest Precedence)

Type	Symbol	Associativity
Exponentiation	**	Right to left
Multiplication, division	* /	Left to right
Addition, subtraction, negation	+ -	Left to right
Relational (all have the same precedence)	.LT. .LE. .GT. .GE. .EQ. .NE.	Left to right
Logical	.NOT.	Left to Right
Logical	.AND.	Left to right
Logical	.OR.	Left to right

The following examples illustrate the evaluation of various relational expressions. These examples assume the following declarations and assignments:

```
CHARACTER KEY
INTEGER I, J, K
REAL X

KEY = 'M'
I = 5
J = 7
K = 12
X = 22.5
```

Expression	Equivalent expression	Value
`I + 2 .EQ. K - 1`	`(I + 2) .EQ. (K - 1)`	`.FALSE.`
`3 * I - J .LT. 22`	`((3 * I) - J) .LT. 22`	`.TRUE.`
`I + 2 * J .GT. K`	`(I + (2 * J)) .GT. K`	`.TRUE.`
`K + 3 .LE. - J + 3 * I`	`(K + 3) .LE. ((-J) + (3*I))`	`.FALSE.`
`'A' .NE. 'B'`	`'A' .NE. 'B'`	`.TRUE.`
`KEY .GT. 'P'`	`KEY .GT. 'P'`	`.FALSE.`
`20.5 .GE. X + 10.2`	`20.5 .GE. (X + 10.2)`	`.FALSE.`

As with arithmetic expressions, parentheses can be used both to alter the assigned operator priority and to improve the readability of relational and logical expressions. Since expressions within parentheses are evaluated first, the following complex condition is evaluated as:

```
(6 * 3 .EQ. 36 / 2) .OR. (13 .LT. 3 * 3 + 4) .AND. .NOT.(6 - 2 .LT. 5)
      (18 .EQ. 18) .OR. (13 .LT. 9 + 4) .AND. .NOT.(4 .LT. 5)
           (True) .OR. (13 .LT. 13) .AND. .NOT.(True)
           (True) .OR. (False) .AND. (False)
           (True) .OR. (False)
                (True)
```

A REAL Problem

A problem that can occur with FORTRAN's relational expressions is a subtle numerical accuracy problem that affects REAL numbers. Due to the way computers store these numbers, tests for equality of REAL values and variables using the relational operator .EQ. should be avoided.

The reason for this is that many decimal numbers, such as 0.1, for example, cannot be represented exactly in binary using a finite number of bits. Thus, testing for exact equality for such numbers can fail. When equality of REAL values is desired it is better to require that the absolute value of the difference between operands be less than some extremely small value. Thus, for REAL operands the general condition

```
operand 1 .EQ. operand 2
```

should be replaced by the condition

```
ABS(operand1 - operand2) .LT. 0.000001
```

where the value 0.000001 can be altered to any other acceptably small value. Thus, if the difference between the two operands is less than 0.000001 (or any other user-selected amount), the two operands are considered essentially equal. For example, if X and Y are real variables, a condition such as

```
(X/Y .EQ. 0.35)
```

should be programmed as

```
( ABS(X/Y - 0.35) .LT. 0.000001 )
```

This latter condition ensures that slight inaccuracies in representing real numbers in binary do not affect evaluation of the tested condition. Since all computers have an exact binary representation of zero, comparisons for exact equality to zero don't encounter this numerical accuracy problem (see, for example, Programs 6-7 and 6-8).

Exercises

1. Determine the value of the following expressions. Assume that all variables are integers and A = 5, B = 2, C = 4, D = 6, and E = 3.
   a. `A .GT. B`
   b. `A .NE. B`
   c. `A * C .NE. D * B`
   d. `D * B .EQ. C * E`
   e. `A * B`
   f. `MOD(D,B) .NE. MOD(C,B)`
   g. `MOD(A,B) * C .EQ. D`
   h. `MOD(C,B) * A .EQ. 0`
   i. `MOD(B,C) * A .EQ. 0`
2. Write relational expressions to express the following conditions (use variable names of your own choosing):
   a. A person's age is equal to 30.
   b. A person's temperature is greater than 98.6.
   c. A person's height is less than six feet.

d. The current month is 12 (December).
e. The letter input is K.
f. A person's age is equal to 30 and the person is taller than six feet.
g. The current day is the 15th day of the 1st month.
h. A person is older than 50 or has been employed at the company for at least 5 years.
i. A person's identification number is less than 500, and the person is older than 55.
j. A length is greater than two feet and less than three feet.

3. Determine the value of the following expressions, assuming that all variables are integers and that A = 5, B = 2, C = 4, and D = 5.

a. `A .EQ. 5`
b. `B * D .EQ. C * C`
c. `MOD(D,B) * C .GT. 5 .OR. MOD(C,B) * D .GT. 7`

4. Using parentheses, rewrite the following expressions to correctly indicate their order of evaluation. Then evaluate each expression assuming all variables are integers and that A = 5, B = 2, and C = 4.

a. `A / B .NE. C .AND. C / B .NE. A`
b. `A / B .NE. C .OR. C / B .NE. A`
c. `MOD(B,C) .EQ. 1 .AND. MOD(A,C) .EQ. 1`
d. `MOD(B,C) .EQ. 1 .OR. MOD(A,C) .EQ. 1`

6.2 The IF-ELSE Structure

The IF-ELSE structure directs the computer to perform a series of one or more instructions based on the result of a comparison. For example, the state of New Jersey has a two-level state income tax structure. If a person's taxable income is less than $20,000, the New Jersey State income tax rate is 2 percent. For incomes exceeding $20,000, a different rate is applied. The IF-ELSE structure can be used in this situation to determine the correct tax based on whether the taxable income is less than or equal to $20,000. The general form of the IF-ELSE structure is:

```
IF (condition) THEN
   statement 1
   statement 2
      .
      .
      .
   statement n
ELSE
   statement n+1
      .
      .
      .
   statement m
ENDIF
```

This structure is formally constructed using three separate FORTRAN statements, each of which must reside on a line by itself: a block IF statement having the form IF (*condition*) THEN, an ELSE statement consisting of the keyword ELSE, and an ENDIF statement consisting of the keyword ENDIF.

The condition in the block IF statement is evaluated first. If the condition is True, statements 1 through *n* are executed. If the condition is False, the statements after the keyword ELSE are executed. Thus, one of the two sets of statements (either statement 1 through statement *n* or statement *n*+1 through statement *m*) is always executed, depending on the value of the condition. The Nassi-Schneiderman and flowchart representations for the IF-ELSE structure are shown in Figure 6-2.

For a specific example of an IF-ELSE structure, we will construct a FORTRAN program for determining New Jersey State income taxes. As previously described, these taxes are assessed at 2 percent of taxable income for incomes less than or equal

Figure 6-2 The IF-ELSE Structure

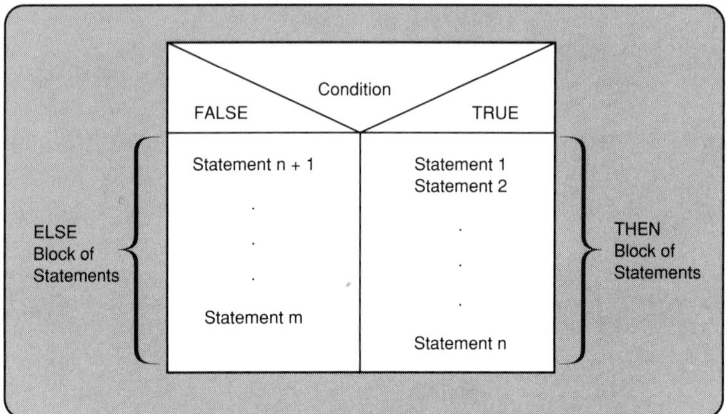

(a) Nassi-Schneiderman Representation

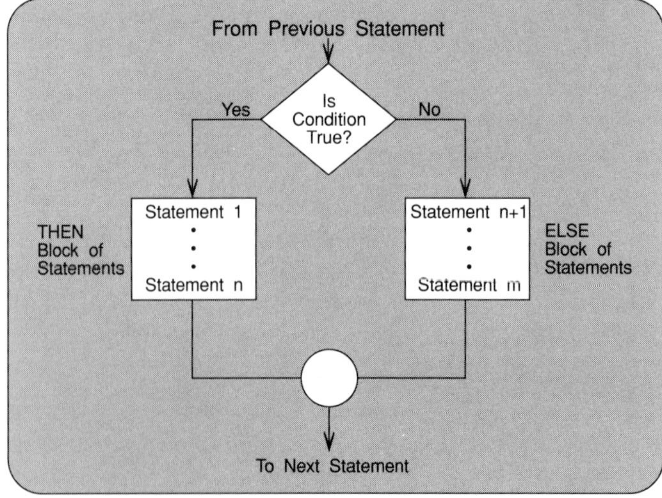

(b) Flowchart Representation

to $20,000. For taxable income greater than $20,000, state taxes are 2.5 percent of the income that exceeds $20,000 plus a fixed amount of $400. Thus, the condition to be tested is whether taxable income is less than or equal to $20,000. An appropriate IF-ELSE structure for this situation is:

```
IF (INCOME .LE. 20000.0) THEN
  TAXES = .02 * INCOME
ELSE
  TAXES = .025 * (INCOME - 20000.0) + 400.0
ENDIF
```

Recall that the relational operator .LE. represents the relation "less than or equal to." If the value of INCOME is less than or equal to 20000.0, the condition is true, and the statement TAXES = .02 * INCOME is executed. If the value of INCOME is not less than or equal to 20000.0, the condition is false, and the statement after the reserved word ELSE is executed. Program 6-1 illustrates the use of this statement in a complete program.

A blank comment line was inserted before and after the IF-ELSE structure to highlight it in the complete program. We will continue to do this throughout the text to emphasize the structure being presented.

Program 6-1

```
      PROGRAM MAIN
        CALL IFTEST
        END
*
      SUBROUTINE IFTEST
        REAL INCOME, TAXES
        WRITE(6,*)'PLEASE TYPE IN THE TAXABLE INCOME: '
        READ(5,*) INCOME
*
        IF (INCOME .LE. 20000.0) THEN
          TAXES = .02 * INCOME
        ELSE
          TAXES = .025 * (INCOME - 20000.0) + 400.0
        ENDIF
*
        WRITE(6,*)'TAXES ARE $ ', TAXES
        RETURN
        END
```

To illustrate the selection provided by the IF-ELSE structure in Program 6-1, the program was run twice with different input data. The results are:

```
PLEASE TYPE IN THE TAXABLE INCOME:
10000.
TAXES ARE $ 200.000000
```

and:

```
PLEASE TYPE IN THE TAXABLE INCOME:
30000.
TAXES ARE $ 650.000000
```

Although the use of FORMAT statements would improve the appearance of the output (see Exercise 3 at the end of this section), observe that the taxable income input in the first run of the program was less than $20,000, and the tax was correctly calculated as 2 percent of the number entered. In the second run, the taxable income was more than $20,000, and the ELSE part of the IF-ELSE structure was used to yield a correct tax computation of:

```
.025 * (30000. - 20000.) + 400. = 650.
```

Although only a single statement was needed in both the IF and ELSE parts of the structure used in Program 6-1, any number of statements could have been included. Program 6-2 illustrates the use of multiple statements within an IF-ELSE structure.

Program 6-2

```
      PROGRAM MAIN
        CALL TEMVER
        END
*
      SUBROUTINE TEMVER
        CHARACTER TYPE
        REAL TEMP, FAHREN, CELSUS
   10   FORMAT(1A)
        WRITE(6,*)'ENTER THE TEMPERATURE TO BE CONVERTED: '
        READ(5,*) TEMP
        WRITE(6,*)'ENTER F IF THIS TEMPERATURE IS FAHRENHEIT'
        WRITE(6,*)' OR C IF THE TEMPERATURE IS CELSIUS: '
        READ(5,10) TYPE
*
        IF (TYPE .EQ. 'F') THEN
          CELSUS = (5.0 / 9.0) * (TEMP - 32.0)
          WRITE(6,*)'THE EQUIVALENT CELSIUS TEMPERATURE IS ', CELSUS
        ELSE
          FAHREN =  (9.0 / 5.0) * TEMP + 32.0
          WRITE(6,*)'THE EQUIVALENT FAHRENHEIT TEMPERATURE IS', FAHREN
        ENDIF
*
        RETURN
        END
```

Program 6-2 checks whether the entered letter is an F. If it is, the two statements within the IF part of the IF-ELSE structure are executed. Any other letter results in execution of the two statements within the ELSE part. Following is a sample run of Program 6-2.

```
ENTER THE TEMPERATURE TO BE CONVERTED:
212
ENTER F IF THIS TEMPERATURE IS FAHRENHEIT
OR C IF THE TEMPERATURE IS CELSIUS:
F
THE EQUIVALENT CELSIUS TEMPERATURE IS    100.000000
```

One-Way Selection: The Block IF and Logical IF Statements

As we have seen, the IF-ELSE structures that we have been using consist of three separate FORTRAN statements: a block IF statement, an ELSE statement, and an ENDIF statement. The block IF statement, IF (*condition*) THEN, can be followed by any number of valid FORTRAN statements. It must, however, always be used with an ENDIF statement. Use of the ELSE statement with a block IF statement is optional. When the ELSE statement is not used, the block IF statement combined with the ENDIF takes the shortened and frequently useful form:

```
IF (condition)  THEN
  statement 1
  statement 2
          .
        .
      .
  statement n
ENDIF
```

The statement or statements following the IF (*condition*) are only executed if the condition is true. The Nassi-Schneiderman and flowchart representations for this combination of statements are illustrated in Figure 6-3.

Program 6-3 uses a block IF statement to selectively display messages for cars that have been driven more than 2000 miles.

As an illustration of its one-way selection criteria in action, Program 6-3 was run twice, each time with different input data. Only the input data for the first run causes the statements within the block IF to be executed.

```
PLEASE TYPE IN CAR NUMBER AND MILEAGE:
56 3742.4

CAR      56 IS OVER THE LIMIT
BY    1742.400000 MILES
END OF PROGRAM OUTPUT.
```

and:

```
PLEASE TYPE IN CAR NUMBER AND MILEAGE:
16 354
END OF PROGRAM OUTPUT.
```

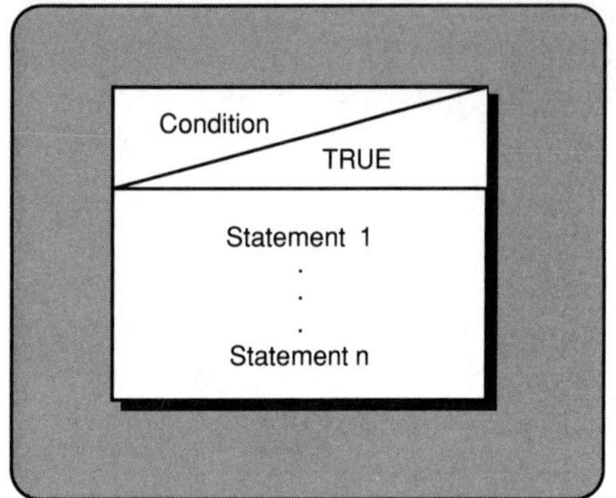

(a) Nassi-Schneiderman Representation

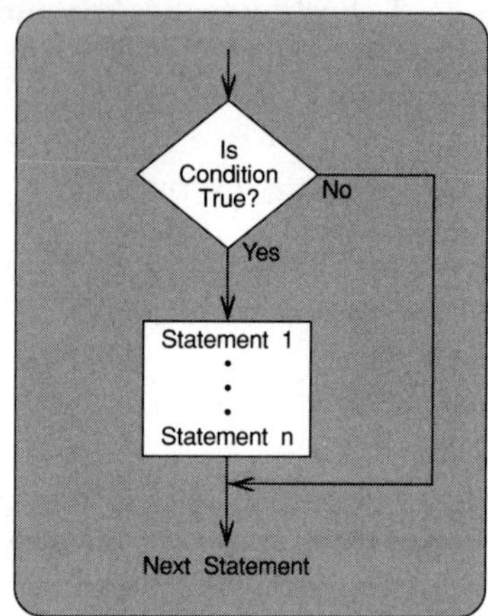

(b) Flowchart Representation

Figure 6-3 The Block IF Structure

Program 6-3

```
      PROGRAM MAIN
        INTEGER IDNUM
        REAL MILES
        CALL IDCAR(IDNUM, MILES)
        CALL CARLIM(IDNUM, MILES)
        END
*
      SUBROUTINE IDCAR(IDNUM, MILES)
        INTEGER IDNUM
        REAL MILES
        WRITE(6,*)'PLEASE TYPE IN CAR NUMBER AND MILEAGE: '
        READ(5,*) IDNUM, MILES
        RETURN
        END
*
      SUBROUTINE CARLIM(IDNUM, MILES)
        INTEGER IDNUM
        REAL MILES
        PARAMETER(LIMIT = 2000.0)
        WRITE(6,*)
*
        IF(MILES .GT. LIMIT) THEN
          WRITE(6,*)'CAR ', IDNUM, ' IS OVER THE LIMIT'
          OMILES = MILES - LIMIT
          WRITE(6,*) 'BY', OMILES, ' MILES'
        ENDIF
*
        WRITE(6,*)'END OF PROGRAM OUTPUT.'
        RETURN
        END
```

A useful alternative to this form of the block IF statement is possible when only a single statement needs to be executed when the tested condition is true. For this case the logical IF statement, having the simplified form:

```
IF (condition) statement
```

can be used. For example, the statements:

```
IF (SPEED .GT. 22896.0) PRINT *, 'THE SPEED IS', SPEED
IF (NUMBER .LT. 0) NEGSUM = NEGSUM + NUMBER
IF (BALNCE .LT. REORD .AND. TIME .GT. 5) READ *, NEWVAL
```

are all examples of logical IF statements. In each case, the single statement following the condition is executed only if the tested condition is true.

In addition to the restriction that only one executable statement may follow the logical IF's condition, this executable statement is further limited in that it may not be another logical IF statement or the DO statement that is described in the next chapter.

Repetition and IF Statements

When IF statements are contained within DO loops they provide an extremely powerful method of "filtering" large amounts of data for subsequent processing. For example, consider Program 6-4, which calculates the total of positive and negative numbers entered by the user:

Program 6-4

```
      PROGRAM MAIN
        CALL REPIF
        END
*
      SUBROUTINE REPIF
        REAL NUM, NEGTOT, POSTOT
        POSTOT = 0.0
        NEGTOT = 0.0
        DO 10 I = 1, 4
          WRITE(6,*) 'ENTER IN A POSITIVE OR NEGATIVE NUMBER:'
          READ(5,*) NUM
          IF (NUM .GT. 0.0) THEN
            POSTOT = POSTOT + NUM
          ELSE
            NEGTOT = NEGTOT + NUM
          ENDIF
 10   CONTINUE
        WRITE(6,*)
        WRITE(6,*) 'THE SUM OF THE POSITIVE NUMBERS IS: ', POSTOT
        WRITE(6,*) 'THE SUM OF THE NEGATIVE NUMBERS IS: ', NEGTOT
        RETURN
        END
```

The DO loop within Program 6-4 is a simple loop which operates four times. Each time through the loop the user is prompted to enter a number, which is then read into the variable NUM. After the number has been "captured" into NUM it is then processed using an IF statement. If the value in NUM is positive, it is added into the total POSTOT, else it is added into the total NEGTOT. Following is a sample run using Program 6-4.

```
ENTER IN A POSITIVE OR NEGATIVE NUMBER:
4
ENTER IN A POSITIVE OR NEGATIVE NUMBER:
-9
ENTER IN A POSITIVE OR NEGATIVE NUMBER:
289
ENTER IN A POSITIVE OR NEGATIVE NUMBER:
-10
THE SUM OF THE POSITIVE NUMBERS IS:       293.000000
THE SUM OF THE NEGATIVE NUMBERS IS:       -19.000000
```

The Nassi-Schneiderman chart for Program 6-4 is shown in Figure 6-4.

Although Program 6-4 is rather simple, it does illustrate the general principle of including an IF statement within a DO loop. By simply changing the unit number in the READ statement to a previously OPENed file, the DO loop can be used to read and then selectively process data directly from a data file.

Data Validation

An important use of FORTRAN's IF statements is to validate data by checking for clearly invalid cases. For example, a date such as 5/33/86 contains an obviously

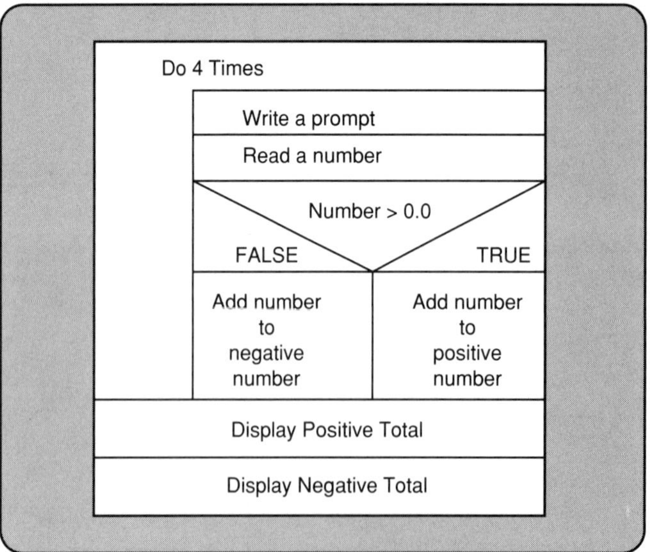

Figure 6-4 Nassi-Schneiderman Chart for Program 6-4

invalid day. Similarly, the division of any number by zero within a program, such as 14/0, should not be allowed. Both of these examples illustrate the need for a technique called *defensive programming*, where the program includes code to check for improper data before an attempt is made to process it further. The defensive programming technique of checking user input data for erroneous or unreasonable data is referred to as *input data validation.*

Consider the case where we are to write a FORTRAN program to calculate the square root and the reciprocal of a user-entered number. Since the square root of a negative number does not exist as a real number and the reciprocal of zero cannot be taken, our program will contain input data validation statements to screen the user input data and avoid these two cases.

The Nassi-Schneiderman chart describing the processing required for our program is shown in Figure 6-5. The pseudocode corresponding to this flowchart logic is:

```
display a program purpose message
accept a user input number
if the number is negative then
   print a message that the square root
   cannot be taken
else
   calculate and display the square root
endif
if the number is zero then
   print a message that the reciprocal
   cannot be taken
else
   calculate and display the reciprocal
endif
```

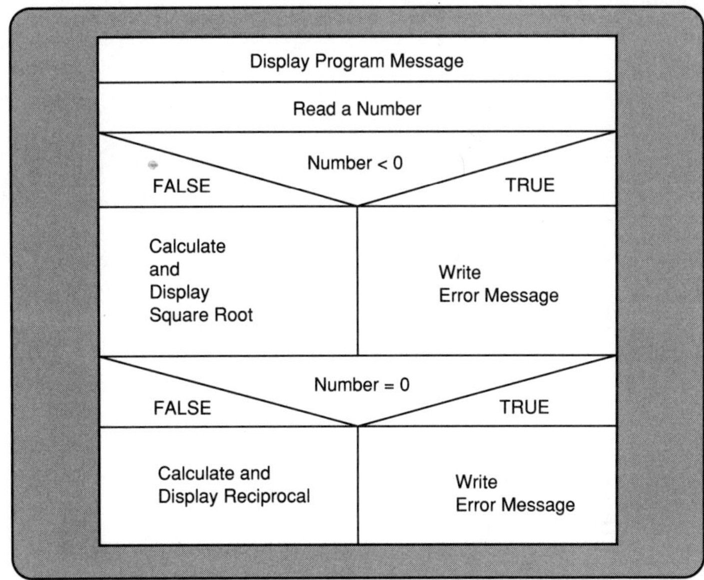

Figure 6-5 Nassi-Schneiderman Chart for Program 6-5

The FORTRAN code corresponding to Figure 6-5 is listed in Program 6-5.

Program 6-5 is a rather straightforward program containing two separate (non-nested) IF-ELSE statements. The first IF-ELSE checks for a negative input number; if the number is negative, a message indicating that the square root of a negative number cannot be taken is displayed, else the square root is taken. The second IF-ELSE statement checks if the entered number is zero; if it is, a message indicating that

Program 6-5

```
      PROGRAM MAIN
        REAL USENUM
        CALL GETNUM(USENUM)
        CALL SQRREP(USENUM)
        END
*
      SUBROUTINE GETNUM(USENUM)
        REAL USENUM
        WRITE(6,*) 'THIS PROGRAM CALCULATES THE SQUARE ROOT AND'
        WRITE(6,*) 'RECIPROCAL (1/NUMBER) OF A NUMBER'
        WRITE(6,*)
        WRITE(6,*) '  PLEASE ENTER A NUMBER: '
        READ(5,*) USENUM
        RETURN
        END
*
      SUBROUTINE SQRREP(USENUM)
        REAL USENUM
        IF (USENUM .LT. 0) THEN
          WRITE(6,*) 'THE SQUARE ROOT OF A NEGATIVE NUMBER'
          WRITE(6,*) '  DOES NOT EXIST.'
        ELSE
          WRITE(6,*) 'THE SQUARE ROOT OF ', USENUM, ' IS ', SQRT(USENUM)
        ENDIF
        IF (USENUM .EQ. 0.0) THEN
          WRITE(6,*) 'THE RECIPROCAL OF ZERO DOES NOT EXIST'
        ELSE
          WRITE(6,*)'THE RECIPROCAL OF ', USENUM, ' IS ', 1 / USENUM
        ENDIF
        RETURN
        END
```

the reciprocal of zero cannot be taken is displayed, else the reciprocal is taken. Following are two sample runs of Program 6-5.

```
THIS PROGRAM CALCULATES THE SQUARE ROOT AND
RECIPROCAL (1/NUMBER) OF A NUMBER

  PLEASE ENTER A NUMBER:
5
THE SQUARE ROOT OF        5.00000000 IS        2.23606801
THE RECIPROCAL OF        5.00000000 IS        0.20000000
```

and

```
THIS PROGRAM CALCULATES THE SQUARE ROOT AND
RECIPROCAL (1/NUMBER) OF A NUMBER

  PLEASE ENTER A NUMBER:
-6
THE SQUARE ROOT OF A NEGATIVE NUMBER
  DOES NOT EXIST.
THE RECIPROCAL OF       -6.00000000 IS       -0.16666667
```

Nested IF Statements

Although a second IF statement may never be included within a logical IF statement, no such restriction is placed on the statements that may be included within a block IF or ELSE statement. The inclusion of one or more IF statements within a block IF or ELSE statement results in a *nested* IF statement. For example, the following nested IF statement includes a logical IF statement nested within the block IF part of an IF-ELSE structure:

```
IF (condition 1) THEN
statement 1
      .
      .
      .
  statement n
ELSE
  IF (condition 2) THEN
    statement n + 1
      .
      .
      .
    statement p
  ELSE
    statement p + 1
      .
      .
      .
    statement q
  ENDIF
ENDIF
```

```
IF (TIME .LT. 9) THEN
  WRITE(6,*) 'SNAP'
  IF (DIST .GT. 6) WRITE(6,*) 'CRACKLE'
ELSE
  WRITE(6,*) 'POP'
ENDIF
```

In this construction, when TIME has a value less than nine, the word SNAP is printed, and the condition in the "inner" logical IF statement is evaluated. If the condition DIST .GT. 6 is also true, the word CRACKLE is displayed after the word SNAP. The word POP is only displayed if TIME is greater than or equal to nine.

The process of nesting IF statements can be extended indefinitely. For example, both the `WRITE(6,*) 'SNAP'` and the `WRITE(6,*) 'POP'` statements may be replaced by any other IF statement. (Since logical IF statements cannot contain other IF statements, the statement `WRITE(6,*) 'CRACKLE'` cannot be replaced with another IF statement.) As always, the indentation we have used is entirely for program readability and is irrelevant as far as the compiler is concerned.

Generally, when one or more IF statements are nested within a single block IF statement or the block IF part of an IF-ELSE structure, the resulting statement tends to be confusing and is best avoided. However, an extremely useful construction occurs when an ELSE statement contains an IF-ELSE structure. This takes the form shown at the left.

The indentation we have used is not required but distinguishes the "inner" IF-ELSE structure from the "outer" IF-ELSE structure. This form of a nested IF statement is so common in programming that FORTRAN provides a special statement, called the ELSEIF statement, to simplify its creation. The ELSEIF statement is the topic of the next section.

Exercises

1. Write appropriate IF statements for each of the following conditions:
   a. If ANGLE is equal to 90 degrees, print the message "THE ANGLE IS A RIGHT ANGLE"; otherwise print the message "THE ANGLE IS NOT A RIGHT ANGLE."
   b. If the temperature is above 100 degrees, display the message "ABOVE THE BOILING POINT OF WATER"; otherwise display the message "BELOW THE BOILING POINT OF WATER."
   c. If the number is positive, add the number to POSSUM; otherwise add the number to NEGSUM.
   d. If the voltage is less than .5 volts, set the variable FLAG to zero; otherwise set FLAG to one.
   e. If the difference between VOLTS1 and VOLTS2 is less than .001, set the variable APPROX to zero; otherwise calculate APPROX as the quantity (VOLTS1 – VOLTS2) / 2.0.
   f. If the frequency is above 60, display the message "FREQUENCY IS TOO HIGH."
   g. If the difference between TEMP1 and TEMP2 exceeds 2.3 degrees, calculate ERROR as (TEMP1 – TEMP2) * FACTOR.

a.

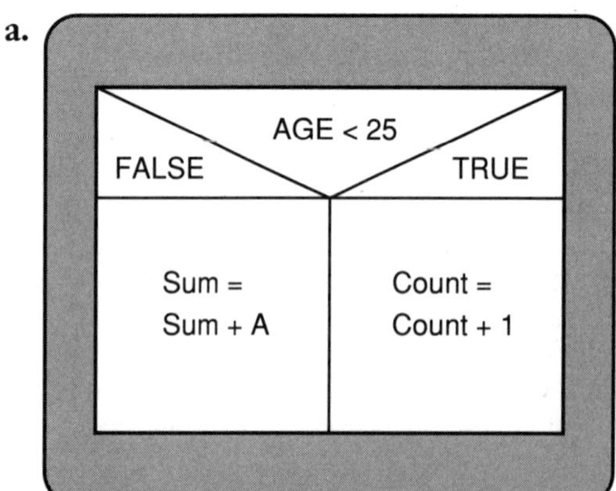

b.

C = 15
FALSE
TRUE
Volts = 5
PWR = 10
Volts = 16
PWR = 25

c.

COUNT = 10
TRUE
AVG = SUM/COUNT
DISPLAY AVG

d.

ID > 22
TRUE
FACTR = 0.7

e.

Is
GRD = 'A'?
No
Yes
Is
WT = 85 ?
No
Yes
BIN = 1
T = S * A

f.

Sum = 0
Is
CNT .LT. 5?
No
Yes
Is
GRD .LT. 50?
No
Yes
Fail =
Fail + 1

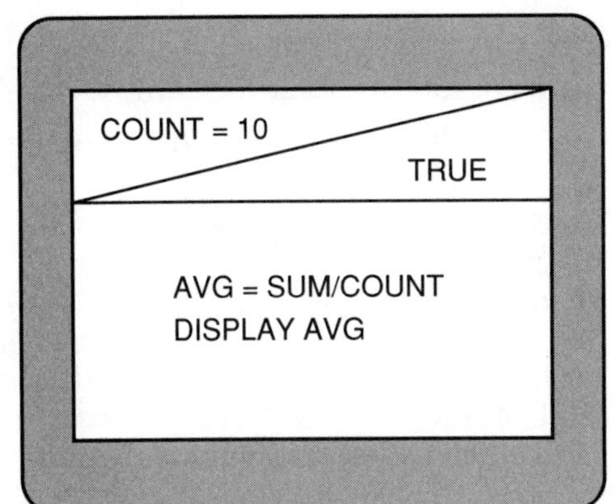

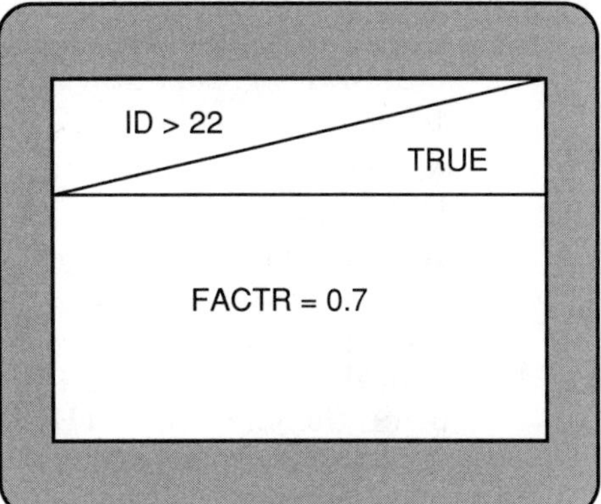

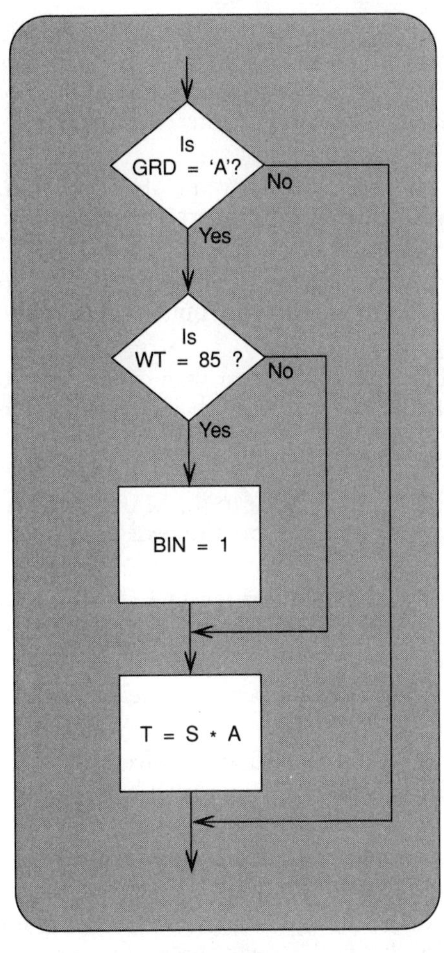

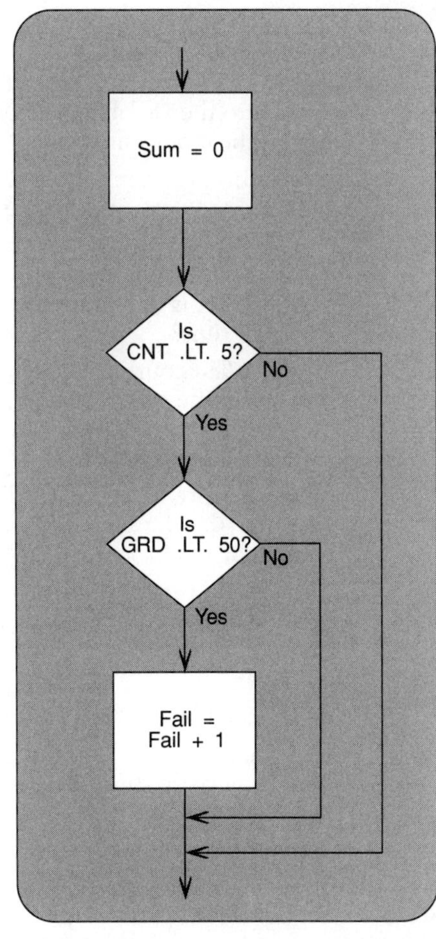

h. If X is greater than Y, and Z is less than 20, read in a value for P.

i. If DIST is greater than 20 and less than 35, read in a value for TIME.

2. Write IF statements corresponding to the conditions illustrated by each of the following Nassi-Schneiderman and flowcharts.

3. Using format statements, rewrite Program 6-1 to have all displayed currency values rounded and displayed to the nearest cent.

4. Write a FORTRAN program that asks the user to input two numbers. If the first number entered is greater than the second number, the program should print the message "THE FIRST NUMBER IS GREATER"; otherwise it should print the message "THE FIRST NUMBER IS SMALLER." Test your program by entering the numbers 5 and 8 and then the numbers 11 and 2. What do you think your program will display if the two numbers entered are equal? Test this case.

Write this program so that the two numbers are input to the MAIN program unit and the determination and display of the appropriate message are performed by a subroutine.

5a. If money is left in a particular bank for more than two years, the interest rate given by the bank is 8.5 percent; otherwise the interest rate is 7 percent. Write a FORTRAN program that uses the READ statement to accept the number of years into the variable NYRS and display the appropriate interest rate depending on the input value.

Write this program so that the number of years is input to the MAIN program unit and the determination and display of the interest rate are performed by a subroutine.

b. How many runs should you make for the program written in Exercise 5a to verify that it is operating correctly? What data should you input in each of the program runs?

6a. In a pass/fail course, a student passes if the grade is greater than or equal to 70 and fails if the grade is lower. Write a FORTRAN program that accepts a grade and prints either the message "A PASSING GRADE" or the message "A FAILING GRADE," as appropriate.

Write this program so that the numerical grade is input to the MAIN program unit and the determination and display of the appropriate message are performed by a subroutine.

b. How many runs should you make for the program written in Exercise 6a to verify that it is operating correctly? What data should you input in each of the program runs?

7a. Write a FORTRAN program to compute and display a person's weekly salary as determined by the following conditions:

If the hours worked are less than or equal to 40, the person receives $8.00 per hour; otherwise the person receives $320.00 plus $12.00 for each hour worked over 40 hours.

The program should request the hours worked as input and should display the salary as output.

Write this program so that the hours worked are input to the MAIN program unit and the determination and display of the weekly salary are performed by a subroutine.

b. How many runs should you make for the program written in Exercise 7a to verify that it is operating correctly? What data should you input in each of the program runs?

8a. Write a program that displays either "I FEEL GREAT TODAY!" or "I FEEL DOWN TODAY #$*!" depending on the input. If the character U is entered in the variable CODE, the first message should be displayed; otherwise the second message should be displayed.

(Recall that a character constant must be entered within apostrophes if a list-directed READ statement is used and without apostrophes if a user-directed READ statement is used.)

Write this program so that the letter code is input to the MAIN program unit and the determination and display of the appropriate message are performed by a subroutine.

b. How many runs should you make for the program written in Exercise 8a to verify that it is operating correctly? What data should you input in each of the program runs?

9a. A senior salesperson is paid $400 a week, and a junior salesperson $275 a week. Write a FORTRAN program that accepts as input a salesperson's status in the character variable status. (Recall that a character constant must be entered within apostrophes if a list-directed READ statement is used and without apostrophes if a user-directed READ statement is used.) If status equals S, the senior person's salary should be displayed; otherwise the junior person's salary should be output.

Write this program so that the letter code is input to the MAIN program unit and the determination and display of the appropriate salary are performed by a subroutine.

b. How many runs should you make for the program written in Exercise 9a to verify that it is operating correctly? What data should you input in each of the program runs?

10. Write a FORTRAN program that accepts a character using the READ statement and determines if the character is an uppercase letter. An uppercase letter is any character that is greater than or equal to A and less than or equal to Z. If the entered character is an uppercase letter, display the message "THE CHARACTER ENTERED IS AN UPPERCASE LETTER." If the entered letter is not uppercase, display the message "THE CHARACTER ENTERED IS NOT AN UPPERCASE LETTER."

Write this program so that the character is input to the MAIN program unit and the determination and display of the appropriate message are performed by a subroutine.

11. Repeat Exercise 10 to determine if the character entered is a lowercase letter. A lowercase letter is any character greater than or equal to a and less than or equal to z.

Write this program so that the character is input to the MAIN program unit and the determination and display of the appropriate message are performed by a subroutine.

6.3 The IF-ELSEIF Structure

The last selection structure provided in FORTRAN 77 uses an ELSEIF statement. An ELSEIF statement can only be used with a block IF statement. When it is included with a block IF and ELSE statement, the complete IF-ELSEIF structure has the form:

```
IF (condition 1) THEN
   statement 1
      .
      .
      .
   statement n
ELSEIF (condition 2) THEN
   statement n+1
      .
      .
      .
   statement p
ELSEIF (condition 3) THEN
   statement p+1
      .
      .
      .
   statement q
ELSE
   statement q+1
      .
      .
      .
   statement r
ENDIF
```

Each condition is evaluated in the order it appears in this structure. For the first condition that is true, the corresponding statements are executed, and the remainder of the structure is not executed. Thus, if condition 1 is true, only statements 1 through *n* are executed; otherwise condition 2 is tested. If condition 2 is then true, only statements *n*+1 through *p* are executed; otherwise condition 3 is tested. The final ELSE statement, which is optional, is only executed if none of the previous conditions are satisfied. This serves as a default or "catchall" case that is frequently useful for detecting an error condition. Although only two ELSEIF statements are illustrated here, any number of ELSEIF statements may be used in the structure, which must be terminated with an ENDIF statement.

Program 6-6

```
      PROGRAM MAIN
        CHARACTER MRCODE
        WRITE(6,*)'ENTER A MARITAL CODE (IN APOSTROPHES): '
        READ(5,*) MRCODE
        CALL DETERM(MRCODE)
        END
*
      SUBROUTINE DETERM(MRCODE)
        CHARACTER MRCODE
*
        IF (MRCODE .EQ. 'M') THEN
          WRITE(6,*)'INDIVIDUAL IS MARRIED.'
        ELSEIF (MRCODE .EQ. 'S') THEN
          WRITE(6,*)'INDIVIDUAL IS SINGLE.'
        ELSEIF (MRCODE .EQ. 'D') THEN
          WRITE(6,*)'INDIVIDUAL IS DIVORCED.'
        ELSEIF (MRCODE .EQ. 'W') THEN
          WRITE(6,*)'INDIVIDUAL IS WIDOWED.'
        ELSE
          WRITE(6,*)'AN INVALID CODE WAS ENTERED.'
        ENDIF
*
        RETURN
        END
```

To illustrate using an ELSEIF statement, Program 6-6 displays a person's marital status corresponding to a letter input. The following letter codes are used:

Marital status	**Input code**
Married	M
Single	S
Divorced	D
Widowed	W

As a further example of an IF-ELSEIF structure, we determine the monthly income of a salesperson using the following commission schedule:

Monthly Sales	**Income**
Greater than or equal to \$50,000	\$375 plus 16% of sales
Less than \$50,000 but greater than or equal to \$40,000	\$350 plus 14% of sales
Less than \$40,000 but greater than or equal to \$30,000	\$325 plus 12% of sales
Less than \$30,000 but greater than or equal to \$20,000	\$300 plus 9% of sales
Less than \$20,000 but greater than or equal to \$10,000	\$250 plus 5% of sales
Less than \$10,000	\$200 plus 3% of sales

Program 6-7

```
      PROGRAM MAIN
        REAL MSALES
        CALL GETSLS(MSALES)
        CALL PAY(MSALES)
        END
*
      SUBROUTINE GETSLS(MSALES)
        REAL MSALES
        WRITE(6,*)'ENTER THE VALUE OF MONTHLY SALES: '
        READ(5,*) MSALES
        RETURN
        END
*
      SUBROUTINE PAY(MSALES)
        REAL MSALES, INCOME
        IF (MSALES .GE. 50000.00) THEN
          INCOME = 375.00 + .16 * MSALES
        ELSEIF (MSALES .GE. 40000.00) THEN
          INCOME = 350.00 + .14 * MSALES
        ELSEIF (MSALES .GE. 30000.00) THEN
          INCOME = 325.00 + .12 * MSALES
        ELSEIF (MSALES .GE. 20000.00) THEN
          INCOME = 300.00 + .09 * MSALES
        ELSEIF (MSALES .GE. 10000.00) THEN
          INCOME = 250.00 + .05 * MSALES
        ELSE
          INCOME = 200.00 + .03 * MSALES
        ENDIF
*
        WRITE(6,10) INCOME
   10          FORMAT(1X,'THE INCOME IS $ ', F8.2)
        RETURN
        END
```

The following statements can be used to determine the correct monthly income, where the variable MSALES is used to store the salesperson's current monthly sales:

```
IF (MSALES .GE. 50000.00) THEN
  INCOME = 375.00 + 0.16 * MSALES
ELSEIF (MSALES .GE. 40000.00) THEN
  INCOME = 350.00 + 0.14 * MSALES
ELSEIF (MSALES .GE. 30000.00) THEN
  INCOME = 325.00 + 0.12 * MSALES
ELSEIF (MSALES .GE. 20000.00) THEN
  INCOME = 300.00 + 0.09 * MSALES
ELSEIF (MSALES .GE. 10000.00) THEN
  INCOME = 250.00 + 0.05 * MSALES
ELSE
  INCOME = 200.00 + 0.03 * MSALES
ENDIF
```

Notice that this example makes use of the fact that ELSEIF statements are executed in sequence only until a true condition is found. Thus, the first condition checks for the highest monthly sales. If the salesperson's monthly sales are less than $50,000, the next ELSEIF statement checks for the next highest sales amount, and so on, until the correct sales category is obtained.

Program 6-7 uses ELSEIF statements to calculate and display the income corresponding to the value of monthly sales input in the READ statement.

A sample run using Program 6-7 is illustrated below.

```
ENTER THE VALUE OF MONTHLY SALES:
44255.80
THE INCOME IS $ 6545.81
```

Exercises

1. Modify Program 6-6 to accept both lowercase and uppercase letters as marriage codes. For example, if a user enters either an m or an M, the program should display the message "INDIVIDUAL IS MARRIED."
2. Modify Program 6-6 to read the marital code using formatted input. What effect does this have on the user?
3. An angle is considered to be an acute angle if it is less than 90 degrees, an obtuse angle if it is greater than 90 degrees, and a right angle if it is equal to 90 degrees. Using this information, write a FORTRAN program that accepts an angle, in degrees, and displays the type of angle corresponding to the degrees entered.
4. The grade level of undergraduate college students is typically determined according to the following schedule:

Number of credits completed	Grade level
Less than 32	Freshman
32 to 63	Sophomore
64 to 95	Junior
96 or more	Senior

Using this information, write a FORTRAN program that accepts the number of credits a student has completed, determines the student's grade level, and displays the grade level.

5. A student's letter grade is calculated according to the following schedule:

Numerical grade	Letter grade
Greater than or equal to 90	A
Less than 90 but greater than or equal to 80	B
Less than 80 but greater than or equal to 70	C
Less than 70 but greater than or equal to 60	D
Less than 60	F

Using this information, write a FORTRAN program that accepts a student's numerical grade, converts the numerical grade to an equivalent letter grade, and displays the letter grade.

6. The interest rate used on funds deposited in a bank is determined by the amount of time the money is left on deposit. For a particular bank, the following schedule is used:

Time on deposit	**Interest rate**
Greater than or equal to 5 years	.095
Less than 5 years but greater than or equal to 4 years	.090
Less than 4 years but greater than or equal to 3 years	.085
Less than 3 years but greater than or equal to 2 years	.075
Less than 2 years but greater than or equal to 1 year	.065
Less than 1 year	.058

Using this information, write a FORTRAN program that accepts the time that funds are left on deposit and displays the interest rate corresponding to the time entered.

7. Write a FORTRAN program that accepts a number followed by one space and then a letter. If the letter following the number is an F, the program is to consider the entered number as a Fahrenheit temperature, convert it to an equivalent Celsius value, and print a suitable display message. If the letter following the number is a C, the program is to consider the number as a Celsius temperature, convert it to an equivalent Fahrenheit value, and print a suitable display message. If the letter is neither an F nor a C, the program is to print a message that the data entered is incorrect and then terminate. Use ELSEIF statements in your program and make use of the conversion formulas:

$$\text{Celsius} = (5.0 / 9.0) * (\text{Fahrenheit} - 32.0)$$
$$\text{Fahrenheit} = (9.0 / 5.0) * \text{Celsius} + 32.0$$

8. Using the commission schedule from Program 6-7, the following program calculates monthly income (note that four of the logical IF statements have been continued across two lines):

```
      PROGRAM MAIN
        REAL MSALES, INCOME
        WRITE(6,*) 'ENTER THE VALUE OF MONTHLY SALES: '
        READ *, MSALES
***
        IF (MSALES .GE. 50000.00) INCOME = 375.00 + 0.16 * MSALES
        IF (MSALES .GE. 40000.00 .AND. MSALES .LT. 50000.00)
     +    INCOME = 350.00 + 0.14 * MSALES
        IF (MSALES .GE. 30000.00 .AND. MSALES .LT. 40000.00)
     +    INCOME = 325.00 + 0.12 * MSALES
        IF (MSALES .GE. 20000.00 .AND. MSALES .LT. 30000.00)
     +    INCOME = 300.00 + 0.09 * MSALES
        IF (MSALES .GE. 10000.00 .AND. MSALES .LT. 20000.00)
     +    INCOME = 250.00 + 0.05 * MSALES
      IF (MSALES .LT. 10000.00) INCOME = 200.00 + 0.03 * MSALES
      WRITE(6,*) 'THE INCOME IS $', INCOME
      END
```

a. Will this program produce the same output as Program 6-7?

b. Do you think that one program is better than the other? Why or why not?

9. The following program was written to produce the same result as Program 6-7:

```
      PROGRAM MAIN
        REAL MSALES, INCOME
        WRITE(6,*) 'ENTER THE VALUE OF MONTHLY SALES: '
        READ *, MSALES
```

```
*
        IF (MSALES .LT. 10000.00) THEN
          INCOME = 200.00 + 0.03 * MSALES
        ELSEIF (MSALES .GE. 10000.00) THEN
         INCOME = 250.00 + 0.05 * MSALES
        ELSEIF (MSALES .GE. 20000.00) THEN
          INCOME = 300.00 + 0.09 * MSALES
        ELSEIF (MSALES .GE. 30000.00) THEN
          INCOME = 325.00 + 0.12 * MSALES
        ELSEIF (MSALES .GE. 40000.00) THEN
          INCOME = 350.00 + 0.14 * MSALES
        ELSE
          INCOME = 375.00 + 0.16 * MSALES
        ENDIF
*
        WRITE(6,*) 'THE INCOME IS',INCOME
       END
```

a. Will this program run?
b. What does this program do?
c. For what values of monthly sales does this program calculate the correct income?

6.4 The CASE Structure

F90

An alternative to the IF-ELSEIF structure presented in the previous section is the CASE structure. This structure was introduced with the new FORTRAN 90 standard, and is unavailable on earlier FORTRAN compilers. The common form of a Fortran CASE structure is:

```
SELECT CASE (expression)
 CASE (value_1)
   statement1
   statement2
       .
       .
 CASE (value_2)
   statementm
   statementn
       .
       .
       .
 CASE (value_n)
   statementw
   statementx
       .
       .
 CASE DEFAULT
   statementaa
   statementbb
END SELECT          ! END OF CASE CONSTRUCT
```

The CASE structure uses three new Fortran statements, a single SELECT CASE statement, one or more CASE statements, and a required END SELECT statement. Let us see how these statements are used. The SELECT CASE statement, which has the general form:

```
SELECT CASE (expression)
```

identifies the start of the CASE construct. The expression in parentheses in this statement is evaluated and the result of the expression compared to various alternative values contained within each CASE statement.

Internal to the CASE construct, the CASE statement, which has the general form:

```
CASE (list of values)
```

is used to identify individual values that are compared to the value of the SELECT CASE expression. The expression's value is compared to each of these CASE values, in the order that these values are listed, until a match is found. When a match occurs, execution begins with the statement immediately following the matching CASE and ends when either the next CASE or END SELECT statement is encountered. The CASE construct is then exited and program execution continues with the statement following the END SELECT statement, which formally "closes off" the CASE construct. Thus, as illustrated in Figure 6-6, the value of the expression determines where in the CASE construct execution actually begins.

Any number of CASE labels may be contained within a CASE construct, in any order; the only requirement is that the values in each CASE statement must be of the same type as the expression in the CASE SELECT statement. If the value of the expression does not match any of the case values, however, no statement within the CASE construct is executed unless a CASE DEFAULT statement is encountered. The word DEFAULT is an optional "value" for the CASE statement that produces the same effect as the last ELSE in an IF-ELSEIF structure. If the value of the SELECT CASE expression does not match any of the CASE values, and the CASE DEFAULT statement is present, execution begins with the statement following the word DEFAULT.

Once an entry point has been located by the CASE construct, all further case evaluations are ignored and execution continues until either a CASE or END SELECT statement is encountered.

When writing a CASE structure, multiple CASE values may be included in the same CASE statement and the DEFAULT case is optional. For example, consider the following CASE structure:

```
SELECT CASE (NUMBER)
  CASE (1)
    WRITE(6,*) 'HAVE A GOOD MORNING'
  CASE (2)
    WRITE(6,*) 'HAVE A HAPPY DAY'
  CASE (3, 5)
    WRITE(6,*) 'HAVE A NICE EVENING'
  CASE (4, 6:10)
    WRITE(6,*) 'HAVE A GOOD NIGHT'
END SELECT
```

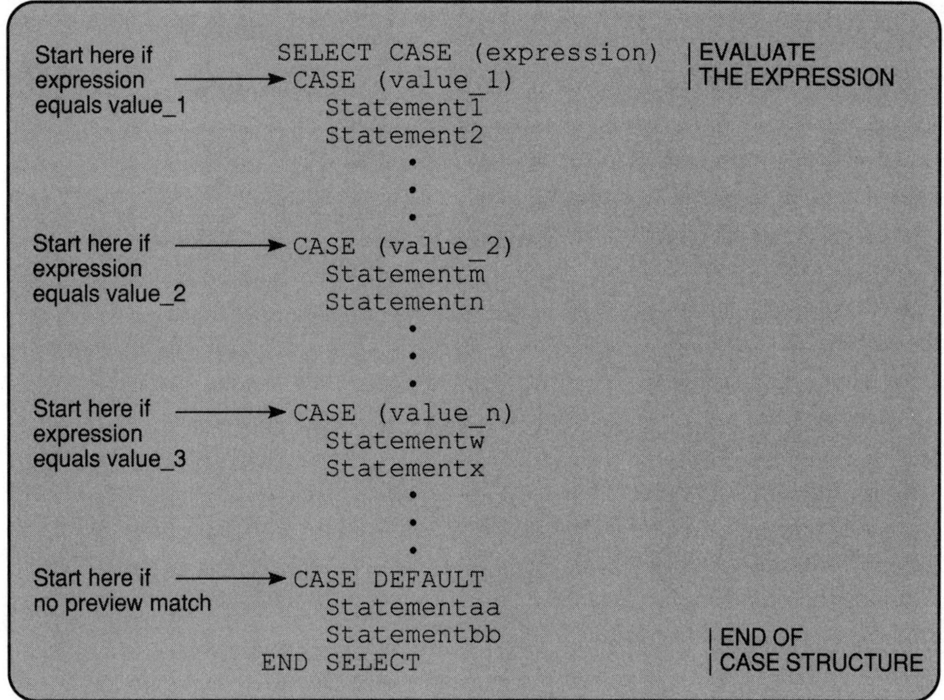

Figure 6-6 The Expression Determines an Entry Point

If the value stored in the variable NUMBER is 1, the message HAVE A GOOD MORNING is displayed. Similarly, if the value of NUMBER is 2, the second message is displayed. The third CASE statement checks for a NUMBER equal to either 3 or 5, in which case the message HAVE A NICE EVENING is displayed. Finally, the last case checks for a value of 4 or any value between 6 and 10, inclusive, which is indicated by the colon (:) between the numbers 6 and 10. When a colon is included between two values, as it is in the last CASE statement, a match occurs if the expression's value is greater than or equal to the lower value and less than or equal to the upper value. Since this sample CASE structure does not include a DEFAULT case, no message is printed if the value of NUMBER is not one of the listed case values. Although it is good programming practice to list case values in increasing order, this is not required by the CASE structure. A CASE structure may have any number of case values, in any order; only the values being tested for need be listed.

Program 6-8 uses a CASE structure to select the arithmetic operation (addition, multiplication, or division) to be performed on two numbers depending on the value of the variable OPSEL.

Program 6-8

```
      PROGRAM MAIN
        INTEGER OPSEL
        REAL A, B
        CALL GETVAL(OPSEL, A, B)
        CALL CALC(OPSEL, A, B)
        END
*
      SUBROUTINE GETVAL(OPSEL, FIRNUM, SECNUM)
        INTEGER OPSEL
        REAL FIRNUM, SECNUM
        WRITE(6,*) 'PLEASE TYPE IN TWO NUMBERS'
        READ *, FIRNUM, SECNUM
        WRITE(6,*) 'ENTER A SELECT CODE:'
        WRITE(6,*)'          1 FOR ADDITION'
        WRITE(6,*)'          2 FOR MULTIPLICATION'
        WRITE(6,*)'          3 FOR DIVISION: '
        READ(5,*) OPSEL
        RETURN
        END
*
      SUBROUTINE CALC(OPSEL, FIRNUM, SECNUM)
        INTEGER OPSEL
        REAL FIRNUM, SECNUM, FINAL
        SELECT CASE (OPSEL)
          CASE (1)
            FINAL = FIRNUM + SECNUM
            WRITE(6,*) 'THE SUM OF THE NUMBERS ENTERED IS', FINAL
          CASE (2)
            FINAL = FIRNUM * SECNUM
            WRITE(6,*) 'THE PRODUCT OF THE NUMBERS ENTERED IS', FINAL
          CASE (3)
            FINAL = FIRNUM / SECNUM
            WRITE(6,*) 'THE FIRST NUMBER DIVIDED BY THE SECOND IS ', FINAL
        END SELECT       ! END OF CASE CONSTRUCT
        RETURN
        END
```

The following display clearly identifies the cases that would be selected in two hypothetical runs of Program 6-8.

```
PLEASE TYPE IN TWO NUMBERS:
12 3
ENTER A SELECT CODE:
        1 FOR ADDITION
        2 FOR MULTIPLICATION
        3 FOR DIVISION:
THE PRODUCT OF THE NUMBERS ENTERED IS 36.000000
```

and

```
PLEASE TYPE IN TWO NUMBERS:
12 3
ENTER A SELECT CODE:
        1 FOR ADDITION
        2 FOR MULTIPLICATION
        3 FOR DIVISION:
3
THE FIRST NUMBER DIVIDED BY THE SECOND IS 4.000000
```

In addition to being used to select a case based on an integer expression, the CASE construct can be used for logical, character, and real valued expressions, as well. For example, assuming that CHOICE is a character variable, the following CASE construct is valid:

```
SELECT CASE(CHOICE)
  CASE ('a', 'e', 'i', 'o', 'u')
    WRITE(6,*) 'THE CHARACTER IN CHOICE IS A VOWEL'
  CASE DEFAULT
    WRITE(6,*) 'THE CHARACTER IN CHOICE IS NOT A VOWEL'
END SELECT
```

Range of Values

As we saw in the first CASE construct example, the values being selected may be included in a range by using a colon to separate the end points of the selected range. Thus, a case value of -1:10 indicates all values between -1 and 10, inclusive, and a case value of 2.2:3.6 indicates all values between 2.2 and 3.6, inclusive. Additionally, case values may take the form *low:* or *:high*, as in the examples 10:, -3.2:, :-2, and :25. When a colon follows a value, as in 10:, and no upper value is listed after the colon, a match occurs if the expression in the SELECT CASE statement is greater than or equal to the value indicated. Similarly, when a colon precedes a value, as in :25, and no lower value is listed before the colon, a match occurs if the expression in the SELECT CASE statement is less than or equal to the value indicated. For example, consider the CASE construct:

```
SELECT CASE (REALNUM)
  CASE (:-1.0)
    WEIGHT = -1
  CASE (1.0:)
    WEIGHT = 1
  CASE DEFAULT
    WEIGHT = 0
END SELECT
```

The first case tested in this CASE construct is whether the value of REALNUM is less than or equal to -1.0, in which case the variable WEIGHT is assigned the value -1. The next case tested is whether the value of REALNUM is greater than or equal to 1.0, in which case WEIGHT is assigned the value 1. Finally, if neither of these two cases is selected, WEIGHT is assigned a value of 0 by the DEFAULT CASE.

Exercises

1. Rewrite the following IF-ELSEIF structure using a CASE construct:

```
IF (LETTER_GRADE .EQ. 'A')
  WRITE(6,*) 'THE NUMERICAL GRADE IS BETWEEN 90 AND 100'
ELSEIF (LETTER_GRADE .EQ. 'B')
  WRITE(6,*) 'THE NUMERICAL GRADE IS BETWEEN 80 AND 89.9'
ELSEIF (LETTER_GRADE .EQ. 'C')
  WRITE(6,*) 'THE NUMERICAL GRADE IS BETWEEN 70 AND 79.7'
ELSEIF (LETTER_GRADE .EQ. 'D'
  WRITE(6,*) 'HOW ARE YOU GOING TO EXPLAIN THIS ONE'
ELSE
  WRITE(6,*) 'OF COURSE I HAD NOTHING TO DO WITH MY GRADE.'
  WRITE(6,*) ' THE PROFESSOR WAS REALLY OFF THE WALL.'
ENDIF
```

2. Rewrite the following IF-ELSEIF structure using a CASE construct:

```
IF (FACTOR .EQ. 1)
  CALL IN_DATA
  CALL CHECK
ELSEIF (FACTOR .EQ. 2)
  CALL DATES
  CALL LEAP_YR
ELSEIF (FACTOR .EQ. 3)
  CALL YIELD
  CALL RESULTS
ELSEIF (FACTOR .EQ. 4 .OR. FACTOR .EQ. 5 .OR. FACTOR .EQ. 6)
  CALL VOLTS
  CALL ROI
  CALL FILES
  CALL SAVE
ENDIF
```

3. Modify Program 6-8 to use a character variable for the select code.

6.5 Applications

In this section we present two applications using IF statements to select appropriate data processing tasks.

Application 1: Solving Quadratic Equations

A *quadratic equation* is an equation that has the form $ax^2 + bx + c = 0$ or that can be algebraically manipulated into this form. In this equation, x is the unknown variable, and a, b, and c are known constants. Although the constants b and c can be any numbers, including zero, the value of the constant a cannot be zero (if a is zero, the equation would become a *linear equation* in x). Examples of quadratic equations are:

$$5x^2 + 6x + 2 = 0$$
$$x^2 - 7x + 20 = 0$$
$$34x^2 + 16 = 0$$

In the first equation, $a = 5$, $b = 6$, and $c = 2$; in the second equation, $a = 1$, $b = -7$, and $c = 20$; and in the third equation, $a = 34$, $b = 0$, and $c = 16$.

The real roots of a quadratic equation can be calculated using the quadratic formula as:

$$\text{root 1} = \frac{-b + \sqrt{b^2 - 4ac)}}{2a}$$

and:

$$\text{root 2} = \frac{-b - \sqrt{b^2 - 4ac)}}{2a}$$

A FORTRAN program that solves for the two roots of a quadratic equation, without any data validation statements, would use the user-entered values of a, b and c to directly calculate a value for each of the roots. However, if the user entered a value of 0 for a, the division by $2a$ would result in an error. Another error occurs when the value of the term $b^2 - 4ac$, which is called the *discriminant*, is negative, because the square root of a negative number cannot be taken. The complete logic for correctly determining the roots of a quadratic equation, including the steps necessary to determine that a valid quadratic equation is being processed, is illustrated in Figure 6-7.

The pseudocode corresponding to Figure 6-7 (a and b) is:

```
display a program purpose message
display a prompt for the coefficients
accept user-input values for a, b, and c
if a = 0 and b = 0, then
   display a message saying that the equation
   is degenerate (has no solution)
else if a = zero then
   calculate the single root equal to –c/b
   display the single root
else
   calculate the discriminant
   if the discriminant > 0 then
      solve for both roots using the quadratic formula
      display the two roots
   else if the discriminant < 0 then
      display a message that there are no real roots
   else
      calculate the repeated root equal to –b/(2a)
      display the repeated root
   endif
endif
```

Notice in both the flowchart and the equivalent pseudocode that we have used nested IF-ELSEIF structures. The outer IF-ELSEIF structure is used to validate the entered coefficients and determine that we have a valid quadratic equation. The inner IF-ELSEIF is then used to determine if the equation has two real roots (discriminant > 0), two imaginary roots (discriminant < 0), or repeated roots (discriminant = 0). The equivalent FORTRAN code for this problem is listed in Program 6-9.

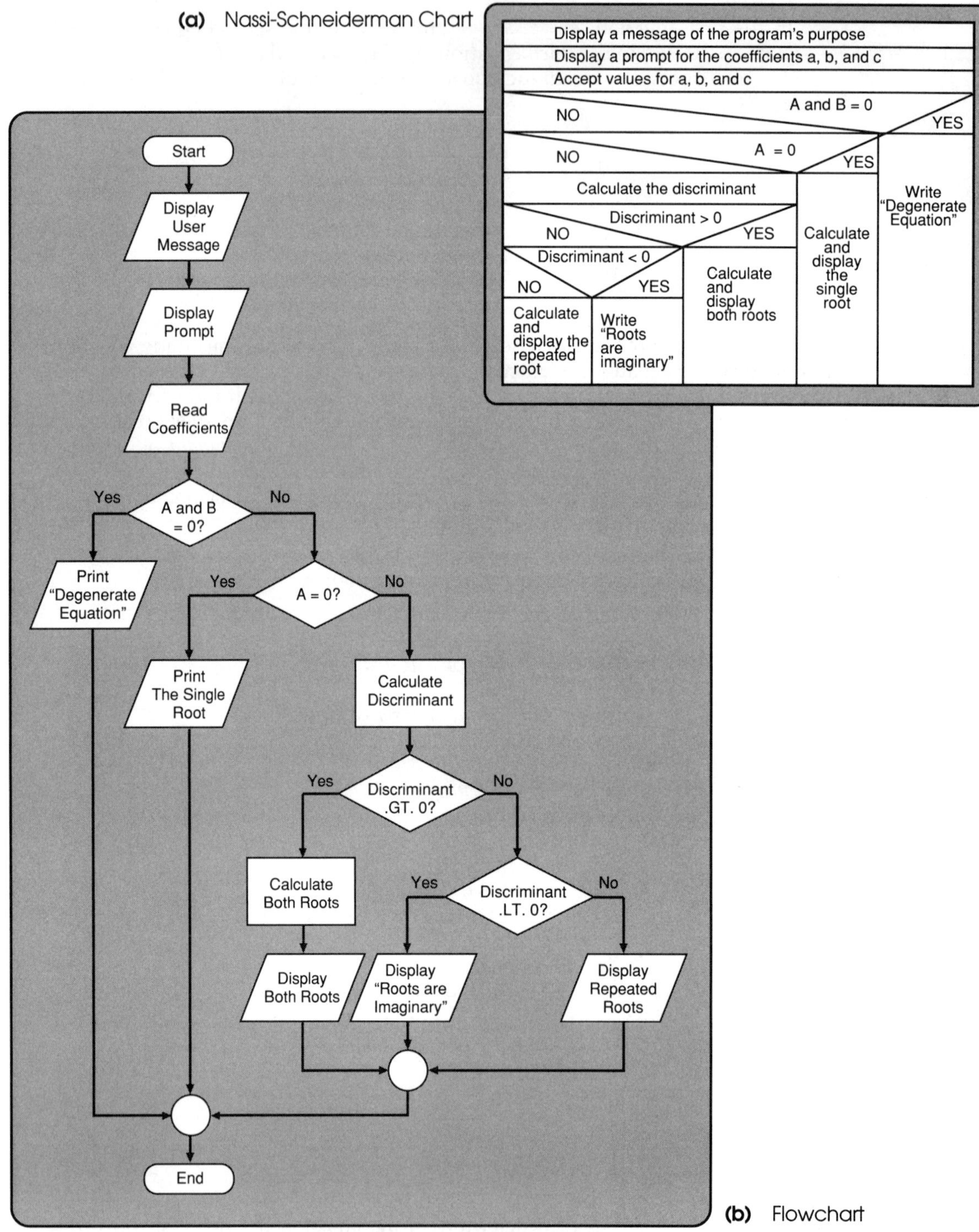

Figure 6-7 Determining the Roots of a Quadratic Equation

Program 6-9

```
* THIS PROGRAM SOLVES FOR THE ROOTS OF A QUADRATIC EQUATION
      PROGRAM MAIN
        REAL A, B, C
        CALL MESSGE
        CALL GETCOF(A,B,C)
        CALL SOLVE(A,B,C)
        END
*
      SUBROUTINE MESSGE
        WRITE(6,*) 'THIS PROGRAM CALCULATES THE ROOTS OF A'
        WRITE(6,*) '    QUADRATIC EQUATION OF THE FORM'
        WRITE(6,*) '            2'
        WRITE(6,*) '          AX + BX + C = 0'
        RETURN
        END
*
      SUBROUTINE GETCOF(A,B,C)
        REAL A, B, C
        WRITE(6,*)
        WRITE(6,*) 'PLEASE ENTER VALUES FOR A, B, AND C: '
        READ(5,*) A,B,C
        RETURN
        END
*
      SUBROUTINE SOLVE(A,B,C)
        IMPLICIT NONE
        REAL A, B, C, DISC, ROOT1, ROOT2
* OUTER IF-ELSEIF STATEMENT
        IF (A .EQ. 0.0 .AND. B .EQ. 0.0) THEN
          WRITE(6,*) 'THE EQUATION IS DEGENERATE AND HAS NO ROOTS'
        ELSE IF (A .EQ. 0.0) THEN
          WRITE(6,*) 'THE EQUATION HAS THE SINGLE ROOT  X = ', -C / B
        ELSE
          DISC = B**2 - 4*A*C
* INNER IF-ELSEIF STATEMENT
        IF (DISC .GT. 0.0) THEN
          DISC = SQRT(DISC)
          ROOT1 = (-B + DISC) / (2*A)
          ROOT2 = (-B - DISC) / (2*A)
          WRITE(6,*) 'THE TWO REAL ROOTS ARE ', ROOT1, ' AND', ROOT2
        ELSEIF (DISC . LT. 0.0) THEN
          WRITE(6,*) 'BOTH ROOTS ARE IMAGINARY'
        ELSE
          WRITE(6,*) 'BOTH ROOTS ARE EQUAL TO ', -B / (2*A)
        ENDIF
      ENDIF
      RETURN
      END
```

Following are two sample runs of Program 6-9.

```
THIS PROGRAM CALCULATES THE ROOTS OF A
   QUADRATIC EQUATION OF THE FORM

          AX² + BX + C = 0

PLEASE ENTER VALUES FOR A, B, AND C:
1 2 -35
THE TWO REAL ROOTS ARE    5.000000 AND    -7.000000
```

and:

```
THIS PROGRAM CALCULATES THE ROOTS OF A
   QUADRATIC EQUATION OF THE FORM

          AX² + BX + C = 0

PLEASE ENTER VALUES FOR A, B, AND C:
0 0 16
THE EQUATION IS DEGENERATE AND HAS NO ROOTS
```

The first run solves the quadratic equation $x^2 + 2x - 35 = 0$, which has the real roots $x = 5$ and $x = -7$. The input data for the second run results in the equation $0x^2 + 0x + 16 = 0$. As this degenerates into the mathematical impossibility $16 = 0$, the program correctly identifies this as a degenerate equation.

Application 2: Coin Toss Simulation

A common use of random numbers is to simulate events using a program, rather than going through the time and expense of constructing a real-life experiment. For example, statistical theory tells us that the probability of having a tossed coin turn up heads is 1/2. Similarly, there is a 50 percent probability of having a single tossed coin turn up tails.

Using these probabilities we would expect a single coin that is tossed 1000 times to turn up heads 500 times and tails 500 times. In practice, however, this is never exactly realized for a single experiment consisting of 1000 tosses. Instead of actually tossing a coin 1000 times, however, we can use a random number generator to simulate these tosses. In particular, we will use the random number subroutine RANDOM( ) developed in Section 4.5, which returns a random number between 0 and 1 and a new "SEED" value.

Using this random number, the algorithm to simulate 1000 coin tosses is given by the pseudocode:

```
Initialize the heads count to zero
Initialize the tails count to zero
Do 1000 times
   get a random number between 0 and 1
   if the random number is greater than .5
      consider this as a head and
      add one to the heads count
   else
      consider this as a tail and
```

add one to the tails count
endif
Endo
Calculate the percentage of heads as
the number of heads divided by 1000 x 100%
Calculate the percentage of tails as
the number of tails divided by 1000 x 100%
Print the percentage of heads and tails obtained

Program 6-10 codes this algorithm in FORTRAN.

Program 6-10

```
*** THIS PROGRAM SIMULATES THE TOSSING OF A COIN 1000 TIMES
      PROGRAM MAIN
        INTEGER SEED
        REAL PERHD, PERTL
        CALL GETSED(SEED)
        CALL SIMUL(SEED, PERHD, PERTL)
        CALL SHOW(PERHD, PERTL)
        END
*
      SUBROUTINE GETSED(SEED)
        INTEGER SEED
        WRITE(6,*)'ENTER AN ODD 6 DIGIT NUMBER NOT ENDING IN 5: '
        READ(5,*) SEED
        RETURN
        END
*
      SUBROUTINE SIMUL(SEED, PERHD, PERTL)
        INTEGER SEED, I, HEADS, TAILS
        REAL FLIP, PERHD, PERTL
        HEADS = 0
        TAILS = 0
*** SIMULATE 1000 TOSSES OF A COIN
        DO 10 I = 1, 1000
          CALL RANDOM(SEED, FLIP)
          IF (FLIP .GT. 0.5) THEN
            HEADS = HEADS + 1
          ELSE
            TAILS = TAILS + 1
          ENDIF
  10    CONTINUE
*** CALCULATE THE PERCENTAGE OF HEADS
        PERHD = (HEADS / 1000.0) * 100.0
*** CALCULATE THE PERCENTAGE OF TAILS
        PERTL = (TAILS / 1000.0) * 100.0
        RETURN
        END
```

(Continued on next page)

(Continued from previous page)

```
*
      SUBROUTINE SHOW(PERHD, PERTL)
        REAL PERHD, PERTL
        WRITE(6,*) 'HEADS CAME UP ', PERHD, ' PERCENT OF THE TIME.'
        WRITE(6,*) 'TAILS CAME UP ', PERTL, ' PERCENT OF THE TIME.'
        RETURN
        END
*
      SUBROUTINE RANDOM(SEED, RANDX)
        INTEGER SEED
        REAL RANDX
        SEED = INT(997.0 * SEED - INT(997.0 * SEED/1.E6)*1.E6)
        RANDX = SEED / 1.E6
        RETURN
        END
```

Following are two sample runs using Program 6-10.

```
ENTER AN ODD 6 DIGIT NUMBER NOT ENDING IN 5:
654321
HEADS CAME UP       49.600000 PERCENT OF THE TIME.
TAILS CAME UP       50.400000 PERCENT OF THE TIME.
```

and

```
ENTER AN ODD 6 DIGIT NUMBER NOT ENDING IN 5:
234567
HEADS CAME UP       53.000000 PERCENT OF THE TIME.
TAILS CAME UP       47.000000 PERCENT OF THE TIME.
```

Writing and executing Program 6-10 is certainly easier than manually tossing a coin 1000 times. It should be noted that the validity of the results produced by the program depends on how random the numbers produced by the random number function actually are.

Additional Exercises for Chapter 6

1a. Write a program that accepts two real numbers and a select code from a user. If the entered select code is 1, have the program add the two previously entered numbers and display the result; if the select code is 2, the numbers should be multiplied; and if the select code is 3, the first number should be divided by the second number.

b. Determine what the program written in Exercise 1a does when the entered numbers are 3 and 0 and the select code is 3.

c. Modify the program written in Exercise 1a so that division by 0 is not allowed and an appropriate message is displayed when such a division is attempted.

2a. Write a program to display the following two prompts:

```
ENTER A MONTH (USE A 1 FOR JAN, ETC.):
ENTER A DAY OF THE MONTH:
```

Have your program accept and store a number in the variable MONTH in response to the first prompt and accept and store a number in the variable DAY in response to the second prompt. If the month entered is not between 1 and 12 inclusive, print a message informing the user that an invalid month has been entered. If the day entered is not between 1 and 31, inclusive, print a message informing the user that an invalid day has been entered.

b. What will your program do if the user types a number with a decimal point for the month? How can you ensure that your IF statements check for an integer number?

c. In a non–leap year February has 28 days; the months January, March, May, July, August, October, and December have 31 days; and all other months have 30 days. Using this information, modify the program written in Exercise 2a to display a message when an invalid day is entered for a user-entered month. For this program, ignore leap years.

3a. The quadrant that a line drawn from the origin resides in is determined by the angle that the line makes with the positive *X* axis as follows:

Angle from the positive X axis	**Quadrant**
Between 0 and 90 degrees	I
Between 90 and 180 degrees	II
Between 180 and 270 degrees	III
Between 270 and 360 degrees	IV

Using this information, write a FORTRAN program that accepts the angle of the line as user input and determines and displays the quadrant appropriate to the input data. (*Note:* If the angle is exactly 0, 90, 180, or 270 degrees, the corresponding line does not reside in any quadrant but lies on an axis.)
Write this program so that the angle is input within the MAIN program unit and the determination and display of the appropriate quadrant are performed by a subroutine.

b. Modify the program written for Exercise 3a so that a message is displayed that identifies an angle of zero degrees as the positive *X* axis, an angle of 90 degrees as the positive *Y* axis, an angle of 180 degrees as the negative *X* axis, and an angle of 270 degrees as the negative *Y* axis.

4a. All years that are evenly divisible by 400 or are evenly divisible by 4 and not evenly divisible by 100 are leap years. For example, since 1600 is evenly divisible by 400, the year 1600 was a leap year. Similarly, since 1988 is evenly divisible by 4 but not by 100, 1988 was also a leap year. Using this information, write a FORTRAN program that accepts the year as a user input, determines if the year is a leap year, and displays an appropriate message that tells the user if the entered year is or is not a leap year.

b. Using the code written in Exercise 4a, redo Exercise 2c such that leap years are taken into account.

5. Based on an automobile's model year and weight, the state of New Jersey determines the car's weight class and registration fee using the following schedule:

Model year	Weight	Weight class	Registration fee
1970 or earlier	Less than 2700 lbs	1	$16.50
	2700 to 3800 lbs	2	25.50
	More than 3800 lbs	3	46.50
1971 to 1979	Less than 2700 lbs	4	27.00
	2700 to 3800 lbs	5	30.50
	More than 3800 lbs	6	52.50
1980 or later	Less than 3500 lbs	7	19.50
	3500 or more lbs	8	52.50

Using this information, write a FORTRAN program that accepts the year and weight of an automobile and determines and displays the weight class and registration fee for the car.

6. Modify Program 6-8 so that the imaginary roots are calculated and displayed when the discriminant is negative. For this case, the two roots of the equation are:

$$x_1 = \frac{-b}{2a} + \frac{\sqrt{-(b^2 - 4ac)}}{2a} i$$

and:

$$x_2 = \frac{-b}{2a} + \frac{\sqrt{-(b^2 - 4ac)}}{2a} i$$

where i is the imaginary number symbol for the square root of –1. (*Hint:* Calculate the real and imaginary parts of each root separately.)

7a. In the game of Blackjack the cards 2 through 10 are counted at their face values, regardless of suit; all face cards (jack, queen, and king) are counted as 10; and an ace is counted as either a 1 or an 11, depending on the total count of all the cards in a player's hand. The ace is counted as 11 only if the resulting total value of all cards in a player's hand does not exceed 21; otherwise it is counted as a 1. Using this information, write a FORTRAN program that accepts three card values as inputs (a 1 corresponding to an ace, a 2 corresponding to a two, and so on), calculates the total value of the hand appropriately, and displays the value of the three cards with a printed message.

b. Modify the program written for Exercise 7a so that the three cards are selected using a random number generator.

8. Modify Program 6-10 so that it requests the number of tosses from the user. (Hint: Make sure to have the program correctly determine the percentages of heads and tails obtained.)

9. (Central Limit Theorem Simulation) Modify Program 6-10 so that it automatically generates 20 simulations, with each simulation having 1000 tosses. Print out the percentage for each run and the percentages for the 20 runs combined.

10a. Write a FORTRAN program that uses a user-entered six-digit integer to produce a random number between 1 and 100. The program should then give the user seven tries to guess the generated random number. If the user guesses the correct number, the message "HOORAY! YOU WIN!" should be displayed. After each incorrect guess the computer should display the message "WRONG NUMBER - TRY AGAIN" and indicate the number of guesses left. After seven incorrect guesses the computer should display the message "SORRY - YOU LOSE". (Hint: To generate a number between 1 and 100 from a random number function RAND(X) that generates numbers between 0.0 and 1.0 requires the use of the expression 1 + INT(100 * RAND(X).)

b. Modify the program written for Exercise 10a to allow the user to run the game again after a game has been completed. The program should display the message "WOULD YOU LIKE TO PLAY AGAIN - 'Y'/'N'?: " and restart if the user enters either 'Y' or 'y'.

6.6 Common Programming Errors

The common programming errors related to FORTRAN's selection statements include the following:

1. Forgetting the periods that must surround all relational and logical operators.
2. Trying to use arithmetic operators, such as =, <, and > instead of the correct FORTRAN relational operators (.EQ., .LE., .GT., etc.).
3. Trying to use a logical operator without a relational expression or logical variable. For example, the expression I .NE. 5 .OR. 10 is invalid. The expression A .NE. 5 .OR. A .NE. 10 in which the .OR. operator connects two relational expressions is valid.
4. Omitting the keyword THEN from a block IF statement or putting it in a logical IF statement.
5. Omitting the final ENDIF from a block IF statement, whether or not the block IF includes either the ELSEIF or the ELSE statement. This can create especially tricky logic problems when two IF statements are placed in sequence. For example, the section of code:

```
IF (AGE .GT. 25) THEN
      .
      .
      .
IF (EMPLYD .LT. 10) THEN
      .
      .
      .
ELSE
      .
      .
      .
ENDIF
```

is missing one ENDIF statement, which will be caught by the compiler when the statement is compiled. Now, however, you must be careful to place the missing ENDIF correctly. Placing an ENDIF immediately before or after the existing ENDIF creates a nested IF-ELSE statement, while placing the ENDIF before the second block IF creates a sequence of two non-nested block IF statements. The correct placement depends on the logic required.

6. This error presents a typical debugging problem. Here an IF statement appears to select an incorrect choice, and the programmer mistakenly concentrates on the tested condition as the source of the problem. For example, assume that the following IF-ELSE statement is part of your program:

```
IF (KEY .EQ. 'F') THEN
  XTEMP = (5.0/9.0)*(TEMP - 32.0)
  WRITE(6,*) 'CONVERSION TO CELSIUS DONE'
ELSE
  XTEMP = (9.0/5.0) * TEMP + 32.0
  WRITE(6,*) 'CONVERSION TO FAHRENHEIT DONE'
ENDIF
PRINT *, 'THE CONVERTED TEMPERATURE IS ', XTEMP
```

This statement will always display "CONVERSION TO CELSIUS DONE" when the variable KEY contains an F. Therefore, if this message is displayed when you believe KEY does not contain an F, investigation of KEY's value is called for. As a general rule, whenever a selection statement does not act as you think it should, make sure to test your assumptions about the values assigned to the tested variables using either PRINT or WRITE statements. If an unanticipated value is displayed, you have at least isolated the source of the problem to the variables themselves rather than the structure of the IF statement. From there you will have to determine where and how the incorrect value was obtained.

7. The last error common to selection statements is a subtle one and is really a numerical accuracy problem relating to REAL numbers. Because of the way computers store these values, tests for equality of REAL values or variables using the relational operator .EQ. should be avoided.

6.7 Things to Remember

1. Relational expressions, which are also called *simple conditions*, are used to compare operands. The value of a relational expression is either .T. (true) or .F. (false). Relational expressions are created using the following relational operators:

Relational operator	**Meaning**	**Example**
`.LT.`	Less than	`AGE .LT. 30`
`.GT.`	Greater than	`HEIGHT .GT. 6.2`
`.LE.`	Less than or equal to	`TAXABLE .LE. 20000`
`.GE.`	Greater than or equal to	`TEMP .GE. 98.6`
`.EQ.`	Equal to	`GRADE .EQ. 100`
`.NE.`	Not equal to	`NUMBER .NE. 250`

2. More complex conditions can be constructed from relational expressions using FORTRAN's .AND., .OR., and .NOT. logical operators.

3. A block IF statement is used to select one or more statements for execution based on the value of a condition. The block IF statement has the form:

```
IF (condition) THEN
```

and must always be used with an ENDIF statement. Additionally, one ELSE statement and any number of ELSEIF statements may be used with a block IF statement to provide multiple selection criteria. The common selection structures that can be created using a block IF statement include the following forms:

a. Form 1: Simple IF-THEN:

```
IF(condition) THEN
   statement 1
   statement 2
        .
        .
        .
   statement n
 ENDIF
```

Here, the statements between the block IF and ENDIF statements are only executed if the condition being tested is true. The block IF and ENDIF statements must be written on separate lines.

b. Form 2: Simple IF-ELSE:

```
IF (condition) THEN
   statement 1
   statement 2
        .
        .
        .
   statement n
ELSE
   statement n+1
        .
        .
        .
   statement m
ENDIF
```

This is a two-way selection structure. Here the ELSE statement is used with the block IF to select between two alternative sets of statements based on the value of a condition. If the condition is true, statements 1 through *n* are executed; otherwise, statements *n*+1 through *m* are executed. The block IF, ELSE, and ENDIF statements must be written on separate lines.

c. Form 3: Simple ELSEIF:

```
IF (condition 1) THEN
  one or more statements in here
ELSEIF (condition 2) THEN
  one or more statements in here
ELSE
  one or more statements in here
ENDIF
```

This is a three-way selection structure. Once a condition is satisfied, only the statements between that condition and the next ELSEIF or ELSE are executed, and no further conditions are tested. The ELSE statement is optional, and the statements corresponding to the ELSE statement are only executed if neither condition 1 nor condition 2 is true. The block IF, ELSEIF, ELSE and ENDIF statements must be written on separate lines.

d. Form 4: Multiple ELSEIFs:

```
IF (condition) THEN
 one or more statements in here
ELSEIF (condition 2) THEN
  one or more statements in here
          .
          .
          .
ELSEIF (condition n) THEN
  one or more statements in here
ELSE
  one or more statements in here
ENDIF
```

This is a multiway selection structure. Once a condition is satisfied, only the statements between that condition and the next ELSEIF or ELSE are executed, and no further conditions are tested. The ELSE statement is optional, and the statements corresponding to the ELSE statement are only executed if none of the conditions tested are true. The block IF, ELSEIF, ELSE and ENDIF statements must be written on individual lines.

4. A logical IF statement is a one-way selection statement that has the general form:

```
IF (condition) statement
```

where the single statement following the condition can be any executable FORTRAN statement except a block IF, logical IF, END, or a repetition statement, described in Chapter 5.

5. Block IF, ELSE, and ELSEIF statements may themselves contain logical IF, block IF, ELSE, and ELSEIF statements. Such constructions are called nested IF statements.

7 Conditional Loops

Chapter 7

7.1 The FORTRAN 77 DO WHILE Structure

7.2 The FORTRAN 90 DO WHILE Construct

7.3 REPEAT UNTIL Loops

7.4 Applications

7.5 Common Programming Errors

7.6 Things to Remember

In addition to creating fixed count loops, using a DO statement, it is frequently convenient to construct a loop that terminates when a specific condition is met. Loops that terminate based on the achievement of a given condition are referred to as *conditional loops*. In FORTRAN 77 these loops are constructed using an IF statement to specify and check the status of the condition, while FORTRAN 90 provides a separate DO WHILE statement. This chapter describes the specifics of constructing conditional loops under both FORTRAN standards.

7.1 The FORTRAN 77 DO WHILE Structure*

A DO WHILE structure is a general repetition construction that can be used in a variety of programming situations. In pseudocode a DO WHILE structure has the general form

```
while (condition) is true
  statement 1
  statement 2
       .
       .
       .
  statement n
endwhile
```

* This section presents a DO-WHILE structure implemented in FORTRAN 77 using a GO TO statement. The next section presents the same material using FORTRAN 90's DO WHILE statement.

The condition contained within the parentheses is evaluated in exactly the same manner as a condition contained in an IF statement; the difference is how the condition is used. As we have seen, when the condition is true in an IF statement, the statements following the condition are executed once. In a DO WHILE structure the statements following the condition are executed repeatedly as long as the condition remains true. This naturally means that somewhere in the DO WHILE structure there must be a statement that alters the value of the tested condition. As we will see, this is indeed the case. For now, however, considering just the condition and the statements following the condition, the process used by the computer in evaluating a DO WHILE structure is:

Step 1. Test the condition

Step 2. If the condition is true
    a. execute the statements following the parentheses
    b. go back to Step 1
  else
    exit the while structure

Notice that Step 2b forces program control to be transferred back to Step 1. The transfer of control back to the start of a DO WHILE structure in order to reevaluate the condition produces the program loop. The DO WHILE structure literally loops back on itself to recheck the condition until it becomes false. The Nassi-Schneiderman and flowchart representations for a DO WHILE structure are illustrated in Figure 7-1.

Construction of a DO WHILE loop in FORTRAN 77 requires the use of a block IF statement. The form of this structure is:

```
k  IF (condition) THEN
      statement 1
      statement 2
          .
          .
      statement n
      GO TO k
   ENDIF
```

Notice that this construction is a standard block IF statement with the addition of the new statement GO TO *k*, where *k* is the value of the statement number corresponding to the beginning of the IF statement. The GO TO statement, which always has the form GO TO *k*, is called an *unconditional transfer of control* statement. Whenever this statement is encountered, execution is automatically transferred to the statement having the label specified in the GO TO statement.

To make this a little more tangible, consider the relational condition `COUNT .LE. 10` and the statement `WRITE(6,*) COUNT`. Using these, we can write the following DO WHILE structure:

```
10 IF (COUNT .LE. 10) THEN
      WRITE(6,*) COUNT
      GO TO 10
   ENDIF
```

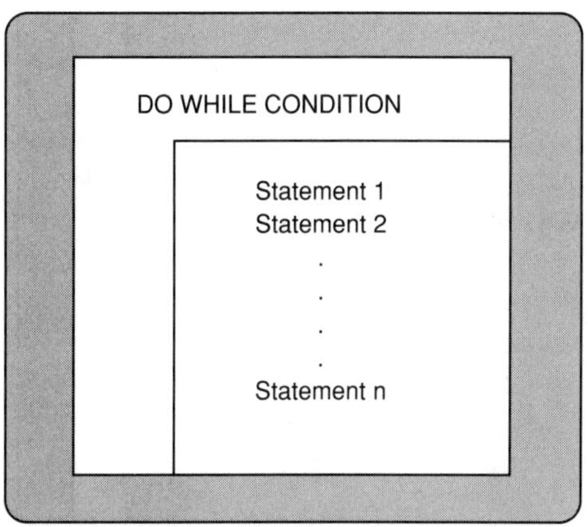

(a) Nassi-Schneiderman Representation

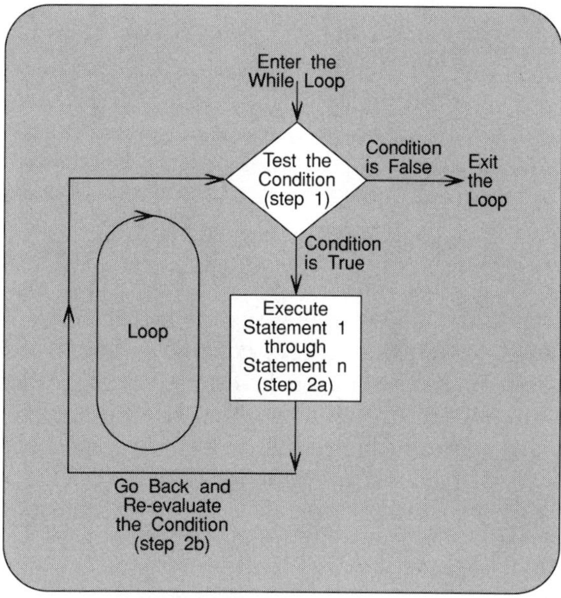

(b) Flowchart Representation

Figure 7-1 The DO WHILE Structure

Although the above structure is valid, the alert reader will realize that we have created a situation in which the WRITE statement either is called forever (or until we stop the program) or is not called at all. Let us see why this happens.

If COUNT has a value less than or equal to 10 when the condition is first evaluated, the WRITE statement is executed. The GO TO statement then causes control to be transferred back to line 10 where the condition is retested. Since we have not changed the value stored in COUNT, the condition is still true and the WRITE statement is re-executed. This process continues forever, or until the program containing this statement is prematurely stopped by the user. However, if COUNT starts with a value greater than 10, the condition is false to begin with and the WRITE statement never is executed.

How do we set an initial value in COUNT to control what the DO WHILE structure does the first time the condition is evaluated? The answer, of course, is to assign values to each variable in the tested condition before the condition is encountered. For example, the following sequence of instructions is valid:

```
      COUNT = 1
10    IF (COUNT .LE. 10) THEN
        WRITE(6,*) COUNT
        GO TO 10
      ENDIF
```

Using this sequence of instructions, we have ensured that COUNT starts with a value of 1. We could assign any value to COUNT in the assignment statement—the important thing is to assign some value. In practice, the assigned value depends on the application.

We must still change the value of COUNT so that we can finally exit the loop. This requires a condition such as COUNT = COUNT + 1 to increment the value of COUNT each time the loop is executed. For example:

```
   COUNT = 1
10 IF (COUNT .LE. 10) THEN
     WRITE(6,*) COUNT
     COUNT = COUNT + 1
     GO TO 10
   ENDIF
```

Let us now analyze this sequence of instructions. The first assignment statement sets COUNT equal to 1. The IF statement is then entered and the condition is evaluated for the first time. Since the value of COUNT is less than or equal to 10, the condition is true and the statements within the IF statement are executed. The first statement within the IF statement causes the WRITE statement to display the value of COUNT. The next statement adds one to the value currently stored in COUNT, making this value equal to 2. The GO TO statement now causes the program to loop back to retest the condition. Since COUNT is still less than or equal to 10, the statements within the loop are again executed. This process continues until the value of COUNT reaches 11. Program 7-1 illustrates these statements in an actual program.

Program 7-1

```
      PROGRAM MAIN
        CALL TESTDW
        END
*
      SUBROUTINE TESTDW
        INTEGER COUNT
        COUNT = 1
 5      IF (COUNT .LE. 10) THEN
          WRITE(6,*) COUNT
          COUNT = COUNT + 1
          GO TO 5
      ENDIF
      RETURN
      END
```

The output for Program 7-1 is:

```
 1
 2
 3
 4
 5
 6
 7
 8
 9
10
```

There is nothing special about the name COUNT used in Program 7-1 or the statement label assigned to the IF line. Any valid integer variable name could have been used and any integer number between one and 99999 could have been used for the statement label.

Before we consider other examples of the DO WHILE structure, three comments concerning Program 7-1 are in order. First, the loop could have been created more simply using a DO statement of the form DO k COUNT = 1, 10, where k is the statement label of a CONTINUE statement. This is because this particular loop is set up to execute a fixed number of times. The usefulness of Program 7-1 is in introducing the key elements of a DO WHILE loop; we will alter it shortly to handle cases that cannot be accomplished with a DO statement. Secondly, the statement COUNT = COUNT + 1 that alters the value in COUNT can be replaced with any other statement that changes the value of COUNT. A statement such as COUNT = COUNT + 2, for example, would cause every second integer to be displayed. Finally, it is the programmer's responsibility to ensure that COUNT is changed in a way that ultimately leads to a normal exit from the DO WHILE. For example, if we replace the statement COUNT = COUNT + 1 with the statement COUNT = COUNT - 1, the value of COUNT will never reach 11 and an infinite loop is created (an infinite loop is a loop that never terminates). The computer will not reach out, touch you, and say, 'Excuse me, you have created an infinite loop.' It just keeps executing over and over (in this case, displaying numbers) until you realize that the program is not working as you expected or the system has a maximum time allocated for each run.

Now that you have some familiarity with the DO WHILE structure, see if you can read and determine the output of Program 7-2.

Program 7-2

```
      PROGRAM MAIN
        CALL TABLE
        END
*
      SUBROUTINE TABLE
        INTEGER NUM
        WRITE(6,*) 'NUMBER     SQUARE      CUBE'
        WRITE(6,*) '------     ------      ----'
        NUM = 1
25      IF (NUM .LT. 11) THEN
          WRITE(6,*) NUM, NUM**2, NUM**3
          NUM = NUM + 1
          GO TO 25
        ENDIF
        RETURN
        END
```

The assignment statement in Program 7-2 initially sets the counter variable NUM to 1. The IF statement then checks to see if the value of NUM is less than 1. While the condition is true, the values of NUM, NUM squared, and NUM cubed are displayed and the value of NUM incremented by 1. When NUM finally equals 11, the condition is false, and the program exits the DO WHILE structure.

When Program 7-2 is run, the following display is produced:*

```
Number      Square      Cube
------      ------      ----
   1           1           1
   2           4           8
   3           9          27
   4          16          64
   5          25         125
   6          36         216
   7          49         343
   8          64         512
   9          81         729
  10         100        1000
```

Note that the condition used in Program 7-2 is NUM .LT. 11 . For the integer variable NUM, this condition can be replaced by the equivalent condition NUM .LE. 10 . The choice of which to use is entirely up to you.

If we want to use Program 7-2 to produce a table of 1000 numbers, all we do is change the condition in the DO WHILE structure from I .LT. 11 to I .LT. 1001. Changing the 11 to 1001 produces a table of 1000 lines—not bad for a simple five-line DO WHILE structure.

Sentinels

In many situations the exact number of items to be entered is not known in advance or the items are too numerous to count beforehand. For example, when entering a large amount of research data we might not want to take the time to count the number of actual data items that are to be entered. In cases like this it is desirable to enter data continuously and, at the end, type in a special data value to signal the end of data input.

In computer programming, a data value used to signal either the start or end of a series of data items is called a *sentinel*. The sentinel value must, of course, be selected so as not to conflict with legitimate data values. For example, if we were constructing a program that accepts a student's grades, and assuming that no extra credit is given that could produce a grade higher than 100, we could use any number higher than 100 as a sentinel value. Program 7-3 illustrates this concept. In this program data is continuously requested and accepted until a number larger than 100 is entered. Entry of a number higher than 100 alerts the program to exit the DO WHILE loop and display the sum of the numbers entered.

* The spacing required to produce alignment of the headings with the column of numbers was determined by trial and error. This, of course, is a disadvantage of list-directed output.

Program 7-3

```
      PROGRAM MAIN
        CALL GRADES
        END
*
      SUBROUTINE GRADES
        REAL GRADE, TOTAL
        GRADE = 0.0
        TOTAL = 0.0
        WRITE(6,*) 'TO STOP ENTERING GRADES, TYPE IN ANY NUMBER'
        WRITE(6,*) ' GREATER THAN 100.'
   10   IF (GRADE .LE. 100) THEN
          WRITE(6,*) 'ENTER A GRADE: '
          READ(5,*)  GRADE
          TOTAL = TOTAL + GRADE
         GO TO 10
       ENDIF
       WRITE(6,*) 'THE TOTAL OF THE GRADES IS ', TOTAL - GRADE
       RETURN
       END
```

Following is a sample run using Program 7-3. As long as grades less than or equal to 100 are entered, the program continues to request and accept additional data. When a number greater than 100 is entered, the program adds this number to the TOTAL and exits the DO WHILE loop. Outside of the loop and within the WRITE statement, the value of the sentinel that was added to the TOTAL is subtracted and the sum of the legitimate grades that were entered is displayed.

```
TO STOP ENTERING GRADES, TYPE IN ANY NUMBER
 GREATER THAN 100.
ENTER A GRADE:
84
ENTER A GRADE:
75
ENTER A GRADE:
93
ENTER A GRADE:
88
ENTER A GRADE:
101
THE TOTAL OF THE GRADES IS     340.00000000
```

Notice that Program 7-3 differs from previous examples in that termination of the loop is controlled by an externally supplied value rather than a fixed count condition. The loop in Program 7-3 will continue indefinitely until the sentinel value is encountered. DO WHILE loops are well suited to handle sentinel values because of the loop's IF statement.

Reading Data Files

DO WHILE loops are especially well suited to reading data files containing large amounts of data. Typically such files do not include a count of the number of records contained in the file; they do, however, have an End of File (EOF) marker that acts as a sentinel. The general form of a DO WHILE loop for reading a file is:

```
n  READ(unit number, fmt, END = k) variable list
                         .
     any other statements in here
                         .
   GO TO n
k  this statement is executed when the file has no more data
```

Notice that the GO TO statement transfers control back to the READ statement. Until the end-of-file has been reached, the READ statement executes as if the END option were not present. When the end of the file is encountered, the END option transfers control to statement number k. Program 7-4 illustrates this loop for reading the TEST.DAT file shown in Figure 7-2.

Program 7-4

```
      PROGRAM MAIN
        CALL SHFILE
        END
*
      SUBROUTINE SHFILE
        INTEGER N
        REAL RESULT
  5     FORMAT(5X,I2,3X,F5.2)
        OPEN(1,FILE='TEST.DAT')
        WRITE(6,*) '      EXPERIMENT'
        WRITE(6,*) '        NUMBER      RESULT'
        WRITE(6,*) '        ------------------'
 10     READ(1, 5, END=30) N, RESULT
          WRITE(6,*) N, RESULT
        GO TO 10
 30     RETURN
        END
```

```
        1    26.50
        2    18.00
        3    44.75
        4    33.25
        5    52.00
123456789111111
         012345
```

└Column Number One

Figure 7-2 The Structure of the TEST.DAT File

The output produced by Program 7-4 is:

```
Experiment
  Number          Result
----------       ---------
     1           26.500000
     2           18.000000
     3           44.750000
     4           33.250000
     5           52.000000
```

Breaking Out of a Loop

It is sometimes necessary to prematurely break out of a loop when an unusual error condition is detected. The means of doing this is provided by the GO TO statement that we have been using to force repetition of the DO WHILE loop. For example, execution of the following DO WHILE loop is immediately terminated if a number greater than 76 is encountered.

```
10    IF (COUNT .LE. 10) THEN
        WRITE(6,*) 'ENTER A NUMBER: '
        READ(5,*)  NUM
        IF (NUM .GT. 76) GO TO 15
        GO TO 10
      ENDIF
15    next statement
```

The use of a GO TO statement in this manner violates pure structured programming principles because it provides a second, nonstandard exit from a loop. Nevertheless, this technique is extremely useful and valuable for breaking out of loops when an unusual condition is detected.

The statement that the "break-out" GO TO statement refers to can be any executable statement within the program, except that it should not be a statement internal to another loop. Can you see why? By entering a loop in the middle, the initializing statements for the variables controlling the loop are skipped, so that there is no control over how the entered loop will terminate.

Programming Exercises

1. Write a program that uses a DO WHILE loop to print the numbers 2 to 10 in increments of two. The output of your program should be:

```
2
4
6
8
10
```

2. Write a program that uses a DO WHILE loop to produce a table of Celsius and equivalent Fahrenheit degrees. The table should start at a Celsius value of -10 and end with a Celsius value of 60, in increments of 10 degrees. Use the formula *Fahrenheit = (9.0/5.0) * Celsius + 32.*

3a. For the following loop, determine the total number of items displayed. Also determine the first and last numbers printed.

```
      INTEGER NUM = 0
20    IF (NUM .LE. 20) THEN
        NUM = NUM + 1
        WRITE(6,*) NUM
        GO TO 20
      ENDIF
```

b. Put the code in Exercise 3a into a working program and run it to verify your answers to the exercise.

c. How would the output be affected if the two statements within the DO WHILE loop structure in Exercise 3a were reversed (that is, if the WRITE statement was made before the NUM = NUM + 1 statement)?

4. Write a FORTRAN program that uses a DO WHILE loop to convert gallons to liters. The program should display gallons from 10 to 20 in one-gallon increments and the corresponding liter equivalents. Use the relationship: liters = 3.785 * gallons.

5. Write a FORTRAN program that uses a DO WHILE loop to convert feet to meters. The program should display feet from 3 to 30 in three-foot increments and the corresponding meter equivalents. Use the relationship: meters = feet / 3.28.

6. A machine purchased for $28,000 is depreciated at a rate of $4,000 a year for seven years. Write and run a FORTRAN program that uses a DO WHILE loop to compute and display a depreciation table for seven years. The table should have the form:

Year	Depreciation	End-of-year value	Accumulated depreciation
1	4000	24000	4000
2	4000	20000	8000
3	4000	16000	12000
4	4000	12000	16000
5	4000	8000	20000
6	4000	4000	24000
7	4000	0	28000

7. An automobile travels at an average speed of 55 miles per hour for four hours. Write a FORTRAN program that uses a DO WHILE loop to calculate and display the distance driven, in miles, that the car has traveled after .5, 1, 1.5, etc., hours until the end of the trip.

8a. An approximate conversion formula for converting Fahrenheit to Celsius temperatures is

Celsius = (Fahrenheit - 30) / 2

Using this formula, and starting with a Fahrenheit temperature of zero degrees, write a FORTRAN program that determines when the approximate equivalent Celsius temperature differs from the exact equivalent value by more than four degrees. (Hint: use a DO WHILE loop that terminates when the difference between approximate and exact Celsius equivalents exceeds four degrees.)

b. Using the approximate Celsius conversion formula given in Exercise 8a, write a FORTRAN program that produces a table of Fahrenheit temperatures, exact Celsius equivalent temperatures, approximate Celsius equivalent temperatures, and the difference between the correct and approximate equivalent Celsius values. The table should begin at zero degrees Fahrenheit, use two-degree Fahrenheit increments and terminate when the difference between exact and approximate values differs by more than four degrees.

9. The value of Euler's number *e* can be approximated using the formula

$$e = 1 + 1/1! + 1/2! + 1/3! + 1/4! + 1/5! + ...$$

Using this formula, write a FORTRAN program that approximates the value of *e* using a DO WHILE loop that terminates when the difference between two successive approximations differs by less than 10 E-6.

10. The value of sin x can be approximated using the formula

$$\text{Sin } x = x - \frac{x^3}{3!} + \frac{x^5}{5!} - \frac{x^7}{7!} + \frac{x^9}{9!} + \ldots$$

Using this formula, determine how many terms are needed to approximate the value returned by the intrinsic SIN( ) function with an error less than 1 E-6, when x = 30 degrees. (Hints: Use a DO WHILE loop that terminates when the difference between the value returned by the intrinsic SIN( ) function and the approximation is less than 1 E-6. Also note that x must first be converted to radian measure and that the alternating sign in the approximating series can be determined as (-1)**(n+1) where n is the number of terms used in the approximation.)

11a. Write, compile, and execute a FORTRAN program that accepts a set of 10 numbers, finds the largest number of the entered values and displays this value after all numbers have been entered.

b. Modify the program written for Exercise 11a to also display the position of the largest entered number (that is, was it the 1st, 2nd, 3rd, etc., number entered?).

7.2 The FORTRAN 90 DO WHILE Construct*

In FORTRAN 90 a DO WHILE structure, which is referred to as a DO WHILE construct, is created using a DO WHILE statement. The general form of this DO WHILE construct is:

```
DO WHILE (relational expression)
  statement_1
  statement_2
     .
     .
  statement_n
ENDDO
```

The DO WHILE construct introduces two new FORTRAN statements, the DO WHILE statement and the ENDDO statement. The general form of the DO WHILE statement, which begins a DO WHILE construct, is:

```
DO WHILE (relational expression)
```

Within the context of a DO WHILE construct, the DO WHILE statement performs as follows: the relational expression contained within the parentheses is evaluated and if the expression is true, the statements between the DO WHILE and ENDDO statements are executed repeatedly as long as the expression remains true. This naturally means that somewhere in the DO WHILE construct there must be a statement that alters the value of the tested expression. As we will see, this is indeed the case. Thus, the process used by the computer in evaluating a DO WHILE construct is:

1. Test the expression

2. If the expression has a nonzero (true) value
   a. execute the statements between the DO WHILE
   and ENDDO statements
   b. go back to step 1
else
   exit the DO WHILE construct and continue
   execution with the statement following the ENDDO statement

* This section presents the same material introduced in Section 7.1 except FORTRAN 90's DO WHILE statement is used to create the DO WHILE loop.

Notice that this is essentially the same sequence of operations listed for the DO WHILE structure introduced in Section 7.1. The transfer of control back to the start of a DO WHILE statement by step 2b forces the DO WHILE statement to recheck its expression and results in a program loop. This looping process was previously illustrated in Figure 7-1, which is reproduced as Figure 7-3.

As an example of a DO WHILE loop, consider the following set of instructions:

```
COUNT = 1
DO WHILE (COUNT .LE. 10)
  WRITE(6,*) COUNT
  COUNT = COUNT + 1
ENDDO
```

The first assignment statement sets COUNT equal to 1. The DO WHILE construct is then entered and the expression in the DO WHILE statement is evaluated for the first time. Since the value of COUNT is less than or equal to 10, the expression is true and the statements between the DO WHILE and ENDDO statements are executed. The first statement within the construct causes the WRITE statement to display the value of COUNT. The next statement adds 1 to the value currently stored in COUNT, making this value equal to 2. The ENDDO statement then causes the program to loop back to retest the condition. Since COUNT is still less than or equal to 10, the statements within the construct are again executed. This process continues until the value of COUNT reaches 11. Program 7-5 illustrates these statements in an actual program.

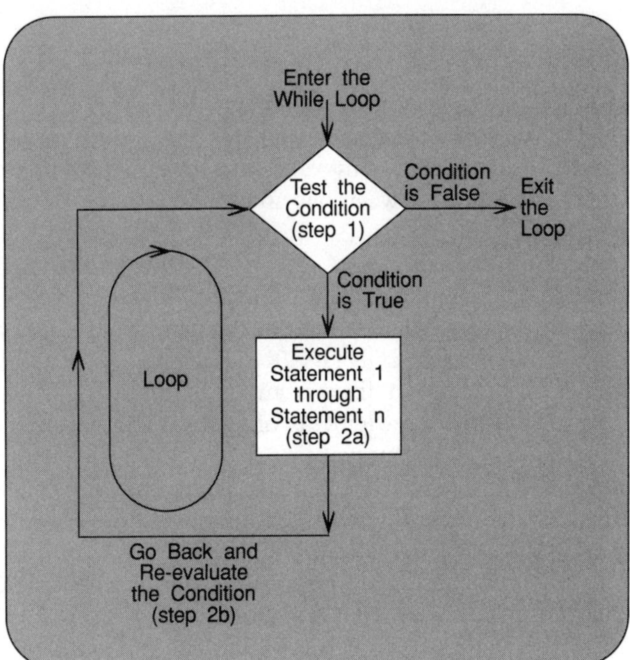

Figure 7-3 Operation of a DO WHILE Loop

Program 7-5

```
      PROGRAM MAIN
        CALL TESTDW
        END
*
      SUBROUTINE TESTDW
        INTEGER COUNT
        COUNT = 1
        DO WHILE (COUNT .LE. 10)
          WRITE(6,*) COUNT
          COUNT = COUNT + 1
        ENDDO
        RETURN
        END
```

The output produced by Program 7-5 is:

```
 1
 2
 3
 4
 5
 6
 7
 8
 9
10
```

There is nothing special about the name COUNT used in Program 7-5 or the statement label assigned to the IF line. Any valid integer variable name could have been used and any integer number between one and 99999 could have been used for the statement label.

Before we consider other examples of the DO WHILE construct three additional comments concerning Program 7-5 are in order. First, the loop could have been created more simply using a DO statement of the form DO k COUNT = 1, 10, where k is the statement label of a CONTINUE statement. This is because this particular loop is set up to execute a fixed number of times. The usefulness of Program 7-5 is in introducing the key elements of a DO WHILE construct; we will alter it shortly to handle cases that cannot be accomplished with a DO statement. Secondly, the statement COUNT = COUNT + 1 that alters the value in COUNT can be replaced with any other statement that changes the value of COUNT. A statement such as COUNT = COUNT + 2, for example, would cause every second integer to be displayed. Finally, it is the programmer's responsibility to ensure that COUNT is changed in a way that ultimately leads to a normal exit from the DO WHILE. For example, if we replace the statement COUNT = COUNT + 1 with the statement COUNT = COUNT - 1, the value of COUNT will never reach 11 and an infinite loop is created (an infinite loop is a loop that never terminates). The computer will not reach out, touch you, and say, 'Excuse me, you have created an infinite loop.' It just keeps executing over and over (in this case, displaying numbers) until you realize that the program is not working as you expected or the system has a maximum time allocated for each run.

Now that you have some familiarity with the DO WHILE construct, see if you can read and determine the output of Program 7-6

Program 7-6

```
      PROGRAM MAIN
        CALL TABLE
        END
*
      SUBROUTINE TABLE
        INTEGER NUM
        WRITE(6,*) '          NUMBER      SQUARE      CUBE'
        WRITE(6,*) '          ------      ------      ----'
        NUM = 1
        DO WHILE (NUM .LT. 11)
          WRITE(6,*) NUM, NUM**2, NUM**3
          NUM = NUM + 1
        ENDDO
        RETURN
        END
```

The assignment statement in Program 7-6 initially sets the counter variable NUM to 1. The WHILE statement then checks to see if the value of NUM is less than 1. While the condition is true, the values of NUM, NUM squared, and NUM cubed are displayed and the value of NUM incremented by 1. When NUM finally equals 11, the condition is false, and the program exits the DO WHILE construct.

When Program 7-6 is run, the following display is produced:*

```
    Number    Square     Cube
    ------    ------     ----
       1         1          1
       2         4          8
       3         9         27
       4        16         64
       5        25        125
       6        36        216
       7        49        343
       8        64        512
       9        81        729
      10       100       1000
```

* The spacing required to produce alignment of the headings with the column of numbers was determined by trial and error. This, of course, is a disadvantage of list-directed output.

Note that the condition used in Program 7-6 is *NUM .LT. 11* . For the integer variable NUM, this condition can be replaced by the equivalent condition *NUM .LE. 10* . The choice of which to use is entirely up to you.

If we want to use Program 7-6 to produce a table of 1000 numbers, all we do is change the condition in the DO WHILE construct from *I .LT. 11* to *I .LT. 1001*. Changing the 11 to 1001 produces a table of 1000 lines—not bad for a simple five-line DO WHILE construct.

Sentinels

In many situations the exact number of items to be entered is not known in advance or the items are too numerous to count beforehand. For example, when entering a large amount of research data we might not want to take the time to count the number of actual data items that are to be entered. In cases like this it is desirable to enter data continuously and, at the end, type in a special data value to signal the end of data input.

In computer programming, a data value used to signal either the start or end of a series of data items is called a *sentinel*. The sentinel value must, of course, be selected so as not to conflict with legitimate data values. For example, if we were constructing a program that accepts a student's grades, and assuming that no extra credit is given that could produce a grade higher than 100, we could use any number higher than 100 as a sentinel value. Program 7-7 illustrates this concept. In this program data is continuously requested and accepted until a number larger than 100 is entered. Entry of a number higher than 100 alerts the program to exit the DO WHILE loop and display the sum of the numbers entered.

Program 7-7

```
      PROGRAM MAIN
        CALL GRADES
        END
*
      SUBROUTINE GRADES
        REAL GRADE, TOTAL
        GRADE = 0
        TOTAL = 0
        WRITE(6,*) 'TO STOP ENTERING GRADES, TYPE IN ANY NUMBER'
        WRITE(6,*) ' GREATER THAN 100.'
        DO WHILE (GRADE .LE. 100)
          WRITE(6,*) 'ENTER A GRADE: '
          READ(5,*)  GRADE
          TOTAL = TOTAL + GRADE
        ENDDO
        WRITE(6,*) 'THE TOTAL OF THE GRADES IS ', TOTAL - GRADE
        RETURN
        END
```

Following is a sample run using Program 7-7. As long as grades less than or equal to 100 are entered, the program continues to request and accept additional data. When a number greater than 100 is entered, the program adds this number to the TOTAL and exits the DO WHILE loop. Outside of the loop and within the WRITE statement, the value of the sentinel that was added to the TOTAL is subtracted and the sum of the legitimate grades that were entered is displayed.

```
TO STOP ENTERING GRADES, TYPE IN ANY NUMBER
 GREATER THAN 100.
ENTER A GRADE:
84
ENTER A GRADE:
75
ENTER A GRADE:
93
ENTER A GRADE:
88
ENTER A GRADE:
101
THE TOTAL OF THE GRADES IS      340.00000000
```

Notice that Program 7-7 differs from previous examples in that termination of the loop is controlled by an externally supplied value rather than a fixed count condition. The loop in Program 7-7 will continue indefinitely until the sentinel value is encountered. DO WHILE loops are well suited to handle sentinel values because of the loop's IF statement.

Reading Data Files

DO WHILE loops are especially well suited to reading data files containing large amounts of data. Typically such files do not include a count of the number of records contained in the file; they do, however, have an End of File (EOF) marker that acts as a sentinel. The general form of a DO WHILE loop for reading a file has the following form:

```
    DO WHILE (.TRUE.)
      READ(unit number, fmt, END = k) variable list
                      .
      any other statements in here
                      .
    ENDDO
k   this statement is executed when the file has no more data
```

The condition, .TRUE., in the DO WHILE statement is always true. This condition creates a loop that will not terminate unless a statement within the DO WHILE construct forces an exit from the loop. This exit is provided by the READ statement, which uses the END option to force an exit out of the loop when the End of File (EOF) marker is encountered. Until the end-of-file has been reached, the

READ statement executes as if the END option were not present. When the end of the file is encountered, the END option transfers control to statement number k. Program 7-8 illustrates this loop for reading the TEST.DAT file shown in Figure 7-4.

Program 7-8

```
      PROGRAM MAIN
        CALL SHFILE
        END
*
      SUBROUTINE SHFILE
        INTEGER N
        REAL RESULT
 5      FORMAT(5X,I2,3X,F5.2)
        OPEN(1,FILE='TEST.DAT')
        WRITE(6,*) '      EXPERIMENT'
        WRITE(6,*) '         NUMBER       RESULT'
        WRITE(6,*) '      ------------------------'
        DO WHILE (.TRUE.)
          READ(1, 5, END=30) N, RESULT
          WRITE(6,*) N, RESULT
        ENDDO
30      RETURN
        END
```

```
      1   26.50
      2   18.00
      3   44.75
      4   33.25
      5   52.00
12345678911111l
         012345
```

└ Column Number One

Figure 7-4 The Structure of the TEST.DAT File

The output produced by Program 7-8 is:

```
Experiment
  Number      Result
---------------------
     1      26.500000
     2      18.000000
     3      44.750000
     4      33.250000
     5      52.000000
```

The EXIT and CYCLE Statements

Two useful statements in connection with FORTRAN's DO statements (both the DO and DO WHILE) are FORTRAN 90's EXIT and CYCLE statements. The general form of the EXIT statement is:

```
EXIT
```

An EXIT statement, as its name implies, forces an immediate EXIT from any DO loop within which it is contained. For example, execution of the following DO WHILE loop is immediately terminated if a number greater than 76 is entered.

```
DO WHILE (COUNT .LE. 10)
   WRITE(6,*) 'ENTER A NUMBER: '
   READ *, NUM
   IF (NUM .GT. 76) THEN
     WRITE(6,*) 'YOU LOSE!'
     EXIT          ! EXIT OUT OF THE LOOP
   ELSE
   WRITE(6,*) 'KEEP ON TRUCKIN!'
   ENDIF
ENDDO
! EXIT FORCES CONTROL TO HERE
```

The EXIT statement violates pure structured programming principles because it provides a second, nonstandard exit from a loop. Nevertheless, the EXIT statement is extremely useful and valuable for EXITing out of loops when an unusual condition is detected.

The general format of a CYCLE statement, which also only can be used in conjunction with DO loops, is:

```
CYCLE
```

When CYCLE is encountered in a loop, the next iteration of the loop is immediately begun. For DO WHILE loops this means that execution is automatically transferred to the top of the loop and reevaluation of the tested expression is initiated, in the same manner as if the ENDDO statement had been encountered.

As a general rule the CYCLE statement is less useful than the EXIT statement, but it is convenient for skipping over data that should not be processed while remaining in a loop. For example, invalid grades are simply ignored in the following section of code and only valid grades are added into the total:

```
DO WHILE (COUNT .LT. 30)
  WRITE(6,*) 'ENTER A GRADE: '
  READ *, GRADE
  IF(GRADE .LT. 0 .OR. GRADE .GT. 100) CYCLE
  TOTAL = TOTAL + GRADE
ENDDO
```

Programming Exercises

1. Rewrite Program 7-5 to print the numbers from -10 to -1 in increments of one.
2. Write a program that uses a DO WHILE loop to produce a table of Celsius and equivalent Fahrenheit degrees. The table should start at a Celsius value of -10 and ends with a Celsius value of 60, in increments of 10 degrees. Use the formula *Fahrenheit* = *(9.0/5.0)* * *Celsius* + *32*.

3a. For the following loop, determine the total number of items displayed. Also determine the first and last numbers printed.

```
         INTEGER NUM = 0
20       DO WHILE (NUM .LE. 20)
           NUM = NUM + 1
           WRITE(6,*) NUM
         ENDDO
```

b. Put the code in Exercise 3a into a working program and run it to verify your answers to the exercise.

c. How would the output be affected if the two statements within the DO WHILE loop construct in Exercise 3a were reversed (that is, if the WRITE statement was made before the NUM = NUM + 1 statement)?

4. Write a FORTRAN program that uses a DO WHILE loop to convert gallons to liters. The program should display gallons from 10 to 20 in one-gallon increments and the corresponding liter equivalents. Use the relationship: liters = 3.785 * gallons.
5. Write a FORTRAN program that uses a DO WHILE loop to convert feet to meters. The program should display feet from 3 to 30 in three-foot increments and the corresponding meter equivalents. Use the relationship: meters = feet / 3.28.
6. A machine purchased for $28,000 is depreciated at a rate of $4,000 a year for seven years. Write and run a FORTRAN program that uses a DO WHILE loop to compute and display a depreciation table for seven years. The table should have the form:

Year	Depreciation	End-of-year value	Accumulated depreciation
1	4000	24000	4000
2	4000	20000	8000
3	4000	16000	12000
4	4000	12000	16000
5	4000	8000	20000
6	4000	4000	24000
7	4000	0	28000

7. An automobile travels at an average speed of 55 miles per hour for four hours. Write a FORTRAN program that uses a DO WHILE loop to calculate and display the distance driven, in miles, that the car has traveled after .5, 1, 1.5, etc., hours until the end of the trip.

8. An approximate conversion formula for converting Fahrenheit to Celsius temperatures is

$$\text{Celsius} = (\text{Fahrenheit} - 30) / 2$$

Using this formula, and starting with a Fahrenheit temperature of zero degrees, write a FORTRAN program that determines when the approximate equivalent Celsius temperature differs from the exact equivalent value by more than four degrees. (Hint: use a DO WHILE loop that terminates when the difference between approximate and exact Celsius equivalents exceeds four degrees.)

b. Using the approximate Celsius conversion formula given in Exercise 8a, write a FORTRAN program that produces a table of Fahrenheit temperatures, exact Celsius equivalent temperatures, approximate Celsius equivalent temperatures, and the difference between the correct and approximate equivalent Celsius values. The table should begin at zero degrees Fahrenheit, use two-degree Fahrenheit increments and terminate when the difference between exact and approximate values differs by more than four degrees.

9. The value of Euler's number *e* can be approximated using the formula

$$e = 1 + 1/1! + 1/2! + 1/3! + 1/4! + 1/5! + \ldots.$$

Using this formula, write a FORTRAN program that approximates the value of e using *a* DO WHILE loop that terminates when the difference between two successive approximations differs by less than 10 E-9.

10. The value of sin x can be approximated using the formula

$$\text{Sin } x = x - \frac{x^3}{3!} + \frac{x^5}{5!} - \frac{x^7}{7!} + \frac{x^9}{9!} \ldots$$

Using this formula, determine how many terms are needed to approximate the value returned by the intrinsic SIN( ) function with an error less than 1 E-6, when x = 30 degrees. (Hints: Use a DO WHILE loop that terminates when the difference between the value returned by the intrinsic SIN( ) function and the approximation is less than 1 E-6. Also note that x must first be converted to radian measure and that the alternating sign in the approximating series can be determined as (-1)**(n+1) where n is the number of terms used in the approximation.)

11a. Write, compile, and execute a FORTRAN program that accepts a set of 10 numbers, finds the largest number of the entered values and displays this value after all numbers have been entered.

b. Modify the program written for Exercise 11a to also display the position of the largest entered number (that is, was it the 1st, 2nd, 3rd, etc., number entered?).

7.3 REPEAT-UNTIL Loops

Both the WHILE and DO loops evaluate a condition at the start of the repetition loop. There are cases, however, where it is more convenient to test the condition at the end of the loop. For example, suppose we have constructed the following WHILE loop to convert Fahrenheit to Celsius temperatures:

```
      WRITE(6,*) 'ENTER A TEMPERATURE: '
      READ(5,*) TEMP
 10   IF (TEMP .NE. SENTNL) THEN
        CELSUS = 5.0/9.0 * (TEMP -32.0)
        WRITE(6,*) 'THE EQUIVALENT CELSIUS TEMPERATURE IS ', CELSUS
        WRITE(6,*) 'ENTER A TEMPERATURE: ' READ *, TEMP
        GO TO 10
      ENDIF
```

Here the variable SENTNL represents an agreed-upon sentinel value. When the user enters this value the loop is terminated. Notice that using this WHILE loop has required us to place a prompt and READ statement before the loop to force initial execution of the statements within the while loop. Once in the loop, these same two statements are then repeated within the loop.

The REPEAT-UNTIL loop structure allows us to execute a set of statements before a condition is evaluated. In many situations this can be used to eliminate the duplication illustrated in the previous example. A general form of a REPEAT-UNTIL loop is:*

```
k    statement 1
     statement 2
         .
         .
         .
     statement n
   IF (condition) GO TO k
```

The important concept with REPEAT-UNTIL loops is that all statements within the loop are executed at least once before a condition is tested. Although we have used a logical IF statement as the last statement in the loop, both IF-ELSE statements and block IF statements can also be used. A flow-control diagram illustrating the operation of the REPEAT-UNTIL loop is shown in Figure 7-5.

* Notice that this pseudocode and Figure 7-5 illustrates a loop that is executed until the condition becomes true.

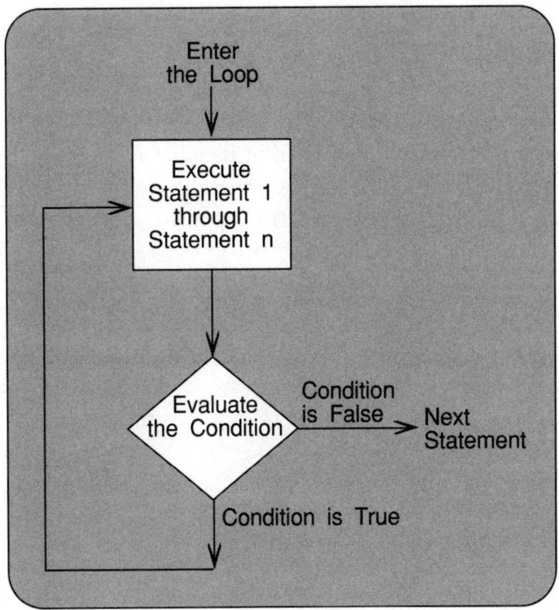

Figure 7-5 The FORTRAN REPEAT-UNTIL Loop

As illustrated in Figure 7-5, all statements within the REPEAT-UNTIL loop are executed once before the condition is evaluated. Then, if the condition is True, the statements within the loop are executed again. This process continues until the condition evaluates to zero. For example, consider the following REPEAT-UNTIL loop:

```
10     WRITE(6,*) 'ENTER A TEMPERATURE: '
       READ(5,*) TEMP
       CELSUS = 5.0/9.0 * (TEMP -32.0)
       WRITE(6,*) 'THE EQUIVALENT CELSIUS TEMPERATURE IS ', CELSUS
   IF (TEMP .NE. SENTNL) GO TO 10
```

Observe that only one PRINT and READ statement is required because the tested condition is evaluated at the end of the loop.

Validity Checks

REPEAT-UNTIL loops are particularly useful in filtering user-entered input and providing data validity checks. For example, assume that an operator is required to enter a valid customer identification number between the numbers 1000 and 1999. A number outside this range is to be rejected and a new request for a valid number made. The following section of code provides the necessary data filter to verify the entry of a valid identification number:

```
 5      WRITE(6,*) 'ENTER AN IDENTIFICATION NUMBER: '
        READ(5,*) IDNUM
       IF (IDNUM .LT.1000 .OR. IDNUM .GT. 1999) GO TO 5
```

Here, a request for an identification number is repeated until a valid number is entered. This section of code is "bare bones" in that it neither alerts the operator to the cause of the new request for data nor allows premature exit from the loop if a valid identification number cannot be found. An alternative that removes the first drawback is:

```
 5      WRITE(6,*) 'ENTER AN IDENTIFICATION NUMBER: '
        READ(5,*) IDNUM
        IF (IDNUM .LT. 1000 .OR. IDNUM .GT. 1999) THEN
          WRITE(6,*) 'AN INVALID NUMBER WAS JUST ENTERED'
          WRITE(6,*) 'PLEASE CHECK THE ID NUMBER AND RE-ENTER'
          GO TO 5
        ENDIF
```

Here we have used a block IF statement to terminate the loop instead of a logical IF statement.

Programming Exercises

1a. Using a REPEAT-UNTIL loop, write a program to accept a grade. The program should request a grade continuously as long as an invalid grade is entered. An invalid grade is any grade less than zero or greater than 100. After a valid grade has been entered, your program should display the value of the grade entered.

b. Modify the program written for Exercise 1a so that the user is alerted when an invalid grade has been entered.

c. Modify the program written for Exercise 1b so that it allows the user to exit the program by entering the number 999.

d. Modify the program written for Exercise 1b so that it automatically terminates after five invalid grades are entered.

2a. Write a program that continuously requests a grade to be entered. If the grade is less than zero or greater than 100, your program should print an appropriate message informing the user that an invalid grade has been entered, else the grade should be added to a total. When a grade of 999 is entered the program should exit the repetition loop and compute and display the average of the valid grades entered.

b. Run the program written in Exercise 2a on a computer and verify the program using appropriate test data.

3a. Write a program to reverse the digits of a positive integer number. For example, if the number 8735 is entered, the number displayed should be 5378. (Hint: Use a REPEAT-UNTIL loop and continuously strip off and display the units digit of the number. For example, if the variable NUM initially contains the number entered, the units digit is obtained as MOD(NUM,10). After a units digit is displayed, integer division by 10 sets up the number for the next iteration. Thus, MOD(8735,10) is 5 and (8735/10) is 873. The REPEAT-UNTIL loop should continue as long as the remaining number is not zero.)

b. Run the program written in Exercise 3a on a computer and verify the program using appropriate test data.

7.4 Applications

In this section two applications are presented to further illustrate the use of conditional loops. In the first application a DO WHILE loop is used to insert a new employee's identification number into an existing file that is maintained in numerical order.

The second application presents an expanded file update procedure. In this application a file containing inventory data, consisting of book identification numbers and quantities in stock, is updated by information contained in a second file. This application requires that identification numbers in the two files be matched before a record is updated.

Application 1: Insertion Update

A common programming problem is to maintain a list in either numerical or alphabetical order. For example, telephone and mailing lists are traditionally kept in alphabetical order, while lists of part numbers are kept in numerical order.

As part of an overall maintenance program, a subroutine is to be written that correctly inserts a 3-digit identification code within a list of numbers that is maintained in increasing order and stored in a data file.

Subroutine Development

Using a top-down development approach, we have:

Step 1: Determine the Desired Output
The required output is a new file of 3-digit codes in which the new code has been inserted correctly into the stored list.

Step 2: Determine the Input Items
The input items for this subroutine are the existing file of identification codes and the new code that is to be inserted into the list.

Step 3a: Determine an Algorithm
To insert a new identification code into the existing list and create a new file:

Open the existing ID code file
Open the new ID code file
Initialize a NOT FOUND flag to .TRUE.
Copy existing ID numbers from the existing file to the new file until the point where the new ID number should be inserted. At this point write the new ID number to the file and then continue copying remaining ID codes from the old to the new file. This is done as follows:

Do While the NOT FOUND flag is .TRUE.
  Read a current ID code from the existing file
  If the current ID code is less than the new code:
    write the current code to the new file
  Else If the current code is equal to the new code:
    write the current code to the new file
    display a message that the new code is aleady in the file
    set NOT FOUND to .FALSE.
  Else if the existing code is greater than the new code:
    write the new code to the new file
    write the current code to the new file
    set NOT FOUND to .FALSE.
Enddo
Do While not EOF for existing file
  Read a current ID code from the existing file
  Write the input ID code to the new file
Enddo
Close both files

Step 3b: Do a Hand Calculation

For our hand calculation assume that the existing file of identification codes consists of the numbers illustrated in Figure 7-6a. If the ID code 142 is to be inserted into this list of numbers, it must be stored in the fourth position in the list, after the number 136.

To insert this new code correctly into the new list the first three codes from the existing file must first be written to the new file. Then the new code is written to the new file, followed by the remaining codes from the existing file. The resulting new file is illustrated in Figure 7-6b.

Step 3c: Select Variable and Argument Names

For this problem we will use the argument names NEWCDE, NEWFIL, and OLDFIL to pass the new code number, new file name, and old file name, respectively, into the subroutine. Internal to the subroutine the name CURRNT will be used to store the ID code that is read from the old file and written to the new file. The logical variable NTFND will be used as a flag to signal that the insertion position for the new code has been found.

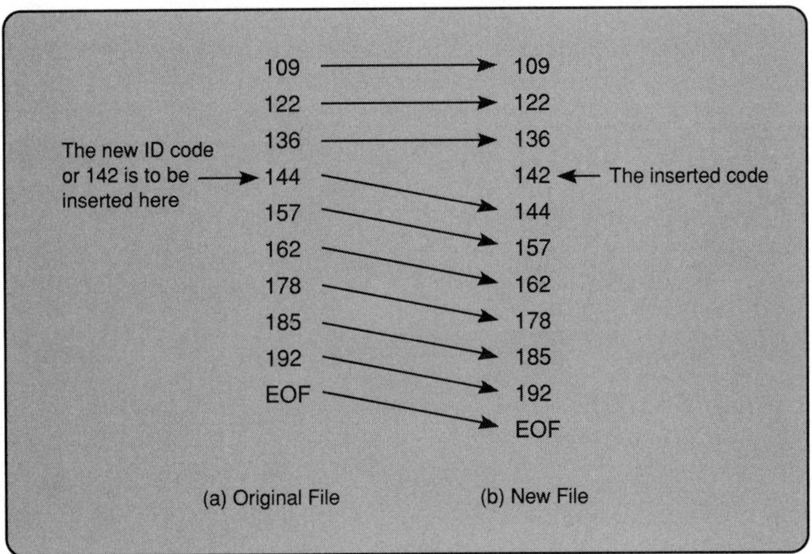

Figure 7-5 Updating an Ordered List of Identification Numbers

Step 4: Write the Subroutine

The subroutine named INSERT performs the required processing. After accepting the new code, new file name, and old file name as the arguments, NEWCDE, NEWFIL, and OLDFIL, respectively, the INSERT subroutine performs the tasks described in the algorithm selected in Step 3a. For this subroutine we have used the FORTRAN 90 DO WHILE statement (If you are using a FORTRAN 77 compiler the two DO WHILE loops in the subroutine would have to be rewritten using IF and GO TO statements as described in Section 7.1). The condition used in the first DO WHILE loop is initially true because the variable NTFND was initialized to a .TRUE. value. When this variable is set to .FALSE. within the loop, the condition, which has the same value as the variable NTFND, becomes false, and the loop is terminated.

```
SUBROUTINE INSERT(NEWCDE, NEWFIL, OLDFIL)
  INTEGER NEWCDE, CURRNT
  CHARACTER*12 NEWFIL, OLDFIL
  LOGICAL NTFND
  OPEN(1,FILE=OLDFIL)
  OPEN(2,FILE=NEWFIL)
  NTFND = .TRUE.
  DO WHILE(NTFND)
    READ(1,*) CURRNT
    IF (CURRNT .LT. NWCDE) THEN
      WRITE(2,*) CURRNT
    ELSE IF (CURRNT .EQ. NEWCDE) THEN
      WRITE(2,*) CURRNT
```

```
          WRITE(6,*) 'THE NEW ID CODE IS ALREADY IN THE FILE'
          NTFND = .FALSE.
        ELSE
          WRITE(2,*) NEWCDE
          WRITE(6,*) 'THE NEW ID CODE HAS BEEN ADDED TO THE FILE'
          WRITE(2,*) CURRNT
          NTFND = .FALSE.
        ENDIF
      ENDDO
      DO WHILE(.TRUE.)
        READ(1,*,END=99) CURRNT
        WRITE(2,*) CURRNT
      ENDDO
99    CLOSE(1)
      CLOSE(2)
      RETURN
      END
```

The first DO WHILE loop in the subroutine determines the correct position for the new code. This is done by reading and writing ID codes while the existing codes are less than the value of the new code.

After the correct position for the new code has been determined, the new code is written to the file followed by the last code read from the file, and the first DO WHILE loop is terminated. The second DO WHILE loop then reads and writes the remaining ID codes from the original file to the new file.

Step 5: Test the Subroutine

Program 7-9 incorporates the INSERT subroutine within a complete program. This allows us to test the subroutine with the same data used in our hand calculation.

Program 7-9

```
      PROGRAM TEST
        INTEGER NEWCDE
        CHARACTER*12 OLDFIL, NEWFIL
        OLDFIL = 'CODES1'
        NEWFIL = 'CODES2'
        NEWCDE = 142
        CALL INSERT(NEWCDE, NEWFIL, OLDFIL)
        END
*
      SUBROUTINE INSERT(NEWCDE, NEWFIL, OLDFIL)
        INTEGER NEWCDE, CURRNT
        CHARACTER*12 NEWFIL, OLDFIL
        LOGICAL NTFND
```

(Continued on the next page)

(Continued from the previous page) page)

```
      OPEN(1,FILE=OLDFIL)
      OPEN(2,FILE=NEWFIL)
      NTFND = .TRUE.
      DO WHILE(NTFND)
        READ(1,*) CURRNT
        IF (CURRNT .LT. NEWCDE) THEN
          WRITE(2,*) CURRNT
        ELSE IF (CURRNT .EQ. NEWCDE) THEN
          WRITE(2,*) CURRNT
          WRITE(6,*) 'THE NEW ID CODE IS ALREADY IN THE FILE'
          NTFND = .FALSE.
        ELSE
          WRITE(2,*) NEWCDE
          WRITE(6,*) 'THE NEW ID CODE HAS BEEN ADDED TO THE FILE'
          WRITE(2,*) CURRNT
          NTFND = .FALSE.
        ENDIF
      ENDDO
      DO WHILE(.TRUE.)
        READ(1,*,END=99) CURRNT
        WRITE(2,*) CURRNT
      ENDDO
99    CLOSE(1)
      CLOSE(2)
      RETURN
      END
```

A test run using Program 7-9, using the file illustrated in Figure 7-6a produced the file illustrated in Figure 7-6b. Although this result agrees with our previous hand calculation, it does not constitute full testing of the program. To be sure that the program works for all cases, test runs should be made that duplicate an existing code, that place a new identification code at the beginning of the list, and that place a new identification code at the end of the list. These tests, and any modifications that might be required as a result of such tests, are left as an exercise (see Exercise 1 at the end of this section).

Application 2: Master/Transaction File Update

A common form of file update occurs when the update data is itself contained in a file. Here, the file to be updated is referred to as a master file, and the file containing the update data is referred to as a transactions file.

As a specific example of this type of update, assume that the current master file, named OLDBK.MAS, contains the book identification numbers and quantities in stock illustrated in Table 7-1.

Table 7-1 Data Contained in the OLDBK.MAS File

Book ID No.	Quantity in Stock
125	98
289	222
341	675
467	152
589	34
622	125

(Format of the Data in the File: I3,3X,I4)

A transactions file, named BOOK.TRN, contains the quantities of each book bought, sold, or returned to stock each day. For purposes of illustration, assume that the BOOK.TRN file is sorted by ID number at the end of each month and contains the data illustrated in Table 7-2.

Table 7-2 Data Contained in the Transaction File Named BOOK.TRN

ID No.	Date	Sold	Returned	Bought
289	1/10/92	125	34	50
341	1/10/92	300	52	0
467	1/15/92	50	20	200
467	1/20/92	225	0	160
589	1/31/92	75	10	55

(Format of the Data in the File: I3,3X,A8,3(3X,I3))

Once the transaction file has been created, there exist two methods of updating the master file. The direct access method, where any record in the master file can be read, updated, and written back to the file directly, is presented in Chapter 11. For the sequential file access that we have been using, each record in the file must be read in the order it is located in the file. Additionally, a record can only be written to the end of the file because writing a record automatically erases all records from that point to the end of the file. This constraint effectively prohibits updating a record within an existing file because an update, by definition, requires that an existing record be rewritten.

The solution to this problem is to use an update algorithm in which all records that need to be are updated at the same time, so that a completely new and updated master file is created when the update is completed. The key to creating this new updated master file is that the records in the transaction file be sorted by ID number to correspond to the order of ID numbers in the master file. Notice in Tables 7-1 and 7-2 that this is indeed the case for the data in the BOOK.TRN and OLDBK.MAS files.

Once the two files are in the same ID number order, the procedure for creating an updated master file consists of reading a master record from the existing master file and one record from the transaction file. If the ID numbers of the two records match, the transaction record's information is applied to the data in the master record and another transaction record is read. As long as the transaction record's ID number matches the master record's ID number, the update of the master record continues. When the transaction record's ID number does not match the master record's ID number, which indicates that there is no further update data to be applied to the master record, an updated record is written to the new master file. Let's see how this procedure works with the two files shown in Tables 7-1 and 7-2.

The first record read from the master file has ID number 125, while the first transaction record has ID number 289. Since the ID numbers do not match, the update of this first master record is complete (in this case there is no update information) and the existing master record is written, without modification, to the new master file. Then the next master record is read, which has an ID number of 289. Since this ID number matches the transaction ID number, the inventory balance for book number 289 is updated, yielding a new balance of 181 books. Because the transaction file can contain multiple update records for the same ID number (notice the two records for ID number 467), the next transaction record is read and checked before writing an updated record to the new master file. Since the ID number of the next transaction record is not 289, the update of this book number is complete and an updated master record is written to the new master file.

This algorithm continues, record-by-record, until the last master record has been updated. Should the end of the transaction file be encountered before the last master record is read from the existing master file, the remaining records in the existing master file are written directly to the new master file with no need to check for update information.

Since this update procedure uses two master files, a notation must be established to clearly distinguish between them. By convention, the existing master file is always referred to as the old master file, and the updated master file is called the new master file. Using these terms, the pseudocode description of the update procedure is:

```
Open the old master file
Open the transaction file
Open the new master file (initially blank)
Read the first old master record
Do for all records in the transaction file
   Read a transaction record
   While the transaction ID does not match the old master ID
      Write an updated master record to the new master file
      Read the next transaction record
   Endwhile
   If the ID numbers do match
      Calculate a new balance
Enddo
```

*** *To get here the last transaction record has just been read*
Write the last updated master to the new master file
While there are any remaining records in the old master file
Read an old master record
Write a new master record
Endwhile
Close all files.

In FORTRAN, this update procedure is described by Program 7-10.

Program 7-10

```
      PROGRAM MAIN
        INTEGER IDM, IDT, BAL, SOLD, RETURN, BOUGHT
        CHARACTER*8 DATE
        OPEN(1,FILE = 'OLDBK.MAS')
        OPEN(2,FILE = 'BOOK.TRN')
        OPEN(3,FILE = 'NEWBK.MAS')
        READ(1,*) IDM, BAL
   10   READ(2,*, END = 20) DATE,IDT,SOLD,RETURN,BOUGHT
***   IF NO MATCH KEEP WRITING AND READING THE MASTER FILE
   15     IF(IDT .GT. IDM) THEN
            WRITE(3,*) IDM, BAL
            READ(1,*) IDM, BAL
            GO TO 15
          ENDIF
***  UPDATE THE MASTER AND GET ANOTHER TRANSACTION
          BAL = BAL + BOUGHT - SOLD + RETURN
          GO TO 10
***   WRITE THE LAST UPDATED MASTER
   20   WRITE(3,*) IDM, BAL
***   WRITE THE REMAINING OLD MASTER FILE TO THE NEW FILE
   25   READ(1,*,END = 30) IDM, BAL
          WRITE(3,*) IDM, BAL
          GO TO 25
   30   WRITE(6,*) '...FILE UPDATE COMPLETE...'
        END
```

The new master file created by Program 7-10 is:

125	98
289	181
341	427
467	257
589	24
622	125

Additional Chapter Exercises

1a. Test Program 7-9 using an identification code of 86, which should place this new code at the beginning of the new file.

b. Test Program 7-9 using an identification code of 200, which should place this new code at the end of the new file. Correct the subroutine to handle this case.

2a. Determine an algorithm for deleting an entry from an ordered list of numbers stored in a file.

b. Write a subroutine named DELETE, which uses the algorithm selected in Exercise 2a, to delete an identification code from the list of numbers illustrated in Figure 7-6a.

3. Assume the following names are stored in a file named NAMES: BRONSON, JONES, KLEIN, MONTROSE, SMITH. Write and test a subroutine named ADNAME, which accepts both the NAMES file and a new name as arguments, and inserts the new name in the correct alphabetical order in a file named NEWNAM array. For this problem assume that the maximum size of each name is fifteen characters.

4. Assume that a data file of test grades exists. Write a subroutine that accepts the name of the file as a formal argument, opens the file, and returns the average of the grades. Additionally, the subroutine should return the number of As, Bs, Cs, Ds, and Fs in the passed grade list. For this purpose assume the following scale:

Numerical Grade	Letter Grade
90 or above	A
greater than or equal to 80 and less than 90	B
greater than or equal to 70 and less than 80	C
greater than or equal to 60 and less than 70	D
less than 60	F

b. Create a file with the following data and test the subroutine written in Exercise 4a using this file: 98 84 67 89 55 65 76 77 85 92 68 76 79 74 68 92 76

5a. A file named POLAR.DAT contains the polar coordinates needed in a graphics program. Currently this file contains the following data:

Distance (Inches)	Angle (Degrees)
2	45
6	30
10	45
4	60
12	55
8	15

Write a FORTRAN program to create this file on your computer system.

b. Using the POLAR.DAT file created in Exercise 5a, write a FORTRAN program that accepts distance and angle data from the user and adds the data to the end of the file.

c. Using the POLAR.DAT file created in Exercise 5a, write a FORTRAN program that reads this file and creates a second file named XYCORD.DAT. The entries in the new file should contain the rectangular coordinates corresponding to the polar coordinates in the POLAR.DAT file. Polar coordinates are converted to rectangular coordinates using the equations

```
x = r cos(theta)
y = r sin(theta)
```

where r is the distance coordinate and theta is the radian equivalent of the angle coordinate in the POLAR.DAT file.

6a. Write a FORTRAN program to create both the OLDBK.MAS file, illustrated in Table 7-1, and the BOOK.TRN file, illustrated in Table 7-2, using the formats listed in the table. (Note: Do not include the column headings in the file.)

b. Using the files created in Exercise 6a, enter and run Program 7-10 to verify its operation.

c. Modify Program 7-10 to prompt the user for the names of the old master file, the new master file, and the transaction file. The modified program should accept these file names as input while the program is executing.

d. Using the BOOK.TRN file create in Exercise 6a, write a FORTRAN program that reads this file and displays the transaction data in it, including the heading lines shown in Table 7-2.

7a. Write a FORTRAN program to create a data file containing the following information:

Student ID Number	Student Name	Course Name	Course Credits	Grade
2333021	BOKOW, R.	NS201	3	A
2333021	BOKOW, R.	MG342	3	A
2333021	BOKOW, R.	FA302	1	A
2574063	FALLIN, D.	MK106	3	C
2574063	FALLIN, D.	MA208	3	B
2574063	FALLIN, D.	CM201	3	C
2574063	FALLIN, D.	CP101	2	B
2663628	KINGSLEY, M.	QA140	3	A
2663628	KINGSLEY, M.	CM245	3	B
2663628	KINGSLEY, M.	EQ521	3	A
2663628	KINGSLEY, M.	MK341	3	A
2663628	KINGSLEY, M.	CP101	2	B

b. Using the file created in Exercise 7a, write a FORTRAN program that creates student grade reports. The grade report for each student should contain the student's name and identification number, a list of courses taken, the credits and grade for each course, and a semester grade point average. For example, the grade report for the first student is:

```
STUDENT NAME: BOKOW, R.
STUDENT ID NUMBER: 2333021

COURSE      COURSE      COURSE
 NAME       CREDITS     GRADE
-------    --------     ------
NS201         3            A
MG342         3            A
FA302         1            A

TOTAL SEMESTER COURSE CREDITS COMPLETED: 7
SEMESTER GRADE POINT AVERAGE: 4.0
```

The semester grade point average is computed in two steps. First, each course grade is assigned a numerical value (A = 4, B = 3, C = 2, D = 1, F = 0) and the sum of each course's grade value times the credits for each course is computed. This sum is then divided by the total number of credits taken during the semester.

8a. Write a FORTRAN program to create a data file containing the following information:

Student ID Number	Student Name	Course Credits	Cumulative Grade Point Average (GPA)
2333021	BOKOW, R.	48	4.0
2574063	FALLIN, D.	12	1.8
2663628	KINGSLEY, M.	36	3.5

b. Using the file created in Exercise 8a as a master file and the file created in Exercise 7a as a transactions file, write a file update program to create an updated master file.

7.5 Common Programming Errors

Eight errors are commonly made by beginning FORTRAN programmers when creating loops. The first three of these pertain to the tested condition and have already been encountered with the FORTRAN's IF statements.

1. Failure to enclose the condition in a WHILE structure within parentheses. (This is the same error encountered using IF statements.)
2. Failure to follow the IF statement used to create a WHILE loop with the keyword THEN. (Again, this is a common error associated with IF statements.)
3. Testing for equality in WHILE and REPEAT-UNTIL loops when comparing real operands. For example, the condition (FNUM .EQ. 0.01) should be replaced by an equivalent test requiring that the absolute value of FNUM - .01 be less than an acceptable amount. The reason for this is that all numbers are stored in

binary form. Using a finite number of bits, decimal numbers such as .01 have no exact binary equivalent, so that tests requiring equality with such numbers can fail.

4. Failure to put the statement label on the WHILE loop's IF statement within columns one through five.
5. Failure to have a statement within a WHILE loop that alters the tested condition in a manner that terminates the loop.
6. Modifying a DO statement's counter variable within the DO loop.
7. Failure to have a statement within a REPEAT-UNTIL loop that alters the tested condition in a manner that terminates the loop.

7.6 Things to Remember

1. The general form of a FORTRAN 77 WHILE loop is:

```
k  IF (condition) THEN
      statement 1
      statement 2
           .
           .
      statement n
      GO TO k
   ENDIF
```

In FORTRAN 90 a DO WHILE loop has the following form:

```
DO WHILE (condition)
      statement 1
      statement 2
           .
           .
      statement n
 ENDDO
```

Since a DO WHILE loop checks its condition at the top of the loop, any variables in the tested condition must have values assigned before the loop is encountered. Additionally, one of the statements within the loop must alter the condition in such a way that the loop ultimately terminates.

2. Sentinels are prearranged values used to signal either the start or end of a series of data items. Typically sentinels are used to create DO WHILE loop conditions that terminate the loop when the sentinel value is encountered.
3. DO WHILE loops evaluate a condition at the start of the loop.

4. REPEAT UNTIL loops check a tested condition at the end of the loop. This ensures that the body of the loop is executed at least once. A general form of a REPEAT-UNTIL loop is:

```
k      statement 1
       statement 2
          .
          .
          .
       statement n
     IF (condition) GO TO k
```

As with the DO WHILE loop, the REPEAT-UNTIL loop must contain a statement that alters its tested condition in such a way that the loop ultimately terminates.

LAB SET FOR CHAPTERS SIX AND SEVEN

LAB ASSIGNMENT 11

1. What values of L and M are displayed when the program below is run?

```
      PROGRAM MAIN
       CALL TEST
       END
*
     SUBROUTINE TEST
       INTEGER I, J, K, L, M
       I = 2
       J = 3
       K = 4
       L = F(I,J,K)
       M = F(J,K,L)
       WRITE (*,*) L, M
       RETURN                            ____________   ____________
       END                               (value of L)   (value of M)
*
     INTEGER FUNCTION F(A,B,C)
       INTEGER A, B, C
       IF (A .GT. C) THEN
         F = A * (B + C)
       ELSE
         F = C * (A + B)
       ENDIF
       RETURN
       END
```

2. Determine the display produced when the following program is run for each of the three cases shown:

```
      PROGRAM MAIN
       CALL TEST
       END
*
     SUBROUTINE TEST
       INTEGER A,B,C,X
       READ(5,*) A, B, C
       IF (A .EQ. B) THEN
         X = A * C
       ELSE
         IF (A .GT. B) THEN
           X = A * B
```

```
    ELSE
      X = B * C
    ENDIF
  ENDIF
  WRITE(*,*) X
  RETURN
  END
```

```
First run : Enter 5, 4, 2  ________
Second run: Enter 3, 3, 6  ________
Third run : Enter 2, 5, 6  ________
```

LAB ASSIGNMENT 12

A Simple beam with a uniform cross section, loaded with a single concentrated force, P, is illustrated in Figure L-4. The deflection of this beam, D, at an arbitrary position X is given by the two part formula:

For X greater than or equal to zero and X less than or equal to A:

$$D = \frac{-PBX}{6EIL} (2L(L-X) - B**2 - (L-X) **2)$$

For X greater than or equal to A and X less than or equal to L:

$$D = \frac{-PA (L-X)}{6EIL} (2LB - B**2 - (L-X) **2)$$

where:

X = position on the beam measured from the origin (inches)
P = applied force (pounds)
L = length of the beam (inches)
A = distance to the load application point measured from the origin (inches)
B = distance to the load application point from the right end (inches) = L - A
E = modulus of elasticity = 3 * 10 ** 7 pounds/ square inch
I = second moment of cross section (inches)
D = deflection of the beam at location X

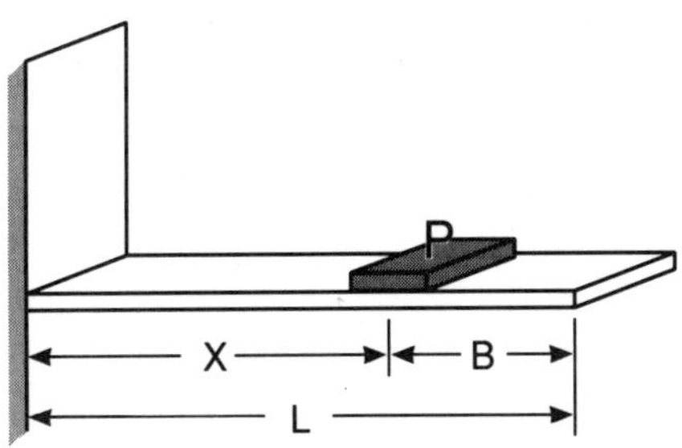

Write a computer program that will perform the following steps for multiple sets of data.

1. Read P, L, A, I, and X from a data file
2. Compute D
3. Write P, L, A, B, I, X, and D to a data file
4. Write a report of the data written to the data file

The program must contain comments. It should also call a subroutine to print your name at the top of your report and triple spaced below this should be your columnar headings. All the headings should be written from a subroutine.

Use a sentinel (dummy) data record with L = 0 to end the program. The following test data should be written to a file and used to test the program:

500	154	65	2.5	46.2
500	154	65	2.5	107.8
250	100	40	3.0	50.0
1000	101.5	51	3.0	20.0
0000	000.0	00	0.0	00.0

The values for D using the first two data sets should be -0.4053 and -0.3761.

LAB ASSIGNMENT 13

The Woonsocket Sprocket Company has fifteen employees. Each employee is paid $10.00/hr. for the first 40 hours of work and $15/hr. for each overtime hour worked. The management wants to know which shift works the most overtime, days, evenings, or graveyard, and the average pay for each shift. Write a program to calculate the total hours worked on each shift by all employees on that shift, and the average weekly pay for employees on each shift.

The input data for this program is the following:

Shift Code	Hours Worked
1	46.0
1	15.0
1	38.0
2	38.0
2	45.0
3	18.0
1	42.0
2	29.0
3	41.0
2	6.0
3	55.0
3	22.0
1	24.0
2	16.0
3	28.0

Processing:

1. All processing must be performed using a programming loop. You may use one of three techniques to end the loop: a.) Use an indexed loop from 1 to 15 records, b.) use the IOSTAT option to end a DO WHILE loop, or c.) use the END option to terminate the loop.
2. Use a PARAMETER statement so that the constants $10.00 and $15.00 and 40 hours are defined as the named constants REGRAT, OTRAT, and REGHRS, respectively. Use these named constants in your processing.

Output:

The output may be in any form you desire but you must output the following:

1. Your name and a page number at the top of the report, which is produced by a call to a subroutine
2. The shift working the most overtime
3. The total hours worked by each shift.
4. The average pay for each shift, using a format having two decimal places.

LAB ASSIGNMENT 14

In this assignment you own a computer store that sells three lines of computers. They are:

Name	Memory (M Bytes)	Cost
Oklahoma Instruments	4	$3,000.
Commander	1	2,600.
HAL	2	2,800.

When a customer asks for your prices, you offer them a discount of 5% on all models if they can pay in cash, or a 10% discount if they use your store's credit card. Next, you find out the amount of memory they want in their computer and how much money the customer has budgeted for the purchase. Finally, you offer them the least expensive computer that meets their memory needs and is one they can afford. If they can't afford any model with enough memory for their needs, you make one last attempt at a sale by giving an additional 5% off the price of the least expensive computer having enough memory. If that is still more than they have budgeted, then you must sadly turn them away.

Since business has been getting busy, you decide to program one of your computers to help deal with customers in the manner described above. Write a FORTRAN program to do this.

Your program should prompt the customer for:

1. Their Name
2. Memory Size Needed
3. Budgeted Funds
4. Form of payment (cash, store credit card, other)

Your program should output the following:

1. Echo all input values entered at the terminal
2. Name of computer, memory size, and cost of the computer if an acceptable model and price is found, else an apology to the customer that you cannot accommodate them.

LAB ASSIGNMENT 15

One of the most important distributions is statistics is the normal distribution, which has the bell-shaped curve shown in Figure L-5.

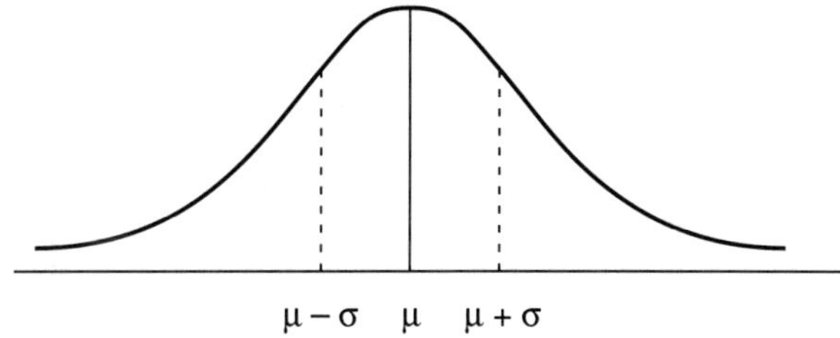

Figure L-5 The Normal Curve

The exact shape of any bell-shaped curve depends on the mean and standard deviation of the underlying distribution of items being sampled. The mean is the average value of the distribution and the standard deviation provides probability information. Specifically, if we select a single item from the distribution there is a .6827 probability that it will fall within the mean plus or minus one standard deviation, there is a .9545 probability that it will fall with the mean plus or minus two standard deviations, and there is a .9973 probability that it will fall within the mean plus or minus three standard deviations. Let us now make this more tangible by applying these statistical concepts to a practical problem.

Assume that the marketing manager of the Radials R Us tire company wants to advertise a new brand of tires as having a guaranteed life of at least 50,000 miles. The company knows that its manufacturing process produces a normal distribution of tires, but would like to verify the average life and standard deviation of a test set of 400 tires. If the mean life of these tires is 56,000 miles with a standard deviation of 2,000 miles, the company will feel secure in providing the 50,000 guarantee, knowing that 99.73% of all tires sold will have a life between 50,000 and 62,000 miles (56,000 plus or minus 3 * 2000).

In this lab you will first simulate a test set of 400 radial tires. After you have created this test set you will determine the percentage of tires that fail to achieve a 50,000 mile life.

Part I. Create the test file.

To create a normal distribution having a mean μ and a standard deviation σ we can make use of the random number generator developed in Section 4.5. Recall that this random number generator produces a uniformly distributed number, where each number has the same probability of occurring. The generation of "pseudo" normally distributed random numbers with mean μ and standard deviation σ from uniformly distributed numbers is accomplished using the following algorithm:

1. *Generate 12 uniformly distributed random numbers and calculate their sum*
2. *Generate the normally distributed number, X, by the following formula:*

$$X = \mu + \frac{\sigma}{2} * \frac{(\text{sum} - 6)}{6}$$

where sum is the sum found in Step 1.

Using this algorithm, write a program to generate and write 400 normally distributed numbers with mean 50,000 and standard deviation 2,000 to a file named TIRES.DAT.

Part II.

Write a program that uses the TIRES.DAT file created in Part I of this lab assignment to create three more files, called STDEV2.DAT, STDEV3.DAT, and REJECT.DAT. Output to STDEV2.DAT all tire values from TIRES.DAT that are within two standard deviations of the mean (that is, those values between 52,000 and 60,000). Similarly, output to STDEV3.DAT all tire values from TIRES.DAT that are within three standard deviations from the mean. Any tire value in TIRES.DAT that is below 50,000 miles should be written to the file named REJECT.DAT. Have your program keep a count of the number of values placed in each output file and report the percentage of values from TIRES.DAT that were placed in these three new files. As a "seed" for your first random number multiply the last five digits of your phone number by 10 and add 1 to the result.

Note: Effectively you are testing how normally distributed the original numbers created in TIRES.DAT really are.

8 Arrays

Chapter Eight

8.1 Single Dimension Arrays
8.2 The DATA Statement and Array Initialization
8.3 Two Dimension Arrays
8.4 Arrays as Arguments
8.5 Applications
8.6 Common Programming Errors
8.7 Things to Remember
8.8 A Closer Look: Sorting Methods

The variables used so far have all had a common characteristic: each variable could only be used to store a single value at a time. For example, although the variables KEY, COUNT, and GRADE specified in the statements:

```
CHARACTER KEY
INTEGER COUNT
REAL GRADE
```

are of different data types, each variable can only store one value of the specified data type. These types of variables are called scalar variables. A *scalar variable* is a single variable that cannot be further subdivided or separated into a legitimate data type.

Frequently, we may have a set of values, all of the same data type, that form a logical group. For example, Table 8-1 illustrates three groups of items. The first

Table 8-1 Three Lists of Items

Temperatures	Codes	Voltages
95.75	Z	12
83.0	C	5
97.625	K	3
72.5	L	55
86.25		16
		6

group is a list of five real temperatures, the second group is a list of four character codes, and the last group is a list of six integer voltages.

A simple list containing individual items of the same scalar data type is called a single dimension array. In this chapter we describe how single dimension arrays are specified, initialized, stored inside a computer, and used. Additionally, we explore the use of single dimension arrays with example programs and present the procedures for declaring and using multidimensional arrays.

8.1 Single Dimension Arrays

A single dimension array, which is also called a one dimension array, is a list of values of the same data type. For example, consider the list of temperatures in Table 8-2.

All the temperatures in the list are real numbers and must be declared as such. However, the individual items in the list do not have to be declared separately. The items in the list can be declared as a single unit and stored under a common variable name called the array name. For convenience, we will choose TEMP as the name for the list in Table 8-2. To specify that TEMP is to store five individual real values requires the declaration statement REAL TEMP(5). Notice that this declaration state-

Table 8-2 A List of Temperatures

Temperatures
95.75
83.0
97.625
72.5
86.25

ment gives the array (or list) name, the data type of the items in the array, and the number of items in the array. Further examples of array declarations are:

```
INTEGER VOLTS(6)
CHARACTER CODE(4)
REAL AMOUNT(100)
```

Each array has sufficient memory reserved for it to hold the number of data items given in the declaration statement. Thus, the array named VOLTS has storage reserved for 6 integers, the AMOUNT array has storage reserved for 100 real numbers, and the CODE array has storage reserved for 4 individual characters. Figure 8-1 illustrates the storage reserved for the VOLTS and CODE arrays.

Each item in an array is called an *element* or component of the array. The individual elements stored in the arrays illustrated in Figure 8-1 are stored sequentially, with the first array element stored in the first reserved location, the second element stored in the second reserved location, and so on, until the last element is stored in the last reserved location.

Some unique means of identifying each element is required to provide access to individual elements in a one dimension array. Since elements in the array are stored sequentially, any individual element can be accessed by giving the name of the array and the element's position. This position is called the element's *index* or *subscript* value (the two terms are synonymous). The first element has an index of 1, the second element has an index of 2, and so on. In FORTRAN, the array name and index of the desired element are combined by listing the index in parentheses after the array name. For example, given the specification REAL TEMP(5), TEMP(1) refers to the first temperature stored in the TEMP array, TEMP(2) refers to the second temperature stored in the TEMP array, TEMP(3) refers to the third temperature stored in the TEMP array, TEMP(4) refers to the fourth temperature stored in the TEMP array, and TEMP(5) refers to the fifth temperature stored in the TEMP array.

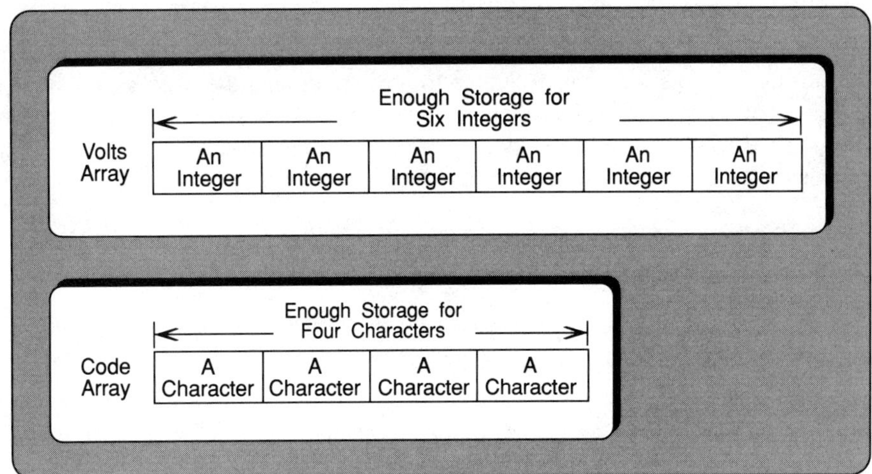

Figure 8-1 The VOLTS and CODE Arrays in Memory

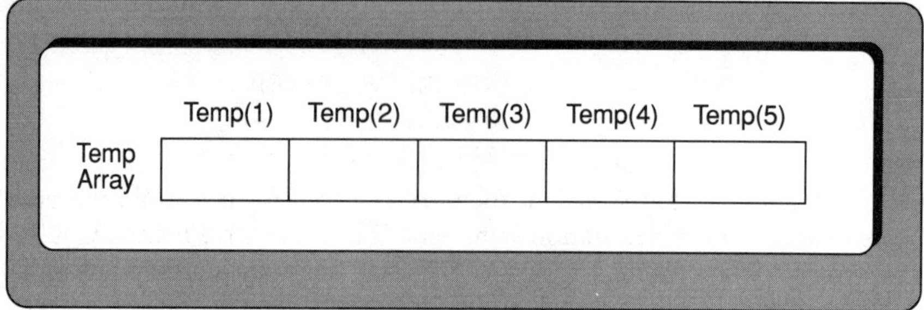

Figure 8-2 Identifying Individual Array Elements

Figure 8-2 illustrates the TEMP array in memory with the correct designation for each array element. Each individual element is called an indexed variable or a subscripted variable, since both a variable name and an index or subscript value must be used to reference the element. Remember that the index or subscript value gives the position of the element in the array, not the element's value.

The subscripted variable TEMP(1) is read as "TEMP sub one." This is a shortened way of saying "the TEMP array subscripted by one" and distinguishes the first element in an array from a scalar variable that could be specified as TEMP1. Similarly, TEMP(2) is read as "TEMP sub two," TEMP(3) as "TEMP sub three," and so on.

Subscripted variables can be used anywhere that scalar variables are valid. Examples using the elements of the TEMP array are:

```
TEMP(1) = 95.75
TEMP(2) = TEMP(1) - 11.0
TEMP(3) = 5.0 * TEMP(1)
TEMP(4) = 79.0
TEMP(5) = (TEMP(2) + TEMP(3) - 3.1) / 2.2
SUM = TEMP(1) + TEMP(2) + TEMP(3) + TEMP(4) + TEMP(5)
```

The subscript contained within parentheses need not be an integer constant, and any expression that evaluates to an integer may be used as a subscript. In each case, of course, the value of the expression must be within the valid subscript range defined when the array is specified. For example, assuming that I and J are integer variables, the following subscripted variables are valid:

```
TEMP(I)
TEMP(2*I)
TEMP(J-I)
```

One extremely important advantage of using integer expressions as subscripts is that it allows sequencing through an array by using a loop. This makes statements such as:

```
SUM = TEMP(1) + TEMP(2) + TEMP(3) + TEMP(4) + TEMP(5)
```

unnecessary. The subscript values in this statement can be replaced by a DO loop counter to access each element in the array sequentially. For example, the code:

```
      SUM = 0
      DO 10 I = 1,5
        SUM = SUM + TEMP(I)
10    CONTINUE
```

sequentially retrieves each array element and adds the element to SUM. Here the variable I is used both as the counter in the DO loop and as a subscript. As I increases by one each time through the loop, the next element in the array is referenced. The procedure for adding the array elements within the DO loop is similar to the accumulation procedure we have used before.

The advantage of using a DO loop to sequence through an array becomes apparent when working with larger arrays. For example, if the TEMP array contained 100 values rather than just 5, simply changing the number 5 to 100 in the DO statement is sufficient to sequence through the 100 elements and add each temperature to the sum.

As another example of using a DO loop to sequence through an array, assume that we want to locate the maximum value in an array of 1000 elements named VOLTS. The procedure we will use to locate the maximum value is to initially assume that the first element in the array is the largest number. Then, as we sequence through the array, the maximum is compared to each element. When an element with a higher value is located, that element becomes the new maximum. The following code does the job.

```
      XMAX = VOLTS(1)
      DO 10 I = 2, 1000
         IF (VOLTS(I) .GT. XMAX) XMAX = VOLTS(I)
10    CONTINUE
```

The search for a new maximum value starts with the second element of the array and continues through the last element. Each element is compared to the current maximum, and when a higher value is encountered it becomes the new maximum.

The DIMENSION Statement*

In addition to creating arrays using explicit declaration statements, as we have done, arrays may also be implicitly declared and sized using a DIMENSION statement. This statement has the form:

```
DIMENSION array name(number of array elements)
```

For example, the statement:

```
DIMENSION LOTTO(6)
```

creates an array named LOTTO having six elements, and the statement:

```
DIMENSION AREA(10)
```

* This topic may be omitted on initial reading without loss of subject continuity.

creates an array named AREA having 10 elements. Since the name LOTTO begins with an L, LOTTO is an integer array unless explicitly declared otherwise (recall FORTRAN's implicit type rule that any variable beginning in I, J, K, L, M, or N is an integer). Similarly, since the name AREA does not begin in either I, J, K, L, M, or N, this is an array of real numbers unless explicitly declared otherwise.

The advantage of DIMENSION statements is that a single DIMENSION statement can be used to specify arrays of different types. For example, the single specification:

```
DIMENSION LOTTO(6), AREA(10)
```

creates both an integer and a real array.

DIMENSION statements can also be combined with explicit typing statements, and this must be done, for example, if a DIMENSION statement is used to create arrays of characters. For example, the statements:

```
CHARACTER CODE
DIMENSION CODE(20)
```

create an array of characters having 20 elements, where each element is a single character. Similarly, the declaration statements:

```
CHARACTER*4 CODE
DIMENSION CODE(20)
```

make each element in the CODE array four characters in length. In these cases, however, it is easier to use one of the following single explicit declarations:

```
CHARACTER CODE(20)
```

or:

```
CHARACTER*4 CODE(20)
```

We will continue to use explicit data typing throughout the text for both scalar and array variables.

Input and Output of Array Values

Individual array elements can be assigned values interactively using the READ statement. Examples of individual data entry statements are:

```
READ(5,*) TEMP(1)
READ(5,*) TEMP(1), TEMP(2), TEMP(3)
READ(5,*) TEMP(4), VOLTS(6)
```

In the first statement a single value will be read and stored in the variable named TEMP(1). The second statement will cause three values to be read and stored in the variables TEMP(1), TEMP(2), and TEMP(3), respectively. Finally, the last READ statement can be used to read values into the variables TEMP(4) and VOLTS(6).

Alternatively, a DO loop can be used to cycle through the array for interactive data input. For example, the code:

```
      DO 15 I = 1,5
        WRITE(6,*) 'ENTER A TEMPERATURE: '
        READ(5,*) TEMP(I)
15    CONTINUE
```

prompts the user for five temperatures. The first temperature entered is stored in TEMP(1), the second temperature entered in TEMP(2), and so on, until five temperatures have been input. Program 8-1 illustrates the use of this code in a complete program.

Program 8-1

```
      PROGRAM MAIN
        CALL TESTAR
        END
*
      SUBROUTINE TESTAR
        INTEGER I
        REAL TEMP(5)
        DO 15 I = 1,5
          WRITE(6,*) 'ENTER A TEMPERATURE: '
          READ(5,*) TEMP(I)
 15     CONTINUE
        WRITE(6,*) 'THE ELEMENTS OF THE TEMP ARRAY ARE:'
        WRITE(6,*) TEMP(1), TEMP(2), TEMP(3), TEMP(4), TEMP(5)
        RETURN
        END
```

Following is a sample run using Program 8-1.

```
ENTER A TEMPERATURE:
96.75
ENTER A TEMPERATURE:
83.0
ENTER A TEMPERATURE:
97.625
ENTER A TEMPERATURE:
72.5
ENTER A TEMPERATURE:
86.25
THE ELEMENTS OF THE TEMP ARRAY ARE:
   96.750000   83.000000   97.625000   72.500000   86.250000
```

Figure 8-3 illustrates the storage of these values in the TEMP array.

Just as a READ statement is used to input values into array elements, both PRINT and WRITE statements can be used to display array elements. Notice in Program 8-1 that a single WRITE statement was used to display the values in the subscripted values TEMP(1) through TEMP(5). Further examples of WRITE statements using subscripted variables are:

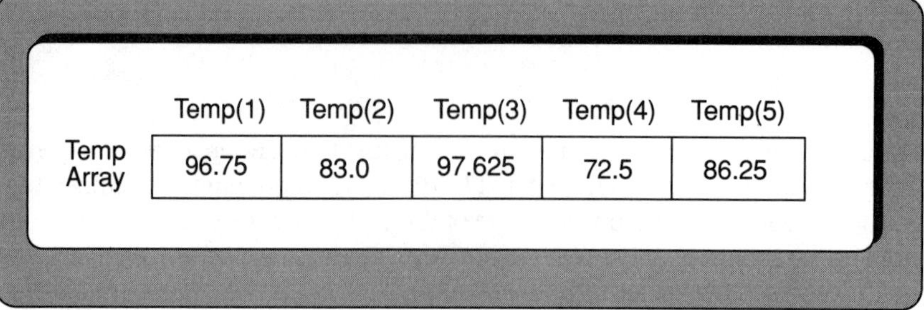

Figure 8-3 The Elements of the TEMP Array

```
      WRITE(6,*) VOLTS(6)
      WRITE(6,*) 'THE VALUE OF ELEMENT ', I, ' IS, TEMP(I)
      DO 25 N = 5, 20
        WRITE(6,*) N, AMOUNT(N)
   25 CONTINUE
```

The first WRITE statement displays the value of the subscripted variable VOLTS(6). The second WRITE statement displays the value of the subscript I and the value of TEMP(I). Before this statement can be executed, I would have to have an assigned value. Finally, the last example includes a WRITE statement within a DO loop. Both the value of the index and the value of the elements from 5 to 20 are displayed.

Program 8-2 illustrates the use of two DO loops: the first to input values into a 10-element array named AREA, and the second to display the values.

Program 8-2

```
      PROGRAM MAIN
        CALL TESTAR
        END
*
      SUBROUTINE TESTAR
        INTEGER I
        REAL AREA(10)
        DO 15 I = 1,10
          WRITE(6,*) 'ENTER AN AREA: '
          READ(5,*) AREA(I)
   15   CONTINUE
        WRITE(6,*) 'THE ELEMENTS OF THE ARRAY ARE:'
        DO 20 I = 1,10
          WRITE(6,*) AREA(I)
   20   CONTINUE
        RETURN
        END
```

Alternative Array Input/Output

Programs 8-1 and 8-2 use similar techniques for the input and display of subscripted variables as used for scalar variables. Two other techniques, called *array name I/O* and *implied DO loops*, are available specifically for the input and output of array elements.

In array name I/O, the name of the array is used to read or display array values without the necessity of using individual subscripts. The general form of the list-directed array name input statement is:

```
READ(5,*)  array name
```

For example, if A is the name of an array, the statement:

```
READ(5,*) A
```

causes the computer to temporarily pause and wait for values of each element in the array to be entered. The first entered value is assigned to A(1), the second to A(2), and so on, until the array has been completely filled with values. Similarly, the list-directed output statement:

```
WRITE(6,*) A
```

causes all of the values in the A array to be displayed, starting with A(1) and ending with the last element in the array. Program 8-3 illustrates the use of these two statements.

Program 8-3

```
      PROGRAM MAIN
        CALL INARRY
        END
*
      SUBROUTINE INARRY
        INTEGER A(5)
        WRITE(6,*) 'ENTER FIVE NUMBERS: '
        READ(5,*) A
        WRITE(6,*) 'THE VALUES FOR A(1) THROUGH A(5) ARE:'
        WRITE(6,*) A
        RETURN
        END
```

Following is a sample run using program 8-3:

```
ENTER FIVE NUMBERS:
36 42 1 18 63
THE VALUES FOR A(1) THROUGH A(5) ARE:
         36           42           1           18           63
```

Notice that in Program 8-3 the statement READ(5,*) is equivalent to the longer statement:

```
READ(5,*) A(1), A(2), A(3), A(4), A(5)
```

and the statement WRITE(6,*) A is equivalent to the longer statement:

```
WRITE(6,*) A(1), A(2), A(3), A(4), A(5)
```

The final technique for inputting and displaying array elements uses implied DO loops. An implied DO loop is simply an alternate form of a standard DO loop in which all returned elements are placed on the same line. For example, WRITE(6,*) (A(I), I=1,5) is equivalent to both WRITE(6,*) A and WRITE(6,*) A(1), A(2), A(3), A(4), A(5).

Similarly, an implied DO loop may also be used on input. Program 8-4 uses an implied DO loop to enter the first, third, and fifth elements of a 10-element array and also to display the array's first 5 elements.

Program 8-4

```
      PROGRAM MAIN
        CALL IMPDO
        END
*
      SUBROUTINE IMPDO
        INTEGER A(5)
        WRITE(6,*) 'ENTER THREE NUMBERS: '
        READ(5,*) (A(I), I=1,5,2)
        A(2) = 17
        A(4) = 2
        WRITE(6,*) 'THE VALUES FOR A(1) THROUGH A(5) ARE:'
        WRITE(6,*) (A(I), I = 1,5)
        RETURN
        END
```

Following is a sample run of Program 8-4.

```
ENTER THREE NUMBERS:
33 26 45
THE VALUES FOR A(1) THROUGH A(5) ARE:
33          17          26          2          45
```

Skill Builder Exercises

1. Write array declarations for the following:
   a. a list of 100 real voltages named VOLTS
   b. a list of 50 real temperatures named TEMPS

c. a list of 30 characters, each representing a single character code, named CODE
d. a list of 100 integer years named YEARS
e. a list of 32 real velocities named VELOCY
f. a list of 1000 real distances named DISTNC
g. a list of 6 integer code numbers named CODE

2. Write appropriate notation for the first, third, and seventh elements of the following arrays:
   a. `INTEGER GRADES(20)`
   b. `REAL VOLTS(10)`
   c. `REAL AMPS(16)`
   d. `INTEGER DIST(15)`
   e. `REAL VELOC(25)`
   f. `REAL TIME(100)`

3a. Write individual READ statements that can be used to enter values into the first, third, and seventh elements of each of the arrays specified in Exercises 2a through 2f.

b. Write a DO loop that can be used to enter values for the complete array specified in Exercise 2a.

4a. Write individual PRINT statements that can be used to print the values from the first, third, and seventh elements of each of the arrays specified in Exercises 2a through 2f.

b. Write a DO loop that can be used to display values for the complete array specified in Exercise 2a.

5. List the elements that will be displayed by the following sections of code:

a.
```
      DO 10 K = 1,5,2
        PRINT A(K)
   10 CONTINUE
```
b.
```
      DO 15 J = 3,10,3
        PRINT B(J)
   15 CONTINUE
```
c. `PRINT *, (A(J), J = 1,5)`

d. `PRINT *, (B(K), K = 3,12,3)`

e. `PRINT *, (C(I), I = 2,10,2)`

Expanding Your Skills

6. All of the array specifications we have used specify only the upper index value of the array. This type of specification, which is the most commonly encountered one in FORTRAN, has the effect of forcing the first array element to have an index value of 1.

It is possible in FORTRAN 77 and 90 to specify a lower as well as an upper index value. For example, the specification REAL VOLTS(–10:7) specifies an array of eighteen elements: the first element is accessed as VOLTS(–10), the second element as VOLTS(–9), the eleventh element as VOLTS(0), and the eighteenth element as VOLTS(7). Although specifying a lower index value is not commonly used, situations may arise that make such a designation useful. For example, in storing population data for the years 1950 through 1990, a specification such as POP(1950:1990) could be used. This specification creates an array named POP consisting of 41 elements, where the first element is accessed as POP(1950), and the last element as POP(1990). For the following array specifications, determine the total amount of elements in each array and the correct notation for the first, third, and seventh elements in the array.

a. `INTEGER GRADES(-10:10)`

b. `REAL VOLTS(-10:5)`

c. `REAL AMPS(-16:0)`

d. `INTEGER DIST(0:15)`

e. `REAL VELOC(-2:25)`

f. `REAL TIME(-5:95)`

Programming Exercises

7a. Write a program to input the following values into an array named VOLTS: 10.95, 16.32, 12.15, 8.22, 15.98, 26.22, 13.54, 6.45, 17.59. After the data has been entered, have your program output the values.

b. Repeat Exercise 7a, but after the data has been entered, have your program display it in the following form:

```
10.95  16.32  12.15
 8.22  15.98  26.22
13.54   6.45  17.59
```

8. Write a program to input eight integer numbers into an array named TEMP. As each number is input, add the numbers into a total. After all numbers are input, display the numbers and their average.

9a. Write a program to input 10 positive integer numbers into an array named FMAX and determine the maximum value entered. Your program should contain only one loop, and the maximum should be determined as array element values are being input. (*Hint:* Set the maximum equal to –10000 before the loop used to input the numbers.)

b. Repeat Exercise 9a, keeping track of both the maximum element in the array and the index number for the maximum. After displaying the numbers, print the two messages:

```
THE MAXIMUM VALUE IS: ___
THIS IS ELEMENT NUMBER ___ IN THE LIST OF NUMBERS
```

Have your program display the correct values in place of the underlines in the messages.

c. Repeat Exercise 9b, but have your program locate the minimum data value entered.

10a. Write a program to input the following integer numbers into an array named GRADE: 89, 95, 72, 83, 99, 54, 86, 75, 92, 73, 79, 75, 82, 73. As each number is input, add the numbers to a total. After all numbers are input and the total is obtained, calculate the average of the numbers and use the average to determine the deviation of each value from the average. Store each deviation in an array named DEVIAT. Each deviation is obtained as the element value less the average of all the data. Have your program display each deviation alongside its corresponding element from the GRADE array.

b. Calculate the variance of the data used in Exercise 10a. The variance is obtained by squaring each individual deviation and dividing the sum of the squared deviations by the number of deviations.

11. Write a program that specifies three single dimension arrays named VOLTS, CURRNT, and RESIST. Each array should be capable of holding 10 elements. Using a DO loop, input values for the CURRNT and RESIST arrays. The entries in the VOLTS array should be the product of the corresponding values in the CURRNT and RESIST arrays (thus, VOLTS(I) = CURRNT(I) * RESIST(I)). After all of the data have been entered, display the following output:

```
VOLTAGE CURRENT RESISTANCE
------- ------- ----------
```

Display the appropriate values under each column heading.

12a. Write a program that allows user inputs of 10 real numbers into an array named RAW. After the numbers are entered into the array, your program should cycle through RAW 10 times. During each pass through the array, your program should select the lowest value in RAW and place the selected value in the next available slot in an array named SORTED. Thus, when your program is complete, the SORTED array should contain the numbers in RAW in sorted order from lowest to highest. (*Hint:* Make sure to reset the lowest value selected during each pass to a very high number so that it is not selected again. You will need a second DO loop within the first DO loop to locate the minimum value for each pass.)

b. The method used in Exercise 12a to sort the values in the array is very inefficient. Can you determine why? What might be a better method of sorting the numbers in an array?

8.2 The DATA Statement and Array Initialization

Array elements can be initialized within a program unit at compile time, using DATA statements. Since DATA statements can also be used to initialize scalar variables, we will consider the scalar case first.

A DATA statement is a specification statement having the general form:

```
DATA   variable list/value list/, variable list/value list/ ...
```

Examples of DATA statements are:

```
DATA LENGTH, WIDTH, RADIUS /22,33.4,86.8/
DATA W,X,Y,Z /6.,8.,10.,12./
DATA I,J,K /1,5,6/,ICOUNT,SUM /23,42.5/
```

The first DATA statement assigns the value 22 to the variable LENGTH, the value 33.4 to the variable WIDTH, and the value 86.8 to the variable RADIUS. The second DATA statement assigns the values 6., 8., 10., and 12., respectively, to the variables W, X, Y, and Z. Finally, the third DATA statement assigns the values 1, 5, and 6, respectively, to the variables I, J, and K, and the values 23 and 42.5 to the respective variables ICOUNT and SUM.

The primary requirement in constructing DATA statements is that there be the same number of values in each value list as there are variables in the corresponding variable list. For example, if the variable list A,B,C,D,E,F,G is used, its associated value list must contain seven values.

Although each value list must contain sufficient values for its associated variable list, the value list can use repeat counts. For example, the value list 3*4.6 is equivalent to the value list 4.6,4.6,4.6. Further examples of repeat counts are listed in Table 8-3.

DATA statements are useful because they permit many variables to be initialized in a single statement rather than in multiple assignment statements. For example, if the variables A, B, C, and D are to be initialized at the beginning of a program unit, a single DATA statement can be used instead of four individual assignment statements. It is important to note that DATA statements must only appear after all declaration statements and should appear before any executable statements. Thus, for example, a DATA statement cannot be used within a DO loop or later in a program unit to subsequently modify the value of a variable. If the variables initialized by a DATA statement must be modified, either assignment or READ statements must be used.

The ability to initialize many variables with a single statement makes the DATA statement particularly useful in initializing arrays. This initialization of array elements can be done by individual element name, by array name, or by using implied DO loops.

Table 8-3 Repeat Count Examples

Using a repeat count	Equivalent value list
/ 5 * 3.2 /	/ 3.2, 3.2, 3.2, 3.2, 3.2/
/ 4 * 2 /	/ 2, 2, 2, 2 /
/ 2 * (1.3, 2), 3 * 1 /	/ 1.3, 2, 1.3, 2,1, 1,1 /

Initialization by Array Element Name

Individual array elements can be initialized using a DATA statement by including the names of the array elements within the list of variables. Examples of this type of array element initialization are:

```
DATA A(1), A(3), A(5) /4.5,6.2,8.3/
```

and:

```
DATA B(1), B(2), B(3) /3*22.6/
```

The first DATA statement initializes the variables A(1), A(3), and A(5) to the respective values 4.5, 6.2, and 8.3, while the second DATA statement uses a repeat count to store the value 22.6 into each of the variables B(1), B(2), and B(3).

Initialization by Array Name

Array elements can also be initialized with a DATA statement by listing the name of the array and sufficient values to fill the complete array. For example, assuming an array named GRADES is specified by:

```
INTEGER GRADES(10)
```

the statement:

```
DATA GRADES/14,24,26,33,35,42,46,19,4,20/
```

initializes GRADES(1) with the value 14, GRADES(2) with the value 24, and so on, until GRADES(10) is initialized to the value 20.

Similarly, the statement:

```
DATA GRADES/10*92/
```

uses a repeat count to initialize all elements to 92, and the statement:

```
DATA GRADES/2*(50,60,70,80,90)/
```

initializes the GRADES array with the repeating sequence of values 50, 60, 70, 80, and 90.

Implied DO Loops

The third method of using DATA statements to initialize array elements is to use an implied DO loop. For example, assuming an array named SLOPES is specified by:

```
REAL SLOPES(15)
```

the statement:

```
DATA (SLOPES(I), I = 1,4)/14,16,18,5/
```

makes the following assignments:

```
SLOPES(1) = 14
SLOPES(2) = 16
SLOPES(3) = 18
SLOPES(4) = 5
```

Repeat counts can also be used with implied DO loops. For example, the statement:

```
DATA (SLOPES(I), I = 1, 15, 2)/8*12/
```

assigns the value 12 to all array elements having an odd subscript value. Notice that the implied DO loop starts with the element SLOPES(1), ends with the element SLOPES(15), and includes eight elements. Thus, the list of values must also contain eight values.

Exercises

1. Write array declarations and initializing DATA statements for the following:
   a. A list of ten integer grades: 89, 75, 82, 93, 78, 95, 81, 88, 77, 82.
   b. A list of five real amounts: 10.62, 13.98, 18.45, 12.68, 14.76.
   c. A list of 100 real interest rates; the first 6 rates are 6.29, 6.95, 7.25, 7.35, 7.40, 7.42.
   d. A list of 64 real temperatures; the first 4 temperatures are 78.2, 69.6, 68.5, 83.9.
   e. A list of 15 character codes; the first 7 codes are G, K, M, Q, R, W, X.
2. Write array and DATA specification statements to store the following values in an array named VOLTS: 16.24, 18.98, 23.75, 16.29, 19.54, 14.22, 11.13, 15.39. Include these statements in a program that displays the values in the array.
3. Write a program that uses a DATA statement to store the following numbers in an array named SLOPES: 17.24, 25.63, 5.94, 33.92, 3.71, 32.84, 35.93, 18.24, 6.92. Your program should locate and display both the maximum and the minimum values in the array.
4. Write a program that uses a DATA statement to store the following values in an array named PRICES: 9.92, 6.32, 12.63, 5.95, 10.29. Your program should also create two arrays named UNITS and AMOUNT, each capable of storing five real numbers. Using a loop and a READ statement, have your program accept five user-input numbers into the UNITS array when the program is run. Your program should store the product of the corresponding values in the PRICES and UNITS arrays in the AMOUNT array (for example, AMOUNT(1) = PRICES(1) * UNITS(1)) and display the following output (fill in the table appropriately):

```
PRICE    UNITS    AMOUNT
-----    -----    ------
 9.92      .         .
 6.32      .         .
12.63      .         .
 5.95      .         .
10.29      .         .
                  ------

TOTAL                .
```

5a. Write an array declaration and DATA initialization statements to store the four strings of characters:

```
' INPUT THE FOLLOWING DATA '
'--------------------------'
'ENTER THE DATE: '
'ENTER THE ACCOUNT NUMBER: '
```

in elements 1 through 4 of an array name MESSGE. (*Hint:* Use the array specification statement CHARACTER*26 MESSGE(4).)

b. Include the array declaration and DATA statements written in Exercise 5a in a program that uses the WRITE statement to display the individual messages. For example, the statement WRITE(6,*), MESSGE(1) should cause the first message to be displayed.

6a. Write an array and DATA specification statement to store the individual characters T, E, S, T, I, N, and G into a character array named STRTST, specified as CHARACTER STRTST(7). Include these specification statements in a program to display the characters using the following loop:

```
      DO 10 I = 1,7
        WRITE(6,*) STRTST(I)
   10 CONTINUE
```

b. Modify the DO loop in Exercise 6a to display only the array characters I, N, and G.

8.3 Two Dimension Arrays

A two dimension array consists of both rows and columns of elements. For example, the array of numbers:

```
 8  16   9  52
 3  15  27   6
14  25   2  10
```

is called a two dimension array of integers. This array consists of three rows and four columns. To reserve storage for this array, both the number of rows and the number of columns must be included in the array's declaration. Calling the array VALS, the correct declaration for this two dimension array is:

```
INTEGER VALS(3,4)
```

Similarly, the declarations:

```
REAL VOLTS(10,5)
CHARACTER*4 CODE(6,26)
```

specify that the array VOLTS consists of 10 rows and 5 columns of real numbers and that the array CODE consists of 6 rows and 26 columns, with each element capable of holding 4 characters.

To make it possible to locate an element in a two dimension array, each element is identified by its position in the array. As illustrated in Figure 8-4, the term

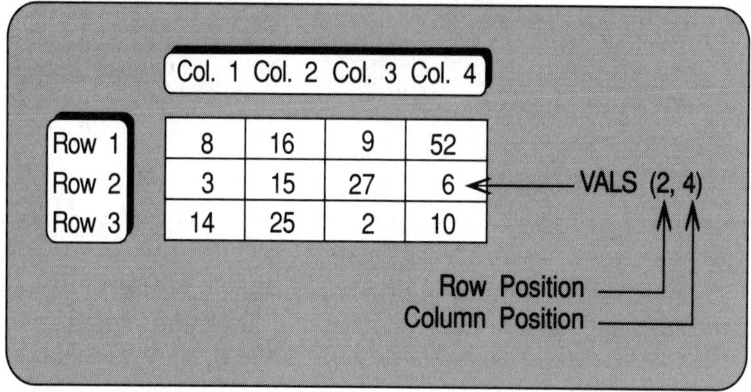

Figure 8-4 Each Array Element Is Identified by Its Row and Column Position

VALS(2,4) uniquely identifies the element in row 2, column 4. As with single dimension array variables, double dimension array variables can be used anywhere that scalar variables are valid. Examples using elements of the VALS array are:

```
WATTS = VALS(2,3)
VALS(1,1) = 62
NEWNUM = 4 * (VALS(2,1) - 5)
SUMR1 = VALS(1,1) + VALS(1,2) + VALS(1,3) + VALS(1,4)
```

The last statement causes the values of the four elements in row 1 to be added and the sum to be stored in the scalar variable SUMR1.

As with single dimension arrays, two dimension arrays can be specified explicitly within a declaration statement or with a declaration statement followed by a dimension statement. For example, both:

```
REAL AREA(3,4)
```

and:

```
REAL AREA
DIMENSION AREA(3,4)
```

produce a real array named AREA having three rows and four columns. This same array is produced using the single specification statement:

```
DIMENSION AREA(3,4)
```

which uses FORTRAN's implied data typing to declare the array (recall that any variable name not beginning in I, J, K, L, M, or N is considered a real variable). As with all FORTRAN type declarations, a single declaration statement can always be used to specify variables of the same type. Thus, for example, the declaration:

```
INTEGER SLOPE, VOLTS(75), TEMPS(52,7)
```

specifies SLOPE to be a scalar integer variable, VOLTS to be a single dimension integer array consisting of 75 elements, and TEMPS to be a two dimension integer array having 52 rows and 7 columns.

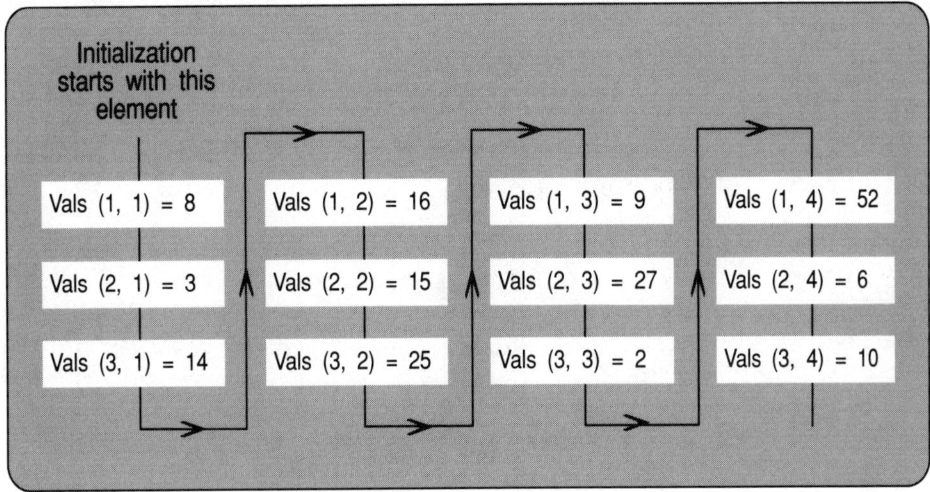

Figure 8-5 Storage and Initialization of the VALS( ) Array

As with single dimension arrays, two dimension arrays can be initialized using DATA statements following the array declaration. For example, the statements:

```
INTEGER VALS(3,4)
DATA VALS/ 8,3,14,16,15,25,9,27,2,52,6,10/
```

create and initialize each element of the VALS array. Figure 8-5 lists the initializations performed by the DATA statement.

As illustrated in Figure 8-5, the initialization of a two dimension array is done in column order. First, the elements of the first column are initialized, then the elements of the second column are initialized, and so on, until the initializations are completed. This column ordering is also the same ordering used to store two dimension arrays. That is, array element (1,1) is stored first, followed by element (2,1), followed by element (3,1), and so on. Following the first column's elements are the second column's elements, and so on for all the columns of the array.

As with single dimension arrays, two dimension arrays may be displayed by individual element notation, by array name, or by using DO loops (either explicit or implied). This is illustrated by Program 8-5, which displays all of the elements of a three-by-four two dimension array using three different techniques.

Program 8-5

```
      PROGRAM MAIN
        CALL TWOARR
        END
*
      SUBROUTINE TWOARR
        INTEGER I, J, VALS(3,4)
        DATA VALS/ 8,3,14,16,15,25,9,27,2,52,6,10/
*** DISPLAY BY EXPLICIT ELEMENT
        WRITE(6,*) 'DISPLAY OF VALS() BY EXPLICIT ELEMENT'
        WRITE(6,*) VALS(1,1), VALS(1,2), VALS(1,3), VALS(1,4)
        WRITE(6,*) VALS(2,1), VALS(2,2), VALS(2,3), VALS(2,4)
        WRITE(6,*) VALS(3,1), VALS(3,2), VALS(3,3), VALS(3,4)
*** DISPLAY BY NESTED DO LOOPS WITH THE INNER LOOP IMPLIED
        WRITE(6,*)
        WRITE(6,*) 'DISPLAY OF VALS() USING NESTED DO LOOPS'
        DO 15 I = 1,3
          WRITE(6,*) (VALS(I,J), J = 1,4)
  15    CONTINUE
*** DISPLAY USING AN ARRAY OUTPUT STATEMENT
        PRINT *
        WRITE(6,*) 'DISPLAY OF VALS() USING ARRAY NAME OUTPUT'
        WRITE(6,*) VALS
        RETURN
        END
```

Following is the display produced by Program 8-5.

```
DISPLAY OF VALS() BY EXPLICIT ELEMENT
          8      16       9      52
          3      15      27       6
         14      25       2      10
DISPLAY OF VALS() USING NESTED DO LOOPS
          8      16       9      52
          3      15      27       6
         14      25       2      10
DISPLAY OF VALS() USING ARRAY NAME OUTPUT
8   3   14  16  15  25   9  27   2  52   6  10
```

The first display of the VALS array produced by Program 8-5 is constructed by explicitly designating each array element. The second display of array element values, which is identical to the first, is produced using a nested DO loop. Nested loops are especially useful when dealing with two dimension arrays because they allow the programmer to easily designate and cycle through each element. In Program 8-5, the variable I controls the outer loop, and the variable J, used within an implied DO loop, controls the inner loop. Each pass through the outer loop corresponds to a single row, with the inner loop supplying the appropriate column elements. After a complete column is printed, a new line is started for the next row. The effect is a display of the array in a row-by-row fashion. The final display was created by the single array output statement:

```
WRITE(6,*) VALS
```

The array output statement is particularly convenient when a quick debugging check of array elements is needed. This same display can be produced by the nested implied DO loop statement:

```
WRITE(6,*) ((VALS(I,J), I = 1,3), J=1,4)
```

Just as implied DO loops and array names can be used for two dimension array output, both of these techniques can be used to initialize two dimension array elements. For example, the statements:

```
READ(5,*)VALS
```

and:

```
READ(5,*) ((VALS(I,J), I = 1,3), J=1,4)
```

require the user to enter 12 data values, which are stored in the VALS array. In both cases the elements must be entered in the column order previously illustrated in Figure 8-5.

Once two dimension array elements have been assigned using either READ, DATA, or assignment statements, array processing can begin. Typically, DO loops are used to process two dimension arrays because, as was previously noted, they allow the programmer to easily designate and cycle through each array element. For example, the first nested DO loop illustrated in Program 8-6 is used to multiply each element in the VALS array by the

Program 8-6

```
      PROGRAM MAIN
        CALL MULTAR
        END
*
      SUBROUTINE MULTAR
        INTEGER I, J, VALS(3,4)
        DATA VALS/ 8,3,14,16,15,25,9,27,2,52,6,10/
*** MULTIPLY EACH ARRAY ELEMENT BY 10
        DO 10 I = 1,3
          DO 5 J = 1,4
            VALS(I,J) = 10 * VALS(I,J)
  5       CONTINUE
 10     CONTINUE
*** DISPLAY THE RESULTING ARRAY ELEMENTS
        PRINT *, 'DISPLAY OF MULTIPLIED ARRAY ELEMENTS'
        DO 15 I = 1,3
          PRINT *, (VALS(I,J), J = 1,4)
 15     CONTINUE
        RETURN
        END
```

scalar number 10. The second nested DO loop uses an implied inner DO loop (the same as that used in Program 8-5) to produce the final array display.

Following is the output produced by Program 8-6.

```
DISPLAY OF MULTIPLIED ARRAY ELEMENTS
              80  160   90  520
              30  150  270   60
             140  250   20  100
```

Larger Dimension Arrays

Although arrays with more than two dimensions are not commonly used, FORTRAN does allow larger arrays to be specified. This is done by listing the maximum size of all indices for the array. For example, the declaration INTEGER RESPON(4,10,6) specifies a three dimension array. The first element in the array is designated as RESPON(1,1,1), and the last element as RESPON(4,10,6).

Conceptually, as illustrated in Figure 8-6, a three dimension array can be viewed as a book of data tables. Using this visualization, the first index value can be thought of as the location of the desired row in a table, the second index value as the desired column, and the third index value, which is often called "rank", as the page number of the selected table.

Similarly, arrays having at most seven dimensions can be specified. Conceptually, a four dimension array can be represented as a shelf of books, where the fourth dimension is used to specify a desired book on the shelf, and a five dimension array can be viewed as a bookcase filled with books, where the fifth dimension refers to a selected shelf in the bookcase. Using the same analogy, a six dimension array can be considered as a single row of bookcases, where the sixth dimension references the desired bookcase in the row. Finally, a seven dimension array can be considered as multiple rows of bookcases, where the seventh dimension references the desired row. Alternatively, arrays of three, four, five, six, and seven dimension arrays can be viewed as mathematical *n*-tuples of order three, four, five, six, and seven, respectively.

Figure 8-6 Representation of a Three Dimension Array

Exercises

1. Write appropriate declaration statements for:
   a. an array of integers with 6 rows and 10 columns named NUMS
   b. an array of integers with 2 rows and 5 columns named NUMS
   c. an array of single characters with 7 rows and 12 columns named CODES
   d. an array of single characters with 15 rows and 7 columns named CODES
   e. an array of real numbers with 10 rows and 25 columns named VALS
   f. an array of real numbers with 16 rows and 8 columns named VALS
2. Determine the output produced by the following program:

```
      PROGRAM MAIN
        INTEGER I, J, VALS(3,4)
        DATA VALS/ 8,3,14,16,15,25,9,27,2,52,6,10/
        DO 10 I = 1,3
          DO 5 J = 1,4
            WRITE(6,*), VALS(I,J)
  5       CONTINUE
 10     CONTINUE
        END
```

3a. Write a FORTRAN program that adds the values of all elements in the VALS array used in Exercise 2 and displays the total.

b. Modify the program written for Exercise 3a to display the total of each column separately.

4. Write a FORTRAN program that adds equivalent elements of the two dimension arrays named FIRST and SECND. Both arrays should have two rows and three columns. For example, element (1,2) of the resulting array should be the sum of FIRST(1,2) and SECND(1,2). The FIRST and SECND arrays should be initialized as follows:

```
FIRST            SECND
16  18  23       24  52  77
54  91  11       16  19  59
```

5a. Write a FORTRAN program that finds and displays the maximum value in a two dimension array of integers. The array should be specified as a four-by-five array of integers and initialized using the statement:

```
DATA NUMS/16,22,99,4,18,-258,4,101,5,98,105,6,15,2,45,33,88,72,16,3/
```

b. Modify the program written in Exercise 5a so that it also displays the maximum value's row and column subscript numbers.

6. Write a FORTRAN program to select the values in a four by five array of integers in increasing order and store the selected values in the single dimension array named SORT. Use the data statement given in Exercise 5a to initialize the two dimension array.

7a. A professor has constructed a two dimension array of real numbers having three rows and five columns. This array currently contains the test grades of the students in the professor's advanced compiler design class. Write a FORTRAN program that uses an array input statement to read 15 array values and then determine the total number of grades in the ranges less than 60, greater than or equal to 60 and less than 70, greater than or equal to 70 and less than 80, greater than or equal to 80 and less than 90, and greater than or equal to 90.

b. Entering 15 grades each time the program written for Exercise 7a is run is cumbersome. What method, therefore, is appropriate for initializing the array during the testing phase?

c. How might the program you wrote for Exercise 7a be modified to include the case of no grade being present? That is, what grade could be used to indicate an invalid grade, and how would your program have to be modified to exclude counting such a grade?

8.4 Arrays as Arguments

An individual array element is passed to a subroutine in the same manner as any scalar variable. For a single array element this is done by including the element as a subscripted variable in a CALL statement's argument list. For example, the subroutine call:

```
CALL FMAX(TEMP(2),TEMP(6))
```

makes the individual array elements TEMP(2) and TEMP(6) available to the subroutine FMAX.

Passing a complete array to a subroutine is in many respects an easier operation than passing individual elements. For example, if TEMP is an array, the statement CALL FMAX(TEMP) makes the complete TEMP array available to the FMAX subroutine.

On the receiving side, the called subroutine must be alerted that an array is being made available. For example, assuming TEMP was declared as INTEGER TEMP(5), a suitable subroutine heading and argument declaration for the FMAX subroutine are:

```
SUBROUTINE FMAX(VALS)
  INTEGER VALS(5)
```

In this subroutine heading, the argument name VALS is local to the subroutine. However, VALS refers to the original array created outside the subroutine. This is made clear in Program 8-7.

Only one array is created in Program 8-7. In PROGRAM MAIN this array is known as TEMP, and in FMAX the array is known as VALS. As illustrated in Figure 8-7, both names refer to the same array. Thus, in Figure 8-7 VALS(3) is the same element as TEMP(3).

The argument declaration in FMAX actually contains extra information that is not required by the subroutine. All that FMAX must know is that the argument VALS

Program 8-7

```
      PROGRAM MAIN
        INTEGER TEMP(5)
        DATA TEMP /2,18,1,27,6/
        CALL FMAX(TEMP)
        END
*
      SUBROUTINE FMAX(VALS)
        INTEGER VALS(5), I, MAX
        MAX = VALS(1)
        DO 10 I = 2,5
          IF (MAX .LT. VALS(I))  MAX = VALS(I)
 10     CONTINUE
        WRITE(6,*) 'THE MAXIMUM VALUE IS ', MAX
        END
```

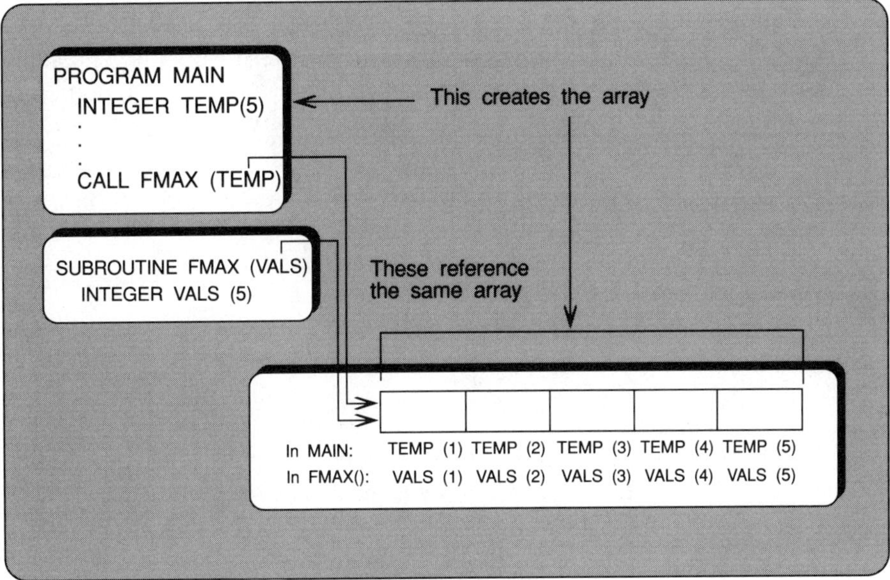

Figure 8-7 Only One Array is Created

references an array of integers. Since the array has been created in PROGRAM MAIN, and no additional storage space is needed in FMAX, the declaration for VALS can omit the size of the array. Thus, an alternative subroutine heading is:

```
      SUBROUTINE FMAX(VALS)
        INTEGER VALS(*)
```

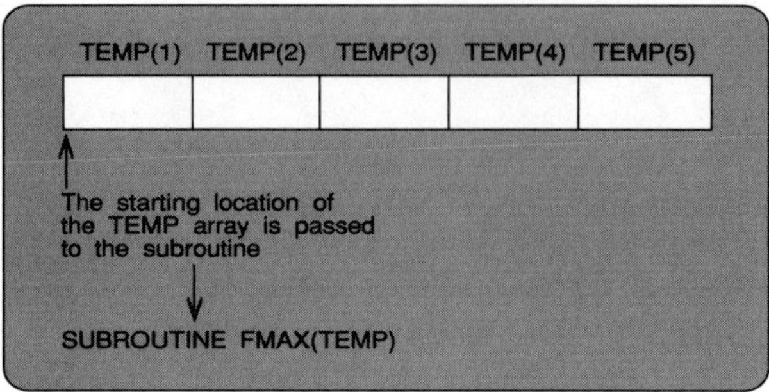

Figure 8-8 The Starting Location of the Array Is Passed

This form of argument declaration is referred to as an *assumed size* array declaration. Assumed size declarations make more sense when you realize that only one item is actually passed to FMAX when the subroutine is called. As you might have suspected, the item passed is the starting location of the TEMP array. This is illustrated in Figure 8-8.

Since only one item is passed to FMAX, the number of elements in the array need not be included in the declaration for VALS. In fact, it is generally advisable to omit the size of the array in the argument declaration. For example, consider the more general form of FMAX, which can be used to find and return the maximum value of an integer array of arbitrary size.

```
      SUBROUTINE FMAX(VALS,NELS,MAX)
        INTEGER VALS(*), NELS, MAX
        INTEGER I
        MAX = VALS(1)
        DO 10, I = 2, NELS
          IF (MAX .LT. VALS(I)) MAX = VALS(I)
10      CONTINUE
        END
```

The more general form of FMAX finds and returns the maximum value in any single-dimensioned integer array passed to it. The subroutine expects that an integer array and the number of elements in the array that must be inspected will be passed into it as arguments. Then, using the number of elements as the boundary for its search, the subroutine's DO loop causes each array element to be examined in sequential order to locate the maximum value. This value is passed back to the calling routine through the third dummy argument in the subroutine's argument list. Program 8-8 illustrates the use of FMAX in a complete program.

Program 8-8

```
      PROGRAM MAIN
        INTEGER TEMP(5), N, MAX
        N = 5
        DATA TEMP /2,18,1,27,6/
        CALL FMAX(TEMP, N, MAX)
        WRITE(6,*) 'THE MAXIMUM VALUE IS ', MAX
        END
*
      SUBROUTINE FMAX(VALS,NELS,MAX)
        INTEGER VALS(*), NELS, MAX, I
        MAX = VALS(1)
        DO 10, I = 2, NELS
          IF (MAX .LT. VALS(I)) MAX = VALS(I)
 10     CONTINUE
        END
```

The output displayed when Program 8-8 is executed is:

```
THE MAXIMUM VALUE IS            27
```

It should be noted that the value of N passed into FMAX need not be the same as the number of elements in the passed array. The passed array is completely declared by the assumed size declaration:

```
INTEGER VALS(*)
```

and the value of N is used to tell FMAX how many elements of this array to examine. Thus, for example, the call:

```
CALL FMAX(TEMP,3,MAX)
```

gives FMAX complete access to TEMP but only specifies that three elements be examined within FMAX.

A third method of passing single dimension arrays to subroutines is to use *adjustable* array declarations. Here, the dimension of the array is passed as a separate argument, which is then used in the dummy argument declaration for the array size. For example, the subroutine heading:

```
SUBROUTINE FMAX(VALS,NELS)
  INTEGER NELS, VALS(NELS)
```

uses an adjustable array declaration to declare the passed array length. It is important to note that a dummy argument, such as NELS, can only be used as an array size if its data type is declared before the array argument's name. Since NELS is declared before VALS, and NELS' value is set by the calling program unit, the size of the VALS array is well defined within the subroutine. Notice, however, that this array declaration method cannot be used in a MAIN program unit using a variable to declare the array size. This is because a value cannot be assigned to the variable prior to the array's declaration.

Passing Multidimension Arrays

Passing multidimension arrays into subroutines is a process identical to passing single dimension arrays. The called subroutine receives access to the entire array. For example, assuming that the following multidimension arrays named TEST, FACTOR, and GRADES are declared as:

```
INTEGER TEST(2,3)
REAL FACTOR(3,5)
REAL GRADES(3,5,10)
```

the following subroutine calls are valid:

```
CALL FMAX(TEST)
CALL SELECT(FACTOR)
CALL AVERGE(GRADES)
```

On the receiving side, the called subroutine must be alerted to the size of the passed array. As with single dimension arrays, this may be done by declaring the exact size of the passed array. For example, suitable subroutine headings and argument declarations for the previous subroutines are:

```
SUBROUTINE FMAX(NUMS)   SUBROUTINE SELECT(VAL)   SUBROUTINE AVERGE(GDS)
  INTEGER NUMS(2,3)        REAL VAL(3,5)               REAL GDS(3,5,10)
```

In each of these subroutine headings, the argument names chosen are local to the subroutine. However, the internal local names used by the subroutine still refer to the original array created outside the subroutine. Program 8-9 illustrates passing a two dimension array into a subroutine that displays the array's values.

Program 8-9

```
      PROGRAM MAIN
        INTEGER VAL(3,4)
        DATA VAL /8,3,14,16,15,25,9,27,2,52,6,10/
        CALL DISPLY(VAL)
        END
*
      SUBROUTINE DISPLY(NUMS)
        INTEGER NUMS(3,4), I, J
        DO 10 I = 1, 3
          WRITE(6,*) (NUMS(I,J), J = 1,4)
 10     CONTINUE
        END
```

Only one array is created in Program 8-9. This array is known as VAL in the MAIN program unit and as NUMS in DISPLY. Thus, VAL(1,2) refers to the same element as NUMS(1,2). The display produced by Program 8-8 is:

```
 8    16     9    52
 3    15    27     6
14    25     2    10
```

The argument declaration for NUMS in DISPLY contains extra information that is not required by the subroutine. The declaration for NUMS can use an asterisk (*) for the column dimension. Thus, an alternative subroutine heading is:

```
SUBROUTINE DISPLY(NUMS)
  INTEGER NUMS(3,*)
```

The asterisk can be used only as the last dimension (this is also true for passing larger-dimensioned arrays). Additionally, as for single-dimensioned arrays, multidimensioned arrays can be passed using adjustable sizing. For example, the heading:

```
SUBROUTINE DISPLY(EXPER, I, J, K)
  INTEGER I, J, K, EXPER(I, J, K)
```

uses adjustable sizing for passing the three dimension EXPER array.

Exercises

1. The following declaration was used to create the MFACTR array:

   ```
   INTEGER MFACTR(500)
   ```

   Write a subroutine header and two different argument declarations for a subroutine named SORTAR that accepts the MFACTR array as an argument named INARRY.

2. The following declaration was used to create the CODE array:

   ```
   CHARACTER CODE(256)
   ```

   Write a subroutine header and two different argument declarations for a subroutine named FINDCD that accepts the CODE array as an argument named SELCT.

3. The following declaration was used to create the WATTS array:

   ```
   REAL WATTS(140)
   ```

   Write a subroutine header and two different argument declarations for a subroutine named POWER that accepts the WATTS array as an argument named WATTS.

4a. Modify the FMAX subroutine in Program 8-8 to locate the minimum value of the passed array.

b. Include the subroutine written in Exercise 4a in a complete program and run the program on a computer.

5. Write a program that has a DATA statement in its main program unit that stores the following numbers into a array named GRADES: 65.3, 72.5, 75.0, 83.2, 86.5, 94.0, 96.0, 98.8, 100. There should be a subroutine call to SHOW that accepts the GRADES array as an argument named GRADES and then displays the numbers in the array.

6a. Write a program that has a DATA statement in PROGRAM MAIN to store the characters 'V','A','C','A','T','I','O','N',' ','I','S',' ','N','E','A','R' into an array named MESSGE.

There should be a subroutine call to DISPLY that accepts MESSGE in an argument named STRNG and then displays the message.

b. Modify the DISPLY subroutine written in Exercise 6a to display the first eight elements of the MESSGE array.

7. Write a program that declares three single dimension arrays named VOLTS, CURRNT, and RESIST. Each array should be declared in PROGRAM MAIN and should be capable of holding 10 real numbers. The numbers that should be stored in CURRNT are 10.62, 14.89, 13.21, 16.55, 18.62, 9.47, 6.58, 18.32, 12.15, 3.98. The numbers that should be stored in RESIST are 4, 8.5, 6, 7.35, 9, 15.3, 3, 5.4, 2.9, 4.8. Your program should pass these three arrays to a subroutine called CALCV, which should calculate the elements in the VOLTS array as the product of the equivalent elements in the CURRNT and RESIST arrays (for example, VOLTS(1) = CURRNT(1) * RESIST(1)). After CALCV has put values into the VOLTS array, the values in the array should be displayed from within the MAIN program unit.

8. Write a program that includes two subroutines named AVERGE and VRANCE. The AVERGE subroutine should calculate and return the average of the values stored in an array named TEST. The TEST array should be declared in the MAIN program unit and include the values 89, 95, 72, 83, 99, 54, 86, 75, 92, 73, 79, 75, 82, 73. The VRANCE subroutine should calculate and return the variance of the data. The variance is obtained by subtracting the average from each value in TEST, squaring the values obtained, adding them, and dividing by the number of elements in TEST. The values returned from AVERGE and VRANCE should be displayed using WRITE statements in the MAIN program unit.

9. The following declaration was used to create the FACTRS array:

```
REAL FACTRS(3,5,10)
```

Write a subroutine header and three different argument declarations for a subroutine named LOCATE that accepts the FACTRS array as an argument named XINARY.

10. Modify Program 8-9 to use adjustable array sizing for the dummy array argument NUMS in DISPLY. The row size should be declared using an argument named ROWSIZ and the column size by an argument named COLSIZ. These two arguments should also be used as final counter parameters in the subroutine's explicit and implied DO loops.

11. Write a subroutine that multiplies each element of a three-row-by-four-column integer array by an integer number. Both the array name and the number

by which each element is to be multiplied are to be passed into the subroutine as arguments.

12. Write a subroutine that adds the values of all elements in a two dimension array that is passed to the subroutine. Assume that the array is an array of real numbers having four rows and five columns.

13. Write a subroutine that adds respective values of two double dimension arrays named FIRST and SECND, respectively. Both arrays have two rows and three columns. For example, element (1,2) of the resulting array should be the sum of FIRST(1,2) and SECND(1,2).

14a. Write a subroutine that finds and displays the maximum value in a two dimension array of integers. The array should be declared as a four-row-by-five-column array of integers in the MAIN program unit.

b. Modify the subroutine written in Exercise 14a so that it also displays the row and column number of the element with the maximum value.

c. Can the subroutine you wrote for Exercise 14a be generalized to handle any size two dimension array?

8.5 Applications

Arrays are extremely useful for plotting data on either a video screen or a standard line printer. In this section we present a simple method of constructing such plots. The first application presents the basic method and uses it to produce modest plots. The second application incorporates data scaling to ensure that the plot fits within the area of the video screen or paper, regardless of the range of data plotted.

Application 1: Curve Plotting

Two basic constraints must be considered in graphing data on either a video screen or a printer. The first constraint is that both devices automatically move in a forward direction, which means that our graphs should avoid the need to "back up" (although there are methods for reversing the cursor motion on a video screen, all of our programs will be constructed to work for both printers and screens). The second constraint is that both printer paper and video displays are restricted in the horizontal direction to displaying a maximum of either 80 or 132 characters. No such restriction exists in the vertical direction because the paper length is effectively unlimited and the video display scrolls forward. For this reason our plots will always be constructed "sideways," with the *Y* axis horizontal and the *X* axis vertical. With these two constraints in mind, consider the plot shown in Figure 8-9.

In Figure 8-9, the graph is plotted with the *Y* axis displayed across the top of the graph and the *X* axis displayed down the side. Omitting, for the moment, the two header lines:

```
                    Y AXIS
+-------------------------------------------->
```

the actual graph of the data points consists of 15 individual lines, as follows;

```
Line 1:   |                                         *
Line 2:   |                                  *
Line 3:   |                            *
Line 4:   |                      *
Line 5:   |                  *
Line 6:   |             *
Line 7:   |    *
Line 8:   | *
Line 9:   |    *
Line 10:  |         *
Line 11:  |              *
Line 12:  |                   *
Line 13:  |                        *
Line 14:  |                              *
Line 15:  |                                      *
```

Notice that individually each line consists of only two printed symbols, a bar (|) and an asterisk (*). The bar is always displayed in column one, and the asterisk is positioned to indicate an appropriate *Y* value. With these points in mind, it is rather easy to construct these 15 lines. To do this we will first construct an exact image of the first line to be printed in an array of characters. After the array is constructed and printed, it will be used to construct an image of the second line. After the second image is displayed, the same array is used to construct an image of the third line, and

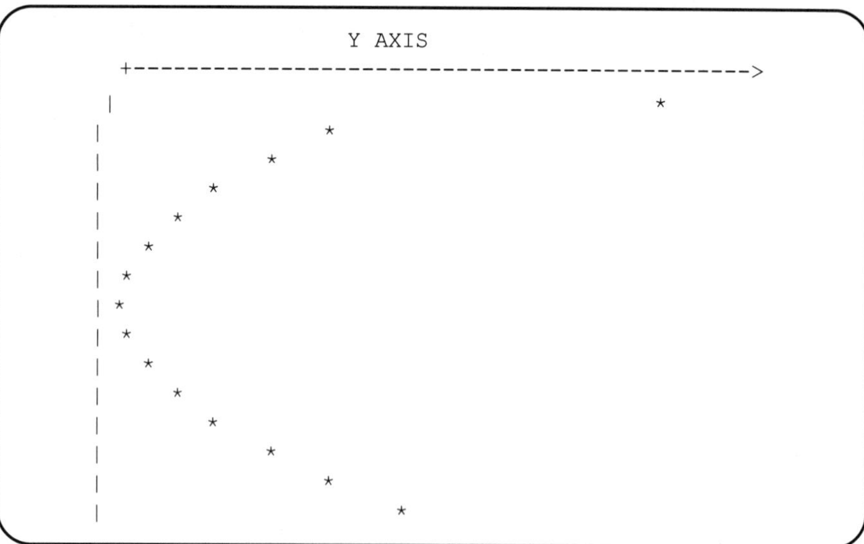

Figure 8-9 A Sample Graph

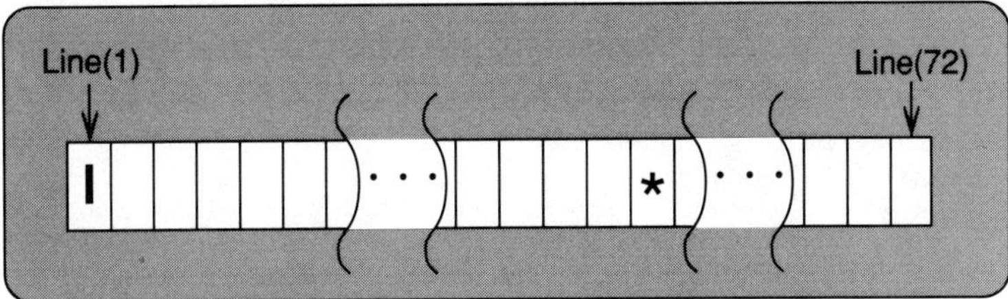

Figure 8-10 The LINE Array

so on, until all 15 lines have been displayed. To make sure that the elements in the array can be displayed on a page with sufficient room for a right-hand margin, the array will be specified as 72 characters long (any value less than the maximum horizontal width of either the paper or video screen can be used).

As illustrated in Figure 8-10, the array, called LINE, is filled with blanks, except for the first element, which stores the bar symbol, and one other element, which stores an asterisk.

Using the LINE array to store the image of each line before it is printed, our graphing approach is:

1. Store an asterisk in the desired array element
2. Print the array
3. Reset the element to a blank
4. Repeat steps 1 through 3 until the required number of lines have been displayed

These four steps are easily implemented using a DO loop having the form:

```
      DO 10 X = 1,15
       calculate a value for Y
       LINE(Y) = '*'
       WRITE(6,*) LINE
       LINE(Y) = ' '
   10 CONTINUE
```

The calculation of the Y value, which is then used as a subscript for the LINE array, depends on the graph being plotted. For the graph illustrated in Figure 8-9, the equation $Y = (X-8)^2 + 3$ was used.* Incorporating this into the DO loop yields:

```
      DO 10 X = 1,15
      Y = (X-8)**2 + 3
      LINE(Y) = '*'
      WRITE(6,*) LINE
      LINE(Y) = ' '
   10 CONTINUE
```

Program 8-10 includes this code within a working program.

* To use the Y value as a subscript for the LINE array requires that this value be an integer between the numbers 0 and 72, inclusive. The curve $Y = (X-8)^2 + 3$ was selected precisely because it yielded Y values within this range. In the next application an algorithm is presented for scaling any Y values into the required range.

Program 8.10

```
      PROGRAM MAIN
        CALL PLOT
        END
*
      SUBROUTINE PLOT
        INTEGER X,Y
        CHARACTER LINE(72)
        DATA LINE/'|',71*' '/
        DO 10 X = 1, 15
          Y = (X-8)**2 + 3
          LINE(Y) = '*'
          WRITE(6,*) LINE
          LINE(Y) = ' '
 10     CONTINUE
        RETURN
        END
```

Notice in Program 8-10 that after the LINE array is specified, a DATA statement initializes LINE(1) with the bar symbol and the remaining 71 elements with blanks. The DO loop then calculates a *Y* value, uses this value as a subscript to locate where the asterisk should be placed in the LINE array, displays the array, and restores a blank in place of the asterisk. This process is repeated fifteen times, resulting in the plot illustrated in Figure 8-11.

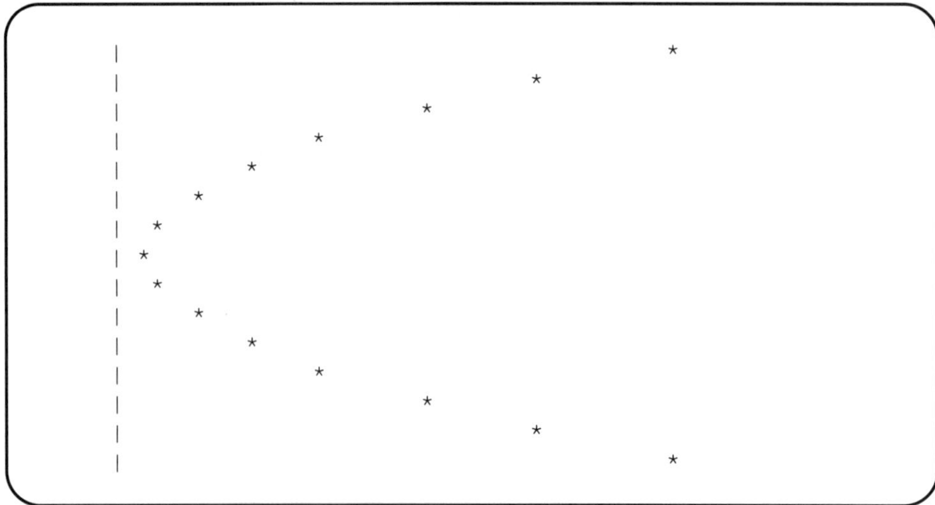

Figure 8-11 The Display Produced by Program 8-10

Program 8-11

```
      PROGRAM MAIN
        CALL PLOT
        END
*
      SUBROUTINE PLOT
        INTEGER X,Y
        CHARACTER LINE(72), YAXIS(72)
        DATA LINE/'|',71*' '/
        DATA YAXIS/'+',53*'-','>',17*' '/
        WRITE(6,*) '                         Y AXIS'
        WRITE(6,*) YAXIS
        DO 10 X = 1,15
          Y = (X-8)**2 + 3
          LINE(Y) = '*'
          WRITE(6,*) LINE
          LINE(Y) = ' '
  10    CONTINUE
        RETURN
        END
```

Two observations must be made about Program 8-10. First, a *Y* axis has not been explicitly included on the output. This is a minor omission that is rectified by Program 8-11.

Notice that Program 8-11 is essentially the same as Program 8-10 with the addition of the YAXIS array specification and initialization and the two WRITE statements. The WRITE statements are placed before the DO loop to display the header lines. Program 8-11 produces the completed plot shown in Figure 8-12.

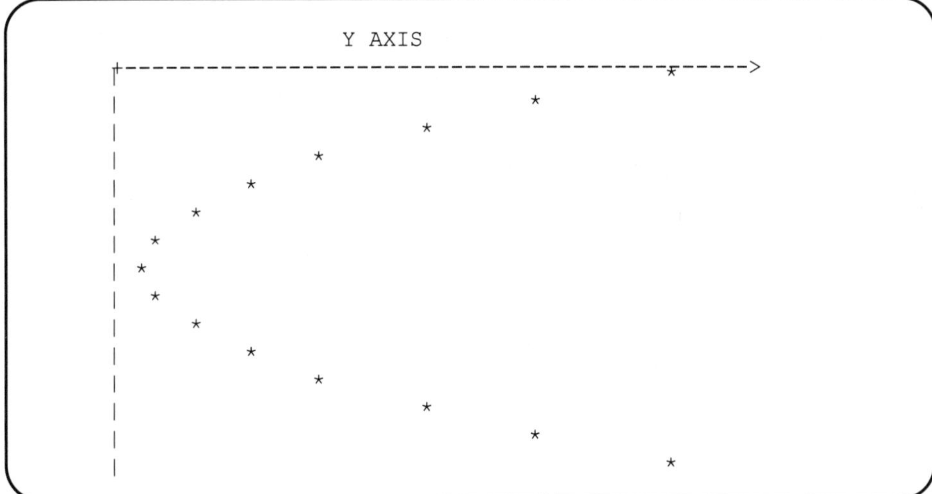

Figure 8-12 The Display Produced by Program 8-11

A more serious problem with both Program 8-10 and Program 8-11 is that negative *Y* values and *Y* values greater than 72 cannot be accommodated as a subscript to the LINE array. Accommodation of graphs with such values requires scaling of the *Y* values to fit within the LINE array's subscript range. The scaling algorithm to do this, which ensures that our plotting program works for any *Y* value, is presented in the next application.

Application 2: Data Scaling

A common problem encountered in plotting data is the need to scale values to fit within the width of the paper or video screen before a plotting routine can be used. Equation 1 provides the required scaling formula:

$$(EQ.1)\ \text{Scaled } Y \text{ value} = \frac{\text{Original } Y \text{ value} - \text{Minimum } Y \text{ value}}{\text{Maximum } Y \text{ value} - \text{Minimum } Y \text{ value}} \times (W-1)$$

where the maximum and minimum values are the respective maximum and minimum values for the complete set of data values being plotted, and *W* is the desired width of the paper or video display.

The term:

$$\frac{\text{Original } Y \text{ value} - \text{Minimum } Y \text{ value}}{\text{Maximum } Y \text{ value} - \text{Minimum } Y \text{ value}}$$

in equation 1 forces each original *Y* value to lie within the range from zero to one, with the minimum data value corresponding to zero and the maximum data value to one. Multiplying this result by the term (W–1) produces values between zero and (W–1), for a total width of *W*.

For example, the second column in Table 8-4 lists *Y* values of the equation $Y = X^3$ for values of *X* between –5 and 5, in increments of 0.5. As shown in column two, the maximum and minimum *Y* values are +125 and –125, respectively.

For purposes of illustration, assume that the width of the display area for plotting each *Y* value in column two is 72 characters wide. Also assume that a single character of this display area, for example, the bar (|), is to be used for an axis symbol. This leaves a total width, *W*, of 71 for the actual data display. Applying equation 1 to the data of column two with $W = 71$ and using the correct minimum and maximum values of –125 and 125, respectively, yields the values listed in column three of the table. Notice that the minimum value of –125 is converted to the value 0.000, and the maximum value of 125 is converted to the value 70.000. The last column in the table is the rounded, integerized values of the scaled numbers listed in the third column. Notice that the values in column four range from 0 to 70, for a total range of 71 possible *Y* values. These values can be used directly by the curve-plotting routine presented in the previous application to create a graph similar to that shown in Figure 8-13.

Program 8-12, which was used to create Figure 8-13, includes the data-scaling algorithm in the curve plotting routine used in Program 8-11.

The MAIN program unit in Program 8-12 is used to declare appropriate variables and initialize the starting value of x, the increment, the number of points to be

Table 8-4 Values of the Equation $Y = X^3$

X	*Y*	Scaled *Y*	Rounded
-5.0	-125.000	0.000	0
-4.5	-91.125	9.485	9
-4.0	-64.000	17.080	17
-3.5	-42.875	22.995	23
-3.0	-27.000	27.440	27
-2.5	-15.625	30.625	31
-2.0	-8.000	32.760	33
-1.5	-3.375	34.055	34
-1.0	-1.000	34.720	35
-0.5	-0.125	34.965	35
0.0	0.000	35.000	35
0.5	0.125	35.035	35
1.0	1.000	35.280	35
1.5	3.375	35.945	36
2.0	8.000	37.240	37
2.5	15.625	39.375	39
3.0	27.000	42.560	43
3.5	42.875	47.005	47
4.0	64.000	52.920	53
4.5	91.125	60.515	61
5.0	125.000	70.000	70

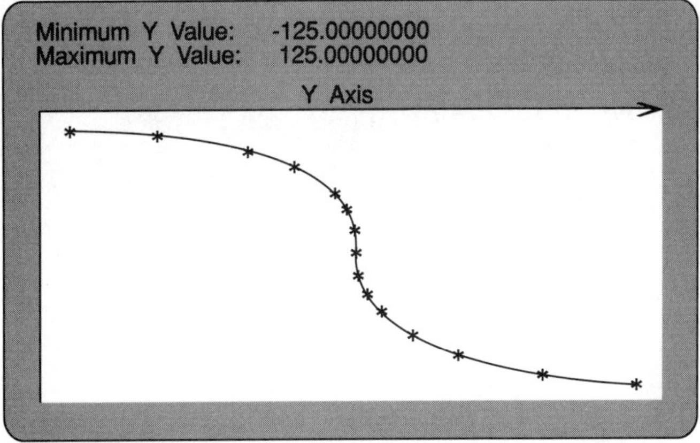

Figure 8-13 The Display Produced by Program 8-12

Program 8-12

```
      PROGRAM MAIN
        IMPLICIT NONE
        INTEGER NPTS, WIDTH, NVAL(100)
        REAL X, XINC, YMIN, YMAX, SVAL(100)
        CHARACTER LINE(72), YAXIS(72)
        DATA YAXIS/'+',70*'-','>'/
        DATA LINE/'|',71*' '/
        DATA YMAX, YMIN /1E-5,1E5/
        DATA NPTS, WIDTH, X, XINC /21, 70, -5.0, 0.5/
        CALL LOADUP(NPTS, X, XINC, SVAL, YMIN, YMAX)
        CALL SCALE(NPTS, WIDTH, YMIN, YMAX, SVAL, NVAL)
        CALL PLOT(NPTS, YMIN, YMAX, NVAL, YAXIS, LINE)
        END
*
      SUBROUTINE LOADUP(NPTS, X, XINC, SVAL, YMIN, YMAX)
        IMPLICIT NONE
        INTEGER NPTS, I
        REAL X, XINC, SVAL(*), YMIN, YMAX
*** LOAD UP THE DATA TO BE PLOTTED AND FIND THE MAX AND MIN VALUES
        DO 10 I = 1, NPTS
          SVAL(I) = X**3
          IF (SVAL(I).GT.YMAX) YMAX = SVAL(I)
          IF (SVAL(I).LT.YMIN) YMIN = SVAL(I)
          X = X + XINC
   10 CONTINUE
        RETURN
        END
*
      SUBROUTINE SCALE(NPTS, WIDTH, YMIN, YMAX, SVAL, NVAL)
        IMPLICIT NONE
        INTEGER NPTS, WIDTH, NVAL(*), I
        REAL YMIN, YMAX, SVAL(*), FVAL
*** SCALE ALL Y VALUES TO BE PLOTTED
        DO 15 I = 1, NPTS
          FVAL = ( (SVAL(I) - YMIN)/(YMAX - YMIN) ) * WIDTH
          NVAL(I) = INT(FVAL + .5)
   15   CONTINUE
        RETURN
        END
*
      SUBROUTINE PLOT(NPTS, YMIN, YMAX, NVAL, YAXIS, LINE)
        IMPLICIT NONE
        INTEGER NPTS, NVAL(*), I
```

(Continued on next page)

(Continued from previous page)

```
      REAL YMIN, YMAX
      CHARACTER YAXIS(72), LINE(72)
*** PRODUCE THE PLOT
      WRITE(6,*)'MINIMUM Y VALUE: ',YMIN
      WRITE(6,*)'MAXIMUM Y VALUE: ',YMAX
      WRITE(6,*)'                                     Y AXIS'
      WRITE(6,*) YAXIS
      DO 20 I = 1, NPTS
        LINE(NVAL(I)+2) = '*'
        WRITE(6,*) LINE
        LINE(NVAL(I)+2) = ' '
   20 CONTINUE
      RETURN
      END
```

calculated, and the width of the display using DATA statements. Once these values are set, the three subroutines, LOADUP( ), SCALE( ), and PLOT( ) are called. Notice that the MAIN program unit and all of the subroutines use the IMPLICIT NONE statement. As described in Chapter 2, this statement disables FORTRAN's implicit data typing and forces all variables to be explicitly declared. For a program that uses many variables, as does Program 8-12, it is useful to employ the IMPLICIT NONE statement to ensure that no variable or argument is inadvertently left out of a declaration statement and mistyped implicitly.

The LOADUP( ) subroutine in used in Program 8-12 to calculate the actual Y values to be plotted and the maximum and minimum of these values. Within this subroutine the values are stored in the local array named SVAL. As the dummy argument names used in the subroutine are the same as the actual argument names used in the CALL statement, and all arguments have the correct data types, the MAIN program unit will have valid data in SVAL, YMIN, and YMAX when LOADUP( ) is finished executing. The values stored in the first 21 elements of the SVAL array are the numbers listed in column two of Table 8-4.

The SCALE( ) subroutine performs the scaling algorithm presented in this application. Using the values in its arguments YMIN, YMAX, and WIDTH, it converts the Y values in the SVAL array to scaled and rounded values in the NVAL array. As with the SVAL array, even though NVAL is declared as having 100 elements in MAIN, only the first 21 elements of the array are used. The scaled and rounded values computed for NVAL correspond to the values listed in column 4 of Table 8-4. Within SCALE( ), the values calculated as FVAL correspond, individually, to the values in column three of Table 8-4.

Finally, the PLOT( ) subroutine is called. This subroutine performs the tasks described in the previous application to produce the graph illustrated in Figure 8-13.

Additional Exercises for Chapter 8

1. Enter and run Program 8-11 on your computer system.
2. Modify Program 8-11 to plot the curve $Y = X^3 - 4X^2 + 3X + 2$ for X equal to 0, 1, 2, 3, 4, 5, and 6.
3. When the switch illustrated in Figure 8-14 is closed at time $t = 0$, the voltage, V, across the capacitor is given by the equation $V = E[1 - e^{-t/(RC)}]$, where E is the voltage of the battery, R is the circuit resistance, C is the value of the capacitance, and t is time in seconds. Assuming that $E = 60$, $R = 2500.5$, and $C = .005$, modify Program 8-11 to plot the voltage across the capacitor from $t = 1$ to $t = 30$, in increments of 1 second.

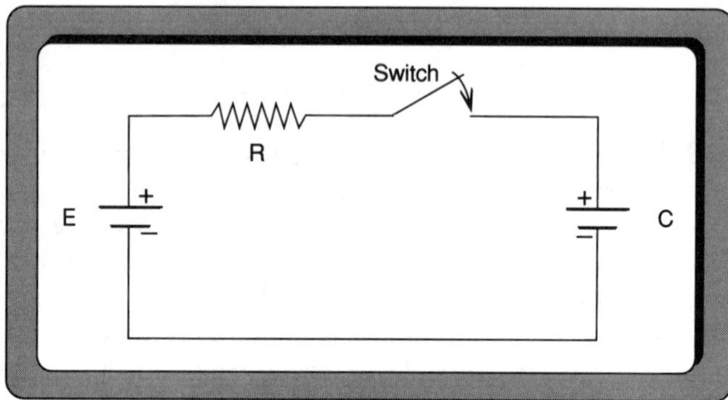

Figure 8-14 A Simple RC Circuit

4. Enter and run Program 8-12 on your computer system.
5. Modify Program 8-11 to plot the curve $Y = X^3 - 4X^2 + 3X + 10$ for X between 1 and +5, in increments of 0.25.
6. Modify Program 8-11 to plot the curve $Y = 4X^3 - X^4$ for X between –10 and +10, in increments of 0.5.
7. Figure 8-15 illustrates a *harmonic oscillator*, which consists of an object of mass M fastened to one end of a spring. The other end of the spring is attached to a wall, and the object is free to slide over a frictionless surface. Assuming the object is initially at rest (that is, the spring is neither stretched nor compressed) and then pulled to position A at time $t = 0$, the position of the mass at any other time, t, is described by the equation $X = A\cos[(\sqrt{k/m})\,t]$, where k is the spring constant, in Newtons/meter; m is the mass, in units of kilograms; and A is the initial displacement, in units of centimeters. Assuming A is 100 centimeters, k is 50 Newtons/meter, and m is 1 kilogram, modify Program 8-12 to plot the displacement of the mass from $t = 0$ to $t = 60$ seconds, in increments of 1 second. (*Hint:* Remember to convert all angles to radian measure.)

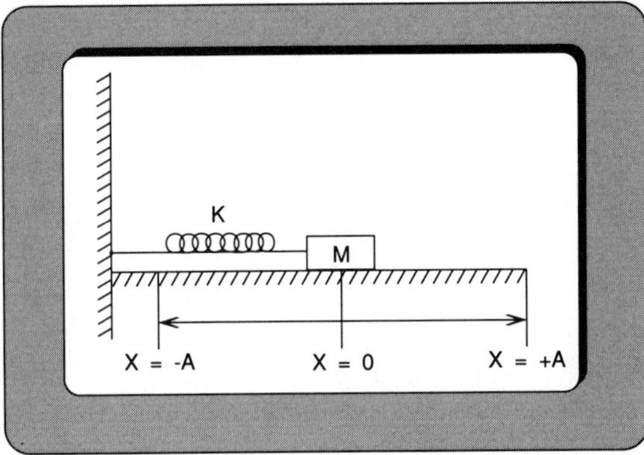

Figure 8-15 A Harmonic Oscillator

8. Modify Program 8-12 to plot the voltage across the capacitor illustrated in Figure 8-14 from $t = 0$ to $t = 30$ seconds, in increments of 1 second. For this problem, assume that $E = 100$ volts, $R = 2500.5$, and $C = .005$.

8.6 Common Programming Errors

There are seven common errors associated with using arrays.

1. The first error is forgetting to declare the array. This error results in a compiler error message equivalent to "SUBSCRIPT USED WITH UNDIMENSIONED VARIABLE" each time a subscripted variable is encountered on the left-hand side of an assignment statement or in a READ statement. When the subscripted variable is used on the right-hand side of an assignment statement, in a PRINT statement, or in a WRITE statement, the compiler interprets the variable as a function. In this case a message such as "UNRESOLVED EXTERNAL" or "UNDEFINED FUNCTION" is displayed.
2. The most common programming error is to use a subscript that references a nonexistent array element—for example, declaring the array to be of size 20 and using a subscript value of 25. This error is typically not detected by most FORTRAN compilers. It will, however, result in a runtime error that results either in a program crash or in a value that has no relation to the intended element being accessed from memory. In either case, it is usually an extremely troublesome error to locate. The only solution to this problem is to make sure, either by specific programming statements or by careful coding, that each subscript references a valid array element.
3. Related to the previous error is not using a large enough terminal value in a DO loop counter to cycle through all the array elements. This error usually occurs when an array is initially specified to be of size *N* and there is a DO loop within the program of the form DO 10 I = 1, *N*. The array size is then expanded, but the programmer forgets to change the interior DO loop

parameters. Using the PARAMETER statement presented in Section 3.4 can ensure that this error will not occur. For example, the statements:

```
INTEGER N
PARAMETER (N=30)
INTEGER NUMS (N)
```

are valid. The DO loop can then be written as:

```
DO 10 I=1,N
```

4. Using a variable name to specify an array. For example, if N is an integer variable, the statements:

```
INTEGER NUMS(N)
N = 30
```

cannot be used to specify an array of size 30. Similarly, the sequence:

```
N = 30
INTEGER NUMS(N)
```

is also incorrect, because all declaration statements must precede any executable statement. The correct method of using N as an array size is to make it a named constant using the parameters statement as illustrated above in error 3.

5. Forgetting to initialize the array. Although many compilers automatically set all elements of integer and real value arrays to zero, and all elements of character arrays to blanks, it is up to the programmer to ensure that each array is correctly initialized before processing of array elements begins.
6. Using the same name for both an array and a scalar variable. Once an array name is declared, this same name cannot be used as a scalar variable.
7. Omitting the comma before setting the subscript parameters in an implied DO loop. For example, writing WRITE(6,*)(A(I) I = 1,5) instead of WRITE(6,*) (A(I), I = 1,5). The reason for this error is that the first comma is not present in the more commonly used DO statement.

8.7 Things to Remember

1. A single dimension array is a data structure that can be used to store a list of values of the same data type. Such arrays are either explicitly data typed and sized using a data declaration statement or implicitly typed using a DIMENSION statement. Explicit array declarations require listing the data type of the array, its name, and the array size. For example, the declaration:

```
INTEGER NUM(100)
```

creates an array of 100 integers. Integer and real arrays can also be data typed implicitly using a DIMENSION statement. For example, the statement:

```
DIMENSION NUM(100), AREA(25)
```

creates an integer array named NUM with 100 elements and a real array named AREA consisting of 25 elements.

2. Array elements are stored in sequential locations in memory and referenced using the array name and a subscript. For example, the variable NUMS(34) refers to the 34th element in the NUMS array. Any integer-value expression can also be used as a subscript.
3. Arrays may be initialized using DATA statements. The general form of a DATA statement is:

```
DATA variable list /value list/, variable list /value list/ ...
```

Each value list must have the same number of values as there are in its associated variable list. For example, the statement:

```
DATA A,B,C,D / 22.4, 16.3, 71.2, 18.6/
```

contains one variable list and one value list, with each list having the same number of items. The first value is assigned to the first variable, the second value to the second variable, and so on, until all variables have been initialized.
4. Arrays may be referenced using implied DO loops. An implied DO loop for a single dimension array has the form:

```
(array name(I), I = initial value, terminal value, increment)
```

where the subscript I may be replaced by any other integer variable name. Implied DO loops may be used with either DATA, READ, PRINT, or WRITE statements for array input and output. Both list-directed and format-controlled versions of the input and output statements can be used with the implied DO loop. Examples of these statements are:

```
READ(5,*) (A(I), I = 1,10)
READ(5,15) (VOLTS(K), K = 2,12,2)
PRINT *, (NUMS(M), M = 5,16)
PRINT 20, (NUMS(J), J = 2,12,2)
WRITE(6,*) (FACTOR(NNN), NNN = 1,15)
WRITE(6,20) (FACTOR(NNN), NNN = 1,15)
```

5. Arrays may also be referenced by name, without any subscript value, in DATA, READ, PRINT, and WRITE statements. For input and output statements, both list-directed and format-controlled versions can be used. When referenced by name in a READ statement, sufficient values must be entered for each element in the array. When referenced by name in either a PRINT or a WRITE statement, all element values are displayed.
6. FORTRAN permits the specification of arrays with a maximum of seven dimensions. For example, a two dimension array is declared by listing both a row and a column size with the data type and name of the array. Thus, the specification:

```
REAL WATTS(5,7)
```

creates a two dimension array consisting of five rows and seven columns of real values. Multidimensional arrays may also be implicitly declared using DIMENSION statements.

8.8 A Closer Look: Sorting Methods

Most programmers encounter the need to sort a list of data items at some time in their programming careers. For example, experimental results might have to be arranged in either increasing (ascending) or decreasing (descending) order for statistical analysis, lists of names may have to be sorted in alphabetical order, or a list of dates may have to be rearranged in ascending date order.

For sorting data, two major categories of sorting techniques exist, called internal and external sorts, respectively. *Internal sorts* are used when the data list is not too large and the complete list can be stored within the computer's memory, usually in an array. *External sorts* are used for much larger data sets that are stored in large external disk or tape files and cannot be accommodated within the computer's memory as a complete unit.

In this section we present two common internal sorts, called the selection sort and the exchange sort, respectively. Although the exchange sort, also known as a "bubble sort," is the more common of the two, we will see that the selection sort is easier and frequently more efficient.

Selection Sort

In a selection sort the smallest (or largest) value is initially selected from the complete list of data and exchanged with the first element in the list. After this first selection and exchange, the next smallest (or largest) element in the revised list is selected and exchanged with the second element in the list. Since the smallest element is already in the first position in the list, this second pass need only consider the second through last elements. For a list consisting of *n* elements, this process is repeated *n*–1 times, with each pass through the list requiring one less comparison than the previous pass.

For example, consider the list of numbers illustrated in Figure 8-16. The first pass through the initial list results in the number 32 being selected and exchanged with the first element in the list. The second pass, made on the reordered list, results

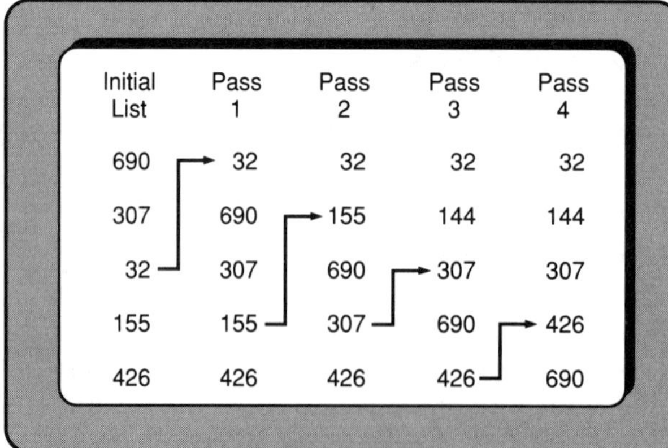

Figure 8-16 A Sample Selection Sort

Program 8-13

```
      PROGRAM MAIN
        INTEGER NUMS(10)
        DATA NUMS/22,55,67,98,45,32,101,99,73,10/
        CALL SLSORT(NUMS)
        END
*
      SUBROUTINE SLSORT(NUMS)
        IMPLICIT NONE
        INTEGER NUMS(*), MOVES, I, J, MIN, MININD, TEMP
        MOVES = 0
        DO 10 I = 1, 9
          MIN = NUMS(I)
          MININD = I
          DO 5 J = I+1, 10
            IF (NUMS(J).LT.MIN) THEN
              MIN = NUMS(J)
              MININD = J
            ENDIF
 5        CONTINUE
*** PERFORM THE SWITCH
          IF(MIN .LT. NUMS(I)) THEN
            TEMP = NUMS(I)
            NUMS(I) = NUMS(MININD)
            NUMS(MININD) = TEMP
            MOVES = MOVES + 1
          ENDIF
10      CONTINUE
        WRITE(6,*) 'THE SORTED LIST, IN ASCENDING ORDER, IS:'
        WRITE(6,*) (NUMS(I), I = 1, 10)
        WRITE(6,*) MOVES, ' MOVES WERE MADE TO SORT THIS LIST'
        RETURN
        END
```

in the number 155 being selected from the second through fifth elements. This value is then exchanged with the second element in the list. The third pass selects the number 307 from the third through fifth elements in the list and exchanges this value with the third element. Finally, the fourth and last pass through the list selects the remaining minimum value and exchanges it with the fourth list element. Although each pass in this example resulted in an exchange, no exchange would have been made in a pass if the smallest value were already in the correct location.

Program 8-13 implements a selection sort for a list of 10 numbers that are stored in an array named NUMS. For later comparison to an exchange sort, the number of actual moves made by the program to get the data into sorted order is counted and displayed.

Program 8-13 uses a nested DO loop to perform the selection sort. The outer DO loop causes nine passes to be made through the data, which is one less than the total number of data items in the list. For each pass, the variable MIN is initially assigned the value NUMS(I), where I is the outer DO loop's counter variable. Since I begins at 1 and ends at 9, each element in the list is successively designated as the next exchange element.

The inner loop is used in Program 8-13 to cycle through the elements below the designated exchange element to select the next smallest value. Thus, this loop begins at the index value I+1 and continues through the end of the list. When a new minimum is found, its value and position in the list are stored in the variables named MIN and MININD, respectively. Upon completion of the inner loop, an exchange is made only if a value less than that in the designated exchange position was found.

Following is the output produced by Program 8-13.

```
THE SORTED LIST, IN ASCENDING ORDER, IS:
           10     22     32     45     55     67     73     98     99    101
           8 MOVES WERE MADE TO SORT THIS LIST
```

Clearly, the number of moves displayed depends on the initial order of the values in the list. An advantage of the selection sort is that the maximum number of moves that must be made is $n-1$, where n is the number of items in the list. Further, each move is a final move that results in an element residing in its final location in the sorted list.

A disadvantage of the selection sort is that $n(n-1)/2$ comparisons are always required, regardless of the initial arrangement of the data. This number of comparisons is obtained as follows: the last pass always requires one comparison, the next-to-last pass requires two comparisons, and so on, to the first pass, which requires $n-1$ comparisons. Thus, the total number of comparisons is:

$$1 + 2 + 3 + \ldots n-1 = n(n-1)/2$$

Exchange Sort

In an exchange sort, successive values in the list are compared, beginning with the first two elements. If the list is to be sorted in ascending (from smallest to largest) order, the smaller value of the two being compared is always placed before the larger value. For lists sorted in descending (from largest to smallest) order, the smaller of the two values being compared is always placed after the larger value.

For example, assuming that a list of values is to be sorted in ascending order, if the first element in the list is larger than the second, the two elements are interchanged. Then the second and third elements are compared. Again, if the second element is larger than the third, these two elements are interchanged. This process continues until the last two elements have been compared and exchanged, if necessary. If no exchanges were made during this initial pass through the data, the data is in the correct order and the process is finished; otherwise, a second pass is made through the data, starting from the first element and stopping at the next-to-last element. The reason for stopping at the next-to-last element on the second pass is that the first pass always results in the most positive value "sinking" to the bottom of the list.

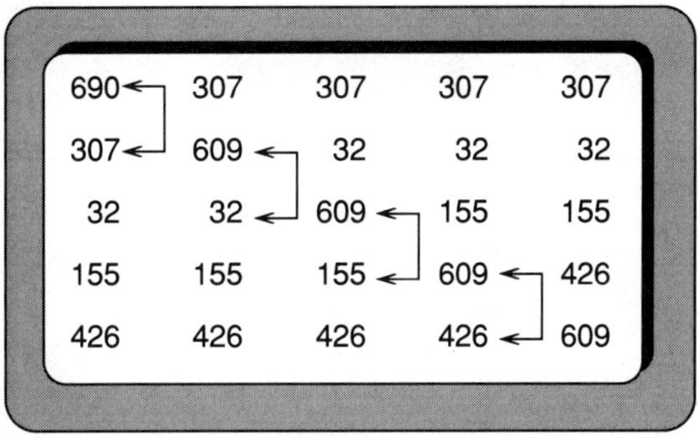

690	307	307	307	307
307	609	32	32	32
32	32	609	155	155
155	155	155	609	426
426	426	426	426	609

Figure 8-17 The First Pass of an Exchange Sort

As a specific example of this process, consider the list of numbers illustrated in Figure 8-17. The first comparison results in the interchange of the first two element values, 690 and 307. The next comparison, between elements two and three in the revised list, results in the interchange of values between the second and third elements, 609 and 32. This comparison and possible switching of adjacent values is continued until the last two elements have been compared and possibly switched. This process completes the first pass through the data and results in the largest number moving to the bottom of the list. As the largest value sinks to its resting place at the bottom of the list, the smaller elements slowly rise, or "bubble," to the top of the list. This bubbling effect of the smaller elements gave rise to the name "bubble sort" for this sorting algorithm.

As the first pass through the list ensures that the largest value always moves to the bottom of the list, the second pass stops at the next-to-last element. This process continues with each pass stopping at one higher element than the previous pass, until either n–1 passes through the list have been completed or no exchanges are necessary in any single pass. In both cases the resulting list is in sorted order.

Program 8-14 implements an exchange sort for the same list of 10 numbers used in Program 8-13. For comparison to the earlier selection sort, the number of adjacent moves (exchanges) made by the program is also counted and displayed.

As illustrated in Program 8-14, the exchange sort requires a nested loop. The outer loop in Program 8-14 is a WHILE loop that checks if any exchanges were made in the last pass. It is the inner DO loop that does the actual comparison and exchanging of adjacent element values.

Immediately before the inner loop's DO statement is encountered, the value of the logical variable OUTORD is set to .TRUE., to indicate that the list is initially out of order (not sorted) and to force the first pass through the list. If the inner loop then detects an element is out of order, OUTORD is again set to .TRUE., which indicates that the list is still unsorted. The OUTORD variable is then used by the outer loop to determine whether another pass through the data is to be made. Thus, the sort is stopped either because OUTORD is .FALSE. after at least one pass has been completed or n–1 passes through the data have been made. In both cases, the resulting list is in sorted order.

Program 8-14

```
      PROGRAM MAIN
        INTEGER NUMS(10)
        DATA NUMS/22,55,67,98,45,32,101,99,73,10/
        CALL EXSORT(NUMS)
        END
*
      SUBROUTINE EXSORT(NUMS)
        IMPLICIT NONE
        INTEGER NUMS(*), I, MOVES, NPTS, TEMP
        LOGICAL OUTORD
        MOVES = 0
        NPTS = 10
        OUTORD = .TRUE.
  5     IF (OUTORD .AND. NPTS .GT. 1) THEN
          OUTORD = .FALSE.
          DO 10 I = 1, NPTS - 1
            IF (NUMS(I).GT.NUMS(I+1)) THEN
              TEMP = NUMS(I+1)
              NUMS(I+1) = NUMS(I)
              NUMS(I) = TEMP
              OUTORD = .TRUE.
              MOVES = MOVES + 1
            ENDIF
 10       CONTINUE
          NPTS = NPTS - 1
          GO TO 5
        ENDIF
        WRITE(6,*) 'THE SORTED LIST, IN ASCENDING ORDER, IS:'
        WRITE(6,*) (NUMS(I), I = 1, 10)
        WRITE(6,*) MOVES, ' MOVES WERE MADE TO SORT THIS LIST'
        RETURN
        END
```

Following is the output produced by Program 8-14.

```
THE SORTED LIST, IN ASCENDING ORDER, IS:
    10     22     32     45     55     67     73     98     99     101
    20 MOVES WERE MADE TO SORT THIS LIST
```

As with the selection sort, the number of moves required by an exchange sort depends on the initial order of the values in the list.

An advantage of the exchange sort is that processing is terminated whenever a sorted list is encountered. In the best case, when the data is in sorted order to begin with, an exchange sort requires no moves (the same for the selection sort) and only n–1 comparisons (the selection sort always requires $n(n-1)/2$ comparisons). In the worst case, when the data is in reverse sorted order, the selection sort does better. Here both sorts require $n(n-1)/2$ comparisons, but the selection sort needs only n–1 moves while the exchange sort needs $n(n-1)/2$ moves. The additional moves required by the exchange sort result from the intermediate exchanges between adjacent elements to "settle" each element into its final position. In this regard the selection sort is superior, because no intermediate moves are necessary. For random data, such as that used in Programs 8-13 and 8-14, the selection sort generally performs equal to or better than the exchange sort.

LAB SET FOR CHAPTER 8

LAB ASSIGNMENT 16

The results of a survey of local households have been entered into a file. Each record contains data for one household and consists of a four digit-integer identification number, the household's annual income, and the number of people in the house. Write a program to read the survey results into three single dimensioned arrays and perform the following tasks:

1. Use a heading subroutine to place your name and page number on your output report.
2. As the data is input, count the number of households included in the survey. Additionally print a three-column table displaying the data being read. Terminate the input of records with the END option. You may assume that no more than 25 households were surveyed when dimensioning your arrays.
3. Calculate the average household income and list the identification number and incomes of all households that exceed the average.
4. Determine the percentage of households having income below the poverty level. The poverty level income, P, for each household may be computed according to the formula:

```
P = $3750.00 + $750.00 * (M - 2)
```

where M is the number of people in a household.

Test your program using the following data:

Identification Number	Annual Income	Household Members
1041	$12,180	4
1062	13,240	3
1327	19,800	2
1483	22,458	8
1900	17,000	2
2112	18,125	7
2345	15,623	2
3210	3,200	6
3600	6,500	5
3601	11,970	2
4725	8,900	3
6217	10,000	2
9280	6,200	1

LAB ASSIGNMENT 17

Read in any number of test scores and store them in an array using the END option. "Echo check" (write out) the entered data. The test scores will be numbers between 0.00 and 100.00 inclusive. You must use subroutines to write your name, page number and the second heading on each page, which can be passed as arguments to the subroutine.

1. Page 1 is to contain:
   a. A heading signifying the programmer and page number.
   b. A second heading with "ECHO CHECK" triple-spaced below the first heading.
   c. Double-spaced below this second heading, a list of the test scores. Single-space each grade.
   d. Illustration of Page 1:

```
YOUR NAME                                         PAGE  1


                         ECHO CHECK

                           XXX.XX
                           XXX.XX
```

2. Page 2 is to contain:
   a. A heading with your name and page number.
   b. A second heading, "GRADES IN DESCENDING ORDER", triple-paced below the first heading.
   c. Double-spaced below this second heading, a list of scores in descending order (highest to lowest). Single-space each grade.
   d. Illustration of Page 2:

```
YOUR NAME                                         PAGE  2


                  GRADES IN DESCENDING ORDER

                          100.00
                          XXX.XX
```

3. Page 3 is to contain:
   a. A heading with your name and page number.
   b. A second heading, "GRADES IN ASCENDING ORDER", triple-spaced below the first heading.
   c. Double-spaced below this second heading, a list of scores in ascending order (lowest to highest). Single-space each grade.

d. Illustration of Page 3:

```
YOUR NAME                                              PAGE  3


                      GRADES IN ASCENDING ORDER

                                 0.00
                               XXX.XX
```

4. Page 4 is to contain:
   a. A heading with your name and page number.
   b. A second heading, "STATISTICAL INFORMATION", triple-spaced below the first heading.
   c. The next lines, double-spaced, consisting of:

```
HIGHEST SCORE =

LOWEST SCORE =

SUM OF SCORES =

AVERAGE SCORE =
```

LAB ASSIGNMENT 18

Write a program to sum the rows and columns of a two dimensional array and search the array for all occurrences of the item stored in the variable MVAL, keeping a count of the occurrences. The array is to be 3 rows by 10 columns. The data from the array is to be input from three records of a data file, with each record having the format specification 10I2. The value of MVAL is to be read from the fourth data record in the file, which has a format specification I2.

The output of the program should be the array elements, in row-order under the format specification 10I5, and the sum of each row and column. Search the values entered from the data file. After the search is complete, write a message that says: "THE VALUE mval OCCURRED IN THE ARRAY nnn TIMES", where mval is the value in MVAL and NNN is the count of occurrences, the sum of each row and column.

```
Data Set 1:   12   4  66  89   5   3  14  36   9  10
              14   3  23  65  14   2   5  28  14   9
               3   5  78  14   8  90   3  14   6   5
       MVAL = 14


Data Set 2:   22  77  68   7   4  55  23  12   1  17
              55   6   8   2   1   6  45  55   1  78
              55  55  55   3  67  55  89   4  55  16
       MVAL = 55
```

LAB ASSIGNMENT 19

For this assignment use the following test data:

STUDENT	TEST 1	TEST 2	TEST 3	TEST 4
9436	100.0	100.0	100.0	100.0
8342	88.5	79.9	83.0	91.2
5311	55.4	63.0	77.5	88.3
4667	100.0	99.6	93.3	88.4
6923	87.4	81.0	83.6	87.5
4283	83.2	0.0	55.3	22.2
0197	88.0	88.0	88.0	88.0
9500	67.9	68.3	69.1	66.6
2042	75.3	85.0	88.0	82.5
7354	55.5	30.9	19.4	55.0
1234	0.0	0.0	0.0	0.0
2945	58.7	63.5	70.1	85.2
9000	90.0	77.3	85.1	95.8
1077	43.1	88.8	68.7	100.0

Using this data, two separate reports are to be prepared. The first report is to echo the data (display exactly as entered) and calculate the average test grade for each student. The second report is to list the student ID and average in sequence with the highest average first followed by the next highest average, etc. (average grades from highest to lowest).

The grades are to be stored in a two dimensional array named GRADES. This array is to be a 30-row by 6-column array, with the sixth column containing the student's average grade. Since there are not 30 students in the existing class, the first number input to your program is the number of students in the class.

Both reports are to contain your name, page number, and a centered title. These items are to be written using a subroutine that accepts the page number and report title as arguments. Following is an illustration of the desired output:

Sample of Page 1:

```
JOHN DOE                                                        PAGE 1


                              FINAL AVERAGES


STUDENT ID     TEST 1     TEST 2     TEST 3     TEST 4      AVERAGE
  XXXX         XXX.X      XXX.X      XXX.X      XXX.X        XXX.X
  XXXX         XXX.X      XXX.X      XXX.X      XXX.X        XXX.X
   .             .          .          .          .            .
   .             .          .          .          .            .
  XXXX         XXX.X      XXX.X      XXX.X      XXX.X        XXX.X
```

Sample of Page 2:

```
JOHN DOE                                                        PAGE 2


                          FINAL RANKINGS

                     STUDENT ID           AVERAGE
                        XXXX               XXX.X
                        XXXX               XXX.X
                         .                   .
                         .                   .
                        XXXX               XXX.X
```

LAB ASSIGNMENT 20

You will be given the length, l, width, w, and height, h, of ten rectangular boxes. For each box you are to calculate:

1. The volume, v, of the box, where v = l*w*h
2. The surface area, sa, of the box, where sa = 2(l*w + w*h + h*l)
3. The length of edges, le, of the box, where le = 4(l + w + h)

Each of the above calculations is to be performed using a statement function. All information about a box must be stored in a two dimensional array. The array is to have ten rows and six columns, using one row for each box and one column for the length, width, height, volume, surface area, and length of edges, respectively.

After the array described above has been filled, your program is to find the boxes having the largest and smallest length, width, height, volume, surface area, and length of edges, respectively. This information should be sorted in either a two dimensional array or in two one dimensional arrays.

Requirements:

1. Your program must use three statement functions.
2. Your program must use one function subprogram that determines the largest value in a set of values passed to it and one function subprogram that deter-

mines the smallest value in a set of values passed to it. (Hint: each function program will be called six times.) Following is a sample of the output:

```
YOUR NAME                                                    PAGE 1

BOX  LENGTH  WIDTH  HEIGHT  VOLUME  SURFACE AREA  LEN. OF EDGES
 1    --.--  --.--  --.--    --.--     --.--         --.--
 2      "      "      "        "         "             "
 .      "      "      "        "         "             "
 .      "      "      "        "         "             "
10    --.--  --.--  --.--    --.--     --.--         --.--


YOUR NAME                                                   PAGE 2

         LENGTH  WIDTH  HEIGHT  VOLUME  SURFACE AREA  LEN. OF EDGES

LARGEST    1       4      6       3         10             8
SMALLEST   2       1      7       5          8             9
```

For your program, use the following test data:

```
BOX  LENGTH   WIDTH   HEIGHT
---  ------   -----   ------

 1     5.25   12.25    8.00
 2     6.78    6.93   10.54
 3    10.86    7.86    4.25
 4    12.54    5.28   11.75
 5     7.89   12.23    5.80
 6     8.26   10.95   12.62
 7    14.00   11.75    6.93
 8     9.75   14.80   13.77
 9     3.46    3.45    7.40
10    11.54    6.54   14.25
```

9 Numerical Techniques and Applications

Chapter Nine

9.1 Solving Simultaneous Linear Equations

9.2 Root Finding

9.3 Numerical Integration

9.4 Common Programming Errors

9.5 Things to Remember

In this chapter we present and apply several programming techniques to solve a variety of commonly encountered numerical applications. The solving of simultaneous equations is presented first. This is followed by root finding and numerical integration techniques.

9.1 Solving Simultaneous Linear Equations

A linear equation in two unknowns, x and y, is an equation of the form:

$$ax + by = k \quad (1)$$

where a, b, and k are known numbers, and a and b are not both zero. For example, the equation $3x + 2y = 10$ is linear because it has the form of equation 1, with $a = 3$, $b = 2$, and $k = 10$. Although we have defined a linear equation for two unknowns, the definition may be extended to include any number of unknowns. For example, the equation $x + 3y + 2z = 5$ is a linear equation in the three unknowns x, y, and z. What makes the equation linear is that each unknown quantity is raised only to the first power and is multiplied by a known number.

Two Linear Equations with Two Unknowns

A simultaneous set of two linear equations in two unknowns are two linear equations having the general form:

$$a_1x + b_1y = k_1$$
$$a_2x + b_2y = k_2$$

where x and y are the unknowns. For example, the equations:

$$2.3x + 4y = 21.75$$
$$3x + 1.5y = 13.5$$

are a simultaneous set of two linear equations in two unknowns. Here the constants a_1, b_1, k_1, a_2, b_2, and k_2 are the numbers 2.3, 4, 21.75, 3, 1.5, and 13.5, respectively, and the unknowns are the values of x and y that satisfy both equations.

The solution to two simultaneous linear equations in two unknowns, if one exists, can easily be solved for using Cramer's rule, which requires the use of determinants. A determinant is a square array of elements enclosed in straight lines, such as:

$$\begin{vmatrix} 3 & 6 \\ 2 & 5 \end{vmatrix}$$

that has the same number of rows as it has columns and can be evaluated to yield a result. The number of rows or columns in a determinant determines its order. For example, the determinant:

$$\begin{vmatrix} 6 & 9 \\ 0 & -2 \end{vmatrix}$$

is a second-order determinant, because it has two rows and two columns. The general form of a second-order determinant is:

$$\begin{vmatrix} a_1 & b_1 \\ a_2 & b_2 \end{vmatrix}$$

where a_1 and b_1 refer to the first and second elements in the first row, respectively, and a_2 and b_2 refer to the first and second elements of the second row, respectively. The value of this determinant is then calculated as $a_1 * b_2 - a_2 * b_1$. Thus, the value of the determinant:

$$\begin{vmatrix} 3 & 6 \\ 2 & 5 \end{vmatrix}$$

is $(3*5) - (2*6) = 3$, and:

$$\begin{vmatrix} 6 & 9 \\ 0 & -2 \end{vmatrix}$$

is $(6*(-2)) - (0*9) = -12$.

Let us now relate the evaluation of determinants to solving sets of two linear equations. Cramer's rule states that the solution of the set of linear equations:

$$a_1x + b_1y = k_1$$
$$a_2x + b_2y = k_2$$

is:

$$x = \frac{\begin{vmatrix} k_1 & b_1 \\ k_2 & b_2 \end{vmatrix}}{\begin{vmatrix} a_1 & k_1 \\ a_2 & b_2 \end{vmatrix}}$$

and:

$$y = \frac{\begin{vmatrix} a_1 & k_1 \\ a_2 & k_2 \end{vmatrix}}{\begin{vmatrix} a_1 & b_1 \\ a_2 & b_2 \end{vmatrix}}$$

As an example using these formulas, consider the set of linear equations:

$$2x + 3y = 130$$
$$10x + 5y = 330$$

Using Cramer's rule, we obtain the solution for this set of equations as:

$$x = \frac{\begin{vmatrix} 130 & 3 \\ 330 & 5 \end{vmatrix}}{\begin{vmatrix} 2 & 3 \\ 10 & 5 \end{vmatrix}} = \frac{(130 * 5) - (330 * 3)}{(2 * 5) - (10 * 3)} = \frac{650 - 990}{10 - 30} = \frac{-340}{-20} = 17$$

$$y = \frac{\begin{vmatrix} 2 & 130 \\ 10 & 330 \end{vmatrix}}{\begin{vmatrix} 2 & 3 \\ 10 & 5 \end{vmatrix}} = \frac{(2 * 330) - (10 * 130)}{(2 * 5) - (10 * 3)} = \frac{660 - 1300}{10 - 30} = \frac{-640}{-20} = 32$$

Notice that the same determinant is used as the denominator in solving for both unknowns. When this denominator determinant is equal to zero, no unique solution can be found that solves the equations. Also notice that the numerator used in solving for x is the same as the denominator, with the first column replaced by the coefficients on the right side of the equations (k_1 and k_2). Likewise, the numerator in the solution for y replaces the second column of the denominator determinant with the coefficients k_1 and k_2. This pattern lends itself to ease of programming and also carries over to the solution of a larger number of equations.

Program 9-1 allows us to enter the numerical coefficients for two linear equations and solve for the two unknowns, x and y, when a unique solution exists. The values of all three determinants required to solve the set of two linear equations are evaluated using a single subprogram function.

Program 9-1

```
      PROGRAM MAIN
        CALL SOLVE2
        END
*
      SUBROUTINE SOLVE2
        IMPLICIT NONE
        REAL A1, B1, C1, A2, B2, C2, X, Y, DET2, VALDET
        WRITE(6,*) 'ENTER A1, B1, C1, A2, B2, C2: '
        READ(5,*) A1, B1, C1, A2, B2, C2
        VALDET = DET2 (A1, B1, A2, B2)
        IF (VALDET .NE. 0.0) THEN
          X  = DET2 (C1 , B1, C2 , B2) / VALDET
          Y = DET2 (A1, C1 , A2, C2 ) / VALDET
          WRITE(6,*) 'THE SOLUTION IS:'
          WRITE(6,*) '      X = ', X
          WRITE(6,*) '      Y = ', Y
        ELSE
          WRITE(6,*) 'A UNIQUE SOLUTION DOES NOT EXIST'
        ENDIF
        RETURN
        END
*
* SUBPROGRAM FUNCTION TO EVALUATE 2X2 DETERMINANT |  A  B  |
*                                                 |  C  D  |
      REAL FUNCTION DET2 (A, B, C, D)
        REAL A, B, C, D
*
        DET2 = A * D - B * C
*
        RETURN
        END
```

Following is the output produced by Program 9-1 when it is used to solve the set of equations:

$$2x + 3y = 130$$
$$10x + 5y = 330$$

```
ENTER A1, B1, K1, A2, B2, K2:
2 3 130 10 5 330
THE SOLUTION IS:
      X =       17.000000
      Y =       32.000000
```

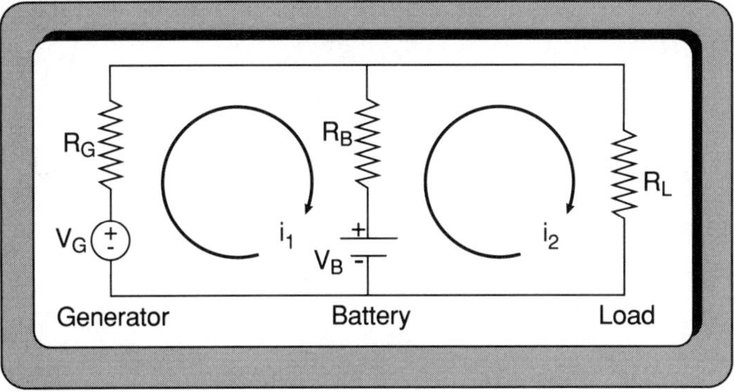

Figure 9-1 Automobile Battery-Charging Circuit

Application: Battery Charger

As an example of solving two equations with two unknowns consider the electrical equivalent circuit of an automobile battery charger, shown in Figure 9-1. The circuit models the car's electrical system after the car has been started. The purpose of the generator (or alternator) is to supply power to (that is, recharge) the battery. A real voltage source, such as a generator or battery, can be modeled by an ideal source in series with a resistor representing the internal resistance of that source. The components shown in the circuit diagram are:

V_G : ideal generator voltage
R_G : generator internal resistance
V_B : ideal battery voltage (for example, 12 volts)
R_B : battery internal resistance
R_L : load resistance (that is, equivalent resistance of all devices drawing energy, such as headlights and radio)

If the component values are known, we can set up two linear equations in terms of the two loop currents, i_1 and i_2. By solving for the two unknowns, we can determine the voltage, current, or power for any source or resistor. By applying circuit laws to the two loops, we obtain the following equations:

$$-V_G + R_G i_1 + R_B (i_1 - i_2) + V_B = 0$$
$$-V_B + R_B (i_2 - i_1) + R_L i_2 = 0$$

These equations result from the fact that the sum of all voltages around a closed circuit path (that is, a loop) is zero, and that the voltage across a resistor (in volts) is equal to its current (in amperes, or amps for short) multiplied by the resistance value (in ohms). We notice that the current through the generator is i_1 flowing upward, and the load current is i_2 flowing downward. The battery has both loop currents circulating through it in opposite directions, so that its current can be specified as $i_1 - i_2$ flowing downward, or equivalently, $i_2 - i_1$ flowing upward.

The equations can be easily rearranged so that they are in the standard form shown previously. This results in:

$$(R_G + R_B)\, i_1 \;\; - R_B\, i_2 = V_G - V_B$$
$$- R_B\, i_1 + (R_B + R_L)\, i_2 = V_B$$

In terms of previous notation we see that:

$$a_1 = R_G + R_B$$
$$b_1 = a_2 = -R_B$$
$$b_2 = R_2 + R_L$$
$$k_1 = V_G - V_B$$
$$k_2 = V_B$$

Suppose we want to determine whether the battery is charging or discharging its energy. If the battery is being charged by the generator, its net current flows downward; that is the case if current i_1 is larger than i_2. Otherwise, if i_2 is larger than i_1, current flows upward, and the battery is discharging. Once i_1 and i_2 have been solved for, a program segment such as:

```
IF (I1 .GT. I2) THEN
  WRITE (6,*) 'BATTERY CHARGING'
ELSE
  WRITE (6,*) 'BATTERY DISCHARGING'
ENDIF
```

displays the battery's status.

Program 9-2 allows us to read in the voltage source and resistor values, calculates the two loop currents, and determines whether the battery is charging or discharging.

The results of two sample runs are shown below, using realistic values for voltages and resistances:

```
ENTER VG AND VB IN VOLTS:
12.5, 12
ENTER RG, RB, AND RL IN OHMS:
0.15, 0.1, 1

GENERATOR CURRENT = 6.603773 AMPS
LOAD CURRENT = 11.50944 AMPS
BATTERY DISCHARGING
```

and:

```
ENTER VG AND VB IN VOLTS:
15, 12
ENTER RG, RB, AND RL IN OHMS:
0.15, 0.1, 1

GENERATOR CURRENT = 16.981130 AMPS
LOAD CURRENT = 12.452829 AMPS
BATTERY CHARGING
```

Program 9-2

```
      PROGRAM MAIN
         IMPLICIT NONE
         REAL VG, VB, RG, RB, RL, I1, I2
         CALL GETVAL(VG, VB, RG, RB, RL)
         CALL CALC(VG, VB, RG, RB, RL, I1, I2)
         CALL DISPLY(I1, I2)
         END
*
      SUBROUTINE GETVAL(VG, VB, RG, RB, RL)
         IMPLICIT NONE
         REAL VG, VB, RG, RB, RL
         WRITE(6,*) 'ENTER VG AND VB IN VOLTS: '
         READ (5,*) VG, VB
         WRITE(6,*) 'ENTER RG, RB, AND RL IN OHMS: '
         READ(5,*) RG, RB, RL
         RETURN
         END
*
      SUBROUTINE CALC(VG, VB, RG, RB, RL, I1, I2)
         IMPLICIT NONE
         REAL VG, VB, RG, RB, RL, I1, I2
         REAL A1, B1, A2, B2, K1, K2, D2, DET2
         A1 = RG + RB
         B1 = - RB
         A2 = - RB
         B2 = RB + RL
         K1 = VG - VB
         K2 = VB
         D2 = DET2 (A1, B1, A2, B2)
         I1  = DET2 (K1 , B1, K2 , B2) / D2
         I2  = DET2 (A1, K1 , A2, K2 ) / D2
         RETURN
         END
*
      SUBROUTINE DISPLY(I1, I2)
         REAL I1, I2
         WRITE(6,*)
         WRITE(6,*) 'GENERATOR CURRENT = ', I1, ' AMPS'
         WRITE(6,*) 'LOAD CURRENT = ', I2, ' AMPS'
         IF (I1 .GT. I2) THEN
           WRITE(6,*) 'BATTERY CHARGING'
         ELSE
           WRITE(6,*) 'BATTERY DISCHARGING'
         ENDIF
         RETURN
         END
*
* SUBPROGRAM FUNCTION TO EVALUATE 2X2 DETERMINANT      | A     B |
                                                       | C     D |
         REAL FUNCTION DET2 (A, B, C, D)
           REAL A, B, C, D
```

(Continued on the next page)

(Continued from the previous page)

```
*
      DET2 = A * D - B * C
*
      RETURN
      END
```

Further analysis of this problem shows that for a 12-volt car battery and the given resistor values, a generator voltage of at least 13.8 volts is required to keep the battery charging. The generator voltage must be higher than the battery voltage to overcome the loss in the internal source resistances.

Three Linear Equations with Three Unknowns

Cramer's rule also applies to the solution of three linear equations in three unknowns, having the general form:

$$a_1x + b_1y + c_1z = k_1$$
$$a_2x + b_2y + c_2z = k_2$$
$$a_3x + b_3y + c_3z = k_3$$

As for the case of two linear equations in two unknowns, each unknown in a set of three linear equations in three unknowns can be evaluated as a ratio of two determinants. In this case, however, each determinant is of the third order. Specifically, for the equations above, the solution is:

$$x = \det_x / \det_3$$
$$y = \det_y / \det_3$$
$$z = \det_z / \det_3$$

where:

$$\det_x = \begin{vmatrix} k_1 & b_1 & c_1 \\ k_2 & b_2 & c_2 \\ k_3 & b_3 & c_3 \end{vmatrix}$$

$$\det_y = \begin{vmatrix} a_1 & k_1 & c_1 \\ a_2 & k_2 & c_2 \\ a_3 & k_3 & c_3 \end{vmatrix}$$

$$\det_z = \begin{vmatrix} a_1 & b_1 & k_1 \\ a_2 & b_2 & k_2 \\ a_3 & b_3 & k_3 \end{vmatrix}$$

$$\det_3 = \begin{vmatrix} a_1 & b_1 & c_1 \\ a_2 & b_2 & c_2 \\ a_3 & b_3 & c_3 \end{vmatrix}$$

As we saw in the two-equation case, the numerator determinant corresponding to each unknown is evaluated by replacing the entries of the appropriate column of the denominator determinant ($\det_3$) by the coefficients on the right side of the

Program 9-3

```
      PROGRAM MAIN
        CALL SOLVE3
        END
*
      SUBROUTINE SOLVE3
        IMPLICIT NONE
        REAL A1,B1,C1,A2,B2,C2,A3,B3,C3,K1,K2,K3
        REAL X, Y, Z, VALDET, DET3
        WRITE(6,*) 'ENTER A1,B1,C1,A2,B2,C2,A3,B3,C3: '
        READ(5,*) A1,B1,C1,A2,B2,C2,A3,B3,C3
        WRITE(6,*) 'ENTER K1, K2, K3: '
        READ(5,*) K1, K2, K3
        VALDET = DET3 (A1,B1,C1,A2,B2,C2,A3,B3,C3)
        IF (VALDET .NE. 0.0) THEN
          X  = DET3 (K1,B1,C1,K2,B2,C2,K3,B3,C3) / VALDET
          Y  = DET3 (A1,K1,C1,A2,K2,C2,A3,K3,C3) / VALDET
          Z  = DET3 (A1,B1,K1,A2,B2,K2,A3,B3,K3 ) / VALDET
          WRITE(6,*) 'THE SOLUTION IS:'
          WRITE(6,*) '    X = ', X
          WRITE(6,*) '    Y = ', Y
          WRITE(6,*) '    Z = ', Z
        ELSE
          WRITE(6,*) 'A UNIQUE SOLUTION DOES NOT EXIST'
        ENDIF
        RETURN
        END
*
* SUBPROGRAM FUNCTION TO EVALUATE 3X3 DETERMINANT |  A  B  C  |
*                                                 |  D  E  F  |
*                                                 |  G  H  I  |
      REAL FUNCTION DET3 (A, B, C, D, E, F, G, H, I)
        REAL A, B, C, D, E, F, G, H, I, DET2
*
        DET3 = A*DET2(E,F,H,I)-D*DET2(B,C,H,I)+G*DET2(B,C,E,F)
*
        END
*
* SUBPROGRAM FUNCTION TO EVALUATE 2X2 DETERMINANT |  A   B  |
                                                  |  C   D  |
      REAL FUNCTION DET2 (A, B, C, D)
        REAL A, B, C, D
*
        DET2 = A * D - B * C
*
        END
```

equations (k_1, k_2, and k_3). As in the two-equation case, when the denominator determinant is zero, no unique solution exists.

The actual evaluation of a third-order determinant can be made by multiplying each element of any arbitrarily chosen row or column by the remaining second-order determinant after removing the row and column corresponding to the element. The selected row or column is called the pivot row or pivot column, respectively, and the resulting evaluation proceeds by alternating additions and subtractions. For example, arbitrarily selecting the first column as a pivot column, the three-by-three determinant:

$$\begin{vmatrix} a & b & c \\ d & e & f \\ g & h & i \end{vmatrix}$$

can be evaluated as:

$$a * \begin{vmatrix} e & f \\ h & i \end{vmatrix} - d \begin{vmatrix} b & c \\ h & i \end{vmatrix} + g * \begin{vmatrix} b & c \\ e & f \end{vmatrix}$$

Program 9-3 uses this evaluation method to compute the determinants required to solve three linear equations in three unknowns. This permits the program to make use of the subprogram function DET2() previously developed for Program 9-1.

Following is a sample run of Program 9-3 used to solve the system of linear equations:

$$\begin{aligned} x + y + z &= 32.5 \\ 10x + 5y + 4z &= 240 \\ 1.5x + 0y + 10z &= 49 \end{aligned}$$

```
ENTER A1,B1,C1,A2,B2,C2,A3,B3,C3:
1 1 1 10 5 4 1.5 0 10
ENTER K1, K2, K3:
32.5 240 49
THE SOLUTION IS:
    X =         16.000000
    Y =         14.000000
    Z =          2.500000
```

Exercises

1. Compile and run Program 9-1 on a computer. Enter the data necessary to solve the linear equations:

$$\begin{aligned} 3x + 4y &= 5 \\ 3x + 5y &= 4 \end{aligned}$$

2a. Notice that the two equations below cannot be solved.

$$\begin{aligned} x + 2y &= 5 \\ 3x + 6y &= 8 \end{aligned}$$

In contrast, the equations:

$$x + 2y = 5$$
$$3x + 6y = 15$$

result in many solutions. Can you see what the problem is?

b. Compile and run Program 9-1 for the equations in Exercise 2a.

3. Modify Program 9-1 to read the coefficients in from a data file COEFF.DAT rather than from the keyboard. Create the data file on a computer with the coefficients from Exercise 1. Then compile and run the modified program and verify the results of Exercise 1.

4. Modify Program 9-1 to evaluate the second-order determinant using a subroutine rather than a subprogram function. Compile and run the modified program, and again verify the result of Exercise 1.

5. Compile and run Program 9-2 on a computer, for a 12-volt battery charger with the following resistor values in ohms:

$$R_G = 0.2 \qquad R_B = 0.2 \qquad R_L = 1.0$$

Noting that 12 must be entered for V_B, enter a higher value of volts for V_G. Rerun the program, varying only the generator voltage. By trial and error, find the minimum V_G required (to one decimal place) to cause the battery to charge rather than discharge.

6a. Modify Program 9-2 to allow you to enter values for V_B, R_G, R_B, and R_L from the keyboard. The currents i_1 and i_2 are to be calculated for all values of V_G ranging from 12.5 to 15.0 volts, in steps of 0.1 volt. Rather than displaying a message as to whether the battery is charging or discharging, print the results in a table with the headings shown below.

```
    VG           I1           I2
 (volts)       (amps)       (amps)
---------     --------     --------
```

b. Compile and run the modified program on a computer. Enter the values:

$$V_B = 12 \qquad R_G = 0.15 \qquad R_B = 0.1 \qquad R_L = 1$$

c. Repeat Exercise 6b for the values used in Exercise 5.

7. Compile and run Program 9-3 on a computer. Enter the data necessary to solve the linear equations:

$$2x + y - 2z = 8$$
$$x - 5y + 3z = 6$$
$$3x - 3y - 2z = 10$$

8. Modify Program 9-3 to read the coefficients in from a data file COEFF.DAT rather than from the keyboard. Create the data file on a computer with the coefficients from Exercise 7, then compile and run the modified program and verify the results of Exercise 7.

9. A common numerical problem is to find the equation of a straight line that best fits a set of N data points, denoted as (x_1,y_1), (x_2,y_2), (x_3,y_3), ... (x_N,y_N). The equation of a straight line is given by $y = mx + b$, where m is the slope of the line, and b is called the y intercept. One technique for determining the values of m and b is called a linear least-squares fit. For such a fit, the unknowns m and b are related by the set of two simultaneous linear equations:

$$Nb + \left(\sum_{i=1}^{N} x_i\right) m = \sum_{i=1}^{N} y_i$$

$$\left(\sum_{i=1}^{N} x_i\right) b + \left(\sum_{i=1}^{N} x_i^2\right) m = \sum_{i=1}^{N} x_i y_i$$

a. Using Program 9-1 as a starting point, write a FORTRAN program that accepts the given x and y values as inputs, determines the coefficients of the two equations, and then solves for the values of m and b. (*Hint:* Accept the number of data points as the first input and store the actual data points in two arrays named X and Y, respectively. A DO loop will be useful in calculating the summations. Test your program using the data points (1,0.5), (2,1.5), (3,1), and (4,2).

b. Using the program developed for Exercise 9a, determine the equation of the straight line that best fits the following data points: (1,3), (2,1), (3,2), (4,1), (6,2), and (8,5).

10. Experimental results on an unknown resistor produced the following table of voltages and currents.

Voltage (volts)	Current (amps)
1	0.018
2	0.043
3	0.056
4	0.085
5	0.092
6	0.100
7	0.102

The equation relating voltage, V; current, I; and resistance, R, is given by Ohm's law, which states that $V = R * I$. Use the program developed in Exercise 9a to assist you in finding the "best" guess at the resistance value, R.

11. Fitting a quadratic curve to a set of N data points, denoted as (x_1,y_1), (x_2,y_2), (x_3,y_3), . . . (x_N,y_N), requires determining the values of a, b, and c for the equation $y = a + bx + cx^2$ that fit the data in some best manner. One technique for determining the values of a, b, and c is called the quadratic least-squares fit. For such a fit, the unknowns a, b, and c are related by the set of equations:

$$Na + b\sum_{i=1}^{N} x_i + c\sum_{i=1}^{N} x_i^2 = \sum_{i=1}^{N} y_i$$

$$a\sum_{i=1}^{N} x_i + b\sum_{i=1}^{N} x_i^2 + c\sum_{i=1}^{N} x_i^3 = \sum_{i=1}^{N} x_i\ y_i$$

$$a\sum_{i=1}^{N} x_i^2 + b\sum_{i=1}^{N} x_i^3 + c\sum_{i=1}^{N} x_i^4 = \sum_{i=1}^{N} x_i^2\ y_i$$

Using Program 9-3 as a starting point, write a FORTRAN program that accepts the given x and y values as inputs, determines the coefficients of the three equations, and then solves for the values of a, b, and c. (*Hint:* Accept the number of data points as the first input and store the actual data points in two arrays named X and Y, respectively.) Test your program using the data points (1,3), (2,1), (3,2), and (4,1).

12a. The official United States population for each census taken since the year 1900 is listed below. The population figures are in millions of people and are rounded off to one fractional digit.

Year	U.S. population
1900	76.2
1910	92.2
1920	106.0
1930	123.2
1940	132.2
1950	151.3
1960	179.3
1970	203.3
1980	226.5

Using the program developed for Exercise 11, determine the equation of the least-squares quadratic curve for this data.

b. Using the equation determined in Exercise 12a, determine an estimate for the population of the United States in the year 2000.

9.2 Root Finding

Although the solution to sets of linear equations can be obtained using methods such as Cramer's rule, presented in Section 9.1, and individual quadratic equations, such as:

$$x2 + 2x - 35 = 0$$

can be solved for x with the aid of the quadratic formula (see Section 6.5), no such computationally simple solutions exist for equations such as:

$$x^4 + 5x^3 + 12x^2 - 7x + 21 = 0$$

and:

$$\sin(5x) - 3x^2 + e^{4.8x} = 12$$

Although both of these equations have only a single unknown quantity, they are extremely difficult to solve because they both are nonlinear equations. By solve, of course, we mean finding values for x that when substituted into the equation yield a value for the equation's left side equal to that on its right side. More formally, such a value of x is called a root of the equation. Not unexpectedly, then, the methods of solving these equations are referred to as root-finding methods.

All root-finding methods require that the equation whose roots are being sought be written as the equation of a curve. In general, this involves the following two steps:

Step 1: Rewrite the equation to have all of the unknowns and constants on one side of the equation and a zero on the other side. For example, the equation $x^2 + 2x = 35$ can be rearranged in this form by subtracting 35 from both sides of the equation to yield $x^2 + 2x - 35 = 0$.

Step 2: Set the side of the equation with the unknowns equal to another variable, such as y. For example, setting $y = x^2 + 2x - 35$ converts the original equation into the equation of a curve. For each value of x in this equation, a value of y can be computed.

Once the given equation has been transformed into the equation of a curve, the root-finding problem reduces to locating values of x for which y is zero. Three such methods are now presented.

All of the methods presented, as indeed do all root-finding methods, rely on guessing at a value of x, finding the corresponding value of y, and then modifying the value of x until a y value of zero is reached. The difference in methods is based on the procedure used to modify each guess until a root is located.

Fixed-Increment Iterations

In the fixed-increment root-finding method, each value of x is obtained from the previous value by adding or subtracting a fixed amount. To understand how this procedure works, consider Program 9-4, which tabulates values of the curve $y = x^2 + 2x - 35$ for integer values of x ranging from -10 to $+10$ (see Section 5.1 to review this use of a DO loop).

Program 9-4

```
      PROGRAM MAIN
        CALL FXINC1
        END
*
      SUBROUTINE FXINC1
        INTEGER X, Y
          WRITE(6,*)'         X VALUE        Y VALUE'
          WRITE(6,*)'         -------        -------'
          DO 20 X = -10, 10
            Y = X ** 2 + 2 * X - 35
            WRITE(6,*) X, Y
 20     CONTINUE
        RETURN
        END
```

The output produced by Program 9-4 is:

```
 X VALUE          Y VALUE
 -------          -------
  -10               45
   -9               28
   -8               13
   -7                0
   -6              -11
   -5              -20
   -4              -27
   -3              -32
   -2              -35
   -1              -36
    0              -35
    1              -32
    2              -27
    3              -20
    4              -11
    5                0
    6               13
    7               28
    8               45
    9               64
   10               85
```

The roots of the curve correspond to those values of x for which the calculated values of y are zero, in this case, $x = -7$ and $x = 5$. Figure 9-2 is a plot of the curve

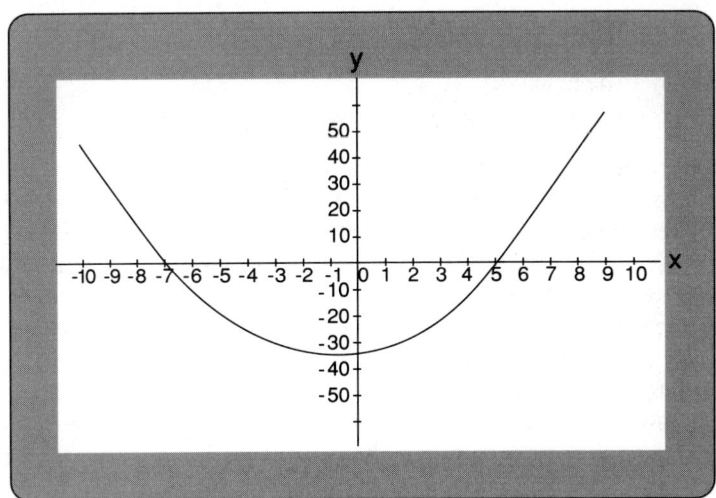

Figure 9-2 The Graph of the Curve $y = x^2 + 2x - 35$

using the tabulated values. The roots are the values of x corresponding to the points where the curve intersects the x axis, namely, at $x = -7$ and $x = 5$.

Now let us modify Program 9-4 to display the two roots without listing the entire table. We do this by eliminating the printing of the headings in Program 9-4 and replacing the WRITE statement inside the DO loop with a conditional WRITE of x only if y is zero. Program 9-5 accomplishes this.

Program 9-5

```
      PROGRAM MAIN
         CALL FXINC2
         END
*
      SUBROUTINE FXINC2
         INTEGER X, Y
            DO 20 X = -10, 10
               Y = X ** 2 + 2 *X - 35
               IF ( Y .EQ. 0 ) WRITE(6,*) 'A ROOT IS AT X = ', X
   20       CONTINUE
         RETURN
         END
```

The output produced by this program is the following:

```
A ROOT IS AT X =           -7
A ROOT IS AT X =            5
```

Of course it should be apparent that Program 9-5 found the solutions to the equation for us because the roots happen to be integers. Noninteger roots cannot be located by this routine because X is declared as an integer, so that only integer values are entered into the equation. To consider the more general case of noninteger roots, we consider the equation:

$$x^2 + 2.1x - 16.96 = 0$$

From the quadratic formula, the roots of this equation are $x = -5.3$ and $x = 3.2$. However, let us assume that we do not know where the roots are, as would be the case for a higher-order equation or one with trigonometric or exponential functions. For this more general noninteger case, the variables X and Y in the program need to be declared as REAL variables. The step size in the DO loop, which defaults to one in Program 9-5, needs to be decreased to enable the finding of noninteger root locations. Also, we need to decide how close to zero the function needs to be to qualify a value as a root (recall from Section 6.1 that, because of round-off errors, exact equality to zero is not always possible for real values). In Program 9-6 the step size used in the loop (called INCR) and the allowable deviation from zero, referred to as the allowable error, are read from the keyboard. The value of Y is calculated within the loop, and the root value is printed out only if the absolute value of Y does not exceed the allowable error.

Program 9-6

```
      PROGRAM MAIN
        CALL FXINC3
        END
*
      SUBROUTINE FXINC3
        REAL X, Y, INCR, ERROR
          WRITE(6,*) 'ENTER STEP SIZE: '
          READ(5,*) INCR
          WRITE(6,*) 'ENTER THE ALLOWABLE ERROR: '
          READ(5,*) ERROR
          DO 20 X = -10.0, 10.0, INCR
            Y = X ** 2 + 2.1 * X - 16.96
            IF (ABS(Y) .LE. ERROR) WRITE(6,*) 'A ROOT IS AT X = ', X
  20    CONTINUE
        RETURN
        END
```

The results of three sample runs using Program 9-6 are:

```
ENTER STEP SIZE:
0.01
ENTER THE ALLOWABLE ERROR:
0.1
A ROOT IS AT X =      -5.309893
A ROOT IS AT X =      -5.299892
A ROOT IS AT X =      -5.289892
A ROOT IS AT X =       3.190131
A ROOT IS AT X =       3.200131
A ROOT IS AT X =       3.210131
```

and:

```
ENTER STEP SIZE:
0.01
ENTER THE ALLOWABLE ERROR:
0.01
A ROOT IS AT X =      -5.299892
A ROOT IS AT X =       3.200131
```

and:

```
ENTER STEP SIZE:
0.01
ENTER MINIMUM FUNCTION ERROR:
0.001
A ROOT IS AT X =      -5.299892
```

The results illustrate the care that needs to be taken in choosing both the step size and the allowable error. The step size determines the total number of iterations that are made, while the allowable error determines the range of y values that are close enough to zero to qualify a given x value as a root. As shown in the first run, too large an allowable error may qualify too many roots, while too small a value, as shown in the last run, may cause valid roots to be missed. In this latter case the root location at 3.2 is not found because of round-off error.

Although the second run correctly locates the two roots of the equation using a step size of 0.01 and an allowable error of the same value, this relationship between step size and allowable error cannot be generalized. However, the problem of selecting too large or small a value for the allowable function error can be eliminated by using a different approach.

Referring to Figure 9-2, notice that the crossing of the x axis by the curve causes the sign of y to change. The table of values printed by Program 9-4 also shows the sign changes. As x is increased from –10, the values of y are positive, and they then change to negative as the root $x = -7$ is passed. The values of y remain negative until the second root, $x = 5$, is reached, whereupon y is again positive for larger values of x. All curves exhibit sign changes in y when a root is encountered, with one exception. The exception is the occurrence of a curve that is tangent to the x axis at some point, whereupon the sign of y will not change even though a root exists (this is referred to as a repeated root).

Taking advantage of the sign change feature allows us to have our program calculate two successive values of y within the loop, corresponding to a value of x and to x plus a chosen increment. If the two values of y differ in sign, then a root is identified. The root, however, is between the two values of x used. Rather than simply use one of the x values, we obtain a more accurate computation of the root using interpolation. In Figure 9-3 a small portion of a curve is shown for both a positive slope and negative slope case; x_1 and x_2 represent two successive values of x between which a root exists. The actual root location, x_r, is approximated by drawing a straight line between the points (x_1, y_1) and (x_2, y_2). Where this interpolation line crosses the x axis determines x_r. From the triangles drawn in Figure 9-3 the slopes of the lines can be equated, resulting in the equation:

$$\frac{y_1}{x_r - x_1} = \frac{y_2}{x_{2r} - x_r}$$

for the negatively sloped case (the equation is the same for the positively sloped case because the minus sign is simply transposed from y_2 to y_1).

By solving the equation above for x_r, the approximate root value is:

$$x_r = \frac{x_2 y_1 - x_1 y_2}{y_1 - y_2} = x_1 + \frac{y_1}{y_1 - y_2}(x_1 - x_2)$$

Program 9-7 incorporates this interpolation formula to locate the roots of the curve $y = x^2 + 2.1x - 16.96$.

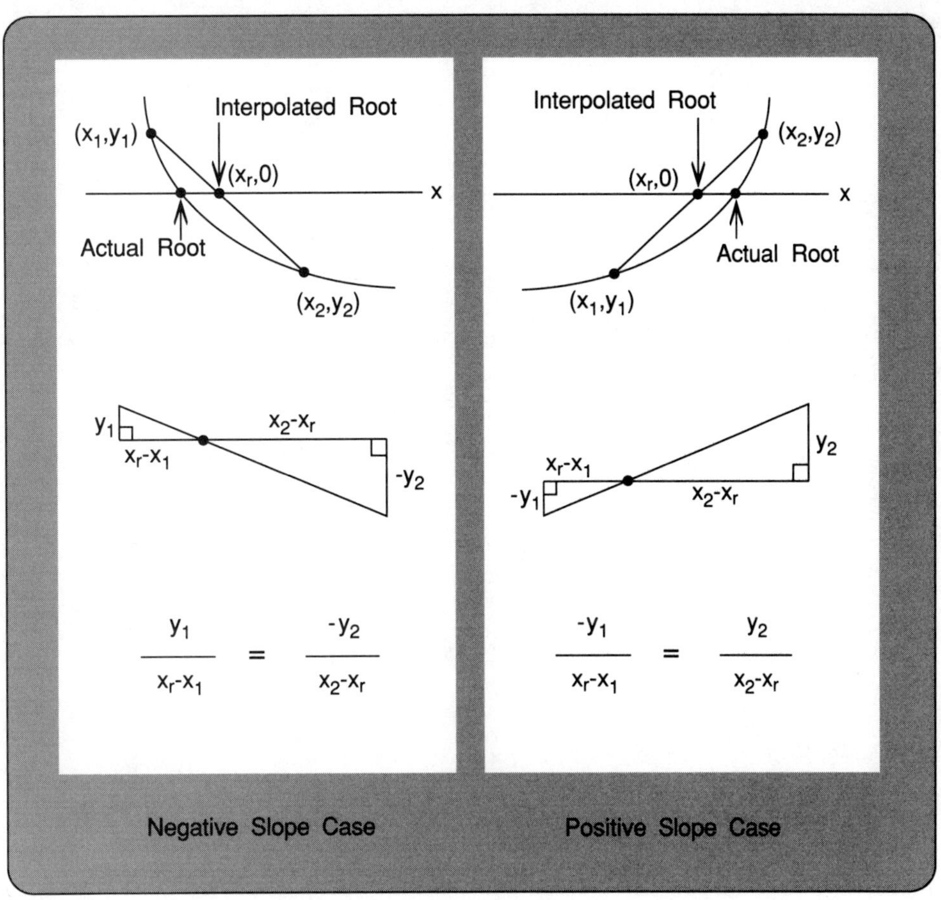

Figure 9-3 Approximating a Root by Interpolation

Following are four sample runs of Program 9-7 using different step sizes:

```
ENTER STEP SIZE:
1
A ROOT IS AT X =        -5.276404
A ROOT IS AT X =         3.182417

ENTER STEP SIZE:
0.5
A ROOT IS AT X =        -5.292857
A ROOT IS AT X =         3.193023

ENTER STEP SIZE:
0.1
A ROOT IS AT X =        -5.300000
A ROOT IS AT X =         3.200000
```

Program 9-7

```
      PROGRAM MAIN
        CALL FXINC4
        END
*
      SUBROUTINE FXINC4
        IMPLICIT NONE
        REAL INCR, X, X1, X2, Y1, Y2, XROOT, YRATIO, F
        F(X) = X ** 2 + 2.1 * X - 16.96
        WRITE(6,*) 'ENTER STEP SIZE: '
        READ(5,*) INCR
        DO 20 X = -10.0, 10.0 - INCR, INCR
          X1 = X
          X2 = X + INCR
          Y1 = F (X1)
          Y2 = F (X2)
        IF (Y1 * Y2 .LT. 0) THEN
             YRATIO = Y1 / (Y1 - Y2)
             XROOT = X1 + YRATIO * ( X2 - X1 )
              WRITE(6,*) ' A ROOT IS AT X = ', XROOT
          END IF
   20   CONTINUE
        RETURN
        END
```

```
ENTER STEP SIZE:
0.01
A ROOT IS AT X =       -5.300000
A ROOT IS AT X =        3.200000
```

The three important points to observe from Program 9-7 are:

1. The calculation of y values for the curve is relegated to a function statement. This statement can easily be changed for different curves.
2. Although two values of x (X1 and X2) and two values of y (Y1 and Y2) need to be calculated inside the loop, care is taken not to change the loop's index value, X. The maximum index value is set to 10-INCR to ensure that X2 does not exceed 10.
3. Since the two values Y1 and Y2 must be of different sign for a root to exist, simply multiplying them and examining the sign of the result provides a conve-

nient test. If both values are positive or if both are negative, the product is a positive number, and the statements within the IF block are ignored.

We see from the results that by testing for a sign change and interpolating to find the root, the accuracy is quite good, and the danger of missing a root has been diminished. Even incrementing X by 1 each time results in roots that are less than 1 percent in error from their true value. For step sizes of 0.1 and lower, the roots rounded to 6 fractional digits are identical to the expected values of –5.3 and 3.2. Clearly, however, a root will be missed if the range of X values used in the DO loop does not include the root.

The Bisection Method

All fixed-increment root-finding algorithms require the computer to iterate through a fixed number of x values, calculate corresponding y values, and identify the roots in some manner. When the step size is small, this can be extremely time-consuming, especially when the general vicinity of the roots is not known. In such cases it may be necessary to search over a wide range of x values to avoid missing a root. For reasons of computational efficiency, various techniques have been developed to permit the search to proceed much more rapidly than is possible when simply incrementing x by a fixed step size. One such method is the bisection method.

The rationale for the bisection method can be better understood by first considering a game called High-Low. In High-Low an integer is selected between 1 and 99, and a player is required to find the number with as few guesses as possible. The game is often played against a calculator or computer, in which case the player must guess a randomly selected integer. Upon each guess, the player is told whether the choice is too high or too low. When the correct number is chosen, the game is over, and the number of guesses is tallied.

If we approach this game as a fixed-step iteration problem, we would begin by selecting 1 as our first guess. If that is incorrect, we will be told that our guess is too low. We would then begin incrementing our guess by 1 each time, proceeding to guess the numbers 2, 3, 4, and so on, until we locate the right number. Clearly, the number of tries is going to equal the selected number. If a low number was selected we are in luck, but in the worst case it could take 99 guesses.

There is, however, a better approach to the game. Rather than selecting 1 as our first guess, let us select a number at the middle of the range, namely, 50. Now, if we are told that the guess is too low, we have instantly eliminated all integers below 50 as well as 50 itself. Conversely, a response of too high removes from further consideration the numbers in the range 50 to 99. In either case the range has been cut approximately in half. Our next guess repeats this strategy: if the new range is 1 to 49, we choose 25, and if the new range is 51 to 99, we choose 75. In either case we again eliminate half of the remaining numbers (assuming that we have not been so fortunate as to hit the number already). You can see that this process will locate the correct number quite rapidly. An illustrative example is shown below:

```
Number selected by opponent:  59
        Range   Guess   Message
        -----   -----   -------
        1-99    50      Too low
        51-99   75      Too high
        51-74   63      Too high
        51-62   57      Too low
        58-62   60      Too high
        58-59   58      Too low
        59      59      Correct
```

Notice that the correct number was identified in seven guesses, without any "lucky" guesses; that is, the number was not identified until it was the only possible one left. It is always the case that the maximum number of guesses required by halving each range is seven, regardless of the number originally selected (recall that the fixed-step iteration method might require 99 guesses).

Let us now apply the underlying strategy of High-Low to root finding. To do this, consider a curve that is known to have a single root, denoted as x_r, between the values $x = a$ and $x = b$, as illustrated in Figure 9-4(a). Although the illustrated curve has a positive slope, the technique works equally well with a curve having a negative slope. Regardless of the curve's slope, the value of the curve at $x = a$ differs in sign from the value at $x = b$.

Using the bisection method, we initially calculate y values corresponding to the left and right bounds on the x axis, namely $x = a$ and $x = b$. Then we select the midpoint of these two x values and replace one of the x values by this midpoint in such a manner that the root lies in the remaining range. For this procedure the midpoint of the values $x = a$ and $x = b$ is calculated as:

$$mid = (a+b) / 2.0$$

If the calculated midpoint lies to the left of the root, as is the case in Figure 9-4(a), the left half of the curve segment (between $x = a$ and $x = mid$) can be discarded; otherwise, the right half between $x = mid$ and $x = b$ can be removed from further consideration. In either case the root is within the reduced interval. Figure 9-4(b) shows the removal of the left half of the curve segment, with the value of a replaced by the previously calculated value of *mid*. The second calculation of *mid*, using this new value of a, results in a value larger than the root. In this case the right half of the remaining segment is discarded, and the value of b is replaced by the newly calculated *mid*. Figure 9-4(c) shows the original segment reduced to one-fourth of its size. A third calculation of *mid* is seen to be smaller than the root, so that the next step would be to replace a by *mid*.

We see that each step of this procedure reduces the interval between $x = a$ and $x = b$ by a factor of two, or in other words bisects the interval. Now we can see the analogy of this procedure with the High-Low game. The initial values a and b correspond to the initial range of integers in the High-Low game, which was 1 to 99 in our illustration. The calculation of *mid* corresponds to the "guessing" of a number

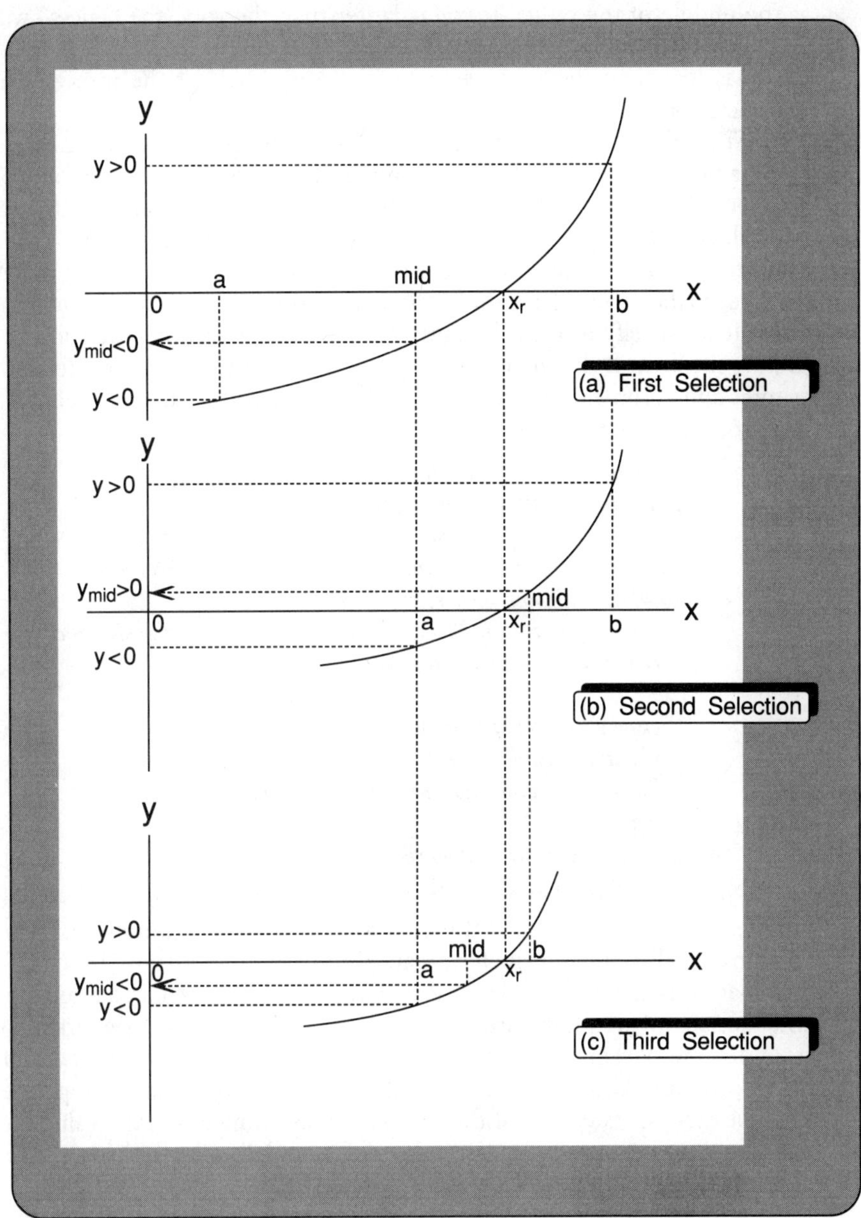

Figure 9-4 Illustration of the Bisection Technique

at the middle of the range. If *mid* is larger than the root, the "guess" was too high, and the upper half of the range is eliminated; alternatively, a low "guess" of *mid*, which is less than the root, removes the lower half of the interval from further consideration.

Since the High-Low game involves only integers, an exact answer will always be obtained after a relatively small number of guesses. Because the roots of equations are generally real numbers subject to round-off error, finding an exact answer, regardless of the root-finding method, is generally not possible. We must, therefore, agree beforehand on an allowable error in the computation of the root. We can also provide further control on the computation time by limiting the number of iterations. If we specify too small an error and too few iterations, we run the risk of not finding the root. If that happens, however, we can then adjust one (or both) of these criteria and rerun the program. With this as background, the pseudocode for the bisection algorithm is as follows:

```
enter an allowable error for the root
  and the maximum number of iterations
initialize left and right bounds of x
repeat until acceptable root found or maximum iterations reached
   calculate midpoint of current interval
   if function value at left bound and at midpoint differ in sign then
     set new right bound to midpoint value
   else
     set new left bound to midpoint value
   if within allowable error
     display root value and number of iterations
     stop
display message indicating no root found
```

Program 9-8 implements this pseudocode for the curve $y = x^2 + 2.1x - 16.96$.

Notice that Program 9-8 uses a loop with a fixed number of iterations that contains an IF statement to terminate the program if a root is found. The actual termination is caused by the STOP statement, which is executed after the root value and number of iterations are printed. (Recall that an END statement, which also stops execution, cannot be used because only one END statement is permitted in the MAIN program. Using END in place of STOP would result in a compiler error, since it is not the last statement of the program.) Also notice that the value of the root is computed by averaging the last values of A and B, which yields a more accurate approximation to the root than either A or B alone.

A disadvantage of the bisection procedure is that two roots within an interval can cause problems because no sign change in *y* values will occur (can you see why?). The solution to this problem is to select an interval that encloses only one root and

Program 9-8

```
      PROGRAM MAIN
        INTEGER N
        REAL XERROR, A, B
        CALL GETVAL(XERROR, N, A, B)
        CALL BISECT(XERROR, N, A, B)
        END
*
      SUBROUTINE GETVAL(XERROR, N, A, B)
        INTEGER N
        REAL XERROR, A, B
          WRITE(6,*) 'ENTER MAXIMUM ROOT ERROR: '
          READ(5,*) XERROR
          WRITE(6,*) 'ENTER MAXIMUM NUMBER OF ITERATIONS: '
          READ(5,*) N
          WRITE(6,*) 'ENTER LEFT AND RIGHT BOUNDS OF X  (A, B): '
        READ(5,*) A, B
        RETURN
        END
*
      SUBROUTINE BISECT(XERROR, N, A, B)
        IMPLICIT NONE
        INTEGER N, I
        REAL XERROR, A, B, X, MID, XROOT, F
        F(X) = X**2 + 2.1 * X - 16.96
        DO 20 I = 1, N
          MID = (A + B) / 2
          IF (F(A) * F(MID) .LT. 0) THEN
            B = MID
          ELSE
            A = MID
          END IF
          IF (B - A .LE. XERROR) THEN
            XROOT = (A+B) / 2
            WRITE(6,*) 'A ROOT IS AT X = ',XROOT
            WRITE(6,*) 'ROOT FOUND AFTER ',I, ' ITERATIONS'
            STOP
          END IF
 20     CONTINUE
        WRITE(6,*) 'NO ROOT FOUND AFTER ',N,' ITERATIONS'
        RETURN
        END
```

then to rerun the program for the additional roots. The sample runs shown below for Program 9-8 illustrate how both roots of the curve $y = x^2 + 2.1x - 16.96$ are found by modifying the range of the search interval.

```
ENTER MAXIMUM ROOT ERROR:
0.0001
ENTER MAXIMUM NUMBER OF ITERATIONS:
30
ENTER LEFT AND RIGHT BOUNDS OF X  (A, B):
-100, 100
A ROOT IS AT X =        -5.299997
ROOT FOUND AFTER             21 ITERATIONS

ENTER MAXIMUM ROOT ERROR:
0.0001
ENTER MAXIMUM NUMBER OF ITERATIONS:
30
ENTER LEFT AND RIGHT BOUNDS OF X  (A, B):
0, 100
A ROOT IS AT X =        3.200006
ROOT FOUND AFTER             20 ITERATIONS
```

In the first run the initial interval includes both roots and the program correctly locates the root at $x = -5.3$ but misses the positive root. The next run locates the positive root at $x = 3.2$ because the search interval includes this root while excluding the negative root.

The Secant Method

The secant method is a variation on the bisection technique just described. Rather than selecting the midpoint of an interval at each step to estimate the root value, the intersection of a secant line with the x axis is used as the next estimate. A *secant line* is a straight line that connects two points on the curve, as illustrated on Figure 9-5.

Figure 9-5 also shows the process of estimating the root location through the use of successive secant lines. The initial interval of the curve is defined by the values x_1 and x_2; notice that these points correspond to points a and b respectively, for the bisection method. In Figure 9-5(a) the first secant line drawn crosses the x axis at x_3; for the curve shown it is to the left of the actual root, but only because of the bending of the curve.

A second secant line, shown in Figure 9-5(b) connects the points of the curve corresponding to x_2 and x_3; the intersection of this secant line with the x axis is then x_4. Again, the last two values of x, namely x_3 and x_4, define the points on the curve corresponding to the next secant line. As shown in Figure 9-5(c), the third secant line intersects the x axis at x_5. The process would then continue, using x_4 and x_5 to define the next curve segment.

Notice that the point x_5 in this illustration falls outside of the interval between x_3 and x_4. This is one difference between the secant method and the bisection method, where each point chosen is halfway between the two previous points. The

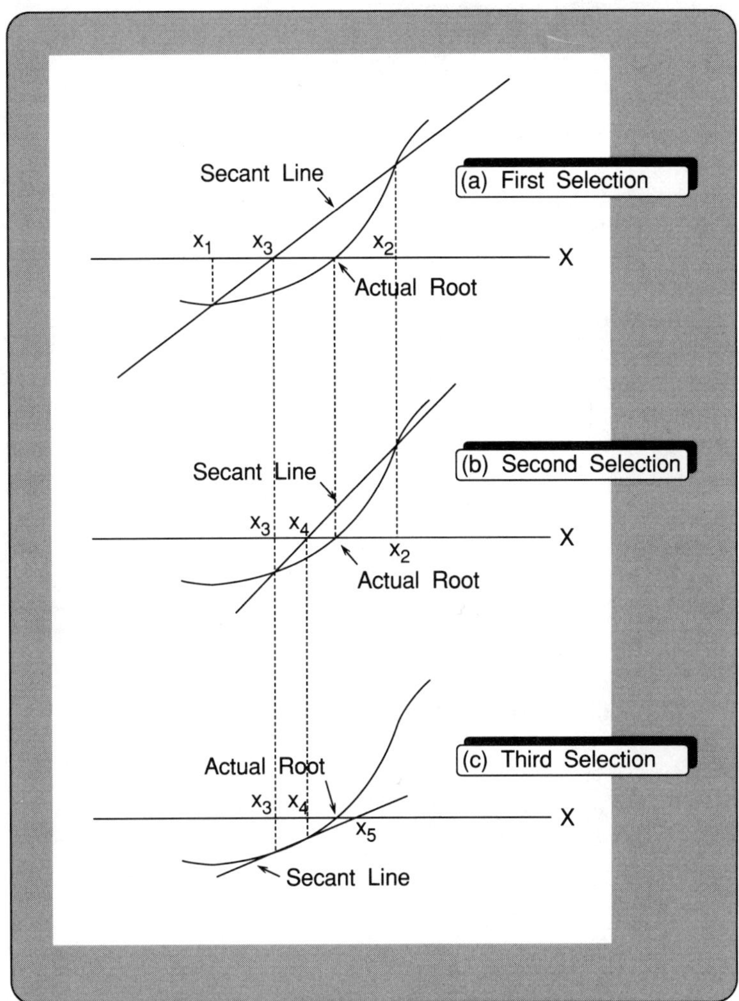

Figure 9-5 Illustration of Root Finding Using Secant Method

fact that a point may fall outside the interval defined by the previous two points does not imply that the secant method is diverging. In fact for most cases it converges more rapidly than does the bisection method, which means that the intersections of the secant lines with the x axis are more rapidly approaching the actual root location. However, as with the bisection method, there are potential problems when multiple roots are involved.

A program to implement the secant method is no more complex than Program 9-9, which implements the bisection method. The secant method requires repeated calculation of the intersection of the line with the x axis in place of the simpler calculation of the midpoint when bisection is used. However, the bisection method includes for each step a test of whether the function value at the midpoint has the

Program 9-9

```
      PROGRAM MAIN
        INTEGER N
        REAL YERROR, X(102)
        CALL GETVAL(YERROR, N, X)
        CALL SECANT(YERROR, N, X)
        END
*
      SUBROUTINE GETVAL(YERROR, N, X)
        INTEGER N
        REAL YERROR, X(*)
        WRITE(6,*) 'ENTER MAXIMUM FUNCTION ERROR: '
        READ(5,*) YERROR
        WRITE(6,*) 'ENTER MAXIMUM NUMBER OF ITERATIONS ( <=100 ): '
        READ(5,*) N
        WRITE(6,*) 'ENTER LEFT AND RIGHT BOUNDS OF X (X(1),X(2)): '
        READ(5,*) X(1), X(2)
        RETURN
        END
*
      SUBROUTINE SECANT(YERROR, N, X)
        IMPLICIT NONE
        INTEGER N, I
        REAL YERROR, X(*), Y(102), XX, XROOT, YRATIO, F
        F(XX) = XX ** 2 + 2.1 * xx - 16.96
        DO 20 I = 1, N
          Y(I) = F (X(I))
          Y(I+1) = F (X(I+1))
          YRATIO = Y(I) / (Y(I) - Y(I+1))
          X(I+2) = X(I) + YRATIO * (X(I+1) - X(I))
          WRITE(6,30) I+2, X(I+2)
 30       FORMAT (' ', 'X (', I3, ') = ', F12.6)
          Y(I+2) = F (X(I+2))
          IF (ABS(Y(I+2)) .LE. YERROR) THEN
            XROOT =X(I+2)
            WRITE(6,*) 'A ROOT IS AT X = ',XROOT
            WRITE(6,*) 'ROOT FOUND AFTER ',I, ' ITERATIONS'
            STOP
          END IF
 20     CONTINUE
        WRITE(6,*) 'NO ROOT FOUND AFTER ',N,' ITERATIONS'
        RETURN
        END
```

same sign as the value at one of the endpoints; the IF-ELSE structure within the DO loop of Program 9-9 implements this test. The test is necessary to determine whether the left or right end of the previous interval is used as a bound for the next interval. Since the secant method always uses the two most recent values of x to define the next interval, regardless of the value of the function at any point, the test is unnecessary.

We can terminate the secant method's root search when the function's value for the most recent value of x is arbitrarily close to zero. As with the bisection method, we can terminate the program before finding a root when a desired maximum number of iterations have been completed.

The pseudocode for the secant method is:

enter acceptable error for root and maximum iterations
initialize left and right bounds of x
do until acceptable root found or maximum iterations reached
  calculate location of secant line intersection with
  x *axis for current bounds*
  use secant intersection value to update bound locations
display root value and number of iterations, or message
indicating no root found

Recall the calculation of the secant line's intersection with the x axis shown in Figure 9-3 and implemented in Program 9-7. Notice that the result of the single calculation of x_r from x_1 and x_2 in Figure 9-3 can be applied to the repeated calculation of $x_3, x_4, x_5, \ldots$ illustrated in Figure 9-5. We are now finding x_{i+2} from x_i and x_{i+1}, starting with $i = 1$, where the first two values x_1 and x_2 are the initial bounds to be entered into our program.

The relationship:

$$x_r = x_1 + \frac{y_1}{y_1 - y_2}(x_2 - x_2)$$

previously shown, now becomes:

$$x_{i+2} = x_1 + \frac{y_i}{y_i - y_{i+1}}(x_{i+1} - x_i) \qquad (i = 1, 2, 3, \ldots)$$

where x_{i+2} is the location of the intersection of the current secant line with the x axis, x_{i+1} and x_i are the previously calculated secant line intersections, and y_{i+1} and y_i are the function values corresponding to x_{i+1} and x_i, respectively.

Program 9-9 implements the secant method for the same quadratic function used previously, namely $x^2 + 2.1x - 16.96$.

It is convenient to use single-dimension arrays in this program to repeatedly calculate the values of x and y. Arrays X and Y have 102 memory locations assigned to them as a result of their declaration statement. This allows us to perform as many as 100 iterations, noting that the first two array elements are reserved for the values entered into X(1) and X(2) and calculated for Y(1) and Y(2). Notice that it is necessary to use a variable name other than X in the function statement to avoid a conflict with the array named X. A function subprogram or subroutine to calculate F would not be subject to this restriction, since the same variable name can be used in different program units.

Another feature to notice is the formatted WRITE statement inside the DO loop. Its purpose is to simply display for us the result of each calculation of the secant line intersection with the x axis. It is a useful aid in debugging such a program and offers some insight into the degree of convergence of this method; it can, of course, be eliminated from the program.

Several sample runs of Program 9-9 are shown below along with comments on the results. For each run the acceptable function error is entered as 0.0001, and a 30-iteration limit is specified.

```
ENTER MAXIMUM FUNCTION ERROR:
0.0001
ENTER MAXIMUM NUMBER OF ITERATIONS (<= 100 ):
30
ENTER LEFT AND RIGHT BOUNDS OF X  (X(1),X(2)):
-100, 100
X (  3) = -4753.829000
X (  4) =   102.191200
X (  5) =   104.479600
X (  6) =    51.223000
X (  7) =    34.021730
X (  8) =    20.146090
X (  9) =    12.482530
X ( 10) =     7.729481
X ( 11) =     5.084414
X ( 12) =     3.772313
X ( 13) =     3.298430
X ( 14) =     3.206143
X ( 15) =     3.200070
X ( 16) =     3.200000
A ROOT IS AT X =          3.200000
ROOT FOUND AFTER            14 ITERATIONS
```

When the same values were entered for the bisection program, the smaller root $x = -5.3$ was found after 22 iterations. Here the larger rather than the smaller root was found, but with fewer iterations. Notice that the large range specified results in the first calculation of X(3) being far removed from the root. This is not surprising in view of the fact that the parabolic function evaluates to about 10,000 for $x = -100$ and for $x = 100$.

```
ENTER MAXIMUM FUNCTION ERROR:
0.0001
ENTER MAXIMUM NUMBER OF ITERATIONS (<= 100 ):
30
ENTER LEFT AND RIGHT BOUNDS OF X  (X(1),X(2)):
100, -100
X (  3) = -4753.829000
X (  4) =   -97.985660
X (  5) =   -96.051970
X (  6) =   -49.123580
X (  7) =   -33.097030
X (  8) =   -20.504140
X (  9) =   -13.506220
X ( 10) =    -9.209970
X ( 11) =    -6.856354
X ( 12) =    -5.735712
X ( 13) =    -5.364632
```

```
X ( 14) =     -5.303129
X ( 15) =     -5.300024
X ( 16) =     -5.300000
A ROOT IS AT X =          -5.300000
ROOT FOUND AFTER             14 ITERATIONS
```

For this run we "fool" the program by reversing the bound numbers entered; despite the prompt message, the right bound is entered before the left bound, and the program has no provision for rejecting the entry. Notice that the first calculation is the same as that for the previous run; a secant line is drawn between the same two points, regardless of which one we choose as X(1). The next calculation, that of X(4), and subsequent ones differ from those from the first run (can you see why?). The result is that the negative root rather than the positive root has been found in the same number of iterations.

```
ENTER MAXIMUM FUNCTION ERROR:
0.0001
ENTER MAXIMUM NUMBER OF ITERATIONS (<= 100 ):
30
ENTER LEFT AND RIGHT BOUNDS OF X  (X(1),X(2)):
-100, 0
X (  3) =      -.173241
X (  4) =      8.802341
X (  5) =      1.438618
X (  6) =      2.400397
X (  7) =      3.437145
X (  8) =      3.176111
X (  9) =      3.199350
X ( 10) =      3.200002
A ROOT IS AT X =          3.200002
ROOT FOUND AFTER              8 ITERATIONS
```

This result illustrates a problem with the secant method when more than one root exists. Only the negative root is enclosed within the initial bound (–100 to 0), yet the positive root is the one found. The problem, as we saw for the curve shown in Figure 9-5, is that the last two secant line intersections with the x axis do not always stay between the root we are searching for. As a result, the process can converge to another root, as is the case for this run.

```
ENTER MAXIMUM FUNCTION ERROR:
0.0001
ENTER MAXIMUM NUMBER OF ITERATIONS (<=100 ):
30
ENTER LEFT AND RIGHT BOUNDS OF X  (X(1),X(2)):
-10, 0
X (  3) =     -2.146835
X (  4) =   -362.119600
X (  5) =     -2.193387
X (  6) =     -2.239640
X (  7) =     -9.375102
X (  8) =     -3.989268
X (  9) =     -4.825817
X ( 10) =     -5.392557
X ( 11) =     -5.294594
```

```
X ( 12) =      -5.299942
X ( 13) =      -5.300000
A ROOT IS AT X =         -5.300000
ROOT FOUND AFTER             11 ITERATIONS
```

For this run we chose the left interval as –10 rather than –100, and the negative root was found. However, the convergence was not as rapid as we might have expected, since an apparently small slope for the second secant line constructed resulted in a large negative value for X(4). This again illustrates that this method is rather sensitive to the nature of the curve.

```
ENTER MAXIMUM FUNCTION ERROR:
0.0001
ENTER MAXIMUM NUMBER OF ITERATIONS (<=100 ):
30
ENTER LEFT AND RIGHT BOUNDS OF X  (X(1),X(2)):
-6, -4
X (  3) =    -5.184810
X (  4) =    -5.321136
X (  5) =    -5.299710
X (  6) =    -5.299999
A ROOT IS AT X =         -5.299999
ROOT FOUND AFTER              4 ITERATIONS
```

For this run it is assumed that we had some knowledge that the negative root was in the vicinity of $x = -5$. By choosing the initial interval to be very narrow in comparison to those used in the previous runs, we converged on the enclosed root quite rapidly.

From the results of these runs, we can conclude that the secant method does indeed converge more rapidly than does the bisection method in most cases, and certainly far more rapidly than the fixed-count iteration method presented at the beginning of this section. However, where more than one root exists, it is not always apparent how to locate all the roots with a very small number of runs. You may want to try other functions with this method to gain more insight into the problem.

Exercises

1a. Modify Program 11-4 to calculate and display a table of integer values of the function:

$$y = x^4 + 4x^3 - 7x^2 - 22x + 24$$

in the interval from $x = -10$ to $x = 10$. Compile and run the program on a computer. Can you determine the roots of this function from your display?

b. Modify Program 9-5 to calculate and display the roots of this function. Compile and run the program.

2. Modify Program 9-6 using the function from Exercise 1. Run the program four times using a step size of 0.01 for each run and allowable errors of 0.1, 0.01, 0.003, and 0.001, respectively.

3. Modify Program 9-7 using the function from Exercise 1. Run the program five times using step sizes of 1, 0.5, 0.499, 0.1, and 0.01, respectively. Explain your results.

4. Consider the function $y = \cos(x)$ in the interval from $x = 0$ to $x = 20$.

   a. Sketch the curve for the function by hand and determine from it the number of roots in this interval and their location.

   b. Modify Program 9-6 using this function and run the program. By trial and error set a step size and an allowable error that will display each root in the interval only once.

5. Modify Program 9-7 using the function from Exercise 4. Run the program four times using step sizes of 1, 0.5, 0.1, and 0.01, respectively. Explain your results.

6. Modify Program 9-8 using the function from Exercise 1. Run the program several times, entering 0.001 for the allowable error and 30 for the maximum number of iterations. For the various runs select left and right bounds to enable you to find all the roots in the interval from $x = -10$ to $x = 10$.

7. Repeat Exercise 6 using the function $y = \cos(x)$ in the interval from $x = 0$ to $x = 20$.

8. Modify Program 9-9 using the function from Exercise 1. Run the program several times, entering 0.001 for the maximum function error and 30 for the maximum number of iterations. For the various runs, select left and right bounds to enable you to find all the roots in the interval from $x = -10$ to $x = 10$. Compare the number of iterations required for the secant method and for the bisection method. Did the presence of multiple roots cause any problems in using the secant method?

9. Repeat Exercise 8 using the function $y = \cos(x)$ in the interval from $x = 0$ to $x = 20$.

10. The equation:

$$2e^{-x} - 1 = 0$$

has a root between $x = 0$ and $x = 1$.

   a. Modify and run Program 9-8 to locate the root using the bisection method, using the interval from 0 to 1 and an allowable error of 0.001, and have your program display the number of iterations made. Then modify Program 9-9 to locate the root using the secant method, using the same allowable error. Compare the number of iterations required by both programs.

   b. Repeat Exercise 10a using an interval from 0 to 5 and determine the number of iterations required to locate the root using both the bisection and secant methods.

   c. Repeat Exercise 10a using an interval from 0 to 10 and determine the number of iterations required to locate the root using both the bisection and secant methods. Note that convergence may be a problem with the secant method.

9.3 Numerical Integration

Integration is a calculus technique that can be used to find the area under a portion of a curve. Frequently, in engineering and statistical problems, the calculated areas correspond to physical quantities. For example, the area under a normal bell-shaped curve in statistical applications is used in calculating probabilities, and the area under a band of frequencies in engineering applications is used to calculate power consumption. As in the root-finding methods discussed in the previous section, there are approximation methods that can be easily programmed on a computer for determining these areas when exact solutions do not exist.

Rectangular Approximations

To illustrate the rectangular approximation method, consider Figure 9-6. As illustrated in this figure, an arbitrary function $y = f(x)$ is shown within an interval bounded by $x = a$ and $x = b$. The area under the curve refers to the area between the curve and the horizontal x axis, bounded by the vertical lines drawn at a and b. An approximation to the true area under the curve can be obtained by dividing the area into N rectangles of equal widths, denoted as w in the figure, and adding the area of each rectangle. The integer N is arbitrary, but larger values chosen for N generally result in more accurate approximations. The width of each subinterval is the total interval width divided by the number of subintervals. Therefore, we have:

$$w = \frac{b-a}{N}$$

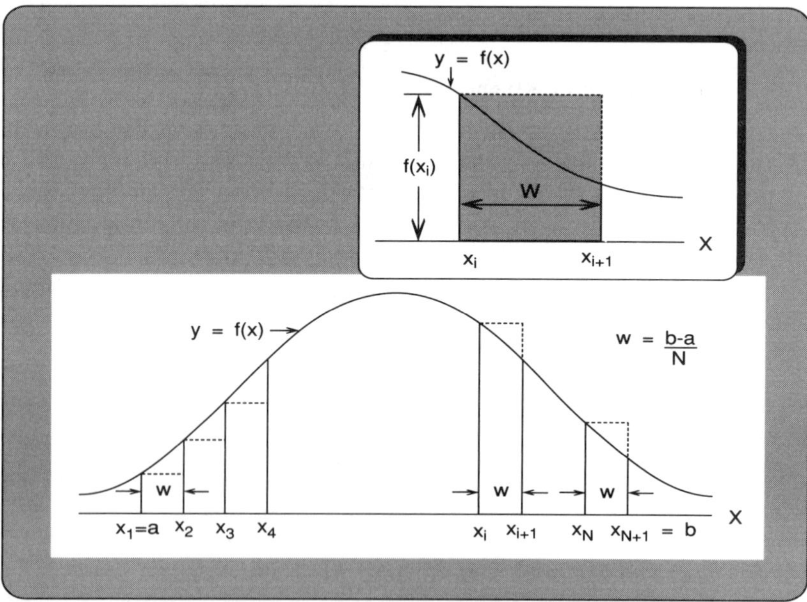

Figure 9-6 Rectangular Approximation to Area Under a Curve

The start of each subinterval is designated by $x_1, x_2, x_3, \ldots x_N$. Using a variable index, i, the start of subinterval i is at x_i where $i = 1, 2, 3, \ldots N$.

The start of the first subinterval, x_1, corresponds to a, and the end of the Nth subinterval, which we can call x_{N+1}, is equal to b. Also, since the subintervals are of equal width:

$$x_{i+1} = x_i + w \qquad \textit{for } i = 1, 2, 3, \ldots N$$

The total area under the curve between a and b is clearly the sum of the areas under the N subintervals. As the name of the rectangular approximation technique implies, it simply approximates the area under each subinterval by that of a rectangle. As seen in the enlarged drawing of the ith subinterval in Figure 9-6, the value of y at the start of the interval determines the height of the rectangle. Since the area of a rectangle is simply width multiplied by height, and the width is w, the area of the ith subinterval can be expressed as:

$$A_i = w * f(x_i)$$

This corresponds to the shaded area shown in Figure 9-6. The total area is then:

$$\text{Area} = A_1 + A_2 + A_3 + \ldots + A_N$$
$$= \sum_{i=1}^{N} A_i$$
$$= w \sum_{i=1}^{N} f(x_i)$$

where:

$$w = \frac{b - a}{N}$$
$$x_1 = a$$
$$x_{i+1} = x_i + w$$

for all i from 1 to N. This result then approximates the area under the curve between limits $x = a$ and $x = b$.

This technique can be programmed with the aid of a looping procedure that calculates each subinterval area and then updates the value of x. The pseudocode for this procedure is given by:

```
enter the left and right bounds (a and b) and the number of subintervals (N)
calculate width (w)
initialize x
set total area to zero
do for all rectangles
    calculate the y value corresponding to x
    calculate the area of the recangle
    add the rectangular area to the total area
    update value of x
enddo
display total area
```

To illustrate this approximation method, we will choose a curve for which the exact area is known, so that we may compare the calculated approximation to the actual area. Figure 9-7 shows a circle centered at the origin of the x–y coordinate system. Consider the area under the portion of the circle in the upper right quadrant, shown by the shaded region in Figure 9-7. From symmetry, the shaded area is one-fourth of the total area of the circle, which we know to be π multiplied by the radius squared (where $\pi = 3.141593$, accurate to six decimal places). Therefore, the exact area of the shaded area is:

$$\text{Area} = \pi * r^2 / 4$$

For a circle of radius equal to 2, the area is then π, or 3.141593.

The equation of a circle centered at the origin is given by:

$$x^2 + y^2 = r^2$$

For a circle with a radius of 2, this becomes:

$$x^2 + y^2 = 4$$

Solving for y, in terms of x, we obtain:

$$y = \sqrt{4 - x^2}$$

To limit ourselves to the upper right quadrant requires that x be bounded by 0 and 2 and the positive (rather than negative) square root be taken for y. The requirement on the sign of the root is no problem, because FORTRAN's square root function (SQRT) always returns the positive root.

Program 9-10 calculates and displays the area of this circle using rectangular approximation.

Notice that although we used subscripted x values in the discussion of the method, the difference between x_{i+1} and x_i is a constant for all i. It is therefore unnecessary to use arrays in the program to store many values of x at once. After each value is used in calculating the area of the subinterval, it is updated by the statement X = X + WIDTH. This calculation in effect replaces each x_i by the next value, x_{i+1}. Notice also the index I in the program simply functions as a counter, allowing the areas of the N subintervals to be summed. The equation of the circle is

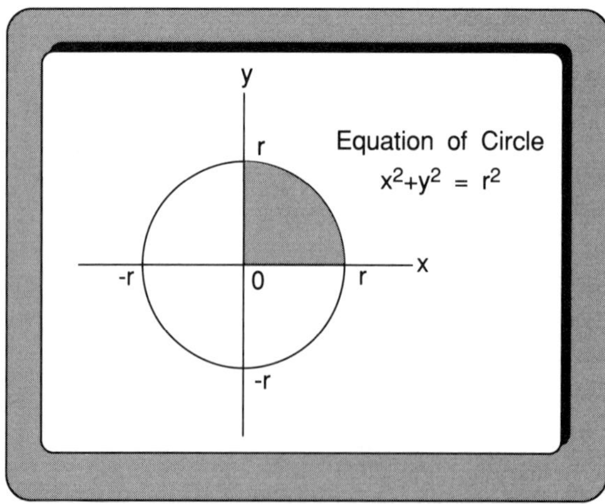

Figure 9-7
Area Under a Circle

Program 9-10

```
      PROGRAM MAIN
        INTEGER N
        REAL A, B, AREA
        CALL GETVAL(N, A, B)
        CALL RECINT(N, A, B, AREA)
        CALL SHOW(AREA)
        END
*
      SUBROUTINE GETVAL(N, A, B)
        INTEGER N
        REAL A, B
        WRITE(6,*) 'ENTER LEFT AND RIGHT BOUNDS OF X  (A, B): '
        READ(5,*) A, B
        WRITE(6,*) 'ENTER NUMBER OF SUBINTERVALS  (N): '
        READ(5,*) N
        RETURN
        END
*
      SUBROUTINE RECINT(N, A, B, AREA)
        INTEGER N, I
        REAL A, B, WIDTH, AREA, X, F
        F(X) = SQRT( ABS(4 - X**2) )
        WIDTH = (B - A) / N
        X = A
        AREA = 0.0
        DO 20 I = 1, N
          AREA = AREA + WIDTH * F(X)
          X = X + WIDTH
   20   CONTINUE
        RETURN
        END
*
      SUBROUTINE SHOW(AREA)
        REAL AREA
        WRITE(6,*) 'APPROXIMATE TOTAL AREA USING RECTANGULAR'
        WRITE(6,*) ' METHOD = ', AREA
        RETURN
        END
```

specified by the function statement placed after the declaration statement. The absolute value intrinsic function (ABS) was inserted to prevent taking the square root of a negative number, a condition that would cause an error.

The sample runs for Program 9-10 are shown below, varying only the number of subintervals, *N*.

```
ENTER LEFT AND RIGHT BOUNDS OF X  (A, B):
0 2
ENTER NUMBER OF SUBINTERVALS  (N):
2
APPROXIMATE TOTAL AREA USING RECTANGULAR
 METHOD =        3.732051

ENTER LEFT AND RIGHT BOUNDS OF X  (A, B):
0 2
ENTER NUMBER OF SUBINTERVALS  (N):
10
APPROXIMATE TOTAL AREA USING RECTANGULAR
 METHOD =        3.304518

ENTER LEFT AND RIGHT BOUNDS OF X  (A, B):
0 2
ENTER NUMBER OF SUBINTERVALS  (N):
50
APPROXIMATE TOTAL AREA USING RECTANGULAR
 METHOD =        3.178269

ENTER LEFT AND RIGHT BOUNDS OF X  (A, B):
0 2
ENTER NUMBER OF SUBINTERVALS  (N):
1000
APPROXIMATE TOTAL AREA USING RECTANGULAR
 METHOD =        3.143558
```

As expected, the accuracy improves as *N* gets larger. For example, if only two subintervals are used the approximated area is about 20 percent greater than the exact area ($\pi = 3.141593$, accurate to six decimal places); however, if 50 subintervals are used, the error is about 1 percent. Obviously, the improved accuracy is gained at the expense of a longer running time for the program.

Modified Rectangular Approximations

A modified form of the rectangular method, called the midpoint method, is illustrated in Figure 9-8. The only difference from the standard rectangular method is that the value of y at the midpoint of the subinterval rather than at the start of the subinterval is used as the height of the rectangle.

From Figure 9-8 it is seen that the midpoint of the *i*th rectangle, m_i, is calculated as:

$$m_i = \frac{x_i + x_{i+1}}{2} = \frac{x_i + (x_i + w)}{2} = x_i + \frac{w}{2}$$

where w is the width of each rectangle. The height of the *i*th rectangle is the y value for $x = m_i$, which is:

$$f(m_i) = f(x_i + \frac{w}{2})$$

and the area of the ith rectangle is then:

$$A_i = w * f(x_i + \frac{w}{2})$$

Finally, the total area under the curve is approximated by:

$$Area = w \sum_{i=1}^{N} f(x_i + \frac{w}{2})$$

where the width, w, of each rectangle is calculated as $(b - a) / N$.

From a programming perspective, this approximation formula for the total area can be programmed using a DO loop that calculates each rectangular area, adds the calculated area to a sum, and then updates the value of x. The pseudocode for this procedure is:

enter the left and right bounds (a *and* b) *and the number of subintervals (N).*
calculate width (w)
initialize x
set total area to zero
do for all rectangles
  calculate the x midpoint and its corresponding y *value*

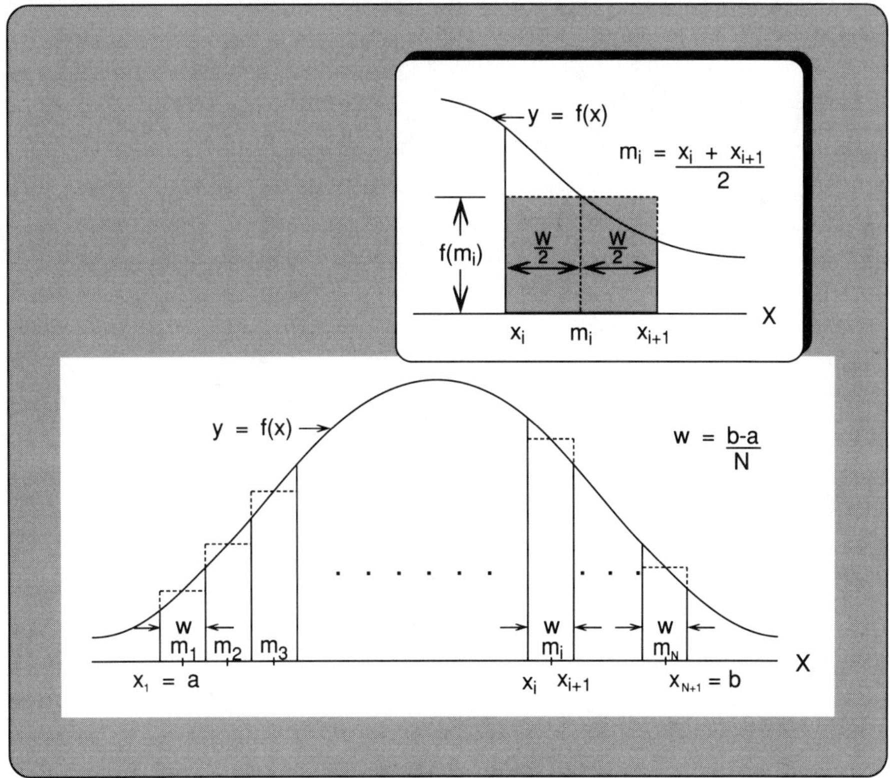

Figure 9-8 Modified Approximation to Area Under a Curve

calculate the area of the rectangle
add the rectangular area to the total area
update the value of x
enddo
display total area

Program 9-11 calculates and displays the area of this circle using the midpoint approximation method. The only difference between Programs 9-10 and 9-11 is the assignment statement for AREA within the DO loop. In this statement the function call F(X) in Program 9-10 is replaced by F (X + WIDTH/2) in Program 9-11.

Program 9-11

```
      PROGRAM MAIN
         INTEGER N
         REAL A, B, AREA
         CALL GETVAL(N, A, B)
         CALL MODREC(N, A, B, AREA)
         CALL SHOW(AREA)
         END
*
      SUBROUTINE GETVAL(N, A, B)
         INTEGER N
         REAL A, B
         WRITE(6,*) 'ENTER LEFT AND RIGHT BOUNDS OF X  (A, B): '
         READ(5,*) A, B
         WRITE(6,*) 'ENTER NUMBER OF RECTANGLES  (N): '
         READ(5,*) N
         RETURN
         END
*
      SUBROUTINE MODREC(N, A, B, AREA)
         INTEGER N, I
         REAL A, B, WIDTH, AREA, X, F
         F(X) = SQRT( ABS(4 - X**2) )
         WIDTH = (B - A) / N
         X = A
         AREA = 0.0
         DO 20 I = 1, N
           AREA = AREA + WIDTH * F(X + WIDTH/2.0)
           X = X + WIDTH
   20    CONTINUE
         RETURN
         END
*
      SUBROUTINE SHOW(AREA)
         REAL AREA
         WRITE(6,*) 'APPROXIMATE TOTAL AREA USING THE'
         WRITE(6,*) ' MODIFIED RECTANGULAR METHOD = ', AREA
         RETURN
         END
```

Notice that after each midpoint value is used to calculate a corresponding *y* value, and the area of each rectangle is computed, this area is immediately added into the total area. Notice also that the index I in the program only acts as a counter, allowing the areas of the *N* rectangles to be summed. The equation of the circle is specified by the function statement placed after the declaration statement.

Four sample runs using Program 9-11 follow, showing the areas calculated when 2, 10, 50, and 1000 rectangles are used.

```
ENTER LEFT AND RIGHT BOUNDS OF X  (A, B): 0, 2
ENTER NUMBER OF RECTANGLES   (N): 2
APPROXIMATE TOTAL AREA USING THE
 MODIFIED RECTANGULAR METHOD =        3.259367

ENTER LEFT AND RIGHT BOUNDS OF X  (A, B): 0, 2
ENTER NUMBER OF RECTANGLES   (N): 10
APPROXIMATE TOTAL AREA USING THE
 MODIFIED RECTANGULAR METHOD =        3.152411

ENTER LEFT AND RIGHT BOUNDS OF X  (A, B): 0, 2
ENTER NUMBER OF RECTANGLES   (N): 50
APPROXIMATE TOTAL AREA USING THE
 MODIFIED RECTANGULAR METHOD =        3.142566

ENTER LEFT AND RIGHT BOUNDS OF X  (A, B): 0, 2
ENTER NUMBER OF RECTANGLES   (N): 1000
APPROXIMATE TOTAL AREA USING THE
 MODIFIED RECTANGULAR METHOD =        3.141631
```

As expected, the accuracy improves as the number of approximating rectangles, *N*, is increased. When using only two rectangles, the approximation differs by less than 5 percent from the exact area (3.141593). This compares to a 20 percent difference using the standard rectangular method. For $N = 50$, the error is less than 0.01 percent of its true value, which compares to an error of 1 percent using the same number of subintervals with the standard rectangular method. Referring again to Figures 9-6 and 9-8, it seems reasonable to expect that using the midpoint for the height of each rectangle method would give a more accurate result than using the endpoint, as in the standard rectangular method. If the curve does not exhibit unusual bending within a subinterval, the use of the midpoint to define the height of the rectangle will give a better approximation to the subinterval area than if the left endpoint of the subinterval (or the right endpoint, for that matter) were used.

Trapezoidal Approximation

In Figure 9-9, which illustrates the trapezoidal approximation method, the interval is divided into subintervals in the same manner as for the rectangular methods. However, the curve is now approximated by connecting a straight line between the points on the curve corresponding to the start and end of the subinterval. As shown by the enlarged drawing of the *i*th subinterval, the approximate area (the shaded portion) is that of a trapezoid made up of a rectangle plus a triangle. Since the area of a triangle is one-half of the product of width and height, the area of the ith subinterval shown in Figure 9-9 is then:

$$\begin{aligned} A_i &= \text{area of rectangle} + \text{area of triangle} \\ &= w f(x_{i+1}) + 0.5w\,[f(x_i) - f(x_{i+1})] \\ &= 0.5w\,[f(x_i) + f(x_{i+1})] \end{aligned}$$

The total area is then:

$$\begin{aligned} \text{Area} &= A_1 + A_2 + A_3 + \ldots + A_N \\ &= 0.5w\,[f(x_1) + f(x_2)] \\ &\quad + 0.5w\,[f(x_2) + f(x_3)] \\ &\quad + 0.5w\,[f(x_3) + f(x_4)] \\ &\quad + \ldots \\ &\quad + 0.5w\,[f(x_N) + f(x_{N+1})] \\ &= 0.5w\,[f(x_1) + f(x_{N+1})] \\ &\quad + w\,[f(x_2) + f(x_3) + f(x_4) + \ldots + f(x_N)] \end{aligned}$$

Since x_1 and x_{N+1} are the interval endpoints a and b, respectively, we can write the total area as:

$$Area = 0.5\,w\,[f(a) = f(b)] + w \sum_{i=2}^{N} f(x_i)$$

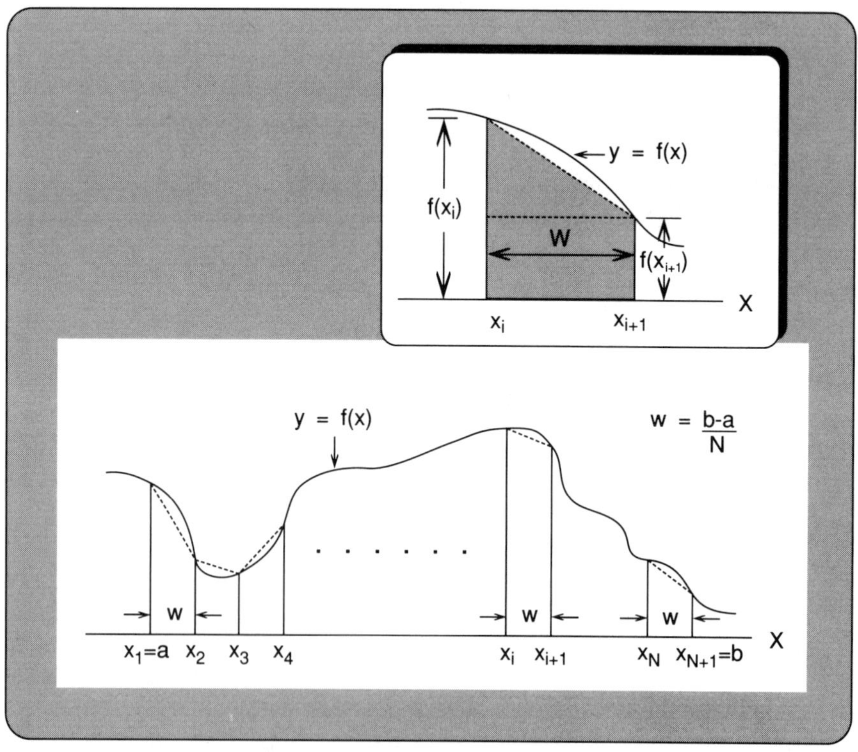

Figure 9-9 Trapezoidal Approximation to Area Under a Curve

where $w = \dfrac{b-a}{N}$ and $x_{i+1} = x_{i+1} + w$.

The computation of the total area can now be done in a manner similar to that used for the rectangular methods. After entering a, b, and N the area can be initialized to:

$$0.5\, w\, [f\,(a) + f\,(b)]$$

and the term $wf(x_i)$ can be added within a loop. Notice that in contrast to the results for the rectangular methods, the summation starts for $i = 2$ rather than $i = 1$. The initial loop index value is therefore 2 for this case. Program 9-12 uses the trapezoidal approximation to compute the area of the quarter circle in Figure 9-7, with radius $r = 2$.

Program 9-12

```
      PROGRAM MAIN
        INTEGER N
        REAL A, B, AREA
        CALL GETVAL(N, A, B)
        CALL TRAPIN(N, A, B, AREA)
        CALL SHOW(AREA)
        END
*
      SUBROUTINE GETVAL(N, A, B)
        INTEGER N
        REAL A, B
        WRITE(6,*) 'ENTER LEFT AND RIGHT BOUNDS OF X  (A, B): '
        READ(5,*) A, B
        WRITE(6,*) 'ENTER NUMBER OF SUBINTERVALS  (N): '
        READ(5,*) N
        RETURN
        END
*
      SUBROUTINE TRAPIN(N, A, B, AREA)
        INTEGER N, I
        REAL A, B, WIDTH, AREA, X, F
        F(X) = SQRT( ABS(4 - X**2) )
        WIDTH = (B - A) / N
        X = A + WIDTH
        AREA = 0.5 * WIDTH * ( F(A) + F(B) )
        DO 20 I = 2, N
          AREA = AREA + WIDTH * F(X)
          X = X + WIDTH
20      CONTINUE
        RETURN
        END
```

(Continued on the next page)

(Continued from the previous page)

```
*
      SUBROUTINE SHOW(AREA)
        REAL AREA
        WRITE(6,*) 'APPROXIMATE TOTAL AREA USING TRAPEZOIDAL'
        WRITE(6,*) ' METHOD = ', AREA
        RETURN
        END
```

As with the rectangular methods, the four sample runs for the trapezoidal method shown below display the approximate area for 2, 10, 50, and 1000 subintervals, respectively.

```
ENTER LEFT AND RIGHT BOUNDS OF X  (A, B):
0 2
ENTER NUMBER OF SUBINTERVALS  (N):
2
APPROXIMATE TOTAL AREA USING TRAPEZOIDAL
 METHOD =        2.732051

ENTER LEFT AND RIGHT BOUNDS OF X  (A, B):
0 2
ENTER NUMBER OF SUBINTERVALS  (N):
10
APPROXIMATE TOTAL AREA USING TRAPEZOIDAL
 METHOD =        3.104518
ENTER LEFT AND RIGHT BOUNDS OF X  (A, B):
0 2
ENTER NUMBER OF SUBINTERVALS  (N):
50
APPROXIMATE TOTAL AREA USING TRAPEZOIDAL
 METHOD =        3.138269

ENTER LEFT AND RIGHT BOUNDS OF X  (A, B):
0 2
ENTER NUMBER OF SUBINTERVALS  (N):
1000
APPROXIMATE TOTAL AREA USING TRAPEZOIDAL
 METHOD =        3.141557
```

The results for this example show that the trapezoidal method is considerably more accurate than the standard rectangular method but not quite as accurate as the modified rectangular (midpoint) method. Although we cannot generalize our conclusions for all curves, the use of the two endpoints of each subinterval should in most cases enable a better approximation of the area than will the use of only one endpoint. This justifies the trapezoidal approach as compared to the standard rectangular method. The midpoint method, unlike the standard method, is actually using the two endpoint values of x in calculating the subinterval's midpoint. We would therefore expect comparable accuracy between the midpoint and the trapezoidal methods. The results for the area of the quarter circle support that conclusion.

Simpson's Method

In addition to obtaining a more accurate estimate of the area under a curve by increasing the number of approximating subintervals, it is frequently possible to increase the accuracy by using a better approximation for the area of each subinterval. Simpson's method effectively achieves this result by fitting a parabolic curve to the endpoints of two successive intervals, as illustrated in Figure 9-10.

Notice that the two subintervals shown in Figure 9-10 share a common endpoint at x_{i+1}, providing three points to which the parabolic curve is being fit. Since two subintervals are being fitted at a time, the total number of subintervals, N, must be an even integer when Simpson's method is used.

The shaded area shown in Figure 9-10 is the approximation to the actual area under curve between the two intervals bounded by $x = x_i$ and $x = x_{i+2}$. The area under a parabolic curve cannot be determined simply as the height times the width, as it can be for a rectangle. With the aid of calculus, however, it can be shown that the shaded area is equal to:

$$A_i + A_{i+1} = \frac{w}{3} * [f(x_i) + 4f(x_{i+1}) + f(x_{i+2})]$$

where A_i is the area of the interval starting at x_i, and A_{i+1} the area of the adjacent next interval, starting at x_{i+1}. Notice that if the curve encompassed within two adjacent intervals is flat (zero slope), then $f(x_i) = f(x_{i+1}) = f(x_{i+2})$, and the shaded area becomes two equal-sized rectangles, each of width w and height equal to $f(x_i)$. In this case the previous expression reduces to:

$$A_i + A_{i+1} = \frac{w}{3} * [f(x_i) + 4f(x_{i+1}) + f(x_i)]$$

$$= \frac{w}{3} * [6f(x_i) + 2wf(x_i)$$

as expected.

The total area under the curve, between the limits $x = a$ and $x = b$, is again a summation of areas A_i for all i from 1 to N. However, since the expression above

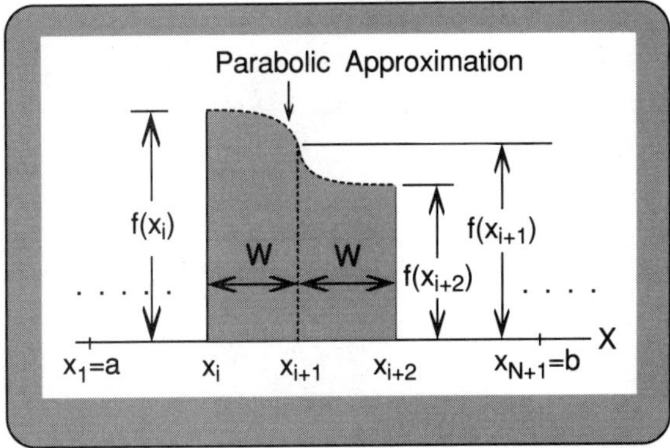

Figure 9-10 Parabolic Approximation to the Area Under a Curve

includes two adjacent intervals, the sum is taken for $i = 1, 3, 5$, and all other odd values of i up to and including $N-1$. That is:

$$Area = \sum_{i=1}^{N-1} (A_i + A_{i+1})$$

(odd i only)

$$= \frac{w}{3} * \sum_{i=1}^{N-1} [f(x_i) + 4f(x_{i+1}) + f(x_{i+2})]$$

(odd i only)

We will find it more convenient to evaluate this expression in its present form using a DO loop than to expand out the expression. As in Program 9-10, a routine to implement Simpson's method must input the values of a and b and the number of intervals (N) and calculate the width (WIDTH). The calculation of the total area is then completed using the following statements:

```
          X = A
          AREA = 0
          DO 20 I = 1, N-1, 2
            TEMP = F(X) + 4 * F(X + WIDTH) + F(X+2*WIDTH)
            AREA = AREA + WIDTH * TEMP / 3
            X = X + 2 * WIDTH
20        CONTINUE
```

Starting with the leftmost interval, X is initialized to A, and AREA to 0. Within the loop, the index advances by two each time, and X is incremented by twice the width, to account for the handling of two intervals at a time. Additionally, a temporary variable (TEMP) is introduced to avoid an overly lengthy statement line for the calculation of AREA.

Program 9-13 includes these statements in applying Simpson's method to approximate the area of the quarter circle with radius $r = 2$.

The sample runs below show the results for 2, 10, 50, and 1000 intervals.

```
ENTER LEFT AND RIGHT BOUNDS OF X  (A, B): 0 2
ENTER EVEN NUMBER OF INTERVALS  (N): 2
APPROXIMATE TOTAL AREA USING SIMPSON METHOD
 =        2.976068

ENTER LEFT AND RIGHT BOUNDS OF X  (A, B): 0 2
ENTER EVEN NUMBER OF INTERVALS  (N): 10
APPROXIMATE TOTAL AREA USING SIMPSON METHOD
 =        3.127031

ENTER LEFT AND RIGHT BOUNDS OF X  (A, B): 0 2
ENTER EVEN NUMBER OF INTERVALS  (N): 50
APPROXIMATE TOTAL AREA USING SIMPSON METHOD
 =        3.140298

ENTER LEFT AND RIGHT BOUNDS OF X  (A, B): 0 2
ENTER EVEN NUMBER OF INTERVALS  (N): 1000
APPROXIMATE TOTAL AREA USING SIMPSON METHOD
 =        3.141579
```

Program 9-13

```
      PROGRAM MAIN
        INTEGER N
        REAL A, B, AREA
        CALL GETVAL(N, A, B)
        CALL SIMPSN(N, A, B, AREA)
        CALL SHOW(AREA)
        END
*
      SUBROUTINE GETVAL(N, A, B)
        INTEGER N
        REAL A, B
        WRITE(6,*) 'ENTER LEFT AND RIGHT BOUNDS OF X  (A, B): '
        READ(5,*) A, B
        WRITE(6,*) 'ENTER EVEN NUMBER OF INTERVALS  (N): '
        READ(5,*) N
        RETURN
        END
*
      SUBROUTINE SIMPSN(N, A, B, AREA)
        INTEGER N, I
        REAL A, B, WIDTH, AREA, X, F, TEMP
        F(X) = SQRT( ABS(4 - X**2) )
        WIDTH = (B - A) / N
        X = A
        AREA = 0.0
        DO 20 I = 1, N-1, 2
          TEMP = F(X) + 4 * F(X + WIDTH) + F(X + 2 * WIDTH)
          AREA = AREA + WIDTH * TEMP / 3.0
          X = X + 2 * WIDTH
   20   CONTINUE
        RETURN
        END
*
      SUBROUTINE SHOW(AREA)
        REAL AREA
        WRITE(6,*) 'APPROXIMATE TOTAL AREA USING SIMPSON METHOD'
        WRITE(6,*) ' = ', AREA
        RETURN
        END
```

Table 9-1 Comparison of Area Approximations for $F(X) = \sqrt{4-x^2}$ Over the Interval X=0 to X=2.

N	Standard rectangular method	Midpoint rectangular method	Trapezoidal method	Simpson's method
2	3.372051	3.259367	2.732051	2.976068
10	3.304518	3.152411	3.104518	3.127031
50	3.178269	3.142466	3.138269	3.140298
1000	3.143558	3.141603	3.141557	3.141579

(Exact area = 3.141593)

Table 9-2 Comparison of Area Approximation for F(X) = SIN(X) Over the Interval X = 0 to X = π

N	Standard rectangular method	Midpoint rectangular method	Trapezoidal method	Simpson's method
2	1.570796	2.221442	1.570796	2.094395
10	1.983524	2.008249	1.983523	2.000109
50	1.999342	2.000329	1.999342	2.000000
1000	1.999998	2.000001	1.999998	2.000000

(Exact area = 2.000000)

Table 9-1 summarizes the results for each of the four numerical integration methods used to approximate the area of the quarter circle with radius $r = 2$.

To further compare the two methods listed in Table 9-1, consider the half-cycle sine wave shown in Figure 9-11. The exact area under the curve from $x = 0$ to $x = \pi$ ($\pi = 3.141593$, accurate to six decimal places) can be shown using calculus to be 2.0. To approximate this value using numerical integration, Programs 9-10 through 9-13 were modified by replacing the function statement in each case by:

```
F(X) = SIN (X)
```

The bounds 0 and 3.141593 were entered when the programs were running. The tabulated results for the sine wave are listed in Table 9-2.

Using Tables 9-1 and 9-2, we can compare the four methods for the two examples, still far too few from which to draw any general conclusions, however. For the quarter circle the standard rectangular method has the poorest accuracy, and the trapezoidal method the next poorest. Both methods have the same accuracy for the half-cycle sine wave, which is coincidental and arises from the special properties of the symmetrical sine wave. For the quarter circle, the modified rectangular and Simpson's methods converge to the correct result equally fast as N increases.

Application: Finding Average and RMS Values

The techniques for finding the area under a curve can also be used to find the average, or root-mean-squared (RMS), value of a waveform described by a function $y = f(x)$. This subject is of importance in electrical instrumentation, in which many voltage- and current-measuring instruments are calibrated to the average or RMS value of a periodic signal (such as a sine wave).

Refer again to Figure 9-6 illustrating the rectangular approximation to the area under a general curve $y = f(x)$. The average value of the function can be approximated by selecting a reasonably large number of equally spaced points on the curve, adding their y values, and dividing by the total number of points selected. Notice that this procedure is analogous to finding the average quiz grade for a class by adding the individual quiz grades and dividing by the size of the class. The average value corresponding to N points on the curve corresponding to $x_1, x_2, x_3, \ldots x_N$ is then:

$$Average = \frac{f(x_1) + f(x_2) + f(x_3) + \ldots + f(x_N)}{N}$$

$$= \frac{1}{N} \sum_{i=1}^{N} f(x_i)$$

where the x values are separated by the fixed interval width:

$$w = \frac{b-a}{N}$$

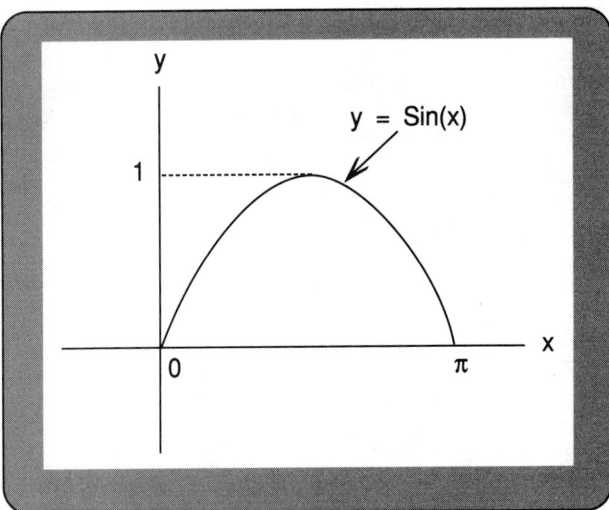

Figure 9-11 Half-Cycle of a Sine Wave

as before. Notice that the expression above can be written as:

$$Average = \frac{1}{Nw} \; w \sum_{i=1}^{N} f(x_i)$$

$$= \frac{1}{b-a} \; w \sum_{i=1}^{N} f(x_i)$$

$$= \frac{\textit{Approximate area under curve}}{\textit{Total interval width}}$$

This should satisfy our intuitive notion that the average height of a curve is the area divided by the base or total width.

The RMS value of a set of function values is also an average or "mean." As the name suggests, the root-mean-squared value is the square root of the average of the individual squared values. For our notation, the RMS value can be written as:

$$RMS = \sqrt{\frac{f^2(x_1) + f^2(x_2) + f^2(x_3) + \ldots + f^2(x_N)}{N}}$$

Program 9-14 is a modification of the rectangular approximation technique shown in Program 9-10. The calculation of AREA has been replaced in the loop by the calculation of the sum of the values of the function (SUM) and the sum of the squared values of the function (SUMSQR). After N iterations we exit from the loop and calculate the average by dividing SUM by N and the RMS value by dividing SUMSQR by N and taking the square root of the result. A sine wave is used for illustration.

Sample runs for Program 9-14 are shown below.

```
ENTER LEFT AND RIGHT BOUNDS OF X  (A, B):
0, 3.141593
ENTER NUMBER OF SUBINTERVALS  (N):
10
APPROXIMATE AVERAGE VALUE =      0.631375
APPROXIMATE RMS VALUE     =      0.707107

ENTER LEFT AND RIGHT BOUNDS OF X  (A, B):
0, 3.141593
ENTER NUMBER OF SUBINTERVALS  (N):
50
APPROXIMATE AVERAGE VALUE =      0.636410
APPROXIMATE RMS VALUE     =      0.707107

ENTER LEFT AND RIGHT BOUNDS OF X  (A, B):
0, 6.283186
ENTER NUMBER OF SUBINTERVALS  (N):
50
APPROXIMATE AVERAGE VALUE =  -4.523840E-08
APPROXIMATE RMS VALUE     =      0.707107
```

Program 9-14

```
      PROGRAM MAIN
        INTEGER N
        REAL A, B, AVERGE, RMS
        CALL GETVAL(N, A, B)
        CALL AVGRMS(N, A, B, AVERGE, RMS)
        CALL SHOW(AVERGE, RMS)
        END
*
      SUBROUTINE GETVAL(N, A, B)
        INTEGER N
        REAL A, B
        WRITE(6,*) 'ENTER LEFT AND RIGHT BOUNDS OF X  (A, B): '
        READ(5,*) A, B
        WRITE(6,*) 'ENTER NUMBER OF SUBINTERVALS  (N): '
        READ(5,*) N
        RETURN
        END
*
      SUBROUTINE AVGRMS(N, A, B, AVERGE, RMS)
        IMPLICIT NONE
        INTEGER N, I
        REAL A, B, WIDTH, AVERGE, RMS, SUM, SUMSQR, X, F
        F(X) = SIN(X)
        WIDTH = (B - A) / N
        X = A
        SUM = 0.0
        SUMSQR = 0.0
        DO 20 I = 1, N
          SUM = SUM + F(X)
          SUMSQR = SUMSQR + F(X) ** 2
          X = X + WIDTH
   20   CONTINUE
        AVERGE = SUM / N
        RMS = SQRT(SUMSQR / N)
        RETURN
        END
*
      SUBROUTINE SHOW(AVERGE, RMS)
        REAL AVERGE, RMS
        WRITE(6,*) 'APPROXIMATE AVERAGE VALUE =', AVERGE
        WRITE(6,*) 'APPROXIMATE RMS VALUE     = ', RMS
        RETURN
        END
```

The first two runs approximate the average and RMS values for the half-cycle sine wave shown in Figure 9-11, from $x = 0$ to $x = \pi$ (where $\pi = 3.141593$). Recall that the exact area under this curve is 2.0, and since the total interval width is π, the actual average value is:

$$\text{Average} = 2 / \pi = 2 / 3.141593 = 0.636620$$

The RMS value can be derived with the aid of calculus and is found to be:

$$\text{RMS} = 1 / \sqrt{2} = 0.707107$$

Notice that the computed average is closer to the exact value for larger *N*, as expected. The RMS value, interestingly, is nearly exact for the smaller as well as the larger value of *N*. As a result of the special properties of the sine function, you will obtain nearly the exact RMS value for any *N* (try it out for yourself!).

The final sample run shown is for a full cycle of the sine wave, from $x = 0$ to $x = 2 * \pi$. The sine wave in the interval from π to $2 * \pi$ has the same shape as in Figure 9-11 but flipped over to the negative direction. The sum of positive and negative values then cancel one another, resulting in an average value of zero. However, the negative values when squared become positive values and the resulting RMS value is the same as for the half-cycle case (do you see why?). The results of the last run support these conclusions.

Exercises

1a. Modify Program 9-10 to approximate the area under the curve:

$$y = x^3 + 2x^2 + 3x + 1$$

in the interval from $x = 0$ to $x = 1$. Run the program four times for $N = 2$, 10, 50, and 1000, respectively. The exact area is:

$$\text{AREA} = 41/12 = 3.416666$$

b. Repeat Exercise 1a using the modified rectangular method (Program 9-11).

2a. Repeat Exercise 1a using the trapezoidal method (Program 9- 12).

b. Repeat Exercise 1a using Simpson's method (Program 9-13).

c. Compare the results of Exercises 1 and 2.

3. Modify Program 9-11 to calculate and display a table of values of area for the quarter circle used in the text examples, for $N = 1, 2, 3, \ldots 10$. Also tabulate for each area the percent error between the approximate area and the exact area of $\pi = 3.141593$. Notice that the input of *N* from the keyboard needs to be replaced by a second loop in the program in which *N* is an index varying from 1 to 10. The original loop in the program should be nested inside this second loop. The output should be displayed using the heading below.

```
N          APPROXIMATE AREA      PERCENT ERROR
---        ----------------      -------------
```

4. The centroid is an important concept in engineering mechanics, as it represents the location of the center of gravity of a body of uniform density and thickness. For a curve described by the equation $y = f(x)$, it can be shown that the centroid is located at a point (x_c, y_c) where:

$$x_c = \frac{\text{Area under function } xf(x)}{\text{Area under function } f(x)}$$

$$y_c = \frac{\text{Area under function } f^2(x)/2}{\text{Area under function } f(x)}$$

Notice that finding the centroid location requires the computation of the areas under three different functions, each related to $f(x)$.

a. Modify Program 9-11 to calculate and display the approximate centroid location for the function:

$$y = x^2$$

in the interval from $x = 0$ to $x = 1$.

b. Compile the program from Exercise 4a and run it for $N = 5$, 10, and 50. Comment on the relative accuracies of x_c and y_c. The exact centroid location is:

$$x_c = 0.75,\ y_c = 0.3$$

5. Repeat Exercise 4 for the function:

$$y = x^4$$

in the interval from $x = 0$ to $x = 1$. The exact centroid location, accurate to six decimal places, is $x_c = 5/6 = 0.833333$, and $y_c = 5/18 = 0.277777$.

6a. Modify Program 9-14 to calculate and display the average and RMS values of the function $y = \sin(2x)$ in the interval $x = 0$ to $x = \pi = 3.141593$. Run the program for $N = 10$ and again for $N = 50$. Compare the results with those obtained from the sample runs shown of Program 9-14 for the function $y = \sin(x)$ in the same interval.

b. Repeat Exercise 6a for the function $y = e^{-x} \sin(x)$.

7. An unusual method of approximating the area under a curve can be made using a Monte Carlo simulation algorithm. To understand this algorithm, consider Figure 9-12, in which a rectangle of base (a,b) is superimposed on the curve $y = f(x)$ such that the height of the rectangle, H, is larger than any y value on the curve.

Now consider throwing N darts at Figure 9-12 and calculating the total number of darts, M, that land in the shaded region. Probability theory states that for a large number of darts, the ratio of the M darts that land in the shaded area to the total number of N darts thrown is the same as the ratio of the shaded area to the total area. That is:

$$\frac{M}{N} = \frac{\text{Shaded area}}{\text{Rectangular area}}$$

Solving this formula for the shaded area under the curve yields:

$$\text{Shaded area} = (M/N) * \text{Rectangular area}$$

Using this information, write a FORTRAN program to approximate the area under the curve:

$$y = \sqrt{4 - x^2}$$

from $x = 0$ to $x = 1$. Generate random values of x and y between 0 and 1 using the random number generation algorithm presented in Section 4.5. If the resultant point (x,y) lies below the curve, the generated point is considered as landing in the shaded region; otherwise, it is considered as landing outside of the shaded region. Run your program using 2, 10, 50, and 1000 random points, respectively, and compare the results obtained with those presented in Table 9-1.

9.4 Common Programming Errors

The common errors associated with the techniques presented in this chapter include the following:

1. Although a real-valued loop index is often used for convenience in root-finding techniques, as it is in Programs 9-6 and 9-7, this practice can lead to problems in determining the exact number of iterations performed. Specifically, due to round-off errors, the real variable index may cause the loop to terminate one step earlier than expected. For example, the loop:

```
      REAL X
      DO 20 X = 0.1, 10.0, 0.1
        .
        .
        .
20    CONTINUE
```

may exit after X = 9.9 rather than X = 10.0 as intended. The reason is that after the last increment of the index, its value may round off to 9.999999, or possibly to 10.000001. In the latter case the loop is exited because the index value exceeds the upper limit of 10.0. This problem can be avoided, when necessary, by using an integer variable as a loop index. For example, using an integer loop counter, the following routine can be used to replace the previous loop.

```
      REAL X
      INTEGER I
      X = 0.1
      DO 20 I = 1, 100
        .
        .
        .
        X = X + 0.1
20    CONTINUE
```

The cost of this solution is the additional complexity of the resultant code.

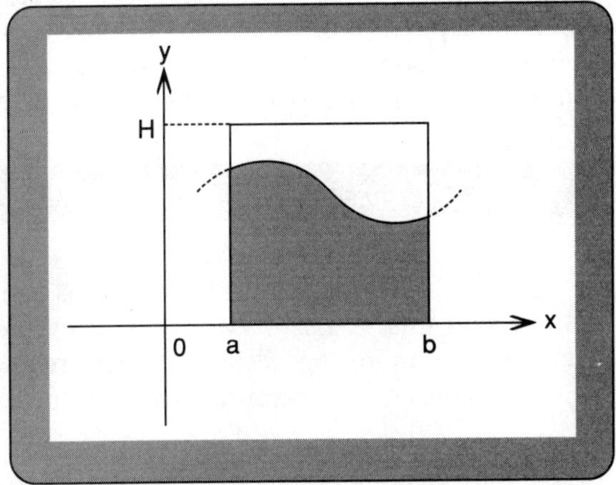

Figure 9-12

2. Unless numerical iteration algorithms are carefully programmed, their execution times can be excessive. Both root-finding and numerical integration programs containing only single loops may exhibit a noticeable delay in completion when the number of iterations is larger than 50. For such programs it is frequently possible to decrease the runtime by performing a calculation outside the loop rather than inside. For example, consider the following segment of code from Program 9-11.

```
      X = A
      AREA = 0
      DO 20 I = 1, N
        AREA = AREA + WIDTH * F (X + WIDTH/2)
        X = X + WIDTH
20    CONTINUE
```

Recall that in this program X represents the start of each interval with the midpoint at X + WIDTH / 2 . Within the loop the function F is repeatedly evaluated at the interval midpoint, requiring WIDTH/2 to be repeatedly added to X. By initializing X to the midpoint of the first interval, however, we can move this calculation outside the loop. Similarly, the returned value of F is multiplied by WIDTH within the existing loop before being added to the previously stored value of AREA. Since WIDTH has a constant value, this multiplication can be done after the loop is exited. The previous segment of code can, therefore, be replaced by:

```
      X = A + WIDTH/2
      AREA = 0
      DO 20 I = 1, N
        AREA = AREA + F(X)
        X = X + WIDTH
20    CONTINUE
      AREA = WIDTH * AREA
```

Since the updating of AREA inside the loop now involves fewer calculations, the program will run faster. For the sake of readability, you may want to use a name other than AREA inside the loop, since the value returned when the loop is exited is not the actual area until it is multiplied by the subinterval width.

9.5 Things to Remember

1. The solution of linear equations with two or three unknowns can be easily programmed. One such method uses *Cramer's rule* and is conveniently programmed using a subroutine function for the calculation of the required determinants. This algorithm is not efficient, however, for larger numbers of equations and unknowns.
2. There are several programming techniques for finding the real roots of an equation $y = f(x)$. In *fixed-increment* techniques the value of x is incremented by a constant step size over a range of values that includes the roots of interest. The value of y is calculated for each x, and a root is assumed to exist wherever the absolute value of y is arbitrarily small. Alternatively, the roots can be located where the function changes sign for two successive values of x. Although fixed-increment methods are easy to program, particularly with the aid of DO loops, such programs generally require a relatively long time to run.
3. The *bisection method* for root finding locates roots more rapidly than do fixed-increment methods. When a bisection algorithm is used, the interval of x is repeatedly bisected. For each bisection the half-interval that maintains the sign change at the endpoints is retained, and the other half interval is discarded from further consideration. The process continues until the interval is arbitrarily small. The presence of multiple roots can cause problems with this method.
4. The *secant method* for root finding is usually more efficient than the bisection method. Rather than bisecting the interval, a secant line is drawn from the points on the function's curve corresponding to the endpoints of the interval. The intersection of the secant line with the x axis is then used as one of the endpoints of the next interval. The process terminates when the absolute value of y is arbitrarily small. Like the bisection method, the secant method may have difficulties handling multiple roots.
5. Numerical integration is a technique for approximating the area under an interval of a curve described by a function $y = f(x)$. The most commonly used techniques divide the interval into N subintervals, where N is an arbitrary number, and adds the subinterval areas in sequence. Within each subinterval the curve can be approximated by a constant value, in which case the total area is a sum of rectangular areas. Alternatively, a straight line can be connected between the endpoints of the subinterval, leading to the addition of trapezoidal areas. *Simpson's method* involves approximating the function in two successive subintervals using a parabolic curve. All of the approximation techniques can be applied to finding the average and root-mean-square (RMS) values of functions.

10 Additional Data Types

Chapter Ten

10.1 Double Precision Data

10.2 Complex Data

10.3 String and Substring Processing

10.4 Data Structures as Parallel Arrays

10.5 Applications

10.6 Common Programming Errors

10.7 Things to Remember

In addition to the four data types we have discussed so far (integer, real, character, and logical), FORTRAN provides two other data types. In this chapter these two additional data types, double precision and complex, are presented. Additional processing techniques are also presented for working with character variables, and the implementation of data structures using parallel arrays is described.

10.1 Double Precision Data

As we discussed in Chapter 1, most FORTRAN compilers provide approximately six significant digits of accuracy. However, there are times when that is not enough—for example, when calculating the angle of intercept of a rocket with a planet 10^9 (1 billion) miles away. An error in the sixth digit in such a calculation could result in the rocket's missing its target by over 1000 miles ($10^{-6} * 10^9$).

In order to gain additional significant digits, FORTRAN provides double precision constants and variables. A double precision constant must be written in exponential notation (see Section 2.1) using a "D" to indicate the exponent. Examples of valid double precision constants are:

```
 4.645D+2
-5.322728D+08
 3.45678D-02
-6.466789039D-03
 1.2345678D5              (same as 1.2345678D+5)
-2.9876D2                 (same as -2.9876D+2)
```

As illustrated by these examples, the plus sign (+) may be omitted immediately following the D when the exponent is positive. In all cases, an exponent must be present as an integer number. The value preceding the D, which is called the *mantissa*, may be either an integer or a real number (some compilers require the mantissa to be real). The number of digits in the mantissa actually stored by the computer is the amount of significant digits retained for the double precision value (see Appendix D for a description of real and double precision number storage).

Examples of invalid double precision constants are:

```
45.3        (missing exponent)
D+4         (missing mantissa)
3.4D-.5     (exponent must be an integer value)
```

Although a double precision constant need not necessarily store twice as many significant digits as are used for real values (often called *single precision* constants), typically they do. Thus, if your compiler retains 6 significant digits for a real number, it typically will retain at least 12 digits for a double precision constant. Even if you specify more digits, only the first 12 (or however many are stored by your compiler) will be retained. Second, execution of arithmetic with double precision values is considerably slower than that with single precision numbers because the extra length of each double precision value must be carried through each computation. Third, since each double precision value typically uses twice the memory space of a single precision constant, the total memory space needed by the program is increased. For these reasons, double precision data should be used only when the additional accuracy they provide is necessary.

Computations using double precision values follow the same rules as computation with reals and integers, with one addition: when an operation is being performed on a double precision number and another number, the other number is first converted to double precision length, and then the arithmetic is executed. For example, the mixed-mode computation 6 * 2.7D4 + 3.0D–1**2 / 3.0 proceeds as follows:

```
= 6 * 2.7D4 + .090000000000 / 3.         (exponentiation performed)
= 162000.000000 + .090000000000 / 3.     (multiplication performed)
= 162000.000000 + .030000000000          (division performed)
= 162000.030000                          (addition performed)
```

Notice that in each case the operand with the highest precision determines the precision to which the other operand is converted. Assuming that the length of a double precision value is 12 digits, each intermediate value in the previous calculation results in a 12-digit number. If the same computation were done using real values capable of holding only 6 significant digits, the value of the final result would be 1.62000E5, and the last 2 digits, 03, corresponding to the seventh and eighth significant digits, would be lost. Similarly, for example, the real computation 2.0/7.0 results in the value 0.285714, while the double precision computation 2.D0/7.D0 results in the value 0.285714285714 (again, the exact number of retained digits is compiler dependent).

The general form of a declaration statement for double precision variables is:

```
DOUBLE PRECISION variable list
```

Thus, the declaration:

```
DOUBLE PRECISION LENGTH, DSTNCE, TOTSAL
```

declares the three variables LENGTH, DSTNCE, and TOTSAL as double precision variables. Assignment statements using double precision variables follow the same pattern as assignment statements using real or integer variables, except that double precision values should be used on the right side of the equal sign. Assuming LENGTH and MEASMT have been declared as double precision variables, the following assignments can be made:

```
LENGTH = 3.75D+05
MEASMT = 4.1567D-10
```

If a real value is assigned to a double precision variable, the real value is padded with zeros to the appropriate length. Conversely, if a double precision value is assigned to a real variable, the double precision value is truncated to the allowed number of significant digits. Similarly, an integer assigned to a double precision variable is first converted to a double precision value, and a double precision value assigned to an integer variable is truncated to an integer.

Intrinsic functions are also available in double precision form (see Appendix F for a complete list of intrinsic functions). All double precision functions begin with the letter D, and most require double precision arguments. For example, DSQRT(DX) returns the double precision square root of its double precision argument DX, and DLOG(DX) returns the double precision natural logarithm of its double precision argument DX.

For formatted READ statements using double precision variables, the F format descriptor must be used. The following program segment, in which a double precision value is read from the standard input unit, illustrates this:

```
  DOUBLE PRECISION A, B
  READ 3, A, B
3 FORMAT (F13.6, 3X, F12.8)
```

For the following input:

```
123456.789098   765.43212345
1234567891111111111222222222
↑         0123456789012345678
```

Column number 1

the value assigned to A is 123456.789098, and the value assigned to B is 765.43212345.

Output of double precision variables can be performed in the same manner as output of real variables and can be made in either exponential or fixed-point form. For display in exponential form, however, double precision values must use a D format specifier rather than the E specifier used for real values. Thus, to display the double precision variables A and B in exponential format on the standard output device, the following statements are valid:

```
     PRINT 4, A, B
4    FORMAT (' ', D18.10, 4X, D15.7)
```

Assuming A and B have the values assigned by the previous READ statements, the output resulting from the PRINT statement is:

```
   0.1234567891D+06       0.7654321D+03
1234567891111111111222222222233333333
↑         012345678901234567890123456 7
```

Column number 1

Here, the value of A is printed in a field of width 18; 10 digits are printed after the decimal, and the D+06 indicates the placement of the decimal in the value of the number. This is followed by 4 blanks (from the 4X). Then B is printed in a field of width 15, with 7 digits after the decimal, and with D+03 indicating that the decimal is placed between the 5 and the 4. When using the D*w*.*d* format specification, as with the E descriptor, the width *w* must be at least 7 more than the number of decimal places *d* in order to allow room for a sign, a leading zero, decimal point, and power of 10. If the width of the field is too small, the field is filled with asterisks. If the field width is too large, the number is right justified in the field.

A double precision variable may also be formatted using an F format specifier; in this case, the output is displayed in decimal rather than exponential notation. For example, A and B (above) can be displayed with the following statements:

```
     PRINT 5, A, B
5    FORMAT( ' ', 2F8.1)
```

The output resulting from these statements is:

```
123456.8   765.4
1234567891111111
↑         0123456
```

Column number 1

Double precision expressions may also be used as subroutine and function arguments, as long as each argument is suitably declared in both the MAIN program and the subprogram. A function will return a double precision value if the name of the function is declared to be double precision. This may be done either in the function header or in a type declaration statement within the body of the function. For example, the following function returns the hypotenuse of a right triangle whose other two sides are declared as double precision arguments:

```
DOUBLE PRECISION FUNCTION HYP (X, Y)
  DOUBLE PRECISION X, Y
  HYP = DSQRT ( X ** 2 + Y ** 2 )
  END
```

Skill Builder Exercises

1. Write each of the following double precision constants in standard decimal notation. Assume the computer retains 12 significant digits.

   a. 0.372D 04
   b. 0.4512D–03
   c. 4.2375D 06
   d. –7.53852D+04
   e. –0.437D+01
   f. –0.242D–05

2. Write each of the following decimal values in double precision scientific notation.

   a. –37654390000.
   b. .00004562000000
   c. 234563.5300
   d. –.002356000000

3. Write each of the following constants in double precision form.

   a. 5/8
   b. 1/6
   c. 0.75
   d. 0.37

4. Assume that the double precision variable DB has been assigned the value 375.26359, and the statement `PRINT 10, DB` is executed. Show the output that is produced by each of the following format statements.

   a. `10 FORMAT (' ', D16.8)`
   b. `10 FORMAT (' ', D10.9)`
   c. `10 FORMAT (' ', D12.5)`
   d. `10 FORMAT (' ', D8.2)`

Programming Exercises

5. Consider the following two equations:

$$X = 3.14159 - .98888 + .98888 - .14159$$
$$Y = X^2 - X - 6.$$

Algebraically, of course, these equations yield $X = 3$ and $Y = 0$. Write a program to calculate the values of X and Y when these variables are declared as single precision, and then display the calculated values. Then change X and Y to double precision variables and rerun the program.

6. Redo Exercise 4 of Section 3.1 using double precision variables and compare the result to that obtained with a calculator.
7. Redo Exercise 5 of Section 3.1 using double precision variables and the double precision square root function. Compare your results to those obtained using single precision variables.
8. Redo Exercise 16 of Section 3.1 with *A*, *B*, and *C* declared as double precision variables.

10.2 Complex Data

A complex number is represented in FORTRAN as an ordered pair of either real or integer numbers that are separated by a comma and enclosed in parentheses. (Some compilers require both components of a complex number to be real values.) Examples of valid complex constants are:

```
(7,5)
(2.5,6.7)
(-.2, 14)
(0, 6)
(3.6, 0)
```

Examples of invalid complex constants are:

```
-3, 5        (missing parentheses)
(4.,)        (missing second component)
(, 7.)       (missing first component)
```

Computation involving complex numbers follows the standard mathematical definitions. For example, (8,10) + (3,4) equals (11,14), and (8,10) – (3,4) equals (5,6). Computation between a complex number and a real or integer value results in the real or integer being converted to a complex number with an imaginary part of 0; complex arithmetic is then performed. For example, 5 + (2,–3) = (5,0) + (2,–3) = (7,–3). Computation between a complex number and a double precision number is not allowed.

The general form of a declaration statement used to declare complex variables is:

```
COMPLEX variable list
```

Thus, the declaration:

```
COMPLEX ROOT1, ROOT2
```

declares that the variables ROOT1 and ROOT2 are complex variables. Complex constants may be assigned to complex variables using assignment statements, as in the assignment statement ROOT1 = (3,–2). If, however, both components of the complex number are not constants, the intrinsic CMPLX function must be used. The following example illustrates this:

```
COMPLEX COM2
REAL X, Y
.
.
.
X = 4.3
Y = 5.2
COM2 = CMPLX (X, Y)
```

Once a variable has been declared as complex, it may be read using either a list-directed or a user-formatted READ statement. Similarly, complex values may be displayed using list-directed or user-formatted PRINT and WRITE statements. The following illustrates the input and output of two complex numbers using list-directed I/O:

```
COMPLEX C, D
READ *, C, D
PRINT *, C, D
```

To input the complex numbers (3.0,–4.0) and (7.0,6.0) the input line should be:

```
(3., -4.)   (7., 6.)
```

When the values of C and D are displayed, they will appear in a similar form, with each number enclosed in parentheses, as follows:

```
(3.00000, -4.00000)    (7.00000, 6.00000)
```

User-formatted input and output of a single complex number require the use of two format descriptors, one for each component of the complex number. Consider the following section of code:

```
     COMPLEX E, F
     READ 3, E, F
3    FORMAT (F5.1, F5.1, F4.1, F4.1)
     WRITE(6,4) E, F
4    FORMAT (' ', 'E:', 2F6.1, 2X, 'F:', 2F6.1)
```

The input format specifies that both components of the first complex number are to be input as real values using an F5.1 format. Similarly, both components of the second complex number are to be input using an F4.1 format. Thus, if the input is:

```
3.5  4.2  2.1 -3.8
123456789111111111
↑        012345678
```

Column number 1

the variables E and F are assigned the values (3.5,4.2) and (2.1,–3.8), respectively.

The output produced by this section of code is:

```
E:    3.5    4.2  F:    2.1  -3.8
123456789111111111122222222223
↑         012345678901234567890
```

Column number 1

Intrinsic functions that operate on complex numbers are included in Appendix F. Descriptions of the more commonly used complex functions follow:

The intrinsic function REAL(C) returns the real portion of the complex number C, while the function AIMAG(C) returns the imaginary portion of C. The intrinsic function CABS(C) returns the magnitude, or absolute value, of C, which is defined to be the square root of the sum of the components squared, and CMPLX(X, Y), as we have already seen, converts two scalar arguments into a complex number.

Exercises

1. Write each of the following FORTRAN complex constants in the algebraic form $a + bi$, where i is the imaginary number equal to the square root of –1.

a. (4.8, 0) c. (0, –8)
b. (3, –7) d. (–2, 5)

2. Assume that the complex variables *CA* and *CB* are assigned the values (3,2) and (4,–5), respectively. For these assignments determine the value of the following expressions.

a. $CA + CB$ e. CA ** 2
b. $CB - CA$ f. REAL (*CA*)
c. CA * CB g. AIMAG (*CB*)
d. CB / CA

3. Assume that C is a complex number with a value of (7,–6), and x is a real variable assigned the value –6. For these values determine the value of each of the following.

a. $C + X$ c. $C * X$
b. $C - X$ d. C / X

4. Assume that *CD* is a complex number with a value of (–2.5, 3.4) and that the statement WRITE(6,15) CD is executed. Show the output that would be produced by each of the following FORMAT statements.

a. `15  FORMAT (' ', 2F6.1)`
b. `15  FORMAT (' ', F5.2, 2X, F5.2)`
c. `15  FORMAT (' ', '(', F5.1, ',', F5.1, ')' )`

Programming Exercises

5. Write a program to compute the value of each of the expressions listed in Exercise 3.

6. If n is an integer greater than zero, the equation $x^n = 1$ has n complex solutions that may be obtained by substituting $k = 0, 1, 2, \ldots n-1$ in the formula:

```
r_k+1 = (cos(2k/n), sin(2k/n))
```

For example, $x^4 = 1$ has 4 roots, which may be found by letting $k = 0, 1, 2$, and 3 in the above formula, as follows:

```
r1 = (cos(2 * 0 / 4), sin(2 * 0 / 4))
r2 = (cos (2 * 1 / 4), sin(2 * 1 / 4))
r3 = (cos (2 * 2 / 4), sin(2 * 2 / 4))
r4 = (cos ( 2 * 3 / 4), sin(2 * 3 / 4))
```

Using this information, write a FORTRAN program to find and display the three roots of $x^3 = 1$. Use complex numbers for all three roots.

10.3 String and Substring Processing

In Chapter 2 we saw that a string is another name for a character constant or character variable consisting of one or more characters. In this section we present techniques for processing strings.

The only specific string operator provided in FORTRAN is the concatenation operator, denoted as //. This operator is used to join two strings into a single string, as illustrated by the following code:

```
CHARACTER*3 CHAR1, CHAR2, CHAR3*6, CHAR4*7
CHAR1 = 'HOT'
CHAR2 = 'DOG'
CHAR3 = CHAR1 // CHAR2
```

Here the variable CHAR3 is assigned the string 'HOTDOG'. To insert a blank space between the words HOT and DOG, the following statement should be used:

```
CHAR4 = CHAR1 // ' ' // CHAR2
```

In addition to being concatenated, strings may be compared for equality or inequality. Recall that each character in a string is stored in binary according to either the ASCII or the EBCDIC code. Although the codes are different, they have some characteristics in common. In each of them, a blank precedes (is less than) all letters and numbers; the letters of the alphabet are stored in order from A to Z; and the digits are stored in order from 0 to 9. (It is important to note that in ASCII the letters come before, or are less than, the digits, whereas in EBCDIC the letters follow, or are greater than, the digits.)

When two strings are compared, if their lengths are unequal the shorter string is padded on the right with enough blanks to make the lengths the same. Then the characters are compared, a pair at a time (both first characters, then both second characters, and so on). If no differences are found, the strings are equal; if a difference is found, the string with the first lower character is considered the smaller string. Thus:

'ABC' is less than 'ABCD', since 'ABC' is padded to 'ABC ', and a blank is less than a D
'SMITH' is greater than 'JONES', because S is greater than J
'123' is greater than '1227', since '123' is padded to '123 ', and 3 is greater than 2
'123' is less than '1237', since '123' is first padded with a trailing blank space, and the blank space is less than 7
'FORTRAN' and 'FORTRAN ' are equal, because the shorter string is first padded with two blank spaces to make its length the same as that of the longer string

Using FORTRAN's relational operators, it is possible to put character data in alphabetical order using a sort in much the same way that we would sort numerical data. Program 10-1 uses an exchange sort to put a list of names in alphabetical order (the exchange sort was presented in Section 6.8).

Program 10-1 Sorting Character Data

```
      PROGRAM NAMSRT
        CHARACTER*10 NAMES(25)
        INTEGER NUMELS
        CALL RDFILE(NAMES, NUMELS)
        CALL SORT(NAMES, NUMELS)
        CALL SHOW(NAMES, NUMELS)
        END
*
      SUBROUTINE RDFILE(NAMES, NUMELS)
        CHARACTER*10 NAMES(*)
        INTEGER NUMELS
        OPEN(UNIT = 20, FILE = 'DATA')
        DO 10 I = 1, 25
          READ(20, 15, END = 99) NAMES(I)
          NUMELS = I
  10    CONTINUE
  15    FORMAT(A10)
  99    RETURN
        END
*
      SUBROUTINE SORT(NAMES, NUMELS)
        CHARACTER*10 NAMES(*), TEMP
        INTEGER NUMELS, I, J
  99    DO 20 I = 1, NUMELS-1
          DO 30 J = 1, NUMELS - I
            IF ( NAMES (J) .GT. NAMES (J+1) ) THEN
              TEMP = NAMES(J)
              NAMES(J) = NAMES(J+1)
              NAMES(J+1) = TEMP
```

Program 10-1 Sorting Character Data (Continued)

```
          ENDIF
 30     CONTINUE
 20   CONTINUE
      RETURN
      END
*
    SUBROUTINE SHOW(NAMES, NUMELS)
      CHARACTER*10 NAMES(*)
      INTEGER NUMELS
      WRITE(6,*) (NAMES(I), I = 1, NUMELS)
 25   FORMAT (' ', A10)
      RETURN
      END
```

In reviewing Program 10-1, notice that each line in the file being read must begin in the same column. For example, if the file consisted of the three lines:

```
JONES
 ZEBEDIAH
  ADAMS
```

the string ' ZEBEDIAH' would be the first name displayed by the program, the string ' ADAMS' would be the next, and the string 'JONES' would be last. This is because blanks have a lower value in both ASCII and EBCDIC codes than do any letters.

Substrings

A *substring* of a character string is a subsection of contiguous characters. For example, all possible substrings of the string 'COMPUTE' are:

```
'C'  'CO'  'COM'  'COMP'  'COMPU'  'COMPUT'  'COMPUTE'
'O'  'OM'  'OMP'  'OMPU'  'OMPUT'  'OMPUTE'
'M'  'MP'  'MPU'  'MPUT'  'MPUTE'
'P'  'PU'  'PUT'  'PUTE'
'U'  'UT'  'UTE'
'T'  'TE'
'E'
```

It is possible to extract a substring from a character constant, character variable, or character array element using the (:) operator. The general form of this operator is:

```
exp1(exp2:exp3)
```

where *exp1* is either a string variable, a string constant, an array element name, or a string expression using the concatenation operator, *exp2* is an integer expression that specifies the leftmost character position of the substring, and *exp3* is an integer expression that specifies the rightmost character of the substring. For example, TEXT(3:8) specifies a substring containing the characters in positions three through eight of the string TEXT. If TEXT contains the string 'A STITCH IN TIME', then TEXT(3:8) equals 'STITCH'.

An error occurs if the value of *exp2* is less than one, the value of *exp2* is greater than the value of *exp3*, or the value of *exp3* is greater than the length of the original string. Additionally, if the value of *exp2* is omitted, a value of 1 is assumed; if the value of *exp3* is omitted, a value equal to the length of the original string is assumed. For example, assuming that DEMO, DEMO1, DEMO2, and DEMO3 are all string variables of length 10 and that DEMO has been assigned the value 'ABCDEFGHIJ', the assignments:

```
DEMO1 = DEMO (3:5)
DEMO2 = DEMO ( :6)
DEMO3 = DEMO (3: )
```

store the third through fifth characters of DEMO to the string DEMO1, the first through sixth characters of DEMO to DEMO2, and the third through last characters of DEMO to DEMO3. In each case the substring is stored left justified and is padded on the right with blanks, if necessary. As with strings, substrings may be concatenated using the concatenation operator.

Skill Builder Exercises

1. Indicate whether the following are true or false.

a. `'ABC' .GT. 'AC'`
b. `'FIFTY' .LT. 'FIVE'`
c. `'48' .GT. '476'`
d. `48 .GT. 476`
e. `'TODAY' .EQ. 'FRIDAY'`

2. For the following FORTRAN statements:

```
CHARACTER*30 ONE, TWO, THREE
ONE = 'THIS IS THE FIRST SENTENCE'
TWO = 'EIGHTH ONE NOT HERE'
THREE = 'HERE''S THE THIRD'
```

a. Determine the result of the following substring extractions.

(1) `ONE(12:17)`
(2) `TWO(8:9)`
(3) `THREE(4:7)`

b. Determine the result of the following concatenations.

(1) `ONE(13:15)//TWO(10:11)//ONE(13:14)//TWO(3:5)//THREE(2:3)`
(2) `ONE(2:4)//TWO(7:8)//THREE(15:15)//'  '//THREE(:3)//'S'`
(3) `ONE(26:)//TWO(:2)//THREE(10:10)`

Programming Exercises

3. Write a program to read in a name having the form first name last name and display it the form *last name, first name*. (*Hint:* After reading the name, check for blank spaces. The first blank indicates the end of the first name, and the second blank indicates the end of the last name. You will want to store the desired output in a second character string, along with the comma and blank, before printing it; use concatenation to do this.)
4. Write a program that reads in a list of names from a file named NAME.DAT, sorts the names in reverse alphabetical order (use any sort other than the bubble sort to do this), and outputs the names in sorted order.
5. A mail order catalog codes its catalog numbers with five digits followed by a letter. The digits indicate the item number, and the letter indicates what additional information is needed, according to the following codes:

```
S       size only
C       color only
B       both size and color
N       no additional information needed
```

Write a program to read in a catalog number, look at the letter in the sixth position, and print a statement of what additional information is needed.

6. Modify the program written in Exercise 5 to accommodate a catalog number consisting of five digits and one letter in any order.

10.4 Data Structures as Parallel Arrays

A data structure is a data type consisting of several elements, not all of which need to be the same data type (recall that an array is a data structure in which all elements are of the same data type). A single data structure consists of a number of individual items, called *fields*. For example, consider Figure 10-1, which illustrates a single structure consisting of a book title, a catalog number, and a price field. The *form* of this structure consists of the three field names, the data types that can be stored in each field, and the arrangement of the fields. The *contents* of each field refers to the actual data stored in the field.

The real usefulness of structures is realized when the same structure form is used for lists of data. In this situation the contents of each structure would contain

Book Title	Catalog Number	Price
PC Tools	CB3027	$28.50

Figure 10-1
A Book Inventory Record

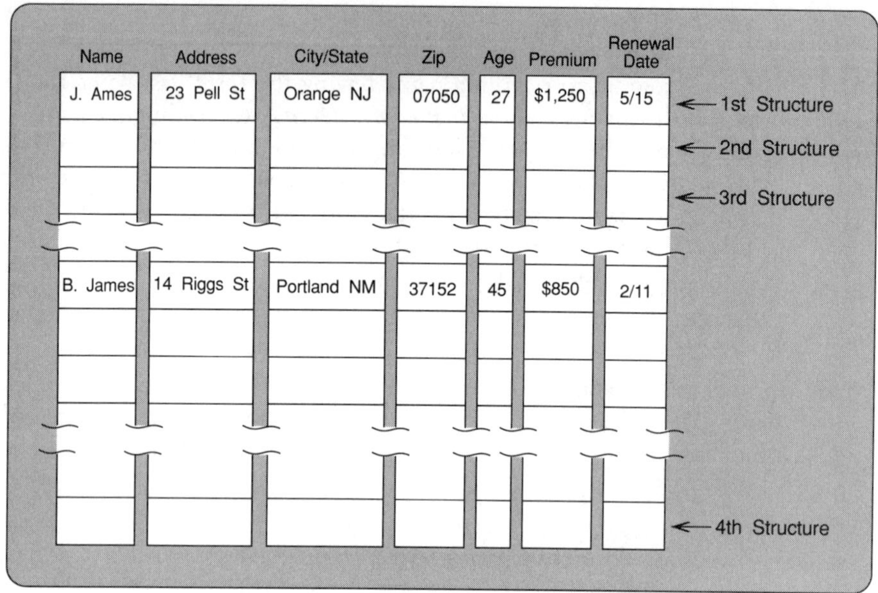

Figure 10-2 A List of Structures

the data for a particular member of a larger group. For example, Figure 10-2 illustrates a list of insurance company structures, where each structure contains the data for a single individual. Notice that the form of each structure is the same and consists of a series of fields to hold the name, street address, city and state, zip code, age, premium amount, and renewal date. Clearly, some of these fields must be character, but some (for example, premium amount) must be numeric.

If an array could hold several types of data, a list of structures could be easily implemented using a two dimension array. Instead, such structures are implemented in FORTRAN 77 using a series of parallel linear arrays*. Each linear array holds a single field; in the example above, we could use a character array for the name, another character array for the street address, and so on, using an integer array for the age and a real array for the premium amount. As shown in Figure 10-3, each individual's data would be stored in the same position in all arrays.

Program 10-2 illustrates the use of parallel arrays for storing and processing data input from a data file containing a maximum of fifty records. Each record in the data file consists of a student name and three test grades. The program inputs all of the records into a set of parallel arrays and then determines and displays the letter grade for each student based on the average of three tests. For each student, the name, three exam grades, the numerical average, and the letter grade are stored using six parallel linear arrays. The data for the first four arrays (name, first test grade, second test grade, and third test grade) are input from the external data file; the data for the fifth and sixth arrays (numerical average and letter grade) are calculated by the program. Figure 10-4a, b, and c provide the appropriate flowcharts for this program.

* In FORTRAN 90, structures can be implemented directly as a derived data type (see Section 12.4).

Program 10-2

```
      PROGRAM MAIN
        IMPLICIT NONE
        CHARACTER*10 NAME(50), GRADE*1(50)
        REAL AVG(50)
        INTEGER EX1(50), EX2(50), EX3(50), NUMELS
        CALL RDFILE(NAME, EX1, EX2, EX3, NUMELS)
        CALL AVERGE(EX1, EX2, EX3, AVG, NUMELS)
        CALL LETGRD(AVG, GRADE, NUMELS)
        CALL SHOW(NAME, EX1, EX2, EX3, AVG, GRADE, NUMELS)
        END
*
      SUBROUTINE RDFILE(NAME, EX1, EX2, EX3, NUMELS)
        IMPLICIT NONE
        CHARACTER*10 NAME(*)
        INTEGER EX1(*), EX2(*), EX3(*), NUMELS, I
        OPEN(UNIT = 22, FILE = 'TESTS.DAT')
        DO 10 I = 1, 50
          READ(22, 15, END = 99) NAME(I), EX1(I), EX2(I), EX3(I)
          NUMELS = I
  10    CONTINUE
  15    FORMAT (A10, 3I5)
  99    RETURN
        END
*
      SUBROUTINE AVERGE (EX1, EX2, EX3, AVG, NUMELS)
        IMPLICIT NONE
        INTEGER EX1(*), EX2(*), EX3(*), NUMELS, I
        REAL AVG(*)
        DO 10 I = 1, NUMELS
          AVG(I) = (EX1(I) + EX2(I) + EX3(I)) / 3.0
 10     CONTINUE
        RETURN
        END
*
      SUBROUTINE LETGRD (AVG, GRADE, NUMELS)
        IMPLICIT NONE
        CHARACTER GRADE(*)
        REAL AVG(*)
        INTEGER NUMELS, I
        DO 10 I = 1, NUMELS
          IF ( AVG(I) .GE. 90) THEN
            GRADE(I) = 'A'
          ELSE IF ( AVG (I) .GE. 80) THEN
            GRADE(I) = 'B'
          ELSE IF ( AVG (I) .GE. 70) THEN
```

Program 10-2 (Continued)

```
            GRADE(I) = 'C'
          ELSE IF ( AVG (I) .GE. 60) THEN
            GRADE(I) = 'D'
          ELSE
            GRADE(I) = 'F'
          ENDIF
   10   CONTINUE
        RETURN
        END
*
      SUBROUTINE SHOW(NAME, EX1, EX2, EX3, AVG, GRADE, NUMELS)
        CHARACTER*10 NAME(*), GRADE*1(*)
        REAL AVG(*)
        INTEGER EX1(*), EX2(*), EX3(*), NUMELS
        DO 20 J = 1, NUMELS
          WRITE(6,25) NAME(J),EX1(J),EX2(J),EX3(J),AVG(J),GRADE(J)
   20   CONTINUE
   25   FORMAT(' ',A, 3X, 3I5, 2X, F6.2, 2X, A )
        RETURN
        END
```

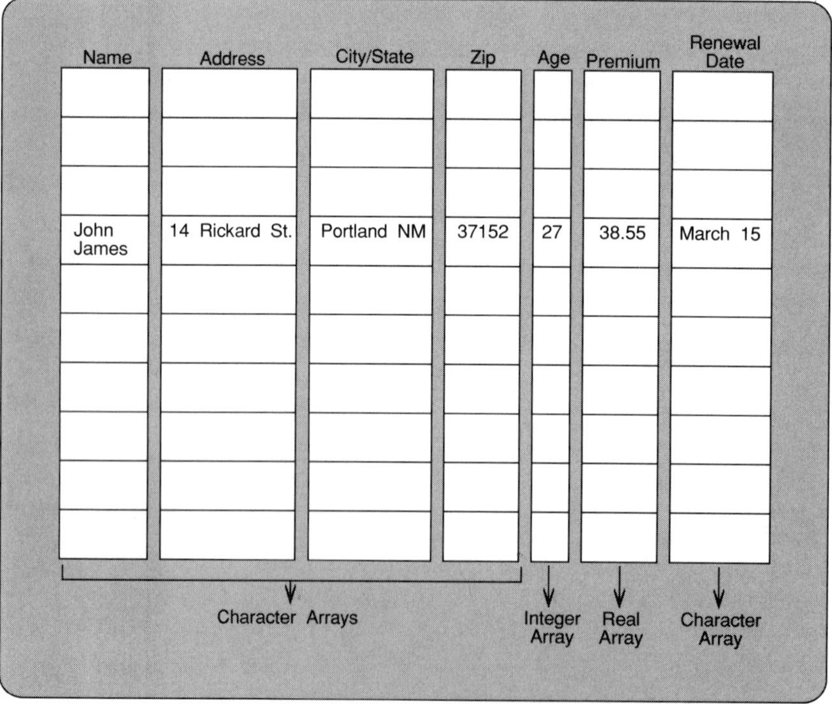

Figure 10-3
A List of Structures Implemented with Parallel Arrays

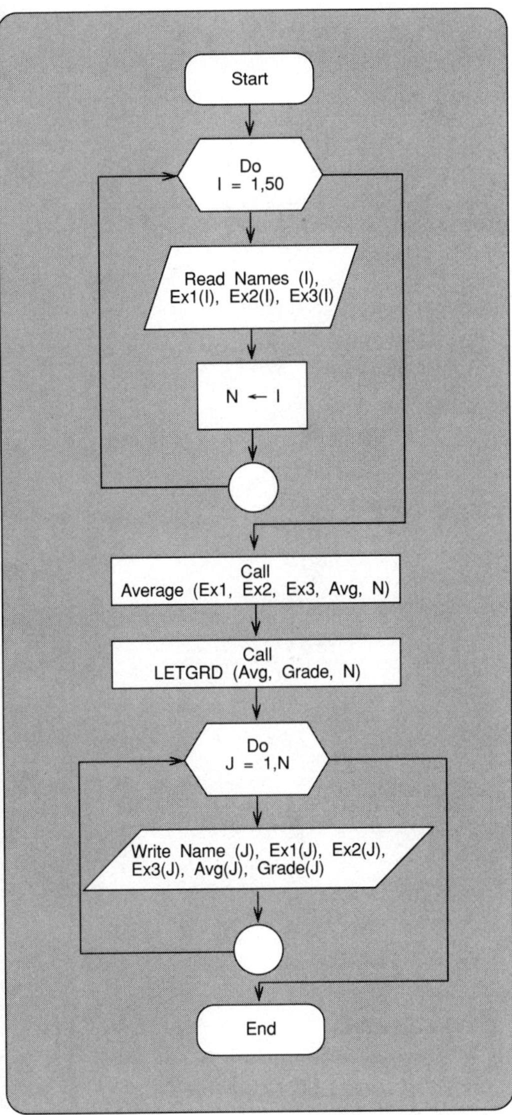

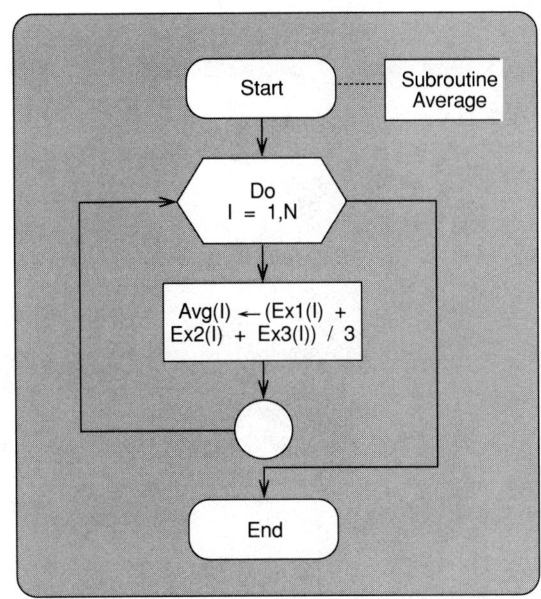

Figure 10-4b

Figure 10-4a
Flowcharts for Program 10-2

Skill Builder Exercises

1. List the fields found on your driver's license.
2. French Creek Marina stores 500 boats for the winter. Records must be maintained on each boat, detailing the owner's name, the length of the boat, the boat license number, the boat slip number, and the warehouse in which the boat is stored. Determine suitable array names and data types that would be required to store this data.

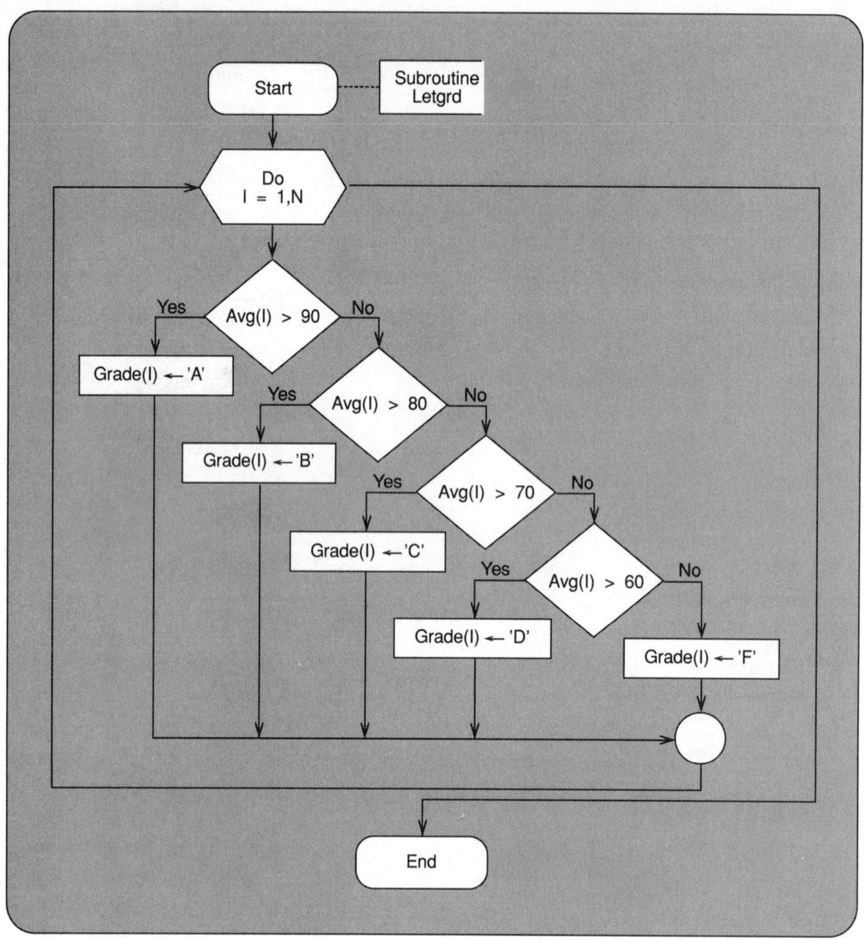

Figure 10-4c

3. Shown is part of a data file that contains student records. Each record consists of the student's name, student's birthday, the number of credits for which the student is registered this semester, and the student's year in school (FR, freshman; SO, sophomore; JR, junior; SR, senior; GR, graduate student). For this data determine a pair of READ-FORMAT statements that could be used to input this data from the data file.

```
JONES, JOHN       011457 15       FR
SMITH, SUSAN      102270 12       SO
COOKE, PAUL       042837  6       GR
MICRO, MARVIN     121867 18       SR
1234567891111111111222222222233333
↑        0123456789012345678901234
```

Column number 1

Programming Exercises

4. Write a program to read in the data given in Exercise 3; add more data so you have a total of at least 20 records representing at least 4 students from each year (FR, SO, JR, and so on). Have your program compute the average number of credits taken and then display the data for all the freshmen, followed by that for all the sophomores, and so on. Additionally, compute the average number of credits for each year, and print that information.

5. The chart below shows the information kept on file by the New Hope Computerized Dating Service. The numbers indicate the number of phone calls each participant received monthly through NHCDS. Write a program to read in the data; then compute the total number of phone calls per month and the total number of phone calls per participant.

NAME	JA	FE	MA	AP	MA	JN	JL	AU	SE	OC	NO	DE
SMOTHERS	3	4	5	2	1	7	8	5	4	3	2	4
JANKE	1	4	2	3	5	6	7	8	3	2	5	6
LIGIN	3	1	2	3	5	3	0	8	6	3	1	2
MELLOW	4	3	1	6	3	0	4	2	8	4	3	1
BILLS	2	4	1	6	4	3	2	7	5	4	2	3
HENRY	1	2	1	0	2	1	3	0	3	4	3	1

6. French Creek Marina (see Exercise 2) needs its bills computed from the data given below. Each record gives the boat owner's name, the boat length, the month the boat went into storage, and the month the boat came out of storage. Storage charges are $1.50 per foot of boat length per month. For example, storage costs for a 20-foot boat that is stored from September until May (9 months) would be $270 (20 x 1.5 x 9). Write a program to read the given data, compute storage costs for each boat, and display the given data as well as each boat's storage costs.

```
KING        22   SEPT   MAY
KING        31   AUG    MAY
KING        18   SEPT   JUNE
ROGERS      18   OCT    JUNE
ROGERS      24   AUG    MAY
SMITHSON    22   AUG    JUNE
SMITHSON    45   SEPT   MAY
CARDWELL    34   AUG    APR
CAUGHEY     42   SEPT   APR
CAUGHEY     18   AUG    MAY
JONES       21   OCT    APR
JONES       45   SEPT   MAY
JONES       15   SEPT   APR
MARTIN      28   OCT    MAY
```

7. Modify the program written for Exercise 6 to calculate and display the total charges for each boat owner.

10.5 Applications

In this section we present two applications of the topics covered in this chapter. First look at a program for analyzing text using the substring (:) operator. Then examine a program that uses parallel linear arrays to simulate data structures.

Application 1: Word Analysis

When writing an article, an author often finds it desirable to have a count of the number of words in the article. The computer can aid in this task. Since each word in a sentence is followed by a blank space, it would seem that we could determine the number of words in a line of text by counting the number of blanks it contains. However, we should look at an example to be sure that this method works. The sentence "this is a sentence" has three blank spaces and four words; so far, the number of words is not equal to the number of blanks. However, if we were to store that sentence (or string) in a character variable called LINE, of length 80, then LINE would look like Figure 10-5. Notice that each word is followed by at least one blank, and the end of the sentence is now followed by more than one blank space. So if the program counted blank spaces, the number of blanks would give us the number of words, as long as we only counted the series of blanks after the last word as a single blank. Our program could check for a blank space using the substring (:) operator to step across the line. Remember that LINE(I:I) looks at the character in the *I*th position, so a DO loop that allowed *I* to run from 1 to the end of the string would look at each character in turn. Using a comparison such as:

```
IF (LINE (I:I) .EQ. ' ')
```

we would be able to locate each blank space in the sentence. Note, again, that if we just counted the blanks in the line, we would think there were more words than there are, because once the sentence is read in, the rest of LINE is padded on the right with blanks. So how do we know when we have reached the end of the series of words? Look at Figure 10-5 again and see that the last word in the sentence is followed by at least two blanks. So two blanks in a row will tell us that the end of the

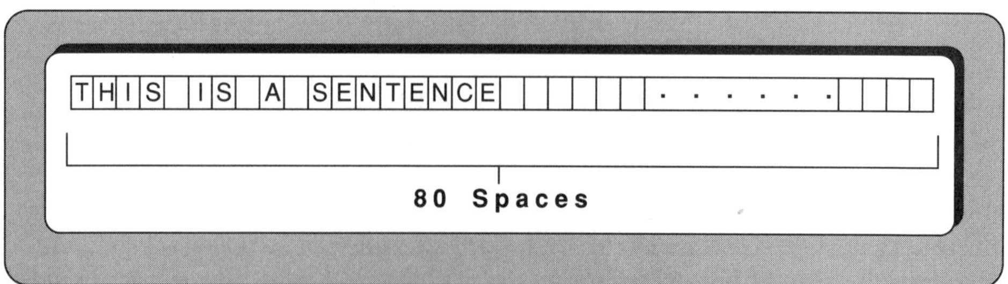

Figure 10-5 A Sample Line of Words

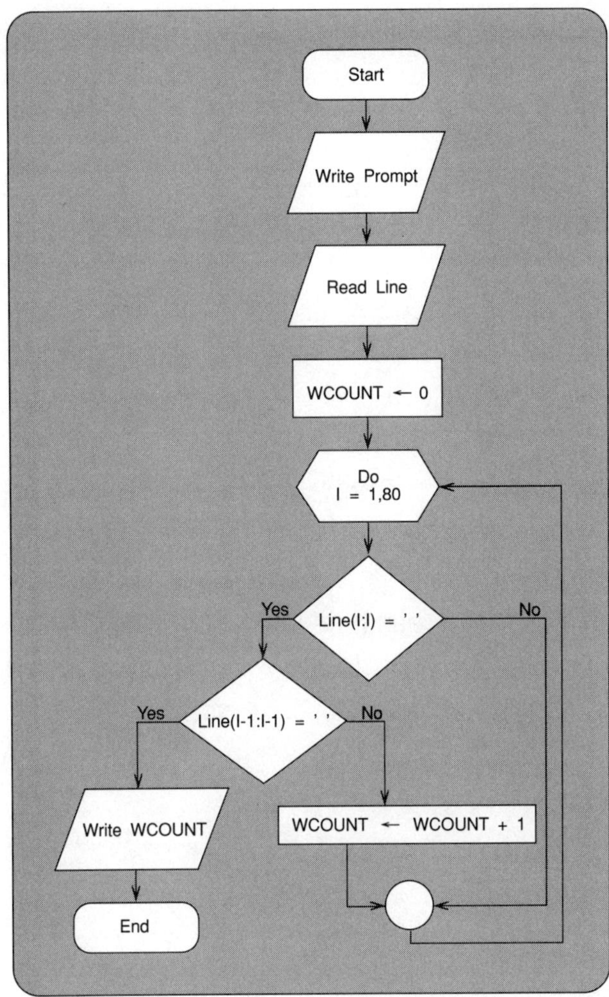

Figure 10-6
Flowchart for Counting the Words in a Single Line of Text

sentence has been reached. When we reach the end of the sentence (as indicated by two blank spaces in a row), the number of blanks (counting the double at the end as a single blank) gives us the number of words. The flowchart for determining the number of words in a single line of text is illustrated in Figure 10-6.

Program 10-3

```
PROGRAM WORDCT
CHARACTER*80 LINE
INTEGER WCOUNT
CALL RDLINE(LINE)
CALL CNTWDS(LINE, WCOUNT)
CALL SHOW(WCOUNT)
END
```

Program 10-3 (Continued)

```
*
      SUBROUTINE RDLINE(LINE)
      CHARACTER*80 LINE
      WRITE(6,*) 'ENTER THE LINE TO BE CHECKED'
      WRITE(6,*) 'DO NOT USE MORE THAN 78 CHARACTERS'
      READ (5,2) LINE
    2 FORMAT(A)
      RETURN
      END
*
      SUBROUTINE CNTWDS(LINE, WCOUNT)
      CHARACTER*80 LINE
      INTEGER WCOUNT, I
***  SEARCH THE LINE FOR BLANKS; AT EACH BLANK, COUNT A WORD
      WCOUNT = 0
      DO 10 I = 1, 80
        IF ( LINE (I:I) .EQ. ' ') THEN
***  CHECK FOR END OF LINE
          IF ( LINE(I-1:I-1) .EQ. ' ') THEN
            RETURN
          ENDIF
***  IF NOT THE END OF LINE, WE HAVE FOUND END OF A WORD
          WCOUNT = WCOUNT + 1
        ENDIF
   10 CONTINUE
      RETURN
      END
*
      SUBROUTINE SHOW(WCOUNT)
      INTEGER WCOUNT
      WRITE(6,10) WCOUNT
   10 FORMAT (' ', 'NUMBER OF WORDS IS', I5)
      RETURN
      END
```

Program 10-3 implements the algorithm shown in Figure 10-6 using FORTRAN code.

When this program is run, the user will first be asked to:

```
ENTER THE LINE TO BE CHECKED
DO NOT USE MORE THAN 78 CHARACTERS
```

The user might now respond with the following:

```
THIS IS A SENTENCE WHOSE WORD COUNT I WANT CHECKED
```

The computer will then respond with the following:

```
NUMBER OF WORDS IS   10
```

The exercises at the end of this section will offer you the opportunity to modify this program by entering a series of lines and counting sentences as well as words.

Application 2: Weight Loss Club

The following data represent individuals at the U-Watch-Ur-Weight Club. The first column contains the initials of the dieter, the second column gives the dieter's initial weight, and the third column gives the dieter's final weight.

```
KLK   132    115
FPD   225    210
DMC   176    154
RJK   165    151
CAJ   182    176
```

We want to write a program to find the weight loss for each individual and the average weight loss for all of the individuals together. To do this, we will read the data into three parallel arrays, one each for the dieter's initials, initial weight, and final weight, respectively. A fourth array will be used to store the weight loss for each individual. The pseudocode for our program is:

Open the data file and input each record into the first three parallel arrays of a four-array data structure
DO for each individual
compute a weight loss and store this value in a fourth array
add the weight loss to a total
Enddo
Calculate the average weight loss
Display the values in the data structure

Program 10-4 is the FORTRAN implementation of this pseudocode. As written, Program 10-4 stores the data from the data file into three parallel arrays, which are named INIT, INITWT, and TERMWT. The program then uses a DO loop to step through the initial and final weight arrays. Each final weight is subtracted from the initial weight, and the result (the weight loss) is stored in the WTLOSS array. The computation of the sum of weight losses is made within the same loop by adding the individual losses into the SUM variable. Finally, the average weight loss is determined by dividing the sum of the weight lost by the number of dieters, and the input data and calculated data are displayed together.

When Program 10-4 is run with the given data as input, the following output is produced:

```
KLK  132  115   17
FPD  225  210   15
DMC  176  154   22
RJK  165  151   14
CAJ  182  176    6
THE AVERAGE WEIGHT LOSS IS  14.8
```

Program 10-4

```
      PROGRAM DIET
        CHARACTER*3 INIT(50)
        INTEGER INITWT(50), TERMWT(50), WTLOSS(50)
        REAL AVG
        CALL RDFILE(INIT, INITWT, TERMWT, NUMELS)
        CALL LOSSWT(INITWT, TERMWT, WTLOSS, NUMELS, AVG)
        CALL SHOW(INIT, INITWT, TERMWT, WTLOSS, NUMELS, AVG)
        END
*
      SUBROUTINE RDFILE(INIT, INITWT, TERMWT, NUMELS)
        CHARACTER*3 INIT(*)
        INTEGER INITWT(*), TERMWT(*), NUMELS, I
        OPEN (UNIT = 7, FILE = 'WEIGHT')
        DO 5 I = 1, 50
          READ (7, 15, END = 99) INIT(I), INITWT(I), TERMWT(I)
          NUMELS = I
   5    CONTINUE
  15    FORMAT(A3, 2(2X,I3))
  99    RETURN
        END
*
      SUBROUTINE LOSSWT(INITWT, TERMWT, WTLOSS, NUMELS, AVG)
        INTEGER INITWT(50), TERMWT(50), WTLOSS(5), NUMELS, I, SUM
        REAL AVG
*  COMPUTE INDIVIDUAL AND TOTAL WEIGHT LOSS
        SUM = 0
        DO 10 I = 1, NUMELS
          WTLOSS(I) = INITWT(I) - TERMWT(I)
          SUM = SUM + WTLOSS(I)
  10    CONTINUE
        AVG = FLOAT(SUM) / FLOAT(NUMELS)
        RETURN
        END
*
      SUBROUTINE SHOW(INIT, INITWT, TERMWT, WTLOSS, NUMELS, AVG)
        CHARACTER*3 INIT(*)
        INTEGER INITWT(*), TERMWT(*), WTLOSS(*), NUMELS, I
        REAL AVG
        DO 30 I = 1, NUMELS
          WRITE(6,25) INIT(I), INITWT(I), TERMWT(I), WTLOSS(I)
  30    CONTINUE
        WRITE(6,35) AVG
  25    FORMAT(' ', A, 3(2X, I3))
  35    FORMAT(' ', 'THE AVERAGE WEIGHT LOSS IS ', F5.1)
        RETURN
        END
```

The first column contains the initials, the second and third columns contain the initial and final weights, respectively, and the fourth column contains the weight loss. The last output line displays the average weight loss.

Additional Exercises for Chapter 10

1. Modify Program 10-3 to accept five lines of input. Have the program count the number of sentences as well as the number of words; assume all the sentences end with periods. Then have the program compute the average number of words per sentence. Test the program on this exercise.
2. Modify the program you wrote in Exercise 1 so that a sentence may end with a period, a question mark, or an exclamation point.
3. Modify Program 10-3 so that it counts the number of letters in each word of a sentence. Have the program then compute the average word length of the sentence.
4. Write a program to read the following city names and temperatures from either the keyboard or a data file into two parallel single-dimensioned arrays.

```
Boston     45        Minneapolis      22
Fresno     66        San Diego        74
New York   51        San Francisco    69
Mobile     73        Houston          70
Madison    -2        Cortland         27
Miami      88        Nashville        65
Chicago    57        Portland         61
Trenton    30        Seattle          54
```

Display the contents of the arrays, with column headings. Calculate and display the average temperature, the minimum temperature, and the maximum temperature.

5. Modify the program written for Exercise 4 to determine the number of balmy days (temperature over 70 degrees Fahrenheit), the number of moderate days (temperature between 50 and 70 degrees Fahrenheit), the number of chilly days (temperature between 25 and 49 degrees Fahrenheit), and the number of cold days (temperature below 25 degrees Fahrenheit). Display this information in a second table, with appropriate headings.
6. Modify the program written for Exercise 4 to display a single table showing the temperatures in decreasing order. Include the names of the cities in the table.
7. Modify the program written for Exercise 4 to display a table that lists the cities in alphabetical order. Include the temperatures in the table.
8. Write a FORTRAN program to read the following student names and grades from either the keyboard or a data file.

```
Adams      94       Turner      66
Baker      88       Lundberg    42
Morris    100       Jeffers     87
```

```
Parker     73       Weston       89
Stine      75       Rogers       96
Godley     54       Feissner     99
```

Have your program display the data in a table with column headings. Also have your program determine and print the average grade, the maximum and minimum grades, and the range (maximum minus minimum).

9. Modify the program written for Exercise 8 to have it determine the distribution of grades, that is, the number of As (90 or above), Bs (80 to 89), Cs (70 to 79), Ds (60 to 69), and Fs (below 60). Display the distribution using appropriate descriptions.
10. Modify the program written for Exercise 8 to produce a table listing the grades in increasing numerical order. Include the students' names in the table.
11. Modify the program written for Exercise 8 to produce a table listing the students' names in alphabetical order. Include the grades in the table.

10.6 Common Programming Errors

The errors commonly associated with the material presented in this chapter are:

1. Forgetting to explicitly declare double precision variables and functions that return a double precision value. If a double precision variable is not explicitly declared, it will be implicitly typed according to its first letter.
2. Using single precision intrinsic functions with double precision arguments or double precision intrinsic functions with single precision arguments.
3. Inadvertently assigning a double precision value to either a real or an integer variable. In such a case the extra precision is lost because the double precision value is either converted to a single precision real value or truncated to an integer value.
4. Forgetting to explicitly declare complex variables and functions that return complex values. If a complex variable is not explicitly declared, it will be implicitly typed according to its first letter.
5. Inadvertently assigning a complex variable or value to a real variable. This results in the loss of the imaginary part of the complex number.
6. Forgetting to explicitly declare all character variables. If a character variable is not explicitly declared, it will be implicitly typed according to its first letter.
7. Confusing a character string of numbers with the number itself. The string '2345' consists of four symbols and is a separate entity from the number 2345. The string '2345' cannot be combined with a numeric variable, nor can it be compared with a numeric.
8. Using the substring operator STRING(I:J) incorrectly. *I* and *J* must be no less than 1 and no greater than the length of STRING. In addition, *I* must be less than or equal to *J*.
9. Attempting to use the concatenation operator (//) with noncharacter data. Only character variables and values may be concatenated.

10.7 Things to Remember

1. In order to achieve greater precision than that provided by real values, FORTRAN provides the double precision data type. A double precision variable must be explicitly declared as DOUBLE PRECISION.
2. A double precision constant must be written in scientific notation using a "D" to indicate the exponent.
3. Intrinsic functions exist for double precision data. Most begin with D, and most require that the argument(s) be double precision.
4. A user-written function that is intended to return a double precision value must be declared double precision in both the calling program and the function itself.
5. A complex number is represented in FORTRAN as an ordered pair of either real or integer numbers that are separated by a comma and enclosed in parentheses. The first number in parentheses is the real part of the number and the second number is the imaginary part. Complex arithmetic in FORTRAN follows the same rules as does complex arithmetic in mathematics.
6. Complex variables must be explicitly declared as COMPLEX.
7. If a complex value is written with a list-directed PRINT or WRITE statement, it is written in ordered pair form. If it is written with a formatted PRINT or WRITE statement, two format descriptors must be given, one for the real part and one for the imaginary part.
8. A function that is intended to return a complex value must be declared complex in both the calling program and the function itself. Additionally, intrinsic functions exist for complex data. Most begin with C, and most require that their argument(s) be complex.
9. Concatenation of strings is accomplished using the concatenation operator (//).
10. A substring is a group of contiguous letters that form part of a string. The substring operator (:) is used to extract a substring from a larger string variable.
11. A single data structure is a collection of fields that need not be of the same data type. A list of structures is implemented in FORTRAN 77 using parallel linear arrays. The FORTRAN 90 standard has a provision for directly implementing structures.

11 Additional Data File Capabilities

Chapter Eleven

11.1 Text (Formatted) Files

11.2 Binary (Unformatted) Files

11.3 File Statements

11.4 Direct Access Files

11.5 Internal Files

11.6 Exercises

11.7 Common Programming Errors

11.8 Things to Remember

The data files we have been using have all been external, sequentially accessed, text files. The term *external* refers to the fact that the data file is stored external to the memory area used for the program. The term *sequentially accessed* refers to the fact that each record, or line, in the file must be accessed sequentially, one after another, starting from the beginning of the file. Thus, the fourth record in a file cannot be read or written until the previous three records have been read or written. Finally, the term *text* file refers to the fact that the data in the file is stored using either ASCII or EBCDIC codes, which permits them to be read like ordinary text.

FORTRAN permits us to change each of these three file characteristics. In place of sequential access, we can create files having direct access, where an individual record anywhere in the file can be accessed without accessing all previous records. In the place of text files, we can create binary files, where numeric data is stored using a binary code rather than a text code. Finally, internal as well as external files can be created. In this chapter we describe each of these capabilities and show how they are implemented.

11.1 Text (Formatted) Files

The files we are familiar with have all been written using either FORTRAN's list-directed formats or specific FORMAT statements containing user-designated formats. Collectively, both list-directed and user-formatted files are referred to as *text* files.

Each character in the formatted files that we have been using is stored using a character code, such as the ASCII or EBCDIC codes introduced in Section 2.1. Both of these codes assign a specific code to each letter in the alphabet, to each of the digits 0 through 9, and to special symbols such as the decimal point and dollar sign. The ASCII and EBCDIC uppercase letter codes were previously listed in Table 2-1. Table 11-1 lists the correspondence between the decimal digits 0 through 9 and their ASCII and EBCDIC representations, in both binary and hexadecimal notation. Additionally, the ASCII and EBCDIC codes for a decimal point, blank space, carriage return, and line feed character are included in the table.

Using Table 11-1, we can determine how the decimal number 67432.83, for example, is stored in a data file using the ASCII code. In ASCII, this sequence of digits and decimal point requires eight character storage locations and is stored using the codes illustrated in Figure 11-1.

The advantage of using ASCII or EBCDIC code for data files is that the file can be read and displayed by any word processing or editor program that is provided by

Table 11-1 Selected ASCII Codes

Character	ASCII Bindary Value	ASCII Hex. Value	EBCDIC Binary Value	EBCDIC Hex. Value
0	00110000	30	11110000	F0
1	00110001	31	11110001	F1
2	00110010	32	11110010	F2
3	00110011	33	11110011	F3
4	00110100	34	11110100	F4
5	00110101	35	11110101	F5
6	00110110	36	11110110	F6
7	00110111	37	11110111	F7
8	00111000	38	11111000	F8
9	00111001	39	11111001	F9
.	00101110	2E	01001011	4B
Blank space	00100000	20	01000000	40
Carriage return	00001101	0D	00001101	0D
Line feed	00001010	0A	00001010	0A

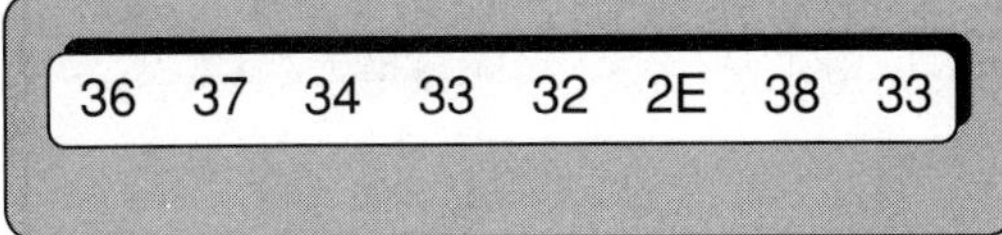

Figure 11-1 The Number 67432.83 Represented in ASCII Code

your computer system. Such editor and word processing programs are called text editors because they are designed to process alphabetical text. The word processing program can read the ASCII or EBCDIC code in the data file and display the letter, symbol, or digit corresponding to the code. This permits a data file created in FORTRAN to be examined and changed by other than FORTRAN programs.

A formatted file is the default file type created in FORTRAN when a sequential file is opened. An option within the OPEN statement permits explicit selection of this file type or selection of the alternative unformatted form. The explicit selection of a formatted (text) file is made by adding the term FORM = 'FORMATTED' within the OPEN statement after the file name is specified. As an example employing this option, assume that the following list of experimental results is to be stored in a formatted file named EXPER.DAT.

Experiment number	**Result**
1	8
2	12
3	497

Program 11-1 opens a file named EXPER.DAT to store this data. Additionally, the OPEN statement uses the FORM option to explicitly create a formatted (text) file.

Program 11-1

```
      PROGRAM MAIN
        CALL TEXTFL
        END
*
      SUBROUTINE TEXTFL
        INTEGER I, RESULT(3)
        DATA RESULT/8,12,497/
        OPEN(1, FILE = 'EXPER.DAT', FORM = 'FORMATTED')
        DO 10 I = 1,3
          WRITE(1,*) I, RESULT(I)
   10   CONTINUE
        CLOSE(1)
        RETURN
        END
```

When Program 11-1 is executed, a file named EXPER.DAT is created and saved by the computer. The file is a formatted file consisting of the following three records:

```
1        8
2       12
3      497
```

The spacing between data items in the file is due to the list-directed formatting invoked by the WRITE statement. This specific formatting can, of course, be changed by having the WRITE statement reference a format control string. In either case, selecting a formatted file requires that some format for the data be designated by the user (hence the name formatted file).

The formatted file created by Program 11-1 contains 73 characters. These characters consist of the codes used to store the required digits (one code per digit or letter, which is the hallmark of a text file) plus the blank spaces before each number, a carriage return and new-line character at the end of each data line, and a special EOF marker placed as the last item in the file when it is closed.

Assuming characters are stored using the ASCII code listed in Table 11-1, the EXPER.DAT data file is stored physically as shown in Figure 11-2. For convenience, the character corresponding to each hexadecimal code is listed below the code. Although the actual code used for the EOF marker is system dependent, the hexadecimal code 00 is commonly used because this code has no equivalent character representation. The number of spaces (Hexcode 20) illustrated is also system dependent.

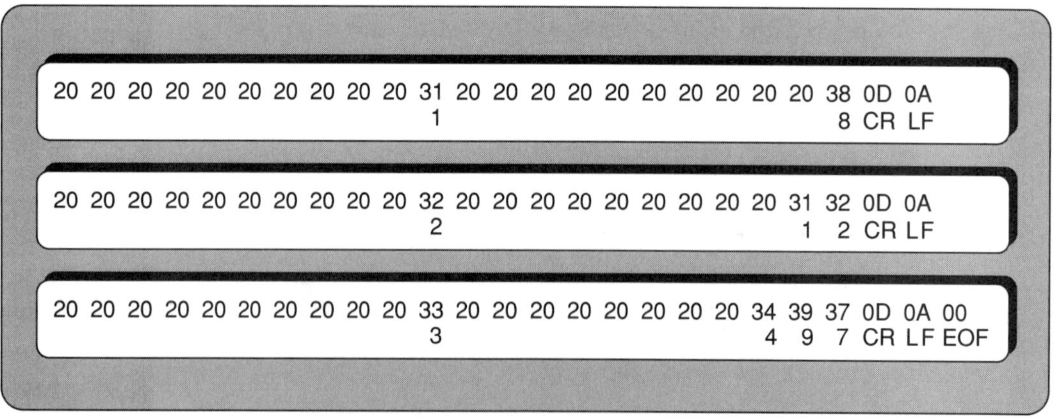

Figure 11-2 The EXPER.DAT File as Stored by the Computer

11.2 Binary (Unformatted) Files*

An alternative to text files, where each character in the file is represented by a unique code, is unformatted files. Unformatted files, also referred to as binary files, store numerical values using the computer's internal numerical code. For example, assume that the computer stores numbers internally using 16 bits in the two's complement format described in Section 1.7. Using this format, the decimal number 8 is represented as the binary number 0000 0000 0000 1000, the decimal number 12 as 0000 0000 0000 1100, and the decimal number 497 as 0000 0001 1111 0001.

The advantages of using this format are that no intermediary conversions are required for storing or retrieving the data (since the external storage codes match the computer's internal storage representation), no format specifications must be supplied, and the resulting file usually requires less storage space than its formatted counterpart. The disadvantages are that the file can no longer be visually inspected using a text-editing program or transferred between computers that use different internal number representations.

The specification for explicitly creating an unformatted file is made by adding the term FORM = 'UNFORMATTED' within the OPEN statement after the file name is specified. For example, the statement:

```
OPEN(1, FILE = 'EXPER.BIN', FORM = 'UNFORMATTED')
```

opens the file named EXPER.BIN as an unformatted file assigned to unit number 1. This OPEN statement is used in Program 11-2 to create a binary file of the EXPER.DAT text file previously created as a formatted file in Program 11-1.

Program 11-2

```
      PROGRAM MAIN
        CALL BINFIL
        END
*
      SUBROUTINE BINFIL
        INTEGER I, RESULT(3)
        DATA RESULT/8,12,497/
        OPEN(1, FILE = 'EXPER.BIN', FORM = 'UNFORMATTED')
        DO 10 I = 1,3
          WRITE(1) I, RESULT(I)
 10     CONTINUE
        CLOSE(1)
        RETURN
        END
```

* This topic assumes that you are familiar with the computer storage concepts presented in Section 1.7.

In reviewing Program 11-2, notice that the WRITE statement does not contain a format specification. In writing or reading an unformatted file, it is essential that no format specification be indicated, because the format has already been set by the FORM option in the OPEN statement. Other than the required omission of a format specification, the WRITE and READ statements for unformatted I/O are identical to their formatted I/O counterparts.

The unformatted file created by Program 11-2 is illustrated in Figure 11-3, which uses hexadecimal values to indicate the equivalent binary values. Although the figure separates the file's records into individual lines, with bars (|) used to distinguish individual items in each record, in actuality the file is stored as a consecutive sequence of codes.

As shown in the figure, each record in a binary file is preceded by a header value and followed by a trailer value. The values in the header and trailer are always equal and contain the number of bytes in the record (each hexadecimal value is one byte in length—review Section 1.7 for a description of a byte). For example, the first record contains 16 bytes, which is indicated by the hexadecimal value 10. Between each header and trailer value are the record's data items. As indicated in Figure 11-3, each record contains two integer values, with each integer stored using four bytes (32 bits). The hexadecimal values shown on the first line correspond to the decimal numbers 1 and 8, the values on the second line to the decimal numbers 2 and 12, and the values on the third line to the decimal numbers 3 and 497. These are the same values previously illustrated in Figure 11-2 using the ASCII code. Although the number of bytes used to store an integer is system dependent, the layout of all binary files corresponds to the form shown in Figure 11-3.

The fact that the EXPER.BIN file uses a binary storage code does not preclude us from displaying the results in a text form. For example, Program 11-3 opens the EXPER.BIN file in the unformatted mode, reads the file using an unformatted READ statement, and displays the data using a list-directed (formatted) WRITE statement. In its most general form, the unformatted READ statement is the same as the formatted READ statement described in Section 5.4, except for the required omission of the format specification.

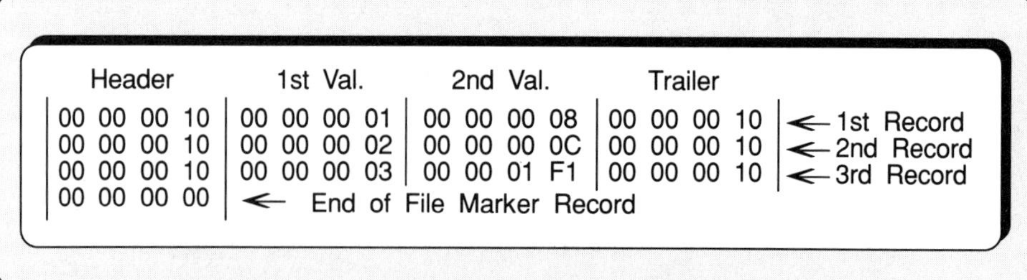

Header	1st Val.	2nd Val.	Trailer	
00 00 00 10	00 00 00 01	00 00 00 08	00 00 00 10	← 1st Record
00 00 00 10	00 00 00 02	00 00 00 0C	00 00 00 10	← 2nd Record
00 00 00 10	00 00 00 03	00 00 01 F1	00 00 00 10	← 3rd Record
00 00 00 00	← End of File Marker Record			

Figure 11-3 The EXPER.BIN File as Stored by the Computer

Program 11-3

```
      PROGRAM MAIN
        CALL READBN
        END
*
      SUBROUTINE READBN
        INTEGER I, N, VALUE
        OPEN(1, FILE = 'EXPER.BIN', FORM = 'UNFORMATTED')
        DO 10 I = 1,3
          READ(1) N, VALUE
          WRITE(6,*)N, VALUE
  10    CONTINUE
        CLOSE(1)
        RETURN
        END
```

The display produced by Program 11-3 is illustrated below:

```
1          8
2         12
3        497
```

11.3 File Statements

In this section we look at all the options available to us in creating and using external data files. As the OPEN statement defines the properties of the external data file being accessed, we begin with this statement.

The OPEN Statement

The OPEN statement established the connection between an external data file and a FORTRAN program. In this operation, the OPEN statement also defines the characteristics of the file and how it must be accessed. As we have seen, in the absence of explicit designations, certain default specifications, such as the form of the file (formatted or unformatted), are supplied by the compiler.

In its most general form, the OPEN statement has the general form:

```
OPEN (UNIT = u, FILE = name, STATUS = stype, FORM = file-type,
 ACCESS = atype, RECL = rln, BLANK = ch, IOSTAT = var, ERR = n)
```

The words UNIT, FILE, STATUS, FORM, ACCESS, RECL, BLANK, IOSTAT, and ERR are optional keywords, called file specifiers, that may be placed in any order within the parentheses. Each of these file specifiers designates a specific file characteristic and is described below. (Blank spaces may be used freely within the parentheses and have no effect on the statement. However, if the statement extends beyond a single line, it must be properly designated as a continuation line.) Except for the UNIT specification, all other file specifiers are optional and may be omitted from the OPEN statement. If the keyword UNIT is not included explicitly in an OPEN statement, the unit number must be the first item listed in parentheses.

File Specifiers

The unit specifier, UNIT = *u*, designates the unit number assigned to the file. The *u* in this specifier may be either an integer expression that evaluates to a nonnegative value or an asterisk, which designates a default system-specified unit. If the term UNIT = is omitted, the unit number must be the first item in parentheses.

The name specifier, FILE = *name*, designates the name of the file being opened, which can be any character expression. If this file specifier is not included in the OPEN statement, a default system-specified file is selected. If a character constant is used for the name, it must be enclosed in apostrophes. For example, the specifier FILE = 'TEST.DAT' identifies the file TEST.DAT as the file to be opened.

The STATUS file specifier, STATUS = *stype*, designates the status of the file. The character expression *stype* must evaluate to one of the values NEW, OLD, SCRATCH, or UNKNOWN. A status of NEW causes a new file to be created. If an existing file has the same name as the file being opened, an error will be reported when the OPEN statement is executed. Files opened as OLD already exist on the system. Files opened as UNKNOWN will be created if they do not exist or opened as OLD files if they do exist. UNKNOWN is the default status selected in the absence of an explicit status designation. A SCRATCH status indicates that the file is temporary and will be deleted upon closing the file or program termination.

The FORM specifier, FORM = *file-type*, designates whether the file is formatted (text) or unformatted (binary). The character expression *file-type* must evaluate to one of the constants FORMATTED or UNFORMATTED, respectively. If this file specifier is omitted, the file is assumed to be FORMATTED if it is a sequential access file or UNFORMATTED if it is a direct access file.

The ACCESS file specifier, ACCESS = *atype*, designates whether the records in a file are accessed in a sequential or a direct manner (see Section 11.4 for a complete discussion of file access methods). The character expression *atype* must evaluate to one of the constants SEQUENTIAL or DIRECT. Files created as SEQUENTIAL must subsequently be opened with this access type and files created as DIRECT also must subsequently be opened using DIRECT access. If the access specification is omitted, the file is opened as SEQUENTIAL by default. If the access specification ACCESS = 'DIRECT' is used, the record length specifier, RECL = *rln*, must be used.

The RECL file specifier, RECL = *rln*, designates the record length of a direct access file. The integer expression *rln* must evaluate to a positive value. This specifier must be present when the ACCESS = 'DIRECT' specifier is used and must be omitted for sequential access files. For formatted direct access files the record length is the number of characters allowed in a record, for unformatted direct access files the record length is typically the number of words allowed in a record. For existing direct access files the record length must always be specified as the same value used when the file was created.

The BLANK file specifier, BLANK = *ch*, determines the interpretation of blank spaces in numeric input fields. The character expression *ch* must evaluate to one of the constants NULL or ZERO, respectively. When BLANK = 'NULL' is specified blank spaces embedded within an input number are ignored. When BLANK = 'ZERO' is specified, embedded blank spaces in a numeric input field are interpreted as zeros. In both cases a completely blank field is assigned the value zero. If the BLANK file specifier is omitted, a NULL default is used. (As noted previously, some compilers are configured to assume a ZERO default.) The BN and BZ format specifiers (see Appendix B) can always be used to override the BLANK file specifier.

The IOSTAT file specifier, IOSTAT = *var*, designates an integer variable that will be assigned an I/O status code. The value assigned to the variable depends on the I/O status produced by the OPEN statement. It is zero if the OPEN statement executed without an error, and it is assigned a computer-dependent positive value for any other detected error condition. The value assigned to the IOSTAT variable may be displayed using either a PRINT or a WRITE statement.

The ERR file specifier, ERR = *n*, designates a statement label to which control is transferred if any error condition is encountered when the OPEN statement is executed.

The WRITE Statement

The WRITE statement, which permits data to be written to a previously opened file, has the following complete form:

```
WRITE(UNIT = integer expression,
        FMT = format specifier,
        ERR = statement label,
        IOSTAT = integer variable,
        REC =  integer expression) expression list
```

Except for the REC option, which is explained in the next section, all of the specifiers in the WRITE statement should be familiar to you: the UNIT, ERR, and IOSTAT specifiers are the same as previously described under the OPEN statement, and the FMT specifier is the same as we have been using throughout the text.

The only file specifiers that are required with a WRITE statement are a unit number and format specification. If the expression UNIT = is omitted, an integer expression defining the file to be written to must be the first item in parentheses. Similarly, if the expression FMT = is omitted, the format specifier must be the second item within the parentheses. Otherwise, the specifiers may appear in any order within the parentheses.

The READ Statement

The READ statement, which permits data to be read from a previously opened file, has the following complete form:

```
READ(UNIT = integer expression,
        FMT = format specifier,
        END = statement label,
        ERR = statement label,
        IOSTAT = integer variable,
        REC =  integer expression) variable list
```

Except for the END option, all of the specifiers in the READ statement are identical to those in the WRITE statement. The END option specifies a statement label to which control is transferred if the end of the file is encountered. The REC specifier, which permits reading a direct access file, is presented in the next section.

The only file specifiers that are required with a READ statement are a unit number and format specification. If the expression UNIT = is omitted, an integer expression defining the file to be read must be the first item in parentheses. Similarly, if the expression FMT = is omitted, the format specifier must be the second item within the parentheses. Otherwise, the specifiers may appear in any order within the parentheses.

The CLOSE Statement

The CLOSE statement disconnects a previously opened file from a program. Its general form is:

```
CLOSE(UNIT = integer expression,
        ERR = statement label,
        IOSTAT = integer variable,
        STATUS = character expression)
```

The only file specifier that is required with a CLOSE statement is the unit number that specifies which file is to be closed. If the expression UNIT = is omitted, an integer expression defining the file to be closed must be the first item in parentheses. Otherwise, the specifiers may appear in any order within the parentheses. The STATUS specifier must be a character expression that evaluates to either 'KEEP' or 'DELETE'. The specification STATUS = 'KEEP' indicates that the file is to be retained after it is closed, while the specification STATUS = 'DELETE' indicates that the file is no longer needed and is to be deleted. The default option, when no STATUS is provided, is to 'KEEP' the file.

The REWIND Statement

The REWIND statement repositions a file to its first record. Its general form is:

```
REWIND(UNIT = integer expression,
       ERR = statement label,
       IOSTAT = integer variable)
```

The only file specifier that is required with a REWIND statement is the unit number that specifies which file is to be rewound. If the expression UNIT = is omitted, an integer expression defining the file to be rewound must be the first item in parentheses. Otherwise, the specifiers may appear in any order within the parentheses.

The BACKSPACE Statement

The BACKSPACE statement repositions a file to the beginning of the preceding record. Its general form is:

```
BACKSPACE(UNIT = integer expression,
          ERR = statement label,
          IOSTAT = integer variable)
```

The only file specifier that is required with a BACKSPACE statement is the unit number that specifies which file is to be backspaced. If the expression UNIT = is omitted, an integer expression defining the file to be backspaced must be the first item in parentheses. Otherwise, the specifiers may appear in any order within the parentheses.

The effect of the BACKSPACE command is listed in Table 11-2.

The ENDFILE Statement

The ENDFILE statement writes an end-of-file record to a file. As this task is automatically performed by the CLOSE statement, the ENDFILE statement is rarely used. Its general form is:

```
ENDFILE(UNIT = integer expression,
        ERR = statement label,
        IOSTAT = integer variable)
```

Table 11-2 Effect of BACKSPACE Command

Current File Position	Effect of BACKSPACE
At start of file	File position not changed
At start of record n	File position changed to start of previous record (normal operation)
In middle of a record	File position changed to beginning of record

The only file specifier that is required with an ENDFILE statement is the unit number that specifies which file is to be used. If the expression UNIT = is omitted, an integer expression defining the file to be used must be the first item in parentheses. Otherwise, the specifiers may appear in any order within the parentheses.

After writing an end-of-file record, the position of the file is at the end of this record. This means that further sequential data transfer is prohibited unless a REWIND or BACKSPACE command is executed. The BACKSPACE command, in this instance, positions the file to the beginning of the end-of-file record. When used on a direct access file, which is described in the next section, an ENDFILE statement erases from access all records beyond the new end-of-file record.

The INQUIRE Statement

The INQUIRE statement returns the values of the various attributes specified when the file was opened. Although it cannot return the attributes of an unopened file, it can determine if an unopened file exists. This statement has two general forms:

```
INQUIRE (FILE = character expression, specifier list)
```

and

```
INQUIRE (UNIT = integer expression, specifier list)
```

where the allowable specifiers are listed in Tables 11-3 and 11-4.

Table 11-3 FORTRAN 77 and FORTRAN 90 INQUIRE Statement Specifiers

File Specifier	Returned Value
ACCESS = *character variable*	'SEQUENTIAL' or 'DIRECT'
BLANK = *character variable*	'NULL' or 'ZERO'
DIRECT = *character variable*	'YES' or 'NO'
ERR = *statement label*	not applicable
EXIST = *logical variable*	.TRUE. or .FALSE.
FORM = *character variable*	'FORMATTED' or 'UNFORMATTED'
FORMATTED = *character variable*	'YES' or 'NO'
IOSTAT = *integer variable*	An integer number
NAME = *character variable*	The opened file's name
NAMED = *logical variable*	.TRUE. or .FALSE.
NEXTREC = *integer variable*	The next record number
NUMBER = *integer variable*	The file's unit number
OPENED = *logical variable*	.TRUE. or .FALSE.
RECL = *integer variable*	Record length
SEQUENTIAL = *character variable*	'YES' or 'NO'
UNFORMATTED = *character variable*	'YES' or 'NO'

Table 11-4 Additional FORTRAN 90 INQUIRE Statement Specifiers

File Specifier	Returned Value
BINARY = *character variable*	'YES' or 'NO'
BLOCKSIZE = *integer variable*	I/O buffer size
MODE = *character variable*	'READ', 'WRITE', or 'READWRITE'
SHARE = *character variable*	The current share status

The INQUIRE statement is particularly useful when prompting a user for a file name, because if the file does not exist the user can immediately be prompted for another name. The subroutine FLOPEN() contained in Program 11-4 illustrates this usage:

Program 11-4

```
      PROGRAM MAIN
        CALL FLOPEN
        END
*
      SUBROUTINE FLOPEN
        CHARACTER*12 FNAME
        LOGICAL EXISTS, NOTDON
        NOTDON = .TRUE.
*
        WRITE(6,*) 'PLEASE ENTER THE FILE''S NAME:'
        READ(5, '(A)') FNAME
*
  10     IF (NOTDON) THEN
          INQUIRE(FILE = FNAME, EXIST = EXISTS)
          IF (.NOT. EXISTS) THEN
            WRITE(6,*) ' THE FILE ', FNAME, 'DOES NOT EXIST'
            WRITE(6,*) 'PLEASE ENTER ANOTHER FILE NAME OR QUIT:'
            READ(5, '(A)') FNAME
            IF (FNAME .EQ. 'QUIT') STOP 'STOPPED BY USER REQUEST'
           GOTO 10
           ENDIF
        ENDIF
        OPEN (UNIT = 2, FILE = FNAME)
        RETURN
        END
```

Following is a sample run using Program 11-4:

```
PLEASE ENTER THE FILE'S NAME:
RICHARD
  THE FILE RICHARD     DOES NOT EXIST
PLEASE ENTER ANOTHER FILE NAME OR QUIT:
WILLIAM
  THE FILE WILLIAM     DOES NOT EXIST
PLEASE ENTER ANOTHER FILE NAME OR QUIT:
QUIT
STOPPED BY USER REQUEST
```

11.4 Direct Access Files

The manner in which records in a file are written and retrieved is called *file access*. All of the files created so far have used *sequential access*, which means that each record in the file is accessed sequentially, one after another. Thus, for example, the fourth record in a sequentially accessed file cannot be read without first reading the first three records in the file, the last record in the file cannot be read without first reading all of the previous records, and no record can be replaced without erasing all subsequent records. Because records within a sequential file cannot be replaced, updating a sequential access file requires using a file update procedure in which a completely new file is created for each update (see, for example, Applications 1 and 2 in Section 5.6). For those applications in which every record in a file must be updated, such as updating a monthly payroll file, sequential access conforms to the way the file must be updated and is not a restriction.

In some applications direct access to each record in the file, where an individual record in the middle of the file can be retrieved, modified, and rewritten without reading or writing to any other record, is preferable. *Direct access* files, also referred to as *random access* files, provide this capability. In this section we will see how to create and use direct access files. Since the access method (sequential or direct) refers to how data in the file is accessed and not to the codes used in storing the data, both sequential and direct access files may be created in both formatted (text) and unformatted (binary) forms.

Unless a file is explicitly specified as a direct access file, it will be opened in sequential access mode. The specification of a direct access file is made by including both the ACCESS = 'DIRECT' and the RECL = *rln* file specifiers in the file's OPEN statement. For example, the statement:

```
OPEN(1, FILE='BK.DAT', FORM='FORMATTED', ACCESS='DIRECT', RECL=20)
```

opens the formatted file named BK.DAT as a direct access file, where each record in the file has a maximum length of 20 characters. If the FORM specifier were omitted, the file would be opened by default as an unformatted file (this is in keeping with the FORM defaults described in the previous section: a direct access file defaults to an unformatted form, and a sequential file to a formatted form). The record length specified for direct access formatted files corresponds to the maximum number of characters that can be stored in a record. Each time a direct access file is opened, the same record length must be specified as when the file was initially created. It is the record length that tells the computer how many characters must be retrieved and written each time a record is accessed.

Once a direct access file has been opened, either as a formatted or an unformatted file, reading and writing to the file are identical to their sequential access file counterparts, with one exception: both the READ and the WRITE statements used must include a REC = *record number* specifier to indicate which record is to be accessed. For example, the statement:

```
WRITE (1, 15, REC = 5) IDNO, QUANTY, PRICE
```

writes the values of IDNO, QUANTY, and PRICE to the fifth record in file number 1 using the format specified in FORMAT statement 15. Similarly, the statement:

```
WRITE (3, *, REC = 226) A, B, C
```

writes the values of A, B, and C to the 226th record of file number 3 using the compiler's list-directed format. For unformatted direct access files the format specification in both READ and WRITE statements, as for unformatted sequential access files, must be omitted.

In general, the record number in both READ and WRITE statements can be any integer expression that evaluates to a positive number. Since records in a direct access file are accessed by record number, applications that use direct access files must contain either an identification number or an account code, to be used either directly or indirectly as a record number, as part of each record. For example, assume that a direct access formatted file that contains the data shown in Table 11-5 is to be created.

Creating a direct access file of the data in Table 11-5, either as a formatted or an unformatted file, requires that five records be written. Each record in the file is used to store a product identification number, the quantity of the product in stock, and the product's selling price. The product identification number has been selected as a four-digit number so that subtracting 1000 from the number yields the correct record number. Thus, the data for product identification number 1001 would be stored in record number 1, the data for product identification number 1002 would be stored in record number 2, and so on. (Converting an identification code to a record number is formally called *hashing*.)

Program 11-5 creates the required file.

Table 11-5 Product Information to Be Stored in a Direct Access File

Product number	Quantity in stock	Selling price
1001	476	28.00
1002	348	32.50
1003	517	51.00
1004	284	23.75
1005	165	35.25

Program 11-5

```
      PROGRAM CREATE
        CALL DIRFL1
        END
*
      SUBROUTINE DIRFL1
        INTEGER RECNO, IDNO, QUANTY, I
        REAL PRICE
        OPEN(1, FILE = 'PRDCT.DAT', FORM = 'FORMATTED',
     +       ACCESS = 'DIRECT', RECL = 20)
        DO 20 I = 1, 5
          WRITE(6,*) 'ENTER THE IDENTIFIATION NUMBER: '
          READ(5,*) IDNO
          RECNO = IDNO - 1000
          WRITE(6,*) 'ENTER THE QUANTITY IN STOCK: '
          READ(5,*) QUANTY
          WRITE(6,*) 'ENTER THE SELLING PRICE: '
          READ(5,*) PRICE
          WRITE (1,15,REC = RECNO) IDNO,QUANTY,PRICE
   15     FORMAT(I5,3X,I3,3X,F6.2)
   20   CONTINUE
        CLOSE(1)
        RETURN
        END
```

The OPEN statement in Program 11-5 opens the PRDCT.DAT file as a formatted direct access file that will be known as unit number 1 within the program. The record length of 20 in the OPEN statement was obtained by adding the field width specifiers in FORMAT statement 15, since it is this format that is used to write each individual record to the file. (*Note:* A larger record length can be specified, but a smaller record length will result in a runtime "direct record overflow" error.) When Program 11-5 is executed, and assuming that the data in Table 11-5 is entered correctly, the file illustrated in Figure 11-4 will be created (since it is a formatted file, it can be listed using any word processing or text editor program).

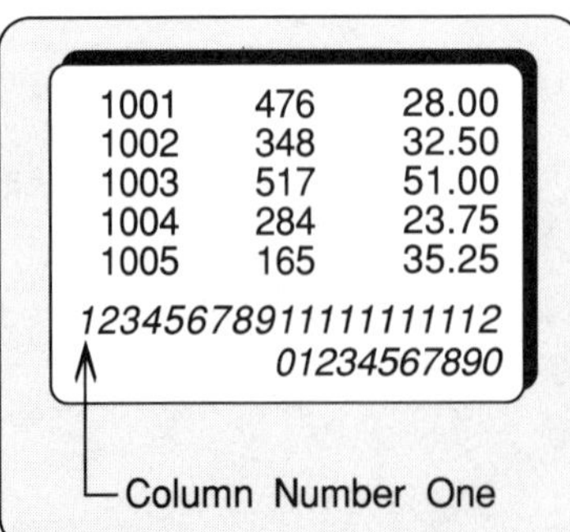

Figure 11-4 The Formatted File Produced by Program 11-5

Program 11-6 illustrates the use of a formatted READ statement to read the data in the direct access file created by Program 11-5. In reviewing this program, notice that the file specifiers used in the OPEN statement are iden-

Program 11-6

```
      PROGRAM MAIN
        CALL READDR
        END
*
      SUBROUTINE READDR
        INTEGER RECNO, IDNO, QUANTY
        REAL PRICE
        OPEN(1, FILE = 'PRDCT.DAT', FORM = 'FORMATTED',
     +       ACCESS = 'DIRECT', RECL = 20)
 5      FORMAT(1X,'                    QUANTITY')
10      FORMAT(1X,'STOCK NO.      IN STOCK     PRICE')
15      FORMAT(1X,'---------      --------    -------')
20      FORMAT(I5,3X,I3,3X,F6.2)
25      FORMAT(2X,I5,10X,I3,7X,'$',F6.2)
        WRITE(6,5)
        WRITE(6,10)
        WRITE(6,15)
        RECNO = 1
30      READ(1, 20, REC = RECNO, END = 35) IDNO, QUANTY, PRICE
          WRITE(6,25) IDNO, QUANTY, PRICE
          RECNO = RECNO + 1
        GOTO 30
35      CLOSE(1)
        RETURN
        END
```

tical to those used when the file was created. Also notice that the READ statement includes a REC = *record number* specifier and uses the same format specification for reading each record in the file as was used when the file was written. The program begins at record number 1 and continuously reads each record in increasing record number order until the end of the file is detected, at which point control is transferred to statement label 35.

The output produced by Program 11-6 is as follows:

```
                  QUANTITY
  STOCK NO.       IN STOCK     PRICE
  ---------       --------    -------
    1001            476       $ 28.00
    1002            348       $ 32.50
    1003            517       $ 51.00
    1004            284       $ 23.75
    1005            165       $ 35.25
```

Notice that although direct access is used in Program 11-6, the data in the PRDCT.DAT file is read in a sequential order, starting from record number 1. The real advantage to direct access files is that records in the file can be read and written in any order. To illustrate this, consider Program 11-7, which requests a user to enter any identification number. If the record corresponding to the desired identification number is located, the user is requested to enter a new quantity in stock number, and the updated data is written to the existing record; otherwise, the user is informed that no record exists for the entered stock number.

In reviewing Program 11-7, notice that the OPEN statement contains the same file specifiers as used in Program 11-5 when the PRDCT.DAT file was created. Also notice the use of the ERR specifier in the READ statement to direct the program to display an error message when the appropriate record is not found.

11.5 Internal Files

As we have seen in the previous chapter, both READ and WRITE statements can be used to read and write data from external data files. In addition these statements can be used to read and write data directly from or to a character string. Character strings used in this manner are referred to as *internal files* because the read and write statements transfer data from one internal location to another. For example, consider the following statements:

```
INTEGER I
REAL VAL1, VAL2
CHARACTER TEXT*15
TEXT = '22.35 17.258 53'
READ(TEXT,*) VAL1, VAL2, I
```

In this section of code the READ statement receives its input directly from the internal variable TEXT, just as it would from the keyboard or an external data file. Thus, the value 22.35 is stored in the real variable VAL1, the value 17.258 is stored in the real variable VAL2, and the value 53 is stored in the integer variable I. Since the input from the string effectively involves converting from either the ASCII or EBCDIC code used to store the string into the data type of the receiving variables, this type of input is also referred to as *in-memory string conversion.*

An extremely useful application of in-memory conversion is its use in "stripping-off" undesirable characters in a data file. For example, assume that a record in a data file contains a price, containing a dollar sign, followed by a description, such as

```
$ 32.50  Right-front light assembly
```

If each record in the file is first read into a character variable named LINE, the price and description in the record can be obtained using the statements:

```
      READ(LINE, 10) PRICE, DESCRP
   10 FORMAT(1X,F5.2,A)
```

In a similar manner, writing to an internal file allows us to "assemble" a string from one or more variables before a complete line is written to either a data file or the standard output device. For example, assuming that TEXT is

Program 11-7

```
      PROGRAM MAIN
        CALL UPDIR
        END
*
      SUBROUTINE UPDIR
        IMPLICIT NONE
        INTEGER RECNO, STKNO, IDNO, QUANTY, CURRNT
        REAL PRICE
    5   FORMAT(I5)
   10   FORMAT(I3)
   15   FORMAT(I5,3X,I3,3X,F6.2)

        OPEN(1, FILE = 'PRDCT.DAT', FORM = 'FORMATTED',
     +       ACCESS = 'DIRECT', RECL = 20)

        WRITE(6,*) 'ENTER AN IDENTIFICATION NUMBER OR 999 TO STOP: '
        READ(5,*) STKNO
   20   IF (STKNO .NE. 999) THEN
          RECNO = STKNO - 1000
          READ(1, 15, REC=RECNO, ERR=25) IDNO, QUANTY, PRICE
***     RECORD HAS BEEN FOUND - ENTER UPDATED QUANTITY
          WRITE(6,*) 'ENTER THE CURRENT QUANTITY IN STOCK: '
          READ(5,*) CURRNT
***     WRITE THE UPDATED RECORD
          WRITE(1,15, REC=RECNO) IDNO,CURRNT,PRICE
   25     IF (STKNO.NE.IDNO) THEN
            WRITE(6,*) 'THERE IS NO RECORD FOR THIS STOCK NUMBER'
            WRITE(6,*) 'PLEASE RECHECK THE NUMBER'
          ENDIF
          WRITE(6,*) 'ENTER ANOTHER STOCK NUMBER OR 999 TO STOP: '
          READ(5,*) STKNO
          GO TO 20
        ENDIF
        CLOSE(1)
        RETURN
        END
```

a character variable of length 14, AMOUNT is an integer variable, and PRICE is a real variable, the statements:

```
      WRITE(TEXT,3) AMOUNT, PRICE
    3 FORMAT(I3,3X,'$',F7.2)
```

would place the values in AMOUNT and PRICE into the TEXT string as the first three and last seven characters, respectively.

11.6 Exercises

1. Write individual OPEN statements that explicitly open files having the following characteristics:
   a. A formatted sequential file named TEST.DAT that is to be assigned to unit number 3.
   b. A file named DESCRI that is a new, direct access file with individual record lengths of 80. The file is to be assigned to unit number 4.
   c. A file named NAMES that is an old, sequential, formatted file that is to be assigned to unit number 1. The I/O status of the file is to be assigned to the variable IOS, and the OPEN statement should transfer control to statement label 850 if an error in opening the file is detected.
   d. An existing formatted sequential file named TYPES that is to be assigned to unit number 4. The I/O status of the file is to be assigned to the variable ISTAT, and the OPEN statement should transfer control to statement label 835 if an error in opening the file is detected.
   e. An existing unformatted sequential file named TYPES that is to be assigned to unit number 4. The I/O status of the file is to be assigned to the variable ISTAT, and the OPEN statement should transfer control to statement label 860 if an error in opening the file is detected.
   f. An existing formatted direct access file with record length 80 named TYPES that is to be assigned to unit number 7. The I/O status of the file is to be assigned to the variable MST, and the OPEN statement should transfer control to statement label 870 if an error in opening the file is detected. Explicitly designate that blank spaces within all numeric fields in the file are to be interpreted as zeros.
   g. Redo Exercise 1f but explicitly designate that blank spaces within all numeric fields in the file are to be ignored.
2. Redo Exercise 1 but omit all explicit file specifiers from the OPEN statement when the desired specifiers are correctly selected by FORTRAN's default values.
3. Write, compile, and run a FORTRAN program that writes the four real numbers 92.65, 88.72, 77.46, and 82.93 to an unformatted sequential file named RESULT. After writing the data to the file, your program should read the data from the file, determine the average of the four numbers read, and display the average. Verify the output produced by your program by manually calculating the average of the four input numbers.

4a. Write, compile, and execute a FORTRAN program that creates an unformatted sequential file named POINTS and writes the following numbers to the file:

```
 6.3   8.2   18.25   24.32    ←  1st record
 4.0   4.0   10.0    -5.0     ←  2nd record
-2.0   5.0    4.0     5.0     ←  3rd record
```

b. Using the data in the POINTS file created in Exercise 4a write, compile, and run a FORTRAN program that reads each record and interprets the first and second numbers in each record as the coordinates of one point and the third and fourth numbers as the coordinates of a second point. Using the formulas given in Exercises 27 and 28 of Section 2.3, have your program compute and display the slope and midpoint of the two points entered. Your program should use the END option of the formatted READ statement.

5a. Write, compile, and run a FORTRAN program that creates an unformatted sequential file named GRADES and writes the following numbers to the file:

```
100, 100, 100, 100
100, 0, 100, 0
86, 83, 89, 94
78, 59, 77, 85
89, 92, 81, 88
```

b. Using the data in the GRADES file created in Exercise 5a, write, compile, and run a FORTRAN program that reads each record in the GRADES file, computes the average for each record, and displays the average.

6. Redo Exercise 12 in Section 5.4 using an unformatted sequential file.

7a. Enter, compile, and execute Program 11-5 on your computer.

b. Modify the record length in the OPEN statement in Program 11-5 to be 10. Run the program and determine the effect produced by this change.

c. What effect do you think will be made if the record length in the OPEN statement in Program 11-5 is changed to 200?

8. Modify Program 11-5 so that an unformatted file is created. (Hint: Typically, an unformatted file requires less space per record than does a formatted file. More generally, the record length for an unformatted file is the number of words needed to store a record in the binary format used by your computer. If the record length is not large enough, a runtime error will occur when the record is being written because of the insufficient storage allocation.)

9. Modify Program 11-6 to read and list the contents of the unformatted direct access file produced in Exercise 8.

10. Modify Program 11-7 to update the unformatted direct access file created in Exercise 8.

11. Modify Program 11-7 so that both the quantity and the price in each record can be modified. Additionally, have your program check that an identification number between 1001 and 9999 has been entered; if a valid identification number is not currently in the file, have your program create a record for the new item.

12. Redo Exercise 12 in Section 5.4 using a formatted direct access file. To do this, you will have to assign product codes that can be translated into record numbers.

11.7 Common Programming Errors

Five programming errors are common when using files. The most obvious of these is incorrect use of the OPEN statement. This statement must include at minimum a unit number and the FILE = '*filename*' specifier.

A second error is omitting the unit number when using a file READ or WRITE statement. Programmers used to writing these statements for standard input and output devices, where a specific file designator is not required, sometimes forget to include a unit number when accessing data files.

A third error is attempting to use the PRINT statement and replacing the list-directed asterisk with a unit number. The PRINT statement can only access the standard output device. If a unit number is used in this statement, the compiler will consider it to be a FORMAT statement label.

A fourth error occurs when a formatted READ or WRITE is attempted on an unformatted (binary) file. This frequently occurs because the programmer is accustomed to writing formatted I/O statements (list directed or user formatted) to standard I/O units.

A fith error occurs when the record number specification is omitted from READ or WRITE statements used with direct access files.

11.8 Things to Remember

1. A data file is any collection of data stored together on an external storage medium under a common name. Formally, each line of data stored on the file is called a *record.*
2. The manner in which records are written to and read from a file is called the file's access method.
   a. In a *sequential access file* each record must be accessed in a sequential manner. This means that the second record in the file cannot be read until the first record has been read, the third record cannot be read until the first and second records have been read, and so on, until the last record is read. Similarly, a record cannot be written until all previous records have been written and a record cannot be replaced without destroying all following records.
   b. In a *direct access file* any record can be read, written, or replaced without affecting any other record in the file. A disadvantage of direct access files is that the record length must be specified. Additionally, each record in a direct access file must contain a value that can be translated into a record number needed for record access.
3. In addition to the access method selected for a file, a file can be either a formatted or an unformatted file.
   a. A *formatted file* is one in which each data item in the file is formatted, using either explicit user-designated formats or the compiler's list-directed format. A formatted file is also referred to as a text file.
   b. An *unformatted file* is one is which each data item in the file is stored using the computer's internal binary code. An unformatted file is also referred to as a binary file.

4. An OPEN statement is required to connect a file name to a program unit number. The most basic form of the OPEN statement is:

```
OPEN(unit number, FILE = 'filename')
```

This form of the OPEN statement, by default, designates the file as both sequential and formatted. If the file does not exist, the OPEN statement creates a file having the indicated name.

   a. Including the specifier FORM = 'UNFORMATTED' in the parentheses opens the file as a binary file.
   b. Including the specifier ACCESS = 'DIRECT' in the parentheses opens the file as a direct access file. If the file is opened for direct access, the record length specifier RECL = *rln* must also be used, where *rln* is the length of an individual record.

5. A file must always be opened using the specifiers with which the file was originally created.
6. Data is written to a file using a WRITE statement.
   a. The basic form of this statement for writing to a sequential formatted file is:

```
WRITE(unit number, format specifier) expression list
```

   b. The basic form of this statement for writing to a sequential unformatted file is:

```
WRITE(unit number) expression list
```

   c. The basic form of this statement for writing to a direct access formatted file is:

```
WRITE(unit number, format specifier, REC = recno)
expression list
```

   d. The basic form of this statement for writing to a direct access unformatted file is:

```
WRITE(unit number, REC = recno) expression list
```

The unit number in all WRITE statements must be either an integer number designating a previously opened file or an integer expression that evaluates to a valid integer file number. The format specifier can be either an asterisk, which specifies a list-directed format, the statement number of a FORMAT statement, or a literal format control character constant surrounded by parentheses and enclosed in apostrophes. For direct access files *recno* can be any integer expression yielding a positive record number.

7. Data is read from an existing file using a READ statement.
   a. The most basic form of this statement for reading from a sequential formatted file is:

```
READ(unit number, format specifier) variable list
```

b. The most basic form of this statement for reading from a sequential unformatted file is:

```
READ(unit number) variable list
```

c. The most basic form of this statement for reading from a direct access formatted file is:

```
READ(unit number, format specifier, REC = recno)
variable list
```

d. The most basic form of this statement for reading from a direct access unformatted file is:

```
READ(unit number, REC = recno) variable list
```

The unit number in all READ statements must be either an integer number designating a previously opened file or an integer expression that evaluates to a valid integer file number. The format specifier can be either an asterisk, which specifies a list-directed format, the statement number of a FORMAT statement, or a literal format control character constant surrounded by parentheses and enclosed in apostrophes. The format used for reading data from a formatted file must be identical to the format used when data was written to the file. For direct access files *recno* can be any integer expression yielding a positive record number.

8. In addition to files opened explicitly within a program, the standard input and output files are automatically opened when a FORTRAN program is executed. The standard input file corresponds to the physical device used for data entry, and the standard output file is the physical device used for data display. Each of these files is assigned a unit number by the system. On many systems an asterisk can be used in place of a unit number to designate the standard I/O device. This asterisk is distinct from the asterisk used to select list-directed formatting.

9. The current position in a sequential file can be altered using the REWIND and BACKSPACE statements. The REWIND statement sets the current position of an internal file pointer to the start of the file. The BACKSPACE statement moves the pointer back one record in the file.

10. Files are formally closed using a CLOSE statement. The most common format of this statement is:

```
CLOSE (unit number)
```

All files are automatically closed when the program they are opened in finishes executing.

12 Additional FORTRAN Features

Chapter Twelve

12.1 COMMON Blocks

12.2 New FORTRAN 90 Features

12.3 Pointers and Targets

12.4 Structures

12.5 Linked Lists

12.6 Things to Remember

In this chapter we look at additional features provided by both FORTRAN 77 and FORTRAN 90. COMMON blocks, described in Section 12.1, are supported in both FORTRAN versions. The remaining features described in this chapter, pointers, targets, data structures, and linked lists using these features, are new to FORTRAN 90.

12.1 COMMON Blocks

As we have seen in Section 4.1, all FORTRAN variables declared within a program unit are local to that unit. In practical terms this means that, unless special provisions are made, one unit's variables cannot be accessed by another unit. One method of providing for the mutual access of variables between a subroutine and its calling unit is to use subroutine argument lists. This method is unwieldy, however, when many variables must be shared among many subroutines. A more suitable approach in this situation is to use the second method provided by FORTRAN for extending the scope of a variable beyond the borders of its originating program unit. This second method is to use a COMMON block.

A COMMON block is a block of memory locations that can be made available to any and all program units. FORTRAN provides two classes of COMMON block types: COMMON blocks that are assigned individual names, called *named* COMMON, and a single unnamed COMMON block. Once an individual variable has been assigned space in a COMMON block, any program unit that needs the variable can gain access to the block by correctly referencing the desired COMMON area.

Unnamed COMMON

Unnamed COMMON, which is also referred to as *blank* COMMON, is created with the COMMON declaration statement:

```
COMMON  list of variables
```

The keyword COMMON must be present and specifies that a common block is being defined. The list of variables defines the variables that are to be included in the COMMON block. For example, the statement :

```
COMMON FACTOR, WEIGHT, MASS, DENSTY
```

places the four variables FACTOR, WEIGHT, MASS, and DENSTY into the computer's unnamed COMMON area. A program unit desiring access to this area must place this declaration statement after the data type declarations for the four variables. If the variables have not been explicitly typed, the compiler assigns data types to COMMON variables using FORTRAN's implicit typing rules.

All program units that desire access to the computer's unnamed common area must include a COMMON declaration. As with arguments, the variable names in each COMMON statement do not have to be the same, but the number, type, and order of the variables in each COMMON statement must be identical. For example, consider the following MAIN program unit and subroutine:

```
PROGRAM MAIN
  INTEGER MASS, N1, N2
  REAL FACTOR, WEIGHT, DENSTY
  COMMON FACTOR, WEIGHT, MASS, DENSTY
   .
   .
   .
  CALL SOLVE(N1,N2)
   .
   .
   .
  END
SUBROUTINE SOLVE(K,J)
  INTEGER K,J
  INTEGER MSS
  REAL SCALE, WT, DN
  COMMON SCALE, WT, MSS, DN
   .
   .
   .
  END
```

In this example the two program units communicate using both arguments and the computer's unnamed COMMON area. As illustrated in Figure 12-1, the variables

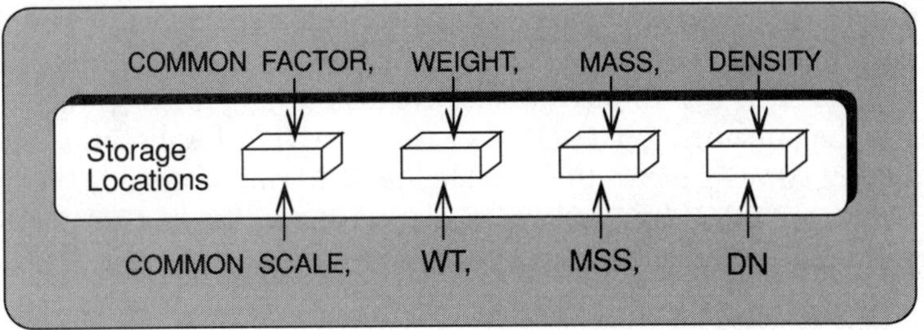

Figure 12-1 Equivalent Variable Designations

FACTOR and SCALE refer to the same memory locations, the variables WEIGHT and WT refer to the same memory locations, the variables MASS and MSS refer to the same memory locations, and the variables DENSTY and DN refer to the same memory locations.

We now include an unnamed COMMON within a working program. Consider, for example, Program 12-1.

Program 12-1

```
      PROGRAM MAIN
        INTEGER FIRNUM,SECNUM
        COMMON FIRNUM
        FIRNUM = 10
        SECNUM = 20
        WRITE(6,*) 'FROM PROGRAM MAIN: FIRNUM = ',FIRNUM
        WRITE(6,*) 'FROM PROGRAM MAIN: SECNUM = ',SECNUM
        CALL ALTVAL
        WRITE(6,*)
        WRITE(6,*)'FROM PROGRAM MAIN AGAIN: FIRNUM = ',FIRNUM
        WRITE(6,*)'FROM PROGRAM MAIN AGAIN: SECNUM = ',SECNUM
        END
*
      SUBROUTINE ALTVAL
        INTEGER FIRNUM, SECNUM
        COMMON FIRNUM
        SECNUM = 30
        WRITE(6,*)
        WRITE(6,*)'FROM ALTVAL: FIRNUM = ',FIRNUM
        WRITE(6,*)'FROM ALTVAL: SECNUM = ',SECNUM
        FIRNUM = 40
        RETURN
        END
```

In this program the unnamed COMMON declaration in the MAIN program unit places this unit's local variable FIRNUM into the system's unnamed COMMON area. This makes this variable available to any other program unit that also specifies the unnamed COMMON area. As the ALTVAL subroutine also specifies the unnamed COMMON block, the variable FIRNUM can be directly accessed within ALTVAL. Since ALTVAL has declared the same name for its COMMON variable, both program units reference the common variable using the name FIRNUM. Additionally, Program 12-1 contains two separate local variables, both named SECNUM. Storage for the SECNUM variable named in PROGRAM MAIN is created by the declaration statement located in PROGRAM MAIN. A different storage area for the SECNUM variable in ALTVAL is created by the declaration statement located in the ALTVAL subroutine. Figure 12-2 illustrates the three distinct storage areas reserved by Program 12-1.

Each of the variables named SECNUM is local to the program unit in which its storage is created, and each of these variables can only be used from within the appropriate subroutine. Thus, when SECNUM is used in PROGRAM MAIN, the storage area reserved by this program unit for its SECNUM variable is accessed; when SECNUM is used in ALTVAL, the storage area reserved by ALTVAL for its SECNUM variable is accessed. The following output is produced when Program 12-1 is run:

```
FROM PROGRAM MAIN: FIRNUM =          10
FROM PROGRAM MAIN: SECNUM =          20

FROM ALTVAL: FIRNUM =          10
FROM ALTVAL: SECNUM =          30

FROM PROGRAM MAIN AGAIN: FIRNUM =          40
FROM PROGRAM MAIN AGAIN: SECNUM =          20
```

Let us analyze the output produced by Program 12-1. Since FIRNUM is in unnamed COMMON declared by both the MAIN program unit and the ALTVAL subroutine, both of these units can use and change its value. Initially, both program units print the value of 10 that PROGRAM MAIN stored in FIRNUM. Before returning, ALTVAL changes the value of FIRNUM to 40, which is the value displayed when FIRNUM is next displayed from within the MAIN program unit.

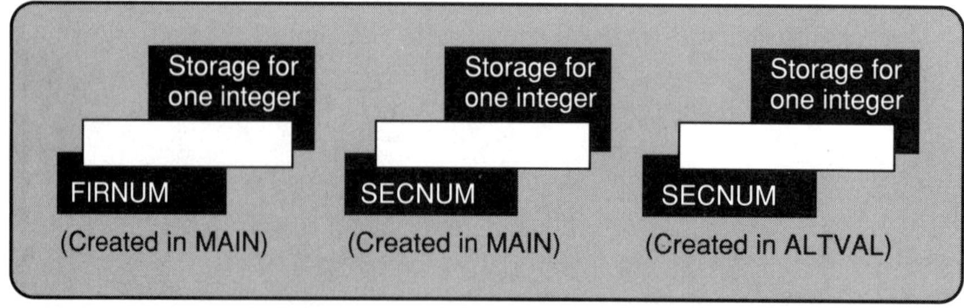

Figure 12-2 The Three Storage Areas Created by Program 12-1

Since each program unit only "knows" its own local variables, the MAIN program unit can only display the value of its SECNUM, and ALTVAL can only display the value of its SECNUM. Thus, whenever SECNUM is displayed from PROGRAM MAIN, the value 20 is output; whenever SECNUM is displayed from ALTVAL, the value 30 is output. The values of the two SECNUM variables are not confused by the computer because only one program unit can execute at a given moment.

Arrays and Unnamed COMMON

In addition to scalar variables, array names may also be included in a COMMON declaration. Doing so places the complete array in the COMMON block. For example, assume that TEST has been declared as an array of real values using the declaration:

```
REAL TEST(500)
```

If TEST is now placed into unnamed COMMON using the statement:

```
COMMON TEST
```

then all 500 elements of the TEST array are made available to any program unit that accesses the unnamed COMMON block.

An additional feature of placing arrays into COMMON areas is that integer and real valued arrays can be dimensioned at the same time they are included in a COMMON statement. For example, the statement:

```
COMMON ARR(100)
```

both dimensions ARR to be an array of 100 elements and places this array into the COMMON area. If another program unit uses the statement:

```
COMMON SEC(100)
```

both ARR and SEC refer to the same array. When dimensioned in this manner, the data type of the array is determined by FORTRAN's implicit typing rules. In this case the array is an array of real values because the initial letter of the array's name does not begin in either I, J, K, L, M, or N.

It must be emphasized that all of the variables and arrays included in an unnamed COMMON statement must match the type, order, and number of the variables and arrays in every other unnamed COMMON statement. For example, if the previous COMMON statement was incorrectly changed to COMMON ITEMP(100), the program unit using this statement would be using the values in the COMMON array as integer values, while the program unit accessing the COMMON array as ARR would think it was dealing with real values. The resulting error would be extremely difficult to find. Retaining the same scalar and array variable names in all unnamed COMMON declarations will help to prevent such an error. Additionally, when a change is made to an unnamed COMMON statement in one program unit, the change must be correctly reflected in every program unit in which the unnamed COMMON statement appears.

Named COMMON Blocks

In addition to FORTRAN's single unnamed COMMON area, multiple named COMMON areas can be established. A named COMMON area is declared using the general format:

```
COMMON /name/ list of variables
```

Examples of named COMMON declarations are:

```
COMMON /GRAPH/ X,Y,Z,FACTOR
 COMMON /PARA/ WATTS, VOLTS, RESIST
 COMMON /PARB/ DENSTY, MASS, WEIGHT, AREA, GRAV
```

The first COMMON declaration establishes a COMMON area named GRAPH, which include the four variables x, y, z, and FACTOR; the second declaration establishes a COMMON area named PARA containing the variables WATTS, VOLTS, and RESIST; and the last declaration creates a COMMON area named PARB containing the variables DENSTY, MASS, WEIGHT, AREA, and GRAV.

The advantage of named COMMON areas is that individual subroutines need reference only those COMMON areas containing variables they need to share. This helps isolate the shared variables between the program units that actually need them and avoids the need to list all COMMON variables in each subroutine.

An individual variable cannot be included in more than one named COMMON block. Thus, if the same variable is required by two subroutines, each sharing a different named COMMON block with the MAIN program unit, either a new COMMON block containing the desired variable must be established or the variable must be passed through each subroutine's argument list. In addition to scalar variables, arrays may also be included in any named COMMON block. When an array is assigned to named COMMON block, it follows the same rules as previously described for unnamed COMMON.

BLOCK DATA Program Units

Scalar and array variables contained within COMMON blocks, named and unnamed, may be initialized in DATA statements. These statements must, however, be collected together within a special type of program unit, called a BLOCK DATA subprogram. This program unit has the form:

```
BLOCK DATA
  variable declarations
  COMMON declarations
  DATA statements
  END
```

An example of a BLOCK DATA subprogram that initializes the named COMMON areas called GRAPH and PARA is:

```
BLOCK DATA
  REAL X,Y,Z,WATTS,VOLTS,RESIST
  COMMON /GRAPH/ X,Y,Z
  COMMON /PARA/ WATTS, VOLTS, RESIST
  DATA X, Y, Z, WATTS, VOLTS, RESIST /3.2,4.6,5.0,5.2,7.8,9.7/
  END
```

To provide for multiple BLOCK DATA subprograms, where each subprogram is used to initialize specific COMMON areas, FORTRAN permits a BLOCK DATA subprogram to be named. An example of a named BLOCK DATA subprogram is:

```
BLOCK DATA PLOT
```

Any valid FORTRAN symbolic name may be selected for a BLOCK DATA subprogram. Although a complete FORTRAN program can contain any number of named BLOCK DATA subprograms, only one unnamed BLOCK DATA subprogram is allowed.

Exercises

1. Assuming that each of the following three COMMON statements are separately contained within their own individual program units, determine the correspondence between variables:

```
COMMON A,B,C,D,I,J,K
COMMON X,Y,Z,P,NCOUNT, MTEMP, LSHOW
COMMON SNAP, CRACLE, POP, PIP, MM, KK, II
```

2. Determine the error in the following program:

```
PROGRAM TEST
  INTEGER I, M, N
  REAL A,B,C,D,E,X,Y,Z,T(100),S(100)
  COMMON E,X,Y,IKOUNT,T,S,A
  CALL CALC
  END
SUBROUTINE CALC
  INTEGER J,K,L
  REAL F,G,H,U(100),V(100),P,Q
  COMMON F,G,H,P,U,V,Q
   .
   .
   .
  END
```

3. Rewrite Exercise 3 in Section 4.1 so that all arguments are exchanged through unnamed COMMON rather than through argument lists.
4. Rewrite Exercise 4 in Section 4.1 so that all arguments are exchanged through unnamed COMMON rather than through argument lists.
5. Rewrite Exercise 5 in Section 4.1 so that all arguments are exchanged through unnamed COMMON rather than through argument lists.

F90

12.2 New FORTRAN 90 Features

The central philosophy in developing a new FORTRAN standard was to modernize FORTRAN so that it continues its long history as a scientific and engineering program language. The major additions to the language provided by the new standard include:

1. *Enhanced array operations.* FORTRAN 77's arithmetic, logical, and character operations and intrinsic functions have been extended to operate on complete arrays. A new intrinsic function, for example, has been specified to sum the elements of an array.
2. *Additional numerical capabilities.* The new standard has specifications for setting the numeric precision of data items and inquiry into the characteristics of numeric representation.
3. *Parameterized character data type.* This feature facilitates the inclusion of additional character sets, such as Chinese or Japanese characters, within the language. It also facilitates the inclusion of mathematical, chemical, and musical character sets.
4. *A new program unit type.* This feature permits a new program unit, called a module, to be accessed by as many or as few other program units as necessary. In its broadest applications this feature permits a singly defined global data area to be accessed by all program units in the same file without the need for further specification. As such, this feature is a generalization and replacement for the block data program unit.
5. *Support for direct implementation of structures.* This feature permits the construction of data structures that can contain elements having differing data types. As such, this feature removes the necessity of constructing parallel arrays of different data types, as described in Section 10.4, to simulate structures.
6. *Inclusion of pointers.* This feature permits the construction of a new type of variable whose content is the memory address of another variable. Since the address effectively "points to" where another variable is located, the name *pointer* is commonly used to describe this new type of variable. Pointer variables are extremely helpful in constructing data lists where each element in the list, unlike in an array, need not be stored consecutively.
7. *A mechanism for language evolution.* A mechanism is included in the new standard for deleting features from a previous standard. This involves defining certain features as obsolete. An obsolete feature becomes a candidate for removal from the next standard.

8. *Addition of new control statements.* The new standard includes a DO WHILE and a CASE statement. The DO WHILE is a repetition statement that can be used to construct WHILE loops (see Section 7.2) without using the block IF, GO TO, and ENDIF statements required for such loops in FORTRAN 77. The CASE statement is a multilevel selection statement that can be used to replace IF-ELSEIF structures (see Section 6.4).

In more general terms, these eight new features are the most significant of many other features added to the new FORTRAN standard. These other features include a new free-form source code more adaptable to keyboard input; increased length of variable names from 6 to 31 characters; an enhanced declaration statement; recursive capabilities; dynamically allocated arrays that can be expanded or contracted during program execution; the addition of binary, octal, and hexadecimal specification of integer constants; the addition of bit manipulation intrinsic functions; new edit descriptors that permit the formatted input and output of binary, octal, and hexadecimal constants; and the extension of READ and WRITE statements to read and write individual characters in a complete input and output record.

Following are descriptions of the new symbolic name capability, the expanded declaration statement, and the new free-form source code. Descriptions of pointers and structures are presented in the remaining sections of this chapter.

Symbolic Names

In the new standard, the length of symbolic names has been increased from 6 to 31 characters, the first of which must be a letter. Additionally, the underscore character, _, has been included in the new character set. Thus, under the new standard the following are all valid symbolic names:

```
A1
NAME_LENGTH
EXPERIMENT
S_P_R_E_A_D__OUT
FINAL_
```

Variable Declarations

In the new standard a variable may have an attribute as well as a data type. To include the attribute, the general form of variable declaration statements has been expanded to:

data type, attribute_1, attribute_2, . . . :: list of variables

where the comma before each attribute and the :: symbol are only required if an attribute is included. For example, since the declaration:

```
REAL SUM
```

has no attributes, the comma after the data type is omitted, and the :: symbol does not have to be included. This symbol can be used, however, resulting in the equivalent declaration:

```
REAL :: SUM
```

Similarly, the declaration:

```
INTEGER, POINTER :: A, B
```

declares two variables, A and B, to have the attribute POINTER and data type INTEGER (the meaning of the POINTER attribute is described in Section 12.3). Notice that multiple variables can be declared using the new declaration statement, as in FORTRAN 77. Thus, in the new standard, the following two declarations can both be used and mean the same thing:

```
INTEGER NUM1, NUM2, NUM3
INTEGER :: NUM1, NUM2, NUM3
```

Another addition is the way in which character variables are specified. Under the proposed standard the length of a character variable can be specified by including the term (LEN = *n*) after the CHARACTER type designation. Thus, the declarations:

```
CHARACTER*20 NAME
CHARACTER(LEN = 20) NAME
CHARACTER*20 :: NAME
CHARACTER(LEN = 20) :: NAME
```

are all equivalent.

Free-Form Source Code

As described in the new standard, "In free source form, each source line may contain from zero to 132 characters and there are no restrictions on where a statement may appear within a line." Although the free-form source code exists in addition to the fixed-form FORTRAN 77 source code the forms may not be intermixed in the same program.

In free-form source entry blanks may be inserted freely within a line, except within designated keywords, such as PRINT, READ, and WRITE. Additionally, blanks must be used to separate names, constants, and labels from adjacent names, constants, and labels. For example, in the statements:

```
INTEGER NUM
READ 10
50 DO I=1,3
```

the blanks are required after the words INTEGER, READ, and DO and after label 50.

The start of a comment in the free-form source code is signified by an exclamation point. For example, the declaration statement:

```
INTEGER NUM  !THIS DECLARES AN INTEGER VARIABLE:
```

contains the comment THIS DECLARES AN INTEGER VARIABLE. In all cases the comment extends to the end of the source line. If the first nonblank character on the line is an exclamation point, the line is called a comment line. A line containing all blanks is also considered a comment line and does not require the ! symbol.

The ampersand character, &, is used to indicate that the current statement is continued on the next line that is not a comment line. Thus, in free-form source entry, the continuation mark is placed on the line being continued rather than on the continuation line, as in the fixed-form source code required in FORTRAN 77. In no case can a statement have more than 39 continuation lines, and comment lines cannot be continued.

Finally, multiple statements may appear on the same line when separated by a semicolon (;). Thus, the line:

```
INTEGER NUM; REAL TOTAL; CHARACTER(LEN = 10) :: CODE
```

contains the three individual statements:

```
INTEGER NUM
REAL TOTAL
CHARACTER(LEN = 10) :: CODE
```

and the single line:

```
NUM = 5; TOTAL = 0.0
```

contains the two statements:

```
NUM = 5
TOTAL = 0.0
```

12.3 Pointers and Targets

F90

As illustrated in Figure 12-3, every variable has two major items associated with it: the value stored in the variable and the address of the variable. Programmers are usually concerned only with the value assigned to a variable (its contents) and give little attention to where the value is stored (its address).

In the new FORTRAN standard, it is possible to store the address of one variable into another suitably declared variable. For example, the statement:

```
NUMADR => NUM
```

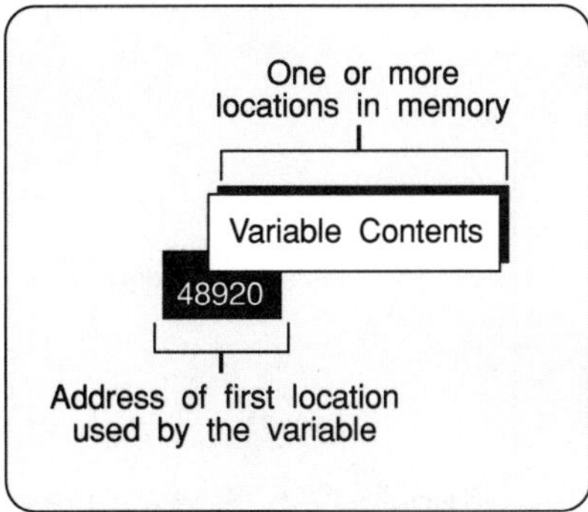

Figure 12-3 A Typical Variable

stores the address corresponding to the variable NUM in the variable NUMADR. Notice that we have introduced a new assignment symbol, =>, which is composed of the two individual symbols, = and >. In the new standard, this new assignment symbol means "store the address of the variable to the right of the symbol in the variable to the left of the symbol." Thus, the statements:

```
D => M

TABPTR => LIST

CHRPTR => CH
```

store the addresses of the variables M, LIST, and CH in the variables D, TABPTR, and CHRPTR, respectively, as illustrated in Figure 12-4.

The variables NUMADR, D, TABPTR, and CHRPTR are all called pointer variables, or pointers. *Pointers* are simply variables that are used to store the addresses of other variables. In programming, another way of saying that one variable contains the address of a second variable is to say that the first variable "points to" where the second variable is located in memory. The variable containing the address is called the pointer variable, or pointer, and the variable whose address is being stored is called the target variable, or target. Thus, for the previous assignment NUMADR => NUM, it is correct to say that the pointer NUMADR "points to" the target NUM, typically shortened to saying NUMADR points to NUM. Similarly, since the address of the variable M was stored in the pointer variable D by the statement D => M, we can say that D points to M. Here D is the pointer and M the target. This interpretation, of course, is reinforced by the notation =>, which can be read "points to."

As we shall see in Section 12.4, when we construct a linked list, the ability to store one variable's address into another variable provides FORTRAN programmers with an extremely powerful programming tool. First, however, we must see how to declare pointer and target variables.

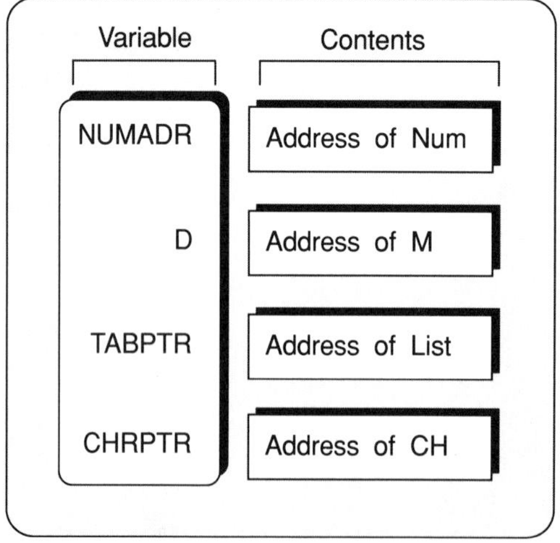

Figure 12-4 Storing Addresses

Declaring Pointer and Target Variables

Like all variables, pointers and targets must be declared before they can be used. FORTRAN requires that we specify the type of variable pointed to when we declare a pointer variable. For example, if the address in the pointer NUMADR is the address of an integer, the correct declaration for the pointer is:

```
INTEGER, POINTER :: NUMADR
```

This declaration is read as "the variable named NUMADR is a pointer to an integer." Notice that the declaration specifies three things: the name of the variable, that the variable will be used as a pointer, and that the variable pointed to by NUMADR is an integer. Similarly, if the pointer TABPTR will be used as a pointer to (contain the address of) a real valued variable, and CHRPTR will be used as a pointer to (contain the address of) a character variable, the required declarations for these pointers are:

```
REAL, POINTER :: TABPTR
CHARACTER, POINTER :: CHRPTR
```

Target variables are declared in a similar manner as pointers except that the keyword TARGET is used instead of the keyword POINTER (both TARGET and POINTER are referred to as attributes in the new standard). Thus, if TABPTR will be used to store the address of the variable LIST, and CHRPTR will be used to store the address of the variable CH, suitable declarations for these two target variables are:

```
REAL, TARGET :: LIST
CHARACTER, TARGET :: CH
```

Once these declarations have been made, the address assignments:

```
TABPTR => LIST
```

and:

```
CHRPTR => CH
```

can be made. In all cases the data type of the pointer must match the data type of the target, or an error will occur. Thus, the data type of the pointer TABPTR must be the same as the data type of the target LIST (they are both REAL variables), and the data type of the pointer CHRPTR must be the same as that of its target, CH (both are character variables of length one).

Using Pointers

Once a pointer has been assigned a target, which means that the address of the target variable has been stored in the pointer, the pointer name may be used in place of the target to access the target's value. For example, consider Program 12-2:

Program 12-2

```
      PROGRAM MAIN
        CALL SHOW_POINTER
        END
*
      SUBROUTINE SHOW_POINTER
        INTEGER, POINTER :: A
        INTEGER, TARGET :: B
        INTEGER C
        A => B       ! STORE B'S ADDRESS INTO A
        B = 22
        WRITE(6,*) A
        WRITE(6,*) B
        A = 15
        WRITE(6,*) A
        WRITE(6,*) B
        C = A
        WRITE(6,*) C
        RETURN
        END
```

The output that would be produced by Program 12-2 is:

```
22
22
15
15
15
```

Let us see how this output is obtained. As previously described, an assignment such as A => B in Program 12-2 causes B's address to be stored in the pointer variable named A. Henceforth, until A is assigned to another target, referencing the variable A automatically forces the computer to use the address in A to locate the desired target. Thus, the statement WRITE(6,*) A causes the computer to use the address in A to locate its target, which in this case is the variable B. It is the contents of the target that is displayed. Thus, the output of the statement WRITE(6,*) A is the value 22, which is the same output produced by the statement WRITE(6,*) B. In the first case the computer "knows" to use the address of A correctly because A has been declared as a pointer. Similarly, the assignment A = 15 is interpreted by the computer to mean "store a 15 in the location pointed to by A," which again is the variable B. Thus, the second set of two consecutive WRITE statements in Program 12-2 both display the value 15. Finally, the variable C is assigned the value pointed to by A. Thus, the value displayed by the last WRITE statement is also 15.

Now we can see why pointer declarations must include the type of value being pointed to. Although it certainly would have been simpler if the pointer A used in

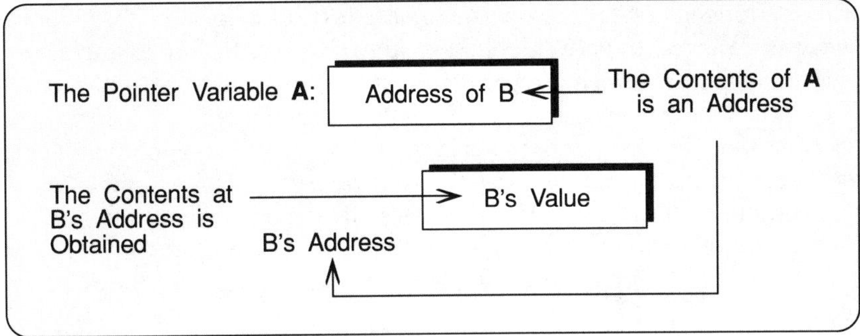

Figure 12-5 Using a Pointer Variable

Program 12-2 could have been declared as POINTER A, such a declaration conveys no information as to the type of variable that ultimately must be accessed. This additional information is essential when the pointer is used in statements such as WRITE(6,*) A and C = A. Here the address stored in A only provides the starting location of the ultimate target and does not tell the computer whether an integer, character, or real valued datum must be accessed. Since these differing data types typically are stored using differing amounts of storage (see both Sections 1.7 and Appendix D for a description of data storage concepts), the computer must know not only that A is a pointer but also the type of data A ultimately references.

When using a pointer variable, as illustrated in Figure 12-5, the value that is finally accessed is always found by first going to the pointer variable for an address. The address contained in the pointer is then used to get the desired contents. Certainly, this is a rather indirect way of getting to the final value, and the term *indirect addressing* is used to describe this procedure.

Since using a pointer requires the computer to do a double lookup (first the address is retrieved; then the address is used to retrieve the actual data), it is worthwhile to ask why you would want to store an address in the first place. The answer must be deferred until we get to a real application, such as presented in Section 12.4, where the use of pointers becomes invaluable. However, given what we know about variables, the idea of storing an address in a variable should not seem overly strange.

12.4 Structures

F90

In Chapter 10 we saw how structures can be represented in FORTRAN 77 using parallel arrays. In the new FORTRAN standard, structures may be defined directly. We first briefly review the concept of a structure and then show how structures may be implemented under the new FORTRAN standard.

In the broadest sense, structure refers to the way individual elements of a group are arranged or organized. For example, a corporation's structure refers to the organization of the people and departments in the company, and a government's structure refers to its form or arrangement. In programming, a structure refers to the way individual data items are arranged to form a cohesive and related unit. For example, consider the data items typically used in preparing mailing labels, as illustrated in Figure 12-6.

Each of the data items listed in the figure is an entity by itself. Taken together, all the data items form a single unit, representing a natural organization of the data for a mailing label. This larger grouping of related individual items is commonly called a structure.

Although there could be thousands of names and addresses in a complete mailing list, the form of each mailing label, or structure, is identical. In dealing with structures, it is important to distinguish between the form of the structure and the data content of the structure.

The *form* of a structure consists of the symbolic names, data types, and arrangement of individual data items in the structure. The *contents* of a structure refers to the actual data stored in the symbolic names. Figure 12-7 shows acceptable contents for the structure illustrated in Figure 12-6.

Using structures requires three steps. The first step requires that we specify the form of the structure. Once a structure form has been specified, variables may be declared to have this form. Specific values can then be assigned to the individual structure elements.

The first step, specifying the form of the structure, requires listing the data types, data names, and arrangement of data items. For example, the declaration:

```
TYPE DATE
  INTEGER MONTH
  INTEGER DAY
  INTEGER YEAR
END TYPE DATE
```

defines the form of a structure. More precisely, a new data type called DATE is created. This new data type consists of three data items, which are called *members of the*

```
Name:
Street Address:
City:
State:
Zip Code:
```

Figure 12-6 Typical Mailing List Components

```
Rochelle Bokow
333 14th Street
NY
10033
```

Figure 12-7 The Contents of a Structure

structure. In this case the structure members consist of three integers, called MONTH, DAY, and YEAR, respectively. Since a structure is derived using other data types for its members, FORTRAN formally refers to a structure as a derived data type.

Once a structure form has been specified, variable names may be declared for this new data type. For example, the declaration:

```
TYPE(DATE) :: BIRTH
```

declares BIRTH to be a variable of the form DATE. As with all FORTRAN data types, multiple variables may be declared in the same declaration statement. Thus, the declaration:

```
TYPE(DATE) :: BIRTH, CURRENT
```

declares both BIRTH and CURRENT to be of type DATE.

Once a variable has been declared as a structure type, assigning actual data values to the individual structure members is called *populating the structure* and is a relatively straightforward procedure. Each member of a structure is accessed by giving both the structure's variable name and the individual member name, separated by a percent sign, %. Thus, BIRTH % MONTH refers to the first member of the BIRTH structure, BIRTH % DAY refers to the second member, and BIRTH % YEAR refers to the third member. Program 12-3 illustrates assigning values to the individual members of the BIRTH structure and displaying the contents of these members.

Program 12-3 Specifying and Populating a Structure

```
      PROGRAM MAIN
        CALL SHOW_STRUCTER
        END
*
      SUBROUTINE SHOW_STRUCTER
        ! SPECIFY A STRUCTURE TYPE NAMED DATE
          TYPE DATE
            INTEGER MONTH
            INTEGER DAY
            INTEGER YEAR
        END TYPE DATE
          ! DECLARE A VARIABLE TO BE OF THE SPECIFIED TYPE
          TYPE(DATE) :: BIRTH
          ! ASSIGN VALUES TO MEMBERS OF THE BIRTH STRUCTURE
          BIRTH % MONTH = 12
          BIRTH % DAY = 28
          BIRTH % YEAR = 52
          ! DISPLAY THE MEMBER VALUES
        WRITE(6,10) BIRTH % MONTH, BIRTH % DAY, BIRTH % YEAR
 10     FORMAT(1X,'MY BIRTH DATE IS: ',I2,'/',I2'/',I2)
        RETURN
        END
```

The output that would be produced by Program 12-3 is:

```
MY BIRTH DATE IS 12/28/52
```

The individual members of a structure are not restricted to being integer data types, as illustrated in Program 12-3. Any valid FORTRAN data type can be used. For example, consider an employee record consisting of the following data items:

```
Name:
Identification number:
Regular pay rate:
Overtime pay rate:
```

A suitable structure specification for these data items is:

```
TYPE PAYREC
  CHAR (LEN = 20) :: NAME
  INTEGER IDNUM
  REAL REG_RATE
  REAL OT_RATE
END TYPE PAYREC
```

Once the form, or template, for PAYREC is specified, a specific structure having the PAYREC form may be declared. For example, the declaration:

```
TYPE(PAYREC) :: EMPLOYEE
```

creates a structure named EMPLOYEE of the PAYREC type. Assignment statements such as:

```
EMPLOYEE % NAME = 'HARRY ROLLBY'
EMPLOYEE % IDNUM = 73562
```

are then valid.

Notice that a single structure is simply a convenient method for combining and storing related items under a common name. Although a single structure is useful in clearly identifying the relationship among its members, the individual members could be defined as separate variables. The real advantage to using structures is only realized when the same structure form is used in a list many times over. Creating lists with the same structure form is discussed shortly.

Before leaving single structures, it is worth noting that the individual members of a structure can be any valid FORTRAN data type, including arrays, structures, and pointers. Accessing an element of a member array requires giving the structure's name, followed by a percent symbol, followed by the array designation. For example, assuming the integer array VAL is a member of an EXPERIMENT structure, EXPERIMENT % VAL(5) refers to the fifth value in the VAL array.

Including a structure within a structure follows the rules for including any data type in a structure. For example, assume that a structure is to consist of a name and a date of birth, where a DATE structure has been declared as:

```
TYPE DATE
  INTEGER MONTH
  INTEGER DATE
  INTEGER YEAR
END TYPE DATE
```

A suitable specification of a structure that includes a name and a date structure is:

```
TYPE INDIVIDUAL
  CHARACTER (LEN = 20) :: NAME
  TYPE(DATE) :: BIRTH
END TYPE INDIVIDUAL
```

Notice that in specifying both the DATE and INDIVIDUAL structures, the symbolic names DATE and INDIVIDUAL are structure types, while the variable BIRTH is a specific structure having the form of a DATE structure. Before individual structure can be used, specific variables must also be declared for this type. Thus, for example, the declaration:

```
TYPE(INDIVIDUAL) :: PERSON
```

declares PERSON to be a variable of type INDIVIDUAL. Here PERSON is the name of a specific structure. Individual members in the PERSON structure are accessed by preceding the desired member with the structure name followed by a percent symbol. For example, PERSON % BIRTH % MONTH refers to the MONTH variable in the BIRTH structure contained in the PERSON structure.

Arrays of Structures

The real power of structures is realized when the same structure is used for lists of data. For example, assume that the data shown in Table 12-1 must be processed.

Clearly, the employee numbers can be stored together in an array of integers, the names in an array of characters, and the pay rates in an array of real values. In organizing the data in this fashion, each column in Table 12-1 is considered as a separate list, which is stored in its own array. Using arrays in this manner, as previously described in Section 10.4, the correspondence between items for each individual employee is maintained by storing an employee's data in the same position in each array.

Table 12-1 A List of Employee Data

Employee number	Employee name	Employee pay rate
12479	ADAMS, C.	5.72
13623	BRENER, D.	7.54
14145	DUNSON, P.	6.56
15987	FRANKLIN, S.	8.43
16203	JAMASON, T.	5.72
16417	KLINE, H.	9.64
17634	OPPER, G.	7.29
18321	SMITH, S.	8.67
19435	VOELMER, L.	5.50
19567	WILSON, R.	7.35

The separation of the complete list into three individual arrays is unfortunate, since all of the items relating to a single employee constitute a natural organization of data into structures, as illustrated in Figure 12-8.

Using a structure, the integrity of the data organization as a whole can be maintained and reflected by the program. Under this approach, the list in Figure 12-8 can be processed as a single array of 10 structures.

Declaring an array of structures is the same as declaring an array of any other variable type. For example, if the structure type PAYREC is specified as:

```
TYPE PAYREC
  INT IDNUM
  CHARACTER (LEN = 20) :: NAME
 REAL RATE
END TYPE PAYREC
```

then an array of 10 such structures can be declared as:

```
TYPE(PAYREC) :: EMPLOYEE(10)
```

This declaration statement constructs an array of 10 elements, each of which is a structure of the type PAYREC. Notice that the declaration of an array of 10 structures has the same form as the declaration of any other array. For example, creating an array of 10 integers named EMPLOYEE requires the declaration:

```
INTEGER EMPLOYEE(10)
```

	Employee Number	Employee Name	Employee Pay Rate
1st structure →	12479	ADAMS, C.	5.72
2nd structure →	13623	BRENNER, D.	7.54
3rd structure →	14145	DUNSON, P.	6.56
4th structure →	15987	FRANKLIN, S.	8.43
5th structure →	16203	JAMASON, T.	5.72
6th structure →	16417	KLINE, H.	9.64
7th structure →	17634	OPPER, G.	7.29
8th structure →	18321	SMITH, S.	8.67
9th structure →	19435	VOELMER, L.	5.50
10th structure →	19567	WILSON, R.	7.35

Figure 12-8 A List of Structures

In this declaration the data type is integer, while in the former declaration for EMPLOYEE the data type is a structure of the form PAYREC.

Once an array of structures is declared, a particular data item is referenced by giving the position of the desired structure in the array followed by a percent symbol and the appropriate structure member. For example, the variable EMPLOYEE(1) % RATE references the RATE member of the first structure in the EMPLOYEE array. Including structures as elements of an array permits a list of structures to be processed using standard array programming techniques. For example, the first five employee structures in the EMPLOYEE array can be displayed using the DO loop:

```
          DO 10 I = 1, 5
            WRITE(6,*) EMPLOYEE(I) % IDNUM
            WRITE(6,*) EMPLOYEE(I) % NAME
            WRITE(6,*) EMPLOYEE(I) % RATE
 10       CONTINUE
```

Finally, extremely useful programs can be constructed when a pointer is included as a member of a structure. The inclusion of a pointer within a structure permits the construction of linked lists, the topic of the next section.

Exercises

1. Specify a structure type named TEMP for each of the following:
   a. A mailing list consisting of the items previously illustrated in Figure 12-6.
   b. A student record consisting of a student identification number, number of credits completed, and cumulative grade point average.
   c. A student record consisting of a student's name, date of birth, number of credits completed, and cumulative grade point average.
   d. A stock record consisting of the stock's name, price, and date of purchase.
   e. An inventory record consisting of an integer part number, part description, number of parts in inventory, and integer reorder number.
2. Declare arrays of 100 structures for each of the structures specified in Exercise 1.
3. Using the specification:

```
TYPE MONTHS
  CHARACTER (LEN = 10) :: NAME
  INTEGER DAYS
END TYPE MON_DAYS
```

   declare an array of 12 structures of type MON-DAYS. Name the array CONVERT. Individual structure elements in the array should be named MONTH_DAYS.

4a. Specify a single structure type suitable for an employee record of the type illustrated below:

```
Number  Name      Rate  Hours
------  ----      ----  -----
23462   BLATT     8.62   40
46793   ERNST     8.83   38
56985   JOHNSON   6.22   45
77834   JONES     9.89   40
78867   SMITHSON  8.43   35
99002   WALTON    9.75   42
```

b. Declare an array of sufficient size to hold all of the data listed in Exercise 4a.

5a. Specify a single structure type suitable for a car record of the following type:

```
Car number   Miles driven    Gallons used
----------   ------------    ------------
25           1450              62
36           3240             136
44           1792              76
52           2360             105
68           2124              67
```

b. Declare an array of sufficient size to hold all of the data listed in Exercise 5a.

F90

12.5 Linked Lists

A classic data-handling problem is making additions or deletions to lists that are maintained in a specific order. This is best illustrated by considering the alphabetical list of names shown in Figure 12-9. We desire to add new names to this list in the proper alphabetical sequence and to delete existing names in such a way that the storage for deleted names is eliminated.

Although the insertion or deletion of ordered names can be accomplished using an array of names, such arrays are not efficient representations for adding and deleting names because arrays are fixed and prespecified in size. Deleting a name from an array creates an empty slot that requires either special marking or shifting up of all elements below the deleted name to close the empty slot. Similarly, adding a name to an array requires that all elements below the addition be shifted down to

```
ADAMS, JOHN
EVANS, MARTHA
KINGSLEY, LEN
NORTON, WILLIAM
ZEBART, HELEN
```

Figure 12-9 A List of Names in Alphabetical Order

make room for the new entry, or the new element could be added to the bottom of the existing array and the array then resorted to restore the proper name order. Thus, either adding or deleting names to such a list generally requires restructuring and rewriting the list — a cumbersome, time-consuming, and inefficient practice.

A linked list provides a convenient method for maintaining a constantly changing list without the need to continually reorder and restructure the complete list. A linked list is simply a set of structures in which each structure contains at least one member whose value is the address of the next logically ordered structure in the list. Rather than requiring each structure to be physically stored in the proper order, each new structure is physically added either to the end of the existing list or wherever the computer has free space in its storage area. The structures are "linked" together by including the address of the next structure in the structure immediately preceding it. From a programming standpoint, the current structure being processed contains the address of the next structure, no matter where the next structure is actually stored.

The concept of a linked list is illustrated in Figure 12-10. Although the actual data for the KINGSLEY structure illustrated in the figure may be physically stored anywhere in the computer, the additional member included at the end of the EVANS structure maintains the proper alphabetical order. This member provides the starting address of the location where the KINGSLEY structure is stored. As you might expect, this member is a pointer.

To see the usefulness of the pointer in the EVANS structure, let us add the name JUNE HAGAR into the alphabetical list in Figure 12-9. The data for JUNE HAGAR is stored in a data structure using the same form as that used for the existing structures. To ensure that the name HAGAR is correctly inserted into the list after EVANS, the address in the EVANS structure must be altered to point to the HAGAR structure, and the address in the HAGAR structure must be set to point to the KINGSLEY structure. This is illustrated in Figure 12-11.

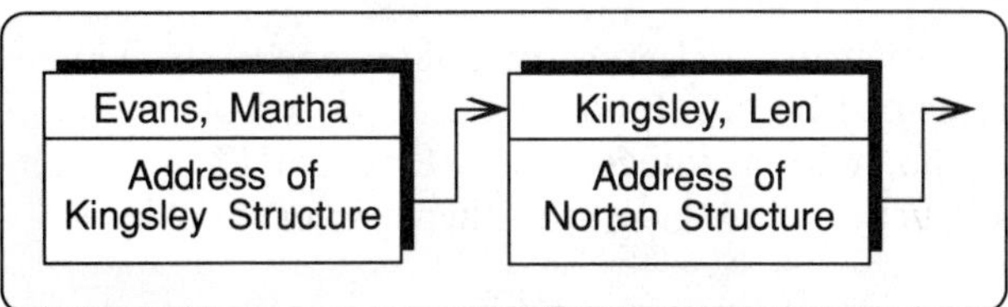

Figure 12-10 Linking Structures with Pointers

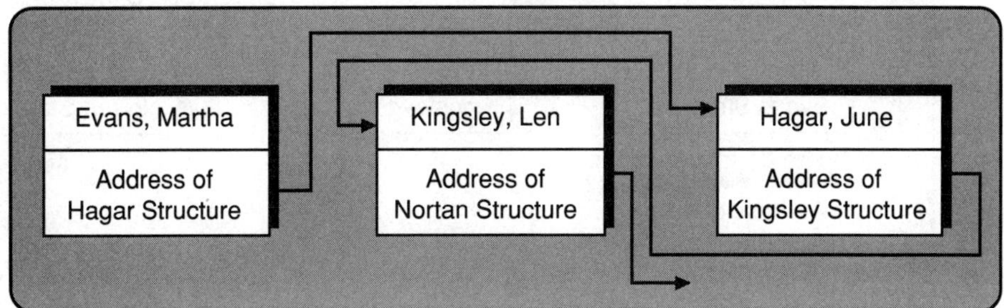

Figure 12-11 Adjusting Addresses to Point to Appropriate Structures

Notice that the pointer in each structure simply points to the location of the next ordered structure, even if that structure is not physically located in order. Removal of a structure from the ordered list is the reverse process of adding a structure. The actual structure is logically removed from the list by simply changing the address in the structure preceding it to point to the structure immediately following the deleted structure.

Each structure in a linked list has the same format; however, it is clear that the last structure cannot have a valid pointer value that points to another structure, since there is none. FORTRAN provides a special pointer value that can be used as a sentinel or flag to indicate when the last record has been processed. This value is placed into a pointer using the NULLIFY statement. This statement has the general form:

```
NULLIFY(list of pointers)
```

For example, if VALPTR and TEMP_ADDR are pointers, the statement NULLIFY(VALPTR, TEMP_ADDR) would set the addresses in these pointers to a system-dependent value indicating that the pointers are not associated with any target variables. Formally, the NULLIFY statement is said to dissociate a pointer.

In addition to dissociating the last pointer, an extra pointer must also be provided for storing the address of the first structure in the list. Figure 12-12 illustrates the complete set of pointers and structures for a linked list consisting of three names.

The inclusion of a pointer in a structure should not seem surprising. As we discovered in the previous section, a structure can contain any FORTRAN data type. For example, the structure declaration:

```
TYPE TEST
   INTEGER :: ID_NUM
   REAL, POINTER :: PT_PAY
END TYPE TEST
```

specifies a structure type named TEST consisting of two members. The first member is an integer variable named ID_NUM, and the second variable is a pointer named PT_PAY, which is a pointer to an integer value. Program 12-4 illustrates that the pointer member of a structure is used like any other pointer variable.

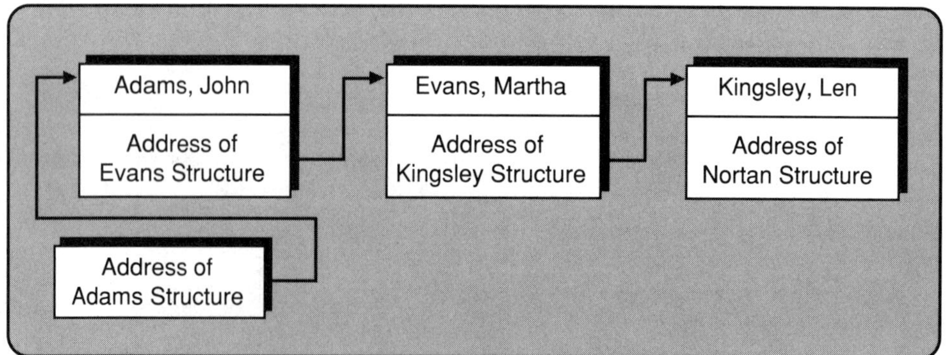

Figure 12-12 A Complete Linked List

Program 12-4

```
      PROGRAM MAIN
        CALL SHOW_A_LINK
        END
*
      SUBROUTINE SHOW_A_LINK
         TYPE TEST
          INTEGER :: ID_NUM
          REAL, POINTER :: PT_PAY
         END TYPE TEST
        TYPE(TEST) :: EMPLOYEE
        REAL, TARGET :: PAY
 *
        PAY = 456.20
        EMPLOYEE % ID_NUM = 12345
        EMPLOYEE % PT_PAY => PAY
        WIRTE(6,10) EMPLOYEE % ID_NUM, EMPLOYEE % PT_PAY
   10        FORMAT(1X,'EMPLOYEE NUMBER ',I5,' WAS PAID $',F6.2)
        RETURN
        END
```

The output that would be produced by Program 12-4 is:

```
EMPLOYEE NUMBER 12345 WAS PAID $456.20
```

Figure 12-13 illustrates the relationship between the members of the EMPLOYEE structure defined in Program 12-4 and the variable named PAY. The value assigned to EMPLOYEE % ID_NUM is the number 12345, and the value assigned to PAY is 456.20. The address of the PAY variable is then assigned to the structure member EMPLOYEE % PT_PAY by the pointer assignment statement EMPLOYEE % PT_PAY => PAY. Since this member has been defined as a pointer to a real value, and PAY was declared as a target variable, having EMPLOYEE % PT_PAY point to PAY (that is, placing the address of the real variable PAY in the variable EMPLOYEE % PT_PAY) is a valid pointer assignment. The use of the pointer variable in the WRITE statement automatically forces the computer to use the pointer correctly to obtain the address of the target variable. It is the contents of this target variable that is ultimately accessed and displayed.

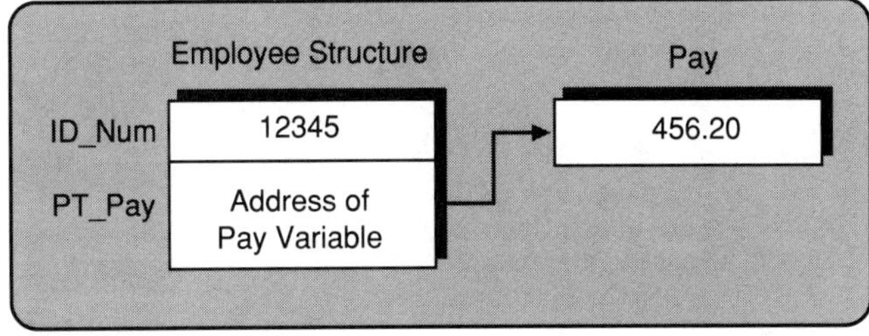

Figure 12-13 Storing an Address in a Structure Member

Although the pointer defined in Program 12-4 has been used in a rather trivial fashion, the program illustrates the concept of including a pointer in a structure. This concept can be easily extended to create the linked list of structures illustrated in Figure 12-12. The following declaration creates a form for such a structure:

```
TYPE TELE_TYP
  CHARACTER (LEN = 30) :: NAME
  TYPE(TELE_TYP), POINTER :: NEXT_NAME
END TYPE TELE_TYP
```

The TELE_TYP form consists of two members. The first member is a character variable suitable for storing a name with a maximum of 30 letters. The second member is a pointer suitable for storing the address of a structure of the TELE_TYP type.

Program 12-5 illustrates the use of the TELE_TYP structure by specifically declaring three structures having this form. The three structures are named T1, T2, and T3, respectively. The name members of each of these structures are assigned the names JOHN ADAMS, MARTHA EVANS, and LEN KINGSLEY, respectively, and the correct structure addresses are assigned using pointer assignments.

Program 12-5

```
      PROGRAM MAIN
        CALL SHOW_A_LINKED_LIST
        END
*
      SUBROUTINE SHOW_A_LINKED_LIST
        TYPE TELE_TYP
          CHARACTER (LEN = 30) :: NAME
          TYPE(TELE_TYPE), POINTER :: NEXT_NAME
        END TYPE TELE_TYP
        TYPE(TELE_TYP), TARGET :: T1, T2, T3
        TYPE(TELE_TYP), POINTER :: FIRST
        ! POPULATE THE NAME MEMBERS
        T1 % NAME = 'ADAMS, JOHN'
        T2 % NAME = 'EVANS, MARTHA'
        T3 % NAME = 'KINGSLEY, LEN'
        ! ASSOCIATE THE POINTERS
        FIRST => T1                  ! STORE T1'S ADDRESS IN FIRST
        T1 % NEXT_NAME => T2       ! STORE T2'S ADDRESS
        T2 % NEXT_NAME => T3       ! STORE T3'S ADDRESS
        NULLIFY(T3 % NEXT_NAME)
        ! USE THE POINTERS TO LOCATE THE NAMES
        WRITE(6,*) FIRST % NAME
        WRITE(6,*) T1 % NEXT_NAME % NAME
        WRITE(6,*) T2 % NEXT_NAME % NAME
        RETURN
        END
```

The output that would be produced by Program 12-5 is:

```
ADAMS, JOHN
EVANS, MARTHA
KINGSLEY, LEN
```

The assignment of member names for each of the structures declared in Program 12-5 is straightforward. The second member of each structure is a pointer. To create a linked list, each structure pointer must be assigned the address of the next structure in the list. Additionally, a pointer variable is provided for storing the first structure in the list. In Program 12-5 this initial pointer is named FIRST. As illustrated in Figure 12-14, the pointer member of each structure contains the address of the next structure in the list.

The three pointer assignment statements in Program 12-5 perform the correct assignments. To link the structures as shown in Figure 12-14, the expression FIRST => T1 stores the address of the first structure in the pointer variable named FIRST. The statement T1 % NEXT_NAME => T2 stores the starting address of the T2 structure into the pointer member of the T1 structure, and the statement T2 % NEXT_NAME => T3 stores the starting address of the T3 structure into the pointer member of the T2 structure. Finally, the pointer member of the T3 structure is nullified because it is the last element in the list.

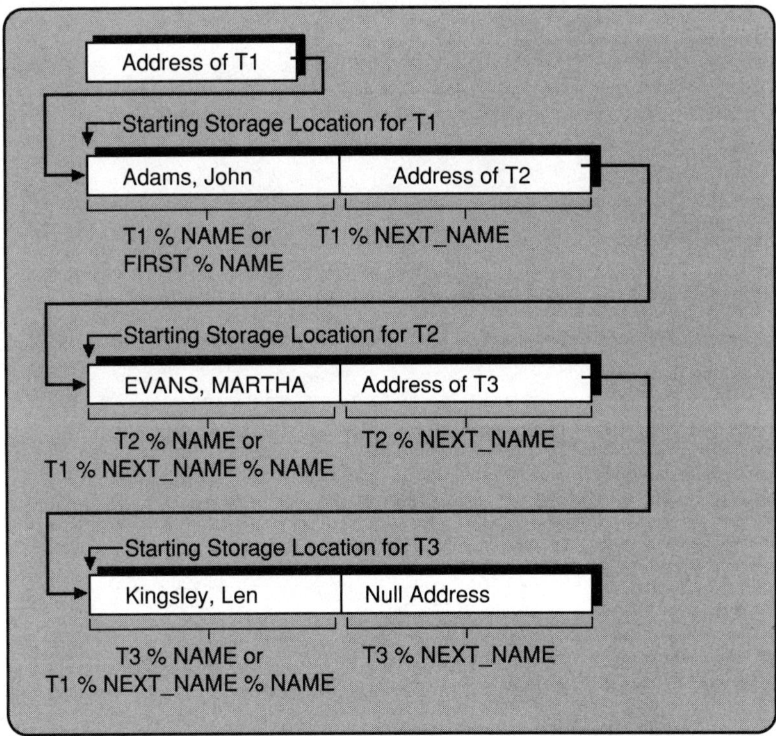

Figure 12-14 The Relationship Between Structures in Program 12-5

Once a value has been assigned to each structure's name member and correct pointer assignments have been made, the addresses in the pointers are used to access each structure's name member. For example, the expression T1 % NEXT_NAME % NAME refers to the NAME member of the structure whose address is in the NEXT_NAME member of the T1 structure. Since T1 % NEXT_NAME contains the address of the T2 structure, the proper name is accessed.

An alternative method for cycling through each structure in a linked list is to continually update a single pointer that is dedicated for pointing to the next structure to be processed, as illustrated in Program 12-6. As each subsequent structure is accessed, it can either be examined to select a specific value or used to print out a complete list. Program 12-6 illustrates the use of a DO WHILE loop that uses the address in a single pointer to cycle through the list and successively display the name stored in each structure.

Program 12-6

```
PROGRAM MAIN
   TYPE TELE_TYP
     CHARACTER (LEN = 30) :: NAME
     TYPE(TELE_TYP), POINTER :: NEXT_NAME
   END TYPE TELE_TYP
   TYPE(TELE_TYP), TARGET :: T1, T2, T3
   TYPE(TELR_TYP), POINTER :: CURRENT
   ! POPULATE THE NAME MEMBERS
   T1 % NAME = 'ADAMS, JOHN'
   T2 % NAME = 'EVANS, MARTHA'
   T3 % NAME = 'KINGSLEY, LEN'
   ! ASSOCIATE THE POINTERS
   CURRENT => T1              ! STORE T1'S ADDRESS
   T1 % NEXT_NAME => T2       ! STORE T2'S ADDRESS
   T2 % NEXT_NAME => T3       ! STORE T3'S ADDRESS
   NULLIFY(T3 % NEXT_NAME)
   ! USE THE CURRENT POINTER TO "WALK THROUGH" THE LAST
   DO WHILE (ASSOCIATED(CURRENT) .EQ. .TRUE.)
     WRITE(6,*) CURRENT % NAME
     CURRENT => CURRENT % NEXT_NAME
   ENDDO
   END
```

Except for the DO WHILE loop in Program 12-6, which introduces a new FORTRAN intrinsic function, the declaration of structures and assignment of pointers are the same as in Program 12-5. Let us, then, examine the DO WHILE construct used in Program 12-6.

The relational expression ASSOCIATED(CURRENT) .EQ. .TRUE. compares the result returned by the proposed intrinsic function named ASSOCIATED with the logical .TRUE. value. The ASSOCIATED function is called with a pointer variable and determines whether or not the address in the pointer is associated with a target. If the pointer is associated with a target, the ASSOCIATED function returns a .TRUE. value; otherwise, a .FALSE. value is returned.

Notice that when the DO WHILE statement in Program 12-6 is first encountered, the address in the pointer CURRENT is the address of the T1 structure. Thus, CURRENT is associated, and the ASSOCIATED function returns a .TRUE. value. Within the DO WHILE loop the name member of the structure pointed to by CURRENT is displayed by the statement WRITE(6,*) CURRENT % NAME. Then the address in CURRENT is set to the target pointed to by the address in CURRENT % NEXT_NAME, which is the T2 structure. The end of the loop is then encountered, and the relational expression is reevaluated by the DO WHILE statement.

For this second reevaluation the address in CURRENT is associated with the T2 structure, so the loop is again traversed. This pass through the loop causes the name member of T2 to be displayed and the address in the T2 structure to be copied into CURRENT. On the third pass through the loop the name member of the T3 structure is displayed, and the address in the pointer member of the T3 structure is copied into CURRENT. This last address, however, is not associated because it was previously nullified. When the last address is passed to the ASSOCIATED function, a .FALSE. value is returned. This makes the relational expression .FALSE., and the DO WHILE loop is exited.

We can make one simple modification to the expression evaluated by the DO WHILE statement. Since the ASSOCIATED function returns either a .TRUE. or a .FALSE. value, the statement:

```
DO WHILE (ASSOCIATED(CURRENT) .EQ. TRUE)
```

can be replaced by the equivalent statement:

```
DO WHILE (ASSOCIATED(CURRENT))
```

When the address in CURRENT is associated with a target, both expressions being evaluated have a .TRUE. value, and when the address in CURRENT is not associated, both expressions have a .FALSE. value.

A disadvantage of Programs 12-5 and 12-6 is that exactly three structures are declared in both programs by name, and storage for them is reserved at compile time. Should a fourth structure be required, the additional structure would have to be declared and the program recompiled. The new FORTRAN standard provides for dynamically allocating and releasing storage for structures as it is required at runtime. Only when a new structure is to be added to the list, and while the program is running, is storage for the new structure created. Similarly, when a structure is no longer needed and can be deleted from the list, the storage for the deleted structure can be relinquished and returned to the computer.

12.6 Things to Remember

1. A COMMON Block is a block of memory locations that can be made available to any and all program units in which they are declared.
2. In Unnamed COMMON, which is also referred to as BLANK COMMON, the common area is declared using the statement:

```
COMMON list of variables
```

The list of variables defines the variables that are to be included in the COMMON block. All program units using this common area must include a COMMON statement having the same number, type, and order of variables in their variable lists.

3. A Named COMMON area is declared using the declaration statement:

```
COMMON /name/ list of variables
```

An individual variable cannot appear in more than one named COMMON block.

4. COMMON blocks and DATA statements initializing variables in the common blocks may be collected together within a BLOCK DATA subprogram. This program unit has the general form:

```
BLOCK DATA optional name
  variable declarations
  COMMON declarations
  DATA statements
  END
```

A FORTRAN program can contain any number of named BLOCK DATA subprograms, but only one unnamed BLOCK DATA subprogram is permitted.

5. All features of FORTRAN 77 are included in the new standard. Additionally, several new features have been added. The major additions include:

a. Enhanced array operations in which FORTRAN 77's arithmetic, logic, character operators, and intrinsic functions have been extended to operate on complete arrays.

b. Additional numeric capabilities that permit the explicit setting of a data item's numeric precision at the bit level.

c. Enhancement of the character set making it possible to include foreign language, mathematical, chemical, and other specialized character sets.

d. A new MODULE program unit that expands the capabilities of the BLOCK DATA program unit.

e. Support for the direct implementation of structures (see item 10 below).

f. Inclusion of pointers (see item 7 below).

g. A mechanism for removing features from future standards. This mechanism involves designating certain features as obsolete, making them candidates for removal from the next standard.

h. Addition of several new control statements, including a CASE and a DO WHILE statement (see Sections 6.4 and 7.2, respectively).

6. Other new features in FORTRAN 90 include a new free-form source code more adaptable to keyboard input; increased length of symbolic names to 31 characters; inclusion of the underscore symbol in the character set; an enhanced declaration statement; recursive capabilities; dynamically allocated arrays; the addition of binary, octal, and hexadecimal integer constants; the addition of bit manipulation intrinsic functions; new edit descriptors for the formatted input and output of binary, octal, and hexadecimal values; and the extension of the READ and WRITE statements for partial record I/O as character streams.

7. A pointer is a variable that is used to store the address of another variable. Variables that will be used as pointers must include the keyword POINTER as an attribute within the variable's declaration statement. For example, the declaration:

```
INTEGER, POINTER :: NAME_ADDR
```

declares that NAME_ADDR is a variable that will be used as a pointer.

8. A target is a variable whose address can be stored in a pointer. Variables that will be used as targets must include the keyword TARGET as an attribute within the variable's declaration statement. For example, the declaration:

```
INTEGER, TARGET :: NAME
```

declares that NAME is an integer variable whose address may be stored in a pointer.

9. The data types of a pointer and its target must agree. A pointer is assigned to a target using the pointer assignment operator =>. Thus, if NAME and NAME_ADDR have been declared as the same data types, where NAME has the TARGET attribute and NAME_ADDR has the POINTER attribute, the pointer assignment:

```
NAME_ADDR => NAME
```

stores the address of NAME into NAME_ADDR. NAME_ADDR is then said to "point to" NAME.

10. A structure allows individual variables to be grouped under a common variable name. Each variable in a structure is referenced by its structure name, followed by a percent symbol, %, followed by its individual variable name.

11. Individual members of a structure can be any valid FORTRAN data type, including structures, arrays, and pointers. When a pointer is included as a structure member, a linked list can be created. Such a list uses the pointer in one structure to "point to" (contain the address of) the next logical structure in the list.

Appendix A

Program Entry, Compilation, and Execution

In this appendix we examine the general steps that must be taken for a FORTRAN program to be entered into a computer, compiled, and executed.

As illustrated in Figure A-1, a computer can be thought of as a self-contained world that is entered by a special set of steps called a log-in procedure. For some computers such as IBM, Apple, and other desk-top computers, the log-in procedure is usually as simple as turning on the computer's power switch. Larger multiuser systems such as DEC VAX and Prime computers typically require a log-in procedure consisting of turning on a terminal and supplying an account number and password.

Once you have successfully logged in to your computer system, you are automatically under the control of a computer program called the operating system (unless the computer is programmed to switch you into a specific application program). The *operating system* is the program that effectively runs the computer. It is used to gain access to the services provided by the computer, including the programs needed for entering, compiling, and executing a FORTRAN program.

Communicating with the operating system is always accomplished using a specific set of commands that are recognized by the operating system. Although each computer system (IBM, Apple, DEC, Prime, and so on) has its own set of operating system commands, all operating systems provide commands that allow you to log in to the system, exit from the system, create your own programs, and quickly list, delete, copy, or rename your programs.

The specific operating system commands and any additional steps used for exiting from a computer, such as turning off the power, are collectively referred to as the log-out procedure. Make sure you know the log-out procedure for your computer at the time you log-in to ensure that you can effectively "escape" when you are ready to leave the system. The operating system command for listing programs typically has a name such as LIST, TYPE, or PRINT; the command for deleting a program typically has a name such as DELETE, DEL, ERASE, UNSAVE, or REMOVE; the com-

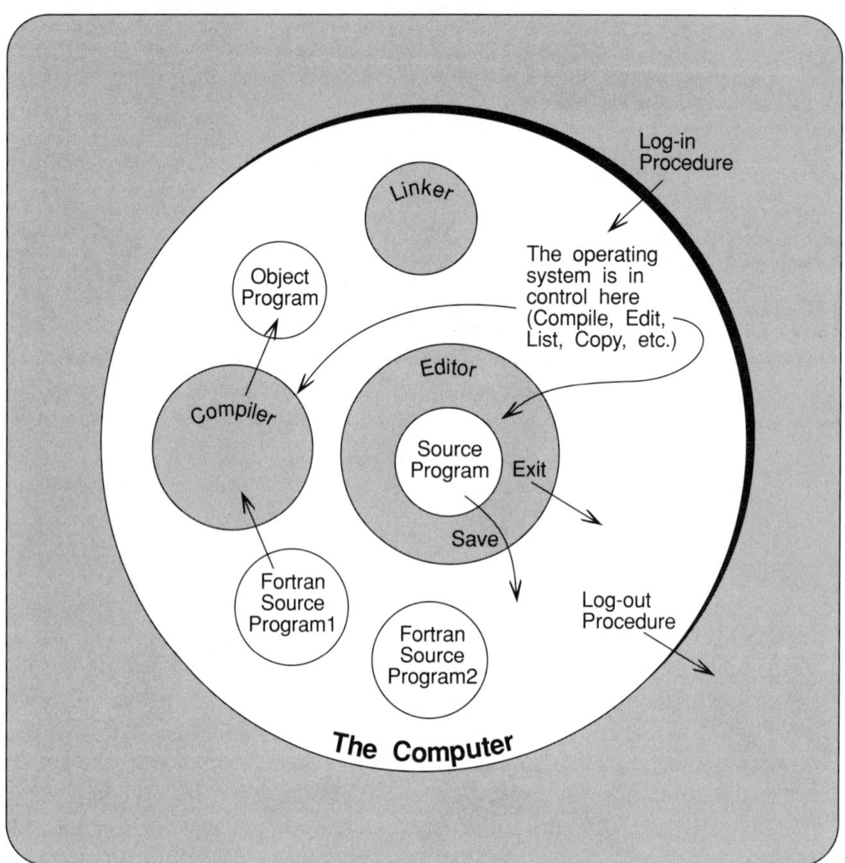

Figure A-1 Viewing a Computer as a Self-Contained World

mand for copying a program typically has a name such as COPY, COP, or CP; and the operating system command for renaming a program typically has a name such as RENAME, REN, or RN. Use Table A-1 to list the specific operating system command names used by your system to perform these tasks.

Table A-1 Operating System Commands (Fill in for Your System)

Task	Command(s)	Example
Log-in procedure		
Log-out procedure		
List a program		
Copy a program		
Delete a program		
Rename a program		

The commands to list, copy, delete, or rename a program are all concerned with manipulating existing programs. Let us now turn our attention to creating, compiling, and executing a new FORTRAN program. The procedures for doing these tasks are illustrated in Figure A-2. As shown in this figure, the procedure for creating an executable FORTRAN program consists of three distinct operations: editing, compiling, and linking.

A.1 Editing

Both the creation of a new FORTRAN program and the modification of an existing FORTRAN program require the use of an editor program. The function of such a program is to allow a user to type statements at a keyboard and to save the typed statements together under a common name, called a *source program file.*

As illustrated in Figure A-1, an editor program is contained within the environment controlled by the operating system. Like all services provided by the operating system, this means that the editor program can only be accessed using an operating system command.

Once the editor program has been requested, the operating system relinquishes control to the editor program. Again, as illustrated in Figure A-1, this means that you temporarily leave the world controlled by the operating system and its commands and enter the world controlled by the editor. The editor, like the operating system, has its own set of services and commands. The services provided by the editor include entering FORTRAN statements, modifying and deleting existing statements in a program, listing a program, naming a program, saving a program, and exiting from the editor back into the operating system with or without saving the program.

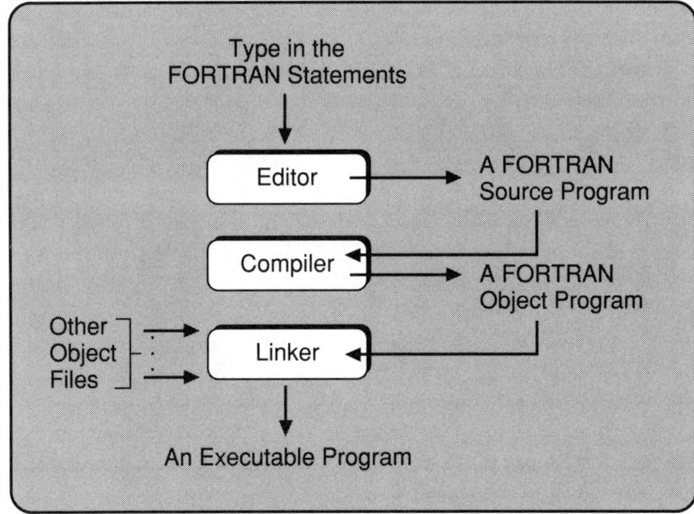

Figure A-2 Creating an Executable FORTRAN Program

When using an editor, you must carefully distinguish between entering a FORTRAN statement and entering an editor command. Some editors make this distinction by using special keys to alert the editor that what is being typed is a command to the editor rather than the line of a program (for example, in BASIC the line number automatically informs the editor that the entered line is a statement, and the absence of a line number informs the editor that the entered line is an editor command). Other editors contain two modes: a text mode for entering and modifying program statements and a command mode for entering editor commands. For the latter type of editor there is always a means of switching from text to command mode and back from command to text mode. In both cases the commands recognized by the editor depend on the editor being used. After filling in the operating system command needed to enter the editor, use Table A-2 to list the specific editor command names or procedures provided by your editor.

```
Operating system command
to enter the editor:______________________________
```

Table A-2 Editor Commands (Fill in)

Task	Command(s)	Example
Save the program and exit from the editor		
Save the program without exiting from the editor		
Exit from the editor without saving the program		
Switch to text mode (if applicable)		
Switch to command mode (if applicable)		
List the complete program from within the editor		
List a set of lines from within the editor		
List a single line from within the editor		
Delete the complete program from within the editor		
Delete a set of lines from within the editor		
Delete a single line from within the editor		
Name a program from within the editor		

A.2 Compiling and Linking

The translation of a FORTRAN source program into a form that can be executed by the computer is accomplished using a program called a compiler. The compiler, like the editor, is accessed using an operating system command. Each operating system uses a different command for calling the compiler into action and giving the compiler the name of the source file to be translated. Determine and then list the command used by your computer for performing this operation.

```
Operating system command
to compile a program:___________________________________
```

The output produced by the compiler is called an object program. An *object program* is simply a translated version of the source program that can be executed by the computer system with one more processing step. Let us see why this is so.

Most FORTRAN programs contain statements that use preprogrammed routines, called intrinsic functions, for finding such quantities as square roots, logarithms, trigonometric values, absolute values, and other commonly encountered mathematical calculations. Additionally, a large FORTRAN program may be stored in two or more separate program files. In such a case, each file can be compiled separately. However, both files must ultimately be combined to form a single program before the program can be executed. In both of these cases it is the task of the linker to combine all of the intrinsic functions and individual object files into a single program ready for execution. This final program is called an executable program.

As with the compiler, the linker program is accessed using a single operating system command. For ease of operation, however, all operating systems provide a single command that both compiles a FORTRAN program and links it correctly with any required other object programs using one command. Determine and then list the command used by your computer for performing this operation.

```
Operating system command
to compile and link a program:___________________________
```

Finally, once the FORTRAN source program has been compiled and linked, it must be run. Determine and then list the command used by your computer for this operation.

```
Operating system command to
execute a compiled and linked program:___________________
```

B Appendix

FORMAT Specifications

A format is used with formatted PRINT, WRITE, and READ statements and provides information that directs the conversion between internal data representations (see Section 1.7 and Appendix D) and external data representations in a file. A format specifier is designated by:

1. an asterisk, which invokes an implicit compiler-defined format
2. the statement number of a FORMAT statement, which contains explicit user-defined format descriptors
3. a literal format control character constant that is enclosed in parentheses and surrounded by apostrophes

Formally, method 1 is referred to as list-directed I/O, and methods 2 and 3 are referred to as user-formatted I/O, usually shortened to the term formatted I/O. The edit descriptors that can be used with user-formatted I/O are listed in Table B-1.

Edit descriptors are interpreted from left to right in a format specification, and input and output records are edited from left to right. If there are insufficient edit descriptors in a format specification for an input or output list, format control is transferred to the first open parentheses in the specification.

Table B-1 Edit Descriptors

Descriptor	Description
*r*Iw	Edits integer data
*r*Fw.d	Edits both real and double precision data in decimal format
*r*Ew.d	Edits real data in exponential format
*r*Dw.d	Edits double precision data in exponential format
*r*Gw.d	Edits both real and double precision data in exponential format
*r*Lw	Edits logical data
*r*Aw	Edits character data
'a . . a'	Specifies a character constant
Tc	Tabs to position c
TLn	Tabs backward n positions
TRn	Tabs forward n positions
nX	Skips over n positions (same as TRn)
/	Causes the current record to be written or the next record to be read
SS	Suppresses printing of plus sign
BN	Ignores blank spaces in a field
BZ	Considers blank spaces in a field to be zeros
*k*P	Multiplies each number by 10^{-k} on input and 10^{k} on output. The scale factor must precede an E, F, D, or G descriptor.

Notes: r is an optional unsigned nonzero positive integer used as repeat count.
w is an unsigned nonzero positive integer that specifies the data field width.
d is an unsigned positive integer that specifies the number of places to the right of the decimal point.
a is any character.
c is an unsigned positive nonzero integer.
n is an unsigned positive nonzero integer.
k is an unsigned positive nonzero integer.

C Appendix

Operator Precedence Table

Table C-1 presents the symbols, precedence, descriptions, and associativity of FORTRAN's operators. Operators toward the top of the table have a higher precedence than those toward the bottom. Operators within each category have the same precedence and associativity.

Arithmetical operations that are undefined mathematically are also undefined in FORTRAN 77. Thus, it is illegal to divide by zero, raise a zero-valued operand to a zeroth or negative power, or raise a negative operand to a real or double precision power.

Table C-1 Summary of FORTRAN Operators

Operator	Description	Associativity
( )	Parentheses	Inner to outer
**	Exponentiation	Right to left
*	Multiplication	Left to right
/	Division	Left to right
+	Addition	Left to right
–	Subtraction	Left to right
//	Concatenation	Left to right
.GT.	Relational	Left to right
.GE.	Relational	Left to right
.LT.	Relational	Left to right
.LE.	Relational	Left to right
.EQ.	Relational	Left to right
.NE.	Relational	Left to right
.NOT.	Logical negation	Left to right
.AND.	Logical conjunction	Left to right
.OR.	Logical inclusion	Left to right
.EQV.	Logical equivalence	Left to right
.NEQV.	Logical nonequivalence	Left to right

Appendix D

Floating Point Number Storage*

The two's-complement binary code used to store integer values was presented in Section 1.7. In this appendix we present the binary storage format typically used to store single precision and double precision numbers. Single precision values are called real values in FORTRAN, and both single and double precision numbers are collectively referred to as floating point values.*

Like their decimal number counterparts that use a decimal point to separate the integer and fractional parts of a number, floating point numbers are represented in a conventional binary format using a binary point for the same purpose. For example, consider the binary number 1011.11. The digits to the left of the binary point (1011) represent the integer part of the number, and the digits to the right of the binary point (11) represent the fractional part.

A code similar to that for decimal exponential notation is used to store a floating point binary number. To obtain this code, the conventional binary number format is separated into a mantissa and an exponent. The following examples illustrate floating point numbers expressed in this exponential notation.

Conventional binary notation	Binary exponential notation
`1010.0`	`1.01 exp 011`
`-10001.0`	`-1.0001 exp 100`
`0.001101`	`1.101 exp -011`
`-0.000101`	`-1.01 exp -100`

In binary scientific notation, the term *exp* stands for exponent. The binary number in front of the exp term is the mantissa, and the binary number following the exp term is the exponent value. Except for the number 0, the mantissa always has a single leading 1 followed immediately by a binary point. The exponent represents a power of 2 and indicates the number of places the binary point should be moved in the mantissa to obtain the conventional binary notation. If the exponent is positive, the binary point is moved to the right. If the exponent is negative, the binary point is moved to the left. For example, the exponent 011 in the number:

```
1.01 exp 011
```

* Reprinted by permission of AT&T from "32-Bit Microprocessors–A Primer Plus" (pages 489–493) by G. Bronson and H. Silver, Copyright 1988, AT&T.

Table D-1 IEEE Standard 754-1985 Floating Point Specification

Data format	Sign bits	Mantissa bits	Exponent bits
Single Precision	1	23	8
Double Precision	1	52	11
Extended Precision	1	64	15

means to move the binary point three places to the right, so that the number becomes 1010. The –011 exponent in the number:

```
1.101 exp -011
```

means to move the binary point three places to the left, so that the number becomes:

```
.001101.
```

In storing floating point numbers, the sign, mantissa, and exponent are stored individually within separate fields. The number of bits used for each field determines the precision of the number. Single precision (32-bit), double precision (64-bit), and extended precision (80-bit) real data formats are defined by the Institute of Electrical and Electronics Engineers (IEEE) Standard 754-1985 to have the characteristics given in Table D-1. The format for a single precision real number is illustrated in Figure D-1.

The sign bit shown in Figure D-1 refers to the sign of the mantissa. A sign bit of 1 represents a negative number, and a 0 sign bit represents a positive value. Since all mantissas except for the number 0 have a leading 1 followed by their binary points, these two items are never stored explicitly. The binary point implicitly resides immediately to the left of mantissa bit 22, and a leading 1 is always assumed. The binary number 0 is specified by setting all mantissa and exponent bits to 0. For this case only, the implied leading mantissa bit is also 0.

The exponent field contains an exponent that is biased by 127. For example, an exponent of 5 would be stored using the binary equivalent of the number 132 (127 + 5). Using eight exponent bits, this is coded as 100000100. The addition of 127 to each exponent allows negative exponents to be coded within the exponent field without the need for an explicit sign bit. For example, the exponent –011, which correspond to –3, would be stored using the binary equivalent of +124 (127 – 3).

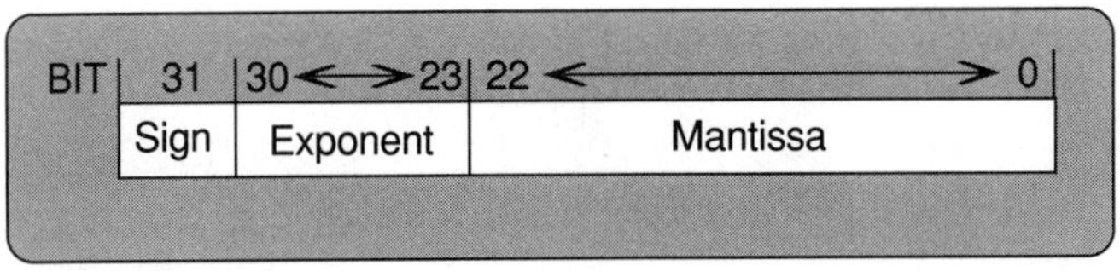

BIT	31	30 ⟷ 23	22 ⟷ 0
	Sign	Exponent	Mantissa

Figure D-1 Single Precision Real Number Storage Format

Figure D-2 illustrates the encoding and storage of the decimal number 59.75 as a 64-bit single precision binary number. The sign, exponent, and the mantissa are determined as follows: The conventional binary equivalent of –59.75 is –111011.11. Expressed in binary exponential notation, this becomes –1.1101111 exp 101. The minus sign is signified by setting the sign bit to 1. The mantissa's leading 1 and binary point are omitted, and the 23-bit mantissa field is encoded as 11011110000000000000000. The exponent field encoding is obtained by adding the exponent value of 101 to 1111111, which is the binary equivalent of the 127_{10} bias value.

$$
\begin{array}{rcl}
1\,1\,1\,1\,1\,1\,1 & = & 127_{10} \\
+\,1\,0\,1 & = & +\,5_{10}
\end{array}
$$

SIGN	EXPONENT	MANTISSA
1	10000100	11011110000000000000000

Figure D-2 The Encoding and Storage of a Decimal Number

Appendix E

Additional Statements

Appendix E

E.1 Additional Subprogram Statements

E.2 Additional Specification Statements

E.3 Additional Selection Statements

E.4 Summary of Additional Statements

The major premise of this text is that FORTRAN programs should be constructed in a modular fashion using structured blocks of code having single-entry and single-exit points. The reason for this, as emphasized throughout the text, is that programs so constructed are more easily written, tested, debugged, modified, and maintained than programs that do not conform to this structure. Simply put, fewer program errors are introduced when programs are designed using a structured, modular approach, and those errors that are coded into such programs can be more easily detected and corrected than those in nonstructured programs.

Except for the first three statements presented in this appendix (the SAVE, EXTERNAL, and INTRINSIC statements), the remaining statements are nonstructured statements that permit programs written in earlier versions of FORTRAN to be compiled using FORTRAN 77 and later compilers. In general, these statements should not be used in a modular FORTRAN program because they violate the principles of structured, modular programming. As such, their use invites numerous program errors and debugging problems that are best avoided by not using these statements.

E.1 Additional Subprogram Statements

This section presents additional FORTRAN statements applicable to subroutine and function subprograms. These include the SAVE, EXTERNAL, INTRINSIC, and alternate subroutine ENTRY and RETURN statements. The first three of these statements provide features that are sometimes required in a particular program application. The last two features, alternate subroutine entry and return, are presented for completeness only. As these two features violate the single-entry, single-exit characteristic of structured program units, their use should be avoided.

The SAVE Statement

When a subroutine returns control to its calling unit, the FORTRAN 77 standard allows the storage for its local variables to be released to the computer's operating system. For example, consider Program E-1, where subroutine TEST is called four times.

Program E-1

```
      PROGRAM MAIN
        INTEGER COUNT
        DO 10 COUNT = 1,4
        CALL TEST
 10     CONTINUE
        END
      SUBROUTINE TEST
        INTEGER NUM
        NUM = 0
        WRITE(6,*) 'THE VALUE OF NUM IS ', NUM
        NUM = NUM + 1
        END
```

The output produced by Program E-1 is:

```
THE VALUE OF NUM IS          0
THE VALUE OF NUM IS          0
THE VALUE OF NUM IS          0
THE VALUE OF NUM IS          0
```

Each time TEST is called, the local variable NUM is created and initialized to zero. When the subroutine returns control to MAIN, the variable NUM is destroyed along with any value stored in it. Thus, the effect of incrementing NUM in TEST is lost.

The initialization used in TEST is called a runtime initialization because the initialization occurs each time the subroutine containing this statement is run. There are cases, however, where we would like a subroutine to retain values between subroutine calls. This usually can be accomplished using the DATA statement introduced in Section 6.2. The DATA statement initializes its variables only once, when the program is first compiled. Thereafter, the value is not reset to zero each time the subroutine is called. To see how this works, consider Program E-2.

Program E-2

```
      PROGRAM MAIN
        INTEGER COUNT
        DO 10 COUNT = 1,4
        CALL TEST
 10     CONTINUE
        END
     SUBROUTINE TEST
       INTEGER NUM
       DATA NUM /0/
       WRITE(6,*) 'THE VALUE OF NUM IS: ', NUM
       NUM = NUM + 1
       END
```

The output produced by Program E-2 is:

```
THE VALUE OF NUM IS:        0
THE VALUE OF NUM IS:        1
THE VALUE OF NUM IS:        2
THE VALUE OF NUM IS:        3
```

As illustrated by the output of Program E-2, the variable NUM is set to zero only once. The subroutine TEST then increments this variable just before relinquishing control to MAIN, and the value that NUM has when TEST is reentered is retained and displayed when the subroutine is next called.

Although the FORTRAN 77 standard ensures that the DATA statement performs a compile-time initialization, it does not require that a subroutine's local variables, such as NUM, retain their values between subroutine calls. This is the purpose of the SAVE statement. This statement has the form:

```
SAVE list of variables
```

and ensures that the variables listed will retain their values between subroutine calls. This means that the last value stored in the variable when the subroutine is finished executing is available to the subroutine the next time it is called.

SAVE variables should always be initialized using a DATA statement (using an assignment initialization defeats the purpose of a SAVE variable by resetting its value each time the subroutine is called). Including a SAVE statement in Program E-2a results in the following program:

Program E-2a

```
      PROGRAM MAIN
        INTEGER COUNT
        DO 10 COUNT = 1,4
        CALL TEST
 10     CONTINUE
        END
      SUBROUTINE TEST
        INTEGER NUM
        SAVE NUM
        DATA NUM /0/
        WRITE(6,*) 'THE VALUE OF NUM IS: ', NUM
        NUM = NUM + 1
        END
```

The EXTERNAL Statement

In certain situations a programmer may want to either rewrite one of FORTRAN's intrinsic functions, use an intrinsic function name for a user-written subprogram, or use a user-written subprogram as an actual argument in a CALL statement. In these situations, an EXTERNAL statement must be used. The general form of this statement is:

```
EXTERNAL list of subprogram names
```

example, the statement:

```
EXTERNAL DSQRT, SIN
```

specifies that when these names are encountered within a program, they do not refer to the intrinsic functions having these names but will be supplied as user-written subprograms (functions or subroutines). This permits the programmer to write versions of these functions that might execute faster or provide more options than those supplied with the intrinsic functions of the same names. For example, Program E-3 uses the EXTERNAL statement to tell the compiler that the name SIN refers to a user-written subprogram rather than to an intrinsic function.

Program E-3

```
      PROGRAM MAIN
***     THIS PROGRAM COMPUTES THE SINE OF THE NUMBERS 0.1 TO 1.0,
***     IN INCREMENTS OF 0.1, USING A USER-WRITTEN SIN FUNCTION
        EXTERNAL SIN
        REAL XNUM, SIN
        INTEGER I
        WRITE(6,*) '  NUMBER       SIN'
        WRITE(6,*) '  ------       -----'
        DO 10 I = 1, 10
          XNUM = I * 0.1
          WRITE(6,20) XNUM, SIN(XNUM)
   10   CONTINUE
   20   FORMAT(4X,F3.1,5X,F8.6)
        END
******
      REAL FUNCTION SIN(VAL)
*       THIS FUNCTION COMPUTES THE SINE OF A NUMBER USING 15 TERMS
*       OF A TAYLOR SERIES. THE FIRST APPROXIMATION IS THE VALUE OF
*       THE PASSED ARGUMENT AND THE NEXT 14 TERMS ARE CALCULATED
*       USING A DO LOOP.
        REAL VAL, FCTORL
        INTEGER I
        SIN = VAL
        DO 10 I = 1, 14
          SIN = SIN + (-1)**I * VAL**(2*I+1) / FCTORL(2*I+1)
10      CONTINUE
        END
******
      REAL FUNCTION FCTORL(NUM)
*      THIS FUNCTION COMPUTES THE FACTORIAL OF A NUMBER
        INTEGER NUM, I
        FCTORL = 1
        DO 10 I = 2, NUM
          FCTORL = I * FCTORL
    10  CONTINUE
        END
```

The SIN function used in Program E-3 uses a Taylor series to approximate the sine of the passed argument (see Section 3.5 for a description of this approximation method). The output produced by this program is:

```
 NUMBER       SIN
-------     -------
     .1     .099833
     .2     .198669
     .3     .295520
     .4     .389418
     .5     .479426
     .6     .564642
     .7     .644218
     .8     .717356
     .9     .783327
    1.0     .841471
```

The interested reader should compare this output to that produced when FORTRAN's intrinsic SIN function is used instead of the user-written version contained within Program E-3.

The INTRINSIC Statement

The intrinsic functions provided by FORTRAN consist of both generic and specific names. For example, the generic name of the square root function is SQRT. Three specific function names exist for this generic square root function: SQRT, DSQRT, and CSQRT. These three specific functions are used for calculating the square roots of integer, real, and complex numbers, respectively.

A useful feature of FORTRAN is that the generic function name can be used in place of all specific function names, and the compiler will select the appropriate version based on the arguments used. For example, using the complex number (25,4) in the statement:

```
WRITE(6,*) SQRT((25,4))
```

automatically invokes the complex version of the square root function and produces the display:

```
(5.015874,3.987341E-01)
```

In this case the compiler "knows" which specific square root function to use because of the argument's data type.

A function's generic name can always be used in place of a specific name. However, when a specific name different from the generic name is used as an argument, the specific name must be declared using an INTRINSIC statement. For example, consider Program E-4:

Program E-4

```
PROGRAM MAIN
  INTRINSIC CSQRT
  WRITE(6,*) SQRT(SQRT((25,4)))
  WRITE(6,*) SQRT(CSQRT((25,4)))
  END
```

In Program E-4, the specific function name CSQRT is used as an argument to another function. As such, this specific function name must be specified using an INTRINSIC statement. The output produced by this program is:

```
(2.241380,8.894835E-02)
(2.241380,8.894835E-02)
```

The results displayed by both WRITE statements are identical because the first statement automatically uses the complex version of the SQRT function due to the data types of the arguments used in the statement. As the second WRITE statement contains the CSQRT function as an argument, this function must be specified using an INTRINSIC statement. The general form of this statement is:

INTRINSIC *funcname-1, funcname-2, . . . funcname-n*

where *funcname* is the name of an intrinsic function that will be used as an actual argument.

The ENTRY Statement

The ENTRY statement permits entry into a subprogram other than at the entry point defined by the header line. The general form of this statement is:

ENTRY *name (list of arguments)*

An ENTRY statement may be placed at any point within a subprogram, and a subprogram may contain multiple ENTRY statements. The list of arguments in the ENTRY statement perform the same function as but are independent of the arguments in a subprogram's header line. This means that an ENTRY statement's arguments do not have to agree in either type, number, or order with the argument list defined in the subprogram header. For example, consider the ENTRY statements contained in the following subroutine:

```
SUBROUTINE FLOW(A,B,D)
      .
      .
      .
ENTRY FLOW1(X,Y)
      .
      .
      .
ENTRY FLOW2(A,X,Z)
      .
      .
      .
END
```

To enter this subroutine at either the program header or alternative entry points designated by the ENTRY statements, a CALL statement must be used. If the CALL statement references the header name, as in the statement:

```
CALL FLOW(FIRST,SECOND,THIRD)
```

the subroutine is entered at the header line, and the actual arguments FIRST, SECOND, and THIRD are equated to the dummy arguments A, B, and C, respectively. As ENTRY statements are nonexecutable, the subsequent two ENTRY statements have no effect on the subroutine's execution. If the CALL statement reference the name listed in the first ENTRY statement, as in the statement:

```
CALL FLOW1(POINT1,POINT2)
```

the subroutine is entered at the entry point designated as FLOW1, and the actual arguments POINT1 and POINT2 are equated to the dummy arguments X and Y, respectively. In this case, subroutine execution begins with the first executable statement following the FLOW1 entry point. Any subsequent ENTRY statements encountered have no effect on the subroutine's execution. Finally, if the CALL statement references the name listed in the second ENTRY statement, subroutine execution begins with the first executable statement following the FLOW2 entry point, and the actual arguments in the CALL statement are equated to the dummy arguments A, X, and Z.

Alternate Subprogram Return

The RETURN statement is used to return program control to the calling program unit. A subprogram can contain multiple RETURN statements. When a RETURN is encountered, control is normally transferred to the first executable statement following the CALL statement that transferred control to the subroutine. If a subprogram contains no RETURN statement, the END statement will return control to the calling program.

In addition to providing this normal return from a subprogram, a RETURN statement can be used to return control to alternative points in the calling program as follows.

The CALL statement used to call a subprogram having alternative return points must contain one or more statement labels in its actual argument list. The statement label must be preceded by an asterisk. For example, the statement:

```
CALL TRY(FIRST, SECOND, *10, *22, *55)
```

contains five actual arguments, including the three statement labels 10, 22, and 55. To accept statement labels as arguments requires that the called subprogram use asterisks as dummy arguments. Thus, a suitable header line for the TRY subroutine is:

```
SUBROUTINE TRY(A, B, *, *, *)
```

This header indicates that the last three dummy arguments will be used to receive statement labels from the calling program unit. The general form of the RETURN statement needed to access the statement labels passed to a subprogram is:

```
RETURN integer expression
```

The value of the integer expression is used to return control to the first, second, third, and so on statement labels designated in the argument list used to call the subprogram. For example, the statement:

```
RETURN 1
```

causes control to be transferred to the first statement label in the actual argument list, and the statement:

```
RETURN 3
```

causes control to be transferred to the third statement label in the actual argument list. A runtime error occurs if the integer expression evaluates to either a nonpositive integer or an integer having no corresponding statement label.

E.2 Additional Specification Statements

The additional specification statements provided by FORTRAN 77 are the EQUIVALENCE and IMPLICIT statements. The capabilities provided by these statements follow.

The EQUIVALENCE Statement

An EQUIVALENCE statement reserves the same area in memory for two or more variables, each of which must be of the same data type. The general form of this statement is:

```
EQUIVALENCE (name-1, name-2, name-3, . . . name-n)
```

For example, the statement:

```
EQUIVALENCE (OHMS, RESIST, VALUE)
```

permits the variable names OHMS, RESIST, and VALUE to be used interchangeably, because all three names refer to the same storage area. Similarly, the statement:

```
EQUIVALENCE (SLOPE, A(5))
```

permits both SLOPE and A(5) to be used interchangeably. The same variable cannot, however, be used in two equivalence statements. Thus, the sequence of statements:

```
EQUIVALENCE (A, B, C)
EQUIVALENCE (A, VAL)
```

is invalid because the variable A has been used twice.

Once two or more variables have been equivalenced, a change to one of the variables included in the EQUIVALENCE statement automatically changes the value referenced by all other variables in the statement (notice that this is the same relationship between an actual and a dummy argument in a subroutine call). For example, assuming that SLOPE and A(5) have been equivalenced, the sequence of statements:

```
A(5) = 20.2
SLOPE = 45.6
WRITE(6,*) 'THE VALUE OF A(5) IS ', A(5)
```

produces the display:

```
THE VALUE OF A(5) IS        45.600000
```

The first statement, A(5) = 20.2, causes the value 20.2 to be assigned to the storage area reserved for this variable. Since both A(5) and SLOPE refer to the same storage area, the next statement, SLOPE = 45.6, causes the value stored in this area to be replaced by the value 45.6. Finally, the WRITE statement causes the value stored in the area referenced by A(5) to be displayed. As the last value assigned to this area is the value 45.6, this value is displayed.

In the early days of FORTRAN, when computer storage was the most costly component of a computer system, the EQUIVALENCE statement provided a means of sharing this expensive resource. This was especially useful when two or more large arrays could use the same storage locations but were accessed by different names. Thus, for example, one array might use the storage area at the start of a program; a second array could use the same storage area later on, when the first array was no longer needed. Inevitably, however, multiple use of the same storage area results in messy debugging problems when the values associated with one usage inadvertently affect the values assumed by the second usage. In the current computer environment, where software costs far exceed hardware costs (see Section 7.7), the potential debugging problems associated with the EQUIVALENCE statement dictate that it should be avoided.

The IMPLICIT Statement*

As described in Chapter 2, the data type of FORTRAN variables can be either explicitly or implicitly declared. In the absence of an explicit declaration, all variables beginning in one of the letters I, J, K, L, M, and N are created as integer variables, and all other variables are created as real variables. This implied data typing can be changed using the IMPLICIT statement. For example, the statement:

```
IMPLICIT DOUBLE PRECISION (A-H,O-P)
```

specifies that all scalar and subscripted variables beginning in the letters A through H and O through P that are not explicitly declared will be created as double precision variables rather than as reals. Similarly, the statement:

```
IMPLICIT INTEGER (A-Z)
```

specifies that all scalar and subscripted variables in a program that are not otherwise explicitly declared will be created as integers. Finally, multiple implicit declarations can be incorporated within the same IMPLICIT statement. For example, the statement:

```
IMPLICIT CHARACTER*8 (C), LOGICAL (L), DOUBLE PRECISION (M-Z)
```

specifies that in the absence of an explicit declaration, all variables beginning in a C will be created as character variables of length eight, all variables beginning in an L will be created as logical variables, and all variables beginning in the letters M through Z will be created as double precision variables.

E.3 Additional Selection Statements

The additional selection statements provided in FORTRAN 77 permit upward compatibility with older versions of the language (such as FORTRAN IV and FORTRAN 66) and permit programs written in these earlier versions to be compiled using a FORTRAN 77 compiler. All of these statements provide multipath selection that are more effectively structured using FORTRAN 77's block IF, ELSEIF, and ELSE statements.

The Arithmetic IF Statement

The arithmetic IF statement is a three-way selection statement, that has the general form:

```
IF (arithmetic expression) n1, n2, n3
```

The *arithmetic expression* in this statement may be any valid arithmetic expression, and n_1, n_2, and n_3 are statement labels of executable statements (the same label may be repeated in this IF statement). The arithmetic expression in the statement is

* The most useful version of this statement is IMPLICIT NONE, which forces all variables to be explicitly declared (see page 63).

evaluated first, and if its value is negative, control is transferred to statement label n_1; if the expression's value is zero, control is transferred to statement label n_2; and if the expression's value is positive, control is transferred to statement label n_3. For example, the statement:

```
IF (POWER - 15.8) 10, 20, 30
```

transfers control to statement label 10 if the expression POWER – 15.8 is negative, to statement label 20 if the expression evaluates to zero, and to statement label 30 if the expression is positive. A complete structure using this specific arithmetic IF statement would typically appear as follows:

```
      IF (POWER - 15.8) 10, 20, 30
10     statements to be executed if the
       expression is negative
       GO TO 40
20     statements to be executed if the
       expression is zero
       GO TO 40
30     statements to be executed if the
       expression is positive
40     CONTINUE
```

Using a block IF statement combined with an ELSEIF and ELSE statement, this can be rewritten as:

```
IF (POWER .LT. 15.8) THEN
   statements to be executed if this
   condition is true
ELSEIF (POWER .EQ. 0.0) THEN
   statements to be executed if this
   condition is true
ELSE
   statements to be executed if the
   previous two conditions are false
ENDIF
```

Besides being easier to read, the block IF version permits the test for exact zero equality to be modified, which avoids the numerical round-off problem described in Section 4.5.

The Computed GO TO Statement

The computed GO TO statement is a multipath selection statement that has the general form:

```
GO TO (n1, n2, n3, . . . n) integer expression
```

where the *n*s are statement labels of executable statements, which may be the same, and the integer expression is any valid FORTRAN integer expression. The integer expression is evaluated first. If its value is 1, control is transferred to statement label n_1; if its value is 2, control is transferred to statement label n_2; if it value is 3, control is transferred to statement label n_3, and so on. For example, assuming ICODE is an integer variable, the statement:

```
GO TO (5, 10, 15, 20) ICODE
```

transfers control to statement label 5, 10, 15, or 20, depending on an ICODE value of 1, 2, 3, or 4, respectively. If ICODE has a value less than 1 or greater than 4, control is transferred to the next executable statement following the computed GO TO statement. A complete structure using this computed GO TO statement would typically appear as follows:

```
          GO TO (5, 10, 15, 20) ICODE
 5          statements to be executed if
            ICODE is 1
            GO TO 40
10          statements to be executed if
            ICODE is 2
            GO TO 40
15          statements to be executed if
            ICODE is 3
            GO TO 40
20          statements to be executed if
            ICODE is 4
40        CONTINUE
```

Using a block IF statement combined with an ELSEIF statement, this can be rewritten as:

```
IF (ICODE .EQ. 1) THEN
   statements to be executed if this
   condition is true
ELSEIF (ICODE .EQ. 2) THEN
   statements to be executed if this
   condition is true
ELSEIF (ICODE .EQ. 3) THEN
   statements to be executed if this
   condition is true
ELSEIF (ICODE .EQ. 4) THEN
   statements to be executed if this
   condition is true
ENDIF
```

Besides being easier to read, the block IF version permits a more varied set of conditions, including a default case, to be incorporated into the selection structure.

The ASSIGN and Assigned GO TO Statements

The last selection statement provided in FORTRAN is composed of two parts: an ASSIGN statement and an assigned GO TO statement. The general form of the ASSIGN statement is:

```
ASSIGN integer constant TO integer variable
```

and the general form of the assigned GO TO statement is:

```
GO TO integer variable (n1, n2, n3, . . . n)
```

where the integer variable in both statements is the same name, and the *n*s are distinct statement labels of executable statements. The integer variable in the assigned GO TO statement must contain a number equal to one of the statement labels in parentheses. This value can only be assigned to the integer variable using the ASSIGN statement. If the integer variable contains a value not equal to one of the *n*s, a runtime error will occur.

The assigned GO TO was used to select a set of statements to be executed based on the value assigned to the integer variable. For example, consider the sequence of instructions:

```
IF (DSCRIM .LT. 0.0) THEN
  ASSIGN 5 TO IFLAG
ELSEIF (DSCRIM .EQ. 0.0) THEN
  ASSIGN 10 TO IFLAG
ELSE
  ASSIGN 15 TO IFLAG
ENDIF
GO TO IFLAG (5, 10 15)
```

In this sequence of statements, the block IF statement is used to assign a value to the integer variable IFLAG, which must be one of the statement label values contained within the assigned GO TO statement. Based on the value assigned, control is transferred to either statement label 5, 10, or 15. As with the previous two IF statements presented in this section, the assigned GO TO statement can be replaced with a block IF statement.

E.4 Summary of Additional Statements

This chapter presents additional program statements provided in FORTRAN 77. Except for the SAVE, EXTERNAL, and INTRINSIC statements, the statements described in this chapter have been retained in FORTRAN 77 to permit programs written in older versions of FORTRAN to be compiled using a FORTRAN 77 compiler. A summary of the statements presented follows:

1. The SAVE statement has the form:

```
SAVE list of variables
```

and ensures that the variables listed will retain their values between subroutine calls. This means that the last value stored in the variable when the subroutine is finished executing is available to the subroutine the next time it is called.

2. The EXTERNAL statement is used to alert the compiler that an intrinsic FORTRAN function name will be used to reference a user-supplied subprogram or that a user-written subprogram is to be used as an actual argument. The general form of this statement is:

```
EXTERNAL list of subprogram names
```

3. When a specific intrinsic function name different from the generic name is used as an actual argument, the specific name must be declared using an INTRINSIC statement. The general form of this statement is:

```
INTRINSIC funcname-1, funcname-2, ... funcname-n
```

where *funcname* is the name of an intrinsic function that will be used as an actual argument.

4. The ENTRY statement permits entry into a subprogram other than at the entry point defined by the header line. The general form of this statement is:

```
ENTRY name (list of arguments)
```

An ENTRY statement may be placed at any point within a subprogram, and a subprogram may contain multiple ENTRY statements.

5. In addition to providing normal return from a subprogram, a RETURN statement can be used to return control to alternative points in the calling program. The general form of the RETURN statement needed to access statement labels passed to a subprogram is:

```
RETURN integer expression
```

The value of the integer expression is used to return control to the first, second, third, and so on statement labels designated in the argument list used to call the subprogram.

6. An EQUIVALENCE statement reserves the same area in memory for two or more variables, each of which must be of the same data type. The general form of this statement is:

```
EQUIVALENCE (name-1, name-2, name-3, ... name-n)
```

7. In the absence of an explicit declaration, all variables beginning in one of the letters I, J, K, L, M, and N are created as integer variables, and all other variables are created as real variables. This implied data typing can be changed using the IMPLICIT statement. This statement has the general form:

```
IMPLICIT data type (default letters)
```

8. The arithmetic IF statement is a three-way selection statement. The general form of this statement is:

```
IF (arithmetic expression) n1, n2, n3
```

where *arithmetic expression* is any valid arithmetic expression, and n_1, n_2, and n_3 are statement labels of executable statements. The same statement label may be repeated within this IF statement.

9. The computed GO TO statement is a multipath selection statement. The general form of this statement is:

```
GO TO (n1, n2, n3, . . . n) integer expression
```

where the *n*s are statement labels of executable statements, which may be the same, and the integer expression is any valid FORTRAN integer expression.

10. The last selection statement provided in FORTRAN is composed of two parts: an ASSIGN statement and an assigned GO TO statement. The general form of the ASSIGN statement is:

```
ASSIGN integer constant TO integer variable
```

and the general form of the assigned GO TO statement is:

```
GO TO integer variable (n1, n2, n3, . . . n)
```

where the integer variable in both statements is the same name, and the *n*s are distinct statement labels of executable statements. The integer variable in the assigned GO TO statement must contain a number equal to one of the statement labels in parentheses. This value can only be assigned to the integer variable using the ASSIGN statement. If the integer variable contains a value not equal to one of the *n*s, a runtime error will occur.

F Appendix

Intrinsic Function Reference

FORTRAN 77's intrinsic functions may be referenced by a specific or generic name. When referenced by specific name, the function requires specific argument data types and returns a value of the specified type. Generally, this returned value agrees with the data type of the arguments. When referenced by generic name, the function returns a value based on the arguments used with the function.

All arguments of an intrinsic function, for both specific and generic forms, must be of the same data type. If arguments of differing data types are used, they will all be converted to the data type of the first argument. Additionally, all angle arguments must be in radians. Table F-1 provides a listing of FORTRAN's intrinsic fucntions by generic and specific name.

Table F-1 FORTRAN 77 Intrinsic Functions

Generic Name	Specific Name	Number of Arguments	Argument Type	Result Type	Description
ABS	IABS	1	1Integer	Integer	Absolute value
	ABS		Real	Real	
	DABS		Double	Double	
	CABS		Complex	Complex	
ACOS	ACOS	1	Real	Real	Arcosine
	DACOS		Double	Double	
ANINT	ANINT	1	Real	Real	Nearest whole number
	DNINT		Double	Double	
ASIN	ASIN	1	Real	Real	Arcsine
	DASIN		Double	Double	
ATAN	ATAN	1	Real	Real	Arctangent
	DATAN		Double	Double	

Table F-1 FORTRAN 77 Intrinsic Functions (continued)

Generic Name	Specific Name	Number of Arguments	Argument Type	Result Type	Description
ATAN2	ATAN2	2	Real	Real	Arctangent of
	DATAN2		Double	Double	(arg_1,arg_2)
CHAR	CHAR	1	Integer	Character	Convert to character
CMPLX	—	1 or 2	Integer	Complex	Convert to complex
	—		Real	Complex	
	—		Double	Complex	
CONJG	CONJG	1	Complex	Complex	Complex conjugate
COS	COS	1	Real	Real	Cosine
	DCOS		Double	Double	
	CCOS		Complex	Complex	
COSH	COSH	1	Real	Real	Hyperbolic cosine
	DCOSH		Double	Double	
DBLE	DFLOAT	1	Integer	Double	Conversion to double
	DBLE		Real	Double	
	DBLE		Complex	Double	(real part only)
DIM	IDIM	2	Integer	Integer	Positive difference
	DIM		Real	Real	(arg_1 - arg_2)
	DDIM		Double	Double	
EXP	EXP	1	Real	Real	Exponential (e**arg)
	DEXP		Double	Double	
	CEXP		Complex	Complex	
ICHAR	ICHAR	1	Character	Integer	Conversion to integer
IMAG	AIMAG	1	Complex	Real	Exact imaginary part
INDEX	INDEX	2	Character	Integer	Return starting position of arg_2 within arg_1
INT	INT	1	Integer	Integer	Conversion to integer
	INT		Real	Integer	
	INT		Complex	Integer	
	IFIX		Real	Integer	
	IDINT		Double	Integer	
LEN	LEN	1	Character	Integer	Length of string
LGE	LGE	2	Character	Logical	True if arg_1 > = arg_2; else False
LGT	LGT	2	Character	Logical	True if arg_1 > arg_2; else False
LLE	LLE	2	Character	Logical	True if arg_1 < = arg_2; else False
LLT	LLT	2	Character	Logical	True if arg_1 < arg_2; else False
LOG	ALOG	1	Real	Real	Natural logarithm
	DLOG		Double	Double	(base e)
	CLOG		Complex	Complex	
LOG10	ALOG10	1	Real	Real	Common
	DLOG10		Double	Double	logarithm (base 10)

Table F-1 FORTRAN 77 Intrinsic Functions (continued)

Generic Name	Specific Name	Number of Arguments	Argument Type	Result Type	Description
MAX	MAX0	> = 2	Integer	Integer	Largest value of all arguments
	AMAX0		Integer	Real	
	AMAX1		Real	Real	
	DMAX1		Double	Double	
	MAX1		Real	Integer	
MIN	MIN0	> = 2	Integer	Integer	Sm allest value of all arguments
	AMIN0		Integer	Real	
	AMIN1		Real	Real	
	DMIN1		Double	Double	
	MIN1		Real	Integer	
MOD	MOD	2	Integer	Integer	Remainder of arg_1 - $(int(arg_1/arg_2)*arg_2)$
	AMOD		Real	Real	
	DMOD		Double	Double	
REAL	REAL	1	Integer	Real	Cert to real (real part only); same as REAL
	REAL		Real	Real	
	REAL		Complex	Real	
	FLOAT		Integer	Real	
	SNGL		Double	Real	
SIGN	ISIGN	2	Integer	Integer	Transfer of sign (sign of arg_1 = sign of arg_2)
	SIGN		Real	Real	
	DSIGN		Double	Double	
SIN	SIN	1	Real	Real	Sine
	DSIN		Double	Double	
	CSIN		Complex	Complex	
SINH	SINH	1	Real	Real	Hyperbolic sine
	DSINH		Double	Double	
	CSQRT		Complex	Complex	
TAN	TAN	1	Real	Real	Tangent
	DTAN		Double	Double	
TANH	TANH	1	Real	Real	Hyperbolic tangent
	DTANH		Double	Double	

Solutions

In addition to the solutions provided on the following pages, source code solutions to selected odd numbered programming exercises are provided on the solutions diskette included with the text. Instructions for accessing these source code solutions are provided below.

Instructions for using the Solutions Diskette:

The individual source code solutions on the diskette all have names of the form EXss-n.FOR, where ss denotes the section number and n the exercise number. For example, the file EX24-7.FOR contains the source code for exercise 7 of section 2.4. Additionally, the source code for all of the individual solved exercises has been stored together in the file named ODDSOL. This file may be displayed or printed to provide a complete manual of solutions.

I. To view or copy the source code for a particular exercise use the following instructions:

Put the solutions diskette into drive A on your computer. Then make the A drive the default drive by typing:

A: <enter>

where <enter> means you press the enter key. This will cause the following prompt to appear on your screen:

A:\>

In response to this prompt use the DOS type or copy commands to access the desired exercise source code. For example, the command:

TYPE EX24-7.FOR

causes the source code for Exercise 7 in Section 2.4 to be displayed on your computer's screen.

II. To view all of the solutions on a computer monitor use the following instructions:

Put the solutions diskette into drive A on your computer. Then type the following command:

a:srnodd <enter>

where <enter> means you press the Enter key. This command will cause the solutions to be displayed on your computer's monitor.

Pressing the Control and Break keys at the same time will cancel the screen display.

(*instructions continued on the next page*)

Instructions for using the Solutions Diskette (*continued*)

Pressing either the Pause key or the Control and S keys at the same time will pause the screen display. Pressing any other key will continue the screen display.

III. To print all of the solutions on your printer use the following instructions:

Make sure you have a printer connected to your computer and that it is turned on and supplied with approximately forty-five sheets of paper. Put the solutions diskette into your computer's A drive and then type following command:

a:prnodd <enter>

where <enter> means you press the Enter key. This command will cause the solutions to be sent to your computer's printer.

Chapter One - Fundamentals

Section 1.1

1. a. A computer program is a sequence of instructions used to operate a computer to produce a specific result. (A more formal definition is that a program is the description of an algorithm using a computer language.)
   b. Programming is the process of writing instructions in a language that a computer can respond to and that other programmers can understand.
   c. A programming language is a set of instructions that can be used to construct a computer program.
   d. FORTRAN is an acronym for FORmula Translation. It was commercially introduced in 1957 as the first high-level computer programming language and is particularly suitable for engineering and scientific applications.
   e. An algorithm is a step-by-step sequence of instructions that describes how a computation or task is to be performed.
   f. pseudocode is a method of describing an algorithm using English-like phrases.
   g. A flowchart is a description of an algorithm using specifically defined graphical symbols for input, output, and processing operations that use flow lines to connect each graphical symbol.
   h. A high-level language is one in which the statements resemble English statements and notation.
   i. A source program is written in a computer language, such as FORTRAN, and must be translated into a computer's machine language before it can be executed.
   j. An object program is the machine language (translated) version of a source program.
   k. A compiler is a program that translates a source program into an object program.
   j. An interpreter executes a source program by translating and immediately executing each instruction in the source program as it is encountered. Using an interpreter, no object program is produced.

3. Step 1: Pour the contents of the first cup into the third cup
   Step 2: Rinse out the first cup
   Step 3: Pour the contents of the second cup into the first cup
   Step 4: Rinse out the second cup
   Step 5: Pour the contents of the third cup into the second cup

5. Step 1: Compare the first number with the second number and use the smallest of these numbers for the next step
   Step 2: Compare the smallest number found in step 1 with the third number. The smallest of these two numbers is the smallest of all three numbers.

7a. Step 1: Compare the first name in the list with the name JONES. If the names match, stop the search; else go to step 2.

   Step 2: Compare the next name in the list with the name JONES. If the names match, stop the search; else repeat this step.

Section 1.2

1. POWER - valid and mnemonic
   DENSITY - invalid, more than six characters
   M123$ - invalid, contains the special symbol $
   1234 - invalid, does not begin with a letter
   ABCD - valid and not mnemonic
   TOTAL - valid and mnemonic
   TANGENT - invalid, too many letters
   ABSVAL - valid and mnemonic
   MARRIED - invalid, too many letters
   B34A - valid and not mnemonic
   34AB - invalid, does not start with a letter
   TAXES$ - invalid, contains the special symbol $
   A2-B3 - invalid, contains the special symbol -
   NEWBAL - valid and mnemonic
   MIN-VAL - invalid, contains the special symbol -
   SINE - valid and mnemonic
   $SINE - invalid, contains the special symbol $
   COSINE - valid and mnemonic
   INVOICES - invalid, more than six characters
   NETPAY - valid and mnemonic
   BALANCE - invalid, more than six characters
   SOLD - valid and mnemonic
   AVERAGE - invalid, more than six characters

3.
```
PROGRAM MAIN
  ITEMS
  SALETX
  BALNCE
  STOP
  END
```

5a. For a case insensitive compiler:
    AVERAG and averag are equivalent
    MODE, Mode, and moDE are equivalent

```
    BESSEL and besseL are equivalent
    Total and total are equivalent
    TeMp and TEMP are equivalent
```

b. In a case sensitive compiler, none of the names are equivalent.

c. AVERAG, MODE, BESSEL, and TEMP

7.
```
Determine the placement of the light fixtures
If you are capable and allowed to do so
  Purchase the necessary materials, including the fixtures
  and wire the lights in accordance with local laws
Else hire a licensed electrician
```

9.
```
Determine the courses needed for graduate school
Take the right courses
Maintain an appropriate grade average
Prepare for the graduate record exam (GRE)
Contact engineering graduate schools for admission
  interview requirements
Establish contacts for letters of recommendation
```

11.
```
Select and reserve a camp site
Prepare a list of items to take along
Purchase needed supplies
Reserve a camper at a rental agency (optional)
Arrange for someone to feed plants and watch house
Make arrangements for pet care, if needed
Check and service automobile
```

Section 1.3

1.
```
123456789<--------------- Column Number
      PROGRAM MAIN
        CALL GROPAY
        CALL TAXES
        CALL NETPAY
        CALL DISPLAY
        STOP
        END
```

3.
```
123456789<-------------- Column Number
* THIS PROGRAM DISPLAYS A FOUR LINE POEM
      PROGRAM MAIN
        CALL POEM
        STOP
        END
      SUBROUTINE POEM
* THE NUMBERS 10, 20, 30, AND 40 IN THE NEXT FOUR STATEMENTS
* ARE STATEMENT LABELS THAT BELONGS IN THE LABEL FIELD
   10   PRINT *, 'COMPUTERS, COMPUTERS EVERYWHERE'
   20   PRINT *, '   AS FAR AS I CAN SEE'
   30   PRINT *, 'I REALLY, REALLY LIKE THOSE THINGS'
   40   PRINT *, '   OH JOY, OH JOY FOR ME'
        RETURN
        END
```

5.
```
123456789<--------------- Column Number
      PROGRAM MAIN
        CALL TEST
        STOP
        END
      SUBROUTINE TEST
* THE NUMBERS 100 AND 200 IN THE NEXT TWO STATEMENTS ARE
* LABELS THAT BELONG IN THE LABEL FIELD
 100    FORMAT(1X,A,2X,A)
 200    FORMAT(1X,I5,2X,F5.3)
* THE FOLLOWING TWO STATEMENTS ARE CALLED DECLARATION STATEMENTS
        REAL VALUE
        INTEGER COUNT
        PRINT 100, 'VALUE', 'SIN'
        PRINT 100, '-----', '---'
        DO 10 COUNT = 1, 20
* FOR APPEARANCE ONLY, BEGIN THE NEXT TWO STATEMENTS IN COLUMN 11
          VALUE = 0.1 * I
          PRINT 200, VALUE, SIN(VALUE)
* THE 10 IN THE NEXT STATEMENT IS A STATEMENT NUMBER
  10    CONTINUE
        RETURN
        END
```

7. PROGRAM is spelled incorrectly

9. The statement number 100 should be placed within columns 1 through 5

11. The statement should begin in column 7 or beyond

13.
```
123456789<--------------- Column Number
C THE NEXT LINE IS AN INITIAL LINE OF A STATEMENT
        PRINT 100, 'THE AVERAGE IS',
C AND THE NEXT LINE IS A CONTINUATION LINE
     1  AVERAGE
```

Section 1.4

1.
```
PROGRAM MAIN
  CALL DISPLY
  STOP
  END
SUBROUTINE DISPLY
  WRITE(6,*) 'JOHN JONES'
  WRITE(6,*) '212 SOMEPLACE STREET'
  WRITE(6,*) 'NONESUCH, NJ, 07078'
  RETURN
  END
```

3. Six PRINT or WRITE statement should be used, one for each line.

Chapter Two - Data and Operations

Section 2.1

1 a. REAL
 b. INTEGER
 c. REAL
 d. INTEGER
 e. REAL
 f. CHARACTER

3.

1.26E2 6.5623E2 3.42695E3 4.8931E3 3.21E-1 1.23E-2 6.789E-3

5a.

M	A	R	T	H	A
01001101	01000001	01010010	01010100	01001000	01000001

b.

M	A	R	T	H	A
11010100	11000001	11011001	11100011	11001000	11000001

7a. 2 * 3 + 4 * 5
 b. (6 + 18) / 2
 c. 4.5 / (12.2 - 3.1)
 d. 4.6 * (3.0 + 14.9)
 e. (12.1 + 18.9) * (15.3 - 3.8)

9.
a. 27 b. 8.0 c. 1.0 d. 220.0 e. 22.5 f. 19.67
g. 6.0 h. 2.0

11. Since all of the operands are integers, the result of each intermediate operation is an integer.
a. 5 b. 10 c. 24 d. 0 (due to truncation)
e. 3 f. -50 g. -2 h. 10 i. 53

15. A program might alert the computer to the amount of storage needed for the various values in the program by specifying how many of each data type will be used by the program.

Section 2.2

1. In FORTRAN 77:
 PROD-A is invalid because of the special symbol -
 C1234 is valid
 ABCD is valid
 -C3 is invalid because of the special symbol -

12345 is invalid because it does not begin in a letter
NEWBAL is valid
WATTS is valid
$TOTAL is invalid because of the special symbol $
NEW$AL is invalid because of the special symbol $
A1B2C3D4 is invalid because it contains more than six characters
9AB6 is invalid because it does not begin with a letter
SUM.OF is invalid because it contains a period
AVERAGE is invalid because it contains more than six characters
GRADE1 is valid
FINGRAD is invalid because it contains more than six characters

3a. INTEGER COUNT
b. REAL GRADE
c. CHARACTER KEYCH

5a. INTEGER FIRNUM, SECNUM
b. REAL PRICE, YIELD, COUPON
c. CHARACTER CH, LET1*3, LET2*3, LET3*7, LET4*9

7. A name and a value

9a. RATE is stored starting at memory location 159
CH1 is stored starting at memory location 163
CH2 is stored starting at memory location 164
CH3 is stored starting at memory location 165
CH4 is stored starting at memory location 166
NUM is stored starting at memory location 167
COUNT is stored starting at memory location 168

11. MILES is stored in byte locations 159 through 162
COUNT is stored in byte locations 163 and 164
NUM is stored in byte locations 165 and 166
KEY is stored in byte location 167
KEY2*3 is stored in byte locations 168, 169, and 170
KEY is stored in byte location 171

Section 2.3

1. CIRCUM = 2 * 3.1416 * RADIUS

3. CELSUS = 5.0 / 9.0 * (FAHREN - 32.0)

5. ETIME = TOTDIS / AVSPED

7. HEIGHT = V**2 * SIN (THETA) **2 / (2.0 * 32.2)

9. FORCE = K * Q1 * Q2 / R**2

11. THE FIRST INTEGER DISPLAYED IS 4
THE SECOND INTEGER DISPLAYED IS 4

13. THE SUM IS   0.000000
THE SUM IS 26.270000
THE FINAL TOTAL IS 28.238000

15. LENGTH is not initialized before it is used in the last statement

17. The last statement should be AREA = LENGTH * WIDTH

19.
```
THE VALUE OF TOTAL IS INITIALLY SET TO 247
  TOTAL IS NOW 247
  TOTAL IS NOW 247
  TOTAL IS NOW 247
  THE FINAL VALUE IN TOTAL IS 247
```

25.
```
      PROGRAM MAIN
        REAL MINRAD, MAXRAD, AREA
        MINRAD = 2.5
        MAXRAD = 6.4
        AREA = 3.1416 * (2 * (MINRAD**2 + MAXRAD**2))**(0.5)
        PRINT *, 'THE AREA IS ', AREA
        END
```

27.
```
      PROGRAM MAIN
        REAL X1, X2, Y1, Y2, SLOPE
        X1 = 3.0
        Y1 = 7.0
        X2 = 8.0
        Y2 = 12.0
        SLOPE = (Y2 - Y1) / (X2 - X1)
        WRITE(6,*) 'THE SLOPE OF THE LINE IS ', SLOPE
        END
```

Section 2.4

1a.
```
   0
123456789
```

b.
```
     7
123456789
```

c.
```
 ****
123456789
```

d.
```
 7.92
123456789
```

e.
```
 5.76
123456789
```

f.
```
82.63
123456789
```

g.
```
*****
123456789
```

```
h. *****
   123456789

i. THE NUMBER IS   26.27
   THE NUMBER IS  682.30
   THE NUMBER IS    1.97
   12345678911111111122
            012345678901

j. 26.27
  682.30
    1.97
  ------
  710.54
  123456789

k.     6.27
     682.30
       1.97
     ------
     710.54
  123456789

l.          34.16
            10.00
           ------
            44.17
    1234567891111
             0000
```

3. Same display as for Exercise 1

7. *Stored as EX24-7.FOR on solutions diskette.*

9. *Stored as EX24-9.FOR on solutions diskette.*

Section 2.5

1a. One output: the dollar amount
 b. Five Inputs: half dollars, quarters, dimes, nickels, pennies
 c. Dollar amount = 0.50 * halfs + 0.25 * quarters + 0.10 * dimes
                  + 0.05 * nickels + 0.01 * pennies

3a. One output : the amount of Ergies
 b. Four inputs: pi, Ì, e, and fergies

5a. One output: distance
 b. Three inputs: s, d, and t

7a. Four outputs: weekly gross and net pay for two people
 b. Four inputs: two hourly rates, income tax rate, and
                 medical rate

9a. One output: the value of y
 b. Four inputs: Ì, r, x, and pi

Section 2.6

5a. *Stored as EX26-5A.FOR on source code solutions diskette.*

7a. *Stored as EX26-7A.FOR on source code solutions diskette.*

9a. *Stored as EX26-9A.FOR on source code solutions diskette.*

11a. *Stored as EX26-11A.FOR on source code solutions diskette.*

13a. *Stored as EX26-13A.FOR on source code solutions diskette.*

Chapter Three - Completing the Basics

Section 3.1

```
1a.  SQRT(6.37)
 b.  SQRT(X-Y)
 c.  SIN(30 * 3.1416/180.0)
 d.  SIN(60 * 3.1416/180.0)
 e.  INT(19.37)
 f.  ABS( A**2 - B**2)
 g.  MOD(7,2)
 h.  EXP(3)

3a.  B = SIN(X) - COS(X)
 b.  B = SIN(X)**2 - COS(X)**2
 c.  AREA = (C * B * SIN(A))/2
 d.  C = SQRT(A**2 + B**2)
 e.  P = SQRT( ABS(M - N) )
 f.  SUM = A*(R**N - 1) / (R - 1)
 g.  X = AMAX1(P,Q,R,S,T)
 h.  Y = AMIN1(P,Q,R,S,T)
```

5. *Stored as EX31-5.FOR on source code solutions diskette.*

7. *Stored as EX31-7.FOR on source code solutions diskette.*

9. *Stored as EX31-9.FOR on source code solutions diskette.*

11. *Stored as EX31-11.FOR on source code solutions diskette.*

13. *Stored as EX31-13.FOR on source code solutions diskette.*

Section 3.2

1.

```
a. READ(5,*) NUMBER  or  READ *, NUMBER
b. READ(5,*) GRADE   or  READ *, GRADE
c. READ(5,*) KEYVAL  or  READ *, KEYVAL
d. READ(5,*) MONTH, YEAR, SCORE  or  READ *, MONTH, YEAR, SCORE
```

e. READ(5,*) CH, NUM1, NUM2 or READ *, CH, NUM1, NUM2
f. READ(5,*) CAPTAL, RATE, AMOUNT or READ *, CAPTAL, RATE, AMOUNT
g. READ(5,*) LETTR1, LETTR2, KEY, NUM1, NUM2, NUM3
   or READ *, LETTR1, LETTR2, KEY, NUM1, NUM2, NUM3
h. READ(5,*) OHMS1, OHMS2, OHMS3, VOLTS1, VOLTS2, VOLTS3
   or READ *, OHMS1, OHMS2, OHMS3, VOLTS1, VOLTS2, VOLTS3

3. Assuming 5 is the standard unit output number, the correct forms are
   a. READ *, NUM1, NUM2, NUM3
   b. READ *, NUM1, NUM2
   c. READ *, NUM1, I4
   d. READ *, TEMP, AMBINT
   e. READ *, VAL1, VAL2
   f. READ *, NUM1, NUM2

5. *Stored as EX32-5.FOR on source code solutions diskette.*

7. *Stored as EX32-7.FOR on source code solutions diskette.*

9. *Stored as EX32-9.FOR on source code solutions diskette.*

11. *Stored as EX32-11.FOR on source code solutions diskette.*

Section 3.3

```
1a. REAL WATTS
 b. REAL TEMP
 c. INTEGER COUNT
 d. INTEGER NUM1, NUM2
    REAL VALUE
    CHARACTER CH1*6
 e. INTEGER COUNT
    REAL VOLTS, OHMS
 f. REAL AVERGE
    INTEGER IFLAG
    CHARACTER*6 KEY, CODE
```

3a. The first field starts at column 1 and ends at column 4
    The second field starts at column 5 and ends at column 9
    The third field starts at column 10 and ends at column 14

 b. The first field starts at column 1 and ends at column 5
    The second field starts at column 6 and ends at column 11
    The third field starts at column 12 and ends at column 19

 c. The first field fills column 1 only
    The second field starts at column 2 and ends at column 6
    The third field starts at column 7 and ends at column 8
    The fourth field starts at column 9 and ends at column 28

 d. The first field fills column 1 only
    The second field starts at column 2 and ends at column 6
    The third field fills column 7 only
    The fourth field starts at column 8 and ends at column 12

```
e. First field: Column 1
   Second field: Columns 2, 3, and 4
   Third field:  Columns 5 and 6
   Fourth field: Columns 7, 8, and 9
   Fifth field:  Columns 10 and 11
   Sixth field:  Columns 12, 13, 14, 15, and 16
   Seventh field: Column 17
   Eighth field:  Columns 18, 19, and 20
   Ninth field:   Column 21
   Tenth field:   Columns 22, 23, and 24
```

5. The program will work. However, it is advisable to display a prompt for the user that explains what input is requested and the format that should be used. It is also generally advisable to use separate FORMAT statements for both input and output statements, so that a change can be made in one of the formats without effecting the other. Note also that the first 1X in the format is used differently on input than it is on output (recall the carriage control character on output).

7a. *Stored as EX33-7A.FOR on source code solutions diskette.*

9a. *Stored as EX33-9A.FOR on source code solutions diskette.*

Section 3.4

1. *Stored as EX34-1.FOR on source code solutions diskette.*

3. *Stored as EX34-3.FOR on source code solutions diskette.*

Section 3.5

3. The mistake in this program is that the output statements for the headings are made before the input prompts. This has the effect of "sandwiching" the input between the desired output, as shown by the following sample run.

```
       SINE         APPROXIMATION    DIFFERENCE
   ------------     -------------   ------------
ENTER AN ANGLE (IN DEGREES)
30
   5.000011E-01     5.236000E-01    2.359891E-02
   5.000011E-01     4.996752E-01    3.258522E-04
   5.000011E-01     5.000032E-01    2.098380E-06
```

5. *Stored as EX35-5.FOR on source code solutions diskette.*

7. *Stored as EX35-7.FOR on source code solutions diskette.*

Chapter Four - Modularity Using Subprograms

Section 4.1

```
1a.  SUBROUTINE TEST(EXPER)              CALL TEST(VALUE)
        REAL EXPER
```

b. SUBROUTINE MINUTE(ITIME) CALL MINUTE(LSECOND)

```
   INTEGER ITIME
```

c. SUBROUTINE KEY(CODE) CALL KEY(CODE)

```
   CHARACTER CODE
```

d. SUBROUTINE YIELD(RATE,N) CALL YIELD(COUPON, IYEARS)

```
   REAL RATE
   INTEGER N
```

e. SUBROUTINE RAND(SEED,RANDNO) CALL RAND(SEED,RVAL)

```
   REAL SEED, RANDNO
```

3b. *Stored as EX41-3B.FOR on source code solutions diskette.*

5b. *Stored as EX41-5B.FOR on source code solutions diskette.*

7b. *Stored as EX41-7B.FOR on source code solutions diskette.*

9b. *Stored as EX41-9B.FOR on source code solutions diskette.*

11b. *Stored as EX41-11B.FOR on source code solutions diskette.*

13. The program causes no problem for the compiler as written.

Section 4.2

1. *Stored as EX42-1.FOR on source code solutions diskette.*

5c. *Stored as EX42-5C.FOR on source code solutions diskette.*

7. *Stored as EX42-7.FOR on source code solutions diskette.*

Section 4.3

1a. The function expects one integer argument to be passed to it.
b. The function must be passed three arguments in the order: one character argument and two real arguments.
c. The function must be passed three arguments in the order: one character argument and two real arguments.
d. The function must be passed three arguments in the order: one character argument and two integer arguments.
e. The function must be passed two real arguments.
f. The function must be passed six arguments in the order: three integers, one character, and two real arguments.
g. The function must be passed four arguments in the order: two character arguments, one real argument, one integer argument.
h. The function must be passed one character argument.

3a. REAL ABNUM
b. REAL ABNUM
c. CHARACTER ABNUM
d. INTEGER ABNUM

5a. *Stored as EX43-5A.FOR on source code solutions diskette.*

7b. *Stored as EX43-7B.FOR on source code solutions diskette.*

9a. *Stored as EX43-9A.FOR on source code solutions diskette.*

11. *Stored as EX43-11.FOR on source code solutions diskette.*

13. *Stored as EX43-13.FOR on source code solutions diskette.*

Section 4.4

1. *Stored as EX44-1.FOR on source code solutions diskette.*

3. *Stored as EX44-3.FOR on source code solutions diskette.*

5. *Stored as EX44-5.FOR on source code solutions diskette.*

7. *Stored as EX44-7.FOR on source code solutions diskette.*

Section 4.5

1. After the declarations and before all executable code.

3. False. Only user-defined functions have their types declared. Intrinsic functions and subroutine names must not appear in data type declarations.

5. No. These are two separate (local) variables as far as FORTRAN is concerned. There is no relationship of one to the other.

7. RESULT could be anything. FORTRAN does not specify what value will be returned by a function that has not been assigned a value.

9. The subroutine exchanges the values in A and B, which produces the following output:

```
5.600000    2.400000
```

11. The SNEEKY function produces unwanted side effects. After each call, the value of N, within the function, is increased by 2. This increased value is passed back to NUM, through the argument list each time SNEEKY is called, producing the output: 5 7 9. (As the order of expression evaluation is undefined in FORTRAN, some compilers may evaluate the calls to SNEEKY from right to left, producing the output 9 7 5.) In general, a function should not alter any of its arguments. If arguments are to be altered, a subroutine should be used.

13. The statement is true. PARAMETERized constants are private (local) to the program unit in which they are declared.

15. The program displays a 0. Notice the spelling of the variable THNBR in the assignment statement within DOIT(). The dummy argument THENBR is never assigned. Assuming the compiler initializes all variables to zero, the incoming value of RESULT, which is 0, is never changed by the subroutine. To avoid this type of error, placing the statement IMPLICIT NONE in each program unit before the variable and argument declarations would alert the programmer to any undeclared names, such as THNBR.

17. *Stored as EX45-17.FOR on source code solutions diskette.*

19. *Stored as EX45-19.FOR on source code solutions diskette.*

21. *Stored as EX45-21.FOR on source code solutions diskette.*

23.
```
      CYLVOL(RAD, HGT) = RAD ** 2 * HGT * PI()
```

25. *Stored as EX45-25.FOR on source code solutions diskette.*
Note: Returning N1 / N2 is not a good idea since N2 can be zero.

27. *Stored as EX45-27.FOR on source code solutions diskette.*

29. *Stored as EX45-29.FOR on source code solutions diskette.*

Chapter 5 -DO Loops and Data Files

Section 5.1

1 For each of these DO statements, the statement label 10 may be replaced by any integer from 1 to 99999.

```
a. DO 10 I = 1, 20   or  DO 10 I = 1, 20, 1
b. DO 10 ICOUNT = 1, 20 , 2
c. DO 10 J = 1, 100, 5
d. DO 10 ICOUNT = 20, 1, -1
e. DO 10 ICOUNT = 20, 1, -2
f. DO 10 COUNT = 1.0, 16.2, 0.2
g. DO 10 XCNT = 20.0, 10.0, -0.5
```

3a. 55
 b. 1024
 c. 75
 d. -5
 e. 40320
 f. .031250

5. The following output is produced by the program:

```
        20
        16
        12
         8
         4
         0
```

7. *Stored as EX51-7.FOR on source code solutions diskette.*

9. *Stored as EX51-9.FOR on source code solutions diskette.*

11. *Stored as EX51-11.FOR on source code solutions diskette.*

Section 5.2

1. The only modification required is to change the DO statement from:

```
DO 50 COUNT = 1, 4
```

to:

```
DO 50 COUNT = 1, 8
```

3. The program will yield the correct average at the completion of the DO loop because the last AVERAGE computed uses the final TOTAL and the correct number of items (NUMS). Except for the final calculation of AVERAGE, all other calculations of this variable are of no use to us; in fact, they are incorrect because NUMS, rather than COUNT is used to calculate them. Since this code computes AVERAGE a number of times within the loop, all of which are not required (and are incorrect) except for the last calculation, this code should not be used. Using a loop to calculate variables that are not required is a sign of bad programming.

5. *Stored as EX52-5.FOR on source code solutions diskette.*

7. *Stored as EX52-7.FOR on source code solutions diskette.*

9. *Stored as EX52-9.FOR on source code solutions diskette.*

Section 5.3

1. *Stored as EX53-1.FOR on source code solutions diskette.*

3. *Stored as EX53-3.FOR on source code solutions diskette.*

5. *Stored as EX53-5.FOR on source code solutions diskette.*

7. *Stored as EX53-7.FOR on source code solutions diskette.*

Section 5.4

3.
```
OPEN(2, FILE = 'MATH.DAT')
OPEN(3, FILE = 'BOOK.DAT')
OPEN(4, FILE = 'RESIST.DAT')
OPEN(7, FILE = 'EXPER2.DAT')
OPEN(8, FILE = 'PRICES.DAT')
OPEN(9, FILE = 'RATES.MEM')
```

5a. *Stored as EX54-5A.FOR on source code solutions diskette.*

5b. *Stored as EX54-5B.FOR on source code solutions diskette.*

7a. *Stored as EX54-7A.FOR on source code solutions diskette.*

7b. *Stored as EX54-7B.FOR on source code solutions diskette.*

9a. *Stored as EX54-9A.FOR on source code solutions diskette.*

9b. *Stored as EX54-9B.FOR on source code solutions diskette.*

Section 5.5

1a. The first field starts at column 1 and ends at column 2
The second field starts at column 3 and ends at column 8
The third field starts at column 9 and ends at column 12

b. The first field starts at column 1 and ends at column 7
The second field starts at column 8 and ends at column 9
The third field starts at column 10 and ends at column 15

c. The first field starts at column 1 and ends at column 5
The second field starts at column 6 and ends at column 10
The third field starts at column 11 and ends at column 17
The fourth field starts at column 18 and ends at column 42

d. The first field starts at column 1 and ends at column 2
The second field starts at column 3 and ends at column 6
The third field starts at column 7 and ends at column 8
The fourth field starts at column 9 and ends at column 12
The fifth field starts at column 13 and ends at column 14
The sixth field starts at column 15 and ends at column 18

e. First field: Columns 1 through 6
Second field: Columns 7 and 8
Third field: Columns 9, 10, and 11
Fourth field: Columns 12 through 17
Fifth field: Columns 18, 19, and 20
Sixth field: Columns 21 and 22
Seventh field: Column 23, 24, and 25
Eighth field: Columns 26 and 27
Ninth field: Column 28, 29, and 30
Tenth field: Columns 31 and 32

5. The program will work. However, it is advisable to use separate FORMAT statements for both input and output statements when the input and output are different devices, such as an external data file and a video screen. (This is not true when the input is from a formatted external data file. In this case the input format for reading the file must be identical to the output format used when the file was written). Note also that the first 1X in the format is used differently on input than it is on output (recall the carriage control character on output).

7. *Stored as EX55-7.FOR on source code solutions diskette.*

9a. *Stored as EX55-9A.FOR on source code solutions diskette.*

9b. *Stored as EX55-9B.FOR on source code solutions diskette.*

Section 5.6

1. *Stored as EX56-1.FOR on source code solutions diskette.*

3. *Stored as EX56-3.FOR on source code solutions diskette.*

Chapter Six - Selection

Section 6.1

1a. True b. True c. True d. True e. 10
 f. False g. False h. True i. False

3a. False b. False c. True

Section 6.2

1a.
```
IF (ANGLE .EQ. 90) THEN
  WRITE(6,*) 'THE ANGLE IS A RIGHT ANGLE'
ELSE
  WRITE(6,*) 'THE ANGLE IS NOT A RIGHT ANGLE'
ENDIF
```

b.
```
IF (TEMP .GT. 100) THEN
  WRITE(6,*) 'ABOVE THE BOILING POINT OF WATER'
ELSE
  WRITE(6,*) 'BELOW THE BOILING POINT OF WATER'
ENDIF
```

c.
```
IF (NUM .GE. 0.0) THEN
  POSSUM = POSSUM + NUM
ELSE
  NEGSUM = NEGSUM + NUM
ENDIF
```

d.
```
IF (VOLTGE .LT. 0.5) THEN
  FLAG = 0
ELSE
  FLAG = 1
ENDIF
```

e.
```
IF (ABS(VOLTS1-VOLTS2) .LT. 0.001) THEN
  APPROX = 0.0
ELSE
  APPROX = (VOLTS1 - VOLTS2)/ 2.0
ENDIF
```

f.
```
IF (FREQ .GT. 60) WRITE(6,*) 'FREQUENCY IS TOO HIGH'
```

g.
```
IF (ABS(TEMP1-TEMP2) .GT. 2.3) ERROR = (TEMP1-TEMP2)*FACTOR
```

h.
```
IF (X .GT. Y .AND. X .LT. 20) READ(5,*) P
```

i.
```
IF (DIST .GT. 20 .AND. DIST .LT. 35) READ(5,*) TIME
```

3. *Stored as EX62-3.FOR on source code solutions diskette.*

5. *Stored as EX62-5.FOR on source code solutions diskette.*

7. *Stored as EX62-7.FOR on source code solutions diskette.*

9. *Stored as EX62-9.FOR on source code solutions diskette.*

11. *Stored as EX62-11.FOR on source code solutions diskette.*

Section 6.3

1. *Stored as EX63-1.FOR on source code solutions diskette.*

3. *Stored as EX63-3.FOR on source code solutions diskette.*

5. *Stored as EX63-5.FOR on source code solutions diskette.*

7. *Stored as EX63-7.FOR on source code solutions diskette.*

9a. The program will run.
b. The program determines whether the monthly sales is less than or greater than 10000. If monthly sales is less than 10000.00 then it determines the correct income. If monthly sales are greater than or equal to 10000.00, regardless of how much greater, the income is calculated as 200.00 + .03 * MSALES.
c. The correct income is calculated for sales less than $10,000 and for sales between $10,000 and $20,000.

Section 6.4

1.
```
  SELECT CASE (LETTER_GRADE)
    CASE('A')
      WRITE(6,*) 'THE NUMERICAL GRADE IS BETWEEN 90 AND 100'
    CASE('B')
      WRITE(6,*) 'THE NUMERICAL GRADE IS BETWEEN 80 AND 89.9'
    CASE('C')
      WRITE(6,*) 'THE NUMERICAL GRADE IS BETWEEN 70 AND 79.7'
    CASE('D')
      WRITE(6,*) 'HOW ARE YOU GOING TO EXPLAIN THIS ONE'
    CASE DEFAULT
      WRITE(6,*) 'OF COURSE I HAD NOTHING TO DO WITH MY GRADE.'
      WRITE(6,*) ' THE PROFESSOR WAS REALLY OFF THE WALL.'
   END SELECT
```

3. *Stored as EX64-3.FOR on source code solutions diskette.*

Section 6.5

1a. *Stored as EX65-1A.FOR on source code solutions diskette.*

3. *Stored as EX65-3.FOR on source code solutions diskette.*

5. *Stored as EX65-5.FOR on source code solutions diskette.*

Chapter 7 - Conditional Loops

Section 7.1

1. *Stored as EX71-1.FOR on source code solutions diskette.*

3a. Twenty-one numbers are printed. The first number printed is 1 and the last number printed is 21.

5. *Stored as EX71-5.FOR on source code solutions diskette.*

7. *Stored as EX71-7.FOR on source code solutions diskette.*

9. *Stored as EX71-9.FOR on source code solutions diskette.*

Section 7.2

1. *Stored as EX72-1.FOR on source code solutions diskette.*

3a. Twenty-one numbers are printed. The first number printed is 1 and the last number printed is 21.

5. *Stored as EX72-5.FOR on source code solutions diskette.*

7. *Stored as EX72-7.FOR on source code solutions diskette.*

9. *Stored as EX72-9.FOR on source code solutions diskette.*

Section 7.3

1b. *Stored as EX73-1B.FOR on source code solutions diskette.*

3a. *Stored as EX73-3A.FOR on source code solutions diskette.*

Section 7.4

1b. *The modified subroutine to correctly handle the case where the new ID code should be placed at the end of the file is Stored as EX74-1b.FOR on source code solutions diskette.*

5a. *Stored as EX74-5A.FOR on source code solutions diskette.*

5b. *Stored as EX74-5B.FOR on source code solutions diskette.*

Chapter Eight - Arrays

Section 8.1

```
1a. REAL VOLTS(100)
 b. REAL TEMPS(50)
 c. CHARACTER CODE(30)
 d. INTEGER YEARS(100)
 e. REAL VELOCY(32)
 f. REAL DISTNC(100)
 g. INTEGER CODE(6)

3a. READ(5,*) GRADES(1), GRADES(3), GRADES(7)
 b. READ(5,*) VOLTS(1), VOLTS(3), VOLTS(7)
 c. READ(5,*) AMPS(1), AMPS(3), AMPS(7)
 d. READ(5,*) DIST(1), DIST(3), DIST(7)
 e. READ(5,*) VELOC(1), VELOC(3), VELOC(7)
 f. READ(5,*) TIME(1), TIME(3), TIME(7)

5a. A(1)
    A(3)
    A(5)

b. B(3)
   B(6)
   B(9)

c. A(1) A(2) A(3) A(4) A(5)

d. B(3) B(6) B(9) B(12)

e. C(2) C(4) C(6) C(8) C(10)
```

7a. *Stored as EX81-7A.FOR on source code solutions diskette.*

7b. *Stored as EX81-7B.FOR on source code solutions diskette.*

9. *Stored as EX81-9.FOR on source code solutions diskette.*

11. *Stored as EX81-11.FOR on source code solutions diskette.*

Section 8.2

```
1a.    INTEGER GRADES(10
       DATA GRADES /89,75,82,93,78,95,81,88,77,82/

1b.    REAL AMOUNT(5)
       DATA AMOUNT /10.62,13.98,18.45,12.68,14.76/

1c.    REAL RATES(100)
       DATA (RATES(I), I = 1,6) /6.29, 6.95, 7.25, 7.35, 7.42/

1d.    REAL TEMPS(64)
       DATA (TEMPS(I), I = 1,4) /78.2, 69.6, 68.5, 83.9/
```

1e.
```
      CHARACTER CODES(15)
      DATA (CODES(I), I = 1,7) / 'G', 'K', 'M', 'Q', 'R', 'W', 'X'/
```

3. *Stored as EX82-3.FOR on source code solutions diskette.*

5b. *Stored as EX82-5B.FOR on source code solutions diskette.*

Section 8.3

1a. INTEGER NUMS(6,10)
 b. INTEGER NUMS(2,5)
 c. CHARACTER CODES(7,12)
 d. CHARACTER CODES(15,7)
 e. REAL VALS(10,25)
 f. REAL VALS(16,8)

3a. *Stored as EX83-3A.FOR on source code solutions diskette.*

5a. *Stored as EX83-5A.FOR on source code solutions diskette.*

7a. *Stored as EX83-7A.FOR on source code solutions diskette.*

Section 8.4

1.
```
SUBROUTINE SORTAR(INARRY)      or      SUBROUTINE SORTAR(INARRY)
  INTEGER INARRY(500)                    INTEGER INARRY(*)
```

3.
```
SUBROUTINE POWER(WATTS)        or      SUBROUTINE POWER(WATTS)
  REAL WATTS(140)                        REAL WATTS(*)
```

5. *Stored as EX84-5.FOR on source code solutions diskette.*

7. *Stored as EX84-7.FOR on source code solutions diskette.*

9.
```
      SUBROUTINE LOCATE(XINARY)
        REAL XINARY(3,5,10)

      SUBROUTINE LOCATE(XINARY)
        REAL XINARY(3,5,*)

      SUBROUTINE LOCATE(XINARY,I,J,K)
        INTEGER I,J,K
        REAL XINARY(I,J,K)
```

11. *Stored as EX84-11.FOR on source code solutions diskette.*

Section 8.5

3. *Stored as EX85-3.FOR on source code solutions diskette.*

5. *Stored as EX85-5.FOR on source code solutions diskette.*

7. *Stored as EX85-7.FOR on source code solutions diskette.*

Chapter Nine - Numerical Techniques and Applications

Section 9.1

1. The solution is $x = 3$, $y = -1$

3. *Stored as EX91-3.FOR on source code solutions diskette.*

5. The minimum V_G required to charge the battery is approximately 14.4 volts.

7. The solution is $x = 5.2$, $y = 0.8$, $z = 1$.

9a. The optimum straight line fit is $y = 0.25 + 0.4x$

11. The optimum parabolic fit is

$$y = 4.25 - 1.75\,x + 0.25\,x^2$$

Section 9.2

Note: The results of some of the root finding exercises are dependent on the roundoff errors generated. Therefore different results may occur when the programs are run on your own computer.

1a. In Program 9-4 replace the assignment statement for Y by

```
Y = X ** 4 + 4 * X ** 3 - 7 * X ** 2 - 22 * X + 24
```

The roots are at $x = -4$, $x = -3$, $x = 1$, and $x = 2$.

b. In Program 9-5 replace the assignment statement for Y as done in Exercise 1a. The four roots are displayed.

3. In Program 9-7 replace the function statement by

```
F(X) = X ** 4 + 4 * X ** 3 - 7 * X ** 2 - 22 * X + 24
```

For a step size of 1 and 0.5 no roots are displayed, since the roots are integers and either x_1 or x_2 fall very close to the roots. Roundoff errors may result in the values of y_1 and y_2 having the same sign, in which case the root is not displayed. All four roots are displayed for the step sizes of 0.499, 0.1, and 0.01. A step size of 0.499 will ensure that all values of x_1 and x_2 do not fall very close to the roots. For smaller step sizes accumulated roundoff error makes it unlikely that values of x_1 and x_2 are very close to the roots.

5. In Program 9-7 replace the function statement by

```
Y = COS (X)
```

The six roots

$x = 1.57, 4.71, 7.85, 11.00, 14.14,$ and 17.28

are displayed for each of the four step sizes.

7. In Program 9-8 replace the function statement by

```
F(X) = COS (X)
```

The six roots are located by selecting the left and right bounds of X shown below. The number of iterations required is also shown.

Left and right bounds of X	Root	Number of iterations
0 to 3	1.571	12
3 to 6	4.712	18
6 to 9	7.854	13
9 to 12	10.995	12
12 to 16	14.137	12
16 to 20	17.279	13

9. In Program 9-9 replace the function statement by

```
F(XX) = COS (XX)
```

When the same bounds of X used in Exercise 7 are entered, the following results are obtained.

Left and right bounds of X	Root	Number of iterations
0 to 3	1.571	3
3 to 6	4.712	3
6 to 9	7.853	3
9 to 12	10.996	4
12 to 16	14.137	3
16 to 20	20.420	5

The first five roots are located much more rapidly than for the bisection method. However, the last run located a root outside the interval (at x = 13 * pi / 2). If the last run is repeated, with 16 and 18 entered as the left and right bounds of X, the root at X = 17.279 is then located after 3 iterations.

Section 9.3

1a. In Program 9-10 replace the function statement by

```
F(X) = X ** 3 + 2 * X ** 2 + 3 * X + 1
```

The results of the four runs are shown below.

N	AREA
2	2.0625
10	3.1225
50	3.3569
1000	3.4136

1b. In Program 9-11 replace the function statement as done in Exercise 1a. The results of the four runs are shown below.

N	AREA
2	3.3438
10	3.4138
50	3.4165
1000	3.4166

3. *Stored as EX93-3.FOR on source code solutions diskette.*

5. In Program 9-11 change the function statement to

```
F(X) = X ** 4
```

The results of the three runs are shown below.

N	x_c	y_c
5	0.8194	0.2545
10	0.8299	0.2718
50	0.8332	0.2775

The value of x_c converges more rapidly than does the value of y_c. This results from the fact that the calculation of x_c requires approximating the area under a fifth order polynomial, while the calculation of y_c involves an eighth order polynomial. The higher order polynomial presents a steeper curve which results in a poorer approximation of area by the modified rectangular method. Nevertheless the error in y_c is only about 2 % for N = 10 and less than 0.1 % for N = 50.

Chapter Ten - Additional Data Types

Section 10.1

1. a. 3720 b. 0.0004512 c. 4237500 d. -75387.2

   e. -4.37 f. -0.00000242

3. a. 0.5D 01/0.8D 01 b. 1.0D 01/6.0D 01

   c. 0.75D 01 d. 0.37D 0

Section 10.2

1. a. 4.8 b. 3 - 7i c. - 8i d. -2 + 5i

3. a. 1 - 6i b. 13 - 6i c. -42 + 36i d. -(7/6) + i

Section 10.3

1. a. false b. true c. true d. false e. false

Section 10.4

1. Answers will vary but may include the following:

```
CHARACTER*15 NAME(1000), STRADR(1000), CITY*10(1000)
CHARACTER*2 STATE(1000), ZIP*5(1000, LICNUM*25(1000)
INTEGER CLASS(1000)
REAL FEE(1000)
```

3.
```
CHARACTER*15 NAME(1200), BDATE*6(1200), YEAR*2(1200)
INTEGER CREDIT(1200)
```

Chapter Eleven - Additional Data File Capabilities

```
1a.     OPEN(1, FILE = 'TEST.DAT', FORM = 'FORMATTED')
 b.     OPEN(4, FILE = 'DESCRI', STATUS = 'NEW', ACCESS = 'DIRECT',
    +          RECL = 80)
 c.     OPEN(1, FILE = 'NAMES', STATUS = 'OLD', FORM = 'FORMATTED',
    +          ACCESS = 'SEQUENTIAL', IOSTAT = IOS, ERR = 850)
 d.     OPEN(4, FILE = 'TYPES', STATUS = 'OLD', FORM = 'FORMATTED',
    +          ACCESS = 'SEQUENTIAL', IOSTAT = ISTAT, ERR = 835)
 e.     OPEN(4, FILE = 'TYPES', STATUS = 'OLD', FORM = 'UNFORMATTED',
    +          ACCESS = 'SEQUENTIAL', IOSTAT = ISTAT, ERR = 860)
 f.     OPEN(7, FILE = 'TYPES', STATUS = 'OLD', FORM = 'FORMATTED',
    +          ACCESS = 'DIRECT', IOSTAT = MST, ERR = 870,
    +          BLANK = 'ZERO', RECL = 80)
 g.     OPEN(7, FILE = 'TYPES', STATUS = 'OLD', FORM = 'FORMATTED',
    +          ACCESS = 'DIRECT', IOSTAT = MST, ERR = 870,
    +          BLANK = 'NULL', RECL = 80)
```

3.
```
      PROGRAM MAIN
        CALL FLTEST
        END
*
      SUBROUTINE FLTEST
        IMPLICIT NONE
        INTEGER I
        REAL VALS(4), TOTAL, AVERGE
        DATA VALS /92.65, 88.72, 77.46, 82.93/
* THIS SECTION OPENS THE FILE AND WRITES THE DATA
        OPEN(1,FILE = 'RESULT', FORM = 'UNFORMATTED')
        DO 50 I = 1, 4
          WRITE(1) VALS(I)
  50    CONTINUE
* THIS SECTION REWINDS THE FILE AND READS THE DATA
        REWIND(1)
        TOTAL = 0.0
        DO 60 I = 1, 4
          READ(1) VALS(I)
          TOTAL = TOTAL + VALS(I)
  60    CONTINUE
        AVERGE  = TOTAL / 4.0
* THIS SECTION DISPLAYS THE RESULTS AND CLOSES THE FILE
        WRITE(6,*) 'THE AVERAGE OF THE DATA READ IS ', AVERGE
        CLOSE(1)
        RETURN
        END
```

5a.

```
      PROGRAM MAIN
        CALL MKFILE
        END
*
      SUBROUTINE MKFILE
        INTEGER I, GRD1, GRD2, GRD3, GRD4
        OPEN(1, FILE = 'GRADES', FORM = 'UNFORMATTED')
        DO 50 I = 1, 5
          WRITE(6,*) 'ENTER FOUR GRADES'
          READ(5,*) GRD1, GRD2, GRD3, GRD4
          WRITE(1) GRD1, GRD2, GRD3, GRD4
 50     CONTINUE
        CLOSE(1)
        RETURN
        END
```

5b.

```
      PROGRAM MAIN
        CALL RDCALC
        END
*
      SUBROUTINE RDCALC
        INTEGER I, GRD1, GRD2, GRD3, GRD4
        REAL AVERGE
        OPEN(1, FILE = 'GRADES', FORM = 'UNFORMATTED')
        DO 50 I = 1, 5
          READ(1) GRD1, GRD2, GRD3, GRD4
          AVERGE = (GRD1 + GRD2 + GRD3 + GRD4) / 4.0
          WRITE(6,*) 'THE AVERAGE FOR RECORD',I,' IS',AVERGE
 50     CONTINUE
        CLOSE(1)
        RETURN
        END
```

11.

```
      PROGRAM MAIN
        CALL UPDIR
        END
*
      SUBROUTINE UPDIR
        IMPLICIT NONE
        INTEGER RECNO, STKNO, IDNO, QUANTY, CURRNT
        REAL PRICE
  5     FORMAT(I5)
 10     FORMAT(I3)
 15     FORMAT(I5,3X,I3,3X,F6.2)
        OPEN(1, FILE = 'PRDCT.DAT', FORM = 'FORMATTED',
     +       ACCESS = 'DIRECT', RECL = 20)
        WRITE(6,*) 'ENTER AN IDENTIFICATION NUMBER OR 999 TO STOP: '
        READ(5,*) STKNO
 20     IF (STKNO .EQ. 999) THEN
          WRITE(6,*) 'PROGRAM WILL END'
        ELSEIF (STKNO .GE. 1001 .AND. STKNO .LE. 9999) THEN
          IDNO = 0
          RECNO = STKNO - 1000
          READ(1, 15, REC=RECNO, ERR=25) IDNO, QUANTY, PRICE
```

```
***       RECORD HAS BEEN FOUND - ENTER UPDATED QUANTITY
             WRITE(6,*) 'THE RECORD HAS BEEN LOCATED'
             WRITE(6,50)  QUANTY
             WRITE(6,60)  PRICE
  50         FORMAT(1X,'THE CURRENT QUANTITY IN STOCK:',2X,I5)
  60         FORMAT(1X,'THE CURRENT PRICE IS: $',F6.2)
             WRITE(6,*) 'ENTER THE NEW QUANTITY AMOUNT:'
             READ(5,*) CURRNT
             WRITE(6,*) 'ENTER THE NEW PRICE'
             READ(5,*) PRICE
             IDNO = RECNO
***       WRITE THE UPDATED RECORD
             WRITE(1,15, REC=RECNO) RECNO, CURRNT, PRICE
  25         IF (RECNO.NE.IDNO) THEN
               WRITE(6,*) 'THERE IS NO RECORD FOR THIS STOCK NUMBER'
               WRITE(6,*) 'A NEW RECORD WILL BE CREATED'
               WRITE(6,*) 'ENTER THE CURRENT QUANTITY'
               READ(5,*) CURRNT
               WRITE(6,*) 'ENTER THE PRICE'
               READ(5,*) PRICE
               WRITE(1,15, REC=RECNO) IDNO,CURRNT,PRICE
             ENDIF
             WRITE(6,*) 'ENTER ANOTHER STOCK NUMBER OR 999 TO STOP: '
             READ(5,*) STKNO
             GO TO 20
             ENDIF
          CLOSE(1)
          RETURN
          END
```

Chapter Twelve - Additional FORTRAN Features

Section 12.1

1. The following variables refer to the same memory locations:
   A, X, AND SNAP
   B, Y, and CRACLE
   C, Z, and POP
   D, P, and PIP
   I, NCOUNT, and MM
   J, MTEMP, and KK
   K, LSHOW, and II

3.

```
    PROGRAM TEST
          INTEGER IQUART, IDIMES, NICKEL, IPENNY
          COMMON IQUART, IDIMES, NICKEL, IPENNY
          IQUART = 26
          IDIMES = 80
          NICKEL = 100
          IPENNY = 216
          CALL TOTAMT
          END
```

```
*
      SUBROUTINE TOTAMT
            INTEGER IQUART, IDIMES, NICKEL, IPENNY
            REAL DOLLAR
            COMMON IQUART, IDIMES, NICKEL, IPENNY
            DOLLAR = (25*IQUART + 10*IDIMES + 5*NICKEL + IPENNY)/100.0
            WRITE(6,*) 'THE AMOUNT OF MONEY IN THE BANK IS $ ', DOLLAR
      RETURN
            END
```

5.

```
      PROGRAM TEST
        INTEGER HOURS, MIN, SEC, TOTSEC
        COMMON TOTSEC, HOURS, MIN, SEC
        TOTSEC = 72345
        CALL TIME
        CALL DISPLY
        END
*
      SUBROUTINE TIME
        INTEGER TOTSEC, HOURS, MIN, SEC, TEMP
        COMMON TOTSEC, HOURS, MIN, SEC
        HOURS = INT(TOTSEC/3600)
        TEMP = TOTSEC - HOURS * 3600
        MIN  = INT(TEMP/60)
        SEC = TEMP - MIN * 60
        RETURN
        END
*
      SUBROUTINE DISPLY
        INTEGER TOTSEC, HOURS, MIN, SEC
        COMMON TOTSEC, HOURS, MIN, SEC
        WRITE(6,*) ' HOURS   = ', HOURS
        WRITE(6,*) ' MINUTES = ', MIN
        WRITE(6,*) ' SECONDS = ', SEC
        RETURN
        END
```

I Index

A format specification 80, 139
ABS function 115
ACCESS specification 542, 548
Accumulating 64, 249
Acid rain 150
ACOS function F-1
Actual arguments 172
Addition operator (+) 43
Addresses 38
Age Norms 214–221
AIMAG function 514
Algorithm 3, 32, 90
ALOG function 115
ALOG10 function 115
Alternate return E–8
ALU (see Arithmetic and Logic Unit)
AMAX0 function F-2
AMAX1 function F-2
American National Standards Institute
AMIN0 function F-3
AMIN1 function F-3
Analysis phase 89, 161
AND operator (.AND.)
ANINT function F-1
ANSI (see American National Standards Institute) 2
Apostrophes 23
Approximations 152
Arguments
  actual 172, 203
  array 418–423
  dummy 173, 200
  formal 173, 200
  of a function 200, 203
  of a subroutine 172, 173
Arithmetic
  expressions 43
  operations 43
Arithmetic and Logic Unit 35
Arithmetic IF statement E-11
Arithmetic operators 43
Array
  as arguments 418–423
  element 397
  in COMMON blocks 563
  initialization 407
  multi-dimension 416
  of structures 577
  single dimension 396–404
  two dimension 411–416
ASCII code 42
ASIN function F-1
ASSIGN statement E-13
Assigned GO TO statement E-13
Assignment
  statement 60–63, 105
  variations 63–65
ASSOCIATED function 587
Associativity 46, 311
Assumed-size array declaration 329
ATAN function F-1
ATAN2 function F-1

BACKSPACE statement 269, 545
Bell control code 298
Binary code 36
Binary files 539–541
Bisection method 471–476
Blank COMMON Statement 560
BLANK specifier 542
BLOCK Data 564
Block IF statement 317
BN format specifier B-2
Bubble Sort 438, 440–443
Buffer 74
Bug 111
Byte 36
BZ format specifier B-2
Call by reference 176
CALL statement 171
Carriage Control 73
Case insensitive 13
Case sensitive 13
CASE statement 334
CASE structure 333
Central Processing Unit 35
CEXP function F-2
CHAR function F-2
Character constant 24, 41
Character data entry 125
CHARACTER statement 54
Character string 515
CLOSE statement 266, 544
Closing a file 266
CMPLX function F-2
Coding 7, 162
Coding form 17
Coding phase 89, 162
Coin Toss Simulation 342–344
Comment 17
Comment line 17
COMMON Block 565
COMMON statement 560, 564
Compilation A-4
Compile time errors 107, 108
Compiler 8
COMPLEX data 512
Computed GO TO statement E-12
Concatenation 515
Condition 308
CONJG function F-2
Connecting a file 264
Constant
  character 41
  complex 512
  double precision 507
  integer 40

logical 42
real 40
Continuation line 18
CONTINUE statement 238
Control codes 297
Control unit 35
COS function 115
COSH function F-2
Counter 23
CPU (see Central Processing Unit)
Cramer's rule 104, 452
CSIN function F-3
CSQRT function F-3
Curve plotting 425–433
CYCLE statement 369

D format specification 508
DABS function F-1
DACOS function F-1
DASIN function F-3
Data file 263–271
Data scaling 430–433
DATA statement 407–409
Data structures
as derived data types 573
as parallel arrays 519
Data validation 320
DATAN function F-3
DBLE function F-2
DCOSH function F-2
DDIM function F-2
Debugging 107, 111
Declaration statement 52–56
Design phase 89, 161
Design checking 107
Determinant 198, 452
DEXP function F-2
DIM function F-2
DIMENSION statement 399
Direct access file 548–551
DIRECT specifier 548
Discriminant 339
DLOG function F-2
DLOG10 function F-2
DMAX1 function F-2
DMIN1 function F-3
DMOD function F-3
DNINT function F-1
DO loop 236–247
DO statement 236
DO WHILE construct 362–370
DO WHILE statement 362
DO WHILE structure 351–360
Documentation 161
DOUBLE PRECISION data 507–511
Double spacing 29, 74
Driver unit 11
DSIGN function F-3
DSIN function F-3
DSINH function F-3
DSQRT function F-3
DTAN function F-3
DTANH function F-3
Dummy arguments 173
Dynamic storage allocation 587

E format specification B-2
EBCDIC code 42
Echo printing 111
Editing A-3
Editor A-4
Element of an array 397
ELSE statement 313, 328
ELSEIF statement 328
END SELECT statement 334
END specifier 358, 367, 544
END statement 27
ENDDO statement 366
ENDIF statement 27
Entry point E-7
ENTRY statement E-7
EQUIVALENCE statement E-9
ERR specifier 543
Errors
compile-time 107, 108
logical 107, 108
runtime 107
syntax 16, 107
Exchange sort 440–443
Executable statement 19
EXIT statement 369
EXP function 115
Explicit data typing 56
Exponent D-2
Exponential notation 41
Expression 43, 45, 307
External file 263
External sort 438
EXTERNAL statement E-4

F format specification 77, 138
FALSE 42
File access 548
FILE specifier 542
FLOAT function 115
Floating point D-1
Floating point storage D-1
Flow of control 307
Flowchart 5
FORM specifier 542
Formal arguments 173
FORMAT specifications B-1
FORMAT statement 73, 74
Formatted files 536, 542
FORMATTED specifier 542
FORTRAN 2
Free-form source code 19, 568
Functions
actual arguments 203
arguments of 197–200
calling 202
dummy arguments 200
evaluation of 198
formal arguments 200
intrinsic 113–117
subprogram 198–205
FUNCTION statement 199

G format specification B-2
Generic function F-1
GO TO statement 352

Hardware 35, 230
Harmonic Mean 256
Hashing 549
Header line 11, 16
Hierarchy of operations 46
Higher index bound 406
High-level language 2
Horizontal spacing 73

I format specification 76, 138
IABS function 115
ICHAR function F-2
IDIM function F-2
IDINT function F-2

IF statement
  block 317, 349
  logical 319, 350
IFIX function F-2
IF-ELSE structure 317, 349
IF-ELSEIF structure 319, 350
Implicit declarations 313–324
IMPLICIT statement E-10
Implied DO loop 404, 409
Indentation 17, 232
Index 398
Indexed variable 398
Indirect addressing 573
Infinite loop 259
Initial value 60
Initialization 60
Inner loop 259
Input Edit descriptor 138
Input/Output Unit 35
Insertion Update 375–379
INT function 115
Integer constant 40
Integer division 46
Integer expression 45
INTEGER statement 52
Integration 484–502
Interactive input 122
Internal file 552–553
Internal sort 438
Interpreted language 7
Interpreter 7
Intrinsic function 113–117
INTRINSIC statement E-6
In-memory conversion 552
IOSTAT specifier 543
ISIGN function F-3
Iterations 464
I/O (see Input/output)

Keyword 11

L format specification B-2
Label field 17
Least squares method 462
LEN function F-2
LGE function F-2
LGT function F-2
Library function 113
Linear equations 104, 451
Linked lists 580–587
List-directed
READ statement 122–129, 267
  PRINT statement 29, 33, 106
  WRITE statement 23, 33, 106, 264
Literal 24
Literal format specification 75
LLE function F-2
Local variable 180
LOG10 function F-2
Logic error107, 108
Logical constant 42
Logical IF statement 319
Logical operators 309
LOGICAL statement 54
Logical unit number 271
Loop
  DO 236–255
  DO WHILE 351–360, 362–370
  REPEAT UNTIL 372–374
Lower index bound 406

Magic numbers 144
Main Program 11
Mantissa 508, D-2
Master File Update 379–383
MAX function F-2
MAX0 function F-2
MAX1 function F-2
Member of structure 574–575
Memory
  address 38
  byte 36
  storage 56
  unit 35
  word 38
Merge 379
Merging files 379
Messages 26
Microprocessor 36
MIN function F-3
MIN0 function F-3
MIN1 function F-3
Mixed-mode expressions 45
Mnemonic 13
MOD function 115
Modular Program Design 89
Module 9, 30
Monte Carlo technique 503
Multidimensional array 416
Multiple entry E-7

Named COMMON 564
Named constant 144
Nested
  IF statements 323
  loops 258–261
Nonexecutable statement 19
NULLIFY statement 582
Numerical integration
  Rectangular approximations 484–491
  Simpson's method 495–498
  Trapezoidal approximations 491–494

Object program A-4
One-dimensioned arrays 396–404
OPEN statement 396–404
Operating system A-1
Operators
  arithmetic 43
  associativity C-1
  logical 309
  precedence C-1
  relational 309
Outer loop 259
Overprint 73

P format specification B-2
Parallel arrays 519
PARAMETER statement 144
Parameters of DO loop 241, 248
Parentheses 46
Pendulum clocks 96
Physical unit number 271
Plotting 425–433
POINTER attribute 571
Pointers 569
Pollen counts 283
Populating a structure 575
Precedence 46, 311
Precision D-2

PRINT statement
  list-directed 29, 33, 106
  user-formatted 72, 106
Priority of operations 46
Procedure oriented 2
Program
  costs 230–233
  development 89
  life cycle 161
  object 8
  source 7
  unit 10
PROGRAM statement 11
Program tracing 111
Program units
  BLOCK DATA 564
  body 16
  function 10, 198–205
  header line 16
  MAIN 11
  subroutine 10, 25, 170–173
  types of 10
Programming language 1
Prompt 124
Pseudocode 5

Quadratic equation 338–341
Queue 284

Random number generation 212–214
Random-access file 548
Reading data files 358–367
READ statement
  list-directed 122–129, 267
  user-formatted 135–137, 277, 544
Real constant 40
Real expression 45
Real function 52
REAL statement 54
REC specifier 543, 549
RECL specifier 542
Record 295
Rectangular approximations 484–491
Refinement 93
Relational expression 307–312
Relational operators 309
Repeat counts 81
REPEAT-UNTIL loops 372–374
Repetition structures236, 351, 362, 372
Reserved word 11
RETURN statement 200
REWIND statement 269, 545
RMS (see Root Mean Square)
Root finding 463–482
Root Mean Square 499
Run-time errors 107

S format specification B-2
SAVE statement E-2
Scale factor B-2
Scalar Variable 395
Scope 180
Secant method 476–482
SELECT CASE statement 334
Selection sort 438–440
Selection structures 317, 319, 323, 328
Sentinel 356, 366
Sequential access 535, 548
Sequential execution 27, 307
Sequential flow of control 307
Simple expression 43
Simpson's method 495–498
Simulation 342, 503
Simultaneous equations 451
SIN function 115
SINE approximation 152
Single precision 508
SINH function F-3
Slash format specification 81
Software 230
Sort
  bubble 438, 440–443
  exchange 440–443
  external 438
  internal 438
  selection 438–440
Source program A-3
Specification statements E-9
SQRT function F-3
Square root 115
Stack 284
Standard deviation 289
Standard input device 123, 127, 137
Standard output device 23, 33
Statements
  Arithmetic IF E-11
  ASSIGN E-13
  Assignment 60–65
  Backspace 269, 545
  Block IF 317
  CALL 11, 171
  CASE 334
  CLOSE 266, 544
  COMMON 559
  COMPLEX 512
  Computed GO TO E-12
  CONTINUE 238
  CYCLE 369
  DATA 408
  Declaration 52–56
  DIMENSION 399
  DO 236
  DO WHILE 362
  ELSE 313, 328
  ELSEIF 328
  END 27
  END SELECT 334
  ENDDO 362
  ENDFILE 545
  ENDIF 313, 317
  ENTRY E-7
  EQUIVALENCE E-9
  EXIT 369
  EXTERNAL E-4
  FORMAT 73, 74
  FUNCTION 199
  GO TO 352
  IF 317
  IF-ELSEIF 328
  IMPLICIT E-10
  INQUIRE 546
  INTRINSIC E-6
  Logical IF 319
  NULLIFY 582
  OPEN 264, 541
  Ordering 148
  PARAMETER 144
  POINTER 571
  PRINT 29, 33, 72
  READ 122. 135, 267, 277, 544
  RETURN 200
  REWIND 269, 545
  SAVE E-2
  SELECT CASE 334

STATEMENT Function 209–210
STOP 27
SUBROUTINE 173
TARGET 571
WRITE 23, 33, 72, 106, 264, 274, 543
Statement categories 19
Statement field 17, 18
Statement function 209–210
Statement number 17
STATUS specifier 542
STOP statement 27
String processing 515–518
Structure 9
Structure diagram 93
Structures 573
Stubs 194
Subprogram functions 198–205
Subprograms 170
SUBROUTINE header 16, 173
Subroutines 25, 170–173
Subscript 358
Subscripted variable 398
Substring 517
Summing 64, 249
Symbolic names 12, 567
Syntax 16, 107
Syntax error 107, 108

Tab FORMAT specifications 82, 140
TAN function F-3
TANH function F-3
TARGET attribute 571
Tc format specifier 82
Telephone switching 98
Testing phase 89, 110
Text files 263–279, 535–538
Three dimensioned arrays 416
TLn format specifier 82
Top-down development 89
Transaction file 379
Trapezoidal approximation 491–494
TRn format specifier 82
TRUE 42
Two's complement numbers 37
Two-dimensional array 411–416
Unconditional GO TO statement 352
Unformatted files 539–541
UNFORMATTED specifier 542
Unit number 33, 72, 123
UNIT specifier 542
Unnamed COMMON 560
Upper index bound 406
User-formatted
READ statement 135–137, 277
PRINT statement 72, 106
WRITE statement 72, 106, 274
User-written function 198

Validity checks 373
Variable 51, 395, 398
Variable declarations 52, 567, 571
Variable parameters 180
Variable scope 180
Vertical spacing 73

White space 24
Width of format specification 76,